Russia's Protectorates in Central Asia: Bukhara and Khiva, 1865-1924

Russian Research Center Studies/54

Great Minaret and Courtyard of the Great Mosque, Bukhara

Russia's Protectorates in Central Asia: Bukhara and Khiva, 1865-1924

Seymour Becker

Harvard University Press   Cambridge, Massachusetts   1968

To My Mother, Lena Saperstone Becker,
and to the Memory of My Father,
Aaron P. Becker 1899-1962

© Copyright 1968 by the President and Fellows of Harvard College

Distributed in Great Britain by Oxford University Press, London

The Russian Research Center of Harvard University is supported by a grant from the Ford Foundation. The Center carries out interdisciplinary study of Russian institutions and behavior and related subjects.

Library of Congress Catalog Card Number 67–30825

Printed in the United States of America

Contents

Illustrations

Maps

Introduction

The inhabited world has since the end of the fifteenth century been undergoing an experience without precedent in history. Beginning with the voyages of Columbus and Vasco da Gama, the West has established contact with all other societies, civilized and primitive alike, on the face of the earth, and its impact has become a vital force in transforming the lives and characters of the non-Western societies. This phenomenon of radical change within non-Western societies, formerly identified as "Westernization" and taken pretty much for granted as a sign of inevitable human progress, has in the past decade increasingly attracted the attention of social scientists and historians under the label of "modernization." Modernization ought not simply to be equated with Westernization, for the precise way in which any society modernizes is always influenced to a considerable extent by its peculiar historical experience—the legacy of attitudes and institutions from the past. The concept of modernization does imply, however, a general course of development, whose basic outlines first emerged in the post-Reformation West and were first brought to the attention of non-Western societies as a result of the expansion of Europe.[1] With respect to modernization, the most significant phase of Western expansion was the New Imperialism of the last third of the nineteenth century, when the leading nations of the West had themselves become more or less modern in their economic, social, and political structures. It was also during this period that Western man completed the process of establishing permanent contact with all his terrestial neighbors, including the inhabitants of the innermost recesses of Asia, Africa, and the Americas.

Russia's role in this world-wide drama has been a unique one—that of both antagonist and protagonist. An object of the first wave of Western expansion in the sixteenth and seventeenth centuries, Muscovite Russia reacted by borrowing from the premodern West the technical, military, and administrative knowledge that her rulers, especially Peter the Great, considered necessary for defense against her Western neighbors. Peter's successors continued this policy, until by the nineteenth century the autocracy and a good part of the bureaucracy and gentry formed a thoroughly Westernized elite in Russian society. Yet the idea of a radical and pervasive transformation of Russian society along the lines indicated by the French and industrial revolutions in the West attracted only the numerically and politically weak intelligentsia, and even they generally rejected industrialization until the late nineteenth century. No Russian government before 1917 would commit itself to a program of modernization: the essential steps in the direction of modernization taken after 1855, such as serf emancipation and railroad construction, were tentative and limited concessions to necessity by an ancien régime that to the end feared social and political change as it feared nothing else.

Despite the essentially traditional and non-Western character of Russian society, the Russian state in the nineteenth century was sufficiently Westernized to be immune to the political and military, if not the economic, weapons of the New Imperialism. Russia, in fact, competed for empire in the Near and Far East and in Central Asia as an equal with the Western powers. To her overland neighbors in Asia, Russia stood in much the same relationship as did the West to her overseas neighbors—as a power whose superior technology and organization left those neighbors virtually helpless before her expansionist drive. In the pre-Petrine period Muscovy had dealt at best as an equal with the Turks and the Chinese; but by the nineteenth century the Westernized Russian state was limited in its designs against the Ottoman and Manchu empires more by the jealousy of its Western rivals than by the inherent defensive capacity of those two societies. In Central Asia, too, Russian power was almost irresistible by the nineteenth century. Beginning in the 1820's, the advance of Russian troops southward from the Siberian forest zone across the arid Kazakh Steppe in search of secure boundaries and reliable neighbors did not cease until the Russian frontier was firmly anchored in the Central Asian oases. One result of this expansion was the reduction of the khanates of Bukhara and Khiva to a state of dependency on their powerful northern neighbor.

Bukhara and Khiva were unique among the possessions of the last three tsars of Russia in that they retained their native rulers and a considerable degree of political autonomy. The two khanates' cultural sophistication (the product of a tradition going back to the eighth century B.C.) and their relative political and social stability gave them an advantage in St. Petersburg's eyes over the primitive and anarchic tribal groups of the Kazakh Steppe and the Kara Kum Desert, all of whom were brought under direct Russian rule. At the same time Bukhara and Khiva, having had no contact with the modern West, lacked the bases for a nationalist movement that could have threatened Russian domination and thereby led, as in the case of Poland and Finland in the latter nineteenth century, to their being deprived of political autonomy. In short, from the point of view of the imperial government Bukhara and Khiva were very nearly the perfect colonies, affording all the political and military advantages of control without requiring any of the costly burdens in men and money to govern them.

As a consequence of St. Petersburg's contentment with having satellites rather than subjects, Bukhara and Khiva were subjected far less to the modernizing influences (technological, institutional, and intellectual) of the New Imperialism than were Russia's other colonies, which in turn lagged far behind the possessions of Britain and France in this respect. In fact, to protect its own interests in the khanates, the Russian imperial government consciously minimized such disruptive influences, so that to a great extent the traditional cultures of Bukhara and Khiva were preserved.

The collapse of the ancien régime in Russia in 1917 radically altered the picture: the Western-oriented intelligentsia took the helm and declared for a thoroughgoing modernization affecting all the peoples of the former empire, although on the vital questions of the precise nature and pace of the transformation there was little agreement among liberals, agrarian socialists, and Marxists. The program of modernization fitfully worked out in the first decade of Bolshevik rule and ruthlessly applied after 1928 has brought to Bukhara and Khiva, along with the rest of the former empire, the benefits and problems of modern society in its distinctive Soviet Communist form. Although still relatively backward compared to the USSR as a whole, Soviet Central Asia in the 1960's is decades ahead of her neighbors Iran and Afghanistan in exchanging the security of old familiar ways for the exciting challenges and opportunities of modernity.[2]

The six decades preceding the beginning of this transformation in Bukhara and Khiva are the setting for the present study. It examines the motives and methods for the extension of Russian control over the khanates, the post-conquest policies followed by the imperial government toward its two protectorates, the reasons for those policies, difficulties they encountered, and the fate of Bukhara and Khiva at the hands of the revolutionary successors to the tsars. The goal has been to achieve a more precise understanding of the manner in which these two traditional societies were brought, through the agency of the Westernized Russian state of the Romanovs and the Bolsheviks, under the influence of the modern West.

I should like to express my gratitude to Professor Richard Pipes, who originally suggested the subject of this study and guided it through its first incarnation as a doctoral dissertation, and to Professor Robert L. Wolff for his helpful reading of the manuscript in its early form. I should also like to thank Miss Mary Balmer of the Douglass College Library for her assistance with interlibrary loans; Mrs. Richard W. Bell, who twice typed the manuscript; Mr. Frank Kelland, who prepared the maps; and Mrs. Virginia LaPlante for her valuable editorial comments and suggestions. Finally, I owe two very large debts: a material one to the Research Council of Rutgers University, which has provided generous financial assistance, and a spiritual one to my wife, Carol Cohen Becker, who not only bore with me but gave me strength and encouragement.

Notes on Dates and Transliteration

All dates through January 1918, except where specifically indicated, are given according to the Julian calendar or Old Style, which lagged behind the Gregorian calendar or New Style by twelve days in the nineteenth century and thirteen days in the twentieth century. In cases where both styles are appropriate, they are given together, separated by a slash. The Bolshevik calendar reform took effect on February 1 (O.S.), 1918; from that date the Gregorian calendar is used exclusively.

The Library of Congress system without diacritical marks and ligatures has been followed in the transliteration of Russian words, with the exception of familiar names and terms, which appear in their Anglicized forms. The transliteration of Turkish, Persian, and Arabic words is based on *The Encyclopaedia of Islam* (4 vols. and supplement; Leyden and London, 1913–1938) and on C. H. Philips, ed., *Handbook of Oriental History* (London, 1951). Geographic names are transliterated from either the Russian or the Turkish, depending on whether or not the place in question was under direct Russian rule. Place names in Bukhara and Khiva thus appear in their Turkish rather than their Russian forms—Shahr-i Sabz, not Shakhri-siabz; Hisar, not Gissar.

Part One / The Russian Conquest

Main Reservoir, Bukhara

1 / The Setting

Central Asia Before the Russian Conquest

If nature, in the phrase of the nineteenth-century historian Soloviev, was a stepmother to Russia, she was hardly more generous to Central Asia. Extending eastward from the Caspian Sea, the Central Asian plain is a forbidding desert relieved only by fertile but scattered oases along rivers fed by the melting snows of the lofty mountains to the southeast and east.[1] And yet, despite nature's niggardliness, Central Asia has in centuries past possessed one tremendous advantage—its location. Situated at the northeastern limit of that part of the Old World where man first invented the techniques of agriculture, animal domestication, and metal-working, and subsequently created the first urban and literate societies, Central Asia was an early participant in these revolutionary developments. After the diffusion of civilization westward and eastward, the most convenient overland routes linking the Mediterranean world, India, and China led through Central Asia. As long as these routes remained the principal arteries of trade and communication among the three main centers of civilized life, Central Asia was assured a leading role in world history. From the second century B.C. to the fifteenth century A.D. the oasis-dwellers of Central Asia profited from their location at the crossroads of Eurasia and twice rose to a position of cultural preeminence—in the tenth and again in the fifteenth centuries. Even the region's location, however, was a mixed blessing: placed between the Iranian Plateau on the southwest, seat of civilized societies since the seventh century B.C., and the Eurasian Steppe on the north, home of fierce nomads until the first half of the nineteenth century, Central Asia was long contested by civilization and nomadism, serving alternately as the northeastern march of the one and the ravaged prize of the other.[2]

Three important events at the beginning of the sixteenth century permanently altered the course of Central Asian history. Most significant was Portugal's opening of the direct sea route from Western Europe to India and China, which robbed Central Asia of its strategic and commercial importance. At the same time the area was invaded by the last of its nomadic conquerors, the Uzbegs, whose arrival brought about a decline in material well-being and cultural activity. The final blow was the conversion of Iran to the Shia heresy, whereby Central Asia was cut off from direct contact with the orthodox Moslem world of the Near East.[3] From the beginning of the sixteenth to the middle of the eighteenth century, Central Asia experienced a steady decline—politically, economically, and culturally.

The Uzbegs were a group of Moslem, Turkic-speaking, nomadic tribes of mixed Turkic, Mongol, and Iranian origin. In the fourteenth and fifteenth centuries they had inhabited the section of the Eurasian Steppe between the Ural and the lower Sir-Darya rivers and owed a loose allegiance to rulers descended from Shaiban, a grandson of Chingiz Khan.[4] During the first decade of the sixteenth century one of these rulers, Muhammad Shaibani-khan, conquered all of Central Asia as far as the Iranian Plateau and the Hindu Kush. After his death in battle against the Persians in 1511 his successors founded two khanates on the ruins of his conquests—Bukhara and Khwarizm. Khwarizm became known as Khiva after the capital was transferred from Kunya-Urgench to Khiva in the seventeenth century. When the Shaibanid dynasties came to an end in Bukhara in 1598 and in Khiva in 1687, political disintegration was added to economic and cultural decline. The outlying areas of both khanates broke away to form independent principalities, while the Uzbeg tribal aristocracy seized power at the center. The various Uzbeg tribes warred among themselves for control of the two governments, for power was actually wielded by a mayor of the palace (*atalik* in Bukhara, *inak* in Khiva), while the dynastic rulers served merely as figureheads. The weak Ashtarkhanid dynasty in Bukhara had been founded by a member of the dispossessed ruling house of Astrakhan, and the rapid succession of khans in Khiva were chosen from among the numerous Chingizid sultans of the Kazakhs.[5] Invasion and temporary occupation by the Persians in the 1740's completed the tale of Central Asia's misfortunes.

The century preceding the Russian conquest was marked by political consolidation and economic revival under new dynasties in the two older states and by the emergence of a third Uzbeg khanate. In Bukhara members of the Mangit tribe served as ataliks from 1747 and succeeded the last Ashtarkhanid on the throne in 1785, taking the sovereign title of emir. In Khiva members of the Kungrat tribe ruled as inaks from 1763 and as khans from 1804. The Mangit and Kungrat dynasties were each to rule until 1920. In the Fergana Valley, traditionally a part of Bukhara, a hundred years of increasing autonomy culminated at the end of the eighteenth century in the emergence of the independent Khanate of Kokand.

In both Bukhara and Khiva the first half of the nineteenth century witnessed the strengthening of royal authority at the expense of the Uzbeg tribal aristocracy. Muhammad Rahim I of Khiva (1806–1825) confiscated the nobles' lands and distributed them to his loyal supporters. Emir Nasr Allah (1826–1860) undermined the power of the Bukharan aristocracy by creating a professional standing army and appointing Persian slaves and Turkomans to high government office.

Centralization was pursued not only within each state but also at the expense of the petty principalities that had sprung up during the eclipse of the central power. Nevertheless, many independent and semi-independent principalities continued to exist into the second half of the nineteenth century. Bukhara under the Mangits was continually plagued by Shahr-i Sabz, a state that not only successfully defended its own independence but also tried to seize Bukharan territory and offered refuge to opposition elements within the khanate. East of Shahr-i Sabz, Hisar and Kulab were only nominally subject to Bukhara, while Karategin and Darvaz stood in the same relation to Kokand.

Other areas served as bones of contention among the major states themselves. Bukhara and Khiva disputed each other's claims to Merv and to the left bank of the lower Sir-Darya. The most important rivalry was that between Bukhara and Kokand. Not only the intervening districts of Djizak, Ura-Tübe, Khodjent, Tashkent, and Turkestan were in dispute, but the very independence of Kokand. In 1839–1842 and again in 1863 Bukhara invaded and occupied the Fergana Valley and temporarily reduced Kokand to the status of a vassal. Hostilities between the two states continued until they were physically separated by the advancing Russian troops. The enduring rivalries among the Central Asian khanates prevented the formation of a united front against the Russian invader, and Bukhara's involvement in Kokand's internal affairs became the immediate cause of Bukhara's conflict with Russia.

The reestablishment of internal political stability in Bukhara and Khiva was accompanied by a substantial economic revival. Urban life flourished again, irrigation systems were repaired and expanded, and in general the economic welfare of Central Asia in the nineteenth century considerably surpassed the level of the previous century. Compared with the Central Asia of the fifteenth century, however, or even with its Moslem contemporaries, Turkey and Persia, Central Asia in the mid-nineteenth century remained at an extremely low level, culturally and economically.

A Brief Description of Bukhara and Khiva

Bukhara and Khiva in the nineteenth century were quite similar and at the same time quite different. Both were autocratic Moslem states composed of a variety of ethnic and, in Bukhara's case, religious groups. In each country Sunnite Uzbegs were in the majority and constituted the political and social elite. Bukhara, however, was the larger, more populous, wealthier, and more urbanized. Commerce and industry played a more important role in her economy. The governments of the two countries differed in their internal structure, and the geographical differences were marked.

Bukhara, which at the end of the nineteenth century embraced an area slightly larger than that of Great Britain and Northern Ireland,[6] was a land with little geographic unity. The western part of the khanate was a plain composed of three oases,[7] each separated from the others by desert. These oases formed the demographic, economic, and political heart of the country. The central part of Bukhara consisted of the fertile valleys of several large tributaries of the Amu-Darya[8] and the intervening mountains. In the eastern region[9] some of the world's highest mountain ranges were interrupted only by deep and narrow gorges, swift-flowing mountain streams, and small, isolated valleys.

Accurate figures on the population of Bukhara did not exist before the late 1920's, since the emir's government felt no need for such data and the inhabitants regarded with suspicion any attempt to collect statistical information. All figures must be regarded as only rough guesses. Bukhara's population at the close of the nineteenth century was usually estimated at two and a half to three million, of whom two-thirds lived in the three western oases. Of the khanate's total population, 65 percent was sedentary, 20 percent seminomadic, and 15 percent nomadic.[10] Between 10 and 14 percent of the population was urban.[11] By far the largest town was the capital, with 70,000 to 100,000 inhabitants. Next in order were Karshi, with 60,000 to 70,000, and Shahr-i Sabz and Chardjui, with 30,000 each, followed by a dozen towns in the 4,000 to 20,000 range.[12]

If Bukhara had little geographic unity, it had even less ethnic homogeneity. The earliest known inhabitants of Central Asia were Iranians, who survived as the Iranian-speaking Tadjiks. The descendants of Turkic conquerors from off the Eurasian Steppe constituted the khanate's two other major ethnic groups. The Turkomans had arrived in the tenth century but still preserved their ethnic and cultural identity and their nomadic way of life. The most recent arrivals were the Uzbegs, who were the ruling group. In Bukhara under the Russian protectorate the Uzbegs constituted a majority of 55–60 percent, and the Tadjiks formed a large minority of about 30 percent. The Turkomans accounted for only 5–10 percent.[13] The Uzbegs were concentrated in the Zarafshan and Kashka-Darya oases and in the river valleys of central Bukhara. The Tadjiks formed local majorities in the mountains of central Bukhara and were the sole inhabitants of the mountainous eastern region. The Turkomans constituted a majority along the Amu-Darya as far upriver as Kelif. Several thousand Kirgiz, a nomadic Turkic people, lived in eastern Karategin, and Persians, Jews, and Indians were present in every important town.

The population of Bukhara was almost exclusively Moslem, the only exceptions being the numerically insignificant, although commercially important, Jews and Hindus. Among the Moslems the great majority were orthodox Sunnites, but among the Tadjiks of central Bukhara there were many Ismaili Shiites, and in the east the entire population was Ismaili.

Bukhara was an autocratic state, ruled by a hereditary monarch in accordance with Moslem religious law and custom. To meet the problem of governing a relatively large and populous country, where the settled districts were separated from each other by deserts and mountains and where communications were slow, especially in the central and eastern regions, Bukhara had developed both a highly organized central administration and a large degree of provincial autonomy.[14] At the head of the administrative complex stood the *kush-begi* (chief minister), to whom, by the second half of the nineteenth century, was entrusted much of the actual business of running the state. He directed the secular and civil branches of the central government, supervised the provincial governors, and administered the capital district. Subject to the kush-begi were the *divan-begi* (finance minister and treasurer) and his subordinate the *zakatchi-kalan* (chief collector of the *zakat*, the tax on movable property). Other important officials in the central government, independent of the kush-begi, were the *kazi-kalan* (supreme judge), who had charge of all religious affairs, justice, and education, his subordinate the *ishan-rais* (chief of police and supervisor of morals), and the *topchi-bashi* (war minister and commander of the army). Each of these officials, from the divan-begi to the topchi-bashi, functioned directly in the capital district and indirectly in the provinces through a network of subordinates. All of the above officials were appointed by the emir and were directly responsible to him. Their respective jurisdictions were not precisely defined, which permitted the emir to retain firm control. Even the kush-begi, whose powers were extensive, could do nothing without the emir's knowledge, no matter how trifling the matter in question.

Bukhara was divided into a capital district and a fluctuating number of *begliks* (provinces).[15] Each beglik was ruled by a *beg* (known as a *mir* in the Tadjik-speaking east), to whom the emir delegated virtually all his authority over the local inhabitants except the power of life and death. Begs were appointed by the emir from among his relatives and favorites; his own sons usually served as begs in some of the more important begliks.[16] The begs ruled as petty princes, maintaining their own courts and troops. The emir often attempted to control the distant begliks of central and eastern Bukhara more closely by naming one of the begs viceroy, with authority over the other begs in the area and the right to impose the death penalty. Each beglik had its zakatchi, kazi, and rais, responsible to their respective superiors in the capital. The numerous provincial officials, each with his separate line of responsibility, were supposed to check each other's abuses, but the system more often worked just the opposite, with the kazi, rais, and zakatchi acting in collusion with the beg for their mutual profit.[17]

The begliks were in turn divided into tax districts (in Russian, *amlakdarstva*), ranging in number from two (Burdalik) to twenty (Hisar), according to the size of the beglik.[18] Each district was ad-

ministered by an *amlakdar*, appointed by the beg from among his
relatives and favorites, and its government repeated in microcosm
the structure of the beglik, with its own zakatchi, kazi, and rais. The
amlakdar, however, was purely a tax collector, with none of the
other governmental functions of the beg. At the lowest level of
government, each *kishlak* (village) elected its own *aksakal* (elder),
who had minor duties and was subject to the administrative hierarchy.

None of the more important members of this vast bureaucracy
received a salary. The dignitaries of the central government depended on the emir's charity, in the form of estates and other gifts,
and on the fees and fines that their offices enabled them to collect
from the populace. The provincial officials lived off the land in a
manner reminiscent of the old Muscovite system of *kormlenie*: each
beg retained for his own use the amount of tax revenue he considered
necessary to maintain himself and his court in their customary style
and forwarded the balance to the emir.

The administrative hierarchy was the almost exclusive preserve
of the Uzbegs. A striking exception was the office of kush-begi, which
from the second quarter of the nineteenth century until 1910 was
always bestowed on a Persian slave or descendant of slaves. In this
way the political power of the Uzbeg aristocracy was diminished,
and the complete dependence of the kush-begi on his royal master
was assured.

Besides the secular and civil hierarchy, there was a semi-official
clerical hierarchy, headed by the kazi-kalan.[19] He appointed the
muftis, experts on the *Sharia* (Moslem religious law), who were
often called in on legal cases. The muftis usually doubled as *mudarrises* (professors) in the *madrasas* (seminaries or colleges). Kazis,
muftis, and *ulemas* (theological scholars) were almost always drawn
from the social class composed of the *saiyids* (real or imagined descendants of the Prophet's daughter) and the *hodjas* (descendants
of the first three khalifs). This clerical body, together with the hereditary social class from which it sprang and the *mullahs* (learned
men who did not necessarily hold clerical posts), formed a powerful
group with a vested interest in the defense of tradition and religious
orthodoxy.

Khiva enjoyed the geographic unity and compactness that her
larger neighbor lacked.[20] The khanate of Khiva consisted of a single
oasis and as much of the surrounding deserts as her rulers could

control. The southern part of the oasis, which was the most densely
populated and intensively cultivated, was the economic and political
center of the country. In the far north was the Amu-Darya delta,
covered by an almost impenetrable growth of thickets and reeds and
crisscrossed by the countless mouths of the great river. Khiva's population in the late nineteenth century was probably in the neighborhood of 700,000 to 800,000,[21] of which 72 percent was sedentary,
22 percent seminomadic, and 6 percent nomadic[22]—approximately
the same proportions as in Bukhara, if allowance is made for the
roughness of these estimates. About 60 percent of the population
lived in the southern part of the oasis.[23] Only 5 percent lived in towns
—less than half the figure for Bukhara—and the towns themselves
were much smaller than those of Bukhara. Sizable permanent populations existed only in the capital, with 19,000, and the commercial
center, Urgench, with a mere 6,000.[24]

Despite her geographic unity, Khiva was no more ethnically
homogeneous than was Bukhara. The Uzbegs constituted a majority
of close to 65 percent in Khiva, and the Turkomans formed a large
minority of about 27 percent, roughly the size of the Tadjik minority
in Bukhara.[25] The Uzbegs dominated the important southern part
of the oasis, while the seminomadic Turkomans occupied the southern and western fringes. In the north two other Turkic groups, the
seminomadic Karakalpaks, constituting about 4 percent of the population, and a slightly smaller number of nomadic Kazakhs, were
concentrated respectively in the delta and on the northwestern edge
of the oasis. In religion Khiva was almost exclusively Sunnite, Shiites
and non-Moslem minorities being nearly nonexistent.

The khan of Khiva exercised the same autocratic powers as did
the emir of Bukhara. But Khiva's administrative structure, while
basically similar to Bukhara's, manifested important differences,
which reflected the geographic differences between the two states.
Because Khiva was a small and compact state, its central government
was able to hold a virtual monopoly of power, leaving a minimum
of delegated authority in the hands of the provincial administration.
Formal organization and differentiation of functions, however, were
weakly developed.[26] The Khivan divan-begi was roughly equivalent to
the Bukharan kush-begi, but he usually served also as commander of
the army and collector of the zakat. The southern and northern
halves of the country were administered by the *mehter* and the kush-
begi, respectively, whose power was limited to the collection of taxes.
In general, the functions and powers of any dignitary depended

more on his personal relationship with the khan than on the particular office he held. Khiva also had a kazi-kalan and a clerical hierarchy, but they exercised much less influence than did their counterparts in Bukhara.

Khiva was divided into a capital district and twenty begliks. The begliks were governed by *hakims,* whose powers were much more limited than those of the Bukharan begs.[27] In Khiva the ethnic minorities enjoyed a system of autonomous local government quite unlike anything in Bukhara. Within each beglik the Turkomans, Karakalpaks, and Kazakhs were ruled by their own tribal elders, who were subject directly to the khan rather than to the local Uzbeg hakim.

On the eve of the Russian conquest both Bukhara and Khiva were classic examples of traditional or premodern societies: the khanates' economic, social, and political systems, their technology, and the intellectual attitudes of their rulers showed no qualitative change from the tenth century. Even the printing press was unknown before the Russian conquest. Central Asia's contacts with the outside world, excluding Russia, were confined to infrequent diplomatic exchanges with Constantinople and, even more rarely, with Persia and China.[28] With Russia, Central Asia had a long history of contact, but it was always limited in nature and produced no significant cultural interchange.

Russia and Central Asia to 1853

Central Asia and the area comprising European Russia have been in intermittent contact with one another since remotest antiquity.[29] The regular exchange of commodities by means of caravans across the intervening steppe dates from at least the eighth century A.D. and was very highly developed during the periods when the Khazar kaganate and the Golden Horde ruled the steppe (the eighth-to-tenth and thirteenth-to-fourteenth centuries, respectively). In the latter period the connection was political as well as economic, for appanage Russia constituted the northwest, and Khwarizm the southeast, march of the Golden Horde. After the decline of the Horde in the late fourteenth century, trade continued on a smaller scale. Bukharan and Khwarizmi merchants brought their goods to Kazan and Astrakhan for sale and trans-shipment to Muscovy and occasionally penetrated even to Nizhnii Novgorod.

Russia's conquest of the Kazan and Astrakhan khanates in 1552

and 1556 cleared the way for direct communication with Central
Asia across the Kazakh Steppe. The year after the fall of Astrakhan
both Bukhara and Khwarizm sent embassies to Ivan IV (1533–1584)
to request permission to trade freely in Russia. In 1558 the English
merchant-adventurer Anthony Jenkinson visited Central Asia as Moscow's first official ambassador to that region. He returned to Russia
the following year accompanied by envoys from Bukhara, Khwarizm,
and Balkh. Thereafter diplomatic relations were maintained at irregular but frequent intervals.

Commerce was the major concern of the embassies from Central Asia in the seventeenth century. Bukharan and Khivan merchants maintained an active trade, carrying their goods to Astrakhan,
Samara, Kazan, Nizhnii Novgorod, Iaroslavl, and Moscow itself. Almost no Russian merchants, however, traded in Central Asia. Bukhara and Khiva were extremely suspicious of strangers, particularly
non-Moslems, and Central Asian merchants jealously guarded their
monopoly of the profitable carrying trade to Russia. Moscow's embassies during this period had two principal aims: liberating Russian
slaves (mostly fishermen and merchants captured by Kazakh and
Turkoman raiders near the Caspian Sea and sold into slavery in
Khiva and Bukhara) and after the middle of the century, collecting
information about trade routes to India. Russia's efforts were equally
unsuccessful on both counts.

The reign of Peter I (1689–1725) marked a temporary change
in the character of Russia's relations with Central Asia. Peter hoped
to take advantage of the "time of troubles" in Bukhara and Khiva
to reduce these states to dependence on Russia, with the ultimate
aim of opening a Russian trade route to India via Central Asia.
Twice during the first decade of the eighteenth century the khan of
Khiva, as a tactical move in his country's traditional rivalry with
Bukhara, requested and received the nominal overlordship of the
Russian tsar. The gesture was a formality without real significance
and did not prevent Peter from sending an armed expedition against
Khiva in 1717, intending to persuade the khan to recognize Russian
suzerainty and permit the stationing of a Russian military guard in
his capital at his own expense. The attempt was a failure, and the
entire expedition was slaughtered by the Khivans.

After Peter the Russian government abandoned his policy of
direct penetration of Central Asia in favor of the more traditional
goals of improving trade relations, freeing Russian slaves, and open-

ing a trade route to India. Although trade increased, Russia failed to make any progress on the other two points. Russian slaves in Central Asia included colonists and soldiers captured by the Kazakhs along the newly established Orenburg fortified line. During the eighteenth century Russia's attention was focused on the pacification of these Kazakh nomads, who were nominally Russian vassals but who continued to raid both the Russian frontier and the trading caravans plying between Russia and Central Asia.

Between 1824 and 1854 Russian troops effectively occupied the Kazakh Steppe, placing the entire steppe for the first time in history under the rule of a sedentary society. The Russian advance greatly aggravated Russo-Khivan tensions by raising the problem of the two powers' conflicting claims to authority over the Kazakhs between the Caspian Sea and the lower Sir-Darya. To the old issues was also added the problem of Khiva's subjecting to harsh legal discrimination the Russian merchants who were just beginning to penetrate Central Asia. In an effort to resolve these problems by force, Russia launched a second attack against Khiva in 1839–40. The attempt was even less successful than that of 1717, for the expedition failed even to reach Khiva because of difficulties of terrain and weather. Rightly fearing a renewal of the Russian offensive, the khan of Khiva in 1840 surrendered a number of Russian slaves and prohibited his subjects from raiding Russian territory or purchasing Russian captives. In 1842 the khan agreed on paper to the demands presented to him by Russian missions in 1841 and 1842, but his promises were never fulfilled.

Russia's aims in Central Asia in the 1840's and 1850's were both political and economic. Bukhara and Khiva had to be persuaded to refrain from any hostile actions against Russia, including possession of Russian slaves and granting asylum to Kazakhs fleeing from Russian justice. Khiva in particular must cease her intrigues among the Kazakhs subject to Russia and her attacks on caravans along the Sir-Darya, while demolishing the forts that had been built along the river to support such attacks. In the commercial sphere Russian merchants had to be allowed to trade freely in Bukhara and Khiva on a basis of equality with native merchants. The khanates must guarantee the safety of the persons and property of Russian merchants, levy no excessive duties (in 1841 Russia demanded that import duties on Russian goods be limited to 5 percent; in 1858 she demanded a limit of 2½ percent), permit unhampered transit of goods and caravans across Central Asia into neighboring states (such as Afghanistan and Kashgar), and allow Russian commercial agents to reside in Bukhara and Khiva. At the end of the 1850's Russia added the further goal of free navigation on the Amu-Darya for Russian ships.[30] None of these aims was realized until both Bukhara and Khiva had been beaten in battle and forced to submit to Russian tutelage.

Not having any pretensions to authority over the Kazakhs of the steppe, and serving in addition as Russia's principal trading partner in Central Asia,[31] Bukhara remained on fairly good terms with Russia as long as the latter confined her activities to the steppe. Russia's relations with Khiva and Kokand, however, were inextricably involved with the problem of her quest for security against the nomads on the southern fringes of the steppe, over whom both Khiva and Kokand claimed jurisdiction. The establishment of a Russian fortress at the mouth of the Sir-Darya in 1847 brought Russia into direct physical contact with Khiva and Kokand for the first time and quickly led to the first instance of Russian territorial aggrandizement at the expense of the Central Asian khanates—the conquest in 1853 of the Kokandian fortress of Ak-Masdjid on the lower Sir-Darya.

Russian troops now stood on the threshhold of Central Asia. As long as the Russian frontier lay in a region inhabited by nomadic and predatory Kazakhs, a halt in Russia's advance and the demarcation of a stable and secure boundary was very unlikely. The task of definitively pacifying nomad raiders who were free to flee across the border to sanctuary in a part of the desert controlled by a foreign state would have been difficult under any circumstances. That the foreign states in question, Kokand and Khiva, were sympathetic on religious, ethnic, cultural, and political grounds to the nomads rather than to Russia made the task virtually impossible. A further Russian advance was inevitable.

Prelude to Conquest

During the years from 1853 to 1864 the groundwork was laid for Russia's conquest of Central Asia. For most of this period Russia's major problem in Central Asia was frontier defense. The system of fortified frontier posts that had been established in the first half of the eighteenth century, stretching in an unbroken arc from the mouth of the Ural River to the upper Irtysh, had been superseded in the mid-nineteenth century by a new, as yet incomplete, frontier at the opposite extremity of the Kazakh Steppe. In the west the recently formed Sir-Darya line extended from the mouth of that river only as far as Ak-Masdjid, renamed Fort Perovsk. On the east the New Siberian line stretched from the Irtysh down to the Ili River. Between Perovsk and the Ili remained a gap of almost 600 miles. From the Aral Sea to the Ural River was no frontier at all—only scattered Russian forts.

The question of closing the gap between Perovsk and the Ili and establishing a single continuous line of forts from the Aral Sea to the Irtysh was first raised in 1853 by General G. Kh. Hasford, governor general of Western Siberia. St. Petersburg, deeply involved in the crisis preceding the outbreak of the Crimean War, would authorize only the extension of the New Siberian line across the Ili River. Vernyi was therefore established in 1854 as the new terminal point of the line.[32] In 1858 General A. A. Katenin, governor general of Orenburg, revived the issue. He protested to the Ministry of Foreign Affairs that the *status quo* was untenable and that unification of the frontier lines and occupation of Turkestan and Tashkent were necessary for the stability of Russia's borders in Central Asia. Katenin further proposed that after the capture of Tashkent a military expedition be launched deep into Bukhara in order to regularize relations with that khanate. The new emperor, Alexander II (1855–1881) and his foreign minister, A. M. Gorchakov—both of whom were cautious men in international affairs—rejected Katenin's proposals.[33] Preoccupation with the emancipation of the serfs during the first years of the new reign undoubtedly played an important role in the decision again to postpone an advance in Central Asia, as did a desire to avoid antagonizing Great Britain so soon after the disastrous Crimean War.

During that war the Central Asian problem had taken on a new dimension in addition to frontier security. The new danger was rival English influence in the area. Anxiety lest Central Asia be denied to Russia by England dated back to the 1830's, when English agents had first penetrated Bukhara and Khiva. England withdrew in 1842, however, after her defeat in the First Anglo-Afghan War and the torture and execution of two English agents by the emir of Bukhara.[34] In 1854 St. Petersburg's fears were reawakened by the activities of Turkish envoys, who attempted to ally the Central Asian khanates with the Porte (thus indirectly with Great Britain, the sultan's protector) against Russia. Turkey's plans were frustrated by the ancient antagonisms among the local powers, but two years later Russia was again disturbed by reports of English agents in Kokand, Khiva, and among the Turkomans. Equally disturbing were conquests achieved in northern Afghanistan at Bukhara's expense in the late 1850's by Dost Muhammad, the emir of Kabul, who had been an ally of Britain since 1855. In the year following the conclusion of the Crimean War the weakness of Russia's position was borne out when Britain applied pressure to Persia, Russia's protégé, forcing her to evacuate the independent state of Herat and grant commercial privileges to British traders.[35]

Colonel N. P. Ignatiev, the bold young Russian military attaché in London, responded to these events with a proposal for the extension of Russian political control to the Amu-Darya. He emphasized the diplomatic and economic advantages to be gained from such a move: only in Asia could Russia fight England with any hope of success, and only in Asia could Russian commerce and industry compete successfully with those of other European states.[36] In 1858 Ignatiev was dispatched to Khiva and Bukhara to attempt to settle Russia's differences with those lands and to strengthen her influence at the expense of Britain's. At the same time the famous orientalist N. V. Khanykov was sent to Afghanistan to convince the Afghan princes of Russia's desire "not to weaken the khanates, but to strengthen them as much as possible; we wish to prove to them that our own interest demands the erection of a bulwark against England's drive for conquest."[37] Yet neither of these diplomatic missions solved the problem of English rivalry in Central Asia. In January 1860 St. Petersburg again received reports of increasing British influence in Afghanistan and Anglo-Afghan pressure on Bukhara.[38]

Two personnel changes in 1861 set the stage for the resumption of Russia's forward movement toward the oases of Central Asia. D. A. Miliutin became minister of war, and Ignatiev, now a general, took over the direction of the foreign ministry's Asiatic Department. Both were strong advocates of military conquest in Central Asia. The actual decision to renew the advance came about in an unforeseen manner. In late 1861 General A. P. Bezak, the new governor general of Orenburg, proposed the immediate unification of the Sir-Darya and New Siberian lines and the occupation of Turkestan and Tashkent. Bezak's plan was discussed in March 1862 and again in February 1863 by a special committee, which included M. Kh. Reutern, minister of finance, as well as Gorchakov, Miliutin, Bezak, Ignatiev, and Kovalevskii, former director of the Asiatic Department. As a result of Reutern's opposition, with which Gorchakov concurred, Bezak's proposals were tabled, despite Miliutin's warm advocacy. Something more forceful than words was necessary to persuade the conservative emperor and government. The committee merely authorized exploration of the region between the terminal points of the two frontier lines by reconnoitering expeditions.[39]

In June 1863 Colonel M. G. Cherniaev, General Bezak's chief of staff and commander of one of these reconnaissance missions, violated his instructions by occupying the fortress of Suzak and declaring it under Russia's protection. Cherniaev's bold move proved to be the catalyst that St. Petersburg needed. Instead of censuring Cherniaev for disobeying orders, Miliutin justified the capture of Suzak to Gorchakov on July 7, 1863, calling it a step toward the unification of the frontier lines. The Minister of War argued that a unified frontier would be more economical to maintain and that the possession of Central Asia would be a valuable diplomatic lever against England: "In case of a European war we ought particularly to value the occupation of that region, which would bring us to the northern borders of India and facilitate our access to that country. By ruling in Kokand we can constantly threaten England's East-Indian possessions. This is especially important, since only in that quarter can we be dangerous to this enemy of ours." The foreign minister had been persuaded by what he termed "the successful activities of Colonel Cherniaev without special expenditures." In his reply to Miliutin on July 16, Gorchakov supported the unification of the frontier. The forward policy championed by the military party (Miliutin, Bezak, Ignatiev) had prevailed over the conservative approach of the ministries of finance and foreign affairs. On December 20, 1863, the emperor instructed Miliutin to proceed during the following year to the unification of the Sir-Darya and New Siberian lines.[40]

Within nine months the emperor's orders were carried out. One detachment advanced from Perovsk and took Turkestan; another, setting out from Vernyi under Cherniaev, captured Aulie-Ata. On September 22, 1864, Chimkent fell to the combined forces of the two detachments. Russia's long-time goal had been achieved: a unified frontier based on a fertile region had supplanted the two dangling lines of outposts in an arid steppe. Cherniaev was made a major general and given command of the New Kokand line, subject to the authority of the governor general of Orenburg.[41]

Although the objective of frontier security had been achieved, the traditional causes of Russia's dissatisfaction with the khanates had not been removed, nor had the threat of English influence. Yet St. Petersburg was content for the time being with the gains made. It was rather the headstrong Cherniaev who would not be bound by the limitations that a cautious government sought to impose. An indication of future events came only five days after the fall of Chimkent, when Cherniaev, without any authorization from his superiors, marched on Tashkent, the largest city and the economic center of the khanate of Kokand. The occupation of Tashkent—although advocated by Katenin in 1858, by Bezak in 1861, and by Ignatiev in 1858 and 1863[42]—was not necessary for the establishment of a unified frontier and thus had not received St. Petersburg's sanction. After news arrived that Cherniaev's attack had been unsuccessful and his forces had withdrawn, Gorchakov reacted by requesting the emperor on October 31, 1864, to order that no future change be allowed in the Russian frontier and that any idea of further conquest in Central Asia be renounced.[43]

On November 21 Gorchakov gave definitive expression to the motives that had led Russia to advance her borders to the fringe of the settled areas of Central Asia. In a circular dispatch to Russian diplomatic representatives abroad, he argued: "The position of Russia in Central Asia is that of all civilized States which are brought into contact with half-savage, nomad populations, possessing no fixed social organization.

In such cases it always happens that the more civilized State is forced, in the interest of the security of its frontier and its commercial relations, to exercise a certain ascendancy over those whom their turbulent and unsettled character make most undesirable neighbors.

First, there are raids and acts of pillage to be put down. To put a stop to them, the tribes on the frontier have to be reduced to a state of more or less perfect submission. This result once attained, these tribes take to more peaceful habits, but are in their turn exposed to the attacks of the more distant tribes."[44] Thus, the civilized state was forced to establish fortified posts deeper and deeper in nomad territory since, "It is a peculiarity of Asiatics to respect nothing but visible and palpable force." This pattern had been followed by the United States in North America, by France in Algeria, by Holland in her colonies, and by England in India—in each case "less by ambition than by imperious necessity."

The Russian foreign minister then enumerated the three courses that Russia wanted equally to avoid: (1) the "continuance of a state of permanent disorder"; (2) the constant repetition of costly punitive expeditions producing no lasting results; and (3) the subjugation, one after another, of small, independent, turbulent states, which would mean following "the undefined path of conquest and annexation which has given to England the Empire of India." Russia's goal was rather the possession of a definitive, continuous, fortified frontier, situated in a country fertile enough to ensure supplies and support the colonization necessary for the future stability and prosperity of the occupied country.

Gorchakov contrasted nomadic and sedentary peoples as neighbors and argued against the conquest of the latter: "the nomad tribes, which can neither be seized or punished, or effectually kept in order, are our most inconvenient neighbors; while, on the other hand, agricultural and commercial populations attached to the soil, and possessing a more advanced social organization, offer us every chance of gaining neighbors with whom there is a possibility of entering into relations. Consequently, our frontier line ought to swallow up the former, and stop short at the limit of the latter . . . any further extension of our rule, meeting, as it would, no longer with unstable communities, such as the nomad tribes, but with more regularly constituted States, would entail considerable exertions, and would draw us on from annexation to annexation with unforeseen complications." The foreign minister concluded with the hope that Russia would have a beneficial influence on the backward civilization and political instability of the states that were her new neighbors. He also promised that Russia, while firmly punishing the misdeeds of her neighbors, would act with moderation and in full respect of their independence.

It would be incorrect to dismiss as hypocritical Gorchakov's justification of the new Russian frontier of 1864 and his declaration that Russia had reached the limit of her expansion in Central Asia. The actions and policy directives of the emperor and the foreign ministry, both before and after November 1864, indicate that Gorchakov's circular was an accurate reflection of official St. Petersburg's motives and intentions. Lord Augustus Loftus, the

British ambassador tò Russia, defined those intentions in the following terms in 1872: "I believe that the Emperor and the Imperial Government are anxious to abstain from extending Russian territory in Central Asia, whilst at the same time they are desirous of obtaining a complete control over the small States of which Central Asia is composed . . . As far as I can learn, the object of the Russian Government is . . . by avoiding collision, to obtain entire influence over Turkestan by conciliatory means through the existing Rulers of the several States."[45] Control and influence through native rulers rather than by outright annexation was St. Petersburg's policy in Central Asia.

It would be inaccurate, however, to suppose that Alexander II and Prince Gorchakov were on principle opposed to following "the undefined path of conquest and annexation which has given to England the Empire of India." Rather, they were deterred by the "special expenditures," the "considerable exertions," and the "unforeseen complications" that such a policy would entail for a country taxed by a decade of military and diplomatic defeat and domestic reform. Although they applauded enthusiastically when a daring commander like Cherniaev took a risk and achieved success with the forces available, they consistently refused to sanction in advance military or political moves that involved great risk or great expenditures.

The events of the next decade—which was to see Bukhara and Khiva partly annexed and reduced to the status of Russian dependencies, and to witness Kokand incorporated piecemeal into the Russian Empire—do not belie these assertions. Gorchakov was guilty not of dissimulation but of underestimating the difficulty of making good neighbors of the Central Asian khanates. Nor did he recognize the impossibility of restraining ambitious commanders in the field, two thousand miles from the capital and beyond the reach of telegraph and railroad,[46] who were not at all anxious to act with moderation and in full respect of the khanates' independence. Throughout the period of conquest the Russian government persisted in adhering to the principles of Gorchakov's circular, although in practice St. Petersburg often willingly sanctioned *faits accomplis* that departed from those principles. The end result was a compromise between the cautious and limited objectives of the emperor and his foreign ministry and the expansive schemes of the military.

Economic Motives for the Conquest

Although repeatedly refuted, the theory that nineteenth century imperialism stemmed primarily from economic motives continues to draw support, not least from Soviet historians, who accept as gospel Lenin's writings on the subject.[47] Since almost all recent historians of the Russian conquest of Central Asia have been Soviet scholars, this particular imperialist episode is invariably presented as having been motivated by economic considerations. "The interest of the ruling circles in Central Asia," so the argument goes, "intensified in the 50's and 60's with Russia's entry into the capitalist period of her history."[48] Russia was becoming a "bourgeois monarchy," in which government policies at home and abroad were increasingly influenced by the interests of the capitalists.[49] Russian capitalists wanted to acquire Central Asia as a colony, for the region was already a valuable supplement to the limited Russian internal market for the products of Russian light industry, and it was an important source of supply for raw cotton. "Economic control" over Central Asia thus "became a historic necessity for Russian capitalism."[50] In other words, the "annexation of Central Asia responded to the needs of the growth 'in breadth' of Russian capitalism."[51] Whether or not Soviet historiography is likely in the future to adopt a less dogmatic view of the subject, Western historians are obliged to treat the problem of economic motivation in a more balanced manner.[52]

Cotton was the most important economic link between Russia and the Central Asian khanates on the eve of the conquest. By the 1850's the Russian textile industry had developed to the point where it produced its own yarn and thus depended on imports of raw cotton.[53] Central Asian cotton found a ready market in Russia: in 1860, 31 percent of the total value of Russia's imports from the khanates consisted of raw cotton.[54] At the same time the Russian textile industry was rapidly developing not only as a consumer of raw cotton imports but as a producer of cotton goods for export, of which about 95 percent was marketed in Asia.[55] In 1860 manufactured cotton goods accounted for 53 percent of the total value of Russia's exports to the khanates of Central Asia.[56]

Until the American Civil War the United States was Russia's largest single supplier of raw cotton. When the war and the Union blockade of Confederate ports disrupted American cotton exports,

Central Asia assumed greatly increased importance as an alternate
source of supply. In 1862, the first year in which the effects of the
war were fully felt, the price of Central Asian cotton on the Russian
market had tripled since 1860; by 1864 it had doubled again.[57] Central Asian producers expanded the acreage devoted to cotton, and the
value of the khanates' raw cotton exports to Russia rose from
713,000 rubles in 1860 to 6,521,000 rubles in 1864. Raw cotton
accounted for 85 percent of the total value of Central Asian exports
to Russia in 1864. Because of the steady rise in the price of cotton,
the figures on the volume of Russian imports of raw cotton from
Central Asia are more telling. These imports rose from 174,059 puds
in 1860 to a high of 459,391 puds in 1864. They accounted for only
6 percent of Russia's total cotton imports from all sources in 1860,
increased their share to a record 40 percent in 1862 (while imports
from other foreign sources declined by 80 percent), and still accounted for a significant 28 percent in 1864. Even after the end of
the American Civil War, Russian cotton imports from Central
Asia continued to increase in absolute terms, although their relative
importance declined as imports from America resumed.[58] Russian
exports to the khanates also experienced a striking increase as the
Russian frontier advanced. Between 1863 and 1867 the annual value
of Russia's exports to Central Asia more than tripled, and the
khanates' share of the Russian export trade to all Asia rose from
22 to 42 percent.[59]

Russia's increased dependence on Central Asian cotton after
1862 and the benefits accruing to Russia's export trade from the
progress of Russian arms are undeniable facts. It is also clear that
at least some groups in the Russian industrial and commercial community were anxious to have the government act on their behalf
in Central Asia. The khanates' discriminatory treatment of Russian
merchants had long been a major point of contention and was not
resolved until after the conquest. Russian manufacturers and traders
in the late 1850's began to complain regularly to the Ministry of
Foreign Affairs about the khanates' discriminatory duties, which kept
all trade in the hands of Central Asian merchants.[60] In 1862, when
cotton from the khanates acquired a new importance for Russian
industry, direct government intervention in Central Asia was warmly
advocated in such influential journals as M. N. Katkov's *Russkii
Vestnik*.[61] Early in the same year fifteen leading Moscow merchants
petitioned the Ministry of Finance to open a consulate in Bukhara

for the protection of the interests of Russian subjects. Despite the foreign ministry's skepticism about receiving from the emir the necessary guarantees for the normal functioning of a consulate in accordance with the rules of international law, two special commissions explored the question in turn and reported favorably. At the end of 1864 further discussion of the issue was postponed at the request of the Asiatic Department, pending a definitive settlement of Russia's relations with Bukhara.[62]

Although Central Asian cotton had acquired a new importance for Russia on the eve of the conquest, and considerable sentiment existed for an advance into Central Asia to protect and promote Russian manufacturing and trading interests, the influence of these factors on policy-formation was minimal. The history of the discussions leading up to the conquest and of the conquest itself indicates that neither in the capital nor among the military commanders in the field were economic considerations of much importance. A case in point is that of M. A. Khludov, owner of one of Russia's largest cotton-spinning mills and a leading Russian exporter to Central Asia, who had been in Bukhara in 1863 and reported to the government in 1867 on trade conditions during the period of uneasy truce with Bukhara. Khludov noted that Central Asia was an extremely profitable market for Russian products but that it was dangerous for Russian merchants to trade beyond the area under Russian administration. He concluded, "it will be very difficult to compete [with the English] even with our government's protection, and completely impossible without it."[63] Rejecting Khludov's conclusion, P. N. Stremoukhov, director of the foreign ministry's Asiatic Department from 1864, observed that it would be to the undeniable advantage of the Russians to make themselves "complete masters of Central Asia, but into the rational solution of this question commercial considerations can enter only as one of the conditions, important but not paramount."[64] Five years earlier the foreign ministry had rejected a similar plea for government support to trade in Central Asia by an expert on the Russian cotton industry, unequivocally asserting that "the government may only consider the interest of the state."[65] In short, Russia was spurred on in Central Asia by a whole complex of motives—the quest for a secure frontier, the provocations offered by unstable neighbors, the fear of being excluded from the area by England, and the temptations of diplomatic leverage, economic profit, and military glory.

Konstantin Petrovich von Kaufman, Governor General of Turkestan, 1867–1882

ties to the formation in Tashkent of a state independent of Kokand and Bukhara but in a state of vassalage to Russia," Cherniaev had all the permission he needed.[4] On April 24 he set out for Tashkent, claiming that the concentration of Bukharan troops at Samarkand and Ura-Tübe posed an immediate threat to Tashkent.[5] Finding that the pro-Russian party within the city was too closely watched by the Kokandian garrison to be an effective instrument of Russian policy, Cherniaev on May 7 laid seige to Tashkent.[6]

Several days later Cherniaev, on his own responsibility, initiated negotiations with Bukhara in an attempt "to divert the emir from interfering in the affairs of Tashkent and to give another direction to his movements which would be more compatible with our interests."[7] In his letter to the emir, Cherniaev officially informed him of Russia's conquest of the northern half of Kokand during 1864 and of the present Russian position before Tashkent. Cherniaev declared that Alexander II had instructed him not to cross the Sir-Darya but wanted the emir to reduce Kokand south of the river to order and tranquillity. The Russian commander further promised to request imperial permission for sending Russian troops to aid in these operations if Muzaffar desired, and he left it up to the emir whether or not to keep Khudayar on the throne of Kokand.[8]

Cherniaev's offers to Bukhara were wholly unauthorized. On May 13 he wrote to Kryzhanovskii, suggesting that Russia take the Sir-Darya as her natural boundary and agree to Bukhara's occupation of southern Kokand, which, he argued, Russia could not at the moment prevent anyway. He also requested permission to initiate negotiations upon this subject with the emir.[9] Cherniaev's request for authorization from above was a mere formality, since he had already written to Muzaffar and could not in any case have waited the two months necessary for a reply from St. Petersburg. The government's answer, of purely academic interest by the time it reached Cherniaev at the end of June or beginning of July, was that the emir's occupation of the remainder of the khanate of Kokand would be considered a hostile act toward Russia and would be met by the suspension of Bukhara's trade with Russia.[10] Although desiring no further territorial gain herself, Russia apparently would not countenance the strengthening of one of her neighbors at the expense of another. St. Petersburg took this opportunity to emphasize that both Tashkent and Kokand ought to be left free from permanent Rus-

sian occupation in order to constitute independent states under
Russian influence, thereby guaranteeing the tranquillity of Russia's
borders and the safety of her trade. Faced with the government's
disapproval, Cherniaev in his report of August 6 minimized the significance of his offer to the emir, claiming that Russia could not
have prevented Bukhara's reduction of southern Kokand in any case
and that the promise of Russian military support obligated Russia
in no way.[11]

Cherniaev's May letter to the emir was inexplicably delayed in
reaching him. The Bukharan party meanwhile gained control in
Tashkent and entered into communication with Muzaffar.[12] Apprehensive of Russia's intentions, the emir marched on Khodjent and
captured that city. But Tashkent fell to Cherniaev on June 17, and
contrary to orders a Russian garrison was installed—in order to prevent civil strife, according to Cherniaev, and to protect the city
against Kokand and Bukhara.[13]

St. Petersburg had meanwhile been considering the policy to be
followed in future toward Bukhara. During May the Ministry of
Foreign Affairs, in consultation with General Kryzhanovskii, drafted
a set of demands asking that Bukhara conduct herself as a good
neighbor and grant Russian merchants "complete security of person
and property, the right to trade freely in all the towns of the khanate
of Bukhara, the payment of the same frontier duties as Bukharan
subjects, and equal rights in Bukharan courts."[14] Russia was still
demanding of Bukhara no more than what she had been asking for
decades.

The Break with Bukhara

Just before the fall of Tashkent to the Russians and after Muzaffar had occupied the capital of Kokand and restored Khudayar to
the throne,[15] he dispatched an embassy to Alexander II with a request for the delimitation of the Russo-Bukharan border. While
awaiting an answer, Bukhara demanded of Cherniaev that he withdraw, at least to Chimkent.[16] Cherniaev responded to the emir's
attempt to deal directly with St. Petersburg by ordering the arrest
of all Bukharan subjects and the sequestration of all Bukharan caravans in the Turkestan Oblast. He then requested his superiors to
extend these measures throughout the Russian Empire.[17] Kryzhanov-

skii was much disturbed at the position in which Cherniaev's move had placed him. Fearing St. Petersburg's disapproval, he nevertheless extended the arrests throughout the Orenburg Government-General rather than make Cherniaev lose face before the natives by rescinding his order or reveal Russian disunity by not applying the order generally.[18] One hundred thirty-eight Bukharan merchants were arrested in the government-general.[19]

Before learning of the arrest of the merchants, Muzaffar finally received Cherniaev's first letter, and in early July he signified his satisfaction by sending presents to the Russian commander and requesting only that the Russians not cross the Chirchik River, which would serve as the temporary frontier until the Bukharan embassy obtained an answer from St. Petersburg.[20] Cherniaev avoided a positive reply, probably because Tashkent was dependent on the district south of the Chirchik for its grain supply.[21] When the emir heard of the arrest of his subjects, his mood chilled, and he immediately sent messengers demanding their release.[22]

St. Petersburg's reaction was dissatisfaction that Cherniaev had taken such an important step without even clarifying his reasons, coupled with determination not to yield an inch to Muzaffar ad-Din. On July 23 Gorchakov complained to the minister of war, Miliutin, about Cherniaev's action, even while affirming, "We cannot retreat now. It is unthinkable to bow before the emir."[23] The foreign minister felt that the situation was rapidly slipping out of the hands of the civil authorities into those of the military but cautioned only that the army be sure of its strength before coming to blows with Bukhara. Although Kryzhanovskii's and Cherniaev's orders were confirmed, they were confined to the Orenburg Government-General pending the arrival of further details. In notifying Kryzhanovskii to this effect, Miliutin added, "it is necessary to maintain our influence and dignity at any price." On July 29 the minister of war expounded the government's policy toward Bukhara at greater length: "the dignity of the Empire and the interests of Russia do not allow us even to consider the possibility of retreat or concession to the Emir of Bukhara's arrogant demands. Our whole future in Central Asia depends on the position in which we place ourselves in regard to Bukhara, and His Majesty the Emperor hopes that Your Excellency will not fail to make every effort to maintain Russia's dignity and our influence in Central Asia."[24] On the same occasion Miliutin conveyed to Kryzhanovskii Gorchakov's admonition to use force only as a last resort and to avoid any military defeats that would cause Russia to lose face.

At the end of July the emir's envoys reached Kazalinsk on the lower Sir-Darya en route to St. Petersburg and were detained there by order of General Kryzhanovskii, who explained to them that Muzaffar must deal with him and not directly with the emperor. Kryzhanovskii at the same time suggested to St. Petersburg that he be authorized to deal with the emir on the subject of Tashkent, which he would make clear was to remain an independent state under Russia's guarantee.[25]

The occupation of Tashkent and the arrest of the Bukharan merchants, both of which had been performed on Cherniaev's initiative, were the immediate cause of the increase in hostility between Russia and Bukhara. St. Petersburg was apprehensive. In September Stremoukhov, director of the foreign ministry's Asiatic Department, reacting to Cherniaev's proposals to annex Tashkent and Kokand north of the Sir-Darya, warned against further involvement in Central Asia.[26] On October 19 in an attempt to reassert the government's control over events the Council of Ministers directed that Kryzhanovskii lift the repressive measures against Bukharan merchants at the earliest possible moment and that no extraordinary measures be taken in the future without the government's sanction.[27]

Meanwhile, events were proceeding in the direction of war. In September Cherniaev ordered his troops to pacify the trans-Chirchik district, thereby in effect rejecting Muzaffar's request of early July to regard the Chirchik as the provisional frontier. In mid-October Cherniaev dispatched an embassy to the emir, led by Court Councillor K. V. Struve of the foreign ministry, to negotiate the reestablishment of friendly relations and trade. At Bukhara the Russians found envoys gathered from Kokand, Khiva, Shahr-i Sabz, and Afghanistan.[28] An anti-Russian coalition seemed to be in the offing. In November Muzaffar arrested not only the Struve mission but all other Russians in Bukhara as well.[29] On December 7 Cherniaev asked the emir for an explanation of the arrests; the latter replied that the Russian mission was being held in retaliation for the detention of the Bukharan embassy (transferred to Orenburg in November) and would be released after the Bukharan envoys had obtained a favorable reply from the emperor personally.[30]

Thinking to frighten the emir, Cherniaev sent a small force across the Sir-Darya at Chinaz on January 12, 1866, but as a result, Muzaffar began to assemble his troops and entered into negotiations with Khiva and the Turkoman tribes. On January 31, therefore, disregarding the instructions of his superiors at Orenburg and in the war ministry, Cherniaev crossed the frozen Sir-Darya in force and moved on Djizak, the strongest fortress on the Bukharan frontier.[31] The governor of the Turkestan Oblast had been decorated for capturing Tashkent and no doubt assumed a similar reward would be his for a campaign against Bukhara, instructions to the contrary notwithstanding. Cherniaev informed Muzaffar that he was crossing the Sir-Darya not for conquest but only to liberate the captive Russian envoys.[32] The emir attempted to prevent a further advance by promising to release the Struve mission, but Cherniaev replied that he would have to continue his advance through the Hungry Steppe[33] until he reached the first watering spot, where he would await his countrymen. The Russians halted about five miles from Djizak, whose beg refused to sell them firewood and hay and opened fire on a Russian detachment sent to collect these materials. It soon became clear that Muzaffar was stalling and did not intend to release his captives. Cherniaev decided against attempting to take Djizak and on February 11 began to withdraw to the left bank of the Sir-Darya. Even before he began to retreat from Djizak, Cherniaev, who had long been at odds with Kryzhanovskii, was relieved of his duties and summoned home to explain his conduct.[34]

The First Bukharan Campaign

Cherniaev's successor as military governor of the Turkestan Oblast was Major General D. I. Romanovskii. Romanovskii was given joint instructions from the ministries of war and of foreign affairs, which were so broad as to leave him in fact a free hand.[35] His instructions directed him "while steadfastly striving not to extend our direct possessions in Central Asia, not to reject, however, for the sake of that goal, such actions and orders as may be necessary for us, and in general to keep in mind, above all, Russia's true interests." St. Petersburg expressed regret that recent events had made an enemy of the emir of Bukhara and urged reestablishment of friendly commercial relations as soon as possible. No specific action toward

this end was recommended, however. On the contrary, his instructions reminded Romanovskii that "the Asiatic respects only armed
force, that the slightest vacillation and indecisiveness, and especially
concession, in response to any kind of inappropriate declarations or
actions on their part, will be taken by them for weakness and thus
not only will not attain its aims but may have a disastrous effect
on the regions newly taken by us as well as on our steppes and on
our former lines." Romanovskii's principal task in regard to Bukhara
was "to compel the emir to understand that we do not wish any
conquests and do not threaten the integrity of his possessions, but
we shall not allow him to extend his possessions in the direction of
our borders."

Less ambiguous evidence of Russia's intentions at this time is
contained in the draft of a treaty with Bukhara drawn up by Kryzhanovskii at the end of 1865. The draft provided for the following:
establishment in Bukhara of a Russian trade agency, equal rights for
Russian merchants in Bukhara, lower Bukharan import and export
duties, recognition by Bukhara of Tashkent's independence, free
navigation on the Sir-Darya for Russian ships, and the possibility
that Russia would support Bukhara's claims against Kokand. Only
after the emir had signed the proposed treaty was his ambassador
to be allowed to proceed to St. Petersburg. Miliutin, acting for
the emperor and the government, approved Kryzhanovskii's draft
on January 14, 1866, but added reciprocal trade privileges for
Bukharans in Russia and again ruled out Bukharan interference in
Kokand.[36]

Romanovskii's own policy, as stated in September 1867, was to
improve Russia's position in Central Asia by weakening Bukhara's
influence as much as possible, occupying only strategic points, and
convincing Russia's neighbors of her peaceful intentions.[37] One of
Romanovskii's first gestures toward weakening Bukhara's influence
was to address the emir as "High Eminence" (*Vysokostepenstvo*)
rather than "Highness" (*Vysochestvo*), as Cherniaev had always
done. The royal title was not again accorded to the emirs of Bukhara until the very end of the nineteenth century, by which time
they had long owed their authority to their Russian protectors.

In March 1866 Romanovskii arrived at the Russian camp at
Chinaz and assumed command. Skirmishes with the Bukharan forces
had been taking place continually, and reports had arrived of Muzaf-

far's request for assistance from Khiva.[38] On April 19 Romanovskii received a Bukharan embassy bringing a letter from the emir, who insisted on Russia's immediate withdrawal beyond the Sir-Darya and evaded the question of the release of the Struve mission.[39] The Russians broke camp on May 7 and on the following day defeated the Bukharan army in a major encounter at Irdjar, Muzaffar himself fleeing from the battlefield.

Instead of using the victory at Irdjar to obtain the release of the Russian hostages and then withdrawing from Bukharan soil in accordance with the spirit of his instructions, Romanovskii proceeded on his own initiative to lay siege to the town of Khodjent, key to the Fergana Valley and now once again in Kokandian hands, which he took on May 24. Romanovskii justified his occupation of Khodjent on strategic grounds: possession of Khodjent was necessary for the defense of the trans-Chirchik district and would sever Kokand from Bukhara and afford the most convenient access to both khanates.[40] Just as Tashkent had formerly been necessary for the defense of Chimkent, and the trans-Chirchik district for the defense of Tashkent, now Khodjent was necessary to protect the trans-Chirchik district. This line of argument has always been dear to the hearts of the military.

The battle of Irdjar and the fall of Khodjent impressed the emir. At the beginning of June he released the Struve mission and dispatched an embassy to Romanovskii to ask the general's promise not to undertake any further action against Bukharan territory. Romanovskii replied that his superior, the governor general of Orenburg, was coming to Tashkent to discuss peace terms. In the meantime, Romanovskii proposed four preliminary conditions of peace. Bukhara was to recognize all of Russia's recent conquests and accept the Hungry Steppe and the Kizil Kum Desert as the Russo-Bukharan boundary, reduce the duty on Russian goods to the level of the duty collected on Bukharan goods in Russia, grant full freedom and safety to all Russian subjects in Bukhara, and pay Russia an indemnity to cover the expenses of the recent campaign. Romanovskii included the point about the indemnity so that further demands might be substituted for it if necessary. As the condition for an immediate cessation of hostilities, Romanovskii demanded the liberation of all Russian merchants together with their goods and promised to solicit the liberation of Bukharans under arrest in Orenburg. Muzaffar subsequently freed all Russian merchants in Bukhara and returned their goods to them.[41]

The summer of 1866 passed uneventfully. The fall of Khodjent terminated hostilities with Kokand, now reduced to the Fergana Valley, although peace was not formally concluded until 1868. The truce with Bukhara was preserved. However, there were ominous signs on the Russian side. In July General Kryzhanovskii, just returned from St. Petersburg, wrote to Romanovskii expressing his dissatisfaction with Romanovskii's handling of the emir and specifically with his petition for the release of the Bukharan merchants at Orenburg. Kryzhanovskii advised Romanovskii, "having beaten the emir as you have done, everything must be demanded of him, nothing conceded to him."[42]

An interesting by-product of the Struve mission was a memorandum addressed to General Romanovskii̇ on July 23 by one of the mission's members, Lieutenant Colonel A. I. Glukhovskoi.[43] Glukhovskoi argued that in order to keep Bukhara and the whole Amu-Darya basin out of England's reach and to secure Bukhara as a vital source of raw cotton, that state had to be brought under Russia's influence. He advised Russia to pursue these aims "by the easiest and cheapest means." Outright annexation, or even the reduction of Bukhara to a state of vassalage, would involve great expenditures. Glukhovskoi suggested instead that Russia make of Bukhara "an independent ally," whose loyalty would be ensured in the following manner. Russia would occupy Djizak, the key to the Zarafshan Valley, the possession of which strongpoint would enable Russia to exert a dominant influence over Bukhara; four or five companies of Russian soldiers would be assigned to the emir to protect him against his domestic enemies; and the Central Asian khanates up to the Amu-Darya would be united to Russia in a customs union. Glukhovskoi's proposal that Bukhara be accorded the role of an independent but subsidiary ally reflected the current thinking in government circles, but its implementation proved neither so easy nor so cheap as he had envisioned.

In August 1866 General Kryzhanovskii arrived in Tashkent and annexed that city, together with the trans-Chirchik district and Khodjent, to the Russian Empire. The war with Bukhara had forced St. Petersburg to abandon its plans for an independent Tashkent.[44] At the end of the month Romanovskii wrote to Muzaffar to inform him that Kryzhanovskii was waiting at Tashkent with full powers to conclude peace. Romanovskii threatened a renewal of hostilities unless the emir immediately sent an envoy to negotiate peace conditions. Muzaffar accordingly dispatched an embassy to Khodjent at the beginning of September with a declaration of his complete readiness to meet all Russia's demands.[45]

The peace terms that Kryzhanovskii presented to the Bukharan envoy were similar to those discussed between Orenburg and St. Petersburg at the beginning of the year. A Russian trade agent must be allowed to reside in Bukhara for the purpose of protecting the interests of Russian merchants, Russian subjects must be permitted to establish caravansaries in any towns of the khanate, Russian merchants must be taxed at the same rates as Bukharans, and the emir must renounce forever any interference in Kokand's affairs and pay a war indemnity of 100,000 *tillas* (about 400,000 rubles).[46]

Despite the Bukharan ambassador's protests that he had no powers to agree to an indemnity, Kryzhanovskii was adamant, true to the advice he had given Romanovskii in July. Muzaffar had not specifically accepted Romanovskii's preliminary conditions of the previous May, and Kryzhanovskii was personally insulted by the meagerness of the gifts the emir had just sent to him. Kryzhanovskii resolved to bring Muzaffar to terms by taking Ura-Tübe and Djizak. On September 5 he wrote to Miliutin that he was renewing the offensive against Bukhara. Eight days later the Bukharan ambassador was told that the emir had just ten days to pay the indemnity or face further military action. Kryzhanovskii knew that it was physically impossible to go from Khodjent to Bukhara (a journey of over three hundred miles), raise such a large sum of money, and return in ten days. On September 20 the Russian troops moved out from Khodjent so as to be on the Bukharan frontier when the ultimatum expired on the twenty-third.[47]

During October the Russians took Ura-Tübe, Djizak, and Yani-Kurgan in that order. In view of the lateness of the season the campaign then ended, and Generals Kryzhanovskii and Romanovskii returned to Tashkent. There was no word from Muzaffar, but shortly after the fall of Djizak on October 18 the begs of Shahr-i Sabz asked the Russians to continue the advance against Bukhara and declared their willingness to cooperate.[48]

The year 1866 had seen considerable new conquests by Russia but without bringing peace and stability to Central Asia. Alexander II and Gorchakov were not slow in registering their dissatisfaction. In November Miliutin reminded Kryzhanovskii that the emperor did "not want any new conquests" and was awaiting the renewal of peace negotiations with Bukhara, "since under the present conditions the pacification of the area and the resumption of trade with our Asian neighbors is more important for us than the most brilliant successes, especially if they require the strengthening of our forces and new expenditures from the state treasury."[49] The following month a memorandum of the foreign ministry critically summed up the events of 1866: "No matter how brilliant the recent successes of our arms, in a political respect they have achieved no satisfactory results whatever."[50]

The Draft Treaty of 1867

In January 1867 India rejected Muzaffar's appeal for help against Russia,[51] so the emir sent another ambassador to Orenburg in May to renew the peace talks. His aim was evidently to secure the return of Ura-Tübe and Djizak and to gain acceptance of the left bank of the Sir-Darya as the frontier, or if that failed, at least win time to prepare for a renewal of hostilities.[52]

While the talks dragged on in Orenburg, the Turkestan Oblast was raised to the status of a government-general,[53] and Romanovskii was replaced by General K. P. von Kaufman. The emperor's grant of powers on July 17 gave Kaufman full authority "to decide any political, frontier and commercial affairs, to send to the neighboring territories trustworthy persons for the conduct of negotiations and the signing of conventions, conditions or regulations affecting the subjects of both parties." The emperor committed himself in advance "to accept everything that will be concluded and signed by virtue of the aforementioned plenary powers."[54] The assignment was to von Kaufman's taste. Vain and ambitious for personal glory, the new governor general enjoyed both the substance and the perquisites of power. The ceremonious display and rigid etiquette with which he surrounded himself in Tashkent so impressed the inhabitants of Central Asia that they called him *Yarim Padishah* (Half-Emperor).

The conflict of views between the central government and its commanders in the field continued unabated. General Manteufel, acting governor of the Turkestan Oblast after Romanovskii's recall, had urged a further advance, this time on Samarkand. Stremoukhov responded on July 29 with an indignant letter to Count F. L. Heiden, chief of the general staff: "Various points in Central Asia have continually been pointed out to us as necessary acquisitions to strengthen our position and serve as a base and a bulwark for our possessions. Chimkent, Tashkent, Khodjent, and Djizak were in turn such points, and now Samarkand has been indicated . . . It has constantly been said that for the glory of Russia, for the raising of her prestige, it is necessary to take some stronghold or other or to smash the Asiatic hordes in the field; strongholds have been taken one after another, the hordes have been utterly defeated, good borders have been attained, and then it has invariably turned out that one more stronghold is lacking, that one more final victory is necessary, that the really perfect frontier lies somewhat farther off, that our prestige is still insufficiently raised by our former successes. Your Radiance rightly will agree that such a form of action ought finally to be ended, because it is compatible with neither the dignity nor the true interests of the government."[55] Stremoukhov was speaking for Gorchakov and the emperor in repudiating the familiar military arguments of strategic necessity.

Upon arrival at his post, General von Kaufman turned to the task of concluding peace with Bukhara. Kryzhanovskii had developed his peace conditions of the previous September into a ten-point draft treaty, which had received the emperor's approval. Kaufman suggested several changes, including stipulations that the emir's relations with Russia be conducted exclusively through the governor general of Turkestan and that Yani-Kurgan be restored to Bukhara. Kryzhanovskii accepted the changes, signed the draft treaty on September 14, 1867, and presented it to the Bukharan ambassador, who had been in Orenburg since May.[56]

The draft treaty established the Russo-Bukharan boundary between Djizak and Yani-Kurgan and thence, in a northwesterly direction, to the mouth of the Sir-Darya. Both Russia and Bukhara were obligated to keep peace along the frontier by suppressing raids against each other's territory. Seven of the treaty's twelve articles were designed to open Bukhara to Russian merchants, who received the right to trade, to establish caravansaries, and to maintain commercial agents throughout the khanate, as well as to reside and acquire real property there, subject to the approval of the governor general of Turkestan. Russians were to pay the same commercial duties as Bukharans. Bukhara was bound to protect Russian caravans against robbers and to leave to the governor general exclusive criminal jurisdiction over all Russians in the khanate. Although expressly forbidding the emir of Bukhara from dealing directly with the imperial Russian government, the treaty in no other way infringed upon Bukhara's sovereignty. Kaufman gave his views on this matter in a letter to Stremoukhov at the time the draft treaty was presented to the Bukharan ambassador: "We did not touch upon some points at all; for example, I considered it both inopportune and superfluous to stipulate that the emir not enter into any political obligations with neighboring khanates, or in general with other nations, without our consent. It would be inopportune because we would betray our apprehension of any kind of Central Asian alliances, or even of the interference of the English; we must not, it seems to me, indicate even imaginary weak spots. It would be superfluous because we will not in any case be in a position to follow up the implementation of such an article in the treaty. Let the emir arrive by himself at the conclusion that his country's every interest demands a close alliance with Russia, and that any malevolent interference from without in our mutual relations will surely reflect in an unfavorable manner first and foremost on himself."[57] In short, the treaty followed St. Petersburg's line of protecting Russian interests in Bukhara without directly asserting Russian control. The emir's envoy in Orenburg signed the treaty, and it was submitted to Muzaffar for ratification.[58]

Russo-Bukharan relations meanwhile deteriorated. The emir renewed efforts to organize a coalition comprising Kokand, Khiva, Kashgar, and Afghanistan and backed by Turkey and Great Britain, but his overtures were everywhere rejected.[59] Russia was further antagonized when, early in September, a Lieutenant Sluzhenko and three other soldiers were captured between Chinaz and Djizak by a robber band organized by a Bukharan frontier beg. Sluzhenko was subjected to torture, threatened with death, and finally forced to embrace Islam and serve the emir as a military instructor.[60] November passed with more frequent raids on the part of the frontier begs but still no reply to the draft treaty from Muzaffar. In December a Bukharan ambassador finally arrived in Tashkent. He came without a signed copy of the treaty, but he also brought no new demands and agreed with everything that was said to him; the emir was obviously stalling for time again. On December 19 Kaufman wrote to Muzaffar requesting ratification and demanding the immediate release of Sluzhenko and his comrades.[61] In preparation for the final reckoning with Bukhara, Kaufman covered his rear by concluding peace with Kokand. The commercial convention, which he signed on January 29, 1868, was ratified by Khan Khudayar on February 13.[62]

The Second Bukharan Campaign

Muzaffar ad-Din had not yet given up all hope of resisting the Russians, and during the winter of 1867–68 he levied emergency war taxes on the merchants and mullahs. His fear of a repetition of the defeats of 1866, however, made him hesitate to renew hostilities. His position at home was also none too secure. Muzaffar had alienated the Uzbeg aristocracy by continuing his father's policy of curbing their activities in the interest of a more strongly centralized state.[63] Now he labored under the additional odium of not having been able to stem the tide of the infidel's advance. The clergy early in 1868 clamored for war, arguing that the emir was obligated to fight because of the war taxes he had collected. By the beginning of March many of the begs and rich merchants had added their voices to the call for war in defense of faith and country. Muzaffar still hesitated. On March 2 Kaufman received a letter from the Bukharan kush-begi, conveying the information that Sluzhenko and his companions had been released but avoiding a positive reply to the terms of the draft treaty of the previous September. Kaufman in turn released the Bukharan envoy who had been in Tashkent since December, in hopes that the treaty would soon be ratified. In late March the war party in Bukhara, led by the clergy, took advantage of the emir's absence from the capital to proclaim a holy war against Russia. In Samarkand the mullahs proved so unruly that the commander of the garrison, a fugitive Siberian Cossack named Osman, was forced to call out the troops to restore order. When Muzaffar returned to the capital, he met with so much hostility that he was forced to withdraw to Kermine, whence he bowed to the war party and proclaimed a holy war. Tashkent learned of these events on April 8.[64]

Kaufman took to the field and defeated the Bukharan army on May 1, the same day that he received the emir's reply to the draft treaty. The reply was unacceptable. Addressed to the emperor personally, the treaty had been rewritten so as to make it appear that Muzaffar freely granted the desired concessions.[65] On May 2 Kaufman occupied Samarkand. Hoping that the emir would now be more compliant, Kaufman halted there and on May 11 proposed the following peace terms: a six-point commercial convention virtually identical to that concluded with Kokand in February and incorporating the essence of the commercial articles of the 1867 draft treaty, cession of the beglik of Samarkand, payment of a war indemnity, and recognition of Russia's title to all gains made at Bukhara's expense since 1865.[66] The peace terms of 1868 differed substantially from the draft treaty of the previous year. No mention was made of the right of Russian subjects to reside and acquire real property in Bukhara, or of the extraterritorial criminal jurisdiction of the governor general over Russians in the khanate. Although Kaufman dropped the article specifically restricting the emir's relations with Russia to the governor general, the restriction had been implied in the plenipotentiary powers granted him at his appointment and had, in fact, been practiced since 1865 when Cherniaev frustrated the emir's attempt to send an embassy to St. Petersburg. The most important change concerned the Russo-Bukharan boundary. By retaining Samarkand, Russia would control the flow of water in the Zarafshan River, upon which Bukhara's life depended, and would thus be in a position to influence decisively the khanate's policies.

Heartened, perhaps, by the suspension of the Russian advance, Muzaffar did not respond to Kaufman's offer; instead, he beheaded one of the two Persians who brought it and threw the other into a pit. On May 16, the expiration date of the ultimatum for accepting peace terms, Kaufman resumed his advance and took Katta-Kurgan. To the Bukharan envoys who contacted him there, he offered a choice of peace terms. Bukhara could either pay an indemnity of 1,150,000 tillas (4,600,000 rubles) over a period of eight years, after which the Russians would return to Bukhara all their conquests from Yani-Kurgan to Katta-Kurgan inclusive, or pay an indemnity of only 125,000 tillas and recognize all Russia's gains since 1865.

On May 23 the envoys agreed to the second course and were given until June 2 to return with 10,000 tillas as the first installment.[67] Yet the Bukharans were not quite ready to give up the struggle: they used the truce to concentrate their forces and on June 2 attacked the Russians in force at Zerabulak, just west of Katta-Kurgan. Muzaffar's army was routed, and a simultaneous revolt in Samarkand was suppressed, which crushed Bukhara's last hopes.

The Treaty of 1868

When the news of the Bukharan defeat reached the capital of the khanate, a new insurrection broke out, and the emir fled into the Kizil Kum Desert. Three days later, after the Russians had withdrawn to Samarkand to quell its revolt and order was restored in his own dominions, Muzaffar appeared in Kermine and decided to give up the struggle. His envoys arrived in Samarkand on June 10 with orders to conclude peace. Two days later a messenger arrived from Kermine bearing the emir's offer of unconditional surrender and abdication and his request for permission to be received by Alexander II and then allowed to go to Mecca as a pilgrim.[68]

The occupation of "Bukhara the Noble," the religious capital of Central Asia, would have greatly enhanced Russia's prestige among her Moslem subjects and neighbors. Kaufman was faced, however, with St. Petersburg's repeated injunctions against increasing the burden of territorial conquests. These injunctions were given added weight by his lack of sufficient troops to occupy the capital of the khanate while adequately protecting Russia's left flank against the threat posed by Shahr-i Sabz, where were gathered all the begs who had become dissatisfied with the emir and wished to continue the war against Russia.[69] The occupation of the remainder of the khanate could probably have been carried out only at great cost and with much bloodshed in view of the anti-Russian feeling in Bukhara and the turbulent internal state of the country.[70] Even with Russian help, it took Muzaffar two years to reassert his control. In these circumstances Muzaffar was probably the most reliable ruler possible for Bukhara, because he had been chastened by his defeats of the past three years and was dependent entirely upon Russia for the retention of his shaky throne. His continued rule would spare Russia the additional financial and manpower burdens against which the

emperor and the foreign and finance ministries were so firmly set.
The desire to avoid diplomatic complications with England, while
undoubtedly contributing to the government's cautious policy, probably did not play a direct role in Kaufman's decision.

General von Kaufman accordingly replied to the emir on June
12: "I have never intended nor desired to destroy the khanate of
Bukhara; I repeat now what I have said previously, that the peace
and tranquillity of Russia's neighbors constitute the goal of my labors
and even of my wars. When I can secure peace, I terminate hostilities."[71] Kaufman advised the emir against the unconditional surrender of his troops, reminding him that they would prove useful in
subduing rebellious begs and hostile members of his own family.[72]
The governor general insisted only on the demands he had made
before the final battle of June 2. Nor did he humiliate the emir by
forcing him to appear in person before his conqueror, as the khan
of Khiva was later compelled to do. On July 18 in Karshi Muzaffar
ad-Din signed the peace conditions submitted to him in May, and
Russia and Bukhara were at peace.

Contrary to the assertions of recent Soviet historians,[73] the 1868
treaty with Bukhara did not in any way limit her sovereignty. The
treaty proper was merely a commercial convention, providing only
for the opening of Bukhara to Russian traders on an equal footing
with native merchants. The supplementary peace conditions defined
the Russo-Bukharan boundary and imposed a war indemnity on Bukhara. The only clause that cast some doubt on Bukhara's sovereignty was Article One of the secret supplement, which declared
that the emir would pay a war indemnity as "a sign of his sincere
desire to live in friendship with the Russian Empire and to acquire
the protection of His Imperial Majesty the Great Emperor of All the
Russias." The treaty itself did not refer to Russian "protection," nor
was it mentioned anywhere else.

In practice, however, Bukhara, like Kokand, had lost much of
its independence of action. Although nothing in their respective
commercial conventions with Russia infringed upon their independence, both states were in fact at Russia's mercy. Bukhara had been
deprived of the middle and upper Zarafshan Valley, while Kokand
had been driven back into the Fergana Valley. Russia had demonstrated the ability to impose her demands at will upon both states,
and both had been forcibly opened to Russian commerce after

decades of resistance. Further opposition to Russia was recognized as futile. In Bukhara especially, the emir's dependence on Russia as his sole reliable source of support against rebellious begs and hostile mullahs, combined with Russia's control over the water of the Zarafshan, made an anti-Russian policy extremely risky. Thus, Bukhara emerged from the war of 1865–1868 in full possession of her legal sovereignty but a *de facto* dependency of the Russian Empire.

Muzaffar ad-Din, Emir of Bukhara, 1860–1885

3 / The Consolidation of Russia's Position in Bukhara

Russo-Bukharan Tensions

Russia's primary interest in the khanates of Central Asia, after 1868 as before, was to ensure the friendly disposition of their governments in order to facilitate the maintenance of law and order along the Russian frontier and to prevent the penetration of British influence into the areas adjacent to that frontier. Russia's policy toward her new dependencies in the first years after 1868 was one of indifference, except on the questions of their attitude toward herself and their ability to maintain political stability within their borders. No advantage was taken of the economic concessions wrung from Bukhara and Kokand. The commercial convention with Bukhara remained a dead letter for several years, and the emir continued to levy discriminatory duties against Russian merchants (the illegal duty thus collected was later returned at Kaufman's demand). Russian trade with the khanates did not appreciably increase. No Russian agents, commercial or political, were maintained in the khanates, although the khan of Kokand several times requested a permanent Russian resident at his court and maintained an agent of his own at Tashkent.[1] Russia conducted relations with her new dependencies by means of the centuries-old method of exchanging occasional embassies. She relied for information of the khanates on the reports of these same embassies, of her frontier military commanders, and of chance travelers and merchants.

In the first years after becoming a dependency Kokand posed no problem for Russia. Khan Khudayar had conceded defeat as early as 1866 and had since remained a faithful ally, even during Russia's war against Bukhara. For a short time in the summer of 1868 St. Petersburg even considered putting him on the throne of Bukhara.[2] Kokand remained Russia's favorite until broken up in the civil strife of 1875–1876. Bukhara, however, continued to be a source of con-

cern to Tashkent and St. Petersburg for several years after the treaty
of 1868 because the emir's devotion to Russia remained in doubt.
Whereas Khudayar was granted the exalted title of "Illustriousness"
(*Svetlost*) in 1872, Muzaffar had to remain content with "High
Eminence" until his death.[3]

The initial reaction of the emperor and Gorchakov to the news
of the 1868 campaign against Bukhara was anxiety over the preservation of the khanate's independence and strong opposition to annexation, with its attendant burdens in men and money and diplomatic
complications vis-à-vis Great Britain.[4] On June 4, 1868, Alexander II
instructed Kaufman, via the foreign ministry's Asiatic Department,
to advance no farther and to withdraw his troops from Bukhara as
soon as possible.[5] Although Kaufman had no intention of annexing
Bukhara proper, the final disposition of Samarkand and Katta-Kurgan (which together with the surrounding rural areas constituted
the Zarafshan *Okrug*) remained in question. From the first Kaufman
urged the permanent retention of Samarkand as the key to the
water supply of the Bukharan oasis, and Miliutin supported this
position in St. Petersburg against the views of the foreign and finance
ministries.[6] In the end Kaufman and Miliutin prevailed, as the military had so often in Central Asia in the preceding decade, and the
district was formally annexed to Russia in 1873.

Russia's respect for Bukhara's integrity was put to the test very
soon after the victory of 1868. During the late summer of that year
the emir's oldest son, Abd al-Malik, the *katta-türa* (crown prince)
and beg of Karshi, revolted. Whereas Muzaffar, already at odds with
the nobles and clergy, had added to his unpopularity by surrendering
to Russia, the katta-türa was popular for his implacable hostility to
the Russians. He took refuge in Shahr-i Sabz, whence he rallied all
the dissident forces in the khanate and posed a serious threat to his
father. General von Kaufman resolved to support the emir in order
to prevent the accession to power of the anti-Russian party and the
reopening of hostilities, as well as to demonstrate to Muzaffar the
tangible advantages of Russian friendship. Kaufman ordered Major
General A. K. Abramov, commandant of the Zarafshan Okrug, to
stage a troop buildup at Djam on the border between Samarkand and
Shahr-i Sabz in order to intimidate the rulers of Shahr-i Sabz, but he
was to refrain from launching an offensive.

Abd al-Malik had meanwhile raised the standard of revolt in
Bukhara and gained allies among the Turkoman and Kazakh tribes

and even in Khiva. At various times the rebels held Nurata, Chi-rakchi, and Karshi. At the end of summer a Russian reconnaissance toward Kitab forced the begs of Shahr-i Sabz to recall their troops from Bukhara and checked the pretender's advance. Yet the danger that the popular, energetic, and hostile Abd al-Malik might replace his unpopular and compliant father remained. Thus, when Muzaffar appealed to Abramov for help, the Russian general moved on Karshi, defeated the katta-türa on October 21, and occupied Karshi two days later. After a brief occupation Abramov handed Karshi over to the emir on October 27. Muzaffar was so pleased with this action of his Russian deliverers that he asked them to capture for him Shahr-i Sabz and Yakkabah; he even offered to pay the military expenses. Shahr-i Sabz, however, was by this time so frightened by Russia's display of power that its begs promised to return Yakkabah to the emir.[7] There the problem of Shahr-i Sabz rested temporarily. Abd al-Malik, after further attempts at revolt had taken him and a small band of loyal followers to Shahr-i Sabz, Hisar, Karshi, and Kermine, fled to Nurata and thence to Khiva at the end of December. He spent the remainder of his life in exile in Khiva, Afghanistan, Kash-gar, and finally India, where he died in Peshawar in 1909.[8]

St. Petersburg reacted unfavorably to the news of General Abramov's expedition against Karshi. On December 28 Stremoukhov admonished Kaufman concerning the undesirability of "armed in-tervention" in "the political affairs of a neighboring khanate" and again urged the necessity "of evacuating as soon as possible Samar-kand and the whole Zarafshan Okrug" and "returning to the eastern side" of the watershed between the basins of the Amu-Darya and the Sir-Darya.[9]

Because of the disruption caused by Abd al-Malik's revolt, Bu-khara lagged behind in payments on her war indemnity to Russia. At the beginning of 1869 a Russian manufacturer and merchant, M. A. Khludov, offered to advance the emir the 276,000 rubles he still owed if the Russian government would guarantee the loan. Kaufman welcomed Khludov's proposal as a means of bringing Bu-khara under the influence of Russian capital and thereby strengthen-ing Russia's political influence as well as her economic links with Bukhara. Probably to avoid just such an expansion of Russian activ-ity in Bukhara, which would have endangered the policy of non-intervention, St. Petersburg suggested that Khludov be content with a guarantee of the loan by the commercial community of Bukhara.

On this rock the scheme foundered. The emir nevertheless brought pressure to bear on his merchants to supply the needed funds, and the last installment on the indemnity was paid in April 1870, only seven months late.[10] The delay may have been due in part to rumors current in Bukhara that Kaufman, who was then in St. Petersburg, was about to be replaced as governor general, with a consequent change in Russian policy.[11]

The belief that the terms imposed upon him in 1868 might be softened died hard with the emir of Bukhara. Immediately after the conclusion of peace in June 1868 Muzaffar had requested permission for his fourth and favorite son, Abd Allah Fattah-khan, to be educated in St. Petersburg. Although Kaufman and the emperor had consented, Abd al-Malik's revolt prevented the execution of this plan. In July 1869, the emir decided to send his favorite, then twelve years old, to St. Petersburg as the titular head of a mission to intercede with the emperor for the return of the Bukharan territories conquered by Russia. Although direct communication between the Central Asian rulers and the imperial government had been refused before the reduction of the khanates, such communication was allowed as a courtesy after the conclusion of the 1868 treaties. Kokand had sent an embassy to St. Petersburg soon after the signing of her treaty in February 1868. Such embassies, however, were restricted to purely ceremonial functions. Kaufman's admonition that he had full authority to settle all matters on the spot was repeated to the Bukharan envoys in St. Petersburg in October 1869. Alexander II and his ministers not only refused the emir's petition but affirmed that relations with neighboring khanates were the province of the governor general of Turkestan and that St. Petersburg would take no direct part in such dealings. In Tashkent on their way home from the imperial court the young prince and the ambassador accompanying him made one last effort in March 1870 to obtain the return of Samarkand, but with no more success.[12]

The return of Samarkand to Bukhara, although much discussed in Russia in the winter of 1869–1870,[13] was an impossible step for St. Petersburg to take at the time in view of the uncertain future of Russo-Bukharan relations. An early cause for the emir's friendship to waver may have been Russia's denial of his request for aid in subjugating Shahr-i Sabz in the fall of 1868. Another factor in the growing tension with Russia was the emir's activities in eastern Bukhara in 1869–1870. After a campaign of six or seven months in 1869

Muzaffar's troops conquered Hisar and Kulab, whose begs had never recognized the emir's authority and had supported Abd al-Malik's revolt.[14] At the beginning of 1870 the Bukharan troops advanced to Karategin. Until the summer of the previous year Karategin had enjoyed de facto independence under one Muzaffar-shah, although the province was nominally subject to Kokand. While Bukhara was extending her control over Hisar and Kulab, Kokandian troops moved into Karategin, sent Muzaffar-shah to Kokand as a prisoner, and installed Shir Ali in his place. After the reduction of Kulab, Bukhara accused Shir Ali of having supported Sari-khan, the former beg of Kulab. Bukharan troops entered Karategin and helped Muhammad Rahim, Muzaffar-shah's nephew, expel Shir Ali. The khan of Kokand complained to Tashkent against Bukhara's encroachment on his dominions. It was important that General von Kaufman, as the representative of the power of which both Bukhara and Kokand were dependencies, avoid an open clash between the two, for the loser would be disaffected toward Russia. Having decided that the letter implicating Shir Ali in Sari-khan's struggle with Bukhara was a forgery, Kaufman advised the emir to restore Karategin to Kokand and urged Khudayar to defer his projected expedition to recover the province. In the meantime, however, Shir Ali had been captured by the Bukharans while attempting to reoccupy Karategin. Kaufman then suggested a compromise. The emir was to free Shir Ali, while Khudayar was to liberate Muzaffar-shah and reinstall him as mir of Karategin. Bukhara and Kokand agreed to Kaufman's plan, but Muhammad Rahim successfully resisted Kokand's attempt to restore his uncle and continued to rule Karategin as an independent state for six more years.[15]

Although Russia's mediation in the Karategin dispute may have increased her influence,[16] it did little to lessen the tensions building up between Tashkent and Bukhara. Kaufman was undoubtedly offended by the emir's attempt to negotiate over his head with St. Petersburg, and according to Miliutin, he was also angered that Muzaffar had undertaken the expedition to Hisar and Kulab without his knowledge and concurrence.[17] Muzaffar for his part was disappointed over the failure of his son's mission to Russia and may also have felt injured at having to restore Kokandian suzerainty over Karategin. Despite an agreement between Kaufman and the emir at the end of 1869 allowing the troops of each state to pursue robber bands onto the other's territory, necessitated by the widespread increase of frontier disorders attendant upon the internal warfare in eastern Bukhara,[18] Tashkent viewed Bukhara with lively suspicion by the spring of 1870.

As early as June 1869 Kaufman reported to Miliutin that anti-Russian feeling was growing in Bukhara and that Muzaffar was vacillating between dread of Russia and fear of Shir Ali, the emir of Kabul and Britain's protégé. Despite Stremoukhov's assurances that a Central Asian coalition against Russia was an "unfeasible fantasy," Kaufman continued to warn in January and February 1870 of Shir Ali's plans to strengthen his position on the Amu-Darya and to draw Bukhara, Shahr-i Sabz, and Khiva into an anti-Russian alliance.[19] During March and April Kaufman kept Miliutin informed of his suspicions that Bukhara was negotiating with Turkey as well as with Khiva and Afghanistan.[20]

Moreover, as of February 1870 the emir had still not paid the balance due on the war indemnity. These and other reasons, such as that a Russian withdrawal from Samarkand might be attributed to weakness by the population of Central Asia, were adduced to justify to Sir Andrew Buchanan, the British ambassador in St. Petersburg, Russia's continued occupation of Samarkand.[21] Kaufman's offer in January or early February to return Samarkand to the emir if he would come to that city and accept it from Kaufman's hands[22] was either designed to humble Muzaffar ad-Din publicly or made in the knowledge that protocol and his own pride would prevent the emir from accepting. At any rate the offer was declined, and Russian administration took firmer hold.

Russo-Bukharan Adjustments

In order to clarify Bukhara's intentions, Kaufman in mid-May 1870 dispatched an embassy under Colonel S. I. Nosovich, commandant of the Djizak *Uezd*. At the same time General Abramov made a conciliatory gesture in Samarkand by timing the release of a large quantity of water in the Zarafshan to coincide with Nosovich's arrival in Bukhara. The khanate was suffering from an acute water shortage after an exceptionally dry winter.[23] The Nosovich mission found in Bukhara a rival embassy from Shir Ali and confirmed that Muzaffar had also been negotiating with Khiva and Turkey. After some hesitation induced by the threats of the Afghans, the emir in early June decided to remain faithful to Russia, perhaps because he was wary that in an anti-Russian alliance he might be left to bear the brunt of the struggle alone.[24] He received Nosovich warmly and requested Russia's help in defending Bukhara against Afghanistan. He specifically wanted a present of four thousand rifles and a technical and military aid mission of Russian cannon-founders, gunsmiths, and officers to instruct his army. Nosovich did not raise the emir's hopes and merely advised him to put his requests in a letter to the governor general. The Russian envoy also impressed upon Muzaffar that General von Kaufman's friendship was more reliable than that of all Bukhara's Moslem neighbors.

Since Russia had been discussing with England for over a year the ideas of a neutral zone or a belt of buffer states in Central Asia, the emir's request for military assistance was refused by Kaufman, and he was cautioned to avoid an open break with Afghanistan and to limit himself to holding the right bank of the Amu-Darya.[25] Nosovich's mission nevertheless temporarily cleared the air. Kaufman reported to Gorchakov on Nosovich's success in optimistic terms: "The emir has firmly decided to adhere to his alliance with Russia. He has repudiated any connection with the schemes of Kabul and Shahr-i Sabz . . . He sees his salvation solely in friendship with his powerful neighbor, toward whom he is prepared to act as a dependent, almost a vassal."[26]

Muzaffar did not have long to wait to reap the benefits of his renewed promise of loyalty to Russia. In late June 1870 a detachment of Cossacks operating out of Samarkand was attacked by unknown raiders. At the same time there was an increase in the number of raids on the frontier areas of the Zarafshan Okrug, which had just been doubled in size by Abramov's reduction of the petty principalities of Kohistan on the upper Zarafshan.[27] Tashkent suspected the begs of Shahr-i Sabz, Djura-beg and Baba-beg, of fomenting the border raids and specifically accused them of sheltering Haidar-beg, the robber chieftain who was believed guilty of the attack on the Cossacks. Kaufman therefore ordered Abramov to capture the twin cities of Shahr and Kitab, which together constituted Shahr-i Sabz, and hand them over to Muzaffar. Almost a year earlier the emir's second request[28] for Russian aid in conquering Shahr-i Sabz had been turned down because at the time Djura-beg and Baba-beg were careful to soothe Russia by meeting all her demands and by handing over fugitives from Russian Turkestan.[29] Now, however, Kaufman believed Shahr-i Sabz to have given provocation, or perhaps he merely pretended to believe so in order to cement his renewed friendship with Muzaffar. On August 14 after a three-day siege Abramov took the twin cities, and on August 16 he formally handed them over to the Bukharan authorities. Djura-beg and Baba-beg fled to Kokand, whose khan delivered them to the Russians. With an eye to the former begs' potential value in the future against a re-calcitrant Bukhara, Tashkent treated them well and granted them commissions in the Turkestan army. Djura-beg retired with the rank of major general, and Baba-beg with that of colonel. Haidar-beg was captured, tried in Samarkand for the attack on the Cossacks, and acquitted.[30]

In the spring of 1871 the cycle of Russo-Bukharan relations began to repeat itself. The crop failure of the previous fall had led to famine in Bukhara. Many Bukharans blamed the crop failure on insufficient water for irrigation and accused the Russians at Samar-kand of neglecting the dam and not supplying enough water to Bukhara. Moreover, because of the high price of grain in Russian Turkestan, Kaufman had prohibited all grain exports. Muzaffar's attempts to have the prohibition lifted in order to relieve the famine were unsuccessful; the most Kaufman would do was to send a gift of fifty-four tons of grain. Bukhara was rife with rumors of conspira-cies against the emir and of renewed negotiations between the emir and neighboring rulers against Russia. Despite Muzaffar's explicit promise of friendship for Russia, the governor general was disturbed over the rumors. In the spring of 1871, therefore, he sent K. V. Struve to report on the state of affairs in Bukhara, to assure the emir of Russia's support, and to sound him out on the question of Russia's projected campaign against Khiva. Struve, the career diplomat who had led the ill-fated embassy of 1865–1866, was from 1868 to 1873 attached to Kaufman as his diplomatic factotum and liaison with the foreign ministry. As a result of Struve's mission, once again the air was cleared. He concluded that the emir was well-disposed toward Russia, and Muzaffar declared his willingness to permit passage through his territory of Russian troops moving against Khiva and to provide these troops with the necessary supplies.[31] In the words of the British ambassador to Russia, Tashkent's relations with Bu-khara were again "entirely satisfactory."[32]

In June, Kaufman again gave concrete proof of Russia's good intentions toward the emir of Bukhara. One of the newly appointed begs of Shahr-i Sabz visited the governor general in Samarkand and showed him the respect that should have been reserved for the emir alone. For this breach of etiquette the beg was deposed by Muzaffar and fled to Samarkand. In the absence of any extradition treaty and in view of the emir's noncompliance with previous Russian requests for the surrender of deserters, Kaufman might well have given asylum in this case. Instead, to prove Russia's intention to uphold the emir's authority over his subjects, General von Kaufman handed over the fugitive, who at Kaufman's suggestion received a pardon from Muzaffar.[33]

During the winter of 1871–1872 the question of the use of the water of the Zarafshan was finally settled. A committee composed of three Russians and three Bukharans, presided over by Major General Abramov, met at Samarkand and decided to replace the old water-control works, which needed annual repairs, with a permanent structure built by the Russian government. The farmers who used the water for irrigation, most of whom were on the Bukharan side of the frontier, had formerly paid an annual tax to cover repairs; these payments were henceforth to be applied to the liquidation of the debt incurred by Russia in constructing the new works. It was also decided that twice a year, if Bukhara reported an inadequate water supply, the irrigation canals in the Samarkand *Otdel* would be ordered closed for two weeks in order to raise the level of the river in the khanate.[34]

Another question raised by the Russian occupation of Samarkand was settled during this period. The Bukharan clergy had formerly derived revenues from a large number of *vaqf* lands (estates belonging to religious and charitable institutions), which were now under Russian rule in the Zarafshan Okrug. Similarly, the clergy of Samarkand possessed many estates in the area still under the emir's rule. Since the revenues from the estates in the khanate were greater than those from the estates in the Zarafshan Okrug, Muzaffar confiscated the former and allowed Kaufman to do the same with the latter.[35]

Kaufman's obliging attitude in the matter of the fugitive beg of Shahr-i Sabz and the settlement of the Zarafshan water and vaqf issues helped to reconcile Muzaffar to his new status as a client of Russia. Even more effective in this respect was the failure of his last desperate appeal to Britain and Turkey for protection against Russia. Embassies dispatched in the summer of 1871 to Calcutta and Constantinople returned the following year with not even so much as a promise of support.[36] In the meantime Bukharan fears of an impending Russian attack were quieted in the spring of 1872 when the emir, at Kaufman's suggestion, sent an envoy to Tashkent to confirm the absence of any hostile preparations on Russia's part. The emir's ambassador was accompanied on his return to Bukhara in late April by N. F. Petrovskii, an official of the finance ministry, whose principal task was to investigate the state of Russian trade with Bukhara.[37]

Despite the radical change in Bukhara's relationship to Russia during the intervening six and a half years, Petrovskii was struck as forcibly as Glukhovskoi had been in 1865 with the highly developed system of espionage, the extreme suspiciousness of the Bukharan authorities, and the restrictions imposed on the movements of official representatives of a friendly power. Although Petrovskii was treated with all outward respect due to a representative of Bukhara's de facto protector, his mission of collecting information on the khanate's trade was obstructed at every turn by official escorts who prevented any contact with the people, by repeated refusals of permission to go about the various towns or even to visit certain towns (Chardjui and Kerki), and by constant surveillance. Petrovskii also gathered reports that Muzaffar had again been in communication with his Moslem neighbors. Envoys from Afghanistan and Khiva had allegedly departed from Bukhara just before Petrovskii's arrival.[38]

Petrovskii proposed the establishment of direct postal communications between the capital of the khanate and the Russian frontier at Katta-Kurgan. The Bukharan government refused, saying there was no need since nothing of this nature had ever existed in the past.[39] Letters continued to be sent with chance travelers for another decade and a half. Bukhara could afford to reject Petrovskii's proposal because there was no official pressure behind it. St. Petersburg's entire policy toward Bukhara consisted of the preservation of peace, friendly relations, the emir's authority in his own country, and the legal rights of Russian merchants. Russia's indifference to everything beyond these limits left Bukhara largely to her own devices.

Petrovskii's mission again illustrated the difficulty Russia encountered in gathering reliable information on her Central Asian dependencies. In the absence of any permanent agents in the khanates, Tashkent had to rely on missions that were dispatched on an average of once a year for specific objects. The success of such missions depended upon the skill of those to whom they were entrusted in circumventing the obstacles invariably placed in their paths by the Bukharan authorities. The Nosovich mission in 1870 remained confined to quarters while in the capital, except for official calls on Bukharan dignitaries. The kush-begi claimed that the emir's government could not take responsibility for the Russians' safety in the streets of the capital unless they were accompanied by an escort. Muzaffar went even further. He refused the mission freedom of movement about the city, arguing that foreigners were not allowed to ride through the streets on horseback and that the Russians would not like to go on foot.[40]

The practice of accepting personal gifts from the emir and provincial governors by the Russian missions conformed to Central Asian usage but undoubtedly limited their effectiveness in conducting relations and obtaining information. The members of Nosovich's mission accepted gifts of *khalats* (native gowns) and horses, and Struve's did the same. Nosovich accepted a gift of 400 rubles, and Struve received 6,000 rubles, although General von Kaufman had forbidden Russian agents to take money. Colonel Kolzakov, who in 1871 conveyed to the emir Russia's condolence on the death of one of his sons, also received various gifts, although he refused to don a khalat over his Russian uniform. Petrovskii accepted khalats and horses and even money from the beg of Kermine.[41]

The ineffectiveness of this method of collecting information was best illustrated by the question of the slave trade. Although the treaty of 1868 did not mention the slave trade, Russia made no secret of her disapproval of a practice by then universally condemned in the West. Thinking to persuade Russia to return Samarkand, the Bukharan ambassador who accompanied the emir's son to St. Petersburg in 1869 announced that Muzaffar had abolished the slave trade in Bukhara in order to please the emperor.[42] L. F. Kostenko, one of the members of Nosovich's mission, confirmed that the slave market in the capital had been closed since 1868, but he had no means of verifying this assertion in person. Struve in 1871 found no evidence of the continuance of the slave trade, but he too was apparently taken in by the Bukharan authorities. Petrovskii reported the following year that the slave trade was still being carried on throughout the khanate and that he had personally visited the largest slave market, in a caravansary in the bazaar in the center of the capital.[43] Eugene Schuyler, the American secretary of legation in St. Petersburg, who visited Bukhara in 1873, confirmed Petrovskii's report and even purchased a slave and brought him back to Russia as proof.[44]

In 1872 the first restriction was placed on the emir's exercise of
his sovereign right to conduct relations freely with states other than
Russia. The peace settlement of 1868 had not in any way limited this
right. Muzaffar continued to exchange envoys with Khiva,[45] Afghanistan, and the Ottoman Empire. But when in the spring of 1872 a
Bukharan envoy appeared in Constantinople seeking Turkish and
British assistance against Russia, Tashkent protested. Muzaffar consequently agreed to renounce his right to communicate directly with
the Porte without the previous knowledge of the governor general
of Turkestan.[46] Apparently the problem did not quite end there, for
in January 1873 the Russian ambassador in Constantinople complained about the activities of another Bukharan envoy.[47]

The Question of a New Treaty

The results of Bukhara's first four and a half years as a Russian
dependency were somewhat disappointing to General von Kaufman.
There had been repeated tensions between Tashkent and Bukhara;
Muzaffar had flirted with the anti-Russian rulers of Afghanistan,
Khiva, and Turkey; his government had tried to hide the continuance of the slave trade; the conduct of relations by means of sporadic
missions had proved unsatisfactory; and the operations of Russian
merchants in Bukhara had not expanded appreciably. In short, because of St. Petersburg's policy of nonintervention in the internal
affairs of the khanates and its extreme reluctance to add to the
burdens of empire, Russia's political and economic ascendency over
Bukhara was far from complete.

As early as 1871 Kaufman proposed to supplement the inadequate settlement of 1868 with a new, more far-reaching treaty. The
governor general's proposal was (1) to make definitive the existing
Russo-Bukharan frontier, leaving the Zarafshan Okrug to Russia;
(2) to establish a Russian commercial agent in Bukhara and a permanent representative of the emir in Tashkent; (3) to regulate the
issuance of commercial visas and passports; (4) to secure for Russian
subjects in Bukhara the right to take up various trades and to exploit
the natural resources of the country; (5) to render obligatory the
surrender of fugitive criminals; and (6) to establish regulations for
the conduct of lawsuits between Russians and Bukharans. Kaufman
also proposed a secret supplement to the new treaty, which would
have (7) bound the emir to follow the instructions of the Russian

government in dealing with his other neighbors; (8) obligated him to follow the governor general's advice in appointing the kush-begi and the begs of the provinces bordering on Russia; (9) pledged the emir not to cede to Afghanistan or any other foreign power the passages of the Amu-Darya; (10) granted to Russia the right to maintain steamship docks on the Bukharan banks of the Amu-Darya; (11) pledged the governor general to aid the emir against his internal and external enemies, as long as Bukhara was not the aggressor; (12) guaranteed the emir's dominions within their existing limits; (13) pledged Kaufman to intercede with the emperor for recognition as the emir's heir of whichever of his sons Muzaffar would designate and for a guarantee of his father's dominions to the heir (the fugitive Abd al-Malik would be expressly deprived forever of the right of succession); and (14) bound Muzaffar, as a favor to the emperor, to forbid the slave trade and to take steps toward the gradual abolition of slavery itself.[48] Kaufman's proposed secret treaty would have drastically curtailed the emir of Bukhara's sovereignty and made him a de jure vassal of the Russian Empire. He would have been deprived of the control of Bukhara's foreign affairs, of the appointment of certain important officials, and of the right to dispose of his own territory, and by implication Russia would have gained a voice in naming his successor.

The governor general's proposals were not at all to the taste of St. Petersburg. A government conference in the capital on November 4, 1872, rejected the more drastic articles and accepted the others only in a watered-down form. Kaufman was instructed (1) to introduce into the Zarafshan Okrug the same system of administration and taxation as had been established in the rest of Russian Turkestan (the old Bukharan administrative system had until then been retained in Samarkand) but to make no public declaration on the definitive annexation of the Zarafshan Okrug; (2) to make clear to the emir that Russia intended to act as a good neighbor and not to annex or subjugate his country, although Russian influence would continue to prevail in the khanate; (3) to conclude a new treaty with the emir when conditions were right, covering the establishment of Russian commercial agents in Bukharan towns and of a permanent Bukharan representative in Tashkent, as well as the drafting of detailed regulations governing commerce, crafts, trades, passports, and fugitives; and (4) to drop the idea of a secret treaty. An engagement to end the slave trade could, if the emir agreed, be included in the new treaty. Advice concerning the emir's foreign relations and his appointment to important offices of persons favorable to Russia could be conveyed to the emir informally by the governor general. If the emir himself should request it, St. Petersburg would not be averse to recognizing one of his sons as his heir.[49]

St. Petersburg was, as always, cautious not to proceed too far or too fast in Central Asia, out of anxiety to avoid straining Russia's finances and military manpower or provoking Britain's open opposition. At this time in particular London's attitude was important: negotiations between Britain and Russia leading toward a détente in Central Asia, which had been going on for over three and a half years, were nearing a successful issue. Russia was also on the verge of launching a new expedition against the still hostile khanate of Khiva, for the success of which England's neutrality was essential. The conclusion of a new treaty with Bukhara, in fact, had to await a settlement with Khiva.

Anglo-Russian Negotiations[50]

Prior to 1869 the British cabinet registered no great concern over the progress of Russian arms and influence in Central Asia. Ever since Britain's unsuccessful attempt in 1836–1841 to force Afghanistan into a state of vassalage like that of the Indian Native States, London's policy had been one of nonintervention in the lands beyond the Indus Valley. Sir John Lawrence, viceroy of India from 1864 and an ardent advocate of the policy of nonintervention, several times during 1864–1867 refused requests of Khudayar and Muzaffar for help against the Russians.[51]

London's and Calcutta's policy was predicated on the maintenance of Afghanistan as an independent buffer state, friendly to Britain and keeping Russia at a safe distance from India's borders. Upon their father's death in 1863, however, the sons of Emir Dost Muhammad began a bloody scramble for his inheritance, which soon threatened to destroy Afghanistan's integrity and raised the specter of Russian interference.[52] As a result of Afghanistan's growing political paralysis and Russia's advance toward the Amu-Darya, a struggle developed in London between the supporters of the established policy, led by Lawrence and Sir Stafford Northcote, secretary of state for India, and the proponents of a "forward policy," led by Sir Henry Rawlinson and other prominent veterans of the Indian service. In an influential article in the *Quarterly Review* for October 1865 Rawlinson argued that Britain must retain complete freedom to advance to Kandahar and Herat in Afghanistan if necessary to defend India against Russia's approach. Upon rejoining the Council of the Secretary of State for India in 1868 after a nine years' absence, Rawlinson went further: in an official memorandum he openly demanded abandonment of the traditional policy of "masterly inactivity" and establishment of a British "quasi-protectorate" over Afghanistan.[53]

Partly in defense against the critics of the government's policy, Lawrence in September 1867 proposed the division of Central Asia into English and Russian spheres of influence. Britain could thus regard without apprehension the extension of Russia's influence over Bukhara and Kokand and could even welcome the "civilizing effect" of such an influence.[54] Although Northcote rejected Lawrence's suggestion as unnecessary, and the prime minister, Lord Derby, doubted whether any understanding with Russia could be relied upon, the viceroy revived his proposal in November 1868 — after Russia's final victory over Bukhara and his receipt of Rawlinson's aggressive memorandum, which Northcote had forwarded to Calcutta.[55] On January 4, 1869, the government of India formally repudiated Rawlinson's proposals, favoring instead "some clear understanding" with Russia by which the latter "might be given to understand, in firm but courteous language, that it cannot be permitted to interfere in the affairs of Afghanistan, or in those of any State which lies contiguous to our frontier."[56] Gladstone, who had launched his first ministry in December 1868, threw the weight of the government behind Lawrence and the established policy. Instead of pressing for a division of Central Asia into spheres of influence, however, Gladstone's foreign secretary, the earl of Clarendon, in February 1869 broached to the Russian ambassador in London, Baron F. I. Brunnow, the possibility of a "neutral territory" between the possessions of Russia and Britain.[57] Prince Gorchakov welcomed the idea (which had first been suggested to the British in 1844 by his predecessor, Count Nesselrode)[58] and proposed Afghanistan for the role of the "independent zone," declaring that Russia regarded that country "as completely outside the sphere within which Russia may be called upon to exercise her influence."[59] Gorchakov thus envisaged a neutral zone beyond a Russian sphere of influence.

London, of course, could not countenance the neutralization of

Afghanistan. In April 1869 under pressure from the government of India, Clarendon rejected Gorchakov's suggestion and proposed instead "that the Upper Oxus [Amu-Darya], which was south of Bokhara, should be the boundary line which neither Power should permit their forces to cross." This seemed like a reversion to Lawrence's original proposal for a demarcation of spheres of influence, but Clarendon was also still thinking in terms of a neutral zone. He pointed out that the line of the upper Amu-Darya "would leave a large tract of country, apparently desert and marked on the map before us as belonging to the Khan of Khiva, between Afghanistan, and the territory already acquired by Russia." Russia would be allowed to cross the Amu-Darya if a punitive expedition against Khiva were necessary, but only on condition that she afterward pull back to the right bank of the river.[60] The two quite different concepts of a neutral zone and a demarcation of spheres of influence were thus thoroughly confused: Clarendon conceived of the neutral zone as lying between the Hindu Kush, which he believed to be Afghanistan's northern frontier, and the Amu-Darya, but he also envisaged that river as the "boundary line" between the British and Russian spheres of influence. The two foreign ministers met at Heidelberg on September 2 but made no progress. When Clarendon renewed his suggestion that the Amu-Darya formed "the most desirable line of demarcation for a neutral ground between the Russian and British possessions," Gorchakov countered by again proposing the neutralization of Afghanistan.[61]

Meanwhile, the earl of Mayo, who succeeded Lawrence in 1869, had continued the pressure from Calcutta for a division of Central Asia into spheres of influence. On June 3 he proposed that, instead of a neutral zone, "a wide border of independent states" be recognized between India and Russia. Afghanistan, Kashgar, and Kalat would constitute Britain's sphere of influence; Khiva, Bukhara, and Kokand would stand in the same relationship to Russia. The two great powers would bind themselves by "a pledge of mutual non-interference" in each other's spheres.[62] To move the negotiations toward an agreement on this basis, Mayo sent T. Douglas Forsyth via London to St. Petersburg, where Forsyth arrived in October.

Forsyth succeeded in steering the talks onto the subject of Britain's and Russia's responsibility for keeping the peace along their respective sides of the Amu-Darya, that is, within their respective spheres of influence. As far back as June 2 Gorchakov had asked Britain to use her influence at Kabul to prevent the possibility of an

Afghan attack against Bukhara, to which London had subsequently agreed.[63] On November 1 Miliutin and Stremoukhov agreed to Forsyth's counter-suggestion that "Russia should exercise all her influence to restrain Bukhara from transgressing the limits of Afghan territory," while Britain should use her influence to see that Afghanistan did not attack Bukhara. In an effort to ascertain the limits of Russia's authority within her sphere of influence, Miliutin and Stremoukhov inquired whether Russia's occupation of Bukhara, if it proved necessary, would "be considered as an infringement of the understanding between Russia and England." Forsyth gave his personal opinion that "so long as the integrity of Afghanistan was preserved, no objection could be made to the chastisement, or even, if properly warranted, the occupation of the country in whole or in part."[64] Russia, and presumably Britain as well, was thus to have full freedom of action within her sphere of influence. London never repudiated Forsyth's interpretation, and Mayo expressed great pleasure with his lieutenant's work. On November 5 the emperor agreed with Forsyth that Russia and Britain, to whom Miliutin and Stremoukhov had been referring as the "patrons" and "protectors" of Bukhara and Afghanistan, respectively, should restrain their clients from aggression. Alexander II perpetuated the confusion, however, by also informing Forsyth that he approved of the "neutral zone" concept.[65]

Actually the concepts of a neutral zone and of twin spheres of influence were compatible if the neutral zone was to be sandwiched in between the two spheres of influence. In November 1869, however, London and Calcutta ruled out the possibility of a neutral zone. Having ascertained that Emir Shir Ali was in effective control of Afghan Turkestan right up to the Amu-Darya, they abandoned Clarendon's original position and claimed the Amu-Darya as Afghanistan's northern boundary, just as it had been in the last years of Dost Muhammad's reign. In February 1870 Sir Andrew Buchanan, Britain's ambassador in St. Petersburg, suggested to Gorchakov and Stremoukhov that Russia follow a policy similar to Calcutta's by creating on the Russian frontier "a series of influential [influenced] but not tributary or neutralized States."[66] When Westmann, Russia's deputy foreign minister, again raised the idea of a neutral zone in November 1872, Lord Augustus Loftus, Buchanan's successor, replied that the term "neutral zone . . . merely referred to those independent States lying between the [southern] frontier of Afghanistan and the

Russian frontier, and that this idea would be perfectly represented by Bokhara in the north, and even, perhaps, by Afghanistan south of the Oxus."[67] Since Lord Granville, who had taken over the foreign office in 1870 on Clarendon's death, specifically approved of Loftus' remarks to Westmann,[68] they may be taken as the official British view of the matter. In London's opinion the neutral zone was in no real sense neutral; it consisted rather of British and Russian spheres of influence on either side of the Amu-Darya.

Russia, however, refused for three years to accept the Amu-Darya as Afghanistan's northern boundary, insisting that Badakhshan, south of the upper reaches of the river, together with its dependency Vakhan, was an independent state—a state, moreover, whose preservation as a buffer was vital to the security of Bukhara, Kokand, and Kashgar.[69] Badakhshan pointed like a dagger into the lands on the right bank of the river. Afghanistan's possession of this strategic wedge would especially endanger Bukhara's recently achieved control over Kulab, whose fugitive former beg was living at the Afghan emir's court.[70] By refusing to recognize the entire length of the Amu-Darya as Afghanistan's boundary, St. Petersburg was in fact holding out for the creation of a neutral zone, even though one restricted to a mountainous region remote from the principal routes between Afghanistan and Bukhara. Russia's insistence on this seemingly minor point was doubtless a tactical move to avoid a binding Central Asian settlement, pending the resolution of Russia's difficulties with Khiva. An agreement with Britain while Khiva remained hostile might well restrict Russia's freedom of action in dealing with the khan. In April 1869 Clarendon had interpreted the proposed understanding as barring any permanent Russian foothold on the left bank of the Amu-Darya at Khiva's expense. Mayo's proposal in June 1869 to assign Khiva specifically to Russia's sphere of influence, while more congenial to Russia's interests, had never been communicated to St. Petersburg as a formal offer. Russia thus had much to lose from a Central Asian settlement while the Khivan question remained unsolved and nothing to gain beyond Britain's recognition of territorial advances already made.

Britain, who had initiated the talks because of anxiety over the approaches to India, finally forced them to a successful issue. In September 1872 Lord Granville correctly surmised that St. Petersburg would be willing to purchase Britain's good will during the impending campaign against Khiva by settling the Afghan frontier on

London's terms.[71] Although Gorchakov once more presented his objections to recognizing Afghan sovereignty over Badakhshan and Vakhan and again suggested Afghanistan as a neutral zone,[72] he yielded shortly after the final decision to attack Khiva. On January 31, 1873, he accepted the Afghan boundary as claimed by Great Britain, with the understanding that Britain would "use all her influence" to induce Kabul to keep the peace and to refrain from further conquest.[73] In effect, any possibility of a neutral zone had been eliminated in favor of contiguous spheres of influence, although for the next several years Russia claimed that the 1873 understanding had created a neutral or intermediate zone in Afghanistan.[74] Not until February 1876, when St. Petersburg became apprehensive over Britain's reaction to its operations against Kokand, did it finally adhere to London's view that Afghanistan formed part of Britain's sphere of influence, as Bukhara did of Russia's.[75]

The Anglo-Russian negotiations of 1869–1873 resulted in an agreement on the boundary between Bukhara and Afghanistan and in an understanding that the two powers would use their influence— Russia's with Bukhara and Britain's with Afghanistan—to protect that boundary from violations by either side. Each power in practice recognized the sphere of influence of the other, beginning on the far bank of the Amu-Darya. Britain thus obtained Russia's promise not to cross Afghanistan's frontier, while Russia secured recognition of her influence over Bukhara and, by inference, Kokand from the only other imperialist power with interests in Central Asia.

Muhammad Rahim II, Khan of Khiva, 1864–1910

4 / The Conquest of Khiva and the Treaties of 1873

Relations with Khiva, 1867–1872

Khiva had traditionally been Russia's most troublesome neighbor in Central Asia. No sooner had Bukhara and Kokand been forced into submission than a showdown with Khiva appeared imminent. Continued difficulties were inevitable, if only because of the total absence of any mutually recognized boundaries between Khiva and the Russian Empire. Further causes of trouble were Khiva's strong natural defensive position as an island in a sea of deserts and Russia's two previous failures to subdue her, which undoubtedly encouraged the khan, Muhammad Rahim II (1864–1910), in his obstinate rejection of Russia's demands.

The immediate effect of Russia's advance up the Sir-Darya and of the resulting hostilities with Kokand and Bukhara was a temporary improvement in Russo-Khivan relations. Khiva abstained from her neighbors' quarrels with Russia, while her merchants profited from the suspension of direct trade between Bukhara and Russia. As Russia's exports to Bukhara declined in value from 4,655,000 rubles in 1864 to 877,000 rubles in 1866, her exports to Khiva rose during the same period from 11,000 to 1,565,000 rubles. In 1867, however, with the renewal of trade between Russia and Bukhara, Russian exports to Bukhara regained their former level, while those to Khiva fell by more than two thirds.[1] Khiva then resumed her traditional practices of raiding the Russian frontier, plundering caravans engaged in trade with Russia, and stirring up trouble among Russia's Kazakh subjects.

On November 19, 1867, General von Kaufman in his first letter to the khan of Khiva announced that Russian troops were being sent across the lower Sir-Darya to punish robbers who had been attacking Russian caravans. The following February the kush-begi, who governed the northern half of the khanate, protested the Russian crossing of the Sir-Darya, which he claimed as the Russo-Khivan boundary.[2] There the question rested, for Russia was not yet ready to turn her attention to Khiva while Bukhara remained openly hostile.

The year 1869 was one of preparation. Although relations with Bukhara had still not been worked out entirely to Russia's satisfaction, they offered little possibility of further armed conflict. Russia's attention was focused primarily on Krasnovodsk Bay on the eastern shore of the Caspian Sea, where as early as 1859 the imperial government had approved the establishment of a fortified trading post. In January 1865 a special government committee again recommended such a post in order to put an end to the depredations of the Turkomans on sea and land and to promote Russian trade with Central Asia by opening a shorter route via the Volga River, the Caspian Sea, and Krasnovodsk Bay. Whereas Orenburg lay sixty-five days distant from Khiva by caravan, Krasnovodsk Bay was only a twelve-day journey.[3] The question was tabled for the duration of the war against Bukhara, but in May 1869 the Society for the Promotion of Russian Industry and Trade petitioned the government to open a trade route from the Caspian to the Amu-Darya. The society argued that only by shortening the trade route and decreasing transport costs could Russian goods compete in Central Asia with English merchandise.[4]

General von Kaufman favored the Krasnovodsk project for other reasons. Khiva was becoming more and more recalcitrant. Its government was encouraging the Adai tribe of Kazakhs, dwelling between the Caspian and Aral Seas, in their revolt against Russia. Khiva also claimed as its frontier the Emba River, and sometimes even the Ural.[5] In the spring of 1869 Kaufman presented his views to P. N. Stremoukhov, director of the foreign ministry's Asiatic Department: "A landing in Krasnovodsk Bay will show the Khivans and the Kirgiz [Kazakhs] that His Highness has decided to halt the spread of the revolt . . . and that, in case Khiva is stubborn, she will be crushed. I think that the khan will not heed my counsels until he sees that measures are being taken for his punishment." On May 31 Stremoukhov protested to Kaufman against this interpretation of the government's plans for Krasnovodsk Bay and insisted that Russia had decided merely to establish a fortified factory, a "station for our squadron, and chiefly, for the development of our trade." Stremoukhov emphasized that no war against Khiva was contemplated: "I am convinced that there will prove to be no need for any foreign expeditions, and I dare say rather that the government ought to make every possible effort to suppress the disorders in the steppe as soon as possible."[6] St. Petersburg and Tashkent viewed the Krasnovodsk project from characteristically different angles. As usual, the foreign ministry wanted to believe in the prospects for peaceful control over Khiva, while the governor general put his faith in military action.

On August 12, 1869, Kaufman wrote to Muhammad Rahim, accusing him of inciting disturbances among nomads subject to Russia, allowing Russians to be held captive at Khiva, and giving refuge to rebels and robbers fleeing from Russian territory. Kaufman demanded a halt to these activities and punishment of the guilty parties, warning, "Similar acts have also taken place on the part of Kokand and Bukhara, the consequences of which are well known to you." On September 20 he again demanded the punishment of robbers, restoration of property stolen by them, and liberation of all Russian and Bukharan captives in Khiva.[7]

On October 10 the minister of war, D. A. Miliutin, notified the Society for the Promotion of Russian Industry and Trade that he supported fully their project for opening a trade route via Krasnovodsk Bay. Miliutin, like Kaufman, was undoubtedly interested in the political and military rather than purely commercial aspects of the project. On October 14 Stremoukhov advised Kaufman that Alexander II had ordered the taking of Krasnovodsk within the month. Although Stremoukhov noted that Russia's establishment at Krasnovodsk would cause "great inconveniences" in the sphere of diplomacy, he thought the move would be beneficial "if only it is to serve the development of our trade and the reduction of Khiva to the same denominator as Kokand and Bukhara, but God preserve us if it is a step toward new conquests."[8] The foreign ministry still hoped that the occupation of the coast of Krasnovodsk Bay would be sufficient to intimidate Khiva into accepting the role of a Russian dependency. But Khiva's submission was not to be purchased so cheaply.

On November 5 a detachment from the Caucasus landed at Krasnovodsk. Two days later General N. A. Kryzhanovskii, governor general of Orenburg, forwarded to the Ministry of War copies of Muhammad Rahim's proclamations to the rebellious Adai Kazakhs. Kryzhanovskii insisted that "this kind of activity must not remain unpunished," and he proposed that, "if it conforms with the government's other aims," Russia "may, making use of the factual proofs of the khan of Khiva's hostile acts, take the cities of Kungrat and Khiva and destroy the khanate of Khiva." At the same time Kryzhanovskii pointed out the disadvantages of such a course of action, particularly the financial burden of administering such an unproductive province. On December 13 he further noted that the safety of the proposed trade route from Krasnovodsk to the Amu-Darya could not be guaranteed without the conquest of Khiva, and Miliutin concurred.[9]

The arguments in favor of a campaign against Khiva were mounting. Already in October and November 1869 the mixed Russo-Bukharan boundary commission had delimited the east-west section of the frontier in the Kizil Kum Desert along a line parallel to, but to the south of, the route from Djizak to the Bukan Mountains and the Khivan border, which would permit Russia to use this route in a future campaign against Khiva.[10]

Having received no answer to his letters of the previous August and September, General von Kaufman again wrote to Muhammad Rahim on January 18, 1870, explaining that the object of the base at Krasnovodsk was to serve as a storage depot for merchandise and to protect caravans against Turkoman attacks. Kaufman warned the khan that Khiva must choose between friendship and enmity toward Russia and insisted on the satisfaction of all Russia's demands, including free entry of Russian merchants.[11] The governor general ended on a threatening note: "Anyone's patience has its limit, and if I do not receive a satisfactory reply, I will [come and] take it." On the same day Kaufman confided to Stremoukhov that, if the khan agreed to his demands, "we may still hope to preserve the status quo for a while." But, Kaufman added, "I am completely convinced that we cannot avoid a clash, sooner or later, with this khanate."[12]

In Khiva, meanwhile, the Russian landing at Krasnovodsk, on soil that Khiva claimed, caused great alarm. Defensive preparations were undertaken. Mild encouragement arrived from Bukhara in the form of a letter from the emir promising in vague terms to renew the struggle against the unbelievers when the time was right. Khiva's response to Russia's demands was determined in part by the internal situation in the khanate. Muhammad Rahim was an affable, easygoing young man in his mid-twenties. He habitually left affairs of state to his advisers, chief among whom was the divan-begi, Muhammad Murad, who was outspokenly anti-Russian. In February 1870 Murad answered Kaufman's letter of the previous August, while the kush-begi answered the Russian's letter of September. Both replies gave no satisfaction, for they rejected the Russian charges and claimed the Sir-Darya as Khiva's frontier. In March Kaufman wrote to the divan-begi, complaining about the khan's refusal to negotiate directly rather than through his ministers and repeating Russia's demands. In April the kush-begi replied to Kaufman's letter of January 18 with a strongly worded protest against Russia's occupation of Krasnovodsk and a warning that Khiva was prepared to resist Russia. Kaufman reacted by proposing to Miliutin an attack on Khiva simultaneously from Russian Turkestan and the Caucasus.[13]

The foreign ministry was now willing to admit the need to take firmer action with Khiva, although not to give the problem top priority. Stremoukhov admitted in March that diplomacy had proved inadequate to bring Muhammad Rahim into line: "Khiva, of course, will not escape its fate (not annexation, I hope, but subordination), but it would scarcely be timely right now to direct our military forces against this country." Stremoukhov believed that the development of trade with Central Asia, the improvement of relations with the Turkomans, and the consolidation of Russian rule in the government-general of Turkestan were matters of more urgency than a Khivan campaign.[14]

In January 1871 the Ministry of War agreed with the foreign ministry that, while decisive action against Khiva was necessary, the time was not yet ripe. In the spring Kaufman's plan for a campaign against Khiva received imperial approval in principle, but the plan's execution was postponed indefinitely because of Russia's preoccupation with events in Sinkiang. Since 1863 China's westernmost province had been the scene of a widespread Moslem uprising, in the course of which Muhammad Yakub-beg, a former Kokandian officer, had carved out a kingdom for himself, with Kashgar as its capital. Yakub-beg, who ruled from 1867 to 1877, followed a generally pro-British policy. Early in 1871 the situation reached a critical point: Yakub-beg was becoming increasingly hostile to Russia, and his northern neighbor, the sultan of Kuldja, was giving refuge to Kazakh fugitives from Russia.[15]

Khiva meanwhile approached Bukhara for an alliance. The emir, whose relations with Russia had just improved as a result of the

Struve mission, detained the Khivan ambassador pending instructions from Tashkent. Since General von Kaufman's projected campaign had temporarily been shelved, he accepted Muzaffar's offer of mediation and sent to Bukhara his conditions for a settlement. Khiva was to surrender all Russian captives, stop protecting robbers, and dispatch an embassy to Tashkent. The emir forwarded these conditions to Khiva with his own envoy. Muhammad Rahim, displeased at this unexpected outcome of his approach to Bukhara, referred the Russian conditions to a committee, which included the divan-begi and the kush-begi. For two months the Bukharan envoy waited in Khiva and only once was invited to attend a session of the committee. The khan finally dismissed him, declaring that the status quo would be preserved until Russia promised to observe the sanctity of Khiva's frontiers.[16]

Although occupied elsewhere, Russia was not entirely inactive on the Khivan front. In the spring and fall of 1870 two reconnoitering expeditions were launched from Krasnovodsk in the direction of the Khivan oasis. In September 1871 a reconnaissance was made from two sides; Russian detachments from Krasnovodsk and Djizak reached Khiva's western frontier at Lake Sari-Kamish, and its eastern frontier at the Bukan Mountains.[17] Khiva's faith in the efficacy of her natural ramparts was thus rudely shattered, and she resorted to diplomacy to avert the impending attack.

Like Bukhara in 1865, Khiva attempted to bypass Tashkent and deal directly with the imperial government. At the end of 1871 the khan dispatched embassies for St. Petersburg and Tiflis to complain about Kaufman's hostile actions, to protest Tashkent's claim to the left bank of the lower Sir-Darya, and to make clear that Khiva would never deliver her captives until the boundary dispute was settled. On orders from St. Petersburg, Khiva's envoys were detained at Orenburg and the Caucasian coast of the Caspian and informed that freeing the captives and sending an envoy to Tashkent were the preconditions of further negotiations.[18] In July 1872 an ambassador from Muhammad Rahim arrived in India to request British mediation between Khiva and Russia, but Calcutta advised compliance with Russia's demands and a friendly attitude toward Tashkent.[19] Lord Northbrook, Mayo's successor, continued the policy of recognizing Khiva as lying within Russia's sphere of influence in Central Asia.

By mid-1872 the problem of Sinkiang had been temporarily solved. During the summer of 1871 Russia occupied Kuldja and the Ili Valley. On June 8, 1872, after he had failed to secure positive support from India, Yakub-beg reluctantly signed a commercial treaty with Russia identical to those Kaufman had concluded four years earlier with Kokand and Bukhara.[20] Yakub-beg nevertheless did not stand in the same dependent power relationship to Russia as did his western neighbors. He had not felt the edge of Russian steel, and Britain was more concerned with Kashgar than with Bukhara and Kokand. After T. D. Forsyth's mission to Kashgar in December 1873, Yakub-beg again gravitated toward India. First he violated the 1872 treaty by renewing the policy of discrimination against Russian trade, then in February 1874 the Russo-Kashgarian treaty was superseded by an Anglo-Kashgarian treaty.[21] Yakub-beg's behavior illustrates that Russia's influence over Bukhara and Kokand after 1868 rested not on a juridical foundation, since those two states were no more closely bound by treaty to Russia than was Kashgar, but on a political relationship which did not exist between Russia and Kashgar.

Having disposed of the problem of Sinkiang, Russia could finally focus on Khiva. A reconnaissance surpassing all previous ones in strength was made from the Caspian to the western fringe of the Khivan oasis in October 1872.[22] On December 4 Kaufman delivered a long report on Central Asia to a special conference presided over by Alexander II. The governor general protested the "unnatural, abnormal and at the same time intolerable order of relations of the khanate of Khiva to us." Khiva would never be brought to reason until the storming of her capital offered dramatic proof of her weakness and Russia's might. The conference commissioned Kaufman to undertake a military expedition. He was at the same time made responsible for seeing "that the khanate of Khiva is not annexed to the empire, but only subjected, like the other neighboring Central Asian countries, to our influence, with a view to the development of our trade interests." The expedition's aims were limited to punishing Khiva and forcing her to comply with Russia's rather moderate demands.[23] Although Prince Gorchakov agreed with these aims, he held out unsuccessfully against the capture of Khiva's capital.[24] He had learned from the experience of the past eight years what outcome to expect from the "temporary" occupation of a Central Asian town.

The plans for the campaign received final imperial approval on December 12, and Kaufman was given the following orders: "His Majesty the Emperor has been pleased to express repeatedly that under no circumstances would he welcome an extension of the empire's borders, and you are enjoined to take His Highness' will as a strict guiding principle in the impending action against Khiva." Kaufman was specifically reminded that, "after Khiva is punished, its territory must be evacuated at once by our troops."[25] Count P. A. Shuvalov, who was being sent to London to arrange the marriage of the tsar's daughter to one of Victoria's sons, was charged with reassuring the English that Russia intended no conquests at Khiva's expense.

The Conquest of Khiva

The attack on Khiva utilized 12,300 Russian troops and was launched from all quarters of the compass—from Tashkent, Kazalinsk, Orenburg, and two points on the Caspian seacoast. Russia was not going to risk a repetition of 1717 or 1839. Before the Russian troops began their advance, Muhammad Rahim attempted to avert the impending catastrophe by liberating twenty-one Russian captives held in Khiva and sending them to Kazalinsk. Russia, however, was not to be deterred from her goal. On May 8, 1873, Kungrat, the most important town in the northern part of the khanate, fell to the Russians. On May 26, with the Russians at the gates of his capital, Muhammad Rahim sent a messenger to Kaufman to say that since the Russian prisoners had already been freed, he did not understand why Kaufman did not withdraw his troops and state his terms. The governor general replied that he would negotiate only in the capital. Two days later the khan sent his cousin to Kaufman, who was then still thirteen miles from the city, to offer unconditional surrender and permanent submission to Russia if Kaufman would order a halt to the attack on the capital launched that day by the troops from Orenburg. Kaufman requested the khan to meet him in person the next morning four miles from the capital. On the morning of May 29 Muhammad Rahim's uncle and brother appeared at the interview to report that the khan had fled to the Turkomans and that they were now regent and khan. Kaufman entered the capital the same day. The news of Khiva's capture was dispatched to Tashkent, whence it was relayed to St. Petersburg as the first message sent over the telegraph line that had just been built from Tashkent to Vernyi.[26]

General von Kaufman refused to deal with the khan's brother Ata-djan-türa, who seemed to have been placed on the throne against his will. Kaufman insisted on the personal submission of Muhammad Rahim, since his proclamations had announced that he was fighting the ruler and not the people of Khiva. Moreover, a peace treaty signed by Ata-djan-türa would have no validity if Muhammad Rahim later returned to power. On June 1, therefore, Kaufman wrote to Muhammad Rahim inviting him to return to his throne and promising him personal security. The next day the khan appeared in the Russian camp before Khiva and surrendered. Kaufman's victory was complete.[27]

During the Russian occupation of Khiva, General von Kaufman took an active hand in the administration of the khanate. Although on June 6 Muhammad Rahim reentered his capital, he was no longer a sovereign ruler. Kaufman had created a *divan* (council), consisting of three Russian officers, a merchant from Tashkent, and three Khivan dignitaries, including the new divan-begi. At Kaufman's insistence the khan had dismissed his anti-Russian advisers, the most important of whom was the divan-begi, Muhammad Murad. The Russians arrested Muhammad Murad and exiled him to Kaluga, about one hundred miles from Moscow. Muhammad Niyaz, the new divan-begi, had belonged to the peace party and was amenable to Russia's interests. The divan was invested with full administrative powers, although judicial authority was left to the khan. The divan became the instrument through which Kaufman ruled the khanate during the Russian occupation. Four of the divan's seven members were appointed by Kaufman, and he had to approve the three remaining Khivan members. Its sessions were held not in the capital but beyond the city walls, in the vicinity of the Russian camp. Finally, it was a temporary body, which ceased to exist upon the termination of the Russian occupation after two and a half months.[28]

The divan's major accomplishment was the abolition of slavery in Khiva. After the Russian capture of the capital the slave population of the khanate, estimated at about 30,000 and mostly Persian, became increasingly restless, and strict measures were taken against disobedience. Acting through the divan, Kaufman prevailed upon the khan to issue a proclamation on June 12 abolishing slavery, granting

full legal equality to former slaves, and permitting them to live anywhere in the khanate or to leave it. By September, 6300 former slaves
had been repatriated to Persia.[29]

For two weeks in mid-July the Russians resumed military operations, not against the khan but against the Yomuts, the most numerous and powerful tribe among Muhammad Rahim's Turkoman
subjects. For reasons that were by no means clear to contemporary
observers,[30] Kaufman imposed a fine of 600,000 rubles on all the
Turkomans of Khiva and gave the Yomuts two weeks, July 7–22, to
pay half this sum, since they accounted for half the total Turkoman
population in the khanate. On July 6 the governor general ordered
his troops to proceed to the Turkoman country west of the capital
and ascertain whether the Yomuts were collecting the required sum.
If they were not, as was highly probable in view of the absence of
a money economy among the Turkomans, the troops were to anni-
hilate the entire tribe and confiscate their property. There ensued
the wholesale slaughter of the Yomuts and their livestock, together
with the devastation of their crops and their settlements by the Cossack troops.[31]

After the conclusion of the campaign against the Yomuts Kaufman was short of money for the return march to Tashkent, so on
July 21 he levied on the other Turkoman tribes their share of the
fine, amounting to 310,500 rubles. He allowed them to pay half
in camels and half in either coin or gold and silver objects. By August
2, the deadline for payment, only 92,000 rubles had been collected,
but in view of their clear intention to pay, Kaufman gave the Turkomans an indefinite extension and took twenty-six hostages.[32]

The Russo-Khivan Treaty

On August 12, 1873, Kaufman and Muhammad Rahim put
their signatures to the treaty that the former had drafted and sent off
by courier to the emperor at the beginning of June.[33] The Khivan
treaty was quite different from the 1868 treaties with Bukhara and
Kokand, both in its terms and in the circumstances under which it
was concluded. Bukhara and Kokand had been defeated in battle
and forced to acquiesce in Russia's annexation of extensive and important provinces, but only Khiva had been subjected to the humiliation of having her khan surrender in person to the White Tsar's
victorious viceroy, her capital occupied, the royal throne shipped off

to Moscow as a trophy, part of the royal archives sent to St. Petersburg, and the government directly controlled by the Russians for two and a half months.[34] The treaty itself was much more far-reaching than the earlier treaties with Bukhara and Kokand, not only because of the circumstances of Khiva's defeat but also because the earlier treaties had proved inadequate as vehicles of Russian domination.[35]

Article one of the treaty reduced Khiva to the legal status of a Russian protectorate.[36] The khan declared himself the "obedient servant" of the Russian emperor and renounced his right to conduct foreign relations or to take up arms against another state without the consent of Tashkent. He was thus deprived of one of the most important attributes of sovereignty.

Article two settled the problem of the Russo-Khivan boundary, giving to Russia the entire Ust-Urt Plateau, the eastern coast of the Caspian Sea, and not only the left bank of the lower Sir-Darya but the right bank of the lower Amu-Darya and the intervening Kizil Kum Desert as well. The advance of the Russian frontier from the Sir-Darya to the Amu-Darya was a flagrant violation of Kaufman's December 1872 instructions and of Shuvalov's assurances to London, but St. Petersburg had yielded to Kaufman's arguments. If it should prove necessary to repeat the campaign against Khiva in the future, outright annexation would be the logical result. In order to avoid this possibility, Kaufman deemed it necessary to establish a Russian post that would serve to protect Russia's frontier, to keep the khan under control, and to support him if need be against his unruly Turkoman subjects. The only spot close enough to Khiva to answer all these needs was the fertile right bank of the lower Amu-Darya. Muhammad Rahim himself had told Kaufman that he could enforce his authority and fulfill his obligations to Russia only if Russia established a fortress and a detachment of troops near at hand. The khan had gone even further and urged that a permanent Russian garrison be placed in his capital.[37] The treaty did not mention Khiva's southern and southwestern boundaries, because Russia's activities did not yet extend into the Kara Kum Desert.

By articles three and four the khan consented to Russia's confiscation without compensation of all estates belonging to him or his officials on the right bank of the Amu-Darya. An exception was made in the case of Muhammad Niyaz, the new divan-begi, who retained large estates there. All right-bank estates belonging to religious institutions on the left bank were confiscated, together with their revenues.[38] The khan also agreed to Russia's transfer of part of the right bank to the emir of Bukhara. Article five granted to Russia complete control over navigation on the Amu-Darya, to the exclusion of all Khivan and Bukharan vessels except such as were licensed to operate by Tashkent. Articles six and seven gave Russian subjects the right to establish wharves and trading posts along the left bank of the Amu-Darya, for whose safety the Khivan government would be responsible. Articles eight through eleven opened the khanate to Russian trade on terms similar to those of the 1868 treaties with Bukhara and Kokand, the principal difference being that trade between Russia and Khiva was exempted on both sides from the zakat or customs duty. Article twelve granted to Russians the right to own real property in Khiva. Articles thirteen through fifteen concerned the settlement of civil cases involving Khivans and Russians: Russian creditors were given priority over Khivan creditors, and cases in which a Russian was the defendant, even if he resided in Khiva, were to be handled by the nearest Russian authorities. Article sixteen obligated Khiva not to admit anyone from Russia without a proper passport and to extradite to Russia all Russian fugitives from justice. By article seventeen the khan promised to continue to enforce his June 12 proclamation abolishing slavery. Article eighteen imposed upon Khiva a war indemnity of 2,200,000 rubles, to be paid over a twenty-year period.

Thus, the treaty of 1873 gave Russia extensive rights in Khiva. Besides a number of valuable commercial privileges, Russia gained control of Khiva's external affairs and of navigation on the Amu-Darya. Russian subjects were granted a special legal status, and the abolition of slavery was made a legal commitment to Russia. The numerous obligations on Khiva's part, including the huge indemnity, afforded ample grounds for intervention if the government of the khanate should prove difficult to handle. Because of St. Petersburg's restraining hand, however, the Khivan treaty did not go quite as far as Kaufman's proposed secret treaty of 1871 with Bukhara. Russia received no right to control the appointment of high Khivan officials nor any implied right to sanction the succession to the throne.

On the very day the treaty was signed, the Russian troops began to withdraw. On August 21 construction was begun on Fort Petro-Aleksandrovsk on the right bank of the Amu-Darya about forty miles from the capital of the khanate. This fort was to be Russia's point of defense, observation, and support vis-à-vis the khan of Khiva.

The Russo-Bukharan Treaty

During the campaign against Khiva the emir of Bukhara pre-served a friendly attitude toward Russia, probably more out of fear than any nobler emotion. Kaufman's route from Tashkent led him across the Bukharan portion of the Kizil Kum. Bukharan envoys met him at the frontier, an ambassador accompanied him during the rest of the campaign, and Muzaffar responded immediately to the governor general's request for fresh grain and camels. On April 23 Kaufman wrote the emir, thanking him for his hospitality and call-ing him Russia's "trustworthy friend and ally." Muzaffar also per-mitted the Russians to build a fort at Khalata on Bukharan soil in order to protect baggage left there for the return march. Despite the fact that the emir was undoubtedly acting from self-interest, as well as that he was reportedly at the same time encouraging the resistance of the Khivan Turkomans, Kaufman professed to believe in Muzaffar's sincerity and rewarded him with a small strip of Khivan territory on the right bank of the Amu-Darya.[39]

After the withdrawal from Khiva, Kaufman on August 28 dis-patched K. V. Struve from Petro-Aleksandrovsk with a new treaty for the emir's signature.[40] Signed on September 28, the new treaty repeated the substance of the 1868 commercial convention, with the single difference that Bukharan caravansaries were to be permitted only in the government-general of Turkestan, not throughout the Russian Empire as formerly. The treaty went much further, however, in line with the proposals discussed between Tashkent and St. Petersburg in 1871–72. The Russo-Bukharan boundary of 1868 was reaffirmed, which ended the emir's hope of regaining the Zarafshan Okrug. The Amu-Darya was opened to Russian ships, Russian sub-jects were permitted to engage in industry and to acquire real estate in Bukhara, the khanate's government was obliged to extradite fugi-tive Russian criminals, the exchange of permanent envoys between Bukhara and Tashkent was arranged, and the slave trade in the khanate was abolished, although no mention was made of slavery itself.

The treaty with Bukhara was in many ways similar to the one just concluded with Khiva, but there were major differences, again reflecting the different circumstances of the conquest. Whereas the Khivan treaty established a Russian protectorate over that country by depriving the khan of control of Khiva's foreign relations, the Bukharan treaty preserved the formal sovereignty of the emir's country. Although in the covering letter sent with the treaty Kaufman referred to "the mighty protection of His Majesty the Emperor of All the Russias" over the emir, in the same letter he promised Muzaffar that as long as he did not violate his treaty engagements to Russia, he would, "as formerly, rule your country independently."[41] The treaty itself in no way infringed upon Bukhara's sovereignty. Although in fact Bukhara had been a dependency of Russia since 1868, in law the khanate continued to exist as a fully sovereign state even after 1873. The legal fiction neither prevented Russia from treating Bukhara as a dependency, nor kept Britain from recognizing Bukhara's inclusion in Russia's sphere of influence.

Other differences between the Khivan and Bukharan treaties may be traced to the basic difference in the legal status of the two countries. In Khiva Russia gained exclusive control over the navigation of the Amu-Darya; in Bukhara Russian and Bukharan vessels enjoyed equal rights of navigation on the river. Russia's right to establish commercial agents in Khiva was one-sided; Bukhara enjoyed a reciprocal right in the government-general of Turkestan. Finally, Russians in Bukhara were to enjoy no such special legal status as did the emperor's subjects in Khiva.

Both of the 1873 treaties remained in force until the 1917 Revolution. In Bukhara, however, beginning in the 1880's the legal differences which distinguished that khanate from Khiva underwent a process of erosion which ended in Bukhara's becoming as much a Russian protectorate as Khiva.

Part Two / *The Period of Neglect*

Khiva

5 / The Stabilization of Khiva and the Expansion of Bukhara

The Khivan Problem, 1873–1877

By 1873 St. Petersburg's limited aims in regard to the Central Asian khanates had been achieved. A defensible frontier had been secured —a frontier, moreover, which placed Russia in a commanding strategic position over Bukhara and Khiva through the possession of Samarkand and the right bank of the lower Amu-Darya. The governments of both Bukhara and Khiva were effectively under Russian control, so that no further hostility was looked for there. Legal discrimination against Russian traders had been abolished, and Russian captives freed. St. Petersburg was satisfied and wished to preserve the status quo: Bukhara and Khiva would gladly be allowed to manage their own affairs and thus save Russia the cost and trouble of ruling them directly. Tashkent, however, regarded the position of the khanates as temporary, to be followed by annexation in the near future. Although St. Petersburg's views took precedence over those of Tashkent, the success of the imperial government's policy depended on the ability of the native regimes to preserve order within their states. Political instability and domestic disorder in the khanates would again disturb the tranquillity of Russia's frontiers and provide a temptation to Britain to interfere. Russia's first task, therefore, was to restore the authority of the native rulers over their subjects, which had been shaken by their defeat at the hands of the Russians. Kaufman had recognized this need in 1868, even if St. Petersburg had not, and had helped Muzaffar defeat the combined opposition forces led by Abd al-Malik. A similar task awaited Russia in Khiva after the conquest, where the deep-seated nature of the problem posed a more serious challenge to St. Petersburg's policy of nonintervention.

The large Turkoman minority in Khiva was continually at odds with the khan's government and the Uzbeg majority. Traditional sources of trouble were questions of taxation and of the distribution of water for irrigation, because the Uzbegs, by virtue of their location to the east or upstream of the Turkomans along the canals leading from the Amu-Darya, had first access to the water on which all agriculture depended. Another problem was the innate hostility between the seminomadic Turkomans, who prided themselves on their military virtues and the purity of their blood, and the sedentary Uzbegs, who had long since fused with the ancient population of the oasis and acquired more peaceful habits.

No sooner had the Russian troops withdrawn from the khanate than the Yomut Turkomans plundered several Uzbeg districts in order to recoup the losses they had suffered in July at the hands of Kaufman's Cossacks.[1] The immediate responsibility for dealing with the Turkoman disturbances rested with Lieutenant Colonel N. A. Ivanov, commander of the garrison at Petro-Aleksandrovsk and also commandant of the Amu-Darya Otdel, formed in 1874 from the territories ceded to Russia by Khiva. The geographic isolation of both Khiva and Petro-Aleksandrovsk from Tashkent[2] made it necessary for Kaufman to delegate to Ivanov much of the responsibility for day-to-day relations with Khiva. Kaufman's instructions to Ivanov of September 12, 1873, defined his principal tasks as: (1) defense of the right bank of the Amu-Darya and its population, now Russian subjects, (2) gathering intelligence about the situation in Khiva, and (3) intervention in the khanate's internal affairs "to the extent that they affect the interests and tranquillity of the territory and population recently acquired by us."[3] Ivanov was thus given a vaguely defined mandate to intervene in Khiva. Kaufman advised a carrot-and-stick policy toward the Turkomans. On September 20 he held out to the Turkomans the promise that he would cancel the balance of the indemnity they owed and return their hostages if they would promise to obey the khan. Eight days earlier Kaufman had directed Ivanov to devastate the territory of two Yomut clans for attacking emancipated Persian slaves and refusing to pay the indemnity. The governor general wished to make of the Yomuts an example for the other Turkomans. During the winter of 1873–1874 Ivanov intervened twice in Khiva. He prevailed upon Muhammad Rahim to remove the hakim of Kipchak, who was suspected of complicity in a Turkoman raid, and in January 1874 he led a detachment of Russian troops on a march among the Turkomans of Khiva from Khodjeili to Khanki.[4]

In view of the khanate's continuing internal difficulties, Ivanov in the fall of 1874 proposed the annexation of Khiva to General G. A. Kolpakovskii, the acting governor general during Kaufman's absence. Kaufman replied to Ivanov from St. Petersburg on October 29, saying he would refer Ivanov's recommendation to the proper authorities in the capital with his endorsement. Kaufman suggested that in the meantime perhaps a second display of Russian armed might among the Turkomans would make annexation unnecessary. The governor general was by this time familiar enough with St. Petersburg's views on territorial expansion in Central Asia to be able to guess the fate of Ivanov's proposal. Foreign Minister Gorchakov soon reiterated those views: he argued that the situation in Khiva was not critical and quoted the emperor on the necessity for preserving Khiva's independence even at the cost of using Russian troops to pacify the Turkomans. On November 10 Minister of War Miliutin informed Kaufman of Gorchakov's position and of his own concurrence. The domestic disturbances in Khiva had not as yet turned into a general uprising against the khan or a civil war among the Khivans. Russian interests had not been directly affected, nor had the tranquillity of the Amu-Darya Otdel been disturbed. Drastic measures were therefore not in order. But if intervention in force should be called for in the future, a temporary campaign on the left bank would be "less burdensome" than the permanent annexation of Khiva.[5] In January 1875 Ivanov again crossed the Amu-Darya with Russian troops and traversed the khanate in a demonstration of force. This time he visited Muhammad Rahim in Khiva and advised him to be firm but fair toward his Turkoman subjects.[6]

In 1876 a new outbreak of Turkoman violence against the khan's tax collectors, the Russian annexation of Kokand in February, and the rivalry between the Russian military authorities in Turkestan and the Caucasus[7] combined to raise anew the problem of the annexation of Khiva. Early in 1876 plans were laid in Krasnovodsk for an expedition to explore the feasibility of turning the Amu-Darya into its supposed ancient bed leading to the Caspian Sea and to build a fort on Khivan territory near Kunya-Urgench. Despite Kaufman's protest to Miliutin that the establishment of such a fort would transfer the dominant influence over Khiva from Tashkent to Tiflis, plans took shape in May for an expedition to leave the Caspian coast in August.[8] On August 18 Ivanov met with Muhammad Rahim at the khan's request at Khanki. The khan objected to the expedition, the projected fort, and the diversion of the Amu-Darya, which would ruin the northern part of the khanate.[9] Ivanov tried to reassure him of Russia's intentions, but Muhammad Rahim was not convinced. He took advantage of the meeting to discuss the dangers to his throne, his powerlessness to preserve order and command obedience among the Turkomans, and his lack of troops and money to enforce his will. The khan proposed various courses of action: a permanent Russian garrison in Khiva, a Russian subsidy for the hiring of native troops, or as a final resort, the annexation of Khiva and the pensioning off of Muhammad Rahim and his family. The khan went so far as to ask where the emperor might allow him to live and how large a pension he might expect. Ivanov reported to Kaufman that the khan had never before been so despondent and was evidently quite frightened.[10]

Nine days after the meeting a delegation of two Khivan Turkomans arrived in Petro-Aleksandrovsk to complain about the khan and his government and to request either permission for all Turkomans to leave the khanate or else Russian annexation. Ivanov reprimanded them for bypassing their legal sovereign and bringing their grievances to him, but he used the two episodes to support his contention to Kaufman that the time was ripe for the annexation of Khiva. Kaufman forwarded Ivanov's recommendations to Miliutin on September 25, but bearing in mind his superiors' previous views on annexation, and hesitant to add Khiva to Kokand on the list of territories reluctantly acquired by the emperor, the governor general expressed reservations about the great expense that its annexation would entail.[11]

The expedition, which had started from Krasnovodsk in early August, reached Kunya-Urgench a month later, remained there five weeks, and then retired.[12] Nothing ever came of the plans for building a fort on Khiva's western frontier or for diverting the Amu-Darya. In early February 1877 Ivanov made a third march among the Turkomans on the left bank, alleging that robber bands had appeared on the Russian side of the river. On this occasion he received another request from a group of Turkomans that Russia save them from the khan's government. Ivanov's report to Kaufman of February 15 summarized for the third time in as many years the arguments for the immediate annexation of Khiva. On March 23 Kaufman forwarded Ivanov's report to Miliutin, observing that although the situation in Europe would probably preclude sending troop reinforcements, the occupation of Khiva would pose no difficulty and could be undertaken at any time. St. Petersburg responded by transferring the persistent Ivanov back to the post he had held prior to 1873—commandant of the Zarafshan Okrug. On May 19 Miliutin replied to Kaufman with orders that Ivanov's successor be directed "not to permit any actions or orders which could lead to the necessity of our troops' occupying Khiva, since such an action would be completely contrary to His Majesty the Emperor's views at the present time."[13]

The question of the annexation of Khiva was thus laid to rest in 1877. The following year the small migration of Khivans into the Amu-Darya Otdel, which had begun in 1875, was halted in response to the Khivan government's complaints over the loss of taxpayers. On November 16 Kaufman ordered that in the future the consent of the khan's government would be necessary for such emigration. Those who had already emigrated were not, however, to be repatriated.[14] Ivanov's successors adopted a much less imperious tone in their relations with the khan, which helped raise his prestige among his courtiers and subjects.[15] The Khivan question was not reopened until the second decade of the twentieth century.

Russo-Bukharan Relations, 1873–1875

In contrast to Khiva, where the commandant of the Amu-Darya Otdel acted as the governor general's deputy and enjoyed a high degree of delegated authority, in Bukhara direct control of all Russian relations with the government was retained by General von Kaufman. Bukhara was much more accessible from Tashkent than was Khiva, and Muzaffar, as a theoretically sovereign ruler, was entitled to deal directly with the governor general. Thus, the commandant of the Zarafshan Okrug, the Russian district that bore the same geographic relationship to Bukhara as the Amu-Darya Otdel did to Khiva, was limited to "the exchange of civilities when necessary" with the emir and the kush-begi, and to the collecting and forwarding to Tashkent of intelligence on the political situation in Bukhara.[16]

Since the commandant at Petro-Aleksandrovsk was only forty miles from the khan's capital, he could deal directly with the Khivan government without need of diplomatic go-betweens.[17] Between Tashkent and the emir's capital, however, there was no such geographic proximity. Articles fifteen and sixteen of the Russo-Bukharan Treaty of 1873 provided for the establishment of a permanent Bukharan ambassador at Tashkent and a Russian counterpart at Bukhara, but these articles were not implemented. Relations between Russia and her dependency continued to be carried on as before, by means of extraordinary missions and embassies.[18] The objections raised against this method of conducting relations in the period

1868–1873 remained equally valid during the ensuing decade. Members of the Russian missions were denied freedom of movement within Bukhara, were kept under constant surveillance, and had difficulty in obtaining accurate information and observing conditions in the khanate, particularly the slave trade. A Russian Tatar envoy sent by General Abramov early in 1874 to locate three sisters from Samarkand who had been abducted and sold into slavery in Bukhara was imprisoned in Karshi for eight weeks. He was set free and permitted to return to Russian Turkestan only by the intercession of N. P. Stremoukhov, who was visiting the khanate on government business.[19] The problems raised by the acceptance of gifts from the Bukharan authorities also remained unsettled. In 1880 Kaufman forbade this practice, and in December 1883 the Minister of War admonished Governor General Cherniaev that it was incompatible with Russia's dignity.[20] Nevertheless, the custom continued down to the 1917 Revolution, undoubtedly because it was favored by the majority of Russian Turkestan's officialdom. V. V. Krestovskii, a member of a Russian embassy to Bukhara in the early 1880's, noted that such embassies invariably accepted many more gifts from Bukharan officials than they could possibly give in return.[21]

Three problems that the treaty of 1873 did not solve and which faced Kaufman almost immediately were slavery, jurisdiction over Russian subjects in Bukhara, and the Turkoman menace along the Amu-Darya. Although the treaty abolished the slave trade in the khanate, it did not, in contrast to the Khivan treaty, abolish the institution of slavery. The circumstances of Bukhara's defeat in 1868 had not given Russia as free a hand there as she obtained in Khiva in 1873. She therefore had to proceed more slowly toward the abolition of slavery. That an institution so universally condemned in the West should continue indefinitely in Bukhara, even though it was purely an internal matter, was inconceivable. The exponents of the Western world's civilizing mission, of whom Russia had her share, would have objected too loudly. Soon after the signing of the new treaty in 1873 Kaufman congratulated the emir for having abolished the slave trade and went on to declare this "the first step toward the final abolition of slavery." The governor general expressed the hope that Muzaffar would effect the gradual emancipation of all slaves in Bukhara within a period of "not more than ten years."[22]

The suppression of the slave trade and the abolition of slavery were not easily effected. Although the public sale of slaves was forbidden, brokers secretly arranged for the sale of Persian slaves brought by Turkomans from the desert. Even the emir's government purchased slaves from these brokers for the purpose of replenishing the ranks of the army. Although such slaves were declared legally free, they were obliged to serve for life in the army.[23] N. P. Stremoukhov accused Muzaffar of violating the 1873 treaty by secretly protecting the slave trade in order to secure recruits for both his army and his harem.[24] In July 1878 one Farat, an agent of the Russian finance ministry, witnessed a slave market in the capital of Bukhara, and as late as 1882 the English traveler Henry Lansdell heard reports of the continuing slave trade.[25] In fact, the effective suppression of the slave trade had to await the abolition of slavery itself.

Muzaffar yielded in late 1873 to Kaufman's suggestion of complete emancipation after a decade but decreed that all slaves were to remain with their current owners until that time. Slaves were granted the almost meaningless right to purchase their freedom before the end of the ten-year period at prices to be set in each individual case by mutual agreement between slave and master. Fugitive slaves were threatened with death, and disobedient slaves with severe punishment. The difficult position of the Bukharan slaves after Muzaffar's edict evoked a prolonged correspondence between Tashkent and Bukhara. There were frequent flights of slaves to Russian Turkestan, who then petitioned the commandant of the Zarafshan Okrug to obtain the release of their relatives remaining in slavery in the khanate. The kush-begi argued that the Bukharan government could not afford to compensate masters for emancipated slaves and that all slaves had to remain in bondage during the decreed ten-year period unless redeemed by their own families. In 1874 Kaufman sent the emir the intelligence that had been collected on the existence of the illicit slave trade and on the harsh conditions under which Bukharan slaves were living. The governor general requested that Muzaffar take decisive measures to terminate the slave trade and to improve the moral and material existence of the slaves during the period of transition to freedom. The emir denied the continuance of the slave trade and ascribed the reports of mistreatment to the insubordinate attitude of the slaves upon learning of their future emancipation. Kaufman closed discussion of the issue in 1876 by directing the commandant of the Zarafshan Okrug to sympathize with the difficulties faced by the Bukharan government during the decade of preparation for emancipation and "in the majority of cases to decline interference in the slaves' affairs."[26]

There the problem rested, not just during the ten-year period set in Muzaffar's decree but until the very end of his reign in 1885. Slavery was, after all, an internal affair of no vital practical interest to Russia. Since the emir's promise of eventual emancipation had been obtained, and in view of his resistance to further pressure, the question was not worth risking the loss of Muzaffar's good will. Bukhara's friendship was particularly necessary during the period of Anglo-Russian hostility in the latter half of the 1870's.

Another problem that arose in the first years after 1873 concerned legal jurisdiction over Russians in Bukhara. The Khivan treaty provided that civil cases in which Russians were defendants should be tried by "the nearest Russian authorities," but the Bukharan treaty contained no equivalent clause, and jurisdiction over civil cases involving Russians was left to Bukhara until the late 1880's. Neither treaty mentioned criminal cases in which Russian subjects were involved, but as a general rule in such cases nineteenth-century imperialist powers had claimed the right to exercise extraterritorial jurisdiction over their nationals in Asian and African countries. Soon after the conclusion of the 1873 treaty, therefore, article fourteen, which obligated Bukhara to extradite to Russia all Russian criminals, received a very broad interpretation. Since the article did not specify that the crime in question had to be committed on Russian territory, the inference was drawn that Russia's jurisdiction extended not only to her nationals committing crimes in Russia and then fleeing to Bukhara but also to Russians committing crimes in Bukhara. Both Tashkent and Bukhara followed this interpretation after 1873. Russians accused of crimes committed either in Russia or Bukhara were tried by the courts of Russian Turkestan. The testimony of Bukharan witnesses was obtained either by summoning them through the kush-begi to the court trying the case or by having the local beg take their depositions on the spot and forward them to the Russian authorities. In some cases a special Russian investigator was sent to Bukhara to collect evidence on a crime committed there by a Russian.[27] Yet because very few Russians actually visited Bukhara in a private capacity before the second half of the 1880's, it is doubtful whether much use was made of Russia's extraterritorial privileges. The khanate also seems to have been a haven for native fugitives from justice from the government-general. Privy Councilor F. K. Giers, who headed an investigation into the affairs of Russian Turkestan in 1883, reported that judicial investigations of half the murders committed in the Katta-Kurgan Otdel, which bordered Bukhara, were impossible because the guilty parties took refuge in the khanate. It took months for an extradition request to go through the proper channels in Samarkand, Tashkent, and Bukhara, and the reply from the emir's government was almost always evasive.[28]

A problem that was covered by the 1873 treaty but which nevertheless proved difficult of solution was the Turkoman raids on trade and travelers along the Amu-Darya. These raids sometimes extended so far into Bukhara as to threaten the road between Karshi and the capital.[29] Since article two of the treaty obligated Muzaffar to ensure safety of movement on the caravan route along the right bank of the Amu-Darya, leading to Petro-Aleksandrovsk, as well as on all other routes between Bukhara and Russian Turkestan, General von Kaufman soon after the conclusion of the treaty demanded that the emir protect the route by erecting fortresses and stationing permanent garrisons at Kabakli and elsewhere on both banks of the river.[30] Muzaffar not only complied with Kaufman's demands but also formed three new begliks in 1873–1874—Kabakli, between Chardjui and the Khivan frontier, and Burdalik and Narazim, between Chardjui and Kerki.[31] Despite these measures and the stationing of one third of the Bukharan cavalry at Chardjui,[32] the Turkomans continued to wreak havoc on both caravans and shipping on the Amu-Darya. The use of Kabakli as a penal colony for Bukharan criminals and as a post to which Bukharan soldiers guilty of misdeeds were assigned probably did not help matters. Travelers in the area continued to run the risk of robbery, capture, and death at the hands of the Turkoman raiders well into the 1880's.[33] Only after the annexation of Merv had completed Russia's pacification of the Kara Kum Desert was the Turkoman menace along the Amu-Darya eliminated.

Bukhara's Conquest of Karategin and Darvaz

Between 1868 and 1875 Kokand was Russia's favorite among the Central Asian khanates. This state of affairs ended abruptly in July 1875, when the internal feuding that had plagued Kokand for decades before Russia's entry into Central Asia broke out anew. The situation was far more serious than the contemporaneous Turkoman troubles in Khiva, for Kokand was faced with a general uprising directed not only against Khan Khudayar but against Russia. The rebels even laid siege to Khodjent. Khudayar fled to Russian Turkestan, and his son Nasr ad-Din was proclaimed khan. Kaufman marched into Kokand, defeated the insurgents, and entered the capital in September 1875. He concluded a treaty that recognized Nasr ad-Din as khan of Kokand, and Nasr ad-Din in turn ceded to Russia the half of the khanate lying on the right bank of the Sir-Darya and promised to pay an indemnity. Kaufman thus gave Kokand one last chance to preserve its autonomy. The new khan, however, was unable to maintain order after the withdrawal of the Russian troops and soon followed his father to Russia. The governor general assigned Major General M. D. Skobelev to occupy the rest of the khanate, and in February 1876 Kokand was annexed to Russian Turkestan as the Fergana Oblast. The first of Russia's three Central Asian dependencies had lost its autonomy because of its inability to meet St. Petersburg's minimum requirement of domestic stability.

Bukhara's attitude during the Kokandian operations of 1875–1876 exhibited the same outward friendliness and watchful waiting that she had displayed during the Khivan campaign. Only after the defeat of Kokand in September 1875 did Muzaffar turn over to Kaufman the letter he had received during the summer from Nasr ad-Din, asking for Bukhara's support in his war against Russia. Contrary to his usual practice, the emir spent the winter of 1875–1876 in Shahr-i Sabz with his army in order the better to observe the course of events in Kokand. He may still have had in mind the recapture of Samarkand in the event of a Russian defeat in the Fergana Valley. Muzaffar's presence in Shahr-i Sabz, combined with the Kokandian insurrection and rumors of an impending attack on Russia by the mir of Karategin, served to provoke local disturbances in the mountainous districts on the upper Zarafshan. These disturbances were serious enough to cause General Abramov to suspend the caravan trade between Samarkand and Bukhara out of fear for its safety. Early in 1876 at Tashkent's request Muzaffar withdrew with his army from Shahr-i Sabz to Bukhara, and the upper Zarafshan was subsequently pacified.[34]

The annexation of Kokand not only raised Muzaffar's prestige by eliminating Khudayar, his rival for Russia's favor, but also made possible the direct incorporation of Karategin and Darvaz into Bukhara. These two remote mountain principalities had for two and a half centuries maintained a de facto independence by playing off against each other their two more powerful neighbors, Bukhara and Kokand. Their independence did not long survive the collapse of Kokand. During the Kokandian troubles the mir of Karategin, Muhammad Rahim, had given asylum to many fugitive rebels and was reportedly preparing to intervene against Russia in Kokand and at Ura-Tübe. After the final annexation of Kokand, General Skobelev, military governor of the new Fergana Oblast, asked Kaufman for permission to invade Karategin and punish Muhammad Rahim. Kaufman refused, for he now recognized Bukhara's suzerainty over both Karategin and its southern neighbor Darvaz.[35] The governor general then demanded of Muzaffar that he replace Muhammad Rahim with someone who would be friendly to Russia and would expel from Karategin all anti-Russian elements. Muhammad Rahim refused the emir's summons to an audience and tried to effect a reconciliation with Kaufman during the spring of 1876. Convinced of the mir's insincerity, Kaufman wrote Muzaffar again on July 6, repeating his earlier demands. By early August the emir was able to enforce his will in the distant province. Muhammad Rahim was sent under arrest to Bukhara, and the emir appointed Muhammad-shah-biy (also called Muhammad Said) ruler of Karategin with instructions to act according to Kaufman's expressed wishes.[36]

The following year for unknown reasons Muzaffar sent his most able general, Khudoi Nazar-atalik, to arrest Muhammad Said and to rule Karategin as a Bukharan beglik. Some members of Karategin's dispossessed ruling family found refuge in Russian Turkestan, where they received pensions from the Russian authorities, who thought they would prove useful against the emir of Bukhara if he should ever make trouble. As long as the emir played his part of the good neighbor and faithful ally, however, Tashkent kept a tight rein on the exiles. In the early 1880's one of the group tried to stir up the population of Karategin against the emir, but Kaufman warned him that he would be turned over to Muzaffar if he did not cease his activities.[37]

Upon Bukhara's asserting her authority over Karategin, Seradj ad-Din, the mir of Darvaz and a relative of Muhammad Said, rejected the emir's claim of suzerainty over Darvaz. At Muzaffar's orders Khudoi Nazar invaded Darvaz in December 1877. By the following spring all of Darvaz was occupied and Seradj ad-Din was carried off to Bukhara as a prisoner. The former mir of Darvaz lived in confinement to the end of Muzaffar's reign in 1885; the governor general then prevailed upon Muzaffar's son and successor to liberate him. The mir's sons were more fortunate, for they managed to escape to Fergana, where they joined the fugitives from Karategin as the recipients of Russian pensions. Two other relatives of Seradj ad-Din,

who had been *amlakdars* (administrators of a subdivision of a beglik) in southern Darvaz on the left bank of the Pandj River, fled to
Badakhshan. One of them tried to seize control of the left bank
in 1882 with Afghan help, but he failed and was executed in Bukhara for his trouble.[38]

In the decade since his defeat by Russia, Muzaffar had par-
tially compensated for the loss of Samarkand by gaining control over
central and eastern Bukhara. Aside from the case of Shahr-i Sabz, he
had accomplished this without Russian help, although Russia was
undoubtedly happy to see the emir occupied in such constructive
activity, for it strengthened his position and thus reduced the
possibility of domestic turmoil in the khanate.

Russian Exploration of Khiva and Bukhara, 1873–1883

Khiva and western Bukhara had been fairly well known to Russians before the conquest through the works of various Russian and
Western visitors. Central and eastern Bukhara, however, had never
been penetrated by any European, and reliable geographic information was consequently almost nonexistent. In the decade after 1873
the store of geographic knowledge about Russia's new Central Asian
dependencies was increased by means of organized scientific expeditions, military reconnaissance of possible routes for the Russian army,
and studies by the geographers and ethnographers who often accompanied Russian embassies and military expeditions.[39]

Between 1874 and 1880 the lower Amu-Darya was the target
of no fewer than five expeditions, sponsored by the Imperial Russian
Geographic Society, the Grand Duke Mikhail Nikolaevich, viceroy
of the Caucasus, the Grand Duke Nikolai Konstantinovich, and the
Ministry of Ways of Communication. They had as their various objects the mapping of the area and charting of the river, collection
of information about the river's suitability for commercial navigation,
and exploration of the putative ancient bed of the Amu-Darya.[40]

Political and military motives played a dominant role in the
exploration of central Bukhara in the period 1875–1880. To remedy
the lack of accurate geographic information on this region, which
lay between Russian Turkestan on the north and Afghanistan and
India on the south, General von Kaufman repeatedly sent out military exploring parties to map the land and river routes. The most
prominent figure in these activities was Lieutenant Colonel N. A.
Maev, a botanist and zoologist, who made five trips into Bukhara in

as many years, ranging from Kelif to Kulab. Maev's Hisar Expedition in 1875 opened much of central Bukhara to Westerners for the first time in history. The military explorations intensified in 1878, coincident first with the Anglo-Russian crisis over the Balkans and the Straits and then with the beginning of the Second Anglo-Afghan War. Maev and later Colonel P. P. Matveev were dispatched to investigate the roads leading south from Samarkand toward Afghanistan and India. Muzaffar, helpless in face of this flurry of Russian exploration within his borders, reacted with a mixture of polite courtesy and suspicion: usually he received in formal audience the explorers about to embark on their travels and consented to their plans while warning them of the difficulties they faced, and he sent along officials to report on the Russians' activities while aiding them in their dealings with the local population.[41]

Russian explorers penetrated eastern Bukhara only after Muzaffar's conquest of Karategin and Darvaz. Since the strategic significance of this remote and mountainous region was minimal, most of the exploration was in the hands of scientists rather than soldiers. In the late summer of 1878 the naturalist V. F. Oshanin became the first European to visit Karategin. The botanist A. E. Regel, sent by the Imperial Russian Geographic Society, achieved the same distinction in Darvaz in 1881, and in the independent principality of Shugnan and Roshan the following year.[42]

Within a decade after the signing of the treaties of 1873 Khiva and Bukhara had yielded up the geographic secrets they had withheld for centuries from the West. A circuit of the entire khanate of Bukhara, made in the spring of 1882 by Captain G. A. Arandarenko, commandant of the Samarkand Uezd, took him to isolated begliks that only seven years before had never seen a European but which in the interim had been visited several times by Russian exploring parties.[43] The scientific mapping of Bukhara and Khiva, begun in the early 1880's, was continued until by 1914 both khanates had been completely mapped.[44] Although foreigners were prohibited from visiting Russian Central Asia in general, and Bukhara and Khiva in particular, without special permission from Tashkent,[45] the khanates did play host in the late seventies and early eighties to several Western travelers—the Englishmen Burnaby and Lansdell, the Frenchmen Bonvalot and Capus, and the Swiss Moser. Yet the travels of these men, while furnishing valuable information on the khanates, contributed little to geographic knowledge because they were confined to the better known areas of western Bukhara and Khiva.

Mikhail Grigorevich Cherniaev, Governor of the Turkestan Oblast, 1865–1866; Governor General of Turkestan, 1882–1884

6 / Anglo-Russian Relations and the Pacification of the Turkomans

Afghanistan, 1875–1880

In the late 1870's and early 1880's Bukhara was of greatest interest to Russia as an instrument in the traditional Anglo-Russian rivalry in Central Asia. That rivalry, which the 1873 understanding had attempted to settle, became intensified after Disraeli replaced Gladstone as prime minister in February 1874. Gladstone's Liberal government had considered an independent Afghanistan under British influence as the best guarantee of India's security against Russia. In the early seventies, consequently, Afghanistan was far less dependent on Britain than Bukhara was on Russia. The Liberals had also readily accepted Kaufman's settlement of the Khivan question, on condition that Russia scrupulously honor her promises in regard to Afghanistan.[1] Disraeli was both more hostile to Russia and more favorable to imperial expansion than Gladstone. The conquest and partial annexation of Khiva was thus taken as evidence that the Russian danger in Central Asia was growing and that a stronger response on Britain's part was needed.

In January 1875 Lord Salisbury, Disraeli's secretary of state for India, sided with the "forward policy" school and launched Britain's new policy for the containment of Russia in Central Asia. Afghanistan, Kashgar, and Kalat were to be converted from independent buffer states under British influence into "dependent, willingly subordinate states."[2] The central feature of the new policy was to be the establishment of a British political agent or agents in Afghanistan. Emir Shir Ali, with an eye to the erosion of the rights of the Indian princes by British resident agents, steadfastly refused to receive such an agent. Disraeli, Salisbury, and Lord Lytton, the new viceroy of India, regarding the reception of a British resident as essential for the protection of Britain's interests, interpreted Shir Ali's refusal as an indication that he was turning toward Russia.

    After Russia's annexation of Kokand in February 1876 Lytton
insisted more strongly that Shir Ali receive a British agent. Further-
more, in September of that year the viceroy asked London to press
St. Petersburg for the termination of all correspondence between
Tashkent and Kabul, which Lytton termed a violation of the 1873
Anglo-Russian understanding. The following month he demanded of
Shir Ali a promise not to communicate with Russia in the future.
General von Kaufman's correspondence with the emir of Afghanistan had begun in March 1870 and continued at irregular intervals
over the intervening six years. Bukhara served as the intermediary
in this correspondence, dispatches being carried at times by the agent
whom Shir Ali maintained at Bukhara and at other times by Muzaffar's own envoys to Kabul. No British official before Lytton had
objected to this correspondence. Shir Ali forwarded Kaufman's letters to Calcutta, whence they were sent to London. Gladstone's
government had actually approved of Kaufman's letters as proof of
Russia's good intentions.[3] Yet Lytton maintained that if the situation were reversed and the government of India opened "similarly
friendly relations with the Khans of Khiva and Bokhara," St. Petersburg would hardly remain indifferent.[4] He was undoubtedly right,
although Khiva was in a somewhat different position, having by
treaty handed over control of her foreign relations to Russia.
    In 1877, while the Anglo-Afghan negotiations dragged on with
little chance of a mutually acceptable settlement, Britain's attention
became focused on the Balkan crisis. The outbreak of the Russo-
Turkish War in April aroused British fears of a Russian seizure of
Constantinople and the Straits. By January 1878, with the Russian
armies sweeping rapidly down upon Constantinople, these fears
seemed about to be realized. London dispatched a fleet to guard
the Turkish capital, and war between Britain and Russia appeared
imminent. Russia decided to answer the British naval demonstration
in the Straits with a land demonstration of her own in Central Asia.
The use of Central Asia as a base for applying pressure on Britain
in India so as to relieve British pressure on Russia in the Near East
was a plan long advocated by many Russian military strategists. Encouraged by the coolness existing between Afghanistan and Britain,
Russia now took steps to implement the plan.[5]
    St. Petersburg at first projected a three-pronged attack on India:
from Fergana via Kashgar, from Samarkand via Kabul, and from
Petro-Aleksandrovsk and Krasnovodsk via Merv and western Afghanistan. By May, however, after Russian troops had been pulled back

from Constantinople and the bellicose Ignatiev had been replaced as ambassador to Turkey, Anglo-Russian tensions lessened. Accordingly, Miliutin informed Kaufman on May 19 that the military plan for Central Asia now envisaged only a demonstration of armed strength on Afghanistan's borders. The route of the Fergana detachment through Kashgar was abandoned in favor of a line of march through Karategin to the Amu-Darya, and the Petro-Aleksandrovsk detachment was to proceed via Chardjui to Kelif rather than to Merv.[6] The route of the Samarkand group remained via Djam to Kelif and Shirabad.

Russia's projected demonstration of military might in Central Asia involved Bukhara,[7] for all three detachments had to cross that khanate in order to reach the borders of Afghanistan. During May Kaufman sent his diplomatic attaché, A. A. Weinberg, to Karshi to secure from Muzaffar permission for the passage of the Russian troops and to lay up supplies of provisions for the men and fodder for the animals. On May 24 Kaufman reported to Miliutin that Weinberg had obtained a pledge of complete cooperation. July 1 was the date set for the crossing of the Russo-Bukharan border.[8]

The Russian troops had not been long on the road when word was received from Miliutin on July 9 that the demonstration was canceled. The Congress of Berlin had succeeded in putting an end to the Balkan crisis. It was perhaps fortunate that the necessity for the demonstration was removed, for the troop movements had not begun auspiciously. The Fergana detachment of 2200 men encountered snowstorms in crossing the Alai Mountains and never reached Karategin. The Petro-Aleksandrovsk detachment, of similar size, was forced to ascend the Amu-Darya in slow native boats because the expected steamboat did not arrive in time; these troops had covered only 87 miles before their recall orders arrived. The main Samarkand detachment, 15,000 strong, never even left Djam, on the Russo-Bukharan frontier.[9]

The abortive Russian demonstration of July 1878 is only the most striking of the numerous examples of Bukhara's central, though passive, role in Central Asian affairs in 1878–1880, imposed by its location between Russian Turkestan and Afghanistan. Even before the Russian troops were set in motion, Muzaffar had played host in Karshi on June 7 to Major General N. G. Stoletov, whom Tashkent was sending to Kabul to negotiate a treaty with Shir Ali. Upon Stoletov's return from Kabul, Muzaffar again received him in Shahr on August 30.[10] The offensive-defensive alliance against Britain that

Stoletov concluded with Afghanistan, followed by Shir Ali's refusal to receive a British embassy, led to the outbreak of the Second Anglo-Afghan War in November 1878. By the following spring Britain had replaced Shir Ali, who received no support from Russia, with his rebellious elder son and established a protectorate over Afghanistan far more complete than were the Russian protectorates over Bukhara and Khiva.

Lord Lytton's triumph was short-lived, however, for the pattern of the First Afghan War was soon repeated. Native hostility caused the downfall of Britain's protégé and forced the British to occupy Kabul and Kandahar, the chief towns, in order to retain control. St. Petersburg now played the trump she had been holding for a decade. Shir Ali's nephew, the pretender Abd ar-Rahman, had been living in Tashkent since 1870. Russia allowed him to leave Tashkent in December 1879 with his retinue of 250 men and a good supply of Russian rifles and ordered Muzaffar to give them free passage through Bukhara. The emir obeyed, although he treated Abd ar-Rahman coldly, just as he had on the pretender's flight from Afghanistan a decade previously. Muzaffar neither received Abd ar-Rahman in audience, as was the custom with foreign visitors, nor appointed any official escort for his trip through Shahr-i Sabz and Hisar.[11] By the spring of 1880 Abd ar-Rahman had made himself master of Afghan Turkestan. In April of that year Gladstone and the Liberals returned to power in England, Lord Lytton was replaced as viceroy of India, and Britain returned to her pre–1875 policy of nonintervention in Afghanistan. Abd ar-Rahman was recognized as emir of Afghanistan, British troops were withdrawn, and all of Lytton's demands were dropped, except that Kabul promised not to maintain foreign relations with any state except Britain.

Afghanistan's loss of the right to maintain relations with foreign states spelled the end of Bukhara's activities in that area, too. After 1873 Bukhara had retained the right to conduct her own foreign relations on condition that she act within the framework of friendship for Russia. In practice, this right was limited to Afghanistan. Since Khiva had been deprived of the right to maintain foreign relations by the treaty of 1873, and Kokand was soon annexed to Russia, Afghanistan was Bukhara's only other independent neighbor. They did in fact exchange envoys quite regularly until 1879,[12] after which Bukhara no longer had any neighbors but Russia with whom to maintain relations. Relations with Turkey had been curtailed at Russia's insistence by 1873. The exchange of envoys with Persia or

China would have been a pointless expense, since Bukhara had no interests in common with these lands; and diplomatic contact with India would have been interpreted by Russia as a hostile act. Thus, without any move on Russia's part to abridge his rights, Muzaffar had ceased to be represented abroad as a sovereign ruler.

Throughout the period of Anglo-Russian tension in the late 1870's Bukhara served as an instrument of Russian policy. Russian troops, Russian envoys to Afghanistan, an Afghan pretender returning from Russia—all were accorded unimpeded passage across Bukhara at Tashkent's request. Whatever his doubts or personal interest in the outcome of Afghanistan's difficulties, Muzaffar had no choice but to comply with the requests of his Russian overlords. Bukhara was proving a docile and useful client and thereby fulfilling the hopes of those Russians responsible for St. Petersburg's policy of nonintervention in the khanate.

Merv, 1881–1884

In the 1870's the area bounded by Khiva, Bukhara, Afghanistan, Persia, and the Russian-held east coast of the Caspian was a political vacuum occupied by various unruly Turkoman tribes. Roaming the Kara Kum Desert and dwelling in the oases strung out along its southern edge, the Turkomans had never been able to establish any stable political order. Into this region Russia eventually had to come, in quest of a stable and defensible frontier.

Whereas Bukhara had served as a passive instrument of Russian policy in regard to Afghanistan, Tashkent assigned Khiva a more active role in the struggle for the Kara Kum. The opponent in this case was not a foreign power but a rival Russian viceroyalty, the Caucasus. The pattern emerged as early as 1875, when some of the Teke Turkomans, who inhabited the western Kara Kum, feeling the pressure of the Russians at Krasnovodsk, sent representatives to the khan of Khiva asking for his protection. They presumably felt that this indirect form of Russian tutelage would be easier to bear than the direct rule imposed by conquest. Muhammad Rahim turned for advice to Colonel Ivanov, commandant of the Amu-Darya Otdel, who told him to send a reliable deputy to rule the Turkomans in Khiva's name. The khan did so, but his action was protested by General Lomakin, commandant of the Transcaspian Otdel, whose jurisdiction extended eastward to the undefined frontier of Khiva. During 1875–1876 Minister of War Miliutin, to whom the protest was referred, urged upon both Kaufman and Lomakin's superiors in Tiflis the need to avoid involvement in Turkoman affairs and the risk of antagonizing Britain at a time when Russia's attention was focused on the Balkan crisis.[13]

Miliutin's intercession did not settle the rivalry between Tashkent and Tiflis for control of the Turkomans. That rivalry became more acute as the Russians in Transcaspia, with St. Petersburg's approval, began a major advance along the line of the southern oases of the Kara Kum in order to pacify the unruly Turkomans and forestall British influence in the area. In the summer of 1877 the Russians took Kizil-Arvat, then after a disastrous setback in 1879 moved forward the following year and captured Geok-Tepe and Askhabad early in 1881. During the campaign of 1880–1881 Khiva and Bukhara acted as secondary sources of supply for camels and provisions. Khiva in particular was important, since she lay on the safest route between Russian Turkestan and the theater of operations in Transcaspia. The troops sent by Kaufman in November 1880, in response to orders from St. Petersburg to join in the attack on Geok-Tepe, crossed Khiva with the khan's permission; and on their return from Geok-Tepe the following March Muhammad Rahim offered the troops his personal congratulations and quartered them for the night on the grounds of his summer palace near the capital.[14] Muhammad Rahim gave further evidence of his good faith to Russia at the end of 1880 when the hard-pressed Teke Turkomans sent envoys to ask his help against the Russians. He replied by advising submission to the White Tsar, as the Russian emperor was known in Central Asia. In April 1881 acting Governor General Kolpakovskii sent the khan a letter of thanks for this friendly act and took the opportunity to ask Muhammad Rahim to exercise his influence with the Turkoman elders of Merv, the easternmost of the Kara Kum oases, to preserve peace in that area.[15] Just as in 1875, the Russians in Turkestan viewed Khiva as the instrument whereby Tashkent might exercise indirect control over a part at least of the Turkomans and thus forestall the extension of Tiflis' jurisdiction.

After the conquests of 1881 the only unorganized Turkoman territory left was that centering on Merv, where several parties among the local population contended for power. In the summer of 1881 one of these parties requested Muhammad Rahim to appoint a Khivan governor for Merv. On the advice of Petro-Aleksandrovsk and Tashkent the khan of Khiva consented, though his experience with the Turkomans of his own khanate must have made him well aware of the difficulties involved in trying to rule the even more anarchic Turkomans of Merv. A Khivan governor would be recognized by only a part of the population, and his authority would be only nominal. Since no Khivan official was anxious to take a post with so many risks and so few rewards, Muhammad Rahim appointed the elderly Yusuf-beg. The following year Yusuf told P. M. Lessar, the Russian engineer, explorer, and later diplomat, that he had been chosen because of his advanced age; if he were killed, it would be no great loss. In fact Yusuf-beg died in Merv of natural causes in October 1882.[16]

After Yusuf's death the pro-Khivan party at Merv sent a large delegation to the khan asking for a new governor. Muhammad Rahim sent the petitioners on to Petro-Aleksandrovsk. At the end of November, acting undoubtedly on Petro-Aleksandrovsk's advice, the khan appointed a new governor and gave him instructions to forbid pillaging by Khiva's vassals at Merv, particularly against the Russians. Merv was also forbidden to maintain relations with Britain, Afghanistan, or Persia, since they were enemies of Russia. During the brief term of office of the new governor, Abd ar-Rahman-beg, there was confused intriguing among the various factions at Merv. The Turkomans were apparently convinced that some form of external control was inevitable, but they seemed incapable of settling the question of who should be the controlling power.[17] Abd ar-Rahman himself established contact with English spies operating among the Sarik Turkomans south of Merv. The governor general of Turkestan, M. G. Cherniaev, who had not been consulted on Abd ar-Rahman's appointment, forced the khan to recall him and took a direct part in the selection of his successor.[18] The new governor, Ata-djan-beg, received Cherniaev's written confirmation of his appointment on April 22, 1883, in Petro-Aleksandrovsk.[19]

Cherniaev was merely continuing the policy of Kaufman and Kolpakovskii with regard to Khiva and Merv. For once Tashkent found support in St. Petersburg, where Foreign Minister Giers in 1882–1883 favored the peaceful exercise of influence over Merv indirectly through Khiva.[20] The turbulence of the Merv Turkomans, however, enabled Tiflis to resolve the matter differently. At the end of 1883 the Russian forces advanced from Askhabad to the Tedjen oasis, seventy-five miles west of Merv, whence they engineered the accession to power in Merv of the pro-Russian faction and then elicited a plea from them for annexation. In March 1884 Russia occupied Merv and annexed it to the Transcaspian Oblast, formed in 1881. Ata-djan-beg had fled to Khiva three weeks earlier.[21]

Tashkent's attempt to restore Merv to Khiva and thus preserve that distant oasis for her own jurisdiction against encroachment from Tiflis ended in failure. The pro-Khivan party at Merv never succeeded in gaining the upper hand, the Khivan governors were never recognized by the other factions, they exercised only nominal authority, and the last governor antagonized the population by attempting to levy heavy taxes.[22] The subjection of Merv to Khiva was further handicapped in that the Turkomans undoubtedly considered it a subterfuge for avoiding any effective control, and as such it did not meet Russia's requirements of frontier security.

Shugnan and Roshan, 1883–1884

During the Russian advance in Transcaspia that area became the primary focus of Anglo-Russian relations in Central Asia, even though Gladstone's government was not especially concerned over Russia's gains against the Turkomans. In the period immediately preceding the annexation of Merv, however, a secondary focus emerged at the other extreme of Afghanistan's northern frontier. The dual principality of Shugnan and Roshan on the upper Pandj River had enjoyed de facto independence for centuries. Its rulers, like the dispossessed dynasties of Kulab, Darvaz, and Badakhshan, claimed descent from Alexander of Macedon.[23] Yet while Badakhshan and Darvaz were falling prey to Afghan and Bukharan expansion and centralization in the 1860's and 1870's, Shugnan, lying even more remote than they among its mountain fastnesses, preserved its independence at the price of a nominal tribute to the mir of Badakhshan. In 1882 the shah of Shugnan, Yusuf Ali, jeopardized his position by receiving the Russian explorer Dr. A. E. Regel for a prolonged stay at his capital, Bar-Pandj. Afghanistan regarded Regel's visit with suspicion. Interpreting it as a sign of official Russian interest in an area that Afghanistan claimed as her own, the mir of Badakhshan sent a small military mission to Bar-Pandj in January 1883 to demand the Russian explorer's departure; Regel accordingly returned to Darvaz the following month. An Afghan garrison was subsequently installed at Bar-Pandj on orders from Kabul, and Yusuf Ali was taken under guard to Badakhshan and finally to Kabul.

When the Russian Pamir Expedition approached the eastern frontiers of Shugnan in the summer of 1883, the Afghans sent a small detachment to occupy Roshan, which was governed by Yusuf Ali's eldest son. Failing to secure a promise of aid from the beg of Darvaz, the population of Roshan sent a delegation to the Pamir Expedition to offer the submission of Shugnan and Roshan to Russia in return for help against Afghanistan. Captain Putiata, leader of the expedition, told the delegation that the distance of their homeland from the Russian frontier and the difficult communications over mountain trails made it impossible for Russia to send troops in time to forestall an Afghan occupation. Putiata advised the people of Roshan to submit to the Afghans unless they could resist the invaders with their own resources.[24]

At the end of August 1883 St. Petersburg learned via Tashkent of Afghanistan's occupation of Shugnan. Shortly afterwards the emir of Bukhara sought Tashkent's help in restoring the status quo ante on the upper Pandj. Governor General Cherniaev soon confirmed the early reports of Afghanistan's move into Shugnan and charged that Bukhara's security was thereby threatened. Cherniaev insisted that the mir of Badakhshan be requested to withdraw his troops and refrain from such hostile acts against Bukhara in the future. In mid-December A. E. Vlangali, Russia's deputy minister of foreign affairs, brought the matter to the attention of the British ambassador in St. Petersburg, Sir Edward Thornton, and charged that Afghanistan had violated the 1873 Anglo-Russian understanding, which had not included Shugnan and Roshan within Afghanistan's frontiers. Vlangali asked the British government, in accordance with the 1873 agreement, to "employ all their influence to induce the Emir of Caboul to withdraw from Shugnan and Roshan as soon as possible the Lieutenant and the Afghan garrison now in that Principality, and to renounce for ever all interference in its affairs."[25]

Although Vlangali's complaint of a violation of the 1873 understanding was on the whole valid, the facts were more complicated than his memorandum indicated. The 1873 agreement, which defined the upper Amu-Darya or Pandj River as the Bukharo-Afghan boundary, had been drawn up by diplomats who lacked accurate information on the geography of the area through which the Pandj flowed and who, on the British side, were more interested in placing the Afghan frontier on a convenient major river than in trying to follow traditional boundaries along the crests of uncharted mountain ranges. Consequently, the 1873 agreement created a number of problems, of which Russia and Britain became gradually aware during the ensuing decade:[26] (1) Vakhan, assigned to Afghanistan by the agreement, included a substantial amount of territory on the right bank of the Pandj, or beyond the Afghan frontier as defined in the agreement; (2) Darvaz, which Bukhara annexed in 1877–1878, lay predominantly on the right bank of the Pandj but also included several districts on the left bank, within the Afghan frontier as defined in the agreement; (3) Shugnan and Roshan, which the agreement did not mention, was regarded by Kabul as a dependency of Badakhshan, which the agreement gave to Afghanistan. Although Shugnan included small stretches of territory on the left bank of the Pandj, and its capital was located there, it lay predominantly on the right bank, beyond the Afghan frontier as defined in the 1873 agreement. Afghanistan's occupation of Shugnan and Roshan in 1883 and the ensuing Russian protest thus brought into the open the problem of Afghanistan's northeastern boundary, which had never really been settled.

London took its time in replying to the Russian memorandum, at first in order to verify the facts of the matter and then because it could not decide what position to take. In October 1883 Rawlinson, who had originally suggested the line of the Pandj in 1869, argued in favor of abandoning it and supporting Kabul's claim to all of Vakhan and Shugnan-Roshan. Calcutta rejected the idea of giving up the convenient and clear line of the Pandj but was unwilling to compel Kabul to observe it by relinquishing right-bank Vakhan and Shugnan-Roshan. Another possibility was to substitute the Murgab River for the upper Pandj as the Afghan boundary, since explorations in 1873–1874 had convinced the British that the Murgab, which flowed through Roshan, was the main branch of the Pandj. Such a substitution would have placed all of Vakhan and Shugnan and half of Roshan in Afghanistan.[27] Lord Ripon, the viceroy of India, did in fact request Abd ar-Rahman in March 1884 to withdraw the troops he had sent into Shugnan and Roshan in violation of the 1873 understanding and warned him not to expect British help in case his trans-Pandj adventures involved him in a collision with Bukhara or Russia.[28] Toward Russia, however, Britain maintained official silence. Meanwhile, Russia rejected a second request for help from the population of Shugnan and Roshan, who were attempting to oust the Afghan garrisons.[29] In March 1884 Britain responded to Russia's annexation of Merv by proposing the delimitation of Afghanistan's northwest boundary. The resulting negotiations on this subject overshadowed the question of the upper Pandj, which was much less important to both Russia and Britain.

On June 9, 1884, the Russian foreign ministry finally reminded Thornton of its memorandum of the previous December and expressed the hope that the British government had not lost sight of the matter.[30] Four days later the British ambassador communicated to Foreign Minister N. K. Giers the contents of Foreign Secretary Granville's instructions of April 17/29. These instructions had not previously been made known to the Russian government, perhaps in the hope that the Shugnan question would be dropped. Britain's belated reply was that the emir of Afghanistan considered Shugnan and Roshan a part of Badakhshan. Since the Indian government did not have sufficient information on the area in question to give an opinion on whether Kabul had violated the 1873 agreement, London proposed that commissioners from England, Russia, and Afghanistan make an on-the-spot investigation.[31] Giers rejected Kabul's claim. He cited Lord Granville's own dispatch of October 5/17, 1872,[32] defining Afghanistan's northern frontier as the Pandj River eastward to its source, and he pointed out that Gorchakov had accepted this definition. Giers once again requested Britain to put pressure on Afghanistan to respect the terms of the 1873 agreement. He declared that he would consult with the governor general of Turkestan on the proposed mixed commission but that the status quo ante would have to be restored first and the commission's powers would have to be limited to tracing the boundary agreed upon in 1872–1873.[33] Britain continued to insist that the joint commission was the only way to determine whether the Afghan claims conflicted with the 1873 agreement or whether the status quo ante had in fact been changed.[34]

Britain knew she was on weak ground, but her principal aim in Central Asia at the time was to get Afghanistan and Russia to agree on Afghanistan's northwest frontier, where Kabul's territories lay wide open to a Russian advance from Transcaspia. At this critical time London refused to run the risk of antagonizing Abd ar-Rahman by pressing him to withdraw from a remote and insignificant principality. Russia, too, was more interested in settling her own border with Afghanistan to the south and east of Merv than in distant Shugnan. The matter was allowed to rest for almost a decade until the Pamirs became of direct interest to Russia and Britain.

Muhammad-biy, Kush-begi of Bukhara, 1870–1889

Muhammad Murad, Divan-begi of Khiva, 1864–1873, 1880–1901

7 / The End of an Era

Russia and Bukhara, 1880–1884

In the early 1880's a conflict arose between Tashkent and St. Petersburg over Bukhara's future, similar to that over Khiva's future in the mid-seventies. Advocates of the annexation of Bukhara had never been lacking. N. P. Stremoukhov cited with approval the alleged opinion of many Bukharans in 1874 that the khanate could not long maintain its independence and would sooner or later be annexed to Russia.[1] The following year Baron A. G. Jomini, senior councillor and acting director of the foreign ministry, told William Doria, Britain's acting chargé d'affaires, that Russia must eventually annex Bukhara and Kokand as India must eventually annex Afghanistan.[2] The annexation of Bukhara was viewed as merely a question of time by the geographer M. I. Veniukov in 1877 and by Captain Putiata and the Swiss traveler Henri Moser in 1883.[3]

Except for Kaufman's support of the annexation of Khiva in the mid-1870's, he in general tolerated the continued autonomy of Bukhara and Khiva because he was convinced of their inevitable collapse. Faced with St. Petersburg's implacable opposition to annexation, Kaufman was willing to wait. He believed that the example of good government and material prosperity set by Russian Turkestan would in the long run give rise to stresses and strains within the khanates that they would not be able to survive.[4] By the beginning of the 1880's Kaufman was able to report with smug satisfaction that Bukhara and Khiva were already disintegrating; the impression made on their populations by Russia's example was so great, in fact, that they must be kept from gravitating too strongly toward Russia. The governor general pointed to the immigration of Bukharans into Russian Turkestan, especially the Zarafshan Okrug, where they made more acute the shortage of irrigated land.[5] Kaufman exaggerated the significance of the Bukharan immigration, for the numbers involved were relatively small, and many were migrant workers who returned to their homes in Bukhara at the end of the harvest season. Moreover, Bukhara received a sizable number of immigrants from Afghan Turkestan and Badakhshan, refugees from the unsettled conditions there.[6] Whereas General von Kaufman could find consolation in the thought that Bukhara and Khiva would collapse in the not too distant future, he could never reconcile himself to the indefinite prolongation of their existence. In his final report on his term as governor general he deplored the "evil economic organization in the khanates which keeps the working mass in desperate poverty, under the permanent oppression of the administration and tax and property abuses." He ascribed the poor condition of the Amu-Darya Otdel to "the oppression and ruin of the work-loving majority of the population under Khivan rule." Finally, he proposed that the expensive "natural subsidy" that Russia provided to the emir of Bukhara in the form of the water of the Zarafshan be decreased so that more water for irrigation would be available to meet Russia's needs in the Zarafshan Okrug.[7]

M. G. Cherniaev, who returned to the scene of his former exploits in 1882 as Kaufman's successor, openly advocated the immediate annexation of Bukhara and Khiva.[8] The internal political situation in Bukhara gave the new governor general a chance to promote his views. The existence of substantial domestic opposition to Muzaffar and the availability of a disaffected eldest son in exile indicated the likelihood of a bitter struggle for succession on the emir's death. Such a contest was a common phenomenon in Central Asia but would be to Russia's disadvantage. As early as September 1881 rumors that the fifty-eight-year-old Muzaffar was very ill filled Tashkent with anxiety over the turmoil that was expected to follow his death.[9]

On June 24, 1882, before going out to Tashkent to assume the duties of his new post, Cherniaev presented his arguments for the annexation of Bukhara to a special conference in St. Petersburg, which included the chief of the general staff, the finance minister, and the new director of the foreign ministry's Asiatic Department, I. A. Zinoviev. In Cherniaev's words: "We can count on the sympathy and cooperation of the so-called Russian party, which consists of the peasants and merchants and sees in Russian rule a reliable guarantee of personal and property security. They have long since desired annexation to Russia, and, in the event of internal disorder, they will certainly turn to us with a request to introduce Russian authority into Bukhara." Pointing to the economic advantages of annexation, the governor general proposed as a first step, "immediately to appoint an official Russian resident in Bukhara, whose duty it would be to observe the course of political events so that we might at the proper time take measures in the event of disorders, and also gradually to prepare the Bukharan population for a peaceful transition to Russian rule." But the conference rejected Cherniaev's proposal, recommending "abstention from any step which might subsequently lead to a change in our relations" with Bukhara. Although recognizing the undesirable elements in the status quo, particularly the latent political instability, the conference pointed both to the great financial burden that annexation would entail, since Russia could never squeeze as much revenue out of Bukhara as could the emir's government, and to the suspicions that annexation would arouse in Britain. The conference recommended, as an alternative to annexation, that Russia officially sanction the succession to the Bukharan throne of that "prince who has the support of the majority of the population and who will promise to stand in the same relationship to Russia as does his father.[10]

At the beginning of 1883 Russian visitors reported the dissatisfaction of the Bukharan population with the emir's government over the question of taxes and administrative abuses, as well as the hostility of the clerical zealots to Muzaffar's pro-Russian policy. Muzaffar himself had stayed away from his capital for over a year in order to avoid the enmity of the populace, stirred up by the clergy. A united opposition seemed to be forming around a nucleus consisting of the adherents of Abd al-Malik, the emir's eldest son, then living in India on a British pension.[11] In order to make her intentions toward Bukhara clear, Russia invited Muzaffar to send as his representative to the coronation of Alexander III in the spring of 1883 the son whom he wished to succeed him, so that the emperor could confirm that son as the emir's heir-apparent. A decade earlier Muzaffar had chosen as his successor his fifth son, Abd al-Ahad, the beg of Kermine, who now went to Moscow and received the imperial confirmation.[12]

This gesture expressing Russia's interest in a peaceful succession did not settle the problem. In fact, after Abd al-Ahad's trip to Russia, during which he had openly admired much of what he saw, the clerical zealots turned increasingly to Abd al-Malik as their last hope.[13] In November 1883 Captain Arandarenko, commandant of the Samarkand Uezd, reported rumors that Abd al-Malik, still hoping to gain the succession, was keeping close watch on the situation in Bukhara and was in contact with the opposition, especially the clergy. At the beginning of the following month Tashkent informed the chief of the general staff, N. N. Obruchev, of its fears that the anti-Russian party in Bukhara would at the first opportunity revolt against Muzaffar or his designated successor. Tashkent's uneasiness was even more apparent in Cherniaev's report of December 12 to the minister of war that he had just received word of rumors that Kulab and Baldjuan had been captured by the former beg of Kulab with Afghan aid. While awaiting instructions from St. Petersburg, Cherniaev reported, "I have ordered General Ivanov [commandant of the Zarafshan Okrug], if the rumors are substantiated, to move immediately two battalions and a battery to Katta-Kurgan for moral support to the emir, with whom the population is dissatisfied, for in case of further Afghan successes in Bukhara, there may be a revolt in favor of the English candidate, the katta-türa."[14] The rumors proved false, but the succession problem continued to trouble Russia until Abd al-Ahad was safely seated on his father's throne.

The struggle between the annexationists and the defenders of nonintervention was waged on another front in the first half of the 1880's, when the unsatisfactory system of conducting relations with Bukhara by means of extraordinary embassies came under serious consideration. Toward the end of his term in office General von Kaufman suggested that a permanent Russian commercial agent be established at Bukhara, who should be charged with the collection of intelligence on Bukhara and Afghanistan. The foreign ministry countered with a proposal for a special diplomatic agent at the emir's court, but Kaufman was firmly opposed. Muzaffar was merely a vassal of the governor general of Turkestan; to accredit to him a member of the Russian diplomatic corps would only encourage him in his pretensions to independence.[15]

Cherniaev's conception of a Russian resident as a means of preparing Bukhara for annexation was not far different from Kaufman's. General N. O. Rosenbach, who succeeded Cherniaev in 1884, differed from both his predecessors in approving of St. Petersburg's policy of nonintervention in the khanates, but he too supported the establishment of a commercial agent subordinate to Tashkent rather than a political agent responsible to the foreign ministry.[16] Despite the opposition from Tashkent, St. Petersburg persisted. In May 1884, shortly after Rosenbach's appointment, the foreign ministry pressed on the new governor general the need for a permanent political agent in Bukhara to protect Russian commercial interests, promote trade, and enforce compliance with the treaty of 1873, in particular the abolition of illegal duties on Russian trade.[17] The Ministry of Foreign Affairs finally had its way a year and a half later, as it usually did in questions of policy decided in the capital.

The atmosphere of Russo-Bukharan relations in the early 1880's was one of imminent change—a change of rulers for the khanate, a change in Russia's method of conducting relations with her dependency, and finally a change toward more rapid communication with the emir's capital. During the previous decade the Russian telegraph network had spread throughout Russian Turkestan, reaching Tashkent in 1873, Khodjent in 1875, Samarkand and Kokand in 1876, and Katta-Kurgan, on the Bukharan frontier, in 1878.[18] General von Kaufman raised the question of a telegraph link to Bukhara several times at the end of the 1870's, but apparently without much insistence and consequently with no effect.[19] In the early 1880's, however, Russia raised in earnest the issue of extending the telegraph from Katta-Kurgan to the capital of Bukhara. Russia may have been motivated by the unstable political situation in the khanate, which required Tashkent to have immediate information on any important turn of events, or by a desire to consolidate and develop her Central Asian territories after the conquest of Transcaspia.

The negotiations over the establishment of a telegraph line between Katta-Kurgan and Bukhara began at Shahr in January 1883. Major General Prince Ferdinand von Wittgenstein, accompanied by Lieutenant Colonel V. V. Krestovskii, had been sent by Cherniaev to secure Muzaffar's agreement to the construction of the line at his own expense. The emir put up as determined a resistance to Russian pressure as he had in the matter of slavery and the slave trade. He argued that Russia could continue to exercise influence over Bukhara and support him against his enemies in the future, as it had in the past, without the telegraph. The telegraph's advantages would therefore be primarily commercial, benefiting only the merchants. But the merchants were a small minority in Bukhara; the great majority of the population were peasants, over whom the emir professed to exercise far less authority than did the clerical hierarchy, and the clergy opposed on religious grounds all innovations such as the tele-

graph. Aware that Russia's policy was to maintain his authority and
to act through him in Bukhara, Muzaffar played his trump. If the
emperor chose to command him in the matter of the telegraph, he
would of course have no choice but to comply, but his authority in
the khanate would thereby be undermined because of the clergy's
hold over the masses. A complete Russian takeover in Bukhara would
be the inevitable outcome. The most Muzaffar could promise Wittgenstein was to try to neutralize the opposition of the clerical
orders.[20]

In October 1883 Prince Wittgenstein was sent to Bukhara again
on the same mission. He was kept waiting two and a half weeks
while Muzaffar attempted to deal directly with Governor General
Cherniaev, who was in Samarkand. After being rebuffed by Cherniaev, the emir received Wittgenstein, and on October 21 he finally
yielded on the subject of the telegraph.[21] As Muzaffar himself had
told Wittgenstein in January, when Russia insisted, Bukhara had no
choice but to obey. The telegraph line was constructed during the
summer of 1884 and inaugurated on August 28. The Bukharan government paid for the building of the line as far as the Russian
frontier and promised to pay for its maintenance and to take responsibility for guarding it and the telegraph office in the capital. Income
from telegrams transmitted over the line in Bukhara was to go to
the emir. Maintenance of the line was contracted out for twelve
years to a Russian merchant from Orenburg named Nazarov.[22] Bukhara thus acquired her first modern link to the outside world. The
telegraph was to prove only a forerunner of the breakdown of Bukhara's isolation from the world of the nineteenth century.

Dependable postal service between Bukhara and Katta-Kurgan
was still nonexistent. The establishment of regular postal communications, first proposed to Muzaffar in 1872 by Petrovskii, had been
resisted by the emir a second time in 1874.[23] Early in 1881 a Russian
Tatar from Tambov, named Burnashev, established with the permission of the Russian government a private postal service between
Bukhara and Katta-Kurgan, but the service was unsatisfactory because of the high price and the insecure conditions of travel in the
khanate.[24] N. V. Charykov, diplomatic attaché to the governor general of Turkestan, who visited Bukhara in the late fall of 1884, noted
the need for regular postal communications, but they had to await
the coming of the railroad.

Attitude of the Native Regimes toward Russia

Muzaffar ad-Din was variously judged by his Western and Russian contemporaries. Some, like the Hungarian orientalist Vámbéry and an unnamed Russian who spent several months in Bukhara just before the Russo-Bukharan War, found the emir a severe but just ruler, who set a frugal and devoutly religious example for his subjects.[25] Others, like Kostenko, Schuyler, and N. P. Stremoukhov, called Muzaffar a despot, who plundered his own subjects and whose weak character made him unfit to rule.[26] Stremoukhov was one of the emir's harshest critics, charging him with neglecting affairs of state for the company of his harem and his *batchas* (boys, eight to fifteen years old, trained as dancers, dressed as girls, and used for homosexual purposes). According to Stremoukhov, neither the wives and daughters nor the property of his subjects were safe from the covetousness of Muzaffar, who also did not hesitate to sell in the bazaar from time to time rare volumes from Tamerlane's library in order to satisfy his need for money.[27] On balance, the emir would seem to have been a typical Central Asian autocrat, regarding his realm as his personal estate entrusted to him by Allah, who fortunately did not demand too close an accounting of his stewardship. Never having been outside his domains, except for campaigns into Kokand, Muzaffar had an extremely parochial outlook and was suspicious of all change. Expediency rather than love dictated his friendship for Russia. He could retain the territories and power left to him only by avoiding an overt demonstration of hostility toward Russia and by preventing his domestic enemies from fomenting civil strife.

Stremoukhov had serious reservations about Muzaffar's reliability as an ally. Not being able to count very far on the loyalty of his own subjects, the emir was forced to maneuver constantly between his more powerful neighbors, Russia and Afghanistan, in order to avert external attacks. According to Stremoukhov, his foreign policy was one of alignment with whichever neighbor was more menacing. In the mid-1870's this meant alignment with Russia, but it offered no guarantee for the future. "It would," Stremoukhov urged, "be a great mistake to depend on him; he is always equally ready to become a staunch friend or a sworn enemy."[28] Captain Arandarenko agreed in 1880 that Muzaffar could not be fully trusted; his continued loyalty would depend on Russia's military strength deployed on his borders.[29]

Muzaffar did indeed zealously defend both the prerogatives and the substance of the authority he retained over his country's internal affairs. He always attempted to get Russian envoys to show their respect by dismounting at the greatest possible distance from the site of their audience with him.[30] In 1869 he tried to establish his right to negotiate with St. Petersburg over Kaufman's head; in 1883 he attempted to bypass Wittgenstein and negotiate directly with Cherniaev; and in 1884 he again demanded permission to deal with the emperor rather than the governor general. Foreign Minister Giers, however, on June 12, 1884, authorized Rosenbach to make clear to the emir that Tashkent was fully empowered to speak for the emperor.[31] On substantive questions Muzaffar successfully resisted Russian pressure on slavery, the slave trade, and postal communications, and he managed for nine months to avoid an agreement on the construction of the telegraph line, the one issue on which Russia was adamant.

In foreign affairs, however, which were of most concern to Russia, the emir proved his loyalty and his usefulness with respect to Russian policy in Khiva and Afghanistan. He was also attentive to public manifestations of friendship for Russia. On February 19, 1880, he marked the silver jubilee of Alexander II's accession by staging a parade and fireworks demonstration in Karshi, at which Captain Arandarenko represented the governor general. In the early 1880's Muzaffar sent one of his younger sons, Mansur, to be educated in the Page Corps at St. Petersburg. In 1883 Abd al-Ahad took to Alexander III's coronation many expensive presents from the emir and 100,000 rubles in gold.[32] Russia was satisfied with Muzaffar's performance, and the commission of inquiry into the state of Russian Turkestan led by Privy Councillor F. K. Giers, brother of the foreign minister, concluded in 1883 that the emir had consistently followed a peaceful policy since 1868 and that there was no serious danger of trouble arising between Russia and Bukhara.[33] Russia showed her appreciation by honoring Muzaffar and Abd al-Ahad with the orders of St. Anna, St. Andrei, and St. Stanislav.[34]

Muzaffar's closest advisers shared his realistic appraisal of Bukhara's position vis-à-vis Russia. The kush-begi, Muhammad-biy, and his family, who occupied positions of the highest importance in the Bukharan bureaucracy, undoubtedly deserve a large share of the credit for Bukhara's pro-Russian orientation.[35] Another leading member of the pro-Russian party at Muzaffar's court was Ali Muhammad

Karataev, a Tatar from Saratov who had lived in Bukhara since 1854. Karataev was the court clockmaker and reportedly exercised "almost unlimited" influence over the emir.[36]

Contemporary estimates of the character of Muhammad Rahim II of Khiva were as varied as those of Muzaffar ad-Din. The American reporter MacGahan and the English army captain Burnaby found the khan an easygoing young man who lived simply, indulged himself mainly by keeping a large harem and a fine stable, and left affairs of state to his advisers. Burnaby described him as quite happy in his status of a Russian vassal.[37] The French traveler Gabriel Bonvalot, however, called Muhammad Rahim a religious hypocrite, devout in public but in private a debauchee and a drunkard, an arbitrary and cruel despot who used the pretext of the Russian war indemnity to fleece his subjects, and an extremely suspicious, fearful man.[38] The evidence of his behavior when faced with the Russian danger in 1873 and the Turkoman threat in the succeeding years attests to Muhammad Rahim's lack of ability as a ruler, but whether his private life was particularly reprehensible, judged by the standards of his time and country, is doubtful. It is indeed true that his interests lay more in the enjoyment of life and in writing poetry than in governing his people.

Because of the khan's lack of interest in affairs of state, Khiva's attitude toward Russia was shaped less by the ruler and more by his advisers than was the case in Bukhara. In 1873 Muhammad Murad, the divan-begi and leader of the war party, was exiled to Russia by Kaufman. The new divan-begi was Muhammad Niyaz, a first cousin of the khan, who had been leader of the peace party and Muhammad Murad's adversary. He was friendly to Russia. In 1875, however, Muhammad Niyaz died in St. Petersburg after undergoing an operation. Muhammad Murad was permitted to return to Khiva in 1879. He soon regained the khan's favor, won the confidence of Petro-Aleksandrovsk, and was reinstated as divan-begi and chief adviser to Muhammad Rahim.[39] As a result of the Khivan defeat of 1873 and his six years in exile Muhammad Murad had gained a more realistic appreciation of Khiva's position vis-à-vis Russia. Unlike Bukhara, Khiva was not caught between Russia and another powerful neighbor and thus lacked both the opportunity and the necessity for political maneuvering. Khiva's only neighbors, other than the Russians, were the anarchic Turkomans of the Kara Kum Desert. Khiva's interest in cultivating good relations with Russia after 1873 was furthered by the realization that only Russian support enabled the khan's government to maintain its authority over the Khivan cousins of those same Turkomans. Khiva was also too small, weak, and poor a country after 1873 to think seriously of antagonizing Russia. Muhammad Rahim's resignation to his new status and his lack of interest in political affairs made the transition to a pro-Russian policy easier in Khiva than in Bukhara, as did the absence of a powerful clerical party. The Khivan government in the 1870's and 1880's punctually met the annual payments owed to Russia on the war indemnity; the divan-begi himself brought the annual installment to Petro-Aleksandrovsk. Russia rewarded the khan for his subservience with the order of St. Stanislav.[40]

Western Influence in Bukhara and Khiva, 1885

Examples of Western influence in Bukhara before 1868 were confined to a few isolated cases connected either with the active trade Bukharan merchants carried on with Russia or with individual Russians who in one way or another found their way to Bukhara. The English agent Burnes in 1833 found the Bukharans of the capital preparing their tea in Russian samovars.[41] Individual bearers of Western culture included a doctor from Vilno, who had been exiled to Petropavlovsk in 1848 for suspected revolutionary activities, had fled to Bukhara, and was practicing medicine there as late as 1870, and a peasant from Simbirsk, who had arrived in Bukhara in 1859 and was making his living there as a small trader fifteen years later.[42] A Westerner who left a permanent memorial was Giovanni Orlando, a prisoner of Nasr Allah who in the late 1840's made a large clock for his captor. Until quite recently Orlando's clock hung in a prominent position over the main gate of the citadel, facing the Rigistan or great square of Bukhara.[43]

In Bukhara, as in many other non-Western societies before and since, the army was the most important vehicle of Western influence. The man responsible for reorganizing the Bukharan army along Western lines was a fugitive Siberian Cossack who took the name Osman in Bukhara. Osman introduced the Russian field manual, Russian words of command, Russian discipline, Russian uniforms, and even Russian military music. He was executed by Muzaffar in 1868, probably for supporting Abd al-Malik's rebellion.[44] Despite Osman's efforts the Westernization of Bukhara's fighting forces remained entirely superficial; all Russian visitors to Bukhara in the 1870's and early 1880's were agreed on this point. Kostenko in 1870 observed that the Bukharan troops knew neither how to shoot nor how to march in step; he termed their drill a parody of the Russian original. Their equipment was in even worse state. Only one out of five infantry soldiers had a rifle, usually an ancient flintlock, which rested on a pedestal while being fired. Of the two hundred field pieces, barely twenty were serviceable.[45] Four years later Stremoukhov concluded that the emir's army was totally useless on account of its lack of discipline, absence of martial qualities, and poor armament.[46] Captain Arandarenko reported in 1880 that an infantry review he had witnessed left an unforgettable memory "of a military comedy whose originality would evoke a smile from the most serious observer."[47] Two years later the English missionary Henry Lansdell noted a great variety in uniforms and arms, some of the latter being muskets dating from the beginning of the nineteenth century.[48] In 1883 Captain Putiata was struck by the ancient flintlocks and even matchlocks with which the infantry was equipped, as well as by the woefully inadequate supply of artillery shells.[49] In 1881 Muzaffar had requested and received Russian military instructors, who attempted to train his army but had little success. The emir also received one thousand up-to-date Berdan rifles and one hundred thousand cartridges from Russia in 1883, but they were not distributed to the troops until after Muzaffar's death.[50]

Despite its obvious shortcomings by Western standards, Muzaffar's army was more effective than contemporary Russian opinions would suggest. It successfully campaigned in central Bukhara in 1869 and in Karategin and Darvaz in 1877–1878, and it maintained internal order after Abd al-Malik's revolt. The army consisted principally of ten to fifteen thousand infantry, theoretically volunteers but in fact often slaves or impressed peasants, poorly paid and consequently forced to hold outside jobs while in service. The officer corps, drawn from the Uzbeg aristocracy and from the emir's relatives and favorites, frequently had little professional training. There was also a small number of cavalry and artillery. The majority of the army doubled as the emir's guard; it was stationed in the capital and accompanied the emir on his annual journey to Karshi and Shahr-i Sabz during the summer and fall. The remainder was garrisoned in Shahr-i Sabz, Hisar, Baldjuan, Kulab, and Darvaz.[51] In addition, each beg maintained his own small body of troops.

If the Westernization of Bukhara's army remained entirely superficial after 1868, such was even more the case in other areas of
Bukharan life. However, Russia's reduction of the khanate to dependent status increased both the opportunities and the incentives
for the adoption of Western ways by the secular ruling class. The
frequent embassies to Tashkent and St. Petersburg exposed many
Bukharan officials to Western civilization. Whereas the 1869 embassy to the Russian capital affected a critical attitude toward European life, the embassy of 1873 was openly impressed by the wonders
of Peter's city.[52] Abd al-Ahad's visit to Moscow in 1883 for Alexander III's coronation produced a similar effect. On his return to
Kermine, the heir apparent organized a personal guard on the Russian model and armed them with the latest Berdan and Remington
rifles.[53] Other evidence of the penetration of Western influence was
noted by European visitors to Bukhara. The beg of Shahr-i Sabz entertained Doctor Iavorskii in 1879 with refreshments served in the
European manner on a table set with a Russian tablecloth, Russian
silverware, and Russian china. Iavorskii observed that the Bukharan
officials present were surprisingly adept at handling forks and
spoons.[54] By the early 1880's several of the begs had acquired a few
articles of European furniture, although these were still so rare, even
in the capital, that Prince Wittgenstein's mission in early 1883 was
preceded on every visit by the same collection of chairs and stools.[55]
In the last years of his reign Muzaffar himself began to manifest a
susceptibility to Western ways. He altered the traditional court ceremonial by receiving Russian envoys seated on a throne given him by
the emperor, garbed in a Russian full-dress coat with gold epaulettes
and adorned with a multitude of medals, both Russian and Bukharan. The emir adopted another European custom by creating
the Order of the Rising Star of Bukhara in 1883 in honor of the
coronation of Alexander III.[56] He also kept a carriage, which he had
received as a present from the Russian emperor, and after the late
1870's resorted for medical treatment to doctors sent out to him
from Tashkent.[57]

Despite these isolated and superficial examples of Westernization, Bukhara remained basically unaffected by Western influence
during Muzaffar's reign. Slaves continued to be owned openly and
sold secretly. Prisoners could still be kept permanently in chains or
confined to vermin-ridden underground pits. Adulteresses were stoned,
while other criminals might be thrown from the summit of the

capital's Great Minaret or hurled into a deep well whose bottom
was strewn with spears. The complete seclusion of women, the total
curfew at sunset, and the humiliating restrictions on Jews continued
to be enforced in Bukhara, as for centuries past. The seductive dances
of the batchas remained the favorite form of entertainment, both in
the bazaars and in the emir's palace. Bukharans were still liable to a
public whipping and a fine if found deficient in knowledge of the
Koran when accosted on the street by a rais. Finally, foreign visitors,
including official Russian envoys, continued to be regarded by the
populace with suspicion and treated by the emir's government as
semiprisoners. Lansdell summed up his impression of Bukhara in the
early 1880's in the observation that after crossing the Hisar Mountains from Samarkand to Shahr-i Sabz, he felt that he had left the
nineteenth century and entered an ancient and exotic world—one in
which, by contrast with Russian Turkestan, the population had not
yet begun to benefit from Russia's civilizing mission.[58]

In Khiva conditions were much the same, and opportunities for
contact with Western culture were even fewer than in Bukhara.
Khiva had never maintained a standing army but had relied in wartime on temporary levies composed mostly of Turkomans. After
1873, when Khiva had been deprived of the right to wage war, the
Turkoman levies were no longer summoned.[59] Thus, the army as a
channel of Western influence did not exist in Khiva. Similarly, Russian trade was less developed with Khiva than with Bukhara. Finally,
Khiva's diplomatic contacts with Russia were normally confined to
the small and isolated military post at Petro-Aleksandrovsk, and
Khivan officials rarely visited Tashkent or St. Petersburg.

Despite these obstacles, both the khan and the divan-begi were
ardent admirers of the West. In 1874 Muhammad Rahim established
a court printing office, which he placed under the direction of one
Ata-djan Adbalov, a young man who had studied in a Russian school
the previous year. Until 1878 Adbalov studied the technique of litho-
graphic printing with a Persian living in Khiva; thereafter Adbalov
worked on his own, publishing the first printed book in Central Asia
in 1880. The court printing office had no impact on Khivan life,
since its publications were not for sale or general distribution but
solely for the use of the court. Poetry, much of it written by Muhammad Rahim himself, was the principal subject matter. After the
khan's death in 1910 the printing office was closed.[60] Muhammad
Rahim's first real exposure to Western life came in 1883 when he

attended Alexander III's coronation in Moscow. While in Russia, the khan learned to smoke cigarettes, and he acquired a telephone in St. Petersburg which he took home with him. Upon his return to Khiva he reduced his harem to nine women and introduced them to corsets and bustles. Even before his trip to Russia Muhammad Rahim had been the proud possessor of a pair of eyeglasses. He told the Swiss traveler Henri Moser in December 1883 that he hoped to get Russia's permission to travel in western Europe. When Moser told him that Prince Wittgenstein had obtained a telegraph concession from Muzaffar, Muhammad Rahim immediately conceived a desire for a telegraph link between Khiva and Kazalinsk. Muhammad Murad was an even more active admirer of Western ways than the khan. The divan-begi maintained in Khiva a house built and furnished like those of the Russians in the government-general, with windows, velvet-covered armchairs, a sofa, tables, and a grand piano that the emperor had sent to the khan.[61]

Beyond the inner circle of the court, however, Western influence was nowhere in evidence. Even the abolition of slavery in 1873 had little effect on the traditional way of life. Since even fewer Russians went to Khiva on government or private business than to Bukhara, the average Khivan had less contact with foreigners than did his Bukharan counterpart. The few Western visitors to Khiva nevertheless noticed a freer attitude toward foreigners than in Bukhara.[62] The suspicion and constant surveillance characteristic of the other khanate were absent, probably because Khiva, having no political pretensions, had nothing to fear from Russia, and because religious fanaticism was traditionally much less marked in Khiva than in Bukhara, the religious capital of Central Asia. Khiva even granted land to a sizable number of Russian Mennonite immigrants in 1879–1880. Of German origin, the Mennonites had left Russia after a century of residence rather than submit to the recently enacted compulsory military service. They settled in several groups near Khiva and at Tashauz and Khodjeili.[63] The Mennonites preserved their traditional culture in Khiva, kept to themselves, and had no effect on the native population of the khanate.[64]

The dozen years following the treaties of 1873 may be called the period of neglect in Russia's relations with Bukhara and Khiva. St. Petersburg continued to pursue the aim of frontier security that had been the major goal during the period of conquest. A secure frontier required friendly neighbors who were able to maintain internal stability. Once the khan of Khiva's position had been strengthened by demonstrations of Russian support against his rebellious Turkoman subjects, the two khanates played their assigned roles well enough so that Russia's official policy of noninterference in their internal affairs seemed justified. The advocates of a more aggressive policy, who were especially influential in Russian Turkestan, made no headway against St. Petersburg's established policy. Even at the end of the period, when the possibility of a disputed succession in Bukhara threatened to disrupt the peace, the imperial government was reluctant to interfere any further than absolutely necessary.

The result of Russia's policy was the continued isolation of Bukhara and Khiva. Western influences, although dating back to the early nineteenth century, were by 1885 still few and weak. Even the 1873 treaties were not fully implemented: no permanent Russian representative was stationed in Bukhara, and practically nothing was done to capitalize on the economic prospects opened up by the treaties. Slavery, and even a clandestine slave trade, were allowed temporarily to continue in Bukhara. In short, Bukhara and Khiva remained almost wholly unaffected internally by their new status as Russian dependencies.

Portents of change were nevertheless not far to seek. In the mid-1870's Russia's third Central Asian dependency, Kokand, disintegrated from internal stresses and was annexed to Russian Turkestan. During the next decade the Turkomans of the Kara Kum Desert were subdued by Russian arms and placed under direct Russian rule. As a result of these new territorial acquisitions, by 1884 Khiva was completely surrounded by the Russian Empire except for a very short common frontier with Bukhara; Bukhara's frontier from the same year marched with Russia's for two thirds of its length. The question of whether the two khanates, now virtual enclaves in Russian territory, could preserve the isolation they had enjoyed when they were merely dependent neighbors of the White Tsar[65] was soon answered in the negative, and Bukhara and Khiva entered upon a new period in their relationship with Russia.

Part Three / *The Russian Presence*

Abd al-Ahad, Emir of Bukhara, 1885–1910

8 / Russo-Bukharan Relations Transformed

The Central Asian Railroad

A new phase in Russia's relations with her Central Asian dependencies dated from St. Petersburg's decision in 1885 to build the Central Asian Railroad. The new period witnessed the ending of the isolation of Bukhara and Khiva and the establishment of a "Russian presence" in the two khanates. A Russian political agency was founded in Bukhara, as were Russian cantonments and civilian settlements. Private Russian commercial activity expanded greatly in both states. They for the first time came into contact with Western civilization on a broad scale. Bukhara was transformed into a Russian protectorate, and the autonomy of both khanates was curtailed in several important respects, although Russia adhered in the main to her policy of nonintervention. The catalyst of change, the Central Asian Railroad, was the most important development in the region since the Russian conquest. As the British statesman Lord Curzon put it after a visit to Central Asia in 1888, Bukhara's "last expiring chance of freedom" from Russian control was lost when the iron rails were laid across the khanate. The same observer reflected, not without some regret, on the probable effect of the railroad on Central Asia: "The present . . . is the blank leaf between the pages of an old and a new dispensation . . . [between] the era of the Thousand and One Nights . . . [and] the rude shock and unfeeling Philistinism of nineteenth-century civilisation."[1] It was typical of Russia's policy in Central Asia that so important a development should have come about in a quite haphazard way.

No sooner had Russia established herself in Central Asia than the problem arose of providing more rapid communication between Russian Turkestan and the heart of the empire. Tashkent was a fifty-to sixty-day journey from Orenburg by caravan, although a special courier could make the trip in half the time.[2] If Russia's new domin-

ions were to be turned to economic advantage, or even if they were
merely to be defended successfully in case of war with Afghanistan
or Britain, a rail link would be necessary. The idea of such a link had
been under discussion since 1854, and by 1880 over forty different
projects had been submitted to St. Petersburg, the majority favoring
the Orenburg-Tashkent route along the Sir-Darya, but some backing
the route across the Ust-Urt Plateau or that eastward from Krasnovodsk.[3] In 1873 Ferdinand de Lesseps, the builder of the Suez Canal,
examined the Orenburg-Tashkent route as a possible link in his project for a seven-thousand mile railroad from Calais to Calcutta. With
the unlimited faith in man's ability to conquer nature with his gran-
diose building schemes so characteristic of the nineteenth century,
Lesseps planned to continue the railroad from Tashkent across the
roof of Asia, via either Bukhara and Afghanistan or Kokand and
Kashgar, to Peshawar, the Indian railhead. Lesseps' project foundered on the opposition of the British government, which did not
care to breach India's natural ramparts and thereby provide Russia
with easy access to the subcontinent. Russia also rejected the scheme
as economically unsound.[4]

General von Kaufman continued to back the idea of a railroad
from Orenburg to Tashkent in the mid-1870's, but with no success.[5]
Two other routes were proposed in 1879—from Tsesarevich Bay in
the northeastern Caspian Sea to Khiva, and from Orenburg to the
northern coast of the Aral Sea.[6] The question remained unresolved
when in 1880 the government began to build a short railroad eastward from the Caspian coast in connection with the campaign
against the Teke Turkomans. This line reached Kizil-Arvat, halfway
to Geok-Tepe, in December 1881—eleven months after the capture
of Geok-Tepe. Faced with the problem of a railroad that led nowhere
and whose strategic purpose had disappeared, various Russian officials proposed extending the line either to the Amu-Darya or, via
Merv and Herat, to Quetta in British Baluchistan. M. G. Cherniaev,
newly appointed governor general of Turkestan, feared that any extension of the Transcaspian Railroad would augment the importance
of Transcaspia at the expense of Turkestan. He therefore supported
with great vehemence a rival scheme for the building of a railroad
from Saratov on the Volga to Kungrat in northern Khiva.[7] In 1883
Cherniaev personally surveyed another shorter route from Petro-
Aleksandrovsk to Kungrat and thence across the Ust-Urt Plateau
to the northeast corner of the Caspian Sea, but this route proved

impractical for a railroad because it debouched on a part of the Caspian that was frozen over from December to March each year and was consequently closed to navigation during that period.[8]

The competition among the several projected railroad routes was finally decided by a completely extraneous event, the clash between Russian and Afghan troops at Penjdeh on March 18/30, 1885, which brought Russia and Britain to the verge of war in Central Asia. By May St. Petersburg had decided to extend the Transcaspian Railroad eastward from Kizil-Arvat, with the dual purpose of strengthening Russia's military position in Central Asia and providing the long sought rail link between European Russia and Russian Turkestan, with steamship connections on the Caspian Sea. The Central Asian Railroad, as the line was called, reached Askhabad in December 1885 and Merv the following July.[9]

Once the decision had been made to build the Central Asian Railroad, it became clear that the line would have to cross Bukhara, which lay athwart the most direct route from southern Transcaspia to Samarkand and Tashkent. In June 1885, only a month after Alexander III had ordered the construction of the railroad, N. V. Charykov, diplomatic attaché to the governor general of Turkestan, was sent to Bukhara to negotiate a railroad convention with the emir. St. Petersburg's primary aim was to secure Muzaffar's cooperation, which promised to be no easy task in view of the prolonged opposition he had offered to the construction of the telegraph line only two years earlier. The problem was to convince the emir of the usefulness, as well as the harmlessness, of the railroad, and also of Russia's continuing intention not to interfere in the internal life of the khanate. If possible, Muzaffar was to be persuaded to pay for the construction of the railroad across Bukhara, or at the very least, to cede without charge the public lands along the right of way and to assist Russia's acquisition of the necessary private lands at a just valuation. The Bukharan government's help was also necessary in hiring laborers and buying building materials, although from the first the foreign ministry adopted the attitude that the emir's moral cooperation was more important than any material help he might give. Material help should be strictly limited to that which would not adversely affect the well-being of the Bukharan population and thereby prejudice it against Russia.[10]

Despite Muzaffar's opposition, Charykov successfully executed his mission, making effective use in an interview with the emir on

June 22 of the point that the railroad would enable Russia better to defend Bukhara against Afghanistan if Kabul continued its hostile attitude. Charykov ironed out the details with the kush-begi, and on June 25 these two signed a protocol in which Bukhara agreed to the construction of the railroad, leaving to Russia the selection of the actual route; promised to donate any public lands needed for the right of way and for buildings connected with the railroad; and undertook to assist in acquiring private land at a just valuation, in purchasing building materials, and in hiring laborers. The protocol received imperial ratification on December 3, 1885. At the emir's request the agreement was not made public, so as to avoid an unfavorable popular reaction in Bukhara. Muzaffar also asked that the railroad pass at least six miles from his capital, again to allay the fears of his subjects. In return for his consent to the railroad, the emir requested that, in case of a Russo-Afghan war, Bukhara be allowed to regain Afghan Turkestan, lost to Kabul a quarter-century before. Charykov subsequently reported Muzaffar's requests to the foreign ministry.[11]

The problem remained of choosing the route of the railroad from Merv to Samarkand. The southern route via Burdalik and Karshi was the most direct and had the strategic advantage of being close to the Afghan frontier. The northern route via Chardjui and the emir's capital, however, would better serve the interests of trade and politics by opening up the economic and political heart of the khanate. Both the foreign ministry and Governor General Rosenbach favored the northern route, which received final approval in October 1885.[12] The railroad reached Chardjui at the end of 1886. Thence it spanned the Amu-Darya, traversed Bukhara, and in May 1888 reached Samarkand, where it halted for a decade. It was extended to Tashkent in 1898. Although the railroad was built and run by the Ministry of War to fill a strategic need, its economic usefulness soon overshadowed its original purpose.

The Accession of Abd al-Ahad

Muzaffar's agreement to the construction of the railroad was his last important act, for his long anticipated death occurred on October 31, 1885, at the age of sixty-two. The emir had customarily spent the summer in Karshi in order to escape the extreme discomfort and unhealthiness of his capital at that time of year, but it was nevertheless in Karshi that he contracted an epidemic disease stemming from bad water and lack of sanitation. Although mortally ill, Muzaffar returned to his villa just outside the capital. On the evening of October 30 the kush-begi, Muhammad-biy, and the emir's half-brother and divan-begi, Astanakul, foreseeing Muzaffar's imminent end and the danger of popular disorders and rebellion once the news got out, took the emir to his palace in the citadel of the capital, which enjoyed greater security. There Muzaffar died.[13] Muhammad and Astanakul kept the emir's death a secret while summoning the heir-apparent, Abd al-Ahad, by messenger from Kermine, fifty-eight miles away. Abd al-Ahad immediately set out for Bukhara with his retinue. After covering only eleven miles, he was lucky enough to overtake Lieutenant General M. N. Annenkov, the builder of the Central Asian Railroad, who was returning from Tashkent to Merv with the final plans for the line. Annenkov accompanied Abd al-Ahad to Bukhara and thereby gave public notice of Russia's support for the prince's succession. Abd al-Ahad entered the capital on November 1 and was crowned three days later.[14]

The news of Muzaffar's death and of Abd al-Ahad's accession reached Tashkent by telegraph from Bukhara on November 1. Charykov promptly produced an order from the Ministry of Foreign Affairs, previously confirmed by the emperor, covering this contingency: it instructed the governor general to recognize Abd al-Ahad immediately and assist him with all available forces. General N. I. Grodekov, governor of the Sir-Darya Oblast and acting governor general in Rosenbach's absence, had no choice but to obey, although he was one of those who favored the annexation of Bukhara. A telegram of congratulation was sent to the new emir; the troops in Samarkand were alerted to march to Bukhara if necessary; military scouts were dispatched to report on the situation in Hisar, Shahr-i Sabz, and Karshi; and a formal embassy was sent to Abd al-Ahad.[15] Russia's military preparations proved unnecessary, for the new emir had the situation well in hand from the first. He removed from their posts two of his brothers, the begs of Hisar and Chardjui, on suspicion of plotting with Abd al-Malik, married off the pretender's childless wives, and imprisoned the other two wives together with their offspring.[16]

Thanks to the precautions of both the Bukharan and the Russian governments, Bukhara had successfully weathered the transition to a new reign, which many observers had long been predicting would prove the khanate's undoing and the pretext for Russian annexation. Abd al-Ahad was safely seated on his father's throne, in part as a result of Russia's previous endorsement and of her prompt demonstration of support.

The Russian Political Agency

St. Petersburg's decision to run the Central Asian Railroad through Bukhara to Samarkand finally settled the long-standing controversy between the foreign ministry and Tashkent over the establishment of a political agent at the emir's court. The enormous number of questions that would inevitably be raised by the coming of the railroad and the consequent influx of Russian subjects in unprecedented numbers demanded the presence of a permanent representative to make immediate, on-the-spot decisions. The foreign ministry thus had its way; on the basis of article sixteen of the treaty of 1873 an Imperial Russian Political Agency, subordinate to the foreign ministry, was established at Bukhara by law on November 12, 1885, effective from January 1, 1886.[17] The same law reduced by 5500 rubles the governor general's allowance for exchanging embassies with the emir and abolished the post of diplomatic attaché at Tashkent. In 1894, however, this post was reestablished.[18]

Despite the foreign ministry's victory, Tashkent had not suffered a complete defeat, for the establishment of the political agency opened a new official channel of communication between Russia and Bukhara without closing the original channel. As the political agent was a member of the Russian diplomatic corps—something more than a consul but less than an envoy to a sovereign power—he was responsible to the Ministry of Foreign Affairs. Thus, in effect, Abd al-Ahad enjoyed the direct relations with the imperial government for which his father had repeatedly striven without success. Yet at the same time the authority of the governor general of Turkestan to conduct relations with neighboring khanates was never abrogated. On the contrary, the Provisional Statute of 1890, which established Transcaspia as an autonomous oblast, specifically confirmed the governor general of Turkestan's jurisdiction over all relations with the emir of Bukhara and the khan of Khiva.[19] After 1885, however, Tashkent acted through the political agency rather than by means of extraordinary embassies to Bukhara. The formation of Russian settlements in the khanate in the late 1880's actually broadened the governor general's responsibility in Bukhara.

By instituting direct relations between the foreign ministry and Bukhara without terminating the governor general's jurisdiction in this sphere, Russia placed on the political agent a dual responsibility —to Tashkent as well as St. Petersburg. In 1893 the governor general was even empowered to invite the political agent to participate in his council in the decision of questions affecting Bukhara.[20] The dual responsibility made the political agent's position particularly difficult because of the traditional differences of opinion between Tashkent and the foreign ministry over policy toward Bukhara. Abd al-Ahad took advantage of the overlapping in lines of authority to obtain greater independence from Tashkent.

The political agent's functions mushroomed over the years, as Russian activities in Bukhara expanded. To his original diplomatic and consular duties were added burdensome administrative and judicial responsibilities. He not only conducted all relations with the Bukharan government and collected intelligence on the situation in Bukhara and Afghanistan but also kept close track of the emir's activities, served as ghost-writer for the emir's formal correspondence with the imperial family and government, and advised the emir on granting Bukharan decorations to Russians. He protected the persons, property, treaty rights, and trade interests of Russian subjects, issued visas and passports, and played host to foreign visitors. He acted as supreme governor, police chief, and censor in the Russian settlements, as judge and chief investigator in legal cases involving Russians, and as notary in registering the land purchases of Russian subjects.[21] One indication of the growth of the political agency's tasks was the expansion of its staff. At first the agency consisted merely of the political agent and a single dragoman. In February 1888 the second member of the agency was promoted to secretary as well as dragoman. A third member, with the simple title of dragoman, was added in August 1892. The addition of a doctor in 1901 and another dragoman two years later raised the staff to five, where it remained until 1917.[22]

The first political agent was N. V. Charykov, a career diplomat who had gained experience in Central Asian affairs as diplomatic attaché to the governor general of Turkestan from October 1883. Charykov visited Bukhara for the first time in the fall of 1884, bearing a letter of introduction to the emir from General Rosenbach. En route to Muzaffar's capital, Charykov visited Abd al-Ahad in Kermine and gave him the governor general's assurance that Russia would support his succession upon his father's death. Charykov's second trip was in June 1885, to negotiate the railroad convention, at which time he also pressed the kush-begi for the abolition of slavery and the closing of the infamous underground prison at Bukhara. Charykov visited the khanate for the third time in November 1885, as a member of the embassy sent from Tashkent to congratulate Abd al-Ahad on his accession and to demonstrate Russia's support of the new emir.[23]

Charykov's first task as political agent was to facilitate the construction of the Central Asian Railroad across Bukhara. When he took up his new post in January 1886, the rails had not yet reached Merv, but by the end of the year they had reached the Amu-Darya at Chardjui. One of his most important functions during the year was to supervise and notarize the deeds of alienation whereby land needed for the railroad was transferred to the Russian government. Some of the necessary land was donated by the emir, but most of it was bought from him or from private owners, who refused paper rubles and had to be paid in silver, brought for the purpose from Hamburg.[24] During 1886 Russian engineers and soldiers were also active in the khanate, surveying the right of way and collecting economic data on the parts of the country to be traversed by the railroad. The collection of the data aroused the suspicion of the natives, who began to fear that the Russians intended to seize their land. In November 1886 crowds of armed peasants prevented a group of engineers from carrying on their work. Governor General Rosenbach prepared to take action to safeguard Russia's rights under the railroad convention. On November 29 he wired the ministers of war and foreign affairs that he proposed to move three infantry battalions and five Cossack squadrons from Samarkand into the khanate in case of continued disorders. The foreign ministry, with the emperor's backing, opposed Rosenbach's plan as not warranted. On December 1 the Chardjui railroad station was opened without incident.[25] On instructions from I. A. Zinoviev, director of the foreign ministry's Asiatic Department, Charykov warned Abd al-Ahad in person of the danger in which the anti-Russian agitation led by clerical zealots placed both him and his country.[26] No further trouble was encountered. The railroad passed eight miles to the south of the capital out

of deference to the attitude of the populace, who called the loco-
motive *Arba-i Shaitan* (Satan's Wagon). Yet within a year or two
the Bukharans had changed their minds and evidenced great delight
in riding the trains.[27] By 1898 it was possible for Abd al-Ahad to
agree to pay the entire cost (500,000 rubles) of a branch line connecting his capital with the railroad. The branch was built in 1900–
1901, and the net profit from its operation went to the emir.[28]

Contrary to article sixteen of the 1873 treaty, which stipulated,
"The Russian plenipotentiary in Bukhara . . . will live in the house
of, and at the expense of, the Russian government," the political
agency was quartered and fed at the emir's expense from 1886 to
1891. According to Bukharan etiquette, all foreigners in the khanate
on official business were the emir's guests. Abd al-Ahad provided the
agency with a large native house and a walled compound in the
capital and supplied its staff, including the guard of twenty Ural
Cossacks, with food, servants, and horses. The emir also assigned a
native official to live in the outer court, where he sat all day and
noted the comings and goings of the Russians and their visitors.
Only after five years did the agency extricate itself from these somewhat "restricted surroundings."[29] In 1891 it moved to new quarters
in the Russian settlement of New Bukhara, which had grown up
around the railroad station south of the capital. There the agency
was on Russian soil instead of being the guest of the emir, which
was more fitting to the dignity of Bukhara's suzerain and protector,
even though one Russian visitor reported that Abd al-Ahad had contributed over 100,000 rubles to the building of the agency's new
quarters.[30]

Anglo-Russian Tensions and the Amu-Darya Frontier, 1885–1888

The prolonged crisis in Anglo-Russian relations, which began in
1885 and prompted the construction of the Central Asian Railroad
and thus indirectly the establishment of the political agency in Bukhara, continued to affect the khanate in the second half of the
1880's. Even after Abd al-Ahad's accession, Tashkent continued
to show concern over possible British interference in Bukhara in
support of Abd al-Malik. In December 1885 Russian frontier commanders reported to Samarkand that rumors were prevalent in Karategin of a conspiratorial gathering in Kulab of partisans of Abd

al-Malik, Sari-khan (the beg of Kulab who had been expelled in 1869), and other dispossessed princes from Kohistan and Kokand, aimed at regaining their lost dominions. In May 1886 the governor of Fergana Oblast warned Tashkent of an Afghan troop concentration in Shugnan and of rumors of a war council in Calcutta between the British viceroy, the emir of Afghanistan, Abd al-Malik, and Abd al-Karim (the pretender to Kokand). The war council was alleged to have decided to use British and Afghan help to restore Bukhara to Abd al-Malik and Kokand to Abd al-Karim, and rumors reached Tashkent of British troop movements into Badakhshan toward the upper Amu-Darya. Finally, in July 1888 a Bukharan merchant from Hisar beglik notified a Russian frontier official that Abd al-Malik and a son of Sari-khan had taken Kulab; the story was duly reported to Samarkand and Tashkent.[31] Although these rumors and reports were greatly exaggerated and often completely unfounded, Russia could not afford to ignore them, since British intrigue was strongly feared during this period of heightened international tension.

Russia did more than merely take note of signs of British support to Central Asian pretenders. During the intense Anglo-Russian crisis following the Penjdeh incident and lasting until August 1885, a repetition of the 1878 military demonstration was decided upon. Troops were to be moved from Russian Turkestan to the Amu-Darya in preparation for action in northern Afghanistan. Muzaffar's consent was obtained for a bridge over the river at some point between Kerki and Patta-Hisar, and the steamboat "Tashkent" was requisitioned from the defunct Aral Sea Flotilla for service on the Amu-Darya.[32] In the fall of 1885 the tension lessened; the immediate threat of war between Russia and Britain gave way to a prolonged crisis over Afghanistan and Bulgaria, which continued until the beginning of 1888. Russian military planners dropped the proposal for an armed demonstration against Afghanistan and turned to the establishment of a strong military position on the Amu-Darya.

Early in 1886 Abd al-Ahad wrote to Governor General Rosenbach complaining that Bukhara was threatened by Britain's arming and training of Afghan troops. Rosenbach replied with an offer to undertake the protection of Bukhara by placing permanent Russian garrisons of one battalion each (eight hundred men) in Chardjui and Kerki. Charykov, newly installed in Bukhara as political agent, took up the negotiations with the emir, who agreed to Rosenbach's proposal but asked for a gift of 12,000 Berdan rifles in return. In

July 1886 a Russian garrison was established in Chardjui and 1000 rifles were sent to the emir.[33] Apparently Abd al-Ahad was not completely satisfied with the bargain, for on November 18 Charykov wired Tashkent requesting an additional 1000 rifles for the emir; whether he ever received them is not clear.[34] The Ministry of War gave its approval on October 28 to the garrisoning of Chardjui and Kerki, citing the need to strengthen Russia's position in Central Asia, to counteract British intrigue in Afghanistan, to protect Bukhara against threats of attack from Afghan Turkestan, and to neutralize British policy in Asia and the Near East.[35] In the beginning of 1887 a road was laid out by native corvée from Chardjui to Kerki along the left bank of the Amu-Darya, at no expense to Russia, and in May 1887 a Russian garrison was installed at Kerki.[36]

In 1886 acting Governor General Grodekov and General Annenkov abandoned the idea of a bridge over the middle Amu-Darya in favor of the establishment of a permanent flotilla on the river, to consist of two fast steamers under the control of the governor general of Turkestan. A flotilla would be much less vulnerable to attack than a bridge three quarters of a mile long; the steamboats would also be useful in maintaining communications with and supplying the proposed garrison at Kerki. Although the 1873 treaties had given Russia exclusive control over navigation on the stretch of the Amu-Darya that formed the Russo-Khivan boundary as well as free navigation rights on the Bukharan portion of the river, Russia had confined her efforts to exploration of the Amu-Darya and had not hitherto attempted to establish regular navigation. Under pressure of the continuing Anglo-Russian tension, Grodekov's and Annenkov's proposal was approved, and at the end of summer, 1887, two armed steamboats arrived in Chardjui via the railroad. They were assembled and launched by November 1887 and began operations the following spring, using Chardjui as their base. Thenceforth, during the nine months of the year when the river was free from ice, the Amu-Darya Flotilla plied between Petro-Aleksandrovsk and Kerki, a distance of 375 miles, serving as the communications and supply link between these remote outposts of empire and the railroad at Chardjui. The flotilla obviated the need for the Chardjui-Kerki road, which fell into disuse and disrepair.[37]

Russia's advanced military position on the Amu-Darya proved useful in the summer of 1888 during the revolt in Afghanistan of Ishak-khan, the governor of Afghan Turkestan and a cousin of Emir

Abd ar-Rahman. Pending the outcome of the revolt, which could have had serious consequences for Britain if Abd ar-Rahman had been overthrown, Russia reinforced her garrison at Kerki. After several months the rebellion was crushed; Ishak-khan and a large number of Afghan Uzbegs fled across the Amu-Darya into Bukhara, Ishak-khan himself taking refuge first in Karshi and then in Samarkand. With the end of the revolt the Russian garrison at Kerki was reduced from four to three battalions; the Chardjui garrison at the time consisted of two battalions.[38]

In the years 1885–1888 the Amu-Darya frontier was also the scene of recurrent minor clashes between Bukhara and Afghanistan. At the end of 1885 some Bukharan Turkomans raided the Afghan frontier and carried off several flocks of sheep. At Britain's insistence Russia prevailed upon the emir's government to have the stolen sheep returned.[39] Afghan troops several times penetrated left-bank Darvaz and crossed the Amu-Darya into Kulab. In January 1887 a report reached Russian Turkestan from Bukhara of Abd ar-Rahman's preparations for a campaign north of the river.[40] Peace was preserved, however, and the most important result of the prolonged Anglo-Russian tension in Central Asia, after the demarcation of the Russo-Afghan boundary, was the strengthening of Russia's military hold over Bukhara.

The Russian Settlements

On the heels of the surveyors for the railroad, even before the line had been built, came private Russian commercial interests. Russian textile manufacturers seeking new sources of raw materials were quick to sense the usefulness of the railroad in providing cheap and rapid transportation for Central Asian cotton to the Russian market and the value of the political agency in protecting their operations. Several such firms proposed to acquire unused Bukharan state lands along the Amu-Darya in Chardjui beglik, to be used for the cultivation of American cotton. Although article twelve of the 1873 treaty had given Russians the right to acquire real estate in Bukhara, no advantage had yet been taken of this provision. Bent on preserving the emir's authority over his country, the imperial government was now faced with the problem of reconciling the private interests of its own subjects with Russia's state interests. In 1886 Abd al-Ahad under the close supervision and guidance of the political agent granted to Russian firms the lands in question along with attractive tax benefits but included conditions protecting Bukhara's interests. Bukhara retained unrestricted access to and use of the towpaths running along the banks of the Amu-Darya; the new owners and lessees were responsible for any losses suffered by their Bukharan neighbors as a result of building dams or changing the direction of the river's channel; and the Russian landowners were forbidden to alienate or mortgage their allotments. This provision ensured that the land actually would be planted to cotton.[41]

The terms of these allotments subsequently served as the basis for a set of general regulations governing the acquisition of land in Bukhara by Russian subjects. In a letter of January 12, 1887, to Governor General Rosenbach, Foreign Minister Giers insisted on the need for well-publicized regulations, which would answer to Russia's political interest in preserving the emir's authority and convince him that the Russian government, far from intending to interfere in the khanate's internal affairs, desired to protect his rights and those of his subjects. Specifically referring to the acquisition by Russians of lands in Chardjui beglik, Giers stipulated that the political agent's role in such transfers "ought in no respect to have the character of pressure, which would be completely at variance with the relations established between us and Bukhara, as well as with the rights of the emir, as the legal proprietor of the territory."[42]

Charykov drew up the required regulations in March 1887, and they were approved by the governor general. The regulations left the negotiation of land grants to the private initiative of Russian subjects, but the political agent was charged with the supervision of all contracts to ensure that they conformed to Russia's aim of maintaining the status quo in the khanate. The political agent was to be particularly cautious in approving purchases of land already under irrigation and cultivation in order to avoid an increase in the number of landless peasants, which would have undesirable implications for the political and economic stability of the country. According to Charykov, "Russian subjects can find sufficient application for their capital and skill in the cultivation of areas now idle." Another feature of the Russian policy with regard to land acquisitions was preference for a limited number of large holdings rather than a large number of small ones. Small holdings were more difficult to keep under observation and control, while their owners, needing less capital, were thought to offer fewer guarantees of permanence and success and greater possibilities of minor unpleasantnesses with the neighboring local population.[43]

Even more important than the arrival of Russian agricultural entrepreneurs in Chardjui beglik was the establishment of the first Russian urban settlement in the vicinity of the railroad station at Chardjui. The station itself, as well as temporary housing for the railroad construction teams and permanent barracks for the Russian garrison, were built in 1886. After the promulgation of the regulations on land purchases during the following year, construction of warehouses and other commercial and industrial buildings and of private homes was undertaken.[44] In 1887 General Annenkov and Charykov selected the site of the Bukhara railroad station, eight miles south of the capital, where another Russian settlement, named New Bukhara, soon arose because of the location's proximity to the political and economic heart of the country.[45]

The Russian government quickly saw the necessity of subjecting the Russian settlements at Chardjui and New Bukhara to regulations controlling their growth and administration in order to avoid the unpleasant friction with Bukhara that might attend uncontrolled development, as well as to ensure that Russia's own material interests—the railroad, the cantonments, and the flotilla—did not suffer from the unsupervised activities of private individuals. Russia's problem was to impose control over the nascent settlements without appearing to weaken the emir's authority over his own territory. Early in 1888 St. Petersburg decided to follow the precedent set in the telegraph and railroad conventions and negotiate a new agreement with Abd al-Ahad to cover the Russian settlements. The foreign ministry drafted the appropriate articles, the governor general of Turkestan was instructed to negotiate with the Bukharan government, and in June 1888 Charykov was charged with securing the emir's approval.

Obtaining the emir's consent to the new agreement proved to be no mere formality. Astanakul-inak, who had just become the zakatchi-kalan and was also the kush-begi's grandson, represented Abd al-Ahad in the negotiations with Charykov. He plainly declared: "Conclusion of a new agreement is a very distressing matter to the emir. The talks concerning the construction of a telegraph in Bukhara continued for three years, and, in the end, his high eminence's late father was compelled, almost by force, to accept the agreement on this subject proposed to him, which his subjects persistently opposed. The late emir also concluded an agreement relative to the construction of a railroad across Bukhara. But this matter ended happily and satisfactorily . . . The emir had hoped that after that no new demands would be addressed to him. But now there has arisen the difficult and complex matter of the settlements. Will not this, moreover, be followed by the need for still more agreements? If the people learn that the emir has concluded another agreement, his authority in the eyes of his subjects will finally be shaken, and his tractability, which stems from his friendly disposition toward the Russians, will be interpreted by his people as proof of his helplessness and complete subservience." Charykov coolly replied that the proposed agreement merely developed certain provisions of the 1873 treaty and the 1885 railroad convention. He insisted that Russia's only aim in requesting the agreement was to avoid possible difficulties in the future by acting in friendly accord with the emir and his government. In response, Abd al-Ahad proved himself fully the equal of his late father in taking advantage of Russia's expressed desire to uphold his authority among his subjects. He repeated to Charykov all the arguments previously presented by Astanakul and added: "I have friends, but also many enemies. There are mullahs and other people here who are not well disposed toward me. My subjects will not understand my consenting. They will construe it to the detriment of my authority. I am alone. What shall I do?"[46]

Unruffled by this plea, Charykov repeated the assurances he had given Astanakul the day before and reminded the emir that he already had proof of the sympathy and good intentions of the emperor and the governor general. Faced with Russia's insistence, Bukhara again had no choice but to capitulate. On June 23 Charykov and Astanakul-inak put their signatures to the protocol, which included the verbatim text of the foreign ministry's draft articles. As in the case of the railroad convention, Abd al-Ahad requested that the agreement be withheld from publication in order to avoid trouble with his subjects. At the political agency on June 30 many Russians, including a sizable number of large firms, received allotments in the settlements at Chardjui and New Bukhara.[47]

The protocol, which was ratified by Alexander III on August 28, 1888, provided that the two existing Russian settlements, as well as any others that might be needed in the future, were to be delimited and subdivided into plots by agreement between the governor general and the emir, who were also to establish detailed regulations covering street layout, building codes, water supply, police, sanitation, and real estate taxes to pay for municipal services. Approval by both the political agent and the Bukharan government was necessary for all purchases of land in the settlements by Russians or Bukharans. Limits on the size of individual holdings were established, and the political agent was charged with issuing building permits.

Since the detailed regulations called for in the protocol had already been drawn up in Tashkent and were attached to the agreement in the form of an appendix, the emir's consent was a mere formality.[48] The principles incorporated in these regulations were: Russia's de facto control over the Russian settlements in Bukhara, with the emir's government having only token representation; subordination of the settlements to the governor general of Turkestan,[49] with the political agent in Bukhara serving as his lieutenant; and extension of the laws and administrative regulations of Russian Turkestan to the settlements.[50] In many respects the Russian settlements in Bukhara were similar to the uezds of the government-general: the settlements collectively constituted a unit akin to an oblast, with the political agent acting as the oblast governor, responsible in this role to the governor general. Municipal administration in New Bukhara was in the hands of a civil governor,[51] appointed by the governor general, and of an advisory council. The council consisted of a local Russian resident selected by the governor and the political agent, the municipal architect, and a representative of the Bukharan government. In Chardjui the commandant of the garrison doubled as head of the municipal administration; he was assisted by an advisory council, as in New Bukhara, but without the municipal architect, which office did not exist in Chardjui. The municipal administrations had charge of private construction, public works, sanitation, public health, taxation to support public services, and police. In New Bukhara the governor general appointed a separate chief of police, while in Chardjui the garrison commandant filled that post, too.

The Russian settlements developed rapidly. Chardjui, as the site of a cantonment and the railroad workshops, the base of the Amu-Darya Flotilla, and the crossroads of the north-south route along the river and the east-west route along the railroad, was the largest settlement. It grew to a total population of 2,500 in 1893, 8,000 in

1910, and 15,000 on the eve of World War I. Although New Bukhara was more important than Chardjui commercially, industrially,
and politically, it grew more slowly, reaching a population of 1,000
in 1891, 3,000 in 1910, and 12,000 in 1917. A third settlement,
established at the end of the 1880's in the vicinity of the cantonment
at Kerki, had only 137 civilians in 1891 but attained a total population, including the garrison, of 5,000 by 1910. In 1897 a Russian
garrison was installed at Termez, 130 miles upriver from Kerki,
where three years later a Russian fortress and settlement were established on thirty-eight square miles of land ceded by the emir at
Russia's request. In the years immediately preceding World War I,
Termez had a total population of 6,000 to 7,000, of whom over one
third were civilians. In Kerki and Termez, as in Chardjui, municipal
administration was assigned to the garrison commandants.[52] New
Bukhara remained the only settlement with a civil governor.

The policy of securing privileges for Russians in Bukhara and
at the same time regulating their activities so as to minimize friction
with the native regime and thus protect St. Petersburg's vital interests also underlay Russia's handling of the trade in alcoholic beverages. In Bukhara, as in all Moslem lands, the manufacture, sale, or
use of strong drink was strictly forbidden. Yet the Russian military
and civilian personnel who settled in the khanate from 1886 brought
with them both a strong thirst and the means to quench it. To
solve the problem, Charykov drafted and sent to the foreign ministry a set of regulations, which received the emperor's approval on
June 25, 1889.[53] The sale of alcoholic beverages was permitted only
in the Russian settlements, at the railroad stations, in railroad dining
cars, and among the Russian troop units in Bukhara, and such trade
was to be conducted only by Russians licensed under the laws of
the government-general. Moslems and Central Asian Jews were forbidden to engage in the trade, nor was it allowed to sell or distribute
strong drink to them. Distilleries were prohibited in the khanate;
Russian subjects were allowed to operate wineries only with the
approval in each case of both the Russian and the Bukharan governments.[54]

Russian Jurisdiction and Extraterritoriality

The unprecedented influx of Russians into Bukhara in the wake
of the railroad posed a judicial as well as an administrative problem

to the imperial government. Because of the tremendous increase in private Russian activity in the khanate, the practice followed since 1873 of extraditing Russians accused of crimes in Bukhara and leaving civil cases in the hands of the Bukharan courts proved no longer expedient. A prompter method than extradition for handling criminal cases was required, and in civil cases Russians could not expect to find justice, as they understood it, in courts that discriminated against non-Moslems and were totally alien in spirit and practice to the courts of Russia and the West.

As Russia's official representative in Bukhara, the political agent was the obvious instrument of judicial authority over his countrymen. On May 20, 1886, within five months of the opening of the political agency, Foreign Minister Giers, with the emperor's approval, endowed the political agent with full criminal jurisdiction over Russians in Bukhara on the model of Russian consular jurisdiction in Persia and Turkey. However, since the article of the Russian criminal code defining that jurisdiction was not specifically extended to Bukhara, the political agent was left in a legally ambiguous position.[55] The ministries of foreign affairs and justice resolved the problem in a proposal incorporated into law on May 27, 1887. Until the definitive settlement of the political agent's judicial duties, he was to have jurisdiction over all crimes and misdemeanors committed by Russians in Bukhara. He was to act as justice of the peace, judge, and procurator on the basis of the authority vested by law in the justices of the peace in the uezds of Russian Turkestan and in the Samarkand oblast court and its procurator.[56]

At the beginning of the following year Charykov raised the question of civil jurisdiction, arguing that the "need of Russian subjects for such jurisdiction is constantly growing, and its absence permits impunity and abuses."[57] Accordingly, on May 11, 1888, civil cases between Russians residing in Bukhara were placed under the jurisdiction of the political agent, who in trying these cases was to be guided by the rules established for the justices of the peace in the government-general. His decisions could be appealed to the Samarkand oblast court. The political agent was to execute the further functions of a justice of the peace in probate and wardship matters.[58]

Within a few months Charykov found his duties as an investigator and a judge beyond his capacity when added to his other functions, such as diplomatic representative, notary, and chief administrator of the Russian settlements. The inauguration of traffic on the Central Asian Railroad to Samarkand in May 1888 also brought a great increase in litigation involving Russians. Charykov began to press Governor General Rosenbach to assign someone from his judicial department on a temporary basis to execute the political agent's judicial functions, arguing that his other duties were at a standstill because of his judicial workload. Rosenbach replied that he was powerless to help because his judicial department was subject to the Ministry of Justice. Charykov finally proposed to Tashkent the establishment of a justice of the peace in Chardjui, charged with the political agent's judicial functions but with the proviso that matters involving the Bukharan government be left to the political agent. Rosenbach forwarded Charykov's proposal to the minister of justice in October 1888.[59]

The result of Charykov's efforts was the law of May 9, 1889, which established a justice of the peace in the Russian settlement at Chardjui. The justice's jurisdiction, subject to the Samarkand oblast court, covered, "All felonies and misdemeanors perpetrated by Russian subjects in the khanate of Bukhara, and equally all civil cases arising between Russian subjects living in this khanate." He was charged with the investigation of crimes in which the victim was a Russian but the identity of the guilty party was unknown. If the investigation revealed that the guilty party was a native, the case was to be handed over to the political agent for trial in the Bukharan courts. Affairs of probate and wardship were also assigned to the justice of the peace.[60] The new law transferred to him all of the political agent's judicial functions without increasing the scope of Russian jurisdiction in Bukhara. Criminal offenses committed by Bukharans against Russians, as well as civil actions between Russians and Bukharans, remained within the jurisdiction of the Bukharan courts.

There the problem rested for almost four years, until a law of March 15, 1893, enlarged the jurisdiction of the justice of the peace and again invested the political agent with judicial functions. Civil cases between Russians and Bukharans were for the first time removed from Bukhara's jurisdiction. Those in which Russians, either alone or with natives, were the defendants were decided by the justice of the peace, while those in which the defendants were natives alone were investigated and tried by the political agent. The political agent was empowered to act as arbitrator in civil cases between Russians and Bukharans if both parties so desired and agreed to be bound by his decision. Crimes and misdemeanors committed by Bukharans against Russians were also removed from the jurisdiction of the Bukharan courts; the political agent was charged with the investigation and trial of these cases, although in accordance with local laws and customs. Finally, the new law accorded to non-Russian Christians residing in Bukhara the same legal rights and duties as Russian subjects, while all non-Christian foreigners were treated legally as if they were Bukharan subjects.[61] The 1893 law marked the culmination of a steady and rapid process of enlargement of Russia's jurisdiction in Bukhara. All legal actions involving Russians in any capacity were now tried according to Russian law before a Russian judge, who in nearly every instance was the justice of the peace. Only criminal and civil cases in which the victim or plaintiff was a Russian and the defendant a Bukharan were reserved for the political agent, since such cases potentially affected Russo-Bukharan relations and thus had political implications. After 1893 only minor additions were made to Russia's jurisdiction, as on May 30, 1894, when civil cases between the recently opened Bukharan branch of the State Bank and private persons were entrusted to the justice of the peace.[62]

Russia's broadened jurisdiction and the growing number of Russians in the khanate led to a rapid development of the Russian judiciary in Bukhara. On November 29, 1893, St. Petersburg ordered the transfer of the justice of the peace from Chardjui to New Bukhara, the center of Russian commercial and industrial activity.[63] On January 15, 1896, the justice of the peace was given jurisdiction over felonies and misdemeanors committed against the property and revenues of the Russian Treasury in Bukhara, and two assistants were assigned to help him cope with the increasing quantity of litigation.[64] Additional justiceships of the peace were created as the needs of the Russian settlements grew. By 1907 there were two justices in New Bukhara and one in Chardjui. The justice in Chardjui also served Kerki and Termez, where he held court twice a year.[65] A fourth justiceship was established in 1909 in Kerki, to serve that town and Termez.[66] During this period the Samarkand okrug court held sessions twice a year in New Bukhara and Chardjui and once a year in Kerki and Termez, each session lasting at least three weeks.[67]

In accordance with government policy, the Russian courts established in Bukhara were careful to protect the interests of the natives. In the days before the creation of the first justiceship of the peace Charykov provoked complaints from Russians in the khanate that he was being too impartial.[68] A decade later two English visitors reported that the Russian courts were so popular with the Bukharans that they would often go to great lengths to have their cases tried under Russian jurisdiction rather than by their own kazis.[69]

The other side of the problem of Russian jurisdiction in Bukhara was the legal status of Bukharans in Russian Turkestan. In 1883 the Giers commission had found no uniformity on this point in the practice of the uezd courts in the government-general. Some judges regarded Bukharans and Khivans as subject to the native courts established for the Moslems of the colony, but the majority held that Bukharans and Khivans were subject to the regular Russian courts. This view raised the difficulty that some crimes punishable under Moslem law were not recognized by the Russian legal code. Giers recommended that Bukharan, Khivan, and Afghan subjects be treated just like Russia's own Moslems and placed under the jurisdiction of the native courts.[70] In 1886 his suggestion was incorporated into article 211 of the Statute on the Administration of the Turkestan Krai, which stipulated, "The regulations on jurisdiction over settled natives apply also to inhabitants of the neighboring khanates while in the Turkestan Krai."[71] Two years later an exception was made for Bukharans and Khivans finding themselves in nomad territory, for the nomads had their own courts, which applied customary law rather than the Sharia. A law of May 17, 1888, provided that in areas of Russian Turkestan where no settled native population and consequently no native courts existed, Bukharans and Khivans were under the jurisdiction of the Russian justice-of-the-peace and oblast courts.[72]

The governor general had summary jurisdiction over Bukharans and Khivans, as well as other aliens, whose presence in Russian Turkestan he deemed harmful or merely undesirable. On March 24, 1892, he was empowered to expel such individuals from Russian soil.[73] Furthermore, in a circular directive to the oblast governors on September 16, 1900, the governor general authorized the uezd commandants, their assistants, and the uezd police to arrest and fine Bukharans and Khivans for civil disobedience, fighting in public places, disturbing the peace, disrespect to persons in authority, and disobedience to parents.[74]

By the end of Charykov's tenure in the post of political agent in March 1890 Russia's presence in Bukhara was firmly established. A railroad had been built across the khanate and remained under the control of the Russian Ministry of War.[75] A Russian political agency had been established in the emir's capital. Russian garrisons had been installed at Chardjui and Kerki, in addition to the troops who operated the railroad and guarded the railroad zone, and a Russian flotilla commanded the Amu-Darya as far as Kerki. Private Russian individuals and firms had begun to invade Bukhara in search of commercial profit, had purchased land, and had laid the foundations for three of the four settlements that were to arise as Russian enclaves on Bukharan soil. Finally, Russians had been accorded the beginnings of a broad extraterritoriality, which by 1893 would result in all legal matters involving Russians being withdrawn from the jurisdiction of the Bukharan courts. A justice of the peace had already been established in Chardjui to exercise this extraterritorial jurisdiction. It was an impressive record for only five years and constituted a veritable revolution in Russia's relations with Bukhara.

This revolution did not signify, however, that the imperial government had abandoned the principles of its traditional policy toward Bukhara—noninterference in the khanate's internal life and maintenance of the emir's authority. The momentous changes of 1885–1890 were the unplanned result of Russia's pursuance of policies that only indirectly involved Bukhara: the rivalry with Great Britain, the need for a rail link between Russian Turkestan and European Russia, and the desire to strengthen the line of the Amu-Darya against Afghan and British designs. The pursuit of these aims opened Bukhara incidentally to the penetration of private Russian interests. Far from being departures from St. Petersburg's traditional policy, the formation of Russian enclaves and the establishment of extraterritorial rights for Russian subjects served rather to limit Russia's role in the internal life of Bukhara. Had Russians in the khanate been left under the administrative and judicial control of the native authorities, continued friction and demands for Russian intervention would have been the inevitable result, to the detriment of the local regime. The only other possible course would have been a ban on private Russian activity in Bukhara, which would have meant surrendering the economic privileges obtained after decades of failure in the treaties of 1868 and 1873. No imperialist power in the late nineteenth century could have openly denied to its subjects the economic advantages that were so often used to justify imperial expansion. Instead, Russia followed the course of abrogating the emir's authority over small parts of his territory and over all Russians and Christians throughout his domain for the sake of maintaining intact his authority over the vast majority of his country and over his own subjects. If the Russian settlements and the railroad zone were privileged enclaves in which the emir's writ did not run, the rest of the khanate was in effect, with rare exceptions, closed to private Russian activity.

Pavel Mikhailovich Lessar, Russian Political Agent in Bukhara, 1890–1895

9 / The Protectorate Completed: Russia and Bukhara

The Amu-Darya Frontier and Russo-Bukharan Relations, 1890–1895

The contact of growing numbers of Russians with Bukhara and Khiva after 1885 and the change in Russo-Bukharan relations, although designed to preserve as much as possible of Bukhara's autonomy, inevitably brought increased pressure for even further curtailment of that autonomy and for eventual annexation. Long-standing advocates of annexation like General L. F. Kostenko of the Turkestan general staff, a leading proponent of Russia's civilizing mission in Asia, spoke out with increased boldness. In 1887 Kostenko charged, "we artificially prolong the lives of state organisms which have already completed their cycle of development. Sooner or later events like those which occurred in the former khanate of Kokand will force us to take the same step [annexation] in regard to Khiva and Bukhara."[1] New voices, like that of Lieutenant Colonel I. T. Poslavskii, a military engineer on service in Bukhara in 1885–1888 in connection with building the railroad, joined in the criticism of the foreign ministry's policy of nonintervention. Poslavskii predicted that sooner or later Bukhara would have to be annexed to Russia and argued that it had been a great mistake to let the khanate retain internal independence after 1868. In peacetime Bukhara presented Russia with moral problems; in wartime, with strategic difficulties. Although he wrote at some length on the correct strategy for capturing the emir's capital, Poslavskii concluded, "The political insect which still bears the name of the khanate of Bukhara will die peacefully on the iron needle with which General Annenkov has pierced it."[2]

P. M. Lessar, who succeeded Charykov as political agent on March 27, 1890, occupied a middle position between the foreign ministry and the annexationists. He subscribed to the foreign minis-

try's policy on the ground that it would be to Russia's disadvantage
to undertake the expense and trouble of administering the khanate
directly.[3] But like many of his countrymen, Lessar also regarded the
Bukharan government—whose exclusive goals were maintenance of
law and order, preservation of religious purity, and collection of a
myriad of taxes for the sole benefit of the country's ruling class—
as an obstacle to the progress of the Bukharan people and of Russian
commerce, as well as a blot on the record of Russian imperialism.
Lessar's conduct of his office was intended to leave no doubt in Abd
al-Ahad's mind that he was a Russian vassal and not an independent
ruler.

The issue that in the early 1890's revived serious discussion of
Bukhara's future relationship with Russia was customs unification.
In 1881 Russian customs posts had been established along the borders of Russian Turkestan with Bukhara and Khiva. Bukharan and
Khivan goods were admitted duty-free, but the import of goods
originating in other countries, primarily India and England, was
prohibited, except for green tea, indigo, and muslin, on which a
high tariff was placed.[4] After the construction of the Central Asian
Railroad Russian goods shipped by rail to the government-general
had to cross the customs frontier twice—upon entering and leaving
Bukharan territory. A more important problem was that the 1881
barriers against English imports applied only to Russian Turkestan
and not to the khanates, as long as the khanates remained outside
the Russian customs frontier. Although the railroad gave Russian
merchants and manufacturers a great advantage over their English
competitors, import restrictions and tariff protection were needed
to secure the Bukharan market to Russia.

In 1887 Minister of Finance I. A. Vyshnegradskii proposed the
inclusion of Bukhara in the Russian customs frontier, but the foreign ministry, as anxious as ever to preserve Bukhara's autonomy,
successfully opposed the idea. In February 1891 Vyshnegradskii revived his suggestion. Lessar supported the finance minister but
pointed out at the same time that Russia ought to find a way to
avoid antagonizing both the emir's government and his people on
this important question. The political agent felt that Abd al-Ahad
was certain to "offer stubborn resistance to such an important interference in the affairs of the khanate as its inclusion in the Russian
customs frontier." Even though the emir would be forced to yield
"once convinced of the inevitability of the imperial government's

will," Lessar did not expect Russia to obtain from the Bukharan government "the sincere cooperation which would be indispensable for the successful operation of the customs control." Lessar predicted that the Bukharan people, too, would react with hostility to inclusion in the Russian customs frontier, since the measure would bring about substantial increases in the price of several necessities. The price of tea, which in the absence of alcohol was even more of a staple in Bukharan life than in Russian, would rise by 30 to 50 percent.[5]

Lessar presented his solution to the problem on April 7, 1891, at a conference in St. Petersburg of members of the finance and foreign ministries, presided over by Vyshnegradskii. The political agent proposed that the customs frontier be moved to the Amu-Darya regardless of the opposition of the emir or his subjects, but that Russia compensate the Bukharan population for the consequent rise in the cost of living. Lessar suggested that the compensation be managed by giving the political agency control over collection of the harvest tax (*heradj*), which, together with part of the customs duties collected on the Amu-Darya, would be spent on public works in the khanate, such as irrigation and communications. He also proposed lightening the tax burden on Bukharans by means of reductions in the size of the army and the bureaucracy. Lessar's views found support in the conference, which agreed to spend part of the customs duties on public works in Bukhara and also to authorize the political agent to supervise the drafting of a state budget for the khanate. Alexander III approved the conference's recommendations on August 7, 1892.[6]

Had Lessar's original proposals, or even the more moderate recommendations of the 1891 conference, been implemented, Russia would have acquired unprecedented authority over the revenues and expenditures of the emir's government and thereby undermined the fiscal basis of Bukharan autonomy. Whether because of subsequent opposition from the foreign ministry or lack of interest in the finance ministry, however, the proposed compensations to the Bukharan people were abandoned when the details of the customs unification were worked out during 1893–1894. V. I. Ignatiev, Lessar's successor, again raised the question of Russian control over Bukhara's finances in 1895, but with no success.[7]

The method of effecting Bukhara's inclusion in the Russian customs frontier became an important factor in the competition among the different views as to the policy to be followed toward the emir. The Ministry of War wanted the customs unification worked out completely and then presented to Abd al-Ahad by the governor general of Turkestan, but a second conference, meeting under Vyshnegradskii's chairmanship on June 15, 1892, did not agree. Instead, in January 1893 the government took advantage of the first visit of a reigning emir of Bukhara to Russia to inform Abd al-Ahad of its plans. On January 15, while the emir was visiting the St. Petersburg mint, S. Iu. Witte, the new minister of finance, made known to him the proposal to move Russia's customs frontier to the Amu-Darya and to spend part of the customs revenue on public works in the khanate. Abd al-Ahad, perhaps forewarned of Russia's intentions, received the news calmly, merely expressing concern over the effect on his poorer subjects of the Russian tariff on Indian tea. Witte promised that only a moderate duty would be imposed on tea of low quality. The emir had been accompanied to Russia by his zakatchi-kalan, Astanakul-parvanachi. Lessar, who had met the Bukharan party in Moscow and escorted them to St. Petersburg, then entered into preliminary explanations with Astanakul on the customs unification.[8]

On June 6, 1894, the project was approved in its final form, and the Bukharan government was informed of the terms. That the transference of the customs frontier was effected unilaterally, rather than by means of another Russo-Bukharan convention, was due to Lessar, who doubtless wanted not only to avoid the wrangling that invariably accompanied negotiations with Bukhara but also to impress upon the emir his subordination to Russia. Abd al-Ahad had no choice but to accept the fait accompli, and on July 24 the kush-begi officially notified Lessar of the emir's consent.[9]

The inclusion of Bukhara in Russia's customs frontier, effective from January 1, 1895, did not establish a customs union between the two states. Bukhara continued to collect the traditional zakat on imports from Russia, and instead of a uniform tariff on the Bukharan-Afghan border, there were actually two tariffs, the Bukharan zakat and the standard Russian duty.[10] What the transference of the customs frontier to the Amu-Darya did accomplish economically was to secure for Russia a virtual monopoly over the Bukharan market. The greatest significance of the new customs frontier, however, was military and political rather than economic, for it was guarded by Russian troops and customs officials. In September 1894 Tashkent sent the steamboat "Tsar" up the Amu-Darya from Chardjui to a point just below Sarai to explore the river crossings, and in the following year Russian customs houses and frontier posts were established along the right bank of the river from Kerki to the western border of Darvaz.[11]

The close connection between the customs frontier and the defense of Bukhara was clear as early as the April 1891 conference in St. Petersburg, where Lessar proposed a reduction in the size of the Bukharan army. Not only was the army a burden on the Bukharan people, but the emir's troops were of only secondary importance in Bukhara's defense, and Russia's assumption of control over the Amu-Darya frontier would reduce their significance still further. As Lessar put it: "The emir cannot . . . count on his army in case of an uprising of his subjects or an invasion of the khanate by the Afghans; he understands that in such circumstances all will depend not on the loyalty and bravery of his soldiers, but on the attitude of the Russian government."[12] A representative of the war ministry at the June 1892 conference observed that the transfer of Russia's customs frontier to the Amu-Darya would significantly aid the defense of Bukhara and Russian Turkestan.[13]

Lessar's recommendation received serious consideration. One proposal was that the army be cut to 5,900 men, with an annual budget of 559,000 rubles.[14] In 1894 the Ministry of War commissioned Cossack Captain P. P. Shubinskii to prepare a study of the Bukharan army for use in discussing the question of its reduction. Despite the fact that in 1889 Abd al-Ahad had supplemented Russia's earlier gifts of arms by purchasing in Russia two thousand rifles for his guard and firearms for part of his cavalry, previously armed mainly with sabers,[15] the Bukharan army had been virtually unchanged since the 1870's. Poslavskii described it as "an even greater anachronism than Bukhara's city wall itself."[16] Shubinskii's report of June 2, 1894, concluded that the emir's army, still armed for the most part with obsolete rifles in poor repair, equipped with useless artillery, and ignorant of the rules of firing, was "nothing but an unorganized mass, totally unprepared for the demands of war, little different with respect to fighting qualities from a simple crowd of armed individuals chosen at random." Acting on Shubinskii's findings, Governor General Baron A. B. Vrevskii, who had succeeded Rosenbach in 1889, argued in his annual report for 1894 that the Bukharan army ought to be reduced in size since it could not be improved in quality.

No substantial improvement was possible without shortening the term of service and increasing the number of trained reserves by means of compulsory military service, but such a step would be contrary to all tradition and repugnant to the population.[17] No overt steps were taken to force a reduction in the size of the Bukharan army, but after the establishment of the Russian customs frontier on the Amu-Darya, Abd al-Ahad did reduce the number of his troops from almost 15,000 to a little over 10,000, probably under informal Russian pressure.[18]

In 1873 Bukhara had been distinguished from Khiva by its enjoyment of a number of legal and political rights that the smaller khanate lacked, being a full-fledged Russian protectorate. Foremost among these rights were that the emir could conduct his own foreign relations and manage the defense of his country. By 1880, however, Bukhara had lost the opportunity, although not the right, to conduct foreign relations. And in 1886–1887 Russia began to assume active military responsibility for Bukhara's defense when it established cantonments at Chardjui and Kerki.[19] In still other ways Bukhara's status vis-à-vis Russia began to resemble Khiva's more closely, as in the expansion of Russia's extraterritorial civil jurisdiction, which by 1893 had progressed even further than in Khiva. From 1895, when Russia undertook the control and protection of the Bukharan-Afghan frontier, Bukhara may be regarded as a de facto Russian protectorate.

There were further developments in the period 1890–1902 that completed the revolution in Russo-Bukharan relations begun in the second half of the 1880's. With the end of Bukhara's isolation, brought about by the building of the Central Asian Railroad and the influx of private Russian interests, the khanate's fate became linked ever more directly to Russia's. Monetary controls and improved communications became necessities. These important changes, like those already discussed, were not part of a long-range scheme to subvert Bukharan autonomy. They came about rather in response to practical problems and in the context of Russia's traditional policy of nonintervention.

In 1895 the foreign ministry demonstrated its unshaken loyalty to the policy of maintaining Bukhara's autonomy during the dispute over a successor to P. M. Lessar, who had gone to London as a counselor of embassy. Governor General Vrevskii, who in 1891 had declared that it was high time "to recognize that the khanate of

Bukhara has lost its political independence and not to regard it as a foreign state," took this opportunity to state his ideas in greater detail: "The position of the emir of Bukhara in his relations to Russia is completely identical with the position of the khan of Khiva. They have both been placed in full and unconditional dependence on Russia and have been granted only the right of internal administration of their khanates. Although they have consequently preserved for themselves all the prestige of independent rulers within the borders of their possessions, they have in fact lost their independence. I cannot therefore regard these two khanates otherwise than as integral parts of the Russian Empire [which are] only temporarily in an exceptional position in regard to their internal situation." What Vrevskii proposed was to abolish the political agency, which he, like his three predecessors, regarded as affording gratuitous support to the emir's delusions of independence. Vrevskii would have replaced the political agent with a Russian resident, who would be directly responsible to the governor general, would have duties roughly equivalent to those of an oblast governor, and would in case of need exert pressure on the Bukharan government to reform the internal administration of the country. In short, the emir would be reduced to carrying out the orders of the Russian resident.[20]

Vrevskii's views were shared by the Ministry of War but met determined opposition from the Ministry of Foreign Affairs, which refused to hand over the conduct of relations with Bukhara to Tashkent and abandon the policy of nonintervention. From the foreign ministry's viewpoint open interference in Bukhara's internal affairs was particularly undesirable in 1895 because it might jeopardize the Pamir boundary agreement recently concluded with Britain.[21] The foreign ministry once again had its way, and V. I. Ignatiev, a member of the Asiatic Department and former diplomatic attaché to the commandant of the Transcaspian Oblast, was named to succeed Lessar.

The Pamir Boundary Settlement

In the late 1870's the British had become aware of the fact that between Afghanistan on the west and Kashgar on the east lay a no man's land that extended right up to the Hindu Kush, India's natural northern rampart. By the end of the 1880's Calcutta was anxiously attempting to get either Kabul or Peking to assert effective control over this political vacuum, comprising the desolate and sparsely inhabited alpine valleys called Pamirs and the intervening mountain ranges.[22] In the meantime Russia, too, had begun to take an interest in this most remote corner of Central Asia, the last region in which her frontiers remained undefined, since the 1873 agreement with Britain over spheres of influence did not extend eastward of the longitude of Lake Sarikol (Victoria). Although the first direct contact in the Pamirs between Russia, in the person of the scientist B. L. Grombchevskii, and Britain, represented by Captain Francis Younghusband, in the fall of 1889 had been peaceful enough,[23] by 1891 the political rivalry between the two powers in this region was out in the open. Aware of Younghusband's efforts to persuade the Chinese authorities in Kashgar to make good their claims to the Pamirs, Tashkent sent Colonel Ianov with the war ministry's approval to annex the Pamirs as far as the Sarikol Mountains on the east and the Hindu Kush on the south. Ianov encountered Younghusband in August 1891 in the upper valley of the Vakhan-Darya, immediately north of the Hindu Kush, informed him of Russia's claim to the area, and forced him to withdraw.[24]

Britain reacted to Russia's advance by occupying Hunza, a small principality on the southern slope of the Hindu Kush, during the winter of 1891–1892; pressing for greater control over Hunza's neighbor to the west, Chitral, into which one of Ianov's exploring parties had already penetrated; and proposing to St. Petersburg a demarcation of boundaries on "the roof of the world."[25] Negotiations toward this end were begun in March 1893, after the victory of the foreign ministry over the war ministry in a prolonged struggle had cleared the way for Russian participation. A delimitation of frontiers necessarily entailed the reopening of the Shugnan-Roshan question, which had been tabled in 1884, since that province lay in the western Pamirs. As early as October 1891, in fact, Russia had raised precisely this issue when it countered London's protests over the Russian advance in the Pamirs by charging Britain with failure to ensure that Kabul observed the 1873 agreement.[26] Now Russia insisted on strict enforcement of that agreement—Afghanistan was to evacuate all right-bank districts of Shugnan, Roshan, and Vakhan, while Bukhara was to evacuate left-bank Darvaz. At the same time St. Petersburg suggested the transfer of the Anglo-Russian demarcation line from the Pamir River, or northern branch of the Pandj, to the Vakhan-Darya, its southern branch. Intent upon keeping the Russian frontier as far north of the Hindu Kush as possible, London reluctantly yielded to Russia's demands in regard to Shugnan-Roshan and in return obtained St. Petersburg's consent at the end of 1893 not only to maintain the Pamir River line of demarcation but to extend it in a roughly eastern direction as far as the Chinese frontier (the Sarikol Mountains). The narrow corridor of territory between the Russian frontier and the Hindu Kush was to be assigned to Afghanistan as a demilitarized zone.[27]

In the fall of 1893 the government of India prevailed upon Abd ar-Rahman, by offering him an increase in his British subsidy and territorial concessions along the Indo-Afghan frontier, to agree to exchange right-bank Roshan, Shugnan, and Vakhan for left-bank Darvaz and eastern Vakhan. Britain undertook to carry out the transfers of territory by agreement with Russia.[28] To obtain the co-operation of Bukhara, Lessar then approached Abd al-Ahad. In March 1895 Astanakul-divan-begi, the zakatchi-kalan, informed Governor General Vrevskii that the emir would be pleased to exchange southern Darvaz, a small and poor district, thinly populated, and producing little revenue, for Roshan, Shugnan, and northern Vakhan, which were by comparison large, populous, and well cultivated. At the same time the Bukharan government granted Russia the right to build forts, station troops, and extend the customs frontier into the new area.[29]

As both Afghanistan and Bukhara had consented in advance, Britain and Russia on February 27/March 11, 1895, signed an agreement in London defining "the Spheres of Influence of the two Countries in the Region of the Pamirs," which formalized the understanding reached at the end of 1893.[30] St. Petersburg ratified the work of the Anglo-Russian boundary commission in March 1896; in October of the same year Shugnan, Roshan, and northern Vakhan, which had been occupied by Russian troops in the spring of 1895, were transferred to Bukhara as Shugnan-Roshan beglik, and southern Darvaz was transferred to Afghanistan.[31] Britain moved quickly to occupy Chitral, just across the Hindu Kush from the great south bend of the Pandj, in 1895. Russia gained direct control of the eastern Pamirs, and although title over the western Pamirs was transferred to Bukhara, Russian garrisons were established in 1897–1898 at Khorog in Shugnan and in two locations on the right bank of the Pandj in Vakhan.[32] Russian control of Bukhara's frontiers was finally complete.

An unforeseen consequence of the 1895 settlement was a sizable emigration from Afghanistan. In 1897 the beg of Darvaz reported that over 700 families had left their homes in left-bank Darvaz after vainly resisting the Afghan takeover there; 100 of these families settled in Bukharan Darvaz, the rest in Kulab and Karategin. In July 1898 Ignatiev reported to Tashkent that the total number of refugees from southern Darvaz had reached 1,164 families. Farther upriver refugees from Badakhshan and Afghan Vakhan began in 1895 to cross the Pandj into Shugnan and Bukharan Vakhan, some continuing on via Roshan to Fergana. In 1897 the Afghan authorities warned that all relatives of fugitives from the left bank would be expelled across the Pandj if the fugitives did not return to Afghanistan. One hundred and three individuals were subsequently transported to one of the islands in the middle of the river, where they remained because the Bukharan authorities in Shugnan refused them permission to land on the right bank. The commandant of the Russian post at Khorog finally interceded with the beg of Shugnan to allow the expatriates to enter Bukhara.[33]

Monetary Controls

Bukhara's and Khiva's close economic links with Russia from the late 1880's required a stable relationship between Russia's currency and that of her protectorates, but in the first half of the nineties a sharp decline in the world price of silver undermined that relationship. The Bukharan and Khivan mints customarily coined into *tangas*, at a commission, all the silver brought to them by private individuals. The Bukharan tanga contained 2.88 grams of silver, worth 20 Russian kopeks in the 1880's but only 10 kopeks by 1894 as a result of the fall in the price of silver. Since the rate of exchange on Bukharan tangas was usually around 20 kopeks, speculators in the early nineties would buy silver bullion in Russia, have it minted into tangas in Bukhara, and then exchange the tangas in Russia for rubles, turning a handsome profit in the process. Such speculation drove the tanga's rate of exchange down to 16 kopeks by 1894, but the difference between the tanga's exchange value and the value of its silver content still encouraged speculation.[34] The Khivan tanga was subject to similar pressures, although on a smaller scale.

Russia tried a variety of solutions. In an effort to discourage speculation, the Ministry of Finance in 1890 announced that Bukharan and Khivan money would no longer be accepted in the government-general of Turkestan in payment of customs duties and taxes after May 1, 1895.[35] In 1893 Lessar prevailed upon Abd al-Ahad to halt the minting of privately owned silver into tangas.[36] In search of a more radical solution, Russia for a time considered permitting the emir to issue 20-kopek pieces with his own name on them and inscriptions in both Russian and Persian, to pass as legal tender in both Russia and Bukhara. The idea was finally rejected on the grounds that placing the emir's name on Russian money would lower Russian prestige in Bukhara.[37] Finally in July 1893, as part of a broader effort to stabilize Russia's currency, the imperial mint discontinued the purchase of silver in any form from private persons for coining into new money; on July 16 the importation of foreign silver money, except Chinese, was forbidden.[38] On October 29, however, an exception was made to allow the import of silver money from Khiva into the government-general of Turkestan, since Khiva had in 1881 received permission to pay off her war indemnity in either Russian paper money or local currency. Khiva paid the last installment on the indemnity in 1900.[39]

In February and March, 1894, a commission set up within the finance ministry under D. F. Kobeko to study the problems of Russian trade with Bukhara and Khiva recommended the unification of the protectorates' monetary systems with that of Russia. The only immediate action taken, however, was to issue orders to both Bukhara and Khiva to halt all minting of new tangas except with the governor general's permission.[40] Beginning in 1895, the New Bukhara branch of the State Bank attempted to stabilize the rate of exchange by buying tangas freely at 12 kopeks, but since the current rate was 14.5 kopeks and higher, the bank had few customers. In 1899 the State Bank raised its purchase price to 15 kopeks, at a time when the rate was 15.4 kopeks.[41] These half-measures did not solve the problem, and Russia slowly came around to the view of the Kobeko commission that monetary unification was the only answer. The difficulty was that the issuance of money was regarded in Central Asia as one of the most important marks of sovereignty; depriving the emir of this right would be hard to reconcile with Russia's policy of maintaining his authority in internal affairs.

At the beginning of April 1901, therefore, I. A. Vyshnegradskii, still an important figure in the Ministry of Finance, was sent to Kermine to obtain, with Ignatiev's help, the emir's consent to an agreement on gradual monetary unification. The memorandum that Vyshnegradskii presented to Abd al-Ahad on April 8 suggested (1) a fixed rate of exchange for the tanga at 15 kopeks, approximately the current rate; (2) the emir's surrender to the New Bukhara branch of the State Bank of his monetary reserves (20 million tangas) as well as of whatever portion of his revenues might be necessary to provide Russia with a sufficient reserve of tangas to maintain the fixed rate of exchange, with the emir receiving in return Russian gold or paper money at the official rate; (3) mutual free acceptance of Bukharan money by branches of the imperial treasury and State Bank in the khanate and the Samarkand Oblast, and of Russian money by the emir's treasury, and the use of Russian money interchangeably with its own by the Bukharan government in meeting expenses; and (4) permanent cessation of the coinage of tangas.[42] Russia aimed for the immediate future at a stable rate of exchange and, ultimately, at the supplanting of Bukharan money altogether by Russian currency.

Abd al-Ahad objected even more strenuously than he had in 1888 over the establishment of the Russian settlements, relying once again on Russia's desire to maintain his authority. In the audience he granted to Vyshnegradskii, the emir argued: "It is well known to everyone that, according to our country's customs and laws, the chief attributes of the authority of the emirs are the right to coin their own money and the pronouncing of their names in prayers in the mosques. Depriving the emir of the right to coin his own money is equivalent to taking away his authority. When they learn of this, the population will no longer recognize the emir as their ruler and will refuse to execute his orders . . . In view of this, I decidedly do not find it possible to renounce forever the right to coin money." Abd al-Ahad subsequently invited Ignatiev to a private talk and desperately appealed to him: "If I am forced to submit to all the demands presented by Vyshnegradskii, and, in particular, the demands forever to renounce the coining of money, then nothing will remain for me but to petition His Majesty the Emperor for permission to go to Mecca in a year or two and settle there for the rest of my life."[43] Ignatiev gave the usual assurances that Russia cared only for the maintenance of the emir's authority and the welfare of

his country and its inhabitants. Then, like one of his subjects hag-
gling in the bazaar, Abd al-Ahad switched from a tone of desperate
outrage to one of sweet reasonableness. His final price was to be
permitted to coin a specified amount of new tangas immediately
and to retain the formal right of coinage for the future, with the
understanding that this right would be exercised only with the prior
approval in each instance of the Russian government.

A compromise was worked out, acceptable both to the emir
and to Finance Minister Witte. Abd al-Ahad agreed to all of Vyshnegradskii's original demands but was granted permission to mint
up to 25,000,000 tangas out of his reserves of silver bullion; the
newly minted money would then be deposited in the State Bank.
In the future the emir could coin tangas only with Russia's permission, out of Russian silver, with the Bukharan mint making no
profit and merely being reimbursed for the expenses of minting.
On April 23, 1901, Astanakul-kush-begi handed to Ignatiev and
Vyshnegradskii a formal letter of consent to the Russian demands.[44]

After 1901 the tanga was stable as a result of Russia's buying
and selling of Bukharan currency at the fixed price, and Russian
money circulated freely in the khanate. Russia's long-range goal of
completely supplanting Bukharan currency with Russian money,
however, was never realized. Although the tangas received by Russian banks and treasury offices in Bukhara were sent to St. Petersburg for reminting into Russian money, the emir continued to mint
new tangas annually. The Bukharan people showed a marked preference for their own money, both out of habit and because it contained 11 kopeks' worth of silver, whereas the Russian 15-kopek
piece contained only 6 or 7 kopek's worth of silver.[45]

The aim set by the Kobeko commission was pursued with even
less success in Khiva. Although the khan was forbidden to mint new
tangas after 1892, and his petition to be allowed to do so was refused
by the governor general in July, 1908, the tanga remained in great
demand in Khiva, and consequently its value remained high. Khivan
tangas were accepted at the Petro-Aleksandrovsk treasury after 1903
at an exchange rate of 15 kopeks, but the current free rate was 19 to
20.5 kopeks. In 1906 and again in 1908 under pressure from Petro-
Aleksandrovsk, Muhammad Rahim decreed the free circulation of
Russian paper money, but his subjects balked at accepting it; in
order to prevent a shortage of specie in Khiva the State Bank in
Tashkent twice had to send 2,500,000 silver rubles to the khanate

—in 1904 and 1908. Senator Count K. K. Pahlen, who conducted a thorough investigation into the affairs of the government-general of Turkestan in 1908, recommended acceptance of the Khivan tanga at the Petro-Aleksandrovsk treasury at the rate of 20 kopeks, the gradual but complete withdrawal of Khivan currency from circulation, and its replacement with Russian money, but his recommendations, although revived in November 1914 by the governor general, were never implemented.[46]

Communications and Public Works

Having undertaken the control of the Amu-Darya frontier, Russia found herself in need of good roads over which to move troops and supplies to her border posts. Except in western Bukhara, roads suitable for wheeled traffic were nonexistent. In 1899 Russia tried in vain to persuade Abd al-Ahad to pay 170,000 rubles for the construction of a post road from the Russian border south of Samarkand via Shahr-i Sabz, Guzar, and Shirabad to Termez, where a Russian garrison had been installed two years previously. The road was finally built at Russia's expense in 1900–1901, at more than twice the cost of the original estimate. Opened to traffic on January 1, 1902, it was Bukhara's most modern road, macadamized in places and with post houses at regular intervals.[47] Another road, built and maintained by native corvée, was begun in 1900 along the right bank of the Amu-Darya and eventually connected all the Russian border posts from Kerki to Chubek, whence the road turned northward from the river to end at Kulab.[48] Early in the twentieth century Russian access to the hinterland of eastern Bukhara was improved by the construction of roads from Samarkand to Karatag, from Fergana to Garm, and from Fergana to Kala-i Khumb.[49]

The coming of the railroad in the 1880's also brought the extension to Bukhara of the Russian postal system, with post offices soon operating in New Bukhara, Old Bukhara, Chardjui, and Kerki.[50] Another result of the construction of the railroad was the extension to Chardjui of the telegraph line, which had been built in 1884 from Katta-Kurgan to Bukhara. In 1896 a new line was established from Chardjui to Kerki and Kelif, and in 1902 another telegraph line was built along the post road from Samarkand to Termez. By 1914 telegraph wires followed the banks of the Amu-Darya from Termez in Bukhara to Urgench in Khiva and to Petro-Aleksandrovsk.[51] In 1896 upon the expiration of the twelve-year contract between Emir Muzaffar and Nazarov, the original telegraph line, which had run along a poorly maintained road that was in places as much as eight miles from the railroad and thus outside the Russian-controlled railroad zone and comparatively inaccessible to repair crews, was transferred at Bukhara's expense to the poles of the railroad telegraph. The emir's government also built a connecting line from Old Bukhara to the railroad telegraph at New Bukhara.[52]

In 1902 the perennial problem of the division of the waters of the Zarafshan River between the Samarkand Oblast and Bukhara for irrigation purposes was finally settled. From time to time various governors general had appointed special commissions to regulate the division of water. In 1902 Governor General N. A. Ivanov designated a new commission, consisting of the governor of the Samarkand Oblast, several other Russians, including the dragoman of the political agency in Bukhara, and representatives of the emir's government, to review the protocol on the division of water drawn up by the previous commission in 1895. Faced with a lack of accurate data on the cultivated acreage in the khanate dependent on the Zarafshan for irrigation, the commission settled on a division of the water between the Samarkand Oblast and Bukhara in the ratio of two to one. The two territorial units shared equally the labor and matériel expenses of regulating the river's flow.[53] The 1902 irrigation settlement stood until the 1917 Revolution, although Bukhara remained unsatisfied with her share, particularly in years of low water.[54]

During his tenure as political agent P. M. Lessar had proposed the appointment of an engineer in charge of irrigation works, to be attached to the political agency but paid by the emir, since his work would benefit Bukhara. He was to superintend administration of the native irrigation system, plan improvements in it, and secure from the emir's government the necessary funds. Lessar's proposal went to Tashkent and thence to the Ministry of War; after almost a decade of bureaucratic delay, it emerged in a modified form. A law of December 11, 1902, established the office of technical assistant to the governor general of Turkestan, to serve in Bukhara. His duties included supervision of the Bukharan irrigation system and of all surveying and construction undertaken by Russia in the khanate as well as execution of the tasks of town architect in the Russian settlements. Bukhara was to pay roughly one third of the expenses of the office. With regard to Lessar's original purpose of forcing the emir to undertake public works for the benefit of his subjects and of Russian trade with the khanate, the office of technical assistant was totally ineffective.[55]

The Bukharan Jews

One problem on which the Russian and Bukharan governments saw eye to eye, although it involved curtailment of the treaty rights of a significant number of the emir's subjects, was treatment of the Bukharan Jews. An offshoot of Middle Eastern and Persian Jewry, the Bukharan or Central Asian Jews had probably been established in the valley of the Zarafshan since the days of the Achaemenid Empire in the sixth century B.C. and had since been reinforced by several waves of immigrants from Persia and Mesopotamia. Numbering some eight or nine thousand, the great majority of them in the capital,[56] the Jews of Bukhara played an important role in the khanate's economic life as merchants and craftsmen. However, a multitude of oppressive restrictions were imposed on them. They were subject to Moslem law, although they were disqualified from testifying against Moslems; they were taxed arbitrarily for the privilege of living and trading in the towns of the khanate; and they needed the emir's permission to buy a house from a Moslem. They were also forbidden to ride, even on donkeys, within the walls of a town and were forced to dress distinctively in a black cap and a dark-colored gown, gathered in at the waist with a piece of rope rather than a belt. Not surprisingly, the Bukharan Jews welcomed the Russian conquerors of Central Asia as their deliverers from Moslem tyranny.[57]

Russia had traditionally treated the Central Asian Jews much more favorably than their European cousins. In 1833 Central Asian Jews were specifically exempted from the laws forbidding Jews in general from living and doing business in Russia beyond the pale of Jewish settlement. Nine years later Jews from Central Asia were granted equal rights with Bukharan and Khivan Moslems to trade in the government-general of Orenburg. Finally, in 1866 an exception was made in the case of Central Asian Jews to the general rule that foreign Jews were not allowed to settle in Russia or to become Russian subjects.[58]

A considerable number of Bukharan Jews took advantage of these privileges and exemptions, as well as of the reciprocal rights granted by the treaties of 1868 and 1873 to all Bukharan subjects to engage in business and own property in Russian Turkestan. During the 1870's and early 1880's many Jews emigrated to the government-general, where their lot was much easier than in the khanate. General von Kaufman regarded the presence of the Bukharan Jews as beneficial to Russian Turkestan and as useful in exerting Russian influence over Bukhara.[59] Not confining their activities to Turkestan, a wealthy colony of Bukharan Jews soon arose in Moscow itself.[60]

In the reign of Alexander III, however, as part of the government's Russification policy, involving a general tightening of restrictions on Jews in Russia, the Bukharan Jews began to lose their favored position. St. Petersburg was particularly concerned over the attraction that Russian Turkestan exercised on the Jews of the khanate: not only was Russia gaining more and more of these undesirable immigrants but the fact that the emir's oppressed Jewish subjects were finding refuge in Russia might react unfavorably on the emir's prestige and authority in Bukhara. The first blow was struck against the right of Bukharan Jews to own real property in the government-general—a right that had been confirmed to all Bukharans by article twelve of the 1873 treaty and by article 262 of the 1886 Turkestan statute. In violation of these previous commitments, Bukharan Jews were by a law of May 23, 1889, legally distinguished from Bukharan Moslems and deprived of the right to own real property in Russian Turkestan.[61] Abd al-Ahad understandably did not protest this infringement on the rights of his Jewish subjects since his own interests were being served.

In 1892 Russia moved more directly to halt the immigration of Bukharan Jews. On January 10 Governor General Vrevskii ordered that Bukharan Jews wishing to travel to Russian Turkestan must first obtain passports from the emir's government. The passports were to be valid for not more than one year and had to be approved by the political agent, who was authorized to withhold his approval in the case of Jews whose presence in Russia he deemed in any way undesirable. At the same time the oblast governors were directed to see that all Bukharan Jews under their jurisdiction had the proper passports and stayed for only one year and to inform the political agent of any Bukharan Jews whom they considered undesirable visitors.[62] These regulations gave the Russian authorities in the khanate and in Turkestan broad powers to curtail the influx of Bukharan Jews into Russia. A law of March 24, 1892, authorizing the governor general to expel from Turkestan any undesirable nationals of the neighboring khanates put teeth into Vrevskii's earlier instructions. The emir's government readily agreed to observe the new regulations and to limit the issuance of passports to its Jewish subjects. The activities of Bukharan Jews in the interior of Russia were severely curtailed in 1893. Formerly they had been allowed free entry from Turkestan into the rest of the empire, but in 1893 a Ministry of Internal Affairs circular announced that henceforth special permission would be needed for such travel.[63]

In 1897 the final blow to Jewish emigration from Bukhara was struck. In that year the emir's government and Ignatiev agreed that Bukharan Jews in general ought not to be granted Russian nationality because it undermined the emir's prestige and authority, diminished his tax revenues, and placed Russia in the awkward position of having to defend the interests of Jews who were former Bukharan nationals against the emir and his Moslem subjects.[64] The privilege that had been accorded Bukharan Jews in 1866 of receiving Russian nationality was never revoked, and in fact as late as 1905 the right of such naturalized Jews to acquire real property in the towns where they were registered was upheld by the Senate.[65] In practice, however, the governor general enjoined the oblast governors to exercise great caution in naturalizing Bukharan Jews, to consult with the political agent as to possible objections, and to investigate carefully the moral character of each applicant. Virtually all such applications were denied on one pretext or another.[66] Finally in 1904 the minister of war issued a circular formally limiting the privilege of naturalization to exceptional cases.[67]

Having effectively halted the flow of Jewish emigration from Bukhara, Russia turned to the problem of the Bukharan Jews settled in Turkestan since the early 1870's, of whom there were over three hundred families. Under the Russo-Bukharan Treaty of 1873 these Jews enjoyed the right to reside anywhere in the government-general, whereas Russian Jews were restricted to a few border towns.[68] In 1900 it was decreed that after January 1, 1906, all "Central Asian Jews of foreign nationality" would be permitted to live and do business only in specified border towns of Russian Turkestan, that is, in the pale already established for Russian Jews.[69] The forced removal of the Bukharan Jews was twice postponed, first until January 1, 1909, and then until January 1, 1910, but it was finally effected.[70] Whether the Bukharan Jews were then in fact permitted to live in the pale or were expelled from Russian Turkestan altogether is unclear. Although they definitely had the right to reside in the designated towns, many of them were probably denied the necessary permits to do so by the local Russian authorities.[71] The pale originally comprised only the small border towns of Osh, Katta-Kurgan, and Petro-Aleksandrovsk, but in 1910 at the urging of the chief rabbi and with the approval of the Council of Ministers it was expanded to include Samarkand, Kokand, and Margelan.[72] Liberal Russian industrialists and newspapers, and even the conservative Minister of Finance V. N. Kokovtsov, protested the government's persecution of Bukharan Jews as harmful to the Russian economy because they played a major role in Russia's trade with Central Asia, but such protests were to no avail.[73]

By 1910 the problem of the Bukharan Jews had been solved by applying to them the same kind of legal restrictions long since established for Russian Jews. This process proceeded in violation of the treaty rights of Bukharan Jews as subjects of the emir but with the approval of the Bukharan government. The closing of the attractive avenue of escape to Russia enabled the emir to keep his Jewish subjects better in hand. Russia was no longer cast in the unwanted role of offering shelter to the oppressed of Bukhara and thus undermining the emir's authority in the khanate.

Gate in the City Wall, Bukhara

10 / Economic Development

Traditional Economy of the Protectorates

The economic impact, as distinguished from the economic motives, of nineteenth-century imperialism is an undeniable fact. All lands affected by this latter-day expansion of Europe were in some degree drawn into the world-wide system of economic relationships that had as its focus the industrialized West. Nor were Bukhara and Khiva exceptions to the rule, despite the fact that the great power which for them represented the West was itself barely and hesitantly beginning to embark on the path of industrialization. Economic development is a relative matter, and between Russia and her Central Asian protectorates there was no comparison.

Before the Russian conquest Bukhara and Khiva had been overwhelmingly agricultural, composed of largely self-sufficient economic regions but with a lively commercial life and some domestic handicraft industry. They retained this basic character even after the important changes that followed the coming of the railroad. In Bukhara the most important crop was wheat for domestic consumption, followed by cotton, rice, barley, and alfalfa. Western Bukhara, the richest agricultural area, was completely dependent on irrigation. The Zarafshan Valley was the center of cotton production and sericulture, while the valley of the Kashka-Darya (Karshi and Shahr-i Sabz) produced a grain surplus that was shipped to the capital. Western Bukhara was also famous for its fruits, particularly apricots, grapes, and melons. Cattle raising was a prosperous industry in Shahr-i Sabz, and the raising of sheep around Karakul was an even bigger enterprise.[1]

Central Bukhara, where rainfall was adequate, particularly in the uplands, had excellent farmlands and pasturage. Wheat, barley, and cattle were shipped in quantity to the capital of the khanate, with Guzar serving as the chief cattle market. Flax was an important secondary crop, and cotton was grown on irrigated land in the southern districts along the Amu-Darya, principally in Shirabad beglik.[2] The mountainous east was a poor region. Although Karategin was relatively self-sufficient, Darvaz had to import grain from Karategin, Kulab, and Baldjuan. There was insufficient arable land and pasturage to support the population, so that during the slack winter season many inhabitants of Karategin and Darvaz sought employment in central and western Bukhara and in the neighboring Fergana Oblast.[3]

Commercial activity was greatest in western Bukhara. The capital was the leading center of internal trade and the only important market for foreign trade. Karshi also played an important role in internal trade. Commerce decreased rapidly toward the east in the khanate. Even in the western begliks most roads were poor and trade relied mainly on camel caravans; east of Guzar no roads suitable for wheeled traffic existed until they were built by the Russians at the beginning of the twentieth century. In remote and mountainous Karategin, Darvaz, and Shugnan-Roshan there was little commercial contact with the rest of the country and only an insignificant local barter trade; money was little used.[4] Bukhara and Karshi were the only important industrial centers, producing primarily cotton and silk textiles, pottery, metal goods, linseed oil, and hides.

In Khiva agriculture was completely dependent on irrigation. The leading crops were wheat, cotton, alfalfa, rice, and barley, and the country normally produced a grain surplus. Fruit growing was also important; sericulture much less so. Cattle raising was confined primarily to the nomadic inhabitants of the khanate.[5] Commerce was much more weakly developed than in Bukhara: whereas Bukhara was the commercial capital of all Central Asia before the Russian conquest, the Hungarian visitor Vámbéry described Khiva in 1863 as a miserable town with few bazaars and little trade, inferior to the smallest provincial market town in Persia. The country's scanty trade and industry was centered in Urgench.[6]

Russo-Bukharan Trade

Long before the conquest of Central Asia, Russia had carried on an important trade with Bukhara. The khanate's major exports to Russia were, in order of importance, raw cotton, karakul skins (also called astrakhan or Persian lamb and much in demand in Russia and the West), and wool, followed by silk, hides, dried fruits, and carpets. Bukhara in turn imported from Russia inexpensive textiles, metal and manufactured goods, sugar, kerosene, and china.[7] The reduction of Bukhara to a Russian dependency did not appreciably affect the volume of Russo-Bukharan trade, for Russian merchants in the 1870's focused their attention on Russian Turkestan, where Tashkent soon surpassed Bukhara as the commercial capital of Central Asia. Bukhara's trade with Russia between 1868 and the mid-1880's did not rise much above the annual level of just over ten million rubles that it had attained during the 1860's.[8]

The construction of the Central Asian Railroad had an immediate impact on Russo-Bukharan trade by making the khanate much more accessible to European Russia both as a source of supply for raw materials and as a market for finished goods. The old caravan route via Kazalinsk to Orenburg was rapidly supplanted by the new rail and water route via Krasnovodsk to Astrakhan; freight costs fell from three rubles a pud to seventy kopeks.[9] Bukhara's annual trade with Russia doubled in value to twenty-three million rubles in the half-dozen years following the opening of the railroad and almost tripled again between the early 1890's and the eve of World War I, when it reached sixty-seven million rubles a year.[10]

Before the conquest Russo-Bukharan trade had been completely in the hands of Bukharan merchants. This situation, too, was little altered until the coming of the railroad. Russian visitors to Bukhara in the 1870's and early 1880's found only two or three Russian commercial representatives in the emir's capital, and only a single Russian company had a permanent branch in the khanate—a freight transportation office opened in 1880.[11] By 1887, however, there were already twenty big Russian merchants, nine large trading firms, and five transportation companies established in Bukhara.[12] The railroad brought to Bukhara not only Russian but also Armenian, French, and Jewish merchants. Although in 1905 the emir's government, with the permission of the political agency, levied a surtax on karakul bought by foreigners (mainly the French) in order to protect the Russian and Bukharan merchants engaged in the trade, five years later Bukhara was still attracting karakul buyers from London, Paris, Berlin, and Constantinople, as well as Moscow.[13]

Despite the changes wrought by the railroad, Russo-Bukharan trade remained small in absolute terms. The vast majority of Bukharans had little purchasing power and little need for foreign products, with the notable exceptions of cheap cotton and metal goods, tea, sugar, and kerosene. Similarly, production in Bukhara was primarily for domestic consumption except in the case of cotton and karakul. Furthermore, the effect of the Central Asian Railroad in promoting Russo-Bukharan trade was limited almost exclusively to the western begliks, which were accessible from the railroad and accounted for the bulk of cotton and karakul production. Central and eastern Bukhara remained almost as remote and economically isolated as ever. The absence of roads and the existence of internal customs duties levied by the provincial authorities were effective bars to trade. Because of transport costs and customs duties, Russian cotton prints sold for as much as 100 percent more in Karategin and Darvaz than in the capital.[14]

Another inhibiting factor, probably less important but certainly more easily altered and consequently the subject of more attention at the time, was the restrictive policy of the Bukharan government and Russia's hands-off attitude toward Russian merchants. Russian traders in Bukhara complained in 1875 that the native authorities were subjecting Russian goods not only to the 2½ percent zakat permitted by the 1873 treaty but also to illegal brokerage fees and trade taxes, which brought the total duty to 10 percent.[15] In the early 1880's Russian merchants in Bukhara were treated with suspicion and their every move closely watched by the government.[16] In the period 1873–1885, however, neither St. Petersburg nor Tashkent made any attempt to see that the 1873 treaty's commercial clauses were observed. More positive measures to promote Russian trade in Bukhara were even further from the thoughts of the imperial government. In December 1884 N. V. Charykov wrote that Russian trade in the khanate would benefit greatly if the post road were extended from Katta-Kurgan to the Bukharan capital, if regular postal service were established between Bukhara and Russian Turkestan, and if a Russian agent were assigned to the khanate to defend the legal rights and interests of Russian traders.[17] Such steps were soon taken, but not primarily with the interests of Russian merchants in mind. Although the radical improvement in communications effected by the railroad, the Amu-Darya Flotilla, and later the new roads was of enormous benefit to Russian trade with Bukhara, this result was quite incidental to the strategic considerations by which Russia was motivated in each case.

Similarly, the establishment of the political agency, although of great value to Russian trade, was the product of long dissatisfaction with the earlier method of conducting relations with the emir, which was finally brought to a head by the decision to build the railroad. The formation of Russian settlements and the broadening of extra-territorial jurisdiction were indeed responses on St. Petersburg's part to the problems raised by the invasion of Bukhara by private Russian interests, but the intention was as much to protect Bukharan autonomy as to promote the business affairs of Russian subjects. The political agency and the justice-of-the-peace courts were solicitous of native interests, and the Russian settlements served to limit Russian activity geographically since the government positively discouraged Russian trade in the Bukharan hinterland. Military as well as economic considerations played a role in the transfer of the customs frontier to the Amu-Darya. Only the institution of monetary controls was intended solely to benefit Russian trade interests.

Toward the close of the first decade of the twentieth century Russia's neglect of the interests of her merchants in Bukhara, along with many other aspects of the situation in the Central Asian protectorates, came under heavy attack. Colonel D. N. Logofet, one of the most persistent and vociferous critics of the situation in Bukhara and Russian policy there, urged that Russia promote the trade of her merchants by further improving communications in the khanate —extending telegraph lines throughout the country and building a railroad from the capital to Karshi, Kerki, and Termez. Logofet also protested that, in violation of the 1873 treaty, Russians were not allowed either to buy land outside of the four Russian settlements and the customs post at Sarai or to build factories outside of these areas and the railroad zone.[18]

In 1908 Count K. K. Pahlen found that Russian trade in Bukhara was still being arbitrarily and illegally taxed by the native authorities, thirty-five years after article six of the 1873 treaty had supposedly put an end to such practices. According to Pahlen, Russian goods were subject to numerous zakats as well as to taxes on buying and selling in the bazaars, on maintaining shops and stalls in the bazaars, and on the compulsory use of the official bazaar weights. In the Russian settlement at Termez, for example, the Bukharan authorities collected not only the legal zakat but also the *aminana* (a tax on the purchase of a commodity by a wholesaler from the producer) and a tax on the use of the bazaar weights. In 1906 Governor General D. I. Subbotich directed the political agent to press the Bukharan government to halt the collection of these illegal imposts in Termez as well as the zakat itself, which Subbotich proposed to replace with regular Russian business taxes. St. Petersburg stepped in at this point to defend Bukhara's right to collect the zakat, and in December 1906 the war ministry instructed the new governor general, N. I. Grodekov, to stop any measures already taken toward the unilateral abolition of the zakat at Termez and to negotiate an agreement with the emir if such abolition was deemed necessary. After both the political agent and the governor general's diplomatic attaché had agreed that the continued collection of the zakat at Termez was sanctioned by the 1873 treaty, the war ministry in March 1909 directed Governor General A. V. Samsonov not to push for abolition of the zakat at Termez but merely to demand of the Bukharan authorities that collection of the other commercial taxes on Russians be halted.[19] Three years later, however, when Samsonov pressed for abolition of the aminana on commodities purchased by Russian wholesalers, Foreign Minister Sazonov, deeming the point not important enough to be made a major issue, yielded to the emir's objections and directed the political agent to drop the matter.[20]

Pahlen reported that not only were the commercial activities of Russian subjects everywhere in the khanate subject to the Bukharan zakat, and sometimes to other, illegal taxes, but that all commercial and industrial activities in the four Russian settlements and in the railroad zone were subject to additional taxation by the administration of the settlements, under laws of the Russian Empire establishing various business taxes and licenses. The "inspecting senator" argued that such double taxation in the areas of greatest Russian activity hindered the development of trade. He also reported the complaints of Russian merchants that the assessment of the value of their goods by the Bukharan authorities for purposes of the zakat was unfair and arbitrary, and that they were usually forced to bribe the authorities in order to obtain a favorable assessment. Pahlen contended that the zakat had become obsolete. When it had been legalized by the treaties of 1868 and 1873, a similar duty had been in force in Russian Turkestan on Bukharan goods, but with the abolition of such duties in 1875 and the inclusion of Bukhara within Russia's customs frontier in 1895, the continued collection of the zakat in Bukhara had lost its justification. Following Subbotich's suggestion, Pahlen proposed abolishing the zakat and all other native taxes on Russian trade and substituting a Russian tax on

Russian business activities throughout the khanate.[21] As with the senator's other recommendations with regard to the Central Asian protectorates, this proposal was filed away and forgotten. Russian trade in Bukhara continued to arouse a minimum of government concern. The Bukharan authorities continued to collect the zakat —not once but several times on the same article as it changed hands —and as late as 1915 the foreign ministry demonstrated its usual reluctance to apply pressure in defense of what were, after all, only private interests. The political agency was similarly unsympathetic in 1916 to a petition of Russian merchants asking for abolition of the zakat levied, in violation of article seven of the 1873 treaty, on the Russian transit trade to Afghanistan.[22]

Bukhara's Trade with Other Countries

If Russia showed little interest in promoting the trade of her own merchants with Bukhara, she did take considerable pains to discourage Bukhara's trade with other countries, primarily India. Long before the conquest Russia had become the leading trade partner of the Central Asian khanates, and Russian manufactures far outnumbered English and other foreign goods in the markets of Bukhara and Khiva. After Bukhara became a Russian dependency, this situation continued to prevail.[23] However, Russia by no means monopolized the Central Asian market, for in the period 1873–1885 her share of Bukhara's total foreign trade was about one third.[24] Bukhara also carried on a lively trade with India, Afghanistan, and Persia. During the 1870's English muslin, cotton prints, calico, and brocade, as well as Indian tea and rice, were widely distributed in Bukhara and to a lesser extent in Khiva.[25]

In 1881 Russia took the first step toward closing the Central Asian market to England. The importation into Russian Turkestan of foreign goods was in general forbidden, and heavy duties were levied on the exceptions: tea, muslin, and dyes imported from India. Bukhara, the traditional middleman in the distribution of Anglo-Indian goods throughout Central Asia, suffered the loss of this valuable trade, which declined by over 50 percent by weight in the period 1881–1884 and virtually disappeared after the coming of the railroad, which gave Russian goods the final advantage over English goods in Turkestan.[26] For her own consumption, however, since she remained beyond the Russian customs frontier and was consequently not covered by the 1881 restrictions, Bukhara continued to import significant quantities of Indian goods, particularly green tea, which the inhabitants of the khanate strongly preferred to the black Russian or Chinese tea. Bukhara imported an estimated 80,000 puds of Indian tea, worth 6.7 million rubles, in 1882, and 70,000 puds in 1887.[27]

The construction of the Central Asian Railroad, which led to a rapid absolute increase in Russo-Bukharan trade, also gave Russia for the first time a preponderant share of Bukhara's total foreign trade. In 1887, the first year of the railroad's operation in the khanate, 83 percent of Bukhara's exports went to Russia, and 63 percent of her imports were derived from the same source.[28] The striking difference between the figures for exports and imports reveals the continuing role played by Bukharan imports from India. Only the transfer of the Russian customs frontier, with its restrictions and protective tariffs, to the Amu-Darya finally succeeded in curtailing these imports, which declined by 75–80 percent in the decade 1895–1905.[29] By 1913 Bukhara's imports from India totalled only 800,000 rubles, as compared with 5,500,000 rubles in 1887.[30] Chinese tea, imported by sea via the Suez Canal and the Straits to Batum, thence by rail and water via Baku and Krasnovodsk to Bukhara, began to compete with Indian tea after 1895; this development was hastened in the early 1900's when the tariff on low quality Indian tea was doubled, raising it to the level of the tariff on Chinese tea.[31] The effect of raising the barriers to Bukharan imports from India is readily apparent in the trade statistics for the period after 1895. At the turn of the century Russia accounted for 86 percent of Bukhara's exports and 72 percent of her imports.[32] By 1913 the corresponding figures were 88 percent and 89 percent.[33]

Russo-Khivan Trade

Khiva's trade with Russia presented much the same picture as Bukhara's, except that its value was only about one third that of the larger khanate's. Khiva exported raw cotton, wheat for the Russian outposts on the east coast of the Caspian and on the lower Sir-Darya, khalats, hides and skins, dried fruits, and fish from the Aral Sea. She imported from Russia manufactured goods, mainly textiles and metal products, tea, sugar, and kerosene.[34] As in the case of Bukhara, Khiva's trade with Russia in the period 1873–1885 showed only a moderate increase over the level of three million rubles that it had attained annually in the early seventies.[35]

Although it passed 230 miles from the khan's capital, the Central Asian Railroad proved a great boon to Russo-Khivan trade, which had nearly tripled by 1898, reaching 11.8 million rubles annually.[36] The old caravan routes to Kazalinsk, Krasnovodsk, and Tsesarevich Bay at the northeast corner of the Caspian Sea yielded much of their traffic to the new routes that connected with the railroad at Chardjui, Merv, and Askhabad.[37] The lack of direct access to Russia by modern means of transportation nevertheless remained a major problem for Khiva. In 1890 two thirds of her cotton, her most important export, still went by caravan via Kazalinsk to Orenburg.[38] The opening in 1905 of the Orenburg-Tashkent Railroad was of further benefit to Khiva's trade, since it gave her an uninterrupted rail route to Russia, although the journey by caravan to the railroad at Kazalinsk was longer than the trip to Chardjui, Merv, or Askhabad. Partly as a result of the new railroad, Russo-Khivan trade in the decade 1898–1908 increased by more than 50 percent to over 18 million rubles a year.[39]

Inaccessibility remained a major obstacle to the further growth of Russo-Khivan trade. The khanate's first direct modern transport link to the outside world was the Amu-Darya Flotilla. In 1894 the Ministry of Finance proposed the establishment of regular commercial navigation on the Amu-Darya, but St. Petersburg decided instead to combine economic with strategic interests. Between 1895 and 1901 the size of the flotilla was increased from two to six steamboats (plus thirteen barges and assorted small craft); the flotilla was permitted to carry private cargoes, and from March to late October a regular sailing schedule was maintained between Petro-Aleksandrovsk and Chardjui, and beyond to Kerki, and later Termez. Although by 1908 the flotilla was transporting annually more than two and a half times as much private cargo as government cargo, most of it originating in or destined for Khiva, the service operated at a heavy loss. Native shipping on the river and camel caravans along its banks continued to carry the bulk of Khiva's trade between the khanate and the railroad at Chardjui. The second attempt to establish a modern transportation link between Khiva and Russia was made by a private Russian joint-stock company, which around 1910 established regular steam navigation on the Aral Sea and the lower Amu-Darya, between the Aralsk station of the Orenburg-Tashkent

Railroad and Chardjui. However, even during the eight months of the year when this route was not blocked by ice, the shallowness of the eastern half of the Aral Sea and of the mouths of the Amu-Darya made navigation difficult and prevented the venture from being an unqualified success.[40]

Russo-Khivan trade was hindered by political as well as physical obstacles. Although Russian merchants were as rare in Khiva before the coming of the railroad as in Bukhara, those who did trade in the khanate were harassed by the native government. Article nine of the 1873 treaty had exempted Russian merchants from the zakat and all other commercial duties, but in the first years after the treaty the khan's government subjected the Russians to the *dallyali*, a tax on the sale of goods by a wholesaler to a retailer. The Khivan government answered the protests of the Russian merchants by claiming that the dallyali was a private brokerage fee. This argument convinced Colonel N. A. Ivanov, commandant of the Amu-Darya Otdel, who in turn persuaded Governor General von Kaufman. In July 1875 Kaufman approved of Ivanov's insistence that Russian traders in Khiva pay the dallyali just as their Khivan competitors did. The khan's government went a step further in 1884 when it levied a zakat of 10 percent ad valorem on green tea imported by Russian merchants from Persia via the Transcaspian Oblast on the grounds that no such article of import from Russia had existed at the time of the signing of the 1873 treaty. Governor General Rosenbach reported this action to the minister of foreign affairs in November 1884 and directed the commandant of the Amu-Darya Otdel not to interfere in the meantime with Khiva's collection of the duty. The foreign ministry never replied to Rosenbach's request for instructions, and the duty continued to be collected for the next eleven years.[41]

The Central Asian Railroad brought a rapidly increasing number of Russian merchants to Khiva, so that a sizable Russian commercial colony soon developed at Urgench. Under these circumstances the illegal Khivan taxes caused increasing discontent. In 1895 the khan's government finally overreached itself when it petitioned Tashkent for permission to subject Russian merchants to various other trade taxes in force in the khanate, such as the tax on the use of bazaar weights and the tax on stalls and shops in bazaars. Acting Governor General Count Rostovtsev rejected Khiva's petition, citing article nine of the 1873 treaty. He also forbade the collection of the dallyali, which had been levied on Russians for twenty years, and in October 1895 directed the commandant of the Amu-Darya Otdel to negotiate with Khiva for the abolition of the zakat on tea.[42]

Despite Rostovtsev's efforts, the Khivan authorities continued to tax Russian trade, often resorting to such subterfuges as levying the zakat on Khivan purchasers of goods from Russians rather than on the Russian sellers. Continuing complaints from Russian merchants led in November 1896 to a meeting in Petro-Aleksandrovsk of a mixed Russo-Khivan commission under the chairmanship of Colonel A. S. Galkin, commandant of the Amu-Darya Otdel, to examine the problem. On the basis of the commission's findings Governor General Vrevskii concluded that Khiva's claims to tax Russian merchants were groundless, and in March of the following year he directed Galkin to protect Russian trade interests in Khiva accordingly. For the guidance of the Russian and Khivan authorities Galkin issued a brochure on the "Rights and Obligations of Russian Subjects Living in the Khanate of Khiva." Galkin's booklet defined the commercial rights of Russians on the basis of article nine of the treaty and explained further that Khivans doing business with Russians and Khivan agents for Russian firms were equally exempt from Khivan commercial taxes. Muhammad Rahim reluctantly agreed to the terms set forth in Galkin's brochure.[43]

Although the steps taken in 1896–1897 should have disposed of the problem, it arose again six years later when Baron Roop, commandant of the Amu-Darya Otdel, interpreted the expression "Russian merchants" in article nine of the treaty as applying only to persons certified as members of the Russian merchant guilds. On August 1, 1903, Roop ordered that all Russian traders not covered by this narrow definition were subject to the zakat and other Khivan taxes. Roop's order remained in force for three years until rescinded by Governor General D. I. Subbotich in August 1906, after the ministries of finance and foreign affairs had found it unjustified.[44] Even then Russia's rights under the 1873 treaty were not fully secured, for on the eve of World War I both a zakat of 2.5 percent and an aminana of 1.5 percent were still being collected in Khiva on Russian goods—often several times on the same article.[45]

Khiva's trade with other countries was quite unimportant compared with her Russian trade, particularly after the Russian advances against the Turkomans in 1881–1884 had virtually surrounded the khanate with Russian territory. Her trade with Bukhara was small, since the two countries had similar rather than complementary economies. In the early eighties, after the enactment of tariffs and restrictions on foreign trade in Russian Turkestan and before the annexation of Merv, Khiva enjoyed a brief period as a center of contraband. Caravans bringing Indian tea and other highly taxed or forbidden commodities from India and Afghanistan via Merv or Bukhara would proceed down the left bank of the Amu-Darya to Khiva and thence enter the Amu-Darya Otdel secretly, avoiding the Russian customs post at the Russo-Bukharan border on the right bank of the river.[46]

The Role of Cotton in Trade and Agriculture

The only group in Bukhara and Khiva that was adversely affected by the growth of trade with Russia was the native craftsmen, who could not compete with the cheap Russian textiles and metal goods, although the extent of the Russian impact is difficult to judge. For the majority of Bukharan and Khivan consumers the trade with Russia meant little except an occasional purchase of cloth or metal goods; in eastern Bukhara even this was rare. The two groups that benefited most from the Russian trade were the merchants and the cotton producers. Although they lost a part of the carrying trade to Russia, taken over by Russian trading firms that established themselves in the khanates after 1886, especially in Bukhara, the merchants quickly adjusted to the new situation. They managed to hold their own in the carrying trade and virtually monopolized the role of middlemen between the small native producers of cotton and karakul and the Russian buyers of those commodities.[47] For the cotton producers, mostly small peasants who grew cotton as a supplementary cash crop, the Russian trade represented a useful source of income.

Cotton was Bukhara's and Khiva's most valuable product, accounting for about three quarters of the total value of each country's exports to Russia. Even before the conquest almost the entire cotton crop had been exported to Russia. As with the total volume of trade, the quantity of cotton exported to Russia in the 1870's and early 1880's showed little increase, remaining in the neighborhood of 400,000 puds annually for Bukhara and 50,000 for Khiva.[48] To feed her growing textile industry during these years, Russia relied overwhelmingly on foreign cotton, primarily from the United States and

Egypt. From 1864 to 1878 foreign cotton entered Russia duty-free, and from 1878 to 1887 only a very low revenue tariff was imposed. Beginning in 1887, however, Russia pursued a policy of tariff protection designed to encourage the production of cotton in her Central Asian colonies and protectorates.[49]

Under the double stimulus of a protective tariff and the opening of the Central Asian Railroad, Russian Central Asia's cotton production expanded fourfold between the middle 1880's and the beginning of the next decade. By the early nineties Central Asia was producing 3.5 million puds of cotton annually and supplying almost 25 percent of Russia's cotton needs, as compared with only 15 percent less than a decade earlier. Bukhara and Khiva participated in this growth, although their share of the total Central Asian cotton crop declined from over 50 percent to less than 40 percent. Bukhara's production expanded two and a half times to one million puds, while Turkestan's increased fivefold and Khiva's, sixfold. From the early 1890's to the eve of World War I the gap widened between Russian Turkestan and the protectorates. Central Asian cotton output rose to 11 million puds a year (50 percent of Russia's needs), but practically all of the increase was in Turkestan, especially the Fergana Oblast. The khanates' share of the total Central Asian cotton crop fell to 15 percent, primarily because Bukhara's cotton exports increased only slightly in those two decades. Although Khiva's exports almost doubled after the turn of the century, owing to the opening of the Orenburg-Tashkent Railroad and to the wider cultivation of the more profitable American cotton, in absolute terms Khiva's cotton exports were too small (600,000 puds a year) to influence the overall figures. World War I further promoted the production of cotton in Central Asia by cutting off Russia's foreign sources of supply. During the war Central Asia's production rose by 50 percent to almost 18 million puds in 1915 (70 percent of Russia's total consumption), and the protectorates registered a relative as well as an absolute gain, increasing to almost 25 percent their share of Central Asia's cotton exports to Russia. Bukhara's cotton exports doubled during the war, reaching 2.6 million puds. Khiva's showed a gain of about 170 percent before production was more than halved in 1916 because of internal disorders.[50]

Despite the two large boosts given to cotton production in Bukhara by the Central Asian Railroad and World War I, the khanate showed no steady growth in the cultivation of cotton and soon yielded to Fergana the leadership in this field. According to a Russian inspector's report in 1904, the reasons for this development were an archaic and inefficient irrigation system, an oppressive and cumbersome tax system, and the emir's lack of interest in rectifying either situation.[51] A meeting of representatives of Russian industry called in Chardjui in 1908 by Count Pahlen claimed that Russian-supervised improvements in the irrigation system could increase cotton acreage by 40 to 50 percent. Perhaps the major hindrance to the more rapid development of cotton culture in Bukhara was the tax system. A Bukharan *dehkan* (peasant) was not allowed to harvest his crops until a government official had come around to assess their value for tax purposes, and the assessors were notorious for taking their time. When ripe, cotton bolls of the native variety remained closed and could thus safely await the coming of the tax assessor before being picked. Cotton bolls of the American variety, however, opened when ripe and had to be picked promptly or the fiber would be ruined. Consequently, peasants preferred to cultivate the coarse native cotton, which also required less water, although American cotton was of higher quality, was more in demand in Russia, and thus commanded a higher price.[52]

American cotton was introduced into Russian Turkestan in the first half of the 1880's and had almost completely supplanted native cotton by the eve of World War I.[53] In Bukhara, although some seeds given to Muzaffar by the Russian government were planted in the early 1870's, the first real attempt to grow American cotton was made unsuccessfully in 1888 on one of the Russian land concessions in Chardjui beglik. At the turn of the century native cotton was still cultivated almost exclusively, and in 1913 the political agent reported only 2,000 *desiatinas* under the American variety, compared with 60,000 under native cotton.[54]

Around 1910 Russian and Armenian merchants from Sarai and Termez introduced American cotton culture into Kurgan-Tübe beglik, where it made slow but steady progress at the expense of the native variety.[55] During World War I American cotton made its greatest gains in central Bukhara. Desperate for more Central Asian cotton to replace the lost foreign imports, Russia insisted in 1915 that the emir purchase seventeen wagonloads of American cotton seed and distribute it to his peasants at a set price. Cotton, 90 percent of it American, was sown for the first time on a large scale in Baisun, Denau, Hisar, Kabadiyan, Kurgan-Tübe, and Kulab begliks.[56]

These provinces plus Shirabad, where cotton culture was already well established, produced almost 800,000 puds of cotton in 1915, out of a total Bukharan harvest of 2,700,000 puds.[57]

In Khiva cotton culture developed more rapidly and more steadily than in Bukhara, owing partly to the wider cultivation of American cotton, especially from the late 1890's. By 1904 half of Khiva's cotton acreage was under the American variety, and by 1914, two thirds.[58]

Bukhara and Khiva never developed the kind of overspecialized, one-crop economy that Fergana had. In the first decade of the twentieth century less than 5 percent of the land under cultivation in Bukhara was planted in cotton, compared with over 50 percent in wheat for domestic consumption. Even in the Zarafshan Valley, which contained 80 percent of the total cotton acreage, only 25 percent of the sown area was under cotton, whereas 40 percent was under wheat.[59] Although Bukhara's cotton acreage increased by 76 percent between 1913 and 1916, the share of total cultivated land under cotton was never much more than 5 percent. By contrast, in the Fergana Oblast, which contained almost two thirds of the cotton acreage of Russian Turkestan and Transcaspia, 36 to 38 percent of the total arable land was planted in cotton in 1915, and in the principal cotton-growing uezds the figure was as high as 95 percent.[60]

In Khiva, although cotton acreage doubled between the early 1880's and the beginning of the nineties, it accounted for only 10 percent of the sown area.[61] By the eve of World War I cotton acreage had doubled again, to 48,900 desiatinas, but constituted only 16 percent of the total cultivated acreage. Even in the southern part of the oasis, the major cotton-producing region, the share of the sown area under cotton was only 18 percent. Wheat accounted for 24 percent of the khanate's cultivated acreage, and alfalfa ranked almost equal with cotton.[62] Thus, Khiva specialized in cotton to a considerably greater extent than did Bukhara but failed even to approach the degree of specialization achieved in Fergana.

In each of Russia's Central Asian protectorates wheat continued to outrank cotton in both acreage and size of harvest, even in the most important cotton-growing districts—the Zarafshan Valley and southern Khiva. Bukhara and Khiva, unlike Fergana, remained self-sufficient in food, and for the most part cotton was raised by small peasants as a supplementary source of income, rather than by specialized producers.[63]

Industrial Development

Modern industry came to Russian Central Asia on a small scale in the wake of the railroad. The sudden large increase in cotton exports to Russia created the need for a local industry devoted to processing raw cotton—ginning and pressing the fiber and extracting oil from the seeds.

In Bukhara until World War I this industrial development was confined entirely to the Russian settlements and the railroad zone, and the mills were owned predominantly by Russians. The first two steam-powered cotton-ginning mills in the khanate, both owned by Russians, were opened in Chardjui in 1889 and in New Bukhara the following year.[64] By 1904 there was a total of nine mills in the country, three of them in New Bukhara, and they had virtually replaced the old native hand-operated machines.[65] Four years later all Bukharan cotton was ginned and pressed locally in seventeen mills, all Russian-owned—nine in New Bukhara, four in Chardjui, and one each in Kermine, Kizil-Tepe, Karakul, and Termez.[66] By 1913 the total was twenty-six, of which nineteen were owned by Russians, three by Russian Tatars, three by the emir of Bukhara, and one by a Bukharan merchant. There were also two oil-pressing mills by 1913, one each in New Bukhara and Chardjui.[67] In 1916 at the height of the wartime cotton boom Bukhara had thirty-five cotton-ginning mills, of which the emir owned four, and three oil-pressing mills. For the first time a ginning-mill had been established beyond the Russian settlements and the railroad zone, at Djilikul on the lower Vakhsh River in central Bukhara, to serve the new cotton-producing regions.[68]

Although cotton processing was by far the dominant industry, a number of minor industries were established in Bukhara in the early twentieth century. By 1913 the khanate contained twenty-four industrial enterprises not connected to cotton processing—including a winery at Karakul; several cigarette factories, a match factory, soap factory, and printing shop at New Bukhara; a wool-processing mill and brickyard at Chardjui; and a flour-grinding mill at Kerki. Oil depots were maintained by the Nobel interests at New Bukhara, Chardjui, Kerki, Termez, and Sarai; and the Russian government operated railroad and flotilla workshops at Chardjui.[69]

Khiva's industrial development was similar to Bukhara's and even kept pace for the first decade and a half with the larger khanate. The first steam-powered cotton-ginning mill was established in

Urgench in 1889, and by the turn of the century there were nine mills, six of them Russian-owned.[70] In 1908 there were eleven steam-powered mills—four in Urgench, three in Tashauz, and one each in Khiva, Khanki, Gurlen, and Mangit.[71] During the next five years two mills were built in Urgench and Khanki. In 1913 only two of the mills were native-owned—one in the capital and one in Khanki. The only other important industrial enterprises in the khanate in 1913 were two Russian-owned tanneries at Urgench and Khanki.[72]

In both Bukhara and Khiva the ownership of the new factories was predominantly Russian, and the management and skilled workers were entirely so. By contrast, the unskilled labor force was drawn from the natives of the two countries. The total number of workers has been estimated at almost 1,300 for Bukhara in 1905, and 400–500 for Khiva in 1917. The factories were generally small, employing usually no more than thirty workers.[73] Count Pahlen in 1908 was highly critical of the factories in the protectorates. He charged that the majority were built, equipped, and run without regard to technical requirements, hygiene, or safety. Steam boilers were installed without having been tested, scarcely any first aid was available to the workers, and the relations of employers to employees were not regulated. Both workers and owners continually requested the intervention of the government engineer of the Samarkand Oblast in cases arising from these conditions. Pahlen recommended the extension to Bukhara and Khiva of the factory inspectorate established in the government-general in 1895, but it is doubtful whether his suggestion was ever followed.[74]

Aside from strictly industrial undertakings, Russians were active, although generally unsuccessful, in gold prospecting and mining in the mountains of eastern Bukhara. On February 24, 1894, out of regard for Bukhara's autonomy the governor general of Turkestan approved regulations that strictly controlled prospecting and mining, excluded all foreigners from those activities, and provided that all gold mined was to be sold to the Bukharan government.[75] Between 1896 and 1917 the emir's government gave thirty-six concessions to Russian gold prospectors, most of which were never operative. The earliest and most persistent prospector was one Zhuravko-Pokorskii, a mining engineer whose operations near Khovaling, east of Baldjuan, after 1894 were never profitable and served primarily to get him into repeated clashes with the local authorities, who wanted to protect, in order to exploit, the local native prospectors. In 1903 Zhuravko-Pokorskii sought the protection of the political agent against the begs of Baldjuan and Hisar. Baron A. A. Cherkasov, secretary of the political agency, was sent to investigate; his report of November 10, 1906, charged that Pokorskii underpaid his workers, defaulted on his debts to Bukharans, interfered with and intimidated the local Bukharan administration, and sublet his concession to Austrians, all of which threatened to undermine Russia's established policy toward Bukhara. Denied foreign capital and forced to pay his debts and raise wages, Zhuravko-Pokorskii witnessed the collapse of his ventures before his death around 1910.[76] His methods were too much at variance with Russia's policy of nonintervention in the internal life of her protectorates.

Russian Capital in Bukhara

Besides being directly invested in the cotton-processing and other industries, Russian capital was active in Bukhara and Khiva in financing small native producers. Most cotton growers were small peasants or sharecroppers who habitually borrowed money at exorbitant rates of interest and bought necessities such as seed, tea, and manufactured goods on credit at inflated prices. Their creditors were the native brokers who purchased their cotton, using the future harvest, grossly undervalued, as collateral. The brokers in turn used as their working capital loans from the Russian banks that sprang up in Bukhara in the 1890's to finance such operations, as well as the activities of Russian merchants and manufacturers in the khanate.[77] The karakul and wool trades were similarly financed to a significant extent. In addition to the New Bukhara branch of the State Bank, which opened in 1894 and twenty years later had assets of 90 million rubles, there were by 1915 branches of seven private Russian banks in New and Old Bukhara with a total capital of 20 million rubles. The Russian Bank for Foreign Trade and the Russo-Asiatic Bank together accounted for 11 million rubles; the latter bank also had a branch in Kerki. The Russo-Asiatic Bank and the Azov-Don Commercial Bank were particularly active in financing the cotton trade, while the Russian Bank for Foreign Trade monopolized the extension of credit to karakul producers.[78] In Khiva the Russo-Asiatic Bank alone maintained a branch, opened in Urgench in 1909, although other banks had agents there.[79]

Russian entrepreneurs and speculators found another source of gain in Bukhara during the last years before the Revolution in concessions from the emir's government of agricultural land, usually beyond the railroad zone and the Russian settlements, for irrigation and cultivation. Between 1912 and 1915 the Bukharan government granted almost 300,000 desiatinas (810,000 acres) of such concessions, or over one percent of the khanate's total area.[80] St. Petersburg had originally been opposed to this type of economic activity because of its potential political consequences. When in 1910 the notorious intriguer Prince M. M. Andronikov secured from Abd al-Ahad a concession of land in the Karshi Steppe for irrigation and development, Acting Foreign Minister A. A. Neratov canceled the arrangements on the grounds that land concessions to private capitalists would violate the emir's sovereign rights over his territory and remove from his control land that would be needed in future by the Bukharan population.[81]

However, the lure of profit and the power of influence in high places proved stronger than considerations of policy, and on February 23, 1912, with Russia's approval, the emir granted a concession of 72,500 desiatinas in Shirabad beglik to A. G. Ananiev, owner of a cotton-ginning mill in Kerki and an oil-pressing mill in Termez. Included in the 99-year concession was the right of eminent domain over any native-owned property necessary for the construction of irrigation works, the right to use the waters of the Surkhan-Darya for irrigation, and exemption from all taxes during the first eight and a half years. After this period a payment in lieu of taxes of 100,000 rubles a year would be due to the Bukharan government. Ananiev soon ran into opposition from the peasants whose lands were intermixed with those of his concession, and he finally ceded his rights to the Shirabad Company, which was financed and controlled by a St. Petersburg bank.[82]

A month after the granting of the Ananiev concession Prince Andronikov, because of his close connections with War Minister V. A. Sukhomlinov, received a concession of 25,000 desiatinas in Karshi beglik, the site of his canceled concession two years earlier. Andronikov met with the same problem as Ananiev—resistance of the local peasants—which prevented completion of the preliminary irrigation surveys and forced him to give up the concession. In March 1913, however, Andronikov obtained a new and larger concession of 80,000 desiatinas, also in Karshi beglik. The emir was undoubtedly pressured into granting such concessions by highly placed Russians like Sukhomlinov in a form of blackmail, since his power depended on the continuance of Russia's favor. The concessions were supposedly empty lands but were in fact often occupied by peasants, whose resistance to the concessions may well have been tolerated and even encouraged by the Bukharan authorities. The concessionaires were frequently men like Andronikov, interested only in selling their rights at a profit to entrepreneurs willing to undertake the necessary irrigation works and to plant cotton. In February 1913 D. F. Stovba, an agent of the Russo-Asiatic Bank, obtained a 10,000-desiatina concession in Kabadiyan beglik, but he forfeited it because he failed to find a buyer to begin work within the allotted period.[83]

In 1915 one Chaev received a concession in Kurgan-Tübe beglik of 65,000 desiatinas, half of which he proposed to settle with Russian colonists, but he was unable to obtain Petrograd's permission before the 1917 Revolution.[84] Russia consistently drew the line at Russian colonization in Bukhara. In February 1899 Political Agent V. I. Ignatiev had argued that Russian agricultural colonies would become privileged oases, protected by Russian law, which would exploit the neighboring Bukharan peasants and thus provoke native hostility. Ignatiev concluded: "In short, the founding of Russian agricultural settlements within the boundaries of the khanate of Bukhara . . . would lead to . . . misunderstandings, the extent and character of which it is difficult even to foresee, and which in a very short time would create the necessity for the forced annexation of the khanate to Russia's dominions."[85] A conference in Tashkent in August 1909 arrived at the conclusion that colonization was out of the question while Bukhara retained her autonomy.[86] At a conference presided over by Governor General A. V. Samsonov in January 1914 the representatives of the concessionaires advocated a broad program of Russian concessions and colonization in Bukhara to strengthen the Russian hold over the khanate, but the conference adhered to St. Petersburg's policy of protecting Bukharan autonomy: it opposed colonization and reaffirmed that the concessions with their irrigation works were to revert to the Bukharan government on the expiration of the original grants.[87]

Railroad Projects

The dramatic impact of the Central Asian Railroad on the economy of Bukhara and Khiva illustrated the protectorates' need for modern transportation facilities. Only a part of Bukhara and none of Khiva were directly accessible from the railroad. Numerous projects were presented over the next three decades for the further development of the railroad system both within the protectorates and between them and Russia, but only one such project came to fruition before 1917.

A feeder line from the Kagan station of the Central Asian Railroad to Termez via Karshi, Kerki, and Kelif was proposed as a government undertaking as early as 1892. It would have both strategic and economic usefulness, enabling Russia to move large numbers of troops quickly to the Afghan frontier and promoting cotton production and Russian trade in Shirabad beglik. A shorter line from New Bukhara to Karshi was proposed in 1898 as a private venture with purely economic significance. During the Anglo-Russian tension over the Far East at the turn of the century the question of a railroad to Termez was raised again. In 1904 a quick survey for such a line was made when Russia, already at war with Japan, faced the possibility of a clash with Japan's ally Britain. Every Russian authority on Bukhara in the early twentieth century advocated building the railroad to Termez. After the Anglo-Russian entente of 1907 had eliminated the strategic necessity for the line, on April 10, 1910, the Council of Ministers decided to let private Russian capital build the railroad. In August of the following year the engineer A. N. Kovalevskii, backed by the Russo-Asiatic Bank, received permission from the Russian government to conduct surveys for a railroad to Termez with a branch from Karshi to Kitab via Guzar, and in 1912 Kovalevskii's plans received the preliminary approval of both Russia and Bukhara, with the emir granting six thousand desiatinas of free land for the right of way and necessary buildings. On May 13, 1913, the kush-begi officially notified the political agent of the emir's consent in a letter that indicated eagerness for the construction of the new railroad, in marked contrast to the opposition three decades before to the Central Asian Railroad.[88] In the intervening years Bukhara's rulers had learned well the value of modern transportation for economic progress and thus higher government revenues. The emir himself was deeply involved in both the cotton and karakul trades, and he was a major stockholder in the new railroad.

On July 13, 1913, Russia granted a charter to the Bukharan Railroad Company,[89] to which Kovalevskii transferred his 1912 concession from the emir. The company was to own the road for eighty-one years from the day of its inauguration, after which period control of the line would pass without compensation to the Russian government. Russia guaranteed the company's bonds, with the emir providing one quarter of the funds for this guarantee.[90] Actual construction began in April 1914. Despite difficulties in finding adequate numbers of native laborers at the low wages the company paid, at the urging of the Russian government the line was completed in July 1916, one year ahead of schedule, partly through the use of labor from Austro-Hungarian prisoners-of-war.[91] American engineers played an important role in directing the construction, having been given special permission by Russia to reside in Bukhara for this purpose.[92] Much of the line was in operation in time to help get the 1915 cotton crop from central Bukhara to market in Russia. After the opening of the railroad the Samarkand-Termez post road was abandoned.[93]

Other railroads were proposed for the protectorates but never built. In 1892 St. Petersburg decided to connect Russian Turkestan with European Russia by a direct rail link. The two possible routes ran from Chardjui via Khiva and the Ust-Urt Plateau to the Russian railhead at Aleksandrov Gai, southeast of Saratov, or from Tashkent down the Sir-Darya and past the Aral Sea to Orenburg. In 1900 Nicholas II sanctioned the second route, which was backed by Minister of War A. N. Kuropatkin, and the Orenburg-Tashkent Railroad was opened to traffic on January 1, 1906.[94] The alternative route, which had been advocated by Cherniaev in the early 1880's, continued to be favored for a second direct rail link, particularly by Russians interested in the economic development of Bukhara and Khiva. This scheme took two forms: a proposal for the immediate construction of a railroad from Kerki to Aleksandrov Gai via Chardjui, Khiva, Kungrat, and the Ust-Urt Plateau; and a less ambitious project, in which Kovalevskii took a leading part, for a line from Chardjui to Kungrat with an eventual extension to Aleksandrov Gai. The supporters of each plan argued that the coming of the railroad to Khiva would lead to the large-scale replacement of grain by cotton in that khanate. They predicted an increase in cotton acreage from 16 percent to at least 40 percent of Khiva's total sown area. After much discussion and many delays caused by the difficulties of financing the projected railroad and the keen rivalry between the backers of the two plans, St. Petersburg finally approved the route from Chardjui to Aleksandrov Gai at the end of 1916, but the Bolshevik Revolution caught the surveyors at their work.[95] The railroad from Chardjui to Kungrat was built only after World War II, and the extension to Aleksandrov Gai was still in the planning stage in the early 1960's.

A further suggestion for promoting Khiva's economic development, put forth by a group of Russian merchants and endorsed by Count Pahlen, called for a rail connection from Petro-Aleksandrovsk to Kazalinsk. Still another was the proposal of Prince V. I. Masalskii, an authority on Central Asian cotton production, for a railroad to link Khiva with the Central Asian Railroad on one side and the Orenburg-Tashkent line on the other. Other proposals called for a railroad from Khiva to the Caspian Sea, either at Krasnovodsk or on the shoreline facing Astrakhan.[96]

A final project was that of Kovalevskii in May 1914 to continue the Bukharan Railroad, not yet built, from Termez in two directions—eastward along the Amu-Darya to Sarai, and northeastward along the Surkhan and upper Kafirnihan rivers to Hisar and Faizabad, with a branch to Shirabad. Kovalevskii's scheme would have opened all of central Bukhara to Russian economic penetration, but the Ministry of Foreign Affairs, anxious to avoid British concern over a further extension of the railroad along the Bukharan-Afghan frontier, vetoed the project.[97]

The striking factor in the economic development of Bukhara and Khiva under the Russian protectorate was the small amount of direct support it received from the Russian government. St. Petersburg did the inescapable minimum to protect and promote Russian private interests in the khanates and acted to restrain those interests when they threatened the foreign ministry's policy of nonintervention. Concern for her own strategic position was more important to official Russia than were the economic interests of her subjects. Fortunately for Russians with a financial stake in Bukhara and Khiva, St. Petersburg's concerns often worked indirectly to their advantage, as in the notable example of the Central Asian Railroad, and thereby promoted in a limited way the khanates' economic development.

Abd al-Ahad's Batchas and Musicians

11 / Bukhara Between Two Worlds

The Impact of the West

With respect to the internal life of Bukhara, 1885 was a much more significant date than 1868. The advent of the railroad, ending Bukhara's physical isolation and bringing an influx of outsiders, signified the beginning of a new period in the life of the khanate. It remained merely a beginning, however, for Bukhara seemed suspended indefinitely between the world of medieval Islam and that of the nineteenth-century West. Although the newcomers brought with them the technology and culture of nineteenth-century Russia, the great majority of the population remained almost totally unaffected by Western influence. The emir's court occupied a position between the two extremes, reflecting an odd mixture of the old and the new.

The most important channel of Western influence in Bukhara was the Russians, who arrived in increasing numbers after 1885, either as soldiers to operate the railway, garrison the cantonments, and guard the Amu-Darya frontier, or as merchants, shopkeepers, and workers. The Russian census of 1897 counted 12,150 Russians in Bukhara.[1] In 1910 the total was estimated at 27,700, and in 1914 at not less than 50,000 (almost two percent of the country's population).[2] In the Russian settlements and military posts the Russians created little islands of Western civilization. Each of the four settlements had broad streets, electric lighting, European-style homes, one or more schools and Orthodox churches, a hospital or dispensary, a postal-telegraph office, and many commercial and industrial enterprises. Kerki, Termez, and New Bukhara had movie houses on the eve of World War I, and New Bukhara also had several small hotels and a library. The first printing press in the khanate was established by a Russian in New Bukhara in 1901.[3] Beyond the four large settlements Western influence was much in evidence wherever Russians lived. Several of the smaller railroad stations, such as Farab on the right bank of the Amu-Darya opposite Chardjui, had Russian churches and schools; at Sarai, 133 miles upriver from Termez, an Orthodox church was built in 1907 to serve the needs of the frontier guard; and even remote Khorog by 1915 boasted a Russian school and electric lighting in the cantonment.[4]

Although the emir's capital had no Russian colony, because of its political and economic importance it could not escape the impact of the Russian presence in Bukhara. In the 1890's the road between the old city and New Bukhara was macadamized, and the political agency in New Bukhara was linked by telephone with the kush-begi's residence in the citadel of Old Bukhara. Electricity from New Bukhara's power plant was supplied to the capital, although few buildings were equipped to use it. By the turn of the century the railroad had reached the walls of the old city. The bazaars of the capital were the principal distribution points for Russian and Western manufactured goods, including such novel articles as kerosene lamps, Singer sewing machines, and American-made phonographs and revolvers.[5]

Striking testimony to the railroad's effect on Bukhara's former isolation is given not only by the influx of Russians for a prolonged residence but also by the change in the number and kind of short-term foreign visitors. Previously this group had been limited to a very few hardy travelers and explorers accustomed to roughing it and facing unknown dangers. After the inauguration of the Central Asian Railroad, however, world travelers and newspaper reporters from the West became frequent visitors, and by the late 1890's sightseeing trips along the railroad by parties of ladies and gentlemen tired of the more usual European tours had become quite fashionable.[6] By 1909 a Russian guidebook was advising the use of extreme caution in purchasing antiques in Old Bukhara, for imitations abounded to snare the rubles of unwary tourists. In the late 1880's Russians and other Europeans could for the first time appear in the main streets of the capital without official escorts, but a foreigner who wandered into the narrow streets leading away from the main bazaar was likely to meet with abusive language, perhaps be pelted with garbage, or even attacked.[7]

In the hinterland Russians and other foreigners were much less common and consequently aroused more suspicion than in the capital and along the railroad. Material evidence of the Russian presence was also much rarer in the provinces, although by 1908 many of the begs of central Bukhara maintained guest quarters furnished in the European manner for Russian visitors.[8]

On balance, the West appeared in Bukhara more as an intruder than as a transformer. Beyond the Russian enclaves along the railroad and the Amu-Darya frontier, the Western impact was confined to a scattering of material objects, such as quantities of Russian cloth, which had slight effect on native life. The Russian enclaves themselves formed a world apart from the native community, with only Bukharan and a few enterprising Russian merchants and native intellectuals serving as intermediaries between the two. It was precisely these Bukharan intermediaries who were instrumental in the emergence of a native reform movement after 1905—the first real sign of a Western impact on Bukharan life.

The Role of the Emir

In a different way Abd al-Ahad also bridged the two worlds. At home he remained the traditional type of Central Asian despot, differing from his father primarily in that he paid more attention to his own enrichment than to the political problems of governing his country. But whereas Muzaffar had never gotten over the shock of his defeat by Russia and had never really adjusted to his new role as a Russian dependent, Abd al-Ahad, who was only nine years old in 1868, had grown up to accept the new order of things. He visited Russia in 1883—a trip that his father never made—and he was visibly impressed by Russian civilization. When the coming of the railroad ended Bukhara's isolation, the new emir introduced into his own manner of living many Western innovations. At the beginning of the 1890's he had electric lights installed in his favorite villa on the road between New Bukhara and the capital, and he furnished both this villa and his palace at Kermine (his principal residence from the mid-1890's) in the European style, although many Russian visitors were appalled at the lack of taste with which the decorating had been done. Abd al-Ahad was also fond of entertaining his Russian dinner guests with European tunes rendered in an almost unrecognizable form by a dissonant brass band playing in the garden.[9] These innovations did not, however, basically affect the emir's mode of life, which remained the traditional one of a Bukharan ruler. His harem was reputed to number one hundred and thirty, with a constant turnover in its membership.[10]

Much more important than the superficial innovations Abd al-Ahad introduced into his manner of living at home was the role he began to play in Russian society. In December 1892 and January 1893 the emir paid another state visit to Russia at Alexander III's invitation, and in 1896 he went to Moscow for Nicholas II's coronation. Thereafter he made almost annual trips to Russia. When in St. Petersburg, he was lodged in the Winter Palace, received at court, honored with dinners and balls and visits from members of the imperial family and government officials. He soon abandoned the traditional summer visits to Karshi and Shahr-i Sabz in favor of the more fashionable, and healthier, attractions of the Caucasus and the Crimea. By the end of the 1890's he had built a villa in the Crimea between Yalta and the imperial villa at Livadia, and he made his trips to Russia in an elegant private railroad car presented to him by Nicholas II.[11]

Having become a familiar figure in Russian society, Abd al-Ahad was careful to cultivate the favor of his Russian masters in a manner befitting an oriental potentate. At every opportunity he bestowed expensive presents on the emperor and empress or other members of the court and government. Neither the governor general of Turkestan nor his wife could pass through Bukhara on the train bound to or from European Russia without being greeted and entertained by the emir either in person or by proxy.[12] Abd al-Ahad was generous in distributing various Bukharan orders among the Russian nobility and military and civil bureaucracy. He added to the Order of the Rising Star of Bukhara, created by his father, two new orders—those of the Sun of Alexander (in memory of Alexander III) and of the Crown of Bukhara. Beginning in the early 1890's, Abd al-Ahad lavished these orders on governors general of Turkestan, political agents, high and low officials of the foreign ministry, and members of the diplomatic corps, from ambassadors to mere vice-consuls, serving in posts from London to Kashgar. He was especially generous in decorating officials in Samarkand and Tashkent.[13] The emir also achieved some renown as a contributor to worthy Russian causes. He donated considerable sums to Russian schools in New Bukhara and Tashkent and to the Russian Red Cross, and during the Russo-Japanese War he presented the Russian navy with a warship, "The Emir of Bukhara," which he had built at Kronstadt.[14] His activities convinced some Russian officials of the emir's sincere affection for his protectors.[15]

The truth, however, was somewhat less engaging. Abd al-Ahad's acquired taste for Western ways, which reputedly extended even to champagne in violation of Moslem law,[16] did not affect his basic dislike for his infidel overlords, although it would have been impolitic to display this feeling in public. At least once the emir was caught off guard. While in Russia for Nicholas II's coronation in 1896, he was assigned as an escort an Arab Christian professor of Arabic, G. A. Murkos. The emir and the professor got along very well until Murkos presented Abd al-Ahad with his book on Damascus, his native city. The emir began to leaf through the pages, skimming the Arabic text, when he suddenly stopped and exclaimed with horror and disbelief over evidence that there were "dogs of Christians" living in Damascus. Murkos not only affirmed that it was true but pointed out to the amazed emir that he was one of those same Christian dogs. Abd al-Ahad was paralyzed with shock and outrage, more at having been caught with his mask off than at the infidels who were defiling holy Damascus with their presence.[17]

Although careful to cultivate Russia's favor, Abd al-Ahad at the same time succeeded in establishing a pose of independence—a pose that Russia herself did much to encourage. Ironically, just when Bukhara had been reduced to a full-fledged protectorate and the limits of her autonomy had been more tightly drawn in the early 1890's, Abd al-Ahad began to act and be treated as though he were the sovereign ruler of an independent state. It was as if Russia was trying to compensate the emir for his lost power and perhaps reassure his subjects of his continuing authority over them. On visits to St. Petersburg the emir received the honors accorded a visiting head of state. In the early nineties Russia abandoned "High Eminence" (*Vysokostepenstvo*) as the form of address for the emir in favor of the more elevated "Illustriousness" (*Svetlost*). By the beginning of the new century "Illustriousness" in turn gave way to the royal "Highness" (*Vysochestvo*), which had last been used in reference to a Bukharan monarch in 1866.[18] The foreign ministry's yearbook for 1893 and all subsequent years listed the emir of Bukhara among the reigning foreign sovereigns and chiefs of state.

Russia further raised Abd al-Ahad's prestige by granting him a series of high orders (St. Stanislav, St. Anna, and the White Eagle) and honorary military ranks (general of cavalry, aide-de-camp to the emperor, ataman of the Terek Cossack Army, and commander of the Fifth Orenburg Cossack Regiment).[19] The political agency was an important instrument in creating the fiction of the emir's sovereignty. After Ignatiev was replaced in 1902, the political agents lacked the influence that their predecessors had exerted on the emir, not primarily because they had a narrower view of their function[20] but because the momentous changes effected in Russo-Bukharan relations in the eighties and nineties were now accomplished facts, and the foreign ministry's emphasis was on strengthening the emir's authority. In pursuit of this aim St. Petersburg cleared with the emir at least two of the last three appointments to the office of political agent, and the appointees themselves were minor diplomats at the rank of consul general with no previous experience in Central Asia, who could be trusted not to take a haughty tone with the emir.[21]

Abd al-Ahad was not slow to take advantage of Russia's concern for the preservation of his authority. When the political agency moved to New Bukhara in 1891, Russia tried to persuade the emir to move out of his old quarters in the citadel of the capital into a new, European-style palace to be built for him next to the political agency in the Russian settlement in order to facilitate close relations. The palace was built, at a cost of 200,000 rubles, but the emir avoided moving in, and Russia did not insist, so that the palace remained an empty and gradually decaying testimonial to Abd al-Ahad's independence. More significant was the emir's permanent desertion of his capital for Kermine in 1897. At Kermine the emir lived miles from the nearest Russian; the political agent was forced to deal with the kush-begi, who remained in occupation of Bukhara's citadel. Abd al-Ahad thereafter received the political agent only when he pleased, usually only a few times a year in Kermine under the most formal circumstances.[22]

In minor ways, too, the emir was jealous of his pose of independence. When early in his reign he was visited by the governor general, he would show his respect for the emperor's representative by meeting him at a distance from his palace. In later years, however, he was accustomed to await the governor general's arrival in his palace, thereby emphasizing his own importance.[23] With Russia's help Abd al-Ahad was so successful in fostering the illusion of Bukhara's independence that in 1907 the authoritative French journal *Revue du Monde Musulman* noted as one of the most remarkable facts of recent Asian history the rebirth of Bukhara as an "effective principality"—an example of the triumph of the Moslem reawakening over Russian imperialism.[24]

The Emir's Government and the Need for Reform

Retaining almost unlimited freedom of action in internal affairs, enjoying St. Petersburg's full support, and moving in both the world of nineteenth-century Russia and that of medieval Bukhara, Abd al-Ahad was in an unrivaled position to help his subjects take advantage of the best that Russian culture and technology had to offer in order to improve their welfare. The emir, however, remained ambivalent toward the world of his political masters, and he showed far more interest in his own enrichment than in the welfare of his subjects.

The bulk of Abd al-Ahad's income came from the state tax revenues, variously estimated at from seven to eighteen million rubles a year, of which 60 to 80 percent found its way into the emir's hands after the amlakdars, begs, and zakatchis had taken what they considered their fair share. State expenditures were minimal, perhaps one million rubles a year for the army and another million for court and other purposes.[25] The balance was sheer profit, to be spent as the emir saw fit, since no distinction was drawn between the state fisc and his own private fortune. That fortune was probably well over fifty million rubles at Abd al-Ahad's death.[26] Aside from tax revenues, the emir derived a large income from his commercial activities. He became the world's third largest trader in karakul and owned three cotton-ginning mills. Producers of karakul and cotton were often forced to sell to the emir's agents at below-market prices.[27]

Abd al-Ahad spent only the unavoidable minimum on public works such as roads, bridges, and irrigation works. He refused to provide the seven million rubles necessary for the execution of Lessar's plan for the irrigation of a large part of the Karshi Steppe by means of a canal from the Amu-Darya.[28] Public health was another area that the emir refused to support. From early in the 1890's he employed as his court physician a Doctor Pisarenko, a former Russian army doctor, but he evidenced no similar concern for the health of his subjects.[29] Malaria, cholera, typhoid fever, and other diseases bred in the stagnant waters of the irrigation and water supply systems were recurrent visitors to Bukhara, and the capital was notorious as the home of *rishta*, an internal worm infection acquired by drinking impure water from reservoirs that served at once for drinking, bathing, and laundering. Abd al-Ahad himself was said to suffer from rishta.[30] A study of the situation by Russian specialists in 1895 led to a plan by civil engineer Kh. V. Gelman to drain the swamps and ponds around the capital into which the irrigation canals emptied, but the emir refused to provide the 120,000 rubles required for the plan's implementation.[31] Individual Russian doctors who practiced in the capital and hospitals in the Russian settlements in which native dispensaries were established met with an enthusiastic response from the people but received little or no support from the emir.[32]

Early in his reign Abd al-Ahad acquired a reputation as a reformer. Bowing to Russia's wishes, he formally abolished slavery on his succession, thereby belatedly fulfilling his father's promise to Russia twelve years earlier to end slavery within a decade. He closed the infamous underground prison in the citadel at Bukhara, ended execution by impalement or hurling from the top of the 200-foot Great Minaret, and prohibited public exhibitions by batchas.[33] The effect of these reforms was slight, however. Slavery lingered on in the form of debtor's bondage and of domestic service as well as in staffing the emir's harem. Inhuman penal conditions, particularly in the provinces, continued to horrify Russian and Western visitors.[34]

Bukhara's fundamental need under the Russian protectorate was a thorough political reform. A system of government that ignored the needs of the country in order to enrich the emir and the fifty thousand members of the Bukharan bureaucracy had served well enough while Bukhara lived in isolation from the modern world, but with the breakdown of that isolation the system became a source of trouble.[35] Its abuses provided Russian annexationists with their strongest argument and even began to arouse dissatisfaction among some Bukharans, who could now contrast their system to Russia's, which by comparison was a model of good government. Bukhara's government not only provided few services beyond the maintenance of a minimum of law and order and the rigorous preservation of religious purity but also drained off the wealth of the country from its producers. The peasants of Bukhara were taxed eight times as heavily as their cousins in Russian Turkestan.[36] Not only were taxes high, but their method of collection was completely arbitrary, with the tax collectors assessing crops and personal property at inflated values. In addition to the taxes prescribed by the Sharia and by customary usage, both the emir and the begs often levied special taxes. The begs in particular were guilty of the practice of imposing special taxes to cover the cost of entertaining visiting Russian officials or the emir himself—in amounts more than sufficient to recompense themselves for the expenses incurred. The acceptance of bribes, the sale of pardons, and the collection of extortionate legal fees were other ways in which Bukharan officials oppressed their charges. In general, the begs were free to squeeze as much as they could from the population under their authority, as long as the emir received his share and the people were not driven to the point of revolt. Complaints to the emir against local officials were actively discouraged, and the very insecurity of his office encouraged a beg to enrich himself as rapidly as possible.[37] If, however, the emir suspected a beg of withholding too large a share of the revenues from his province, that official was liable to lose not only his office but his property and freedom as well.[38]

The emir's active displeasure with an overly avaricious beg on the one hand, and popular revolt or emigration on the other, were the only correctives to this system of legalized plunder. The usual pattern of a peasant revolt was that a band of peasants would attack and perhaps kill a tax collector; then, fired up by their own temerity, they would march on the beg's citadel and maybe even capture it. Within a relatively short time the beg's troops, perhaps with reinforcements from a neighboring beglik, would suppress the revolt, and the leaders would be sent to the emir for execution. After such an insurrection the beg might be replaced to appease the people, but his successor was not likely to be any better. Under the Russian protectorate the most serious peasant uprising was one led by Abd al-Vose in Baldjuan beglik in the late 1880's.[39] After the turn of the century peasant revolts became rarer, primarily because of the presence of Russian troops along the Amu-Darya, ready to come to the rescue of any beg threatened by rebels.[40] Russian border guards also cooperated with the beg of Kulab in 1899 to halt the flow of Bukharans whom his despotic rule had driven to seek refuge across the river in Afghanistan.[41] Russia's policy of supporting the emir's authority thus operated to protect and perpetuate a system of government riddled with corruption and abuses and actually tended to remove whatever restraint the traditional corrective of revolt had provided, even though at the same time contact with Russia was stimulating a native reform movement.

The Origins of a Native Reform Movement

Like all non-Western societies in close contact with the modern West, Bukhara had its Westernizers as well as its xenophobic zealots. The earliest critics of the ancien régime in the khanate were intellectuals, whose contacts with Russian civilization awakened in them a dissatisfaction with the weakness and backwardness of their own country and the injustice prevailing there. The most famous of these early critics was Ahmad Mahdum Donish (1827–1897), a scholar, poet, artist, musician, doctor, and court astrologer to Emir Muzaffar. At least three times—in 1857, 1869, and 1874—Donish was a member of Bukharan embassies to St. Petersburg.[42] His observation of life in Russia during the era of the reforms stimulated him to attack the situation in Bukhara mercilessly in two works, written in Persian and circulated clandestinely in manuscript form among a limited circle of sympathizers. Donish argued that the emir was the servant of his people and was consequently entitled to wealth and power only as long as he met the needs of his subjects. Donish looked to Russia not as a model to be imitated but as a useful source of knowledge and tools with which to rebuild Bukharan society and thus save it from threatened extinction by Western civilization. He envisaged reform from above by an enlightened despot, ruling with the aid of a consultative council composed of people from all classes and through ministries with well-defined functions. He advocated the secularization of education in Bukhara's *madrasas* (seminaries), so that history, literature, and the natural sciences would be taught in addition to the traditional disciplines of Moslem law, theology, logic, and metaphysics.[43]

A small but influential group of contemporaries—perhaps nine or ten in all—shared Donish's views. Among them were the satirical poet Abd al-Kadir Savdo (1823–1873); Shamsiddin Mahmud Shahin (1859–1894), one of Abd al-Ahad's court poets and a bitter critic of Bukharan morals and the treatment of women; Mirza Hayit Sahbo (ca. 1850–1918), a government servant renowned for his honesty; and Siddik-khan, a scholar and poet, brother-in-law of Abd al-Ahad and former beg of Karshi, who was held in the capital under house arrest from Abd al-Ahad's accession.[44]

More influential in the long run in Bukhara than the writings of Ahmad Donish was the movement for educational reform among Russia's Moslems, begun by a Crimean Tatar, Ismail-beg Gasprinskii (1851–1914). In the traditional Moslem seven- or eight-year elementary school (*maktab*) the pupils were taught by rote to read and write Arabic, but little emphasis was placed on understanding the text, which was usually a passage from the Koran. The education thus received was of no practical value, and graduates of the maktab

who pursued their studies no further soon forgot what little they
had learned. In Bukhara, where over 100,000 pupils were enrolled
in maktabs in the early twentieth century, the literacy rate was only
two percent.[45] Gasprinskii's "new-method schools," first established
in 1884 at Bakhchisarai in the Crimea, applied European pedagogical
methods to the teaching of reading, writing, and Arabic grammar
and added to the curriculum such secular subjects as mathematics,
history, and geography, as well as Russian. Schools that followed his
system were far more effective in producing literate graduates with
a fund of useful knowledge, and in a briefer period, than the traditional maktabs.

The movement to establish new-method schools at first made
little headway in Bukhara, despite Gasprinskii's unremitting efforts
to win Abd al-Ahad's favor. Gasprinskii visited Bukhara in 1893
and secured the emir's promise not to block the establishment of
new-method schools in the khanate, but Abd al-Ahad remained suspicious of educational reform. Gasprinskii did not lose hope: he
often visited the emir on the latter's trips to the Crimea and the
Caucasus and eulogized him in his newspaper as the "defender of
Central Asian Islam."[46] Three new-method schools were opened in
succession in the period 1900–1902 in and around New Bukhara,
but each one closed after only a few months, either because of lack
of financial support or under pressure from the Bukharan clergy.
Like those established in Russian Turkestan, the first new-method
schools in Bukhara were meant not for the native Uzbeg children but
for the children of the Russian Tatars, who formed an important
commercial community in Central Asia. From the beginning, however, the drive for educational reform aroused the enthusiasm of the
small group of Bukharan liberals as well as many Bukharan merchants, whose dealings with the Russians had pointed up the inade-
quacies of the traditional education.[47]

Educational reform was for Gasprinskii only the means to a
more important end—the political and cultural awakening of the
Turko-Tatar peoples and the modernization of Islamic life, including
the emancipation of women. This entire program came to be known
as Djadidism, from *usul-i djadid* (new method), the term originally
applied to the system of instruction used in the reformed schools.
Gasprinskii's newspaper *Tardjuman* (The Interpreter), established
at Bakhchisarai in 1883, was the voice of the Djadid movement and
circulated on a limited scale even in Bukhara, where newspapers

were forbidden to be read in public. Followers of Ahmad Donish, advocates of educational reform, and other liberals received the paper, copies of which were passed from hand to hand.[48]

Whereas the stirrings of the Bukharan reform movement were just barely noticeable at the beginning of the twentieth century, the external events of 1905–1908 gave rise to an organized movement with clearly defined goals. The Russian Revolution of 1905 was the first of these events. Revolutionary activity in the khanate was confined almost exclusively to the Russian population. The skilled Russian workers in the railroad shops and flotilla dockyard at Chardjui were the most active: Chardjui was the scene of a two-day railroad strike in February 1905, it participated during October 16–27 in the general strike that paralyzed Russia, and it witnessed a dockyard strike and sailors' mutiny on November 13.[49] Native Bukharans were involved in the revolution only to the extent that unskilled workers participated in the strikes involving the cotton-ginning mills—most notably the general strike of November 19–December 5, provoked by the government's suppression of a mutiny in Tashkent on November 15. In general, the Bukharan mill workers were less politically conscious than the Russian railroad workers, and their demands were purely economic.[50]

In the latter half of November 1905 the Russian authorities in the khanate lived in fear that the native population might be tempted by Russia's temporary paralysis to rise against the Russians in their midst. The Russian settlements were placed in a state of emergency on November 30, and Ia. Ia. Liutsh, the political agent (1902–1911), requested troop reinforcements to remind the Bukharans of Russia's power.[51] Actually the effect of the revolution on Bukhara was not to shake Russia's hold over the khanate but rather to encourage the native liberals, who were inspired by the political awakening of Russia's Moslems in 1905.

In the first years after 1905 the Bukharan reform movement continued to move along its previous path, focusing its attention almost exclusively on the establishment of new-method schools and looking for leadership to Gasprinskii and the Russian Tatars. *Tardjuman* and other Turko-Tatar journals were much more widely circulated and read in Bukhara after 1905 than before. In 1907 two new-method schools were opened in Old and New Bukhara for Russian Tatar children. The following year Gasprinskii visited the khanate and tried to persuade Abd al-Ahad to transform the school in

Old Bukhara into a state-supported institution for both Tatar and Bukharan children, but the emir refused under pressure from the clerical zealots. In October 1908 the first new-method school entirely for Bukharan pupils was opened, and a "Society of Bukhara the Noble" was established to provide the school with textbooks. During the following year the progress displayed in public examinations by the pupils of the Bukharan and Tatar new-method schools won much favor for the institutions but at the same time aroused the hostility of the clergy, who succeeded in closing first the Bukharan and then the Tatar schools by the end of 1909. A final attempt in 1910 to reopen a Tatar school in New Bukhara provoked from the emir first an order prohibiting the enrollment of Bukharan pupils and then a request to the governor general of Turkestan to abolish all new-method schools for Russian subjects in Bukhara. Tashkent complied in 1911, from which time the schools were forced to operate clandestinely in private homes. At the outbreak of World War I about half a dozen new-method schools were being conducted in this manner.[52]

The Bukharan Djadids

Frustrated by the opposition of the emir's government to educational reform, the Bukharan liberals soon broadened their aims and began to look elsewhere than to Russia's Moslems for leadership in their attempt to modernize Bukhara. Their attention was attracted by the liberal revolution in Persia in 1906 and even more by the liberal nationalist Young Turk revolution in Turkey in 1908. These two revolutions endowed Persia and Turkey with a semblance of constitutional government on the Western model and gave hope that the Moslem world might yet be rejuvenated by reformers willing to learn from the West. The aims of the Bukharan liberals remained essentially educational, but in a broader sense than before. They set themselves the task not only of eliminating illiteracy and ignorance in the khanate but also of educating the people to an awareness of the uselessness and the reactionary role of the clergy, of government arbitrariness and illegality, and of the emir's appropriation for his own use of state revenues that ought properly to be spent on the needs of the country.[53]

To accomplish these aims, the Bukharan liberals for the first time began to organize. Late in 1909 a group of Bukharan exiles in

Constantinople founded the Bukharan Society for the Dissemination of Knowledge (*Bukhara Tamim-i Maarif*), whose goals were to found schools in the khanate and to finance the sending of Bukharan students to study in Constantinople.[54] Within Bukhara itself a secret organization called the Society for the Education of Children (*Gamiyati Tarbiye-i Atfal*) was formed toward the end of 1910, with the aims of disseminating knowledge and literature among the population, fighting government abuses, and waging antigovernment agitation.[55] This group operated like a conspiratorial organization in order to escape government suppression. New members were carefully screened, sworn to secrecy, moral purity, abstention from alcohol, and devotion to enlightenment and reform, and only gradually initiated into the society's secrets. The organization's existence was kept secret even from the Bukharans from whom money was solicited to further its purposes.[56]

Although it probably never numbered more than thirty members, the Society for the Education of Children counted among its membership the leading Bukharan liberals and in the brief period of its active existence (1911–1914) achieved an impressive record. It cooperated with the Constantinople group to send fifteen Bukharan students to the Turkish capital in 1911 and thirty in 1913. It supported and protected the clandestine new-method schools already in existence and helped to open new ones in Shahr-i Sabz, Karakul, Kerki, and elsewhere in the provinces. Its most notable achievement was publication of the khanate's first two newspapers, printed at the privately owned Russian printing press in New Bukhara. Two members of the society persuaded A. S. Somov, the political agent (1911–1913), of the usefulness of a local newspaper the better to acquaint Bukharans with Russia; Somov consented to the publication on condition that he act as censor, and he obtained the agreement of the emir's government not to hinder the newspaper's circulation. A Persian-language daily, *Bukhara-i Sharif* (Bukhara the Noble), was published from mid-March to mid-July, 1912, under the editorship of a Moslem from Baku. In July a second paper, the Uzbeg semiweekly *Turan*, was launched under the editorship of a Bukharan who had been educated in Constantinople. *Bukhara-i Sharif* continued on a reduced schedule, appearing four times, and later twice, a week. During their brief lives the two newspapers brought into the open for the first time discussion of such problems as the political order and school reform, formerly confined to private conversation. The Bukharan government could not long tolerate such freedom of expression: at the emir's request the political agent closed both papers on January 2, 1913. In other fields the work of the society went forward, and in 1914 a bookshop and a manufacturing company were established as fronts for the conduct of political propaganda.[57]

Both the Djadid group in the khanate and the Constantinople organization shared common aims and to some extent a common membership.[58] The spokesman for both groups was Abd ar-Rauf Fitrat, who left Bukhara for Constantinople in 1910 and there became the best-known propagandist for reform in the khanate and the acknowledged ideological leader of the Bukharan reform movement. His writings, published in Persian in Constantinople and widely circulated among the small group of liberals in Bukhara, advocated educational reform, attacked the Moslem clergy, and called for an Islamic revival.[59]

The Bukharan Djadids had barely gotten organized when on December 23, 1910, Abd al-Ahad died at the age of fifty-one.[60] He was succeeded without incident by his son and designated heir, Saiyid Mir Alim, born in 1880. Alim had an even closer familiarity with Russian life than his father, for during his teens he had spent four years in the Nikolaevskii Cadet Corps in St. Petersburg. He stocked his library with Russian authors and, like his father, was a frequent visitor to Russia and a benefactor of Russian causes.[61] At home he was a far weaker ruler than Abd al-Ahad and was much more subject to the influence of others. For the first three and a half years of his reign Alim tried to steer a middle course between the clerical zealots and the advocates of reform—not so much the few native critics of the regime as its many Russian critics. On the one hand, he asked the political agent to suppress the Djadid newspapers in 1912 and did not permit the new-method schools to operate openly. On the other hand, he made no attempt to close the clandestine schools, although their existence was common knowledge. Further, at his accession Alim decreed a number of reforms aimed at eliminating government corruption. He prohibited the giving of presents to the emir, his courtiers, or civil servants; kazis were forbidden from accepting more than the legal fees to which they were entitled; and the wages of soldiers and all salaried clerical and secular officials were raised. The manifesto announcing these reforms made a good impression in the khanate and in Russia, but although the pay of government employees was raised, the other points were never enforced; the manifesto was never even made public in central and eastern Bukhara. Early in 1911 Alim responded to a students' petition by ordering the kazi-kalan to investigate and correct abuses in the administration of the madrasas, but the vehement opposition of the *mudarrises* (professors) forced the emir to abandon this attempt at reform. The clergy seemed finally to have gotten the upper hand over the regime's critics when it persuaded the emir on July 5, 1914, to order the closing of the five or six new-method schools operating semi-secretly in the khanate.[62]

The outbreak of World War I two weeks after the order closing the reformed schools brought a temporary suspension of Djadid activities. The close connections of the reformers with the Ottoman Turks, who in November 1914 entered the war on the side of the Central Powers, made them suspect in Russia's eyes, even though a large part of the Bukharan student and emigré colony in Constantinople, Fitrat included, left for Tashkent.[63] The governor general of Turkestan established a special department of political police in Bukhara to carry out searches and arrests, and A. K. Beliaev, the political agent (1913–1916), tried unsuccessfully to discover the membership of the secret society, whose existence was suspected. During the war the group was forced to meet much less frequently than twice a month, which had been its custom.[64]

As an orthodox Moslem state, Bukhara itself was embarrassed by the sultan-khalif's proclamation of holy war against the Allies. Emir Alim demonstrated his loyalty to Russia by donating several million rubles to the Russian war effort; in September 1916 he journeyed in person to the front to present the emperor with a gift of one million rubles.[65] At home the Bukharan government proved its loyalty by suppressing all opposition and forbidding the reading of newspapers or the discussion of current events. In the summer of 1915 when the Russian army was in rapid retreat all along the front from Courland to Galicia, the kush-begi summoned fifteen of the leading Bukharan liberals, severely lectured them for discussing politics and the Russian defeats, and made them promise in writing to refrain from reading newspapers. A year later, during the widespread native rebellion in the government-general of Turkestan the emir's agents were everywhere in Bukhara, and it was strictly forbidden even to speak of the uprising across the border.[66] Alim was probably as anxious to avoid any suspicion on Russia's part that Bukharans were supporting the revolt as he was to prevent its spread to the khanate.

The reform movement that developed in Bukhara during the reigns of Abd al-Ahad and Alim, particularly after 1905, was the first attempt on the part of Bukharans to solve the problem of their country's suspension between the worlds of medieval Islam and the modern West. Although Bukhara's economic development after 1885 prepared the way for the reformers by linking Bukhara's fate ever more closely with Russia's, the native reform movement was much more a cultural than an economic phenomenon. The leaders as well as most of the members of the movement were disaffected intellectuals—writers, poets, educators, students—drawn primarily from the urban lower middle class and awakened to their country's backwardness through contact with Russia or, later, Turkey. The movement found both moral and financial support in the group of merchants, shopkeepers, and minor officials who functioned as intermediaries between the Russian world and the Bukharan and who were therefore aware of the need for educational, clerical, fiscal, and administrative reforms.[67] The development of such a movement, however limited its numbers and however restricted its view of the necessary degree of modernization, was one of the more significant facets of Russia's impact on her Central Asian protectorates.

Alim, Emir of Bukhara, 1910–1920

12 / Nonintervention under Attack: Russia and Bukhara

Russian Critics

After the turn of the century Russia found that her traditional policy of nonintervention in Bukhara's internal affairs was in danger of being undermined both by the increasingly vociferous group of critics of the situation in the protectorate and by developments in Bukhara demanding limited intervention in order to protect St. Petersburg's political interests in Central Asia. Significant as were the Bukharan liberals to the history of Bukhara after the collapse of the Romanov Empire, it was the Russian critics of the ancien régime in the khanate who were of immediate importance in the period before 1917. Since the 1870's critics had never been wanting, particularly advocates of annexation among the military in Russian Turkestan. Only at the turn of the century, however, after many individual Russians had acquired first-hand experience of conditions in Bukhara and direct economic interests there, did anything like a concerted campaign for reform or annexation develop.

The few serious studies made of Bukhara in the early twentieth century were unanimous in condemning the emir's rule and proposing that Russia take a much more active hand in running the country. Lieutenant Colonel, later Major General, M. V. Grulev of the Russian general staff complained at the end of the 1890's that after a generation of Russian protection Bukhara was a land hardly surpassed in misery by any other Asian country. Disease, depravity, and corruption were the rule rather than the exception. Grulev argued that the time had long since come for Russia to compel the emir to introduce reforms under her guidance. The drafting of a regular budget and reorganization of the army into native auxiliaries officered by Russians on the Anglo-Indian model were uppermost on Grulev's list of necessary reforms.[1]

A. Gubarevich-Radobylskii, a student of Bukhara's economy who lived in the khanate for six years at the turn of the century, emphasized the fact that the emir's government spent nothing on the needs of the country or its inhabitants, either for irrigation, roads, education, or anything else. The emir did not even spend very much on his court, which would have been an indirect means of returning some of the tax revenues to the economy. He merely hoarded his ever-growing fortune, so that sizable sums of money were withdrawn annually from circulation. Gubarevich-Radobylskii complained that Russia's policy toward her protectorate lacked a clear understanding of the interests of the Bukharan people. Since the political agent was burdened by too many varied duties to be able to perform any of them effectively, Gubarevich-Radobylskii suggested his replacement by a military resident subject to the governor general of Turkestan. The resident would provide active guidance for the Bukharan government in internal as well as external matters; one of his first tasks would be to assist in drafting a state budget that would set aside 20 percent of total revenues for items such as public works and education.[2] Gubarevich-Radobylskii's ideas drew heavily upon the defeated proposals of Political Agent Lessar and Governor General Vrevskii in the early 1890's.

Undoubtedly the most influential—although certainly not the most original, perceptive, or reliable—critic of the situation in Bukhara in the early twentieth century was Colonel D. N. Logofet of the Amu-Darya border guard, who lived more than ten years in the khanate. Between 1907 and 1913 Logofet published four books and at least two series of articles on Bukhara, which contained much valuable information along with a good deal of misinformation, all presented with the author's strong bias in favor of drastic Russian intervention in Bukhara's internal affairs.[3] Writing after the establishment of a quasiconstitutional regime in Russia in 1906, Logofet was the first to formulate a general indictment of conditions in Bukhara and of Russian policy toward her protectorate. His first book, published in St. Petersburg in 1909 under the sensational title *Strana bezpraviia* (Land of Lawlessness), had a great impact on the Russian reading public as well as in government circles.

Logofet claimed that Russia was protecting and perpetuating in Bukhara a system of "savage despotism [and] complete lawlessness" by which three million people were kept in a position "incomparably worse than serfdom."[4] He painted a shocking but barely exaggerated picture of the oppressiveness, corruption, and arbitrariness of the Bukharan administrative and judicial systems, the government's lack of attention to the needs of the country and its people, and the preoccupation of the emir and his officials with enriching themselves at the expense of the people. Logofet criticized the Russian foreign ministry for not interfering and even bolstering the emir's prestige. Like Grulev before him, Logofet pointed out that the emir's gifts to Russians responsible for dealing with Bukhara were obstacles to reform.[5]

Logofet proposed that the Russian Duma, to whom he dedicated *Strana bezpraviia*, take the lead in introducing basic reforms in Bukhara, with a view to preparing the country for annexation by Russia in the near future. Specifically, Logofet urged the revision of the 1873 treaty to bring Bukhara under direct Russian control and the establishment of a Russian civil administration to take over the government of the country from the emir and the begs. The director of this new administration, who would be subject to the governor general of Turkestan and would replace the political agent, was to be assisted by Russian officials at the national and beglik level and by elected native officials at the district level. The Russian administration would collect all taxes, deposit them in branches of the Russian treasury to be established throughout the khanate, and appropriate annually the necessary funds for maintenance of the emir's court, the clergy, the native schools, and public works. Immediate attention would be given to expansion of the road and railroad networks and of postal and telegraphic services. The judicial system would be reformed on the model of Russian Turkestan, with native courts for the Bukharans, Russian justice-of-the-peace courts in all major towns, and an okrug (circuit) court at Bukhara. A force of native auxiliaries officered by Russians would replace the Bukharan army, as Grulev had suggested. Finally, Logofet proposed promoting Russian colonization and the development of unused agricultural land in Bukhara.[6] In effect, Bukhara was to be reduced to an oblast of Russian Turkestan, and the emir to a mere figurehead.

In 1911 Logofet incorporated his criticisms and his suggestions for reform into a greatly expanded work with the sober title, *Bukharskoe khanstvo pod russkim protektoratom* (The Khanate of Bukhara under the Russian Protectorate).[7] Logofet claimed to be concerned about Russia's moral obligation to the three million people of her protectorate, but in his two major works he was preoccupied both with the threat posed to Russia's prestige by the foreign ministry's policy of enhancing the emir's authority and with the right of Russian nationals to exploit and colonize the khanate freed of the restrictions that stemmed from the foreign ministry's policy of preserving Bukharan autonomy.[8]

Prince V. I. Masalskii, the last Russian thoroughly to describe Bukhara before the 1917 Revolution, relied heavily on Logofet for factual material and adopted his point of view. Masalskii regretted that the existence of a political agency subject to the Ministry of Foreign Affairs gave support to the view that Bukhara was a foreign power when actually it was merely "a part of the empire ruled by an hereditary emir." Masalskii called "abnormal" the existence of Bukhara and Khiva as "semi-independent khanates" and urged that immediate steps be taken to extend the blessings of Russian government and Russian culture to the two protectorates.[9]

After the appearance of *Strana bezpraviia* liberal Russian Moslems, discouraged by Abd al-Ahad's opposition to all reform, began openly to condemn conditions in the khanate. On May 3, 1909, the Baku satiric journal *Mullah Nasreddin* featured on page one a cartoon that depicted the emir and the kazi-kalan holding down a sheep labeled "Bukhara the Noble," which was being sheared by a European.[10] The liberal Orenburg Moslem newspaper *Vakt* (Time) in 1910 printed several unfavorable articles on the situation in Bukhara.[11] After a visit to Central Asia in the same year S. Maksudov, head of the Moslem caucus in the third Duma, declared that conditions in the khanate, compared with those in Russian Turkestan, were intolerable. Writing in *Tardjuman* in June 1909, Ismail-beg Gasprinskii looked to Russia to effect reforms in Bukhara: "If only Tashkent and Petersburg would try seriously, it would be possible to make of Bukhara a better organized and cultured land with a well-adjusted administration."[12]

M. A. Varygin, a Russian visitor to Bukhara at the beginning of World War I, presented squarely the choice facing Russia if she did not want to go on being responsible for the impossible conditions in the khanate by closing her eyes to the activities of the native regime. Either Russia must take positive steps toward political reform and the promotion of economic growth, or she must grant Bukhara full independence and thereby at least secure the good will of the people.[13] The Russian government was not likely to make such a difficult choice as long as the traditional policy toward Bukhara promised more advantages than disadvantages. Developments in the khanate, however, were already raising doubts as to the continued effectiveness of the foreign ministry's policy.

The West Pamir Question, 1896–1905

Although the emir's friendship toward Russia could be taken for granted from the 1880's, the policy of nonintervention also presupposed the existence of a native government able to command the respect and obedience of its subjects. Despite Russia's conscious bolstering of the emir's prestige, the reality of Russian strength and Bukharan weakness could not be disguised. Both the Bukharan government and the Bukharan people turned increasingly to Russia for support against each other. This problem came to a head in the western Pamirs, where popular hostility to the Bukharan authorities was highest.

Annexed to Bukhara in 1896 as a result of the Anglo-Russian agreement of the previous year on the Pamir boundary, Shugnan, Roshan, and northern Vakhan were the poorest districts in the khanate. Twelve years of Afghan rule had left their mark on a region already poorly endowed by nature.[14] The introduction of Bukharan administration proved a further burden, although Abd al-Ahad promised Russia in 1895 to postpone the collection of taxes in the area until October 1, 1899. Added to the material grievances of the inhabitants was the religious antipathy between the Sunnite ruling class and the local Ismaili Shiite population. The latter lost no time in complaining against their oppressive Bukharan masters to the Russian troops stationed at Khorog, in Vakhan, and in the Russian eastern Pamirs.[15]

Friction in the western Pamirs between the local population and the Bukharan authorities was especially undesirable from Russia's point of view because of the region's strategic location near the northern border of India. In May 1897 Tashkent instructed the commander of the Pamir Detachment at Khorog to use his moral influence with the Bukharan officials to secure just treatment for the population of the western Pamirs.[16] This type of informal supervision having failed to solve the problem, Governor General S. M. Dukhovskoi in December 1898 sent Lieutenant Colonel Kuznetsov to Bukhara to discuss the situation in the western Pamirs and to propose that the Russian military authorities in the area assume responsibility for its administration. Abd al-Ahad was agreeable, observing that since its annexation the region had brought him much trouble and expense but no profit. He argued, however, that since Lessar had forced him to accept Shugnan-Roshan in exchange for southern Darvaz, he could not now turn the region over to Russia without suffering a tremendous loss of prestige among his subjects, unless he were to receive some suitable compensation. Political Agent Ignatiev, in his report of February 1899 to Dukhovskoi, supported Abd al-Ahad's request for compensation on the grounds that if Russia did not compensate the emir for his loss, she would be undermining his authority.[17]

Ignatiev subsequently went a step further and advocated the outright annexation of the western Pamirs to Russia. He called intolerable the system of diarchy that had resulted from the interference of the local Russian military authorities in the area's internal affairs: "The appeals of the inhabitants for the intercession of the commander of the Pamir Detachment and their requests to be received as Russian subjects are a result not so much of the severe oppression under which the population of these regions lives as of the completely abnormal relationship which has existed from the very beginning between our officers and the Bukharan authorities and the inhabitants. Having demonstrated open hostility to the Bukharan authorities, our officers began to interfere in the government of the principalities and openly gave the inhabitants to understand that they could always rely on the commander of the Pamir Detachment to intercede with the emir's functionaries, and that all their grievances would be received with full sympathy."[18] Yet, as Ignatiev subsequently argued, once Russia had committed herself to the protection of the local population, she could not afford to back down, so annexation was the only solution.[19]

The foreign ministry consented in March 1899 to Russia's annexation of the western Pamirs, provided that the emir be compensated with the title of "Highness" and either the rank of full general or membership in the order of Andrei the First Named. The foreign ministry also insisted that the territorial transfer be effected through a secret treaty with Bukhara in order to avoid embarrassing explanations to Britain and Afghanistan.[20]

For once it was Tashkent who objected. Dukhovskoi opposed immediate annexation of the western Pamirs because Britain might demand compensation in the form of territorial gains elsewhere in the area, which was the game then being played by the great powers in China. Dukhovskoi believed the question would be better postponed until a more favorable time. Accordingly, Ignatiev informed the emir that the issue had temporarily been dropped. Bukhara then requested formal permission to begin collecting taxes in Shugnan-Roshan, and Ignatiev supported the request on the grounds that Russia could not very well refuse if she intended to leave the western Pamirs in Bukhara's hands. A solution was worked out early in 1900, which perpetuated the unwieldy system of diarchy to which Ignatiev had objected: the emir and the beg of Shugnan-Roshan were permitted to collect taxes under the supervision of the governor general of Turkestan and the commander of the Pamir Detachment. Famine resulting from a crop failure the previous fall, however, led the commander of the Pamir Detachment to recommend in July 1900 the postponement of tax collections for another year in order to prevent large-scale emigration to Afghanistan.[21]

With Russia's permission Bukharan officials finally began to collect taxes in Shugnan-Roshan in March 1903, and they immediately met with opposition from the inhabitants, who had just weathered a particularly severe winter with great losses of cattle and crops. The Russian authorities at Khorog and Tashkent tried to steer a middle course between the population and the Bukharan officials, persuading the inhabitants not to revolt or flee while prevailing upon the emir's government to ease the tax burden. Russia's efforts were to no avail, and open rebellion occurred in Vakhan, where the intervention of Russian troops from a nearby Russian frontier post was necessary to free ten Bukharan tax collectors and to suppress the disorders. The Russians arrested the rebel leaders and turned them over to the Bukharan administration. Governor General N. A. Ivanov sent his diplomatic attaché, A. Polovtsev, to investigate the disturbances and explain to the population that Russia expected them to obey their own government and would not tolerate any failure to do so. Ivanov meanwhile departed from the policy of his predecessor by urging the immediate annexation of Shugnan-Roshan.[22]

Nothing daunted, the inhabitants of the western Pamirs continued to bombard the political agency and the commander of the Pamir Detachment with their complaints against the Bukharan government. On June 15, 1904, the secretary of the political agency, Baron A. A. Cherkasov, was sent on a fact-finding tour of the region. He collected much information on the area's poverty and on the oppressiveness of the Bukharan officials and also determined that religious persecution had much to do with the unrest. Cherkasov concluded that the only solution to Shugnan-Roshan's problems was its administration by Russia.[23]

In the face of continued unrest, suspected British intrigue, and the possibility of mass emigration from Vakhan across the Hindu Kush, Russia finally moved to take control of the western Pamirs. Ivanov's successor, General N. N. Teviashev, favored such a course, to which Abd al-Ahad again gave his consent. A special conference in Tashkent in 1905, attended by Cherkasov and the commander of the Pamir Detachment, decided to assume de facto control of the region while leaving formal sovereignty to Bukhara in order not to antagonize Britain. The commander of the Pamir Detachment was to administer Shugnan, Roshan, and Vakhan through an official appointed by the emir or by the viceroy of central and eastern Bukhara and residing in Khorog, the Russian military headquarters. All taxes were to be abolished except for one, which was retained as a token of Bukharan sovereignty.[24]

Chronic maladministration and popular discontent had finally resulted in the transfer of a part of Bukhara's territory to Russian control. True, the area in question had never been integral to the khanate, and the emir was quite willing to part with it because it had been consistently unprofitable. Yet Russia's assumption of the burdens of government in one part of the emir's territory in order to preserve political stability in a strategic zone was an admission that the policy of nonintervention was no longer producing the desired results.

The Riots of January 1910

In 1910 Russia was forced to intervene to preserve political stability not in the emir's most distant province but in his very capital. Following in the footsteps of his grandfather Muhammad-biy, Astanakul, Abd al-Ahad's zakatchi-kalan since 1888, was appointed kush-begi in 1906 or 1907. He immediately began to appoint his fellow Shiites to many important posts in the administration and the army which had traditionally been reserved for Sunnites. In 1908 he went a step further, granting the Shiites permission openly to celebrate their most important festival, which commemorates the martyrdom of Husein, the second son of Muhammad's cousin and son-in-law Ali, whom the Shiites regard as the Prophet's rightful successor. Astanakul's flaunting of the Shiites' power irritated the religious susceptibilities of the orthodox majority in the khanate, and on January 9, 1910, the last day of Husein's festival, a group of madrasa students insulted a Shiite procession in the capital. In the ensuing riot one of the students was killed. When his comrades appealed to the kush-begi to punish the killers, Astanakul arrested the students instead. This act was all that was needed to release the pent-up dissatisfaction of the Sunnite populace, who stormed the citadel until repelled by a volley of gunfire from the guards.[25]

On the following day, January 10, a mob of Sunnites invaded the Shiite quarter and was met by armed resistance; there were rumors of Shiite attacks on mosques and madrasas. By evening an uneasy quiet had descended on the city. A small body of Russian troops, normally stationed in New Bukhara, took up positions near the railroad station and the Karshi gate. Their orders were to take no offensive action against the mobs unless requested to do so by the Bukharan government. From the beginning the kush-begi took the view that the disorders were purely an internal matter. Political Agent Liutsh agreed, but on orders from the foreign ministry he sent one Schultz, a member of his staff, to Abd al-Ahad in Kermine to demand that the Bukharan government take steps to restore order. Liutsh meanwhile insisted that the Russian troops were not to interfere.[26]

January 11 was relatively quiet, with only a few sporadic clashes between Sunnites and Shiites as both sides gathered arms and organized their forces. Russian troop reinforcements from Katta-Kurgan arrived at New Bukhara, but the Bukharan government still made no move. On the morning of the twelfth Major General Lilienthal arrived to take command of the Russian troops and demanded that the kush-begi take positive steps to pacify the population. Around 11 A.M. major rioting broke out. Lilienthal repeated to Astanakul his demands for action and offered the assistance of the Russian troops at New Bukhara. By evening the riots had subsided, but Lilienthal warned both Astanakul and Liutsh that he would occupy the city on the following day if the disturbances were renewed. At the news that several thousand Sunnites and Shiites were marching on the capital from the surrounding villages to support their co-religionists, the kush-begi lost his nerve and, apparently on his own initiative, requested Liutsh in writing to order the Russian troops to occupy the city on the morning of the thirteenth.[27]

The arrival of Russian troops in force in the capital on January 13 restored order. Lilienthal proclaimed that the troops would act immediately to halt any further outbreaks of violence. Bukhara had now been subjected to the crowning indignity—Russian occupation of her capital; even Muzaffar ad-Din in the dark days of June 1868 had been spared this humiliation. Not Russian aggression but the emir's inability to keep his own subjects in order had brought the khanate to this pass. After the Russian troops had already moved into Old Bukhara, Schultz wired from Kermine that Abd al-Ahad refused to go to the capital in person but was sending his son and heir, Mir Alim; the emir requested the Russians not to occupy the city. Astanakul and Liutsh thereupon urged Lilienthal to withdraw his troops, but he refused on the grounds that a withdrawal before order was completely restored would damage Russia's prestige. Since Liutsh continued to press for a withdrawal, Lilienthal asked Tashkent for instructions. Governor General A. V. Samsonov ordered him to keep the troops in the city until there was no longer any danger of disorders.[28]

The heir-apparent arrived in the capital late on the thirteenth. The following day he and Lilienthal cooperated to restore the confidence of the populace in the government. Alim dismissed the kush-begi and several of his followers from office, and Astanakul was escorted to Kermine on the night of the fourteenth by an armed guard of Russian soldiers. On January 15 the leaders of the Sunnite and Shiite communities were publicly reconciled in Lilienthal's presence. Life soon returned to normal. A few days later the Russian troops evacuated the capital, although they remained at the railroad station in the old city and also in New Bukhara a while longer. At the end of the month Abd al-Ahad went to St. Petersburg, as planned, to celebrate the twenty-fifth anniversary of his accession.[29]

The main importance of the riots was not in their effect on Bukhara, which was quite minor: although Nasr Allah, the new kush-begi and former beg of Shahr-i Sabz, was relatively liberal, no important shift in government policy occurred.[30] The significance of the events of January 1910 lay rather in the evidence they gave of the failure of Russia's policy of nonintervention in Bukhara's internal affairs. The temporary occupation of the capital of her protectorate might be considered a cheap price for Russia to pay for escaping the constant drain in men and money that the direct administration of Bukhara would entail. Nevertheless, the necessity for armed intervention on a large scale to restore order was a token of the emir's diminishing ability to maintain the political stability that was a sine qua non of nonintervention. In the next few years further evidence of this inability was provided by several minor uprisings —such as one in Kulab in 1910 and another in Hisar in 1913—which were suppressed only with the aid of Russian troops.[31]

Russian Policy Reappraised, 1909–1914

The criticism leveled both at conditions in Bukhara and at Russian policy, as well as the developments in the khanate necessitating Russian intervention, forced the Russian government to reexamine its traditional policy of nonintervention. The publication of Logofet's *Strana bezpraviia* encouraged Tashkent to initiate the first open discussion of that policy in official circles since 1895. Governor General P. I. Mishchenko convoked a conference in Tashkent on February 2, 1909, attended by Political Agent Liutsh, which dealt with a whole range of matters concerning Bukhara. On the crucial questions of whether the governor general of Turkestan should be given control over the actions of the Bukharan government in internal affairs and whether the political agent should be subordinated to the governor general, the conference reached no decisions. A majority of the conferees favored the gradual abolition of the Bukharan army, although Mishchenko advocated sending Russian instructors to reform the army so that it could be entrusted with the defense of the railroad and the Samarkand-Termez post road in case of war in Central Asia (presumably against Britain). The conference also favored further development of the Russian settlements and full freedom of trade for Russians in the khanate but opposed Russian colonization in the immediate future. Apparently the conference's only practical result was a decision to instruct the political agent to bring to Abd al-Ahad's attention the plight of his people and the need for reforms.[32]

Quite different was the tenor of a second conference held in Tashkent on August 10–11 of the same year under the chairmanship of General A. V. Samsonov, the new governor general. Samsonov's position was that Bukhara should not be pressed to adopt reforms and that Tashkent should simply wait until St. Petersburg decided to annex the khanate. He put it to the meeting frankly: "Our basic aim is to absorb Bukhara." General Galkin, governor of the Samarkand Oblast, seconded Samsonov's views, but Liutsh and V. F. Minorskii, a diplomat and Persian and Central Asian expert, presented the foreign ministry's view that immediate annexation would be premature; Gubarevich-Radobylskii, who was also present, agreed. Samsonov did advocate one change in Bukhara in the period before annexation—liquidation of the emir's army and use of the money thus saved to maintain additional Russian troops there and to construct public works. Minorskii favored an alternative proposal, based on the ideas of Grulev and Logofet, for the reorganization of the Bukharan army as a body of native auxiliaries officered by Russians and stationed in small groups all over the khanate so as to be easily controlled by Russia. Samsonov rejected this plan as too dangerous in case of war with Afghanistan, and the conference went on record in favor of abolishing the army. Galkin advocated Russian colonization in central Bukhara, but Samsonov tabled discussion of that issue on grounds that it would raise too many complications as long as the khanate retained autonomy. In submitting the protocols of the conference to the ministries of war and foreign affairs, the governor general insisted on the annexation of both Bukhara and Khiva as the best solution to the protectorates' problems.[33]

On January 28, 1910, hard on the heels of Russia's intervention to restore order in Bukhara, the Council of Ministers in St. Petersburg took up the problems previously discussed in Tashkent. Governor General Samsonov, who was present for the occasion, delivered a report which concluded that substantial improvement in Bukhara's political and economic life was impossible without annexation. P. A. Stolypin, chairman of the Council, agreed that annexation was in the long run inevitable but argued that for the foreseeable future it was premature. Annexation would entail large and unnecessary expenditures at a time when "all the nerves of the empire are strained to the task of internal improvement." Russia's prime minister thus by 1910 envisaged Bukhara's eventual annexation. The failure of nonintervention to produce the desired political stability and the growing attacks of Russian critics undoubtedly underlay his attitude. At the same time, in the absence of any pressing need for immediate action the Council of Ministers would go no further than to endorse the foreign ministry's plan for putting pressure on the emir to effect reforms in the budget, army, and taxation with Russia's assistance.[34]

The foreign ministry, however, had only slightly more interest in reform than the Bukharan government itself, and the history of Russo-Bukharan relations since the 1870's had shown that in cases where Russia had no vital interests at stake, Bukhara could with impunity ignore the wishes of her protector. Emir Alim's abortive reforms of early 1911 were a case in point. Samsonov, having altered his views on the desirability of reforms, kept the issue alive by proposing to St. Petersburg a series of necessary changes: placing the entire native administration on salary, substituting a proportional land tax for the traditional *heradj* (harvest tax), and abolishing the zakat and the aminana, whose collection was subject to so many abuses. On March 11, 1913, a conference in the foreign ministry discussed Samsonov's suggestions, but no action was taken.[35] In fact, the foreign ministry, while appearing to give ground to its critics on the subject of reform, never really retreated from its view that nonintervention in Bukhara was in Russia's best interests. As Foreign Minister S. D. Sazonov put it on June 20, 1913: "The khanate of Bukhara, autonomous in its internal affairs, is in a very special position. While we do not impart an international or diplomatic character to our relations with the government of the khanate, we nevertheless maintain in Bukhara a special representative in the person of the imperial political agent, in whose hands exclusively are concentrated both our relations with the emir and his government and also the supervision of the khanate's internal life. The latter task is most complex and requires very prudent handling in view of the absolute necessity for us not to undermine the emir's authority in his subjects' eyes and carefully to avoid anything that might bear the character of direct interference on our part in the internal affairs of the khanate."[36]

The State Duma twice debated briefly Russia's relations with her Central Asian protectorates. On May 23, 1912, the Duma took up the report of its Committee on Judicial Reforms favoring the enactment of a draft law, submitted four years earlier by the minister of justice, which would extend to Khiva the same rules of extraterritorial jurisdiction in force in Bukhara. Count A. A. Uvarov, a member from Saratov *guberniia* (province), took the opportunity to condemn native justice in the khanates as resting on the purely arbitrary decisions of government officials. He claimed that Britain would never have tolerated the existence of such a system in her vassal Indian principalities for forty years, and that for Russia to have allowed Bukhara and Khiva to retain so large a degree of autonomy for this long was a political mistake. Uvarov proposed that the Duma consider the question of introducing the Russian legal system into the protectorates for the native as well as the Russian population. After Uvarov had finished speaking, the chairman of the Duma closed the discussion, and the law was approved in the form recommended by the minister of justice.[37]

A broader discussion of the Bukharan problem took place in the Duma on the very eve of World War I. On June 14, 1914, the Duma received the report of its Committee on Legislative and Budgetary Proposals on a plan presented by the foreign ministry to enlarge the staff of the political agency and raise the ranks, salaries, and expense accounts of its members. The foreign ministry's draft had been approved with only minor changes by the committee members, but not before they had denounced the situation in Bukhara, specifically the medieval character of the government and the conditions giving rise to popular dissatisfaction. The committee's report declared that Bukhara's system of government was retarding the cultural and economic growth of the country and hindering the activities of Russian subjects, and that the only solution was the active supervision of the native regime by the Russian authorities. The committee recommended that the foreign ministry take positive steps to force the emir to introduce the necessary reforms in the near future.[38]

M. A. Karaulov, a member from the Terek Cossack Army, opened debate on the report by moving that the Duma seize the opportunity offered by the bill on the political agency to go on record in favor of greater definition of Russo-Bukharan relations and the reorganization of Bukhara's judicial and administrative institutions. The Kadet leader P. N. Miliukov opposed Karaulov's motion on the grounds that the question was too complicated to dispose of with a well-meaning but ineffectual resolution and that a more thorough examination of the problem would mean an unnecesary delay in the passage of the bill under consideration. Rzhevskii, chairman of the budgetary committee, also opposed the motion, arguing that the question had already been discussed at length in committee. The Duma approved the bill but rejected both Karaulov's motion and the committee's expression in favor of internal reforms in Bukhara.[39]

Although challenged in the Duma and in the older organs of the imperial government, the traditional policy of nonintervention remained unchanged. It would take more than criticism, no matter how widespread, more even than a few cases of temporary political instability requiring Russian intervention, to impel Russia to assume greater responsibility for the government of her Central Asian protectorates. It would in fact take a complete breakdown in the political order of the khanates, such as had happened in Kokand in 1875–1876 and was soon to occur in Khiva.

Isfendiyar, Khan of Khiva, 1910–1918, and His Suite

13 / Nonintervention Abandoned: Russia and Khiva

Khiva, 1885–1912

From the 1870's Khiva was the less important of Russia's Central Asian protectorates. Bukhara was larger and richer, of greater value to the Russian economy, and of more strategic importance. It was to Khiva, however, that Russia's attention turned in the last years of the empire, when the domestic problems that had troubled the khanate in 1873–1877 returned in more serious form.

Khiva's internal life was even less affected by the Russian protectorate than was Bukhara's. No railroad ran through Khiva; there were no Russian enclaves, civil or military, no Russian extraterritorial courts, and no Russian customs and frontier posts. Although an unofficial colony of Russian merchants developed at Urgench in the 1890's, the total number of Russians in the khanate remained small —3,951 by the census of 1897, and 6,150 in 1912—and was concentrated in Urgench.[1] Urgench had a number of modern commercial and industrial enterprises, a telegraph office, and a branch of the Russian treasury, but no Russian schools, churches, hospitals, or hotels, and no separate administration.[2] The schools, hospitals, and legal institutions of the Amu-Darya Otdel served also the Russian residents of Khiva.

The khan of Khiva played a much less important role in Russian society than did the emir of Bukhara. Russia made Muhammad Rahim a major general in the Orenburg Cossack Army and bestowed several high orders on him, but as a consequence of Khiva's loss of formal independence by the treaty of 1873, Russia did not treat the khan, as it did the emir, like an independent ruler. The foreign ministry's yearbooks never listed the khan of Khiva among the reigning foreign sovereigns and chiefs of state. He was addressed and referred to formally merely as "High Eminence" until 1896, when he was granted the slightly higher dignity of "Radiance" (*Siiatel-*

stvo). In 1902 the khan was accorded the title of "Illustriousness," given to Abd al-Ahad a decade earlier, but it remained for Muhammad Rahim's son and successor, Isfendiyar, finally to attain the title of "Highness."[3] The khan of Khiva visited Russia much more rarely than did the emir, maintained no villas there, and did not travel to Russia in a private train. He was not nearly so wealthy as the emir and consequently could not afford the same expensive presents and philanthropic donations.

Under the Russian protectorate the centuries-old hostility between Khiva and Bukhara continued. On the few occasions when the khan or the heir-apparent did go to Russia, as for Nicholas II's coronation, they went by way of Chardjui and the railroad, but they always preferred to stay overnight on the steamboat that had brought them up the river rather than to be the emir's guests in Chardjui.[4]

Khiva's government attracted less criticism than Bukhara's both because fewer Russians were interested in Khiva and because the government itself was probably a little less oppressive than Bukhara's. Taxes were lower, and the government spent proportionately more for such public works as roads and bridges. As in Bukhara, much of the revenue stayed in the hands of the hakims and tax collectors. Total annual revenue in the 1870's was about 400,000 rubles.[5] This figure rose after 1885 as Khiva benefited from the expanded trade with Russia, but a large share of the khan's revenues went to Russia in payment of the 1873 war indemnity. By treaty the annual payments on the indemnity were to increase gradually until by 1881 they would attain a level of 200,000 rubles, where they were to remain until the indemnity was paid off in 1893. Actually Khiva fell behind in her payments, which continued until 1900.[6] In 1912 Khiva's state revenue was estimated at one million rubles, of which somewhat over half reached the khan.[7]

Muhammad Murad, the divan-begi, continued to be the most powerful figure in the Khivan government until his death in 1901. For the next nine years the government was in the hands of the several dignitaries who comprised the khan's council.[8] Muhammad Rahim died of a heart attack on August 16, 1910, at the age of sixty-five and was succeeded by his fourth son Isfendiyar, born in 1873, whom Russia had confirmed as heir-apparent in 1891.[9] Like his father, Isfendiyar left affairs of state primarily to his ministers and advisers, the most important of whom in the first few years was Islam-hodja, the divan-begi and a grandson of Muhammad Murad.

Since Islam-hodja was relatively liberal, and Khiva's clerical hierarchy was not as powerful as Bukhara's, the pressure that Russia exerted on Isfendiyar at his accession to introduce basic reforms produced slightly more results than the similar pressure exerted on Emir Alim at about the same time.

A report on the possibility of increasing cotton acreage in Khiva, made at Governor General Samsonov's orders in late 1910, criticized the situation in the khanate, particularly the population's lack of rights, the arbitrariness of the government, the inequitable system of taxation, the lack of modern medical and communications facilities, and the poor condition of the irrigation network. The report advocated only minor reforms to promote cotton production, but on the general subject of reforms it recommended that Khiva's autonomy not be allowed to work to the detriment of the native population, of the interests of Russian subjects, or of Russia's prestige. As a result of such criticism, Russia pressed the new khan to introduce reforms at the time of his confirmation on the throne in January 1911. On January 22 Isfendiyar publicly proclaimed his support of a broad range of reforms, including establishment of a state budget, placing of all government servants on salary, tax reform, improvement and extension of the irrigation network, and establishment of hospitals, dispensaries, and new-method elementary schools. The tax reform was expected to raise government revenue to about two million rubles a year, of which one million was to be spent on projects such as schools and hospitals—about five times the current expenditure for those purposes.[10]

In fact, however, few of the reforms were ever effected. Islam-hodja built a school and a hospital in the capital and founded a reformed madrasa, and new-method schools were encouraged.[11] But the attempt to change the tax structure, including the introduction of a proportional land tax, opened a Pandora's box of troubles for Khiva because of opposition from the Yomut Turkomans.[12]

The Turkoman Revolt of 1912–1913

The problem of the chronic insubordination of the khan's Turkoman subjects had never been permanently solved. The period 1880–1905 was marked by repeated minor disturbances among the Khivan Turkomans, usually over taxes or water rights. Major trouble recurred in 1912, when to the ancient dispute over the division of water for irrigation and the traditional cultural antagonism between Turkomans and Uzbegs were added Isfendiyar's attempts to reform the tax structure. The reforms enacted in 1912 meant a doubling and tripling of the Turkomans' taxes. Only a spark was needed to ignite an open rebellion. The khan's officials provided that spark in December 1912 by killing a rich and influential Turkoman who had refused to hand over a criminal who was his guest and was thus, by custom, entitled to his protection. Shammi-kel led other tribal chieftains in playing on the discontent of the masses. On December 12 a Turkoman band attacked and plundered a caravan traveling from Tashauz to Takhta; on December 17 and 26 the Turkomans raided Uzbeg settlements.[13]

The Khivan government was deeply split over the policy to be followed in regard to the Turkomans. Islam-hodja headed a group that favored a compromise settlement of the Turkomans' grievances. He was opposed by a group led by the war minister, Sheikh Nazar-beg, which had formerly been in disgrace because of their resistance to Islam-hodja's reform policy but had recently been restored to favor by the khan at the insistence of the commandant of the Amu-Darya Otdel. Nazar-beg's party advocated the use of force to crush the rebels. The war party finally prevailed, and Isfendiyar ordered a punitive expedition, led by Nazar-beg himself, against the Turkomans.[14] The expedition met with stubborn resistance from the three hundred to five hundred Turkoman warriors who occupied a strongly fortified defensive position between Takhta and Ilyali and was held off for twenty days. Meanwhile, Colonel N. S. Lykoshin, commandant of the Amu-Darya Otdel, who did not approve of the khan's decision to attack the Turkomans but had nevertheless not interfered to halt the punitive expedition, proceeded to Khiva with a Cossack escort on orders from Tashkent and distributed ammunition to the khan's militia. Evidently impressed by this show of Russia's support for Isfendiyar, Shammi-kel and the other Turkoman leaders, although as yet undefeated, decided to make peace. Assisted by Lykoshin, Islam-hodja on January 25, 1913, concluded a peace agreement with the Turkomans at Kunya-Urgench, whereby the khan abandoned the new taxes but levied a fine of 110,000 tillas (198,000 rubles) on the Turkomans. The rebel leaders went to Khiva as voluntary hostages for the payment of the fine.[15]

The revolt of 1912–1913 had unfortunate results for Khiva. On Isfendiyar's orders Islam-hodja was assassinated in 1913, probably at the instigation of his enemy Nazar-beg. Tashkent, which had backed Khiva's tough policy toward the Turkomans, was disgusted with Isfendiyar's leniency toward the defeated rebels. On November 6, 1913, Governor General Samsonov advised the khan through Colonel Lykoshin that it would be dangerous to liberate the hostages, but Isfendiyar did so anyway, perhaps out of fear of another uprising if he did not. Samsonov subsequently directed the commandant of the Amu-Darya Otdel not to interfere directly in future disputes between the khan and his Turkoman subjects unless Russian subjects were attacked or the capital or the khan was in immediate danger.[16]

World War I brought further problems for Khiva. When Governor General Samsonov was transferred to an active command at the front in August 1914, his place in Tashkent was taken by General F. V. von Martson, who as acting governor general administered Russian Turkestan for the next twenty-two months. Martson, who favored the annexation of Khiva, followed the curious policy of taking bribes from Isfendiyar while at the same time favoring the Turkomans against him. Over a two-year period the Russian military in Turkestan and Petrograd extorted more than a quarter of a million rubles from Isfendiyar under the guise of contributions to the war effort, leading the khan to understand that this money would secure him favor in high places in Russia and, more concretely, arms for his militia. Colonel Kolosovskii, Lykoshin's successor at Petro-Aleksandrovsk, acted in this unsavory business as agent both for himself and his superiors. About three quarters of the total extorted from the khan, or 187,000 rubles, went into Kolosovskii's own pockets. At least 40,000 rubles went to Minister of War V. A. Sukhomlinov. Other recipients of large sums, besides Martson, were Lieutenant General A. S. Galkin, the governor of Sir-Darya Oblast, and General Tseil, a member of the war ministry. In order to pay these exactions, Isfendiyar resorted to new taxes, which were in part responsible for the next outbreak among the Turkomans.[17]

The Turkoman Revolt of 1915

During the latter half of 1914 occurred a new series of incidents over the perennial problems of water and taxes. On one occasion Isfendiyar ordered the water supply of the Turkoman peasants around Takhta and Ilyali cut off. On another occasion some Turko-

mans killed a Khivan tax collector near Takhta. In January 1915
with Martson's approval the khan sent another punitive expedition
against the Turkomans and imposed a new fine of 611,000 tillas
(almost 1,100,000 rubles).[18] There was no open resistance, but the
Turkomans were growing increasingly restless. Two months later
Isfendiyar finally provoked an open rebellion by arresting one of the
Yomut chieftains, Bakhshi Shah Murad, after a series of robberies
in the steppe. On March 22 the Turkomans attacked the capital of
the khanate itself under the leadership of Djunaid-khan, another
Yomut chief. Martson ordered Colonel Kolosovskii to go to Khiva
in person to liberate Bakhshi Shah Murad and to offer Isfendiyar
refuge in Petro-Aleksandrovsk if the need arose. Russia's intervention on the side of the Turkomans encouraged them to renew their
rebellion, and by April 9 several Khivan towns were in their hands.
Hoping to turn Russia against the Turkomans, Isfendiyar tried to
blame the uprising on German agitators, but Russia found no evidence to support the charge. Martson suggested to Kolosovskii that
he use both promises and threats to persuade the Turkomans to end
their rebellion. Martson himself toyed with the idea of Isfendiyar's
removal as a means of pacifying the rebels, but the foreign ministry
warned that it would be extremely dangerous to Russia for the khan
to be forced out of his country by Turkoman threats.[19]

At the beginning of May 1915 Isfendiyar sent an embassy to
Tashkent to request either arms or Russian troops to help suppress
the revolt. In execution of a previous promise to the khan, Minister
of War Sukhomlinov had already dispatched two thousand late-model
rifles and four hundred thousand cartridges, but Martson, who was
opposed to the arming of Khiva, held up the arms shipment at
Chardjui. On May 8 Sukhomlinov wired Kolosovskii "to suppress
with fire and sword the revolt of the Khivan Turkomans."[20] A week
later the war minister instructed Martson to the same effect, arguing
that since the khan could not rely on the Turkomans to keep the
peace, Russia must either give him arms to enforce their obedience
or herself undertake the task of maintaining order in Khiva. That
task would be an unwelcome addition to Russia's burdens because
her military strength was already strained to the utmost by the war
against Germany and Austria-Hungary. Martson nevertheless ignored
Sukhomlinov's instructions, which had the foreign ministry's backing, and continued to withhold the arms from Isfendiyar, while
urging on St. Petersburg the justice of the Turkomans' case against
the khan.[21]

Early in June Martson again sent Kolosovskii to Khiva to arbitrate a settlement of the three-month-old revolt. Kolosovskii summoned the Turkoman representatives to the capital for peace negotiations, but being distrustful of Isfendiyar, they halted twenty miles northwest of Khiva with their escort of five hundred armed cavalry. There on June 7 the Turkomans were attacked without provocation by fifteen hundred of the khan's troops, whom they soon put to flight. Although no further hostilities took place, Tashkent sent Major General Geppener, an aide to the governor of the Samarkand Oblast, to Khiva with plenipotentiary powers to pacify the country. Geppener, who arrived in Khiva on June 22, concluded that the khan and his government were chiefly, if not wholly, to blame for the khanate's troubles. After promising the Turkomans that Russia would take steps to remove the causes of their discontent, Geppener on June 30 arranged a peace agreement between the rebels and the khan.[22]

The settlement that Martson and Geppener imposed on Khiva after the revolt of 1915 marked an important departure from the principle of nonintervention. A small body of Russian troops was stationed permanently in the capital for the khan's protection, with Isfendiyar paying 150,000 rubles for the construction of barracks. Isfendiyar's Russian bodyguard—the realization after two centuries of Peter the Great's ambition—differed from the troops quartered in Bukhara in that it was intended solely to defend the khan against his domestic enemies. Geppener appeased the Turkomans by exiling two of the most aggressively anti-Turkoman members of the government, including Sheikh Nazar-beg. The Turkomans were allowed to determine what compensation they owed for the material losses their rebellion had caused. Geppener told the Turkomans that they should feel free to bring their grievances to him, to the khan, or to the commandant of the Amu-Darya Otdel. Finally, the Turkomans were allowed to retain their arms.[23]

Russia interfered in 1915 to an unprecedented extent in the internal affairs of her protectorate on the grounds that the khan was unable to restore order on his own—at least not without the arms Martson withheld from him. By strengthening the hand of the Turkomans without finding permanent solutions to their grievances, however, Martson and Geppener actually ensured the continuance of political instability in Khiva. This may very well have been what they were intending. Martson's idea of a permanent solution was annexation: he argued that the Turkomans' grievances would never

be settled in any other way, and on September 4, 1915, he urged
Petrograd to abolish the "semi-independence of Khiva." The foreign
ministry nevertheless persisted in defending Khiva's autonomy. On
January 12, 1916, Foreign Minister Sazonov reminded the minister
of war that the time was hardly propitious for assuming the burdens of government in Khiva and Bukhara.[24] On January 14 the
foreign ministry's representative in Tashkent, V. F. Minorskii, the
governor general's diplomatic attaché, reported his conviction that
the pro-Turkoman policy of Martson, Geppener, and Kolosovskii
was systematically undermining the khan's prestige and encouraging
the Turkomans to persist in their insubordination.[25]

The Turkoman Revolt of 1916 and the Russo-Khivan Agreement

At the very moment that Minorskii was drafting his report,
trouble was again brewing in Khiva, this time among the Uzbeg
population as well as among the Turkomans. Forced collection of
taxes, disputes over water rights, and a levy of girls for the khan's
harem were the immediate causes of the new wave of discontent,
in which the hakim of Khodjeili, Ovez-hodja, cooperated with
Djunaid-khan in an attempt to depose Isfendiyar and his divan-begi,
Muhammad Vafa Bakalov. On January 10, 1916, a crowd of five
to six hundred men led by Ovez-hodja began a march on Khiva
from Khodjeili. Other Uzbegs from Kipchak, Mangit, Shah-abat,
Urgench, Manak, and Gurlen joined the marchers, who then
totaled two to three thousand. On January 18 three thousand Turkomans joined the march near the capital. The marchers demanded
that the divan-begi listen to their grievances, but Khiva's Russian
garrison soon dispersed the demonstration.[26]

The new uprising was merely beginning. In early February
Djunaid-khan led the Turkomans in open revolt and declared himself khan of Khiva. On February 13 Djunaid defeated Isfendiyar's
Russian guard, seized the capital, and deposed the khan. A ransom
of sixty thousand rubles was collected from Isfendiyar, while three
of his ministers, including Bakalov, were killed. The city itself was
plundered for three days by the Turkomans.[27]

The new revolt, the most serious in Khiva under the Russian
protectorate, finally influenced Petrograd to overrule Tashkent's policy of favoring the Turkomans against the khan. On February 11

the ministers of foreign affairs and war wired General von Martson reprovingly: "Since the present uprising of the Turkomans is apparently a result of the gentleness shown them earlier, it seems necessary now to teach them a severe lesson . . . Take care to strengthen the khan's authority, which has been undermined." Lieutenant General A. S. Galkin, governor of Sir-Darya Oblast, led a punitive expedition to Khiva and on February 15 expelled the Turkomans from the capital. A month later the rebels gave battle for the last time, after which Djunaid-khan fled across the Kara Kum Desert to Persia and thence to Afghanistan. For two and a half months, from mid-March until early June, Galkin systematically laid waste the Turkoman districts and levied a huge indemnity of 3,500,000 rubles.[28] General von Kaufman's methods were thus repeated after forty-three years as Russia tried again to ensure the political stability of her Khivan protectorate.

The 1916 revolt in Khiva not only put an end to Tashkent's pro-Turkoman policy but also made clear Khiva's need for a more permanent solution to her troubles than the unsatisfactory arrangement of 1915. The khanate's primary need was for reforms to correct the conditions underlying the discontent of both Uzbegs and Turkomans. General A. N. Kuropatkin, Turkestan's last governor general, recognized this need, and upon taking office in the spring of 1916 he presented a plan to establish a military commissar in Khiva responsible to Tashkent and charged with aiding the khan to pacify the country and to raise the well-being of the population. Kuropatkin also uncovered the corruption and extortion practiced by the military in Turkestan since 1914. On December 16, 1916, Isfendiyar himself revealed to the commandant of the Turkestan *okhrana* (secret police) the extent of the sums he had been forced to pay.[29]

Kuropatkin's project for a military commissar in Khiva, which was approved in principle by Nicholas II on July 17, 1916, was similar to the proposals that Logofet and others had been advocating for Bukhara since the 1890's. The governor general's plan took final form in the agreement that he concluded with Isfendiyar on January 29, 1917.[30] The commissar's duties were to keep the Russian authorities in Turkestan informed on the situation in the protectorate, to exercise close supervision over the Khivan administration, and to aid the khan in carrying out the reforms that Isfendiyar had recognized as necessary in January 1911 but which had never been implemented. The khan promised: to take all necessary steps to meet the

needs of the population, both Uzbegs and Turkomans, and to reconcile the two groups; to improve the roads and river crossings and
to build feeder lines when a railroad was finally constructed through
the khanate; and to give special protection to the undertakings of
Russian subjects. At Isfendiyar's request Russian troops were to remain temporarily in Khiva to ensure domestic order. The khan was
to pay for the maintenance of these troops as well as of the military commissar and his staff. Until Khiva had made some progress
toward internal reorganization and development, however, the khan's
contribution toward the maintenance of the military commissariat
would be limited to 156,000 rubles a year, and Russia would continue to bear the expense of keeping troops in the country.

The Russo-Khivan agreement was a landmark in the development of Russia's relations with her Central Asian protectorates. St.
Petersburg's policy of nonintervention had proved unworkable in the
face of the khan's continuing inability to provide Khiva with the
political stability that was a precondition of that policy. Still hoping
to avoid the burdens of annexation, Russia followed a third course—
close supervision of the khan's government and active participation
in the introduction of necessary reforms. This course was not entirely new, for it had been foreshadowed by the decision of the
Council of Ministers in 1910 with regard to Bukhara, but it had
been rendered ineffective on that occasion by the foreign ministry's
commitment to nonintervention. In Khiva in 1917, however, the
execution of the new policy was entrusted to the governor general
of Turkestan, acting through a military commissar in Khiva, and
Tashkent was traditionally much less hesitant to interfere in the
khanates. It could well be argued that the Russian military was
hardly the best instrument for achieving political and economic
reform in a backward and dependent country, but no other organ
of the imperial government was likely to undertake the task. If the
new course had been successful in Khiva, it might well have been
followed eventually in Bukhara as well. But the time for experiments
was over. Twenty-nine days after the signing of the agreement between General Kuropatkin and Khan Isfendiyar, the empire of the
Romanovs was no more. The ultimate fate of Khiva and Bukhara
was to be decided by Russians who owed no allegiance to the policies of the past.

Part Four / Revolution

Rigistan and Entrance to the Citadel, Bukhara

14 / The Provisional Government and the Protectorates

The February Revolution and Central Asia

The sudden collapse of the autocracy in February 1917 inaugurated for Russia a period of great expectations but limited accomplishments, in the field of imperial policy as elsewhere. As both moderates and radicals were dedicated to the achievement of equal rights for all citizens, on March 20 the Provisional Government swept away all of the old regime's legal restrictions on members of minority nationalities. Beyond that basic point, however, there was little concern among the intelligentsia, to whom political power had passed so unexpectedly, over the problems posed by the multinational character of the Russian state. To liberals and socialists alike the national problem was a transitory one—a by-product of autocracy, according to the Kadets, or of class oppression, according to the Social Democrats. The solution of the national problem would likewise be a by-product of either the liberals' democratic society or the socialists' classless society. Neither wing of the intelligentsia was prepared to preside over the dismemberment or serious weakening of the Russian state along ethnic lines. Socialists especially, although liberals as well, saw themselves as bearers of a universal mission: the fate of the new Russia and of all its peoples, including the inhabitants of Russia's two Central Asian protectorates, properly belonged in the hands of the revolutionary government.[1]

In Central Asia the fundamental relationship of colony to metropolis thus remained unaltered, although, as befitted a regime committed to the democratization of Russian political life, the Provisional Government attempted to remodel the colonial machinery. On April 7 Petrograd replaced the military governor general in Tashkent with a civilian Turkestan Committee, consisting of five Russians and four natives, with one of the Russians serving as chairman. Kuropatkin, the last governor general, had been arrested by the Tashkent Soviet a week earlier. The powers and responsibilities of the Turkestan Committee were essentially those of the former governors general, including authority "to act in the name of the Provisional Government" within the old government-general "and also in Khiva and Bukhara."[2]

Responsibility for diplomatic relations with Bukhara continued as it had under the Romanovs, being shared between Tashkent and the foreign ministry; the only change was to rename the Imperial Russian Political Agency in Bukhara, which became the Russian Residency on March 17. A. Ia. Miller, the last tsarist appointee to the office, suggested the change in title to allay the "mistrust" evidenced toward him by "the mass of the local Russian population" in the khanate.[3] Foreign Minister P. N. Miliukov concurred in the change, observing that "resident" was as apt as "political agent" in describing an official whose functions were analogous to those of the English representatives to vassal Indian courts, who sometimes bore the one title and sometimes the other.[4] The change in title was purely formal and no more signified a change in Petrograd's policy than did the subsequent remodeling of the office of governor general.

At the level of local government the new Russian regime introduced somewhat more significant changes. On March 8 Governor General Kuropatkin, acting on instructions from Petrograd, invited the householders in all towns to elect municipal dumas of twelve to fifteen members, half of whom in each case were to be Russians. Each duma would in turn elect a three-to-five-member executive committee to administer local affairs. The four Russian settlements in Bukhara responded by setting up the new local organs of government promptly—Chardjui and New Bukhara by March 12, Kerki and Termez during the next few weeks. Moslem residents of the four settlements, even though they might be Russian nationals, were barred from voting for the new bodies.[5] The executive committees took over civil administration of the settlements from the civil governor in New Bukhara and from the garrison commandants in the other three towns. The democratic revolution had reached even the remote outposts of Western civilization along the Amu-Darya.

When the political agency was renamed on March 17, it was divested of its civil authority over the settlements, which had dated from their foundation. The residency maintained informal contact, however, with the new municipal institutions in the person of P. P. Vvedenskii, who had been attached to the political agency since 1916 and was also a member of the New Bukhara Executive Committee. The political agent's former authority over the settlements as a group was entrusted to an oblast executive committee (subordinate to the Turkestan Committee) established by the First Oblast Congress of Executive Committees of the Russian Settlements at the beginning of May. A month later Vvedenskii, by then deputy director of the residency, was appointed to the newly created post of oblast commissar of the Russian settlements.[6] Thus, after a lapse of less than three months, civil authority over the four settlements was again entrusted to a member of Russia's diplomatic mission in the khanate. The Provisional Government had by this time recognized that the affairs of the Russian settlements had a potentially vital bearing on Russia's relations with her protectorate and ought therefore to be subject to the supervision of the agency charged with handling those relations.

That the affairs of the settlements had assumed such importance was a result of the extension to Central Asia, along with the local organs of the Provisional Government, of the local counterparts to that government's powerful rival—the Petrograd Soviet. Within less than a week of the arrival of the news of Nicholas II's abdication, the Russian population of Turkestan and Bukhara had begun to imitate the example of their cousins at home by forming extralegal soviets. Soviets of workers' and soldiers' deputies were created in Chardjui and New Bukhara on March 9 and 10; soldiers' soviets were organized in the garrison at Kerki within a month and at Termez by the beginning of May. The Bukharan soviets held their own oblast congresses and participated in the Turkestan krai and all-Russian congresses as well.[7] Led by SR's and Mensheviks, as were their Russian counterparts, the soviets in the khanate enjoyed from the beginning a good deal of support among the Russian population—often more than the municipal dumas and executive committees with whom the soviets were frequently at odds. That the local representatives of the Provisional Government were often, like Miller and Vvedenskii, holdovers from the old regime encouraged the soviets to interfere in policy-making and administration.[8] The formation of representative political institutions, particularly the soviets, among the Russian population of Bukhara created a new and effective source of pressure for modernizing reforms.

The Emir's Manifesto

The members of the small native reform movement in Bukhara were as quick to react to the news of the autocracy's collapse as were the Russians who lived in their midst. Previously, when the emir had turned a deaf ear to their pleas for reform, there had been nowhere else to turn. Now, suddenly, there was a new regime in Petrograd, committed to a new order in Russia and, they hoped, willing to use its power to compel the emir to act accordingly. The Bukharan Djadids lost no time in wiring the Provisional Government and N. S. Chkheidze, chairman of the Petrograd Soviet, to put pressure on the emir to grant the reforms so long awaited.[9] Emir Alim, meanwhile, anxiously conveyed to Miller and directly to Tashkent and Petrograd his congratulations on the formation of the new government, his protestations of loyalty and friendship, and most important, his hopes for the continuance of the traditional relationship between Russia and Bukhara.[10]

Petrograd responded to the appeals from the Djadids and the emir by informing Alim that the new order in Russia was incompatible with the continued existence in her Bukharan protectorate of "a people without rights."[11] Both of the traditional schools of thought on the Bukharan question were already finding new spokesmen in the Russian capital. Minister of Justice A. F. Kerensky was inclined toward the annexation of Bukhara and Khiva, while Miliukov, relying perhaps on the professional personnel of the foreign ministry's Central Asiatic Department, favored allowing the native rulers to adjust to the "new trends" by promulgating reforms and perhaps even initiating a very limited form of representation for the propertied classes in Bukhara.[12]

Yielding to the pressure from Russia, Alim on March 18 promised Miller that he would begin the reforms by declaring an amnesty, lightening criminal punishments, establishing a printing press, and permitting the publication of newspapers. Alim also authorized his kush-begi, the relatively liberal Nasr Allah, to meet with Miller and N. A. Shulga, first secretary of the residency, to work out plans for basic fiscal, administrative, judicial, and educational reforms. Nasr Allah spoke for the emir in insisting that all reforms be based strictly on the Sharia to avoid provoking the mullahs' hostility against Alim and Russia, and from the beginning Miller heartily endorsed the wisdom of this approach, citing "the extreme backwardness and fanaticism of the local population." By March 20 Miller and his staff had worked out, in consultation with the emir's government, a draft manifesto in which Alim was to announce to his subjects the impending changes. The manifesto promised "the eradication of abuses and irregularities" in the Bukharan government and its reform on the basis of the Sharia and in the light of "progress and useful knowledge." Specifically, the document promised judicial and tax reform, promotion of economic development and education, a salaried civil service, prohibition of bribe-taking among government officials, representative self-government for the capital city, separation of the state treasury from the emir's private fortune, a government budget, a government printing office to produce "publications of social utility," and a general amnesty.[13]

For two and a half weeks after dispatching the draft manifesto to Petrograd for the Provisional Government's approval, Miller anxiously awaited permission from the foreign ministry for Alim to promulgate the announcement of reforms. The situation in the Bukharan capital grew daily more tense as the mullahs learned of the impending changes and began to express their concern for the faith and the established order. Their fears were heightened when Alim, at Miller's urging, replaced Burhan ad-Din, the ultraconservative kazi-kalan, and the ishan-rais with men more acceptable to the Djadids and more sympathetic to the cause of moderate reform. While urging upon Petrograd the necessity for quick action to avoid trouble in Bukhara, Miller tried through the emir's government to reassure the clergy and personally attempted to hold the Djadids in check.[14]

Not yet one month old, the Provisional Government was occupied with much more pressing matters than the question of reform in Bukhara: general democratic reforms such as the abolition of all legal disabilities based on faith or nationality; the first stirrings of agrarian revolt in mid-March; the acute problem of keeping the cities and the army supplied with food; and the dilemma of maintaining discipline in the army and of continuing to wage a war whose annexationist goals were rejected by the Petrograd Soviet and the masses. However, the Provisional Government had found time by the end of March to consider the Bukharan question and submit to Miller its suggestion for including in the manifesto some sort of representative legislative body or *madjlis*. Citing Bukhara's backwardness as an argument against the introduction of representative government, the resident predicted that "a majority of the madjlis would consist of fanatical reactionaries" and warned that "the creation of a madjlis and the granting of self-determination to the local elements, a majority of whom, I repeat, are opponents of reforms, would lead to anarchy and the overthrow of the emir as an apostate and to an anti-Russian movement on a pan-Islamic base."[15]

While Miller's draft manifesto was still under consideration, Governor General Kuropatkin offered his advice on the Bukharan question. Kuropatkin, whom Miller had kept informed on developments in the khanate, approved of the resident's draft but suggested to Miliukov that Russia could best avoid the necessity of annexing Bukhara and maintain her as an "autonomous region, subordinate to Russia, ruled by an emir" by giving the resident formal supervisory authority over the Bukharan government. In short, Kuropatkin proposed applying to Bukhara "the system, with necessary changes, which I have projected for a military commissariat in Khiva." Miller was as adamantly opposed to Kuropatkin's suggestion as he had been to Petrograd's proposal for a madjlis. In view of the existence in Bukhara of an "organized liberal group," small but vocal and growing in influence, Miller felt that it would be a serious mistake for Russia to arrogate to herself the direct execution of reforms. Such a course would turn against Russia both the advocates and the opponents of change in the khanate. It would be much more politic to work with the emir's officials and attempt to reconcile both liberals and conservatives to reforms undertaken by their own government.[16]

While impatiently awaiting Petrograd's approval of the draft manifesto, Miller elaborated his own plans for the machinery to implement the reforms. Alim had indicated his intention of creating local commissions, composed of prominent Bukharans from private life, to work out fundamental reforms, but Miller agreed with the Djadids that such commissions would be inadequate to such an enormous undertaking and would need Russian guidance if the cause of reform were to be successful—"without our people on the scene all proclaimed reforms will remain a dead letter," the resident bluntly told Petrograd. Miller proposed that Russian technical advisers in New Bukhara staff centralized departments of agriculture, finance, trade and industry, education, post and telegraph, public works, and public health. The Russian resident would preside over a council composed of the leading personnel of the various departments, whose task would be to work out and supervise all necessary reforms. Final approval of reforms would be obtained by the resident from the emir's government. The departments would work together with the native commissions while gradually replacing them. At the local level, representatives of the seven central departments would be present "to see that the reforms are actually realized"; and as a further guarantee, the resident would delegate six regional inspectors, stationed throughout the khanate, to head a system of thirty-four Russian Tatars who would serve as directors of chancellery under each of the provincial begs, which would in effect deprive the begs of any independent authority. Funds from the Russian customs revenue collected on the Bukharan-Afghan frontier or, alternatively, from the Bukharan treasury would pay for the maintenance of this rather extensive body of Russian "advisers."[17] Despite Miller's strong objections to Kuropatkin's proposal for extending to Bukhara his earlier plan for Khiva, the resident had devised administrative machinery which, even in the absence of any formal supervisory power over the emir's government, would have resulted in Russia's involvement in the internal life of Bukhara to fully as great a degree as under Kuropatkin's plan.

After increasingly anxious pleas from Miller for immediate promulgation of the manifesto in order to prevent trouble from both reactionaries and reformers, which would place the Russian community in the khanate in an extremely vulnerable and defenseless position, Petrograd finally approved both the draft manifesto and Miller's proposed machinery for implementing reforms with Russian "advisers."[18] In effect, the Provisional Government thus decided to continue and apply more broadly the policy of supervised reform in its Central Asian protectorates that the tsarist regime had adopted toward Khiva in its last weeks. On April 7, 1917, Emir Alim signed the manifesto as Miller had drafted it with the single addition, to placate the democrats in Petrograd, of a vague promise to support "the further development of self-government in the khanate of Bukhara to the extent that there proves a need for this."[19]

The Aftermath of the Manifesto

An invited audience of some two hundred clerics, dignitaries, and merchants, plus a few Russians representing the residency and the soviets of New Bukhara and Samarkand, attended the formal reading of the manifesto in the citadel in Bukhara on the morning of April 7. In the afternoon the Djadids, attended by representatives of the Samarkand Soviet, met to discuss their future course of action in the light of the emir's apparent acceptance of all their demands. The rift that had for several years been growing within the Djadid movement between moderates in favor of cultural activities and radicals clamoring for political action now took the form of a division between those who favored cooperation with their reforming monarch and those who, distrusting Alim, wanted to remain an opposition group. The immediate problem was whether to stage a public demonstration on the following day. Abd al-Vahid Burkhanov, a writer and petty official who was chairman of the Djadid central committee, led the moderates in opposing a demonstration on the ground that it might frighten the emir into the arms of the conservatives and serve as a pretext for reneging on his promises of reform. The radicals, led by Faizullah Khodzhaev, nineteen-year old son of a wealthy merchant long associated with Djadidism, and Abd ar-Rauf Fitrat, the writer, feared that the passivity of the Bukharan masses would allow the emir to escape with purely insignificant reforms unless something was done to prevent this. A demonstration thanking Alim for the manifesto could serve to publicize the points of the manifesto, as yet but little known to the masses, and thereby commit the emir to the cause of reform. Despite Miller's sharp warning against any demonstration, the radical minority, with the assistance of the guests from the Samarkand Soviet, persuaded all but a hard core of the moderates to go along with the demonstration.[20]

On April 8 over a thousand demonstrators marched in the emir's capital, but they soon discovered that they had competition from a considerably larger counterdemonstration organized by the clerical forces, which manifested violent hostility to the proponents of reform, including the recently appointed kazi-kalan and ishan-rais. The fact that the proreform demonstrators included numbers of Shiites and Bukharan Jews further incensed their opponents. To avoid an open clash, the Djadids dispersed their followers and dispatched a three-man delegation to the kush-begi to assure him of their peaceful intentions. These three were the first of approximately thirty Djadids arrested and imprisoned in the citadel during the next few hours. The prisoners were subjected to the traditional Bukharan methods of punishment, which in the case of several meant seventy-five lashes of the whip.[21]

The arrest of some of the Djadids and the flight of the majority from the capital to New Bukhara did not immediately halt the mass protest, led by the clergy, against the reformers and the manifesto. Popular disorders continued in the capital throughout April 8 and 9. During the night of the eighth Miller, backed by the New Bukhara Soviet, requested a company of troops from Samarkand (about 150 miles by rail from New Bukhara), and the following morning, because of the continuing disorders, he raised the request to a regiment armed with machine guns. By the afternoon of the ninth the company first requested had arrived in New Bukhara, accompanied by a delegation from the Samarkand Soviet led by I. V. Chertov, the Socialist Revolutionary chairman of the Samarkand Oblast Soviet. Miller had meanwhile sent a note to the Bukharan government demanding the restoration of order, charging the emir and his officials with responsibility for the safety of Russians in the capital as well as of the Djadids, and requesting the expulsion from the city of Burhan ad-Din, the former kazi-kalan and a leader of the ultra-conservatives. Not until the troops from Samarkand arrived, however, did the situation return to normal. Impressed by this show of force, Alim yielded to Miller's demand that the ten Djadids still under arrest be released. Not trusting the native regime, the newly arrived troops formed a fifty-man escort, which was allowed to enter the citadel and liberate the prisoners. On April 10 in an audience with the emir Miller and representatives of the New Bukhara and Samarkand soviets placated him with a promise to ban all demonstrations in the future.[22]

The abortive demonstration of April 8 and its repercussions shattered the precarious groundwork Miller had been laying for the past month. The hostility between the Djadids and the clerical zealots was now in the open. Relations between the residency and the Russian element in the khanate had also been irreparably damaged. Backed by the radical Djadids, the representatives from the Samarkand Soviet began to press for the dismissal of Miller and Shulga, charging that the residency was in league with the emir's government to thwart reform. At first reluctant, the New Bukhara Soviet eventually joined the attack. Miller requested the recall of Chertov and his group and an official investigation of their charges, but he also offered his resignation to Petrograd, claiming that his usefulness in the post had been destroyed.[23]

The Djadids, now referred to more and more frequently as

Young Bukharans, were thoroughly disorganized in the wake of their unsuccessful demonstration. The moderates hastily elected a new central committee, headed by Muhiddin Mansur, a wealthy merchant and old Djadid who had recently returned from exile in Transcaspia. Blaming the radicals for the April 8 fiasco, the moderates devoted all their energy to negotiating with the emir through Miller to obtain an amnesty for themselves, an end to persecution of advocates of reform, and the legalization of political activity in the khanate. Although pessimistic about the chances for a rapprochement between the Djadids and the native regime, Miller agreed to try.[24] He obtained the government's promise to allow the Djadids to return to the capital and also persuaded the kush-begi to take advantage of the Djadids' peace overture by staging a public reconciliation and appealing to the conservatives to submit to the emir's will on the question of reform. The gathering called for this purpose began as planned on the afternoon of April 14 in the citadel, with Miller, Vvedenskii, and Shulga present to witness the emir's sincerity. The mullahs and mudarrises in the audience, however, disrupted the proceedings with their outcries of concern for the faith and of hostility to the manifesto of April 7. Alim left the audience chamber, and Miller and Vvedenskii spent the next several hours in vain trying to persuade the mullahs and officials of the manifesto's complete compatibility with the Sharia and Islam in general, while a hostile mob gathered outside the citadel to demand the execution of the apostate Djadids. The Djadids themselves believed that the emir, with Miller's assistance, had treacherously trapped them. In the face of the kush-begi's attempts to get them to repudiate their commitment to broad reforms, the Djadids stood fast. The residency's Cossack escort meanwhile prevented the mob from breaking into the citadel, and by 10:30 P.M. Miller, after having telephoned to New Bukhara for troop support, escorted the Young Bukharans out of the citadel and back to the Russian settlement.[25]

The attempt of Miller and the moderate Djadids at a rapprochement with the emir's government had failed, giving rise instead to even greater hostility and tension. Miller's position was now thoroughly compromised, the moderate Djadids were discredited, and the emir was less inclined to think seriously of reform. The conduct of the kush-begi on the fourteenth having convinced Miller that he was deeply involved with the opponents of reform, the resident demanded his replacement the following day. Nasr Allah, who no

longer commanded the confidence of either reformers or conservatives, was in fact relieved of his duties on April 15 and formally
dismissed a week later, but the choice of an ultraconservative as his
successor indicated that Miller's influence at the emir's court had
declined sharply. Petrograd's dilatoriness in demonstrating its support for Miller's draft manifesto, the residency's inability to prevent
the April 8 demonstration, and the rising distrust by the Djadids and
the soviets toward the residency had combined with the violence
of the clerical and popular opposition to convince Alim that he was
unwise in attaching so much importance to the demands of the new
regime in Russia and so little to the feelings of his own subjects.
Over the protest of the Young Bukharans, Alim on the twenty-
second appointed Nizam ad-Din Urgandji as the new kush-begi and
at the same time selected several other ultraconservatives for high
office.[26]

Nizam ad-Din made little effort to hide his sympathy with the
clerical zealots. Before his appointment he had favored the assassination of the leading Djadids, and once installed as kush-begi, he
distributed funds from the state treasury to support the reactionaries.
With such support from the government and with encouragement
from Moslem clerics in Turkestan and elsewhere in Russia, the Bukharan mullahs and clergy became bolder. In April they agitated
among the peasantry for a holy war against the Russians and their
Young Bukharan allies. On June 7 they wrecked the printing office
that the emir had just opened. In mid-July they campaigned successfully for the restoration to office of the former kazi-kalan, Burhan
ad-Din, whose dismissal Miller had secured in late March.[27]

While yielding to pressure from the opponents of change, Alim
found himself in an ever more difficult position. Until the very confused situation in Russia should clear up, he felt the necessity of continuing to convince the residency and Petrograd of his commitment
to implement reforms, albeit "prudently and gradually." The emir
even went so far as to introduce standardized legal fees and regular
salaries for the bureaucracy in early May and to set up the first printing press in history in his capital at the end of the same month.
Although Alim did not comply with the residency's demand for
the dismissal of Nizam ad-Din, he deprived the kush-begi of jurisdiction over the state treasury and appointed a deputy kush-begi to
serve as a check on him.[28] Whereas such gestures served to pacify
Russia, they weakened the emir's credit among the clerical zealots,

who by mid-May were beginning to discuss Alim's replacement by a more staunchly conservative member of the ruling house. Caught between the opposing forces, Alim longed to escape. He considered a trip to the Caucasus for his "health" but was dissuaded by S. V. Chirkin, Miller's successor, who warned that the emir's return to Bukhara could not be guaranteed. Alim then decided to take a summer vacation in Kermine, his father's old retreat, away from the tensions of the capital; this time the conservatives, over Chirkin's protests, forced him to abandon any idea of leaving.[29]

The effectiveness of the residency as a vehicle of influence over the Bukharan government continued to diminish. The tension between Miller and the Samarkand mission headed by Chertov had reached a peak on April 16, when in the aftermath of the resident's disastrous failure to reconcile the emir and the Young Bukharans, the Samarkand group finally prevailed on the New Bukhara Soviet to place Miller under house arrest, while Chertov and his assistants took over the residency, ignoring the protests of the Russian business community in the khanate.[30] The conflict was resolved only after the arrival on the eighteenth of P. I. Preobrazhenskii and Major General A. A. Davletshin, members of the Turkestan Committee sent from Tashkent to clear up the confused situation in Bukhara. Preobrazhenskii's and Davletshin's investigation confirmed the views of the Turkestan Committee, which had already expressed its complete confidence in Miller's handling of the situation. Yet since the soviets' hostility had undermined Miller's continued usefulness in office, he was allowed to depart for Petrograd, and the residency was temporarily turned over on April 22 to Chirkin, a career diplomat, until a new resident could be appointed.[31]

Assisted by Vvedenskii and backed by Tashkent, Chirkin continued along the course marked out by Miller. Although continuing to express confidence in the emir as an agent of reform, Chirkin and Vvedenskii repeatedly urged Petrograd to select and send out in the immediate future the advisers without whom significant reforms were unthinkable. Even with the help of such advisers, Miller's successors recognized that fundamental reform would be a prolonged and gradual process. They agreed with Miller, whom the events of April 14 had convinced that except for about two hundred Young Bukharans, there was no support among the native population for changes in the traditional life of Bukharan society. To implement a program of reform in the face of such overwhelming opposition would require the backing of a substantial number of Russian troops, which was not feasible at a time when Russia's armed forces were being taxed to the limit on the German and Austrian fronts; moreover, the use of Russian troops might provoke a general uprising throughout the Moslem areas of Russia and raise the threat of Afghan intervention in Russian Central Asia. Chirkin and Vvedenskii not only took this same pessimistic view of the situation but went even further: they attempted to placate the native conservatives by reducing the number of Russian troops at New Bukhara from four companies to one.[32]

Relations between the residency, on the one hand, and the Young Bukharans and the New Bukhara Soviet, on the other, continued to be strained after Miller's departure. The soviet kept pressing the residency to explain why the promised reforms were being delayed, while the residency in turn urged the removal from the khanate of native radical leaders like Faizullah Khodzhaev. In July the oblast congress of soviets in New Bukhara signified its lack of confidence in the residency by establishing, over Chirkin's angry protests, a committee on Bukharan affairs. In desperation Chirkin and Vvedenskii asked Petrograd with increasing urgency for the immediate dispatch of a new resident and the promised advisers so that a start could be made on the long discussed and much delayed reforms. Only thus, the residency argued, could Russia rescue the emir from the clerical zealots and the irresponsible revolutionaries among his own subjects and in the New Bukhara Soviet and thereby avoid the necessity of occupying the khanate in force.[33]

From Petrograd, where the Provisional Government's own position was far from secure as the revolution broadened and deepened, no decisive action on the Bukharan problem was forthcoming. The foreign ministry, in the hands of the wealthy industrialist M. I. Tereshchenko after May 5, seemed to be having second thoughts on the program of reform, for by the beginning of July Petrograd was proposing a complete reconsideration of the April 7 manifesto by the liberal and conservative Moslem clerics of both Bukhara and Russian Turkestan. Chirkin reacted coldly to the prospect of altering the manifesto; such a move could only be a step backward. Feeling itself in no position to pursue with any vigor a new policy toward Bukhara, Petrograd fell back on the preservation of the status quo. In May Tereshchenko had made it clear that the Provisional Government had no intention of relaxing Russia's hold over Bukhara and Khiva; by July it was equally clear that Petrograd opposed a more complete integration of the two protectorates into the Russian body politic, for they were not to be represented in the projected Constituent Assembly. While marking time on the Bukharan problem, the Provisional Government continued to treat the emir much as its predecessors had, even submitting to him for his comments the names of candidates for the role of advisers on the execution of reforms.[34]

On September 30 New Bukhara finally welcomed the new resident, V. S. Elpatievskii—a lawyer, a Kadet, and one of the original members of the Turkestan Committee. By then the Provisional Government's hesitant attitude had encouraged Alim openly to request that the implementation of the promised reforms be put off indefinitely. With the assistance of the first two Russian advisers, who had arrived in August, Elpatievskii spent October trying without success to work out with the emir a preliminary plan for proceeding with the work of modernization, being always careful not again to provoke the clerical zealots. The opponents of change were considered the major threat to the emir and hence to Russia, since once more Russia's position in Bukhara was identified with the stability of the emir's throne, as it had been under the Romanovs.[35]

In the light of Russia's difficulties closer to home—the July Days, the Kornilov revolt, the war, land reform, and the general economic and political disorganization—it is not surprising that the Provisional Government found just as little time and energy at the end of its brief life as at the beginning to devote to the situation in its Central Asian protectorates. Petrograd was guided in this area primarily by the professional personnel it had inherited from the tsarist regime, who by 1917 were agreed on introducing a measure of political modernization, although not democracy, in Bukhara, if this could be done without provoking civil strife in the khanate. Most of the Provisional Government's own suggestions were in the direction of representative government for the khanate, or at least for its capital, but they were dropped in the face of opposition from the residency.[36] Russia's definition of her interests in Bukhara remained unchanged through the February Revolution: maintenance of internal law and order in the khanate so as to preclude both the necessity of a costly occupation and the possibility of foreign intervention from south of the Amu-Darya.

But the encouragement that the revolution had given to the

Young Bukharans, the formation of soviets in the Russian settlements, and the Provisional Government's own commitment to a new
political and social order meant that the necessity for fundamental
reform in Bukhara was felt much more acutely than it ever had been
before. At the same time the cause of reform was prejudiced by the
weakness of the Young Bukharans in comparison with the strong
hold of the clergy over both government and populace. Reform was
finally doomed by the indecisive behavior of the Russians, on whom
the Young Bukharans and the cause of reform depended. Incapable
of holding the confidence of either the native reformers or the Russian workers and soldiers who supported the soviet, lacking the necessary backing from Petrograd in the form of authority and men to
carry out its program, the residency ended as a completely ineffective
instrument of Russian policy, unable to compete successfully with
the clerical zealots for influence over a weak monarch.[37] The Young
Bukharans, internally divided and disillusioned with the Provisional
Government, ceased to play any significant role within the country;
Mansur and a small group of rightists seceded from the movement,
while the bulk of the membership nursed its wounds in New Bukhara under the protection of the soviet.[38]

Khiva in 1917

The February Revolution found Khan Isfendiyar wintering in
the Crimea. He returned to his country in early March, escorted by
a detachment of Russian troops under Major General Mir Badalev,
sent as Tashkent's plenipotentiary to keep order in the troubled protectorate during the transition to a new order in Russia. Isfendiyar
soon faced an unaccustomed situation. Following the example of
their counterparts in Bukhara, the Khivan Djadids, who numbered
fewer than fifty, allied themselves with the soviet formed in mid-
March in the Russian garrison at Khiva and pressed the khan to
grant freedom and reforms to his subjects. Influenced by Mir
Badalev's advice and Bukhara's example, the khan accepted the
demands of the Djadids and on April 5 promulgated a manifesto
composed for him by Husein-beg Matmuradov, the Djadid leader.
The manifesto promised civil liberties, a constitutional regime with
a madjlis and a council of *nazirs* (ministers), an electorate based on
a property qualification, a government budget and strict fiscal accounting, a salaried judiciary, new-method schools, a railroad, and

expanded telegraph and postal service. Three days later the Khivan Madjlis assembled for the first time. It was composed of thirty members, one from each beglik and ten from the capital, drawn from the clerical and propertied classes; the Djadids formed a majority of seventeen. The Madjlis promptly elected Matmuradov as prime minister and another Djadid leader, Muhammad Karim Baba Ahun, as speaker. During the next few months the Madjlis busied itself with plans for the modernization of the khanate's administration and communications and the reform of education. At the same time in each beglik a four-man committee was elected to act as a check on the hakim.[39]

The Djadids soon stumbled over the very problem that had been plaguing Khiva for decades and since 1912 in an acute form— the enmity between Turkomans and Uzbegs. All of the Djadids were Uzbegs, and at first they opposed giving the Turkomans any special representation in the Madjlis. At the urging of Mir Badalev, however, seven Turkoman tribal chieftains were eventually added to the legislative assembly. This concession did not appease the Yomut Turkomans. Encouraged by Russia's preoccupation with revolution at home and by Isfendiyar's helplessness before his Uzbeg subjects, and angered by the Djadids' lack of concern for the water and tax problems that lay close to the Turkomans' hearts, the leaders of the 1916 uprising, Shammi-kel and Kosh-mamed-khan, were by the end of May 1917 again leading their Yomut tribesmen on pillaging forays against the sedentary Uzbeg inhabitants of the khanate. With Mir Badalev's approval the Madjlis responded by voting to collect the unpaid balance of the 3,500,000-ruble indemnity levied on the rebels in the spring of 1916 by the Russian punitive expedition and to disarm the Turkomans, with force if necessary. Early in June the Madjlis turned to Russia for assistance against the Turkomans, sending a delegation of its Djadid members under Baba Ahun to Tashkent to request ammunition and troops.[40]

The Djadids' inability to cope with the perennial Turkoman problem, coupled with the Provisional Government's reluctance to get deeply involved in Khivan affairs, encouraged the conservative forces in the khanate. Led by the hakims, who resented the interference of the local elected councils, the conservatives persuaded Isfendiyar to stage a *coup d'état* during the absence of Baba Ahun and his delegation. The khan arrested most of the Djadid leaders, including Matmuradov, outlawed the party, and packed the Madjlis with conservatives. Mir Badalev apparently consented to the coup, perhaps in the belief that the Djadids' unyielding attitude toward the Turkomans was heading the khanate toward disaster.[41] Alarmed by this unfavorable turn of events, hampering the further development of representative government in Khiva, the Turkestan Committee in June dispatched a three-man commission to investigate. After conferring with Isfendiyar and Mir Badalev, the commission decided it would not be wise to attempt to undo the results of the coup.[42]

The events of June 1917 demonstrated the inadequacy of the native reform movement to the enormous tasks of political and social modernization without strong Russian backing. In the aftermath of the Djadids' failure the Turkestan Committee took up the problem of the khanate's future, and on July 25 they decided in principle to implement the agreement Kuropatkin had concluded with Isfendiyar in January for a military commissar to supervise the khan's government and the execution of necessary reforms. During the next six weeks Tashkent worked out a draft statute for the commissariat and a set of fundamental laws.[43] Khiva was to be endowed with a constitutional monarchy on the Western model, complete with the rule of law, full civil liberties, legal equality of citizens, universal suffrage, and a parliamentary system with ministerial responsibility. The Madjlis was to enjoy full control over the budget, including the khan's household and personal expenses, and was to share with the local elected councils control over the hakims. At the same time Russia was assured a permanent position of dominance in the khanate's internal affairs, and the Russian military commissar was assigned an intimate supervisory role over all branches of the Khivan government. Neither the accession of a new khan nor the amendment of the fundamental laws was legal without Russia's approval. The khan could not dissolve the Madjlis or set a date for new elections without the consent of the Russian commissar, who could also require the khan to call the Madjlis into special session. The speaker of that body was to make daily reports to the commissar, and each hakim was accountable for financial and military matters to the commissar as well as to the Madjlis. In cases of impeachment against Khivan officials, the commissar would appoint the president of the special court to hear the charges as well as the Russian judges who must constitute at least half the total membership of the court. These extensive powers, as well as his authority to call on the Russian garrison in Khiva if necessary to maintain order, were designed to enable the commissar effectively to supervise the implementation of reforms in the areas of administration, the judiciary, taxation and public finance, education, public health, irrigation, transportation, and Uzbeg-Turkoman relations.[44]

Tashkent was proposing a Western-type constitutional system with broad civil and political rights for a population to whom such notions were entirely alien. At the same time it was reposing ultimate authority in none of the organs of the Khivan government but in the Russian commissariat. The draft constitution is a testimonial to the Provisional Government's dedication to Western political and social ideals, while the statute on the commissariat indicates an awareness of the difficulty of realizing those ideals in the setting of Khiva's traditional society. Together the proposals bear witness to the Provisional Government's belief in the message of the February Revolution for the non-Russian peoples of the former empire. They were formally submitted for Petrograd's approval on September 13.

In contrast to Bukhara, the situation in Khiva could not await the deliberations of overworked ministers in Petrograd. The Turkoman raids had been gaining in intensity since the end of May and demanded Russia's immediate attention. In mid-July a regiment of Orenburg Cossacks was ordered to Khiva to pacify the Turkomans. While this regiment was in Tashkent in August en route to the khanate, the Turkestan Committee designated its commanding officer, Colonel I. M. Zaitsev, as acting military commissar in Khiva as well as commander of all Russian troops in Khiva and the Amu-Darya Otdel.[45] Upon his arrival in the khanate at the beginning of September, Zaitsev launched punitive expeditions against the troublesome Turkomans. When Djunaid-khan returned from exile in Afghanistan a week or two later and offered his services against his old rivals Shammi-kel and Kosh-mamed-khan, Zaitsev accepted him as an ally. Despite this unexpected assistance, Zaitsev made little headway against the Turkomans, in part because of the rapidly deteriorating morale of his own troops. The rank and file of the Russian garrison in Khiva, already organized in a soldiers' soviet, grew increasingly disobedient toward its officers: discipline virtually disappeared, and the soldiers were continually drunk and frequently attacked the native population. Cossack replacements for the garrison reached Tashkent en route from Orenburg on September 20, but the local authorities detained them in order to cope with the mounting insubordination of the Tashkent Soviet and the soldiers of the fortress at Tashkent.[46] The replacements never did reach Khiva.

In presenting its proposals for political reform under Russian control to Petrograd on September 13, the Turkestan Committee urged their approval by the beginning of October, so that the permanent commissar and his staff could arrive in Khiva before the close of navigation on the Amu-Darya toward the end of that month. Prompt action was necessary, Tashkent argued, to deal with the continuing disorder in the khanate. But on October 5 the proposals were just being forwarded by the war ministry to the Juridical Conference, and on the twenty-fifth they were still in the hands of the latter body.[47] By the following day the Provisional Government was no more.

Walls of the Citadel, Bukhara

15 / The Bolshevik Revolution and the Independence of the Khanates

Bolshevik Nationality Policy before October

There was little room for nationalism in the system of Karl Marx. A world view that regarded mankind as differentiated into economic classes had little tolerance for an attitude that persisted in regarding nations as groupings of individuals with common interests. At most, Marx's "scientific" socialism might support nationalist movements that advanced capitalist society along the road to proletarian revolution, but such movements must involve nations with a well-developed bourgeoisie and be aimed at the formation of larger, rather than smaller, states, for capitalism needed an extensive market.[1] Late nineteenth-century Marxists, however, shared the positive attitude toward national aspirations in general that characterized their age: the Second International at its London Congress in 1896 adopted a resolution favoring "the full autonomy of all nationalities." Following the lead of the Western Marxists, the Second Congress of the Russian Social Democratic Labor Party went on record in 1903 in favor of "the right of self-determination [*samoopredelenie*] for all nations forming part of the state."[2]

Within the Russian party there was little agreement as to the interpretation and implementation of the right to self-determination. The overwhelming majority of Russian Marxists regarded nationalism as an obstacle, to be either rendered harmless or overcome directly. Those who wished to neutralize nationalism—and by 1917 this group included most of the Mensheviks—were drawn to the program of cultural or nonterritorial autonomy proposed at the end of the nineteenth century by the Austrian Marxists Renner and Bauer. The more aggressive course was favored by Georgii Plekhanov and by Rosa Luxemburg and the Polish Social Democrats, who openly repudiated the right of self-determination. Only a small minority led by Lenin regarded nationalism as a force capable of being exploited in the interest of the Marxists' struggle for power. Lenin fulminated tirelessly against both the "Austrian heresy," for fear it would transform the party into an ineffectual confederation of national parties like the Jewish Bund, and the "Polish heresy," which would deprive the party of the use of a potentially popular selling point—the right of self-determination. He evolved instead a doctrine of nationalism which was at bottom a "combination between the recognition of a formal right of national self-determination and the recognition of a real need for unity in pursuit of common social and economic ends."[3]

In his first statement on the national question in 1903, Lenin laid down the axiom that the right of self-determination was a right possessed only by the proletariat of a nation and not by the nation as a whole.[4] Stalin, Lenin's pupil in this area, stated the corollary implicit in his teaching: the obligation of the party, as the proletariat's leader and guide, was to influence the use that the proletariat made of its right of self-determination, for Lenin had very early made clear that the general right of self-determination must not be confused with the expediency of a given nation's exercise of that right.[5] The goal of a socialist society would be furthered by the closest international unity of the working class, not by its division into artificial national units. In fact, as Lenin himself admitted, what he advocated was merely the *recognition* of the right of self-determination, not the *exercise* of that right.[6]

Before 1913 Lenin never troubled to explain precisely what he meant by the term self-determination. At the beginning of that year Stalin, having occupied himself at Lenin's orders with a study of the national question, defined self-determination as the right "to autonomy and federation, as well as to separation."[7] Although this broad definition was in keeping with Lenin's previous vague usage, the Bolshevik leader corrected his pupil six months later by narrowly defining self-determination as simply the right to political secession and independence.[8] This new definition again implied the undesirability of any nation's exercising the right. Lenin consistently argued that the large centralized state, as both a condition and a product of mature capitalism, was a necessary stage on the road to socialist revolution. The political and economic fragmentation of large states into smaller ones could only delay the day when a fully developed capitalism on a worldwide basis would give way to Marx's apocalyptic society. Nationalist movements, therefore, which attempted to undermine the political unity of existing large, centralized states, to set one nation against another at a moment when history demanded greater international unity as a precondition for socialism, could only be regarded as manifestations of "bourgeois nationalism" and combated as such.[9] Only in the exceptional case where national oppression prevented economic development would the "interests of capitalist development" and of the class struggle justify the exercise of the right of secession.[10]

Of what use was a right that ought virtually never to be exercised? A multinational state like the Russian Empire would, according to Lenin, acquire new strength if its various nationalities cooperated freely and without compulsion, which they could do only if they were granted the right to secede. On a world scale, freedom of secession was an essential right during the period when human society was in transition from the feudal and capitalist past, when nation oppressed nation, to the socialist future, when all nations would be merged in a common mankind. Possession of the right to secede would enable a formerly oppressed nation to overcome its sense of insecurity and distrust of other peoples and thereby prepare itself for life under socialism. Consequently, the Marxist mentors of the proletariat in oppressor nations must demand freedom of secession for all oppressed nations, although Marxists in the oppressed countries must struggle not for independence but for the complete unity of their own proletariat with that of the oppressor nation.[11]

However impressive as a display of intellectual gymnastics, and however successful as a propaganda tool after February 1917, Lenin's nationality policy was "neither consistent nor practical."[12] He had attempted to reconcile the irreconcilable, for in the Russian situation the requirements of a socialist revolution, as interpreted by Lenin, were incompatible with the desires of the various nationalities. The Bolshevik position seemed to offer the oppressed nationalities of the Russian Empire a choice of unacceptable alternatives— either to sever all connection with Russia or else to lose their identity as nations within a unitary Russian state.[13] In the two months after the February Revolution, however, when Lenin and Stalin were for the first time competing for popular support in an open society, they shifted their position and held out the promise of broad regional autonomy, although Lenin was careful to add that the workers of all nationalities in Russia must participate in common proletarian organizations.[14]

Bukhara and Khiva attracted little attention from the Bolsheviks before their seizure of power in Russia. Lenin had at various times over the years compared the two protectorates to Manchuria, Korea, and France's colonies—the point always being that the khanates, too, were the objects of capitalist exploitation. As such, they were entitled to the same freedom of secession from Russia as were Turkestan, the Ukraine, Poland, or Finland. In June 1917 at the First All-Russian Congress of Soviets, Lenin insisted that Russia must not forcibly retain her quasicolonies, Bukhara and Khiva, for "all nations must be free." Two months earlier, however, he had told the Seventh Party Conference, an audience before whom he could afford to be more candid, "We are for a fraternal union of all peoples . . . We certainly do not want the peasant in Khiva to live under the khan of Khiva. By developing our revolution we shall influence the oppressed masses."[15] Given this attitude, the logical product of Bolshevik nationality policy as it had developed over the previous decade and a half, the overthrow of the Provisional Government by the Bolsheviks in October 1917 boded no good for Emir Alim and Khan Isfendiyar.

Bukhara and the October Revolution

In the first three months following the October Revolution the Bolsheviks grappled with the problem of how to implement the principles of their nationality policy now that they were in power. Petrograd repeatedly proclaimed its adherence to the ideal of self-determination, even to the point of secession and independence, for all the peoples of Russia, while at the same time never ceasing to emphasize its real goal of a "voluntary" union of the peoples of Russia, welding the workers and peasants of all nationalities into a single revolutionary force.[16] Stalin, now people's commissar for nationalities, continually reminded the country that Petrograd would not permit the counterrevolutionaries to abuse the right of self-determination; its only proper use was by the proletariat of a national region wishing to establish an independent republic.[17] Dropping their old abhorrence of the term federation, the Bolsheviks in January 1918 declared that the new Russian Soviet Republic was a voluntary federation of national regions. The new masters of Russia adopted the forms but never the essence of federalism and thus remained faithful to the spirit of Leninism.

All the public pronouncements by the new Russian government in favor of the workers and peasants of the national borderlands taking their destiny into their own hands, setting up republics, and federating with Soviet Russia confirmed the initial reaction of the rulers of Bukhara and Khiva to the October Revolution. In the Romanovs they had found benevolent and not very demanding protectors, and in the Provisional Government a relatively weak regime that could be turned aside from its goal of modernizing the khanates. But in the Soviet government Alim and Isfendiyar sensed a potentially serious threat. Their major consolation was the expectation that the Bolshevik regime was destined for a short life.

Soviet power was definitively established in Tashkent on November 1, when the municipal soviet, composed of Bolsheviks and Left SR's, arrested the Provisional Government's Turkestan Committee. Ever since September 13 when the Tashkent Soviet, supported by the soldiers of the Tashkent garrison, had first proclaimed its assumption of authority over all of Russian Turkestan, it had been locked in a power struggle with the Turkestan Committee and General Korovichenko, whom Kerensky had sent to restore order. Most of the other soviets in Central Asia, including those of the Russian settlements in Bukhara, regarded as premature the attempt of the Tashkent Soviet to seize power. By the end of October, however, with the arrival of the news of the proclamation of a soviet government in Petrograd, the soviets of Turkestan and Bukhara fell into line behind Tashkent. On November 20 the Turkestan Krai Soviet was renamed the Sovnarkom (Council of People's Commissars) of the Turkestan Krai, with the Bolshevik F. I. Kolesov, a former railroad worker, as chairman. Within the week a soviet regime was established in the Russian settlements in Bukhara: the oblast soviet abolished the four executive committees and the municipal dumas and occupied the residency in New Bukhara. On December 2 the Second Oblast Congress of Soviets elected a Council of People's Commissars of the Russian Settlements, subordinate to the congress itself and to the Tashkent Sovnarkom. Thus, in less than six weeks from the Bolshevik takeover in Petrograd, a soviet government in miniature had been created for the Russian inhabitants of Bukhara.[18]

Despite its resounding proclamations, the new Russian regime

was forced at first to adopt quite a conservative policy toward the
emir's government. At the time the Bolsheviks seized control, Central Asia had already been cut off from direct overland contact with
European Russia: on October 17 Ataman A. I. Dutov and his Cossacks had seized Orenburg and halted communications and traffic
along the Orenburg-Tashkent Railroad. In late November, just as
the Bolsheviks were establishing their authority over the Russian
settlements in Bukhara, Tashkent faced another serious threat. On
November 28, by way of reply to the Tashkent Sovnarkom's rejection of territorial autonomy for Turkestan and of Moslem participation in its government, the Fourth Congress of Turkestan
Moslems proclaimed the autonomy of the region within a Russian
federation and set up in Kokand a rival government to Tashkent.
Faced with matters of such urgency, Kolesov's regime was reluctant
to create any new problems over Bukhara. Accordingly, Tashkent
implicitly recognized Bukhara's independence on November 29 and
instructed the residency and the New Bukhara Soviet merely to ask
the emir to abolish the death penalty and all forms of corporal punishment. The Provisional Government's elaborate scheme of reform
under Russian guidance had been reduced to these two polite
requests, and even they were ignored by the emir, who was now
completely under the influence of Nizam ad-Din and the ultra-
conservatives. Tashkent strictly forbade the Russian authorities in
the khanate to create any popular disturbances against the Bukharan
government, and Alim was assured of Soviet Russia's friendship in
return for his loyalty and the preservation of internal order.[19] The
Bolsheviks' initial policy toward Bukhara more closely resembled that
of the imperial regime than it did that of the Provisional Government. For the moment, implementation of Lenin's nationality policy
was out of the question.

Bukhara's response was cautious in the extreme. The Bolsheviks'
reputation as radicals and the weakness of their hold over Russia and
Turkestan persuaded the emir to have nothing to do with them. He
prevented the execution of Tashkent's order nationalizing the banks
and Russian-owned industries in the settlements, began to put his
army in a state of readiness to ward off a Russian attack, and refused
either to recognize the government in Tashkent or to receive the
three-man collegium that replaced the residency in December. Alim
preferred to deal with Soviet Turkestan indirectly, via Vvedenskii
and the other members of the former residency.[20] At the same time

the emir refused to receive emissaries from the liberal Moslems in Kokand who hoped to obtain his armed support against Tashkent.[21] The situation was much too confused to risk involvement; Bukhara preferred to look to her own defenses and see what the future would bring. Cautious as ever, Alim was fully aware of the vulnerability of Bukhara's position. Russian troops garrisoned New Bukhara, New Chardjui, Kerki, and Termez and were stationed along the railroad and the Bukharan-Afghan frontier. Soviet territory cut off Bukhara from the outside world on three sides; only from Afghanistan was there any chance of obtaining material support in case of war. Finally, profiting from Kaufman's foresight in annexing Samarkand, the Bolsheviks held the key to the water supply of every Bukharan beglik from Khatirchi to Karakul, including the capital itself. In this vulnerable position Bukhara could hardly risk an open break with Russia except as a last resort to prevent a Bolshevik conquest of the khanate, or unless Russia became sufficiently paralyzed by her own internal troubles so as to make probable a Bukharan victory.

Tashkent's situation improved with the new year. With the defeat of Dutov and recapture of Orenburg on January 18–20, 1918, communications with Europe were restored; and on February 19 (N.S.), Kokand fell to Tashkent's troops. Bukhara was consequently not eager to risk a trial of strength. She nevertheless found herself compelled to do so, with surprisingly successful results.

The Kolesov Campaign

Their confidence shattered by the events of April 1917, and hounded ever since by the emir's government, the Young Bukharans at first took a dim view of the October Revolution. They knew the Bolsheviks only vaguely as German agents and traitors to the democratic February Revolution. With an air of hopelessness the Young Bukharans in November commissioned Fitrat to draft a minimal program around which the party could reunite. Fitrat's program called for the usual reforms but not for any type of representative government.[22]

This mood of demoralization did not last long, for by the beginning of December the Young Bukharans had been persuaded by Bolshevik representatives that they had a common enemy in the emir. With the radicals once again in the ascendant, the central committee early in December sent Faizullah Khodzhaev to Tashkent at the head of a delegation to obtain Russian support for an uprising in the khanate. The aim of the revolt was to establish a Young Bukharan government with effective control over the emir; Tashkent was to send in Russian troops if necessary to secure its success. Kolesov approved of the proposals but advised postponing the uprising until after the liquidation of the Kokand regime. In New Bukhara the central committee began laying the groundwork for the revolt, but as January gave way to February and Kolesov kept postponing delivery of the promised arms and ammunition, disillusionment spread among the conspirators. After the capture of Kokand, however, Kolesov turned eagerly to Bukhara. Underestimating the strength of the emir's regime and army and attaching little importance to the uprising being planned by the Young Bukharans, Kolesov thought that the Bukharan question could be solved with a whiff of Russian grapeshot. Early in March (N.S.) 1918 he appeared unannounced in New Bukhara and informed the Young Bukharans that Tashkent would attack the emir in five days. Kolesov promised to bring with him at that time as many arms as he could spare for the conspirators. The Young Bukharans thereupon abandoned their plans for a large-scale uprising, for which there would be neither time nor sufficient arms, formed a revolutionary committee headed by Faizullah Khodzhaev, and armed the two hundred or so loyal followers in New Bukhara for whom there were weapons.[23]

On the night of March 13 Kolesov returned to New Bukhara with an escort of forty-six soldiers to take command of the five or six hundred Russian troops stationed there. He conferred with Khodzhaev's committee and they together on the afternoon of March 14 sent a twenty-four-hour ultimatum to the emir. Alim was to dismiss his ministers, disarm his troops, and hand over full authority to an executive committee composed of Young Bukharans, who would advise him on the choice of a new government. In the probable event that the emir should refuse their terms, Kolesov and the Young Bukharans planned to attack the capital. Presented with such an ultimatum, Alim had no choice but to fight. To surrender himself to the tutelage of the Young Bukharans and their Bolshevik allies would provoke a civil war in which the majority of his subjects would follow the clerical zealots, who could be expected to raise up a rival candidate for the throne. The chances of the Russians' being either willing or able to furnish Alim with effective support in such a situation, as they had his grandfather in 1868, were slim, given the Bolsheviks' revolutionary aims and the shakiness of their position in Russia. Alim's only hope was to rely on his own troops and on the demonstrated antipathy of his subjects for the renegade Young Bukharans and their infidel supporters. Having made this decision, the emir proceeded to play for time in order to marshal his forces. He agreed in principle to implement the Young Bukharans' demands but argued, as he had many times in the past year, that the ignorance and fanaticism of his subjects would permit only the most gradual reforms. As a feeble gesture of compromise, he replaced his notorious kush-begi, Nizam ad-Din, with the equally reactionary but less well-known Osman-beg.[24]

Neither Kolesov nor the Young Bukharans were so easily put off. Early in the morning of March 15 they began an advance on the old city and won an initial skirmish less than a mile from its walls. His first attempt at delaying tactics having failed, Alim made another try: he asked for a truce and declared his readiness to agree to all demands. The attackers withdrew to New Bukhara where they received the emir's representatives, who not only accepted the ultimatum but also declared Alim's intention to proclaim full civil liberties and abolish corporal punishment, the death penalty, and several inequitable taxes. Alim's envoys asked only that he be allowed three days to persuade his fanatical troops to disarm. Kolesov gave the emir one day instead, and a five-man delegation with a cavalry escort of twenty-five went to the capital to supervise the disarming of the troops. During the night the delegation was assaulted in its quarters by a mob and killed—whether at the government's orders or merely with its connivance is not clear. Only two members of the cavalry escort escaped to report the fate of their comrades to Kolesov in New Bukhara.

The emir had used the short respite to bring up reinforcements and order the destruction of portions of the railroad and telegraph linking New Bukhara to Russian Turkestan. Finding themselves cut off from all assistance on March 16, the Russians in desperation shelled the old city for a day and a half until their ammunition gave out, but they scored no hits. Their poor marksmanship was proclaimed by the Bukharan clergy as a sign of divine intervention. On March 17 Kolesov ordered a retreat toward the Soviet frontier at Katta-Kurgan. Fearful of reprisals at the hands of the native regime, several thousand Russian and Bukharan inhabitants of New Bukhara, as well as the Young Bukharan revolutionary committee, joined the retreating Russian troops. The soldiers and the fugitives covered only thirty miles in the first two days because of the destruction of the railroad (they often had to take up the rails over which they had passed and lay them down again ahead) and harassment from Bukharan cavalry units. On the nineteenth Kolesov halted at Kizil-Tepe and sent a delegation to the emir asking to be allowed to depart from the khanate in peace. Not wishing to risk any more of his men, Kolesov dispatched on this mission Vvedenskii and Mir Badalev, who as officials of the tsarist and provisional regimes were considered expendable. Alim responded by demanding the surrender of Khodzhaev, Fitrat, and Burkhanov, the leading members of the revolutionary committee, but Kolesov rejected this condition over the protests of many civilian refugees.

Kolesov's overtures proved unnecessary, for on the seventeenth Tashkent had heard of his plight and ordered all available troop units along the railroad from Samarkand to Kizil-Arvat to his rescue. Two days later a two-hundred-man unit from Samarkand captured Kermine and its beg, Alim's uncle, and scouts from this unit made contact with Kolesov at Kizil-Tepe. Faced with the prospect of a massive Russian attack, the emir sued for peace. Kolesov was only too happy to extricate himself from an adventure that had turned into a near disaster. After two days of negotiations a treaty of peace was signed on March 25. It was a one-sided treaty in that it imposed obligations on Bukhara exclusively, but it was also a victory for Bukhara in that no more was heard of the ultimatum of Kolesov and the Young Bukharans, and Russia temporarily abandoned all efforts to extend the revolution to the khanate.[25] In the treaty the emir promised to demobilize his army and disarm his subjects; to compensate Russia for the damage caused to the railroad, pay for its restoration, and in future protect it along with the postal service and the telegraph line; to exchange prisoners of war with Russia; not to place on the lower classes the burden of paying for the recent military expenditures; to receive Soviet Russia's diplomatic representatives and protect all Russian citizens in the khanate; to preserve strict neutrality in any hostilities between Russia and her enemies; to guarantee free movement of Russian troops on the railroad; and to hand over to Russia all counterrevolutionaries who had taken refuge in Bukhara. Short of another resort to military coercion, however, Russia had no way of guaranteeing that the emir would fulfill these promises, and it would be some time before Tashkent was again willing to risk a direct trial of strength.

Soviet-Bukharan relations were thus established on a formally correct, although far from cordial, basis. Tashkent's first attempt to solve the Bukharan problem by an armed attack had failed miserably, primarily because the forces allotted to the campaign and the preliminary planning had been woefully inadequate, but also because the emir received widespread support from his subjects in the face of this undisguised attempt at invasion by infidel troops. These two lessons were taken to heart in Tashkent and Moscow, where the Soviet government had moved on the eve of Kolesov's campaign, and the mistakes of March 1918 were carefully avoided in September 1920.

Khiva and the October Revolution

Smaller, poorer, and weaker than her sister protectorate, Khiva nevertheless enjoyed even greater freedom from Russian interference in the wake of the Bolshevik coup and escaped having to fight to maintain her new independence. There were no Russian enclaves in Khiva to serve as privileged bases for the spread of revolution. The Russian garrison, especially the Cossacks, and the Russian business community in Urgench were for the most part anti-Bolshevik. Since Urgench had a much smaller proportion of workers among its Russian inhabitants than did either Chardjui or New Bukhara, its workers' soviet was far less influential than theirs. Finally, Khiva did not bestride the Central Asian Railroad. In the first months after October Tashkent paid almost no attention to Khiva. Tashkent did appoint a new commander of the Russian garrison in Khiva when Colonel Zaitsev refused to recognize Soviet authority, but it made no attempt actually to remove Zaitsev from power.[26] All thought of implementing the project for constitutional government under the supervision of a military commissar was abandoned: constitutional government was a bourgeois game, intended to mask capitalism's exploitation of the proletariat.

In effect, the October Revolution meant that Khiva was left to her own devices. Khan Isfendiyar, backed by Colonel Zaitsev and Djunaid-khan, the real powers in the khanate, took advantage of his new freedom to hunt down the native reformers. On November 21 he ordered the trial of the seventeen Djadids arrested in June, and the packed Madjlis appointed a special court of kazis to judge the accused on charges of having violated the Sharia. Whether or not the trial actually took place is unclear. Either because of protests from the soldiers' soviet or, more likely, because of pressure from Zaitsev, the prisoners were for the time being saved from execution.[27]

Khiva's internal situation continued to deteriorate. The Turko-man raids did not abate, and within the Russian garrison morale and discipline were virtually nonexistent. Zaitsev sent the infantry units, which were most heavily pro-Bolshevik, to Petro-Aleksandrovsk in order to be rid of them. He had originally planned to remain in Khiva until spring and then lead his Cossacks to the lower Ural River to join the anti-Bolshevik camp of Ataman Dutov, but restless-ness among his Cossacks and the formation of an anti-Soviet govern-ment in Kokand, which sought his help, led him to adopt a new plan. Early in January he withdrew with his troops from Khiva to Chardjui, where he arrested the local soviet and received reinforce-ments from Cossack units formerly stationed in Persia. His intention was to attack the Tashkent regime from the rear while it was pre-occupied with the struggle against Kokand. Advancing along the railroad, Zaitsev's forward units occupied Samarkand, whose small Red garrison had withdrawn toward Djizak. On February 14 at Ro-stovtsevo station, across the Zarafshan from Samarkand and fifteen miles to the east, Zaitsev's men encountered the Soviet troops return-ing with reinforcements from Tashkent and Fergana. At this point Bolshevik agitators persuaded the demoralized Cossacks to surrender their arms. Zaitsev himself fled in disguise to Askhabad, where the Bolsheviks arrested him on February 20, the day after the fall of Kokand.[28]

The departure of the Russian garrison left Isfendiyar at the mercy of Djunaid-khan, who commanded the only remaining armed forces in the khanate that supported the government. Acting through Isfendiyar, Djunaid-khan proceeded to consolidate his hold on the country by abolishing the Madjlis and ordering numerous arrests and executions. Among his victims were the Djadid leaders arrested the previous year; they were shot in May 1918. Of the remaining Djadids, who had led an underground existence since June 1917, as many as were able escaped to Tashkent, where they formed a Young Khivan revolutionary committee-in-exile.[29]

The initial triumph and consolidation of Soviet power in Turkestan during the winter of 1917–1918 was accompanied by the establishment in Bukhara and Khiva of regimes openly hostile to the Bolsheviks and enjoying a degree of independence not known in either khanate since the 1860's. The right of self-determination, even to the point of breaking long established ties to Russia, was exercised by governments that in Leninist terms represented not the proletariat nor the poor peasantry, nor even the bourgeoisie, but the feudal aristocracy. Such a development was clearly the product not of Bolshevik design but of Russian weakness. The future of the khanates was inevitably bound up in the larger question of the future of Soviet power in Central Asia.

Mikhail Vasilevich Frunze, Commander of the Turkestan Front, 1919–1920

16 / The Civil War and the Second Russian Conquest

The Military Situation and Russo-Bukharan Relations, 1918–1919

From the revolt of the Czech corps in May 1918 to the repulse of Generals Denikin and Yudenich in late October 1919, Soviet Russia was engaged in a life-and-death struggle against its various enemies in the south, east, north, and west. During this period the Soviet government at Tashkent was fighting its own war of survival, for the most part in isolation from European Russia. By early June 1918 the Czech revolt embraced an area extending from Siberia along the northern periphery of the Kazakh Steppe and across the Volga River to Penza in the west. Coming just two months after Dutov's Ural Cossacks had overthrown Soviet authority along the lower Ural and Emba rivers, the Czech revolt blocked all overland routes between Turkestan and the rest of Russia. Tashkent's isolation from the center of Communist power was made complete on July 16 when an anti-Bolshevik government was established at Askhabad, thereby interrupting the land-and-water route via Krasnovodsk to Astrakhan. Organized opposition formed on a third front in September with the creation of a White army in Semirechie just north of the Ili River. Nor was all quiet behind the lines, for after the dispersal of the Kokand government in February 1918 an anti-Russian guerrilla movement had developed in Fergana, composed of bands calling themselves Basmachis. Of the three fronts across which Tashkent faced regular bodies of enemy troops, the Transcaspian was the most troubling for the greater part of the period 1918–1919. Askhabad's forces were the closest to Tashkent; they alone would have to be defeated by Tashkent unassisted by any Soviet armies in the enemy's rear, and they alone were in receipt of material assistance from the Allies, in this case Great Britain. The urgency of the threat from

Transcaspia placed Bukhara right in the midst of the civil war, for Tashkent's lines of communication, supply, and reinforcement to Chardjui, headquarters of the Transcaspian front, necessarily traversed the khanate. Chardjui itself, although a Russian enclave, was still technically Bukharan territory. Should the emir decide to throw in with the Askhabad regime and the British, the Soviet troops at the front would be cut off from their base, and the war would be brought to Tashkent's doorstep.

Still smarting from the defeat of March 1918, the Fifth Turkestan Congress of Soviets, meeting at the beginning of May to organize the former government-general into an autonomous soviet republic within the Russian federal republic, formally recognized the independence of Bukhara and Khiva and, as a sign of Bukhara's restored sovereignty, abolished the Russian customs frontier on the Bukharan-Afghan border.[1] The product of Soviet weakness and defeat, such gestures could not be counted upon to moderate the cold hostility existing between Bukhara and Soviet Turkestan. Hard pressed on all sides and lacking sufficient military forces to deal with the khanate, Tashkent was in a continual state of alarm over reports—the great majority of them inaccurate and based on rumor—of Bukhara's dealings with Afghanistan, with Britain, and with various White elements all the way from Askhabad and Fergana to the Ukraine and Siberia. Any defensive preparations in the khanate itself were invariably interpreted in Tashkent as evidence of an imminent Bukharan attack on Soviet Turkestan.

Yet the attack never came. Had Alim's intentions toward Russia been as single-mindedly aggressive as the contemporary Soviet regime in Tashkent believed, and as Soviet historians have ever since insisted, he surely ought to have launched such an attack in late July 1918, when Askhabad's troops were only five miles from Chardjui and the bridge over the Amu-Darya. Tashkent half expected him to do so. Indeed, six weeks earlier the Russian diplomatic representative in Bukhara had caused a major war scare in Tashkent with his reports of the emir's preparations for an offensive.[2] However, Askhabad hoped in vain for help from Bukhara in July, and in the absence of such support the White forces were driven back by a Soviet counteroffensive, which took Merv and was halfway to Askhabad itself by the end of August.[3]

Regardless of his hostility to the Bolsheviks, Alim was in no hurry to provoke an attack from Tashkent merely for the sake of advancing Askhabad's cause. If the Communists saw few differences among their enemies in the civil war, regarding them all as capitalists and imperialists united in a common crusade against the proletarian revolution, it is equally true that Bukhara and Khiva regarded the various parties in the civil war as all Russians, with little to choose among them. The emir's performance in 1918–1919 indicates that he probably hoped to be able to do business with whichever group finally came out on top in Russia, unless he could escape from Russia's orbit entirely, which was highly desirable but never seemed likely to prove feasible. In the Bolsheviks' favor was the fact that they controlled the greater part of Russia's former colonial domain in Central Asia, including the Russian settlements in Bukhara, the railroad zone that cut through the heart of the khanate, and Samarkand, the key to western Bukhara's water supply. These were strong arguments for not provoking Tashkent; no equally forceful arguments could be made for allying with Kokand, Askhabad, or any other center of opposition to Communism. When the Bolsheviks were doing poorly in the war, Alim was not displeased, but he always waited to see whether their bad luck would continue. When it turned, as it always did, the emir professed friendship for Tashkent and shrank from commitments to the Bolsheviks' enemies.

Bukhara's neutrality in July 1918 did nothing to allay the anxiety of the Bolsheviks in Tashkent, who during August lived in constant fear that should the Soviet troops in Transcaspia suffer defeat, Bukhara would attack.[4] The Soviet drive toward Askhabad was in fact halted at the end of August with the aid of Anglo-Indian troops from Persia, who had crossed into Transcaspia in the middle of the month at Askhabad's invitation. Britain's purpose in intervening in Russian Central Asia was to forestall a possible advance into this strategically situated area by the Germans and Ottoman Turks, who were already entrenched in Transcaucasia.[5] Having chosen to support Askhabad as the only available bulwark against German and Turkish expansion toward Persia and India, Britain soon found that she had no choice but to help Askhabad defend itself against the Soviet forces to the east. Whereas Askhabad was primarily concerned with the threat from Soviet Turkestan, Britain's attention was focused on Transcaucasia and the Caspian Sea. Once the World War had ended, and with it the German and Turkish occupation of Transcaucasia, the British were left in an awkward position. Although the original reason for their presence had disappeared, in the meantime Askhabad had come to rely heavily on their support; the British hesitated to assist the Bolsheviks by withdrawing that support but were not inclined to become more deeply involved. Britain's dilemma was reflected in Delhi's directive at the end of November forbidding Major General Wilfrid Malleson, commander of the Transcaspian expeditionary force, to advance east of Merv, the last point occupied by the combined White and British forces in their offensive begun in mid-October.[6] Without British assistance the Whites were unable to advance further, and the front remained static until May 1919.

The British intervention in Transcaspia did not materially alter Bukhara's situation. The emir had established a consulate at Merv in the fall of 1918 as an observation post and channel of communication with Askhabad. Through his representative in Merv, Alim made contact with Malleson in January 1919 to sound out Britain's intentions in Central Asia. If ever Bukhara were to escape from the Russian orbit, it would have to be with British help. But Malleson was in no position to encourage any such hopes the emir might have entertained. The British commander was bound by his orders not to commit his troops east of Merv, nor was he certain how long the British forces would remain in Transcaspia. With Delhi's permission Malleson sent to Bukhara in February a small quantity of arms as a token of friendship, but he also sent a letter urging Alim not to provoke Tashkent.[7] His contact with the British thus served merely to confirm the emir in his policy of watchful neutrality.

The caravan bearing the arms from Malleson reached Bukhara in March, and for the next year Tashkent's pulse was kept racing by reports of hundreds of British military instructors in the khanate; the sole factual basis for these reports was the presence of two Indian noncommissioned officers who had been in charge of the arms shipment and who remained in Bukhara until the end of 1919.[8] The arrival of the arms also gave rise in the spring of 1919 to an endless stream of false rumors in Tashkent of additional arms deliveries to Bukhara from the British, from Afghanistan, and from Askhabad.[9] In fact, although the emir's army had grown to thirty thousand men in preparation for a possible renewal of Russian aggression, modern arms and ammunition were as scarce as in the past. Malleson's gift was not repeated, and neither Afghanistan, preoccupied from March through July 1919 with her war against Britain, nor Askhabad, hard pressed to defend itself after the British evacuation in March, was willing or able to help Bukhara.

An additional cause for concern in Tashkent in early 1919 was the concentration in Bukhara of anti-Communist fugitives, including Basmachis from Fergana and Osipov, the former commissar of war in Turkestan and leader of an abortive anti-Soviet uprising in Tashkent in January. Bukhara ignored Turkestan's demands for the surrender of all fugitives as provided in the Treaty of Kizil-Tepe. Tashkent, again cut off from European Russia in mid-April by Dutov's capture of Aktiubinsk on the Orenburg-Tashkent Railroad and by Kolchak's great offensive toward the Volga, was powerless to enforce compliance.[10]

The evacuation of the British troops, ordered in early February and completed on April 1, altered the balance of military power in Transcaspia in the Communists' favor. They began their final gradual advance toward the Caspian Sea in May and recaptured Merv on the twenty-third. Askhabad made a desperate attempt from May 13 to 17 to halt the new offensive by sending a detachment around the main body of Red troops to besiege the fortress of Kerki in their rear. Believing the local Bukharan officials to be collaborating with the besiegers, the Soviet garrison in the fortress occupied the native town and then, having lifted the siege, found themselves blockaded by the emir's troops. A mixed Russo-Bukharan commission arranged a truce at Kerki between the garrison and the beg on July 10, and the last remnants of Askhabad's units were expelled from the rural areas of Kerki beglik on the nineteenth, but the blockade continued for at least another month.[11]

While the crisis at Kerki lasted, Russo-Bukharan relations reached their lowest point since the Kolesov campaign. In June, Emir Alim again demanded the withdrawal of all Soviet troops from the khanate and the transfer of the railroad zone to Bukharan control.[12] On June 20 the first Soviet embassy to Afghanistan, en route from Tashkent via the Amu-Darya to Kabul, was twice fired upon just downriver from Kerki, with losses of two killed and eighteen or more wounded. Russia's representative in the khanate registered an outraged protest, without noticeable effect, while the embassy retreated to Chardjui and then proceeded via Merv to Herat.[13] The settlement of the Kerki crisis did not lessen the tension significantly. As late as September 2 the Russians felt it necessary to take the most elaborate precautions in transferring troops via the Central Asian Railroad from the Transcaspian to the Aktiubinsk front, lest any untoward incident between the troops and the native population serve the emir as a pretext for launching the expected attack on Turkestan: the troop train was to be sealed while crossing the khanate, no soldiers were to be in evidence, and the distance from Chardjui to Katta-Kurgan was to be covered nonstop and, insofar as possible, at night.[14]

Tashkent's anxiety over an invasion from Bukhara was as exaggerated as ever. After withdrawing to Meshed in Persia, Malleson on June 20 repeated to Alim his earlier advice to maintain complete neutrality for the time being. The tone of Malleson's letter indicates that he hardly regarded the emir as a fervent anti-Communist, straining at the leash to have a go at Tashkent. On the contrary, Malleson's note betrays considerable concern that Bukhara not abandon its neutrality for an alliance with the Bolsheviks or the Afghans. Malleson assured the emir that Meshed was in close touch with the political and military situation in European Russia and that the overthrow of the Bolsheviks was at hand.[15] The British general's warnings against a Bukharan rapprochement with Tashkent were superfluous, and his assurances regarding the Bolsheviks' impending collapse must have left the emir either puzzled or wryly amused. The Red Army took Askhabad on July 15; by then Kolchak's retreat from the Volga had turned into a full-fledged rout, and in his wake Soviet troops advanced southeast from Orenburg along the railroad, taking Aktiubinsk on September 2 and linking up with Tashkent's forces north of the Aral Sea eleven days later.[16] Whatever news may have reached the khanate about Denikin's conquest of the Ukraine in July and August must have been outweighed by these significant Communist victories on fronts that more directly concerned Bukhara.

By the end of summer 1919 Alim had no more reason to like or trust the Bolsheviks than he had a year and a half earlier, but the Soviet victories in Transcaspia and along the Orenburg-Tashkent Railroad meant that in Central Asia at least the balance had shifted definitively in favor of Moscow and Tashkent. Now only a complete overthrow of the Soviet government in its European base could free

Bukhara from the necessity of finding a modus vivendi with the Bolshevik successors to the tsars. Yet Moscow did nothing during 1918–1919 to indicate that it believed coexistence with the emir's government was possible. Stalin, people's commissar for nationalities, consistently maintained that the Communists were prepared to recognize the autonomy of only those borderlands in which the native bourgeoisie had been overthrown and deprived of political rights and in which power belonged to the workers and peasants, organized in soviets. Lenin put the matter somewhat more subtly to the Eighth Party Congress in March 1919: in the case of backward nations, Moscow must first accord the right of self-determination to the entire nation, then wait for the class differentiation of proletariat from bourgeoisie to develop, and finally assist the proletariat to overthrow its exploiters.[17] Bukhara was obviously in the second stage. But could a group as inherently voluntaristic as the Bolsheviks be expected to resist for long the temptation to give history a push, especially if hostile forces within the khanate and in the Allied camp were conspiring to hinder the march of history?

That such was Moscow's intention in 1919 would have been obvious from a careful reading of *Zhizn Natsionalnostei*, official organ of Stalin's commissariat. From the pages of this journal it was clear that Moscow regarded Bukhara as a bulwark of reaction and counterrevolution, which Kolesov's campaign had "unfortunately" failed to liquidate. Britain's hold over the Bukharan ruling elite was observed to be growing stronger, and the khanate becoming a major base for British agents conducting anti-Soviet propaganda. It was argued that the future of the oppressed masses of Central Asia and India hinged on Bukhara's becoming the leader of a series of revolutions in that part of the world. In March *Zhizn Natsionalnostei* published the appeal of the Moscow "Socialist Committee of Young Bukharans" to the Bukharan masses to rise up, along with the other peoples of the East, and liberate themselves with the fraternal support of Russia's workers and the Bolshevik government. In August the journal noted with satisfaction that Afghanistan's new independence from Britain and the recent Soviet victories in Transcaspia had cut Bukhara off from her British masters, leaving her helpless before a mass liberation movement. As *Zhizn Natsionalnostei* had earlier pointed out, since Bukhara had no industrial proletariat to provide leadership for the peasant masses, who themselves lacked class consciousness, the only chance for overthrowing the emir was "the development of the international revolution"—in other words, the intervention of Russia's workers and peasants in the persons of their champions, the Red Army.[18] As Kolesov's campaign had shown, however, a successful military intervention must first neutralize the resistance of a population who still viewed the world in terms of believers and infidels.

The Bukharan Political and Economic Scene

In the wake of Kolesov's retreat in March 1918 the core of the Young Bukharan movement, some 150 to 200 members, had emigrated to Tashkent and Samarkand with its leaders. In exile the movement at first lacked any organized existence; for six months the group's energies were taken up with efforts to ward off starvation and with endless recriminations and disputes over the March fiasco. Some members became politically inactive; others deserted to join the Russian political parties in Turkestan, the Left SR's or the Communists. The former leaders, blamed by many for the ruin of the party's fortunes in the khanate, retired temporarily from the scene; Faizullah Khodzhaev went to Moscow. For the duration of the civil war in Central Asia the Young Bukharans' hopes and prospects remained dim, reviving only at the end of 1919 when Moscow began actively to prepare for intervention in Bukhara.[19]

After the exodus of the Young Bukharans the only organized political party in the khanate was the Communists, who had cells in the four settlements with a membership drawn from the Russian civilian and military population. Chardjui and New Bukhara, where party organizations had been formed at the end of 1917, were the centers of Communist activity. Chardjui was one of twelve party organizations represented at the First Congress of the Communist Party of Turkestan (CPT) in June 1918, and Chardjui and New Bukhara were represented jointly with Samarkand Oblast at the Eighth Congress of the Russian Communist Party (RCP) in March 1919. By the fall of 1919 total membership in the four settlements was almost nine hundred.[20]

As a purely Russian party confined to the Russian enclaves, the Communists had little influence among the native population. To remedy this situation in April 1918 P. G. Poltoratskii, commissar of labor and chairman of the Economic Council of the Turkestan Republic, persuaded some of the Young Bukharan emigrés in Tashkent to break with their old party and form a Bukharan Communist Party (BCP). The organizational work lagged, undoubtedly a reflection of the general mood of despondency among the Bukharan exiles; the party held its first congress in late November in the capital of Soviet Turkestan and subsequently joined the Comintern. In December the BCP adopted a program calling for the emir's overthrow and establishment of a "Bukharan People's Soviet Republic." Within a few months the party had legal branches in Samarkand, Katta-Kurgan, and Merv; in the khanate illegal cells sprang up in the Russian settlements and elsewhere, including the emir's capital.[21]

The recent and superficial conversion to Communism of most of the BCP's members, including its leaders, was evident in both the party's aims and its methods. The party program included respectful references to the Sharia; the members were dedicated to the achievement of equality for all social classes rather than the establishment of the dictatorship of the proletariat; and they resorted heavily to terrorist practices, including political assassination and raids on the Bukharan mails. Under the prodding of the CPT at the Bukharan party's second congress in Tashkent on June 26–27, 1919, these doctrinal and tactical errors were denounced, along with the slow progress in developing a mass following. The congress reaffirmed the central committee's decision to purge the party of reformist and bourgeois elements and received from the CPT a pledge of 200,000 rubles to promote the work and raise the flagging spirits of the BCP.[22] Despite the efforts of the Communists of Turkestan, by the fall of 1919 the Bukharan exiles had failed to develop into a political force enjoying any significant degree of popular support among the Bukharan population. The experiences of 1917 and the spring of 1918 were too disheartening, the fate of the revolution in Turkestan too unsure, and the repressive policies of the emir's government too effective for the small number of politically conscious Bukharans to make any headway.

Emir Alim's attitude toward the domestic opposition became even more hostile after the failure of Kolesov's campaign. Not only Young Bukharan sympathizers but all Bukharans with a Western education or who read newspapers were subject to persecution and execution. A wave of xenophobia gripped the country and its government, presided over by Nizam ad-Din, the former kush-begi and still a power in the khanate, and Burhan ad-Din, the kazi-kalan. A special tribunal tried and condemned to death fifteen to twenty prominent advocates of reform, including seven clerics belonging to the older generation of Djadids. Larger numbers were executed without benefit of trial, like the seventy victims hanged in Kerki beglik after the Treaty of Kizil-Tepe. Others, like the Russians remaining in Old Bukhara after Kolesov's withdrawal, were massacred by excited mobs.[23]

Although the emir's government profited from its new independence of Russia on the domestic political front, the same is not true of the economic sphere. Communications with European Russia, the area responsible for nine tenths of Bukhara's foreign trade on the eve of World War I, were interrupted from the summer of 1918 until the fall of 1919. Even after the restoration of communications Russian industry was in no condition to resume its former role as consumer of Bukharan cotton, karakul, and wool and supplier of cotton textiles and other manufactured goods for the Bukharan market. Although Soviet Turkestan and the khanate agreed on December 19, 1918, to establish trade relations, the agreement remained a dead letter—in part because of the hostility existing between the two regimes and Bukhara's reluctance to accept Soviet paper currency, in part because the economies of Russia's former protectorate and her Central Asian colony were competitive rather than complementary. Both had served metropolitan Russia before the revolution as suppliers of raw materials, primarily cotton, and as protected markets for Russian manufactures. Turkestan had no need for Bukhara's cotton and could not supply even the khanate's limited demand for manufactured goods. Any trade between the two areas would have benefited Turkestan far more than Bukhara, for Bukhara was at least self-sufficient in foodstuffs, whereas Turkestan was not. Cut off from her usual sources of grain, Turkestan was in desperate straits for much of 1918 and 1919 and tried repeatedly, with little success, to purchase grain in Bukhara.[24]

Although Bukhara renewed her old trading relations with Afghanistan and Persia, the main articles of Bukharan export to those lands were the products of local craftsmen, not the raw materials that had been the staples of the Russian trade. The export of raw cotton via those countries to England, a possible customer, would have involved prohibitive transportation costs. By 1919 cotton had ceased to be king among Bukhara's marketable natural resources: cotton exports to Russia had fallen to a mere 5 percent of the 1917 level (the figures for karakul and wool were 10 percent and 17 percent, respectively). With the virtual disappearance of its sole market, cotton lost popularity as a cash crop. Cotton acreage in Bukhara and Khiva together in 1919 was only 38 percent of the 1913 figure; the total cotton harvest in the khanates in 1919 was a mere 18 percent of the 1913 level.[25] Many small producers, especially in western Bukhara and southern Khiva, who had raised cotton as a supplementary, income-producing crop, suffered financial distress as they shifted their fields from cotton to grain for home consumption.

Even more important than the collapse of the cotton trade as a source of economic hardship and social unrest was the burden of the ever-growing Bukharan army. Taxes to support the army increased as the number of troops increased, and taxes, as well as the recruitment of soldiers, bore most heavily upon the peasant masses. Popular resentment over taxation and the levying of recruits motivated a succession of ill-organized uprisings in the Zarafshan and Kashka-Darya oases from the end of 1918 throughout the following year. Old Bukhara itself was the scene of a major riot on July 2, 1919; over sixty of the participants were executed in the Rigistan the following day.[26] In this growing popular discontent the Russians and the Bukharan reformers and revolutionaries found encouragement for their attempts to alienate the Bukharan masses from their rulers. At the very least, it would permit the neutralization of the native population and thereby deprive the emir of popular support in the face of a second Soviet assault on the khanate.

Khiva under Djunaid-khan

Of the two former Russian protectorates, it was Bukhara that gave Tashkent more cause for anxiety but Khiva that actually gave more trouble. Unlike the cautious emir of Bukhara, trying as best he could to safeguard his inherited power and wealth in unsettled times, Djunaid-khan was an adventurer who had achieved power by taking risks and exploiting the possibilities presented by the political instability of the period, and he continued to do so. Djunaid spent the spring and early summer of 1918 consolidating his hold on Khiva. He established a system of government through local military commanders (*atli-bashis*) who were directly responsible to him rather than to the khan, although he generously allowed Isfendiyar a share of the tax revenue. The atli-bashis exercised power in the begliks through the hakims and other royal officials, who were retained for their experience and literacy. Djunaid's residence at Bedirkent near Takhta, where he began the construction of a palace, became the de facto capital of the country. Under his rule taxes increased, with the heaviest burdens falling on the Uzbegs. Uzbeg peasants were subjected to compulsory labor service in cleaning the irrigation canals, while Turkoman peasants were required to arm themselves at their own expense for militia duty. Popular disturbances were a recurrent problem, but the only serious domestic threat came in April 1918 from Djunaid's old rivals among the Yomut tribal leaders. Their revolt flagged after the death of Shammi-kel in July and ended on September 1 with the surrender of Kosh-mamed-khan.[27]

On September 20 Djunaid's troops raided Urgench and confiscated the money and goods of the Russian firms and banks there, despite the Russian business community's support for him in the absence of any practical alternative at the time of Zaitsev's departure. On the same day the Russian garrison at Petro-Aleksandrovsk was strengthened by the arrival of sixty to one hundred Red Guards under N. A. Shaidakov, a Bolshevik and former sailor, now military commissar of Chardjui. Shaidakov demanded through the Petro-Aleksandrovsk Soviet the release of the Russians arrested in the raid on Urgench. Djunaid complied, but he refused to restore the confiscated money and property and warned Shaidakov against interfering in Khiva's affairs. Apprehensive lest Isfendiyar turn to Shaidakov for help, Djunaid on September 30 sent his eldest son to the capital to assassinate the khan. Isfendiyar's brother Abd Allah succeeded to the throne, where he proved a satisfactory puppet in Djunaid's hands.[28]

Toward Soviet Turkestan Djunaid-khan pursued an openly aggressive policy. He regarded the Communists as enemies, not because they were Marxists or revolutionaries but because they, like the tsarist troops in 1916, stood in the way of his ambition. Although he was no one's tool, and in August 1918 refused Askhabad's plea to slow down the Soviet advance in Transcaspia by attacking the Reds at Petro-Aleksandrovsk, three months later he felt strong enough to attack Russia in pursuit of his own personal ends. As long as the Amu-Darya Otdel remained in Russian hands, Khiva was not secure against invasion: Petro-Aleksandrovsk was a foreign foothold inside the desert perimeter that was Khiva's natural line of defense. Defended by only a small garrison and isolated during the winter when navigation on the Amu-Darya was suspended, Petro-Aleksandrovsk looked like an easy prize. On November 25 Djunaid's troops crossed the river at six points and began to occupy the right bank. Despite the lateness of the season, a steamboat carrying reinforcements from Chardjui managed to get through to Petro-Aleksandrovsk and helped lift an eleven-day siege; Djunaid's Turkomans retired in disorder to the left bank.[29] The ensuing lull in the war ended the following March. On the twenty-eighth Russian troops from Chardjui again defeated Djunaid's men, this time near Pitniyak on the Khivan side of the river. The Petro-Aleksandrovsk Soviet urged the annexation of Khiva, but Tashkent, in order to free as many troops as possible for the impending offensive on the Transcaspian front, had already decided to make peace with Djunaid. After suffering defeat in several more small skirmishes, Djunaid received the Russian peace mission and concluded the Treaty of Takhta with them on April 9, 1919. The treaty provided for an immediate end to hostilities, Russia's reaffirmation of Khiva's independence, the establishment of normal diplomatic relations, a mutual guarantee of free movement of trade, and a Russian amnesty for all Turkoman citizens of Russia charged with anti-Soviet activity.[30]

Russo-Khivan relations remained far from cordial after the fighting had ceased. In late May Chardjui asked Djunaid to supply seven hundred horsemen for the offensive against Askhabad, but since Djunaid set impossible conditions for their pay and equipment and stipulated that his men not be used in action against fellow Moslems, the matter was dropped. Djunaid's relations with Tashkent were strained almost to the breaking point in July when he refused to receive the permanent Russian diplomatic representative whom Turkestan had appointed in accordance with the peace treaty. Incensed at this rebuff, which contrasted so pointedly with the cordial reception Djunaid gave immediately afterward to a Bukharan embassy, Tashkent demanded that its envoy be received, that Djunaid restore the telegraph line connecting Chardjui with Petro-Aleksandrovsk, which he had destroyed the previous November, and that Khiva extradite fugitive Russian criminals and sell grain to Turkestan. Djunaid complied only to the extent of permitting the Russians to restore the telegraph line but even then would give no guarantees for its future safety. The other points he rejected.[31]

During the summer Russo-Khivan relations were further complicated by the revolt of a squadron of Ural Cossacks stationed at Chimbai in the Amu-Darya Otdel. By mid-August the Cossacks, aided by the local Karakalpak population, were in control of the entire delta from the Aral Sea south to Nukus, across the river from Khodjeili. Shaidakov, who returned to Petro-Aleksandrovsk on August 19 as commander of the newly formed Khivan army group of the Transcaspian front, attempted to quell the uprising but soon discovered that he had to contend with more than Cossacks and Karakalpaks. His steamboat was fired upon from the left bank by Djunaid's patrols as it carried the Russian troops up and down the Amu-Darya. After retaking Nukus, Shaidakov was forced to retire to Petro-Aleksandrovsk at the beginning of September to protect his headquarters against a possible Khivan attack. Djunaid-khan had already in late August cut the telegraph line to Chardjui again and begun discussions with Chimbai leading toward a joint attack on Petro-Aleksandrovsk. By mid-September Tashkent expected Khiva to open hostilities at any moment.[32]

While Djunaid oppressed his countrymen at home and planned the extension of his power to the right bank of the Amu-Darya, the Young Khivan emigrés in Turkestan dreamed of his overthrow. At the end of 1918 Mullah Djumyaz Sultanmuradov organized the Petro-Aleksandrovsk Committee of Young Khivans. Although composed of only ten to fifteen members at first, the group expanded with the aid of an increasing flow of refugees from Djunaid's fiscal and manpower levies. By the end of 1919 the Young Khivans could boast a party militia of five hundred and an underground cell in the khan's capital. Like its Bukharan counterpart, the Young Khivan movement by the beginning of 1919 had a Communist faction, led by Russians from the Petro-Aleksandrovsk party organization.[33]

The Overthrow of Djunaid-khan

In the fall of 1919 the military situation shifted definitively in favor of the Communists. The Orenburg-Tashkent Railroad was reopened in mid-September, and during the next four weeks Soviet troops from Europe destroyed Dutov's army at Kustanai on the northern edge of the Kazakh Steppe while Tashkent's forces took Kizil-Arvat, halfway between Askhabad and the Caspian Sea. By October 22 the Red Army in Europe had lifted Yudenich's second siege of Petrograd and launched its final drive against Denikin with the recapture of Orel, two-hundred miles south of Moscow. Soviet Russia was free for the first time to consolidate its position in Central Asia and regain control of Bukhara and Khiva. Early in October Moscow established the Commission for the Affairs of Turkestan under the All-Russian Central Executive Committee of the Congress of Soviets and the Council of People's Commissars as the new de facto government of Turkestan. *Izvestiia* published an appeal from the foreign commissariat in Moscow to the workers and peasants of Bukhara and Khiva to overthrow their rulers and ally themselves with the workers and peasants of Turkestan and Russia in the name of liberty, equality, and fraternity. The Fourth Congress of the CPT declared its support of the Young Bukharans and the Young Khivans in the common struggle to destroy the hold of British imperialism over the khanates.[34]

That Tashkent and Moscow decided to settle the fate of Khiva before turning to the bigger and more important problem of Bukhara was due to Djunaid-khan's openly aggressive behavior—his repeated assaults against Russian territory and troops and his undisguised support of the Cossack revolt in the Amu-Darya delta—as well as to the relatively less stable political situation in the smaller khanate. At the beginning of November Djunaid's old rival, Koshmamed-khan, in alliance with another Turkoman tribal leader, Gulam Ali, launched a new revolt in the Khodjeili and Kunya-Urgench region in the northern part of the Khivan oasis and then turned to the Russians at Petro-Aleksandrovsk for support. Although the Russians were primarily concerned with the suppression of the Cossack revolt, they realized that the solution of the problem hinged on the overthrow of Djunaid-khan. The decision to intervene in Khiva on the side of the opposition to Djunaid was taken on November 18 by the Revolutionary Military Council of the Turkestan Front, and G. B. Skalov, the council's newly appointed representative for Khiva and the Amu-Darya Otdel, was sent to Petro-Aleksandrovsk at the beginning of December to organize the invasion of the khanate. Late in November Shaidakov, commander of the

Khivan army group, had been besieged in Nukus by a combined force of Cossacks and six hundred of Djunaid's troops; he was rescued only by a relief force from Chardjui. During December the Russians had to repulse several attempts by additional Khivan units to cross into the delta to support the Cossack rebels.[35]

On December 23, the preparations completed, Skalov proclaimed to the troops poised to invade the khanate that the goal of the impending campaign was to secure for Khiva its independence and the right of self-determination. The proclamation characterized Djunaid-khan as a tyrant, an ally of the counterrevolutionary Cossacks of Chimbai, and an agent of British imperialism. The rescue of the Khivan people from Djunaid and his armed brigands was the sole aim of the Soviet troops; after the destruction of the tyrant the Khivans would be free to set up whatever form of government suited them. Skalov's reason for focusing on Djunaid and not Khan Abd Allah as the target of Russian intervention was Moscow's desire to mobilize as broad a coalition as possible for the attack, including the Khivan Communists on the left, the Young Khivans in the center, and the anti-Djunaid Turkoman chieftains on the right. Once the revolution in Khiva had been accomplished, there would be time enough for Russia to reveal her intention of only permitting the establishment of a regime that was subservient to her commands.[36]

The Russians launched their invasion on December 25 with a column of 430 men, which took Khanki and Urgench without a fight but was then besieged for three weeks in Urgench by Djunaid's troops. A second column of 400 men led by Shaidakov defeated the Cossacks and Karakalpaks near Chimbai and then crossed into Khiva and captured Khodjeili on December 29. Kosh-mamed-khan, Gulam Ali, and the other insurgent Turkoman chieftains joined forces with Shaidakov, and Kunya-Urgench fell on January 2, 1920. Djunaid-khan was soon cornered in his headquarters at Bedirkent, near Takhta, by the northern column advancing from Kunya-Urgench and the southern column that had broken out of Urgench. After a two-day battle Takhta and Bedirkent fell on the evening of January 23, and Djunaid fled into the Kara Kum Desert. While Shaidakov's men returned to the Amu-Darya Otdel and finally suppressed the Cossack revolt, the southern column occupied the remainder of the Khivan oasis, taking the khan's capital on February 1.[37]

Abd Allah implored Russia's pardon, alleging his helplessness in Djunaid's hands, but the Russians forced the khan to abdicate in favor of a revolutionary committee, composed of two Young Khivans, two Turkoman chieftains, and one cleric and headed by Sultanmuradov, chairman of the Petro-Aleksandrovsk Young Khivan Committee. During February Djunaid's atli-bashis and the royally appointed hakims were replaced with local revolutionary committees and soviets whose members were designated by the new regime. Neither the Young Khivans nor the Turkomans had previously called for the replacement of the monarchy with a soviet republic, but the Russians were now the ultimate source of authority in the country. On February 8 the Communist faction of the Young Khivan party, a numerically insignificant group, formally requested Soviet Russia to help Khiva establish a workers' and peasants' dictatorship on the Russian model, and on April 1 a political mission from Tashkent arrived in Khiva to conduct elections to a nationwide congress of soviets. The elections were duly held under Tashkent's auspices, and at the end of the month the First All-Khorezmi Kurultai (Congress) of Soviets met, elected Lenin its honorary chairman, abolished the khanate, proclaimed an independent Khorezmi People's Soviet Republic under a Council of People's Nazirs, adopted a constitution for the new republic, and sent a delegation to Moscow to conclude treaties of alliance and assistance.[38] Since a soviet republic without a Leninist party to furnish proper direction was unthinkable, a Khorezmi Communist Party was established at the end of May, which by summer claimed a membership of six hundred organized in twenty cells. So weak were the party's local roots that the leadership was composed almost exclusively of Communists from Russia and Turkestan; a Russian Tatar served as chairman of the central committee.[39] Russia's promise to secure for Khiva the right of self-determination was thus fulfilled along Leninist lines, with the Bolsheviks making certain that the right was exercised so as to strengthen, not weaken, the revolutionary government in the Kremlin.

The Overthrow of Emir Alim

While Russia solved the Khivan problem, suppressed the revolt in the Amu-Darya delta, and liquidated the Transcaspian and

Semirechie fronts in February and March 1920, Russo-Bukharan relations continued substantially as before, with a maximum of mutual suspicion but few overtly hostile acts. The Soviet conquest of Khiva frightened Alim into making a number of minor concessions, such as permitting Russian citizens free entry into Old Bukhara for the first time since Kolesov's attack and banning the importation of British goods via Afghanistan. On March 30 M. V. Frunze, the gifted young commander of the Turkestan front and a member of the Turkestan Commission, obtained from the emir an agreement to exchange diplomatic representatives and settle all outstanding questions; Tashkent subsequently returned to Bukhara six cannon carried off as trophies by Kolesov two years earlier. These gestures did not, however, affect Russia's view of the Bukharan problem: several visits to the khanate during March and April by Frunze and other members of the Turkestan Commission confirmed that the influence of the clerical zealots over the emir was unbroken, that Alim was more concerned with expelling Young Bukharan agitators from the Russian settlements than with introducing political and social reforms, and that Bukhara had no intention of establishing normal trade relations with Turkestan.[40]

Worse yet, Tashkent was becoming more and more alarmed at reports of preparations by Bukhara and Afghanistan for a joint attack on Russia. After successfully asserting Afghanistan's independence in the Third Anglo-Afghan War (March to July 1919), Emir Amanullah began to demonstrate an interest in his newly independent northern neighbor—primarily for its value as a buffer against Russia but also, perhaps, as a member of a league of Central Asian Moslem states under Kabul's leadership. In July 1919 Alim had requested material support from Amanullah, who responded in October by sending to Bukhara sixty military instructors, half a dozen experts in arms production, and six cannon. In January 1920 Afghanistan established a permanent embassy in Alim's capital, and Bukhara opened a consulate at Mazar-i Sharif in northern Afghanistan. By April reports were flowing into Tashkent that Alim had fifteen hundred Afghans on his payroll, who were helping to prepare his army for war against Russia. On the fourteenth Frunze warned Lenin that as Bukhara and Afghanistan were both arming feverishly, Soviet Turkestan was in serious danger. During May Lenin received urgent requests from both Tashkent and the foreign affairs commissariat in Moscow to send troop reinforcements to protect Turkestan against an expected Bukharan-Afghan attack.[41]

Preoccupied from late April to early July with the Polish invasion of Russia and Baron Wrangel's seizure of the southern Ukraine, Moscow could give no assistance to Tashkent, but once again the Bukharan attack failed to materialize. Alim was still reluctant to try his luck in war against Russia, even though the prospects for a permanent modus vivendi were far from promising. Lenin's "Theses on the National and Colonial Questions," published on July 14 in the journal *Kommunisticheskii Internatsional,* prescribed the liberation of backward colonial lands by a united front of bourgeois liberals, peasants, and workers against the clergy and other reactionaries who back the "khans, landowners, mullahs, etc." Whether or not this open threat caught Alim's attention, he could not have failed to take note of the reception in Tashkent in June of a Khorezmi embassy en route to Moscow, on which occasion Frunze and his chief political commissar, V. V. Kuibyshev, had promised that Bukhara and the other oppressed Eastern lands would soon be liberated in the same manner as Khiva. But there was little the emir could do: a war against Russia would be an unequal contest, which would only make certain the fate that Alim dreaded. In desperation he initiated an exchange of diplomatic politenesses with Foreign Commissar G. V. Chicherin in June and dispatched an embassy to Moscow at the end of the month to reassure the Russians of his good will and desire for an understanding.[42]

By late June, however, Frunze was already taking steps preparatory to a Russian invasion of Bukhara. On the twenty-fourth he ordered the defenses of Kerki and Termez strengthened and moved one regiment upriver to Kerki and another by rail to Karshi.[43] The ostensible purpose of these measures was to guard the New Bukhara-Karshi-Kerki railroad, but actually, as Frunze frankly told Moscow on July 12, they were preparations for the emir's overthrow. In his reports to the Turkestan Commission on June 30 and to supreme headquarters in Moscow on July 12 Frunze urged the immediate "integration of Bukhara into the Soviet system." Bukhara's continued independence under the emir posed a direct military threat to Russia and, by keeping alive the hopes of counterrevolutionaries, made the definitive pacification of Turkestan impossible.

Frunze agreed that the emir's overthrow would have to be accomplished in the guise of an internal revolt led by a Bukharan revolutionary council and aided by armed units of Bukharan emigrés already forming on Russian soil, but he candidly asserted that the decisive factor would be the Red Army. At the end of July Frunze informed Lenin that Russia might wait for the revolutionary movement within the khanate to develop to the point where it could accomplish the emir's overthrow, but that this would not happen in the near future because of poor organization among the revolutionaries and the backwardness of the masses. "If the liquidation of the emirate as soon as possible is believed necessary (on this point, I think, there can be no disagreement), then there remains the second course, *i.e.*, the organization of a revolution by means of the direct participation of our forces." On August 10 the Politburo provisionally approved of Frunze's invasion plans but insisted that Tashkent make every effort to avoid the appearance of blatant foreign intervention, which had worked to Kolesov's disadvantage in 1918: the army of liberation must have a strong Moslem element, drawn from the population of Russian Turkestan and from the Bukharan emigrés and deserters, and the attack must be preceded by a clear invitation from the Bukharan revolutionary leadership.[44]

To strengthen the native revolutionary movement for the coming campaign, the Orgburo of the RCP had already decided to force the BCP and the Young Bukharans into a coalition. The consolidation of Soviet power in Turkestan in the fall of 1919 and the conquest of Khiva had revived the hopes of the two groups for the overthrow of the emir with Russia's assistance. The two parties differed little in membership or in goals. The BCP was composed of recent and superficial converts to Communism; the party newspaper, for instance, was in the hands of Sadriddin Aini and Abd al-Vahid Burkhanov, both former moderate Djadids. At the same time the Young Bukharans, led by radicals like Faizullah Khodzhaev since the winter of 1917–1918, made every effort to appear acceptable to Russia, upon whose help the success of their cause wholly depended. The Young Bukharans published for the first time the program Fitrat had written for them two years earlier, after first doctoring it with phrases about the unity of the workers and peasants of the whole world, a democratic republic for Bukhara, and universal suffrage except for counterrevolutionaries. The party applied unsuccessfully for admission to the Comintern. Both parties tried to capitalize on the existing disaffection in the khanate toward the emir's government, the Young Bukharans appealing to all groups, while the BCP concentrated on the lower classes, although neither party achieved much of a mass following.[45]

The two parties were intensely hostile, and the BCP repeatedly protested against Russia's encouragement of its rival. Moscow argued that in the short run the liberal nationalist Young Bukharans were "a progressive factor, cooperating in the overthrow of the despotic power of the emir and the begs," and would prove useful even after the revolution, given their superiority over the BCP in terms of personal talent and the hostility or apathy of the Bukharan population to the cause of socialism. During August 4–6 Kuibyshev presided over a conference that achieved a reconciliation of the Young Bukharans and the BCP, in spite of the BCP's greater reluctance. The Young Bukharans promised to cooperate with the BCP in making the revolution and to join the BCP after the emir's overthrow. To further strengthen the Bukharan revolutionary movement, Tashkent early in August recalled from Khiva the cadres of RCP and CPT members who had been sent to establish the Khorezmi Soviet Republic.[46]

During August 16–19 the Bukharan Communist Party held its fourth congress in the Russian enclave at Chardjui, where it reluctantly ratified the alliance with the Young Bukharans and discussed plans for the imminent overthrow of the emir. A "spontaneous" uprising in Chardjui beglik was to serve as the signal for Russian intervention. In anticipation, Tashkent sent two hundred rifles to the BCP congress to help arm the rebels; Frunze had already designated the Russian garrison at Chardjui as one of the units in the campaign ahead. On August 23 the new members of the Turkestan Commission, whom Moscow had dispatched with the power to approve or alter the plans for the Bukharan campaign, reached Tashkent and unanimously endorsed the decisions already taken by Frunze.[47]

That same day the planned revolt began among the Turkomans of Chardjui beglik, and on the twenty-fifth Frunze issued to his troops their marching orders: beginning on the night of August 28, they were to attack the western part of the khanate from their bases at Chardjui, New Bukhara, Katta-Kurgan, and Samarkand, occupy-

ing all the major towns and sealing off all possible routes by which
the emir and his government might escape to Afghanistan or central
Bukhara. The delay of five days between the start of the revolt and
the Russian intervention was designed to lend credence to the fiction
of a spontaneous revolution. As the Turkestan Commission reassured
the Central Committee of the RCP on the twenty-sixth, every effort
had been made to ensure the success of the campaign: Tashkent had
been particularly careful to present its intervention as a measure
both of self-defense against a hostile and aggressive neighbor and
of assistance to a genuine revolutionary movement rooted in the
native population of Central Asia. The troops to be launched against
the emir were half Moslem, including two regiments of Bukharans.[48]

The long and careful preparations finally bore fruit. On the
night of August 28 the beg of Chardjui was deposed by a Bukharan
Revolutionary Committee, which immediately summoned the entire population of the khanate to join the struggle against the emir
and in their name invited the assistance of the Red Army. Frunze
launched the invasion according to plan: the emir's capital was attacked by troops from Chardjui, New Bukhara, and Katta-Kurgan;
Guzar was taken on August 31 by units from Samarkand and Karshi;
and troops from Chardjui, Kerki, and Termez, with the aid of the
Amu-Darya Flotilla, effectively sealed off the possible escape routes
to Afghanistan. After a fierce struggle the Russians occupied Old
Bukhara on September 2. The anti-Russian leaders Burhan ad-Din
and Osman-beg were arrested—to be tried and shot before the year's
end—and three of the emir's sons, including his heir, were sent to
Moscow as hostages.[49] Alim himself had escaped the city on August
31 and with a small body of loyal troops made his way to central
Bukhara.

The victors formed a new Bukharan government on September
2. It consisted of a Revolutionary Committee and a Council of People's Nazirs, each having nine men. Faizullah Khodzhaev, the most
prominent and capable of the native revolutionaries, became chairman of the Council, headed the foreign nazirat (commissariat), and
served on the Revolutionary Committee. Khodzhaev honored his
written pledge to the Russians, to whom he owed his new power,
by leading the Young Bukharans into a full merger with the BCP
under the name, organization, and program of the Communist group
on September 11.[50] On October 6 the First All-Bukharan Kurultai

of Soviets formally abolished the four-century-old khanate and established the Bukharan People's Soviet Republic. Bukhara, like Khiva, had now exercised its right of self-determination with the assistance of, and in the manner prescribed by, the Communist rulers of Russian Central Asia.

Faizullah Khodzhaev, Premier of Bukharan People's Soviet Republic, 1920–1924

Soviet Policy and the Structure of Dependence

The reduction of Khiva and Bukhara by Russian troops in 1920 transformed the centuries-old khanates into "people's soviet republics." Ostensibly sovereign and independent states, in the course of the next four years they made the transition from the status of subordinate allies of Soviet Russia to that of thoroughly controlled satellites and finally to political annihilation through absorption into the Soviet Union. Although the creation of the two republics would not have been possible in 1920 without Russian armed intervention, the establishment of the new regimes satisfied the long frustrated wishes of the small group of local nationalist and liberal reformers who assumed power in place of the deposed khan and emir. Four years later, power having passed into the hands of men more devoted to Russia and more committed to Communism, the two republics liquidated themselves upon orders from Moscow.

That Soviet Russia never intended Bukhara and Khiva, whatever their form of government, to enjoy more than the appearance of independence was made clear almost immediately after the revolution in Bukhara. Writing in *Pravda* on October 10, 1920, Stalin once again emphasized that Bolshevik policy toward the non-Russian areas of the former empire was based on the subordination of national aspirations to the cause of proletarian revolution. He insisted that the experience of the past three years had shown that Russia and her "border regions" were dependent upon each other for victory in the struggle against imperialism: while Russia could not survive without the raw materials, fuel, and foodstuffs of the border regions, those areas "would inevitably be doomed to imperialist bondage without the political, military and organizational support of more developed central Russia." According to Stalin, the border regions had but two courses open to them—either "an intimate, indestructible union" with the Russian revolutionary center, which would be to the advantage of both parties, or the path of secession, which would run counter to "the interests of the mass of the people in both the center and the border regions." Clearly, the quest for union and not the exercise of the "inalienable" and "unquestionable" right of secession must guide the relations between Moscow and the border regions. Although Finland, the Baltic states, and Poland had been lost to Russia by October 1920, the Red Army had thwarted a number of efforts at secession, including the attempt of the Bukharan and Khivan khanates to pursue an independent course; Armenia and Georgia still maintained their independence, but their days were numbered. In the other borderlands Moscow had since the winter of 1918–1919 been carefully concentrating in its own hands all the important levers of control—the army, transportation and communications networks, public finance, and economic affairs.[1]

In his October 1920 statement Stalin envisioned the specific forms of union between the center and the border regions as varying in individual cases all the way from a "narrow, administrative autonomy" to "the highest form of autonomy—to treaty relations." Stalin cited Azerbaidzhan as an example of a region enjoying treaty relations with Moscow. The terms of the treaties concluded by the RSFSR with Azerbaidzhan in September 1920 were repeated in the virtually identical treaties with the Ukraine in December and with Belorussia a month later.[2] Bukhara and Khiva enjoyed this "highest form of autonomy" to an even greater extent, at least on paper. Whereas the other republics ceded to the RSFSR full authority over the commissariats of war, supply, finance, and transportation and communications, as well as all organs of domestic and foreign trade, the Bukharan and Khorezmi republics retained some control in these areas. Their privileged status was due in part to their unique historical experience as self-governing protectorates under the tsars and to the problems thus posed for their integration into the Russian body politic. More important was Moscow's desire to preserve for a time the appearances of a genuine local revolution against the despotism of khans and mullahs, to serve as an example for the colonial East beyond Russia's borders.

The formal treaty relations entered into in 1920–1921 by the RSFSR on the one side and the Khorezmi and Bukharan People's Soviet Republics (KhPSR and BPSR) on the other were the concrete expression of a policy toward the minority nationalities that

Stalin subsequently defined as comprising the recognition of the right of the non-Russian nations to independence, the renunciation of all tsarist claims and rights in the regions inhabited by these nations, Russian assistance for the cultural and economic development of the relatively backward border nations, and the voluntary military and economic union of the borderlands with central Russia.[3] In recognition of the full independence of Khorezm and Bukhara, Moscow abrogated all treaties and agreements concluded with the khans and emirs by former Russian governments and renounced all of Russia's former rights in the two states.[4] All property, land concessions, and rights of usage formerly held in the khanates by the Russian government, Russian nationals, or Russian business firms were turned over without compensation to the governments of the people's republics.[5] Moscow handed over to a joint Khorezmi-Bukharan authority the steamboats and barges of the Amu-Darya Flotilla, also without compensation, and returned to full Bukharan jurisdiction the four Russian settlements held as enclaves since the 1880's.[6]

Nor was the RSFSR laggard in committing itself to assist the cultural and economic development of Khorezm and Bukhara. Less than five months after the Khivan revolution the Turkestan Commission resolved to help the KhPSR by sending teachers and textbooks, medical and public health personnel, medicines and hospital equipment—in addition to one thousand rifles, two hundred thousand cartridges, two airplanes, and twenty military instructors.[7] In the September 1920 treaties with Khorezm Moscow assumed the obligation of helping to wipe out illiteracy and raise the cultural level of its population by supplying teachers, textbooks, literature, printing facilities, and schools. To hasten the KhPSR's economic development, Russia promised to supply technicians and machinery; a start was made with a grant of five hundred million rubles for cultural and economic development.[8] By 1923 Russia had helped Khorezm to establish a university, a teachers' college, thirty-five schools, fifteen adult schools, three newspapers, and two journals; to launch a major campaign against illiteracy; and to build bridges, telegraph lines, and twenty-four major irrigation works.[9] In September 1920 and March 1921 Russia made similar promises to Bukhara of money (two hundred million rubles), personnel, and matériel for her economic and cultural development.[10]

Along with formal independence, political equality, and economic and cultural aid programs, Moscow's nationality policy included one more promise to the borderlands: "voluntary" union with revolutionary Russia. Never once forgetting the strategic and economic value of Khorezm and Bukhara, nor the danger of British penetration into Central Asia, Moscow bound the two people's republics into "an intimate, indestructible union," both military and economic, with their former suzerain and new-found helper. Common plans for defensive and offensive military operations and for raising and equipping troops, with final authority resting in the Russian supreme command, ensured that the Bukharan and Khorezmi armies would be little more than local units in a unified military machine directed from Moscow. Even the appointment of the Bukharan nazir of war and the work of his department were subject to the approval of the Revolutionary Military Council of the Turkestan Front. The economies of the two people's republics were linked somewhat more loosely to that of the RSFSR: Russia became a partner in the management and development of the irrigation and communications networks; the Russian commissariats for foreign trade and foreign affairs received close supervisory authority over foreign trade; and Khorezm and Bukhara gave Russia preference in marketing their exports and in granting commercial, industrial, and mining concessions—in no case were such concessions to be granted to governments, companies, or individuals of a third state, unless Moscow gave its permission.[11]

In addition to the many provisions for military and economic control, Moscow took more direct precautions to make of the new republics compliant instruments of Soviet policy. In June 1920 the Turkestan Commission charged its representatives in Khiva with "the removal of counterrevolutionary elements who are hindering the work of Soviet construction in the Khorezmi Republic." Former Khan Abd Allah was arrested on July 10 after a series of anti-Soviet demonstrations and taken to Russia, where he shortly afterward died in a prison hospital. In Bukhara, too, Russia took direct responsibility for internal security: on September 5, 1920, Tashkent ordered the establishment of a Bukharan Cheka (secret police) as a branch of the "Special Section" of the Turkestan Front. The numerous Russian personnel sent to aid in the development of the young republics were added insurance of Russian control, especially since Russians in Bukhara and Khorezm enjoyed not only all the civil rights of local citizens but full political rights as well.[12]

Formal independence and equality, economic and cultural development, all within the framework of a close and unequal partnership with the RSFSR, was the concrete form taken by Bolshevik nationality policy in the Central Asian people's republics. However, one important element was lacking, for the implementation of that policy always assumed "the complete emancipation of the peasants and the concentration of all power in the hands of the laboring elements of the border nations."[13] As of the fall of 1920, notwithstanding their Soviet form of government and their subordination to Russia, Khorezm and Bukhara were still, as Moscow saw it, in the hands of the liberal and nationalist representatives of the bourgeoisie.

Eclipse of the Young Khivans and Young Bukharans, 1920–1921

Young Khivans headed ten of the fifteen nazirats in Khorezm's first republican government, elected in April 1920 by the First All-Khorezmi Kurultai of Soviets. The premier was Palvan-hadji Yusupov, chairman of the Young Khivan central committee and a wealthy merchant. His three deputies were Muhammad Karim Baba Ahun, speaker of the Madjlis in 1917; Mullah Djumyaz Sultanmuradov, former chairman of the Young Khivan committee in Petro-Aleksandrovsk; and the Turkoman chieftain Kosh-mamed-khan. The republican government did not move nearly fast enough on the problem of land reform to satisfy Russia, nor was it sufficiently anticlerical. Its most serious failure involved the familiar Turkoman problem. The Young Khivans, Uzbegs all, regarded the Turkoman minority as a potential fifth column in league with Djunaid-khan and his followers, who were still at liberty in the Kara Kum Desert. As early as April 1920 the Young Khivans pressed for the disarming or expulsion of the Turkoman troops who had helped overthrow the khanate, despite Frunze's pleas for an end to ethnic tensions. In mid-September Yusupov's government had its way: it tricked six hundred Turkoman soldiers into disarming, executed Kosh-mamed-khan without benefit of trial, and arrested and shot approximately one hundred other Turkomans. The following month the Young Khivan regime dispatched punitive expeditions against Turkoman villages suspected of aiding Djunaid's guerrilla bands.[14]

Alarmed at the direction events were taking in Khorezm, the Turkestan Commission on October 19 sent an extraordinary investigating commission headed by Valentin Safonov—a Bolshevik, former commandant of troops in Fergana, and now Russian plenipotentiary in Khorezm. The situation Safonov found at Khiva was very discouraging from the point of view of Moscow and Tashkent: not only were the Young Khivans in full possession of the state machinery, but they also had at the beginning of November seized control of the infant Khorezmi Communist Party, electing Sultanmuradov chairman of the central committee. Safonov instituted a purge of the party ranks and engineered the election of a new central committee in December. He next turned to the Turkoman minority for support and convoked a Turkoman congress in January 1921, which elected an executive bureau to administer Turkoman affairs. Safonov's report to the Turkestan Commission in February charged the Young Khivans with responsibility for the September executions and in general for unjust treatment of the Turkomans. The struggle against the Young Khivan faction finally came to a head on March 10 when Safonov, working with the Red Army garrison in Khiva and the Turkoman tribal leaders, staged a mass demonstration against the government. Yusupov and the other Young Khivan officials bowed to the inevitable and fled. Some of them, including Sultanmuradov, joined forces with Djunaid-khan, whose following quadrupled as a result of Safonov's coup.[15]

Under Communist supervision a provisional revolutionary committee took over the government and conducted elections to the Second All-Khorezmi Kurultai of Soviets, which met in May to elect a new government that would correct the mistakes of the Young Khivans. The kurultai proclaimed an amnesty for the Turkoman rebels and asserted the right of each nationality to local self-government, to schools and courts using the native language, and to an equal share in the country's land and water resources. The Central Executive Committee (TsIK) which the kurultai created included a Turkoman Section elected by the Turkoman congress. The kurultai also amended the constitution to disfranchise large landowners and wealthy merchants, clerical dignitaries, and all those who exploited the labor of others; in fact, the second kurultai had itself been elected on the basis of just such a restricted suffrage, imposed after the March coup.[16]

From the spring of 1921 the Russians retained close control of the situation in Khorezm, purging at will both the local Communist Party and the ostensibly independent republican government. The party was reduced to a hard core of sixty members in May (a 97 percent drop), and the first purge of the government occurred in the fall, when several officials were arrested for alleged counterrevolutionary activities. The chairman of TsIK and the nazir of foreign affairs, faced with similar charges, fled to Djunaid's camp in the Kara Kum.[17]

In Bukhara as well Russia found it irksome to deal with liberal nationalists not subject to Moscow's strict party discipline. Bukhara was in the hands of the Young Bukharans, in spite of their formal merger with the BCP in September 1920. The first chairman of TsIK, a post equivalent to president of the republic, was Abd al-Kadir Muhiddin, one of the leaders of the Young Bukharans during their years in exile and a son of Muhiddin Mansur, the moderate who had headed the Young Bukharan central committee in the spring of 1917. Mansur's other three sons also held prominent government posts, one serving as ambassador to Moscow. Faizullah Khodzhaev was premier and foreign nazir. Following the 1920 revolution the Young Bukharan-dominated government split with the Central Committee of the BCP, which urged an immediate start on the transformation of Bukhara into a socialist society. This time Russia, in the person of Kuibyshev, her plenipotentiary representative in Bukhara, intervened on the side of the government, and a more moderate central committee was installed. By April 1921, however, the balance of power in Bukhara had shifted too far to the right for Moscow's taste, with Muhiddin leading a group that took an antisocialist and anti-Russian position on such issues as the presence of Soviet troops in the country. Bowing to pressure from Russia, the more moderate members of the regime, led by Faizullah Khodzhaev, replaced Muhiddin in September with another Young Bukharan, Osman Hodja, formerly nazir of finance.[18]

To further complicate relations between the Young Bukharans and their Russian patrons, a strong Basmachi resistance movement developed in the central and eastern *vilayets*, as the begliks had been renamed under the republic. The initial Soviet conquest of the outlying parts of Bukhara during the winter of 1920–1921 met with no effective opposition from a population that had little cause to defend the old regime and, in any case, lacked the organization and arms to halt the Russians. Emir Alim and his retinue, having escaped from the capital and suffered a defeat in battle at Guzar, forsook the western plains for the mountains and valleys of central Bukhara,

where they took refuge in ever more remote provincial centers—
Baisun, Hisar, and finally Kurgan-Tübe. By February 1921, when
the Russian advance had reached Düshambe and Faizabad in the
upper reaches of the river valley adjacent to the emir's refuge, Alim
resolved to abandon his dominions. Flight to India was impossible,
for the Russians were in possession of Khorog and the western
Pamirs; Afghanistan was the only avenue of escape.[19] At the end of
February Alim crossed the Pandj above the former Russian post at
Sarai and found asylum in Kabul, as so many Bukharan political
refugees had before him. After its successful winter campaign the
Red Army handed over central Bukhara to the administrators and
militia of the BPSR. The withdrawal of the Soviet troops encouraged
the development of open resistance to the republican government
created by the Russians and run by their Young Bukharan allies.
Local rebel leaders appeared, who received moral and material support from the former emir in Afghanistan. By the fall of 1921 most
of central and eastern Bukhara was in the hands of the insurgent
Basmachis.[20]

These developments placed the Young Bukharan regime in an
awkward situation, increasingly at odds with its Russian patrons over
the pace and direction of social change and at the same time openly
defied by its own people. In the summer of 1921 a prominent Young
Bukharan, Muhiddin Mahzun, went over to the Basmachis. His desertion was an indication of the difficult choice of allies soon to face
the republican leaders: either the Russians or the rebels, behind
whom stood the deposed emir. For some the conflict was resolved by
the arrival in Bukhara on November 8 of Enver Pasha, the Ottoman
military hero and leader of the Young Turk regime before 1918. In
exile since Turkey's defeat by the Allies, Enver Pasha had offered
his services to Moscow, which hoped to use his popularity to stir
up enthusiasm among the Central Asian Moslems for the struggle
against the Basmachis in Bukhara and in Turkestan. Enver quickly
decided that he had more to gain personally as unifier and leader
of the divided and quarrelsome rebels than as an agent of Soviet policy. He deserted to the Basmachis on November 11 and took with
him several eminent Young Bukharans, including the president of
the republic, Osman Hodja, and the nazirs of war and the interior.[21]

Enver Pasha nevertheless proved unable to subordinate more
than three thousand of the sixteen thousand Basmachis in central
and eastern Bukhara to his leadership, and he ended by quarreling

with Alim and with Ibrahim-beg, the former emir's lieutenant in Bukhara; these divisions within the rebels' ranks were a major factor in their defeat. Enver's capture of Düshambe and siege of Baisun in February 1922 marked the high tide of the Basmachi advance, for the rebels were unable to take Baisun and break through onto the western plains. In mid-June the Red Army launched a decisive coun- teroffensive, cutting the Basmachis' supply routes from Afghanistan by the seizure of Kurgan-Tübe and Kulab, and surprising and killing Enver himself near Baldjuan on August 4. By late summer of 1923 the back of the rebellion had been broken with the fall of Garm and Kala-i Khumb to the Reds, although Ibrahim-beg did not finally abandon guerrilla warfare until 1926, when he joined Alim in Kabul.[22]

The desertion of Osman Hodja and other prominent Young Bukharans to the Basmachis in November 1921 left the government of the BPSR in the hands of those who, like Faizullah Khodzhaev, chose to depend on Russian support in order to retain power rather than to join the anti-Soviet camp. For most of them the choice was the lesser of two evils, and they still hoped to be able to pursue an independent, liberal-nationalist policy; only Khodzhaev seems sin- cerely to have adopted the Marxist faith of Russia's new masters. But increased dependence *on* Russia inevitably meant increased subordination *to* Russia. Although at the end of 1921 the Young Bukharans still governed, Bukhara was fully as much at Russia's disposal as was Khorezm after the March coup.

An End and a Beginning

After expelling the Young Khivans from power and gaining an effective hold over what remained of the Young Bukharans, Moscow found that its means of controlling its two Central Asian depen- dencies were still far from satisfactory. Khorezmi and Bukharan leaders, including the Communists, lacked the proper revolutionary background to compensate for the fact that their countries, even more than Russia herself, lacked the economic and social precon- ditions for socialism. On December 31, 1921, the Russian Politburo ordered the Turkestan Commission to investigate and recommend means by which the Bukharan government, still in the hands of the Young Bukharans, might be altered from a merchants' to a workers' and peasants' government. A month later the Politburo and the

Orgburo jointly created a commission consisting of Stalin, Foreign Commissar Chicherin, and Kuibyshev to study the Turkestan Commission's report. That report included recommendations for a merger of the BCP with the parent party in Russia and for closer economic cooperation among Bukhara, Khorezm, and Turkestan in a new Central Asian Economic Council, on which the RSFSR would also be represented. In May 1922 the Politburo approved the merger of both the Bukharan and Khorezmi parties with the RCP, established in Tashkent a Central Asian Bureau of the Russian party's Central Committee, and dispatched G. K. Ordzhonikidze (chairman of the party's Caucasian Bureau and ruthless conqueror of Transcaucasia) to Central Asia to "strengthen" both party and state by means of an intensive purge in Bukhara and Khorezm.[23]

A year later Stalin could claim before the Central Committee of the RCP that the Bukharan party had already been reduced in membership from sixteen thousand to "not more than a thousand" and that the purge in process in Khorezm would reduce party membership from "several thousand" to "not more than some hundreds." Stalin justified such a drastic rate of expulsion by pointing out that only a few years earlier 50 percent of the Khorezmi party had been "merchants and the like." Even after the purges the situation was still far from satisfactory, for Stalin complained that in the Bukharan government, both in its composition and its policies, he found "nothing either of a people's or a soviet character."[24] The Politburo immediately sent Ia. E. Rudzutak, one of the original members of the Turkestan Commission and now a secretary of the Central Committee, to Central Asia to complete the process of sovietization. Under Rudzutak's direction the Bukharan governmental apparatus was thoroughly purged at all levels: most of the remaining Young Bukharan officials, including Fitrat, the nazir of education, were arrested and deported to Russia. Faizullah Khodzhaev alone of the former Djadids remained in power; unlike most of the others he had become a convinced Communist and was at the time a member of the All-Russian Central Executive Committee and of the Revolutionary Military Council. Rudzutak completed his assignment by directing the amendment of the Bukharan constitution to disfranchise all former officials of the emir's government and members of the upper bourgeoisie and to extend broader political rights to the urban proletariat and poor peasantry. In October 1923 the Fourth Kurultai of Soviets elected a new TsIK, handpicked by Rudzutak.

The BCP underwent a final purge at the same time that worker and peasant members were being actively recruited.[25]

By the fall of 1923 both Bukhara and Khiva had been transformed from subordinate allies into docile satellites, whose leaders were merely the instruments for executing policies formulated in Moscow. That even this state of affairs was not the ultimate fate envisaged by the Politburo for the former khanates had been made clear a year earlier when the creation of the USSR gave final form to the existing "intimate, indestructible union" of the several soviet republics. *Pravda* quoted Stalin on November 18, 1922, as granting that "Bukhara and Khorezm, not being socialist, but only people's soviet republics, may, perhaps, remain outside this union until their natural development transforms them into socialist republics." The following month Stalin reassured the Tenth All-Russian Congress of Soviets on the same point: "Two independent soviet republics, Khorezm and Bukhara, which are not socialist, but people's soviet republics, remain for the time being outside this union solely and exclusively because these republics are not yet socialist. I have no doubt, comrades, and I hope that you too have no doubt, that, as they develop internally towards socialism, these republics will also join the union state which is now being formed."[26]

To allay any lingering doubts among the assembled comrades, the Bukharan and Khorezmi observers at the congress affirmed their hope of eventually gaining admission to the USSR. In fact, Bukhara and Khorezm moved with astonishing rapidity toward socialism— if socialism be taken to mean simply the elimination of all but dependable Communists from their ruling elites. Once the state and party purges had been completed, Khorezm in October 1923 and Bukhara the following September were officially restyled as soviet socialist republics, qualifying them for membership in the USSR.[27]

There had been little social or economic change to justify the change of name in either republic. Far from having experienced the kind of economic development that would have increased the size and strength of their minute proletariats, Bukhara and Khorezm in the early 1920's saw even their traditional economies reduced to ruins. Cotton production for export to Russia, the key index to the economic vitality of Central Asia, fell in each of the people's republics during 1920–1922 to less than 5 percent of the 1913 level. By 1924 a substantial recovery had been achieved, but production was still only 40 percent of the 1913 figure in Bukhara, and 29 percent in Khorezm. The situation with respect to karakul skins was similar: exports to Russia in 1924 were five times the 1921 figure but only 25 percent of the pre-1917 level.[28] Nor had popular attitudes changed substantially since the second Russian conquest: two months after it had proclaimed a soviet socialist republic, the Khorezmi government faced a serious revolt against new taxes and secular schools. Besieged in its capital for three and a half weeks by ten to fifteen thousand Uzbeg and Turkoman rebels supported by Djunaid-khan's bands, and defended only by the troops of the Russian garrison, the regime was rescued early in February 1924 by a cavalry regiment from Soviet Turkestan. The rebellion was suppressed, but at Moscow's orders the newly purged Khorezmi government lowered the objectionable tax, freed over two hundred political prisoners, and reestablished the maktabs, madrasas, and religious courts.[29] In Central Asia, as in Russia itself, the cause of socialism seemed best served for the moment by retreat and concessions. The Basmachi bands in the Kara Kum Desert posed no serious threat after a six-week campaign by Russian troops in February and March 1924, although they did not actually disband until Djunaid fled to Persia in the fall of 1928.[30]

Even while the purges of 1922–1923 were transforming Bukhara and Khorezm into "socialist" republics, steps were being taken toward their integration into the USSR. In March 1923 the Central Asian Economic Council, which had been recommended a year earlier by the Turkestan Commission, was established. Bukhara and Khorezm agreed to merge their economic planning, postal and telegraph systems, and foreign trade activities with those of Soviet Turkestan, to adopt the monetary system of the USSR, and to place their transportation systems under the RSFSR Commissariat for Communications. *Pravda* and *Izvestiia* hailed the economic unification of the people's republics with the USSR as an important preparatory step toward complete incorporation.[31] The following month Moscow regained direct control of the Amu-Darya Flotilla, which had been turned over to Bukhara and Khorezm in September 1921. In May the RSFSR concluded a customs union with Bukhara, under which Russian customs officials and Russian troops, just as in tsarist days, assumed control of the Bukharan-Afghan frontier.[32]

By the fall of 1923 the stage had been set for the final act, on which the curtain was raised by the petition in October of the Fourth All-Khorezmi Kurultai of Soviets for admission to the USSR.

But on what basis were Bukhara and Khorezm to be included? There had always been an element of the anomalous in Moscow's extension to these two lands of the formal rights of nationalities as prescribed by Lenin and Stalin, for Stalin's own definition of a nation clearly indicated that Bukhara and Khorezm were multinational states. And yet the commissar for nationalities had himself referred in recent years to a Bukharan and a Khivan nationality.[33] The inconsistency stemmed from the necessity of justifying in terms of Bolshevik nationality policy the creation of the BPSR and the KhPSR, which had in fact been dictated by considerations of expediency, *i.e.*, Moscow's desire to control the former khanates at minimum cost while consolidating its position in Russia and Central Asia. As the time arrived when Moscow no longer felt the need of two nominally independent republics in Central Asia, the inconsistency was resolved by abandoning the fiction of a Bukharan and a Khivan nationality. In the spring of 1923 Stalin was already denouncing "Uzbeg chauvinism directed against the Turkomans and the Kirgiz [Kazakhs] in Bukhara and Khorezm."[34]

In fact, Moscow had already decided upon the institutional forms most suitable for the strengthening of Communist rule in Central Asia: a completely new system of national republics and national oblasts to replace the traditional political divisions in the area.[35] Not only Bukhara's and Khorezm's nominal independence but their very political existence was to be terminated in the process. Early in 1924 the Communist parties of the four republics involved (Bukhara, Khorezm, Turkestan, and Russia) approved the proposed "national delimitation" of Central Asia, and in September and October the respective governments gave their formal assent to the new order. Bukhara and Khorezm thereby lost their political identity; their territories, together with those of the Turkestan Republic, were divided approximately along ethnic lines; and the new political formations were all included within the USSR, receiving varying degrees of formal autonomy. Bukhara, except for the Turkoman districts along the Amu-Darya, became the nucleus of the Uzbeg Soviet Socialist Republic, which also included Samarkand, Tashkent, the Fergana Valley, and a fragment of Khorezm contained within the triangle Gurlen-Khiva-Pitniyak. Central and eastern Bukhara constituted the Tadjik Autonomous SSR within the Uzbeg republic. The former Kabakli, Chardjui, Burdalik, Kerki, and Kelif begliks of Bukhara, together with southern and western Khorezm as far north as Kunya-Urgench, were incorporated into the Turkoman SSR, whose core was the old Transcaspian Oblast. The remainder of Khorezm, including Kungrat, Khodjeili, Kipchak, and Mangit, along with the Amu-Darya Otdel and the eastern half of the Ust-Urt Plateau, formed the Karakalpak Autonomous Oblast within the Kirgiz [Kazakh] ASSR of the RSFSR.[36]

The dismemberment of Bukhara and Khiva, carried out with the cooperation of their own governments, was a strangely peaceful end for two countries that had known so much turbulence over the centuries. It was a foretaste of the radical changes in store for these ancient lands under their new rulers. Political modernization, following the Soviet Russian model and effected in stages under Moscow's direction between 1920 and 1924, proved to be the first step in Russia's program for the wholesale transformation of Bukhara and Khiva in the image of a political, social, economic, and moral order, whose inspiration derives from the history and thought of the modern West. For this transformation the six decades covered by this study were a period of gradual, albeit unconscious, preparation.

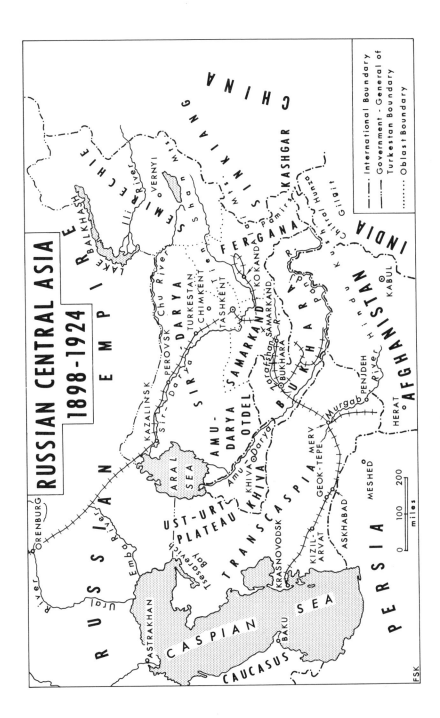

RUSSIAN CENTRAL ASIA
1898-1924

International Boundary
Government - General of
Turkestan Boundary
Oblast Boundary

CHINA

SINKIANG

SEMIRECHIE

LAKE BALKHASH

Ili River

VERNYI

Chu River

Tien Shan

KASHGAR

FERGANA

Pamir

Chitral Hunza

Gilgit

PEROVSK

SIR-DARYA

Syr-Darya

TURKESTAN

CHIMKENT

TASHKENT

KOKAND

SAMARKAND

SAMARKAND

Zarafshan

BUKHARA

BUKHARA

Panj R.

Hindu Kush

INDIA

KABUL

KAZALINSK

ARAL
SEA

AMU-
DARYA
OTDEL

Amu Darya

KHIVA

KHIVA

PENJDEH

HERAT

AFGHANISTAN

RUSSIAN EMPIRE

ORENBURG

Ural River

Emba River

Tsesarevich Bay

UST-URT
PLATEAU

TRANSCASPIA

KRASNOVODSK

KIZIL-
ARVAT

GEOK-TEPE

MERV

Murgab

ASKHABAD

MESHED

PERSIA

ASTRAKHAN

CASPIAN   SEA

BAKU

CAUCASUS

0   100   200
miles

FSK

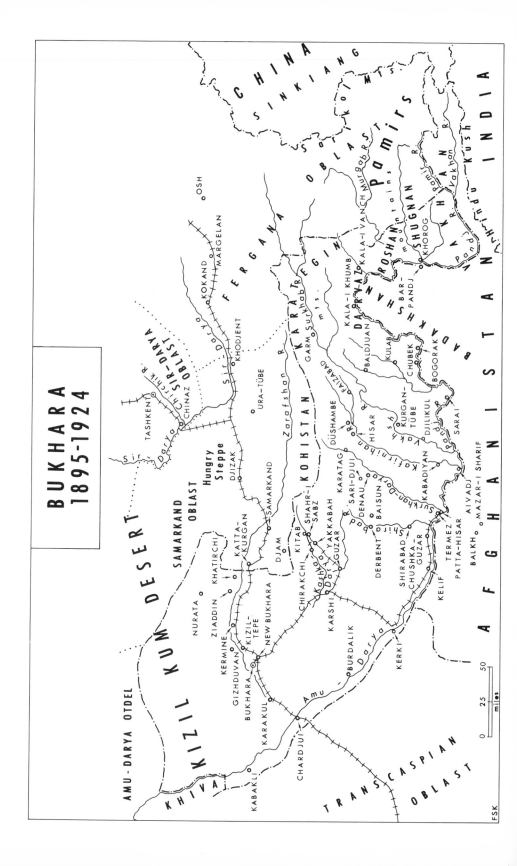

BUKHARA
1895-1924

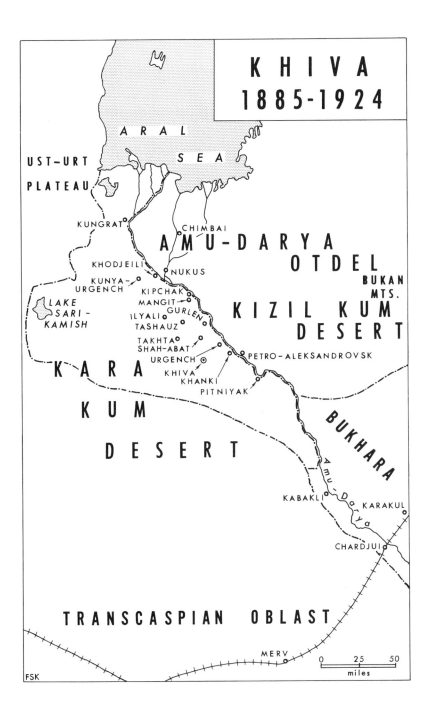

KHIVA
1885-1924

ARAL
SEA

UST-URT
PLATEAU

KUNGRAT
CHIMBAI
AMU-DARYA
OTDEL
KHODJEILI
NUKUS
BUKAN
MTS.
KUNYA-
URGENCH
KIPCHAK
MANGIT
GURLEN
KIZIL KUM
ILYALI
LAKE
SARI-
KAMISH
TASHAUZ
DESERT
TAKHTA
SHAH-ABAT
URGENCH
PETRO-ALEKSANDROVSK
KARA
KHIVA
KHANKI
PITNIYAK

KUM
BUKHARA

DESERT
Amu-Darya

KABAKLI
KARAKUL

CHARDJUI

TRANSCASPIAN OBLAST

MERV
0   25   50
miles

FSK

Appendix 1

Russo-Bukharan Commercial Convention of 1868
From *Pravitelstvennyi Vestnik*, October 31/November 12, 1872

1. All Russian subjects, whatever their religion, are granted the right to travel for purposes of trade wherever they wish in the khanate of Bukhara, just as all subjects of the emir of Bukhara have always been, and will in future continue to be, permitted to trade throughout the Russian Empire.

2. His High Eminence the Emir pledges himself strictly to guard the security and safety of Russian subjects, their caravans, and, in general, all their property within the borders of his dominions.

3. Russian merchants will be permitted to have caravansaries in which to store their merchandise in any Bukharan towns they wish. Bukharan merchants will enjoy the same right in Russian towns.

4. Russian merchants are granted the right to maintain, if they so desire, commercial agents (*caravan-bashi*) in all the towns of the khanate of Bukhara to look after the regular course of trade and the legal collection of duties. This right is also granted to Bukharan merchants in the towns of the Turkestan Krai.

5. The same duty will be levied on all goods going from Russia to Bukhara or from Bukhara to Russia as is levied in the Turkestan Krai, *i.e.*, 2½ percent ad valorem; in any case, the duty will not be more than that collected from Moslem subjects of Bukhara.

6. Russian merchants and their caravans are granted free and safe passage across Bukharan territory into adjacent lands, just as Bukharan caravans are permitted to cross Russian territory.

These conditions dispatched from Samarkand, May 11, 1868. (Signed) Adjutant General von Kaufman I, Governor General of Turkestan and Commander of the Troops of the Turkestan Military Okrug. The Emir affixed his seal in Karshi, June 18, 1868.

Appendix 2

Russo-Khivan Peace Treaty of 1873
From *Pravitelstvennyi Vestnik*, November 30/December 12, 1873

1. Saiyid Muhammad Rahim Bohadur Khan acknowledges himself to be the obedient servant of the Emperor of All the Russias. He renounces the right to maintain direct and friendly relations with neighboring rulers and khans and to conclude with them any commercial or other treaties; he will not undertake any military actions against them without the knowledge and permission of the supreme Russian authority in Central Asia.

2. [Article two traces the Russo-Khivan boundary on the east, north, and west of the khanate.]

3. The entire right bank of the Amu-Darya and the lands adjoining it, until now considered Khiva's, shall pass from the khan into the possession of Russia together with all their settled and nomadic inhabitants. The plots of land on the right bank that are at present the property of the khan and have been granted by him to the dignitaries of the khanate for their use shall at the same time become the property of the Russian government, free of any claims on the part of the former holders. It is left to the khan to compensate their losses with lands on the left bank.

4. If, by the imperial will of His Majesty the Emperor, a part of the right bank should be transferred into the possession of the emir of Bukhara, the khan of Khiva will recognize the emir as the legal ruler of this part of his former possessions and renounce any intentions of restoring his authority there.

5. Russian steamboats and other Russian ships, governmental as well as private, are granted free and exclusive navigation on the Amu-Darya. Khivan and Bukharan ships may enjoy the right of navigation only with special permission from the supreme Russian authority in Central Asia.

6. Russians have the right to construct wharves in those places on the left bank of the Amu-Darya where it may prove necessary and convenient. The Khivan government is responsible for the security and safety of these wharves. The approval of the places selected for wharves rests with the supreme Russian authority in Central Asia.

7. Aside from these wharves, Russians are granted the right to maintain trading posts on the left bank of the Amu-Darya for the deposit and

storage of their goods. In those places indicated by the supreme Russian authority in Central Asia, the government of the khanate promises to allot for trading posts a sufficient amount of unpopulated land for wharves and for the construction of shops, of lodgings for those serving in the trading posts and those having business with the trading posts, premises for mercantile offices, and land for the establishment of farms. These trading posts, together with all the people living on them and all the goods stored on them, will be under the direct protection of the government of the khanate, which will be responsible for their safety and security.

8. In general all the towns and villages of the khanate of Khiva are henceforth open to Russian trade. Russian merchants and Russian caravans may travel freely throughout the khanate, and they shall enjoy the special protection of the local authorities. The government of the khanate is responsible for the security of caravans and warehouses.

9. Russian merchants trading in the khanate are exempt from the payment of zakat and any other kind of commercial duties, just as Khivan merchants have not for a long time paid zakat, either on the road through Kazalinsk, in Orenburg, or in the ports of the Caspian Sea.

10. Russian merchants are granted the right of duty-free passage for their goods across Khivan territory into all neighboring lands.

11. In Khiva and in the other towns of the khanate, Russian merchants are granted the right to maintain, if they wish, agents (*caravan-bashi*) for handling relations with the local authorities and for superintending the conduct of commercial affairs.

12. Russian subjects are granted the right to have real property in the khanate. Such property is subject to the land tax by agreement with the supreme Russian authority in Central Asia.

13. Commercial obligations between Russians and Khivans shall be held sacred and inviolable on both sides.

14. The government of the khanate pledges itself to investigate without delay the complaints and claims of Russian subjects against Khivans and, if they prove well-founded, to satisfy them immediately. In a case where debts are due to Russian subjects and to Khivans, the claims of the Russians shall have priority.

15. The complaints and claims of Khivans against Russian subjects, even in cases where the latter are within the borders of the khanate, shall be handed over to the nearest Russian authorities for examination and satisfaction.

16. In no case will the government of the khanate admit persons coming from Russia without exit permission from the Russian authorities, whatever their nationality may be. Should any criminal who is a Russian subject take refuge from the law within the borders of the khanate, the government of the khanate promises to apprehend and deliver him to the nearest Russian authorities.

17. Saiyid Muhammad Rahim Bohadur Khan's proclamation, published the 12th of June last, concerning the emancipation of all slaves in the khanate and the abolition for all time of slavery and the trade in

human beings, shall remain in full force; the government of the khanate pledges itself to follow up with all the means in its power the strict and conscientious execution of this matter.

18. An indemnity in the amount of 2,200,000 rubles is imposed upon the khanate of Khiva to defray the expenses of the Russian treasury for the conduct of the recent war, provoked by the government of the khanate and by the Khivan people. [The remainder of article eighteen concerns the payment of the war indemnity plus interest at the rate of 5 percent per annum, in Russian paper currency or Khivan coin, in annual installments due each November 1 according to the following schedule: 1873—100,000 rubles; 1874—100,000 rubles; 1875—125,000 rubles; 1876—125,000 rubles; 1877—150,000 rubles; 1878—150,000 rubles; 1879—175,000 rubles; 1880—175,000 rubles; 1881–1892—200,-000 rubles per year; 1893—73,557 rubles.] (Signed) Governor General of Turkestan, Adjutant General von Kaufman. Saiyid Muhammad Rahim Khan signed the Turkish text of this treaty by affixing his seal in the presence of the Governor General of Turkestan, Adjutant General von Kaufman I, on the 12th day of August, 1873.

Appendix 3

Russo-Bukharan Friendship Treaty of 1873
From *Pravitelstvennyi Vestnik*, December 18/30, 1873

1. [Article one concerns the Russo-Bukharan and Bukharan-Khivan boundaries.]

2. Since the separation of the right bank of the Amu-Darya from the khanate of Khiva, all caravan routes leading from Bukhara northward into Russian territory pass through Bukharan and Russian lands exclusively. Both the Russian and the Bukharan governments, each within its own borders, will guard the safety of movement of caravans and trade along these routes.

3. Russian steamboats and other Russian ships, governmental as well as private, are granted free navigation on an equal basis with Bukharan ships on that part of the Amu-Darya River which belongs to the emir of Bukhara.

4. Russians have the right to construct wharves and warehouses for goods in those places on the Bukharan banks of the Amu-Darya where it may prove necessary and convenient. The Bukharan government takes upon itself to guard the security and safety of these wharves and warehouses. The approval of the places selected for wharves depends on the supreme Russian authority in Central Asia.

5. All towns and villages of the khanate of Bukhara are open to Russian trade. Russian merchants and Russian caravans may travel freely throughout the khanate, and they enjoy the special protection of the local authorities. The Bukharan government is responsible for the security of Russian caravans within the borders of Bukhara.

6. In Bukhara a duty of 2½ percent ad valorem will be levied on all goods, without exception, belonging to Russian merchants and going from Russia to Bukhara or from Bukhara to Russia, just as one-fortieth part is levied in the Turkestan Krai. No supplementary duties will be levied above this zakat.

7. Russian merchants are granted the right of duty-free transport of their goods across Bukharan territory into all neighboring lands.

8. Russian merchants will be permitted to have in Bukharan towns, where it proves necessary, their own caravansaries in which to store their goods. Bukharan merchants will enjoy the same right in the towns of the Turkestan Krai.

9. Russian merchants are granted the right to have commercial agents in all Bukharan towns to supervise the regular course of trade and the legal collection of duties, and also for relations with the local authorities on mercantile matters. This right is granted also to Bukharan merchants in the towns of the Turkestan Krai.

10. Commercial obligations between Russians and Bukharans shall be held sacred and inviolable on both sides. The Bukharan government promises to see to the conscientious execution of all commercial transactions and the conscientious conduct of commercial affairs in general.

11. Russian subjects in Bukhara are granted the right to engage in the various industries and handicrafts permitted by the Sharia on an equal basis with Bukharan subjects; Bukharan subjects in Russia enjoy the same right in regard to industries and handicrafts permitted under Russian law.

12. Russian subjects are granted the right to have immovable property in the khanate, *i.e.*, to buy houses, gardens, and fields. This property is subject to the land tax on an equal basis with the property of Bukharan subjects. Bukharan subjects will enjoy the same right within the boundaries of the Russian Empire.

13. Russian subjects shall enter Bukharan territory with passports issued to them by the Russian authorities; they have the right to travel freely throughout the khanate, and they enjoy the special protection of the Bukharan authorities.

14. In no case will the Bukharan government admit persons coming from Russia without exit permission from the Russian authorities, whatever their nationality may be. Should any criminal who is a Russian subject take refuge from the law within Bukhara's borders, he will be apprehended by the Bukharan authorities and delivered to the nearest Russian authorities.

15. In order to maintain an uninterrupted, direct relationship with the supreme Russian authority in Central Asia, the emir of Bukhara will appoint from among his retinue an agent to act as his permanent envoy and plenipotentiary in Tashkent. This plenipotentiary will live in Tashkent in the emir's house and at the emir's expense.

16. The Russian government may likewise have its own permanent representative in Bukhara at the court of His High Eminence the Emir. The Russian plenipotentiary in Bukhara, like the emir's envoy in Tashkent, will live in the house of, and at the expense of, the Russian government.

17. To please his Majesty the Emperor of All the Russias, and for the greater glory of His Imperial Majesty, His High Eminence the Emir Saiyid Muzaffar has decreed that henceforth and for all time the shameful trade in human beings, which is contrary to the laws of humanity, is abolished within the borders of Bukhara. In accordance with this decree, Saiyid Muzaffar shall at this time circulate to all his begs strict orders to the following effect: if, despite the emir's injunction about the end of the slave trade, slaves should be brought from neighboring countries to

Bukharan frontier towns for sale to Bukharan subjects, said slaves will be taken from their masters and immediately set free.

18. His High Eminence Saiyid Muzaffar, desiring in all sincerity to develop and strengthen the good neighborly relations that have now existed for five years to Bukhara's benefit, shall be guided by the seventeen articles set forth above, which constitute a treaty of friendship between Russia and Bukhara. This treaty has been signed in two copies, each in the two languages, Russian and Turkish. As a sign of his ratification of this treaty and of his acceptance of it as a guide for himself and his successors, Emir Saiyid Muzaffar has affixed his seal. In Shahr, the 28th day of September, 1873, the 19th day of the month of Shagban, 1290.

Abbreviations Used in Bibliography and Notes

(I)RGO	(Imperatorskoe) russkoe geograficheskoe obshchestvo
NKID	Narodnyi komissariat inostrannykh del
PSZ	*Polnoe sobranie zakonov Rossiiskoi imperii*
SAGU	Sredneaziatskii gosudarstvennyi universitet (Tashkent)
SMPA	*Sbornik geograficheskikh, topograficheskikh i statisticheskikh materialov po Azii* (St. Petersburg)
SU	*Sobranie uzakonenii i rasporiazhenii pravitelstva*

Bibliography

1. Bibliographies and General Histories

Two excellent general bibliographies are Richard A. Pierce, *Soviet Central Asia: A Bibliography* (Berkeley, 1966), and N. Ia. Vitkind, *Bibliografiia po Srednei Azii* (Moscow, 1929). The first volume of V. I. Mezhov, *Bibliografiia Azii*, 3 vols. (St. Petersburg, 1891–1894), is an indispensable guide to the periodical literature, both Russian and foreign, on Central Asia down to about 1888. Mezhov's *Turkestanskii sbornik sochinenii i statei*, 3 vols. (St. Petersburg, 1878–1888), is a valuable index to the collection of books and articles gathered in Tashkent under the sponsorship of Governors General von Kaufman, Cherniaev, and Rosenbach. The Soviet literature is covered in the following:

Istoriia SSSR. Ukazatel sovetskoi literatury za 1917–1952 gg., 2 vols. and 2 supplements (Moscow, 1956–1958).

Bibliografiia izdanii Akademii Nauk Uzbekskoi SSR. Sistematicheskii ukazatel knig i statei (1943–1952) (Tashkent, 1956), and *(1953–1957)* (Tashkent, 1959).

Istoriia Uzbekistana. Bibliograficheskii ukazatel knig i statei v izdaniiakh Komiteta Nauk pri Sovete Narodnykh Komissarov UzSSR, Uzbekistanskogo filiala Akademii Nauk SSSR, i Akademii Nauk UzSSR (1933–1957 gg.) (Tashkent, 1960).

Sistematicheskii ukazatel k izdaniiam Sredneaziatskogo Gosudarstvennogo Universiteta im. V. I. Lenina (s 1922–1956 gg.), 2nd ed. (Tashkent, 1958).

The following are all good general histories of Central Asia:

Bartold, V. V., *Istoriia kulturnoi zhizni Turkestana* (Leningrad, 1927).
Istoriia narodov Uzbekistana, 2 vols. (Tashkent, 1947–1950).
Istoriia tadzhikskogo naroda, 3 vols. in 5 (Moscow, 1963–1965).
Istoriia Uzbekskoi SSR, 1 vol. in 2 (Tashkent, 1955–1956).

Wheeler, Geoffrey, *The Modern History of Soviet Central Asia* (London and New York, 1964).

2. Geographic, Ethnographic, and Historical Background

A. Geography and Ethnography

The most exhaustive treatment of Central Asia's geography is E. M. Murzaev, ed., *Sredniaia Aziia. Fiziko-geograficheskaia kharakteristika* (Moscow, 1958).

Also excellent are L. S. Berg, *Natural Regions of the USSR* (New York, 1950), and S. P. Suslov, *Fizicheskaia geografiia SSSR: Aziiatskaia chast* (Moscow, 1954). The Commission on the Districting of Central Asia's *Materialy po raionirovaniiu Srednei Azii,* 3 vols. (Tashkent, 1926), is also useful.

Much valuable ethnographic information on Central Asia is contained in S. A. Tokarev, *Etnografiia narodov SSSR* (Moscow, 1958), and Stefan Wurm, *Turkic Peoples of the USSR* (London, 1954).

B. Central Asia Before the Conquest

The major authority on Central Asian history is still the great Russian orientalist V. V. Bartold, whose works are currently being republished in the Soviet Union in a complete edition. René Grousset, *L'empire des steppes* (Paris, 1939), is a useful survey, and there is much valuable information on the Uzbeg khanates in P. P. Ivanov, *Ocherki po istorii Srednei Azii* (*XVI–seredina XIX v.*) (Moscow, 1958). Mary Holdsworth, *Turkestan in the Nineteenth Century: A Brief History of the Khanates of Bukhara, Kokand and Khiva* (London, 1959), is drawn largely from recent Soviet monographs. The only full-length history of Bukhara is the out-dated study by Arminius Vámbéry, *History of Bokhara* (London, 1873). L. Sobolef, *Latest History of the Khanates of Bokhara and Kokand* (Calcutta, 1876), covers the late eighteenth and the first third of the nineteenth century; it is translated from articles that appeared in the *Turkestanskie Vedomosti* (Tashkent).

The best contemporary description of Bukhara before the Russian conquest is N. V. Khanykov, *Opisanie Bukharskago khanstva* (St. Petersburg, 1843), translated as *Bokhara: Its Amir and Its People* (London, 1845). For Khiva in the same period, Colonel G. I. Danilevskii, "Opisanie Khivinskago khanstva," IRGO, *Zapiski,* V (1851), 62–139, is the standard contemporary description. Arminius Vámbéry's *Travels in Central Asia* (London, 1864) and *Sketches of Central Asia* (London, 1868) are unsurpassed travel accounts by a Western savant who visited Khiva and Bukhara in 1863 disguised as a Moslem pilgrim. Other contemporary descriptions, in addition to the accounts of English visitors listed in Chapter 1, note 34, are:

"Bukharskii emir i ego poddannye," IRGO, *Izvestiia,* II (1866), 64–65.

Galkin, M., "O Shegri-Sebzskoi oblasti Bukharskago khanstva," IRGO, *Izvestiia,* I (1865), 131–135.

Nashi sosedi v Srednei Azii. I. Khiva i Turkmeniia (St. Petersburg, 1873).

Spalding, Captain H., trans., *Khiva and Turkestan* (London, 1874).

C. Russia and Central Asia

S. V. Zhukovskii, *Snosheniia Rossii s Bukharoi i Khivoi za poslednee trekhsotletie* (Petrograd, 1915), is the basic work. Also valuable is the more general study by V. V. Bartold, *Istoriia izucheniia vostoka v Evrope i v Rossii,* 2nd ed. (Leningrad, 1925), available in translation as *La découverte de l'Asie, Histoire de l'orientalisme en Europe et en Russie* (Paris, 1947). The nineteenth century is ably covered in John Wentworth Strong, "Russian Relations with Khiva, Bukhara, and Kokand, 1800–1858," unpub. diss. Harvard University, 1964. M. K. Rozhkova, "Iz istorii torgovli Rossii so Srednei Aziei v 60-kh godakh XIX v.," *Istoricheskie Zapiski*, LXVII (1960), 187–212, and her *Ekonomicheskie sviazi Rossii so Srednei Aziei. 40–60e gody XIX veka* (Moscow, 1963) are indispensable for the economic aspect of the relationship on the eve of conquest. Other works are:

Bunakov, E. V., "K istorii snoshenii Rossii s sredneaziatskimi khanstvami v XIX veke," *Sovetskoe Vostokovedenie*, II (1941), 5–26. Primarily economic relations in the early nineteenth century.

Fioletov, N., "Bukharskoe i Khivinskoe khanstva i otnosheniia ikh s Rossiei," *Istoricheskii Zhurnal*, 1941, No. 3, pp. 68–79. A popular account covering the whole period from the sixteenth century to the 1920's.

G[agemeister, Iu. A.], "O torgovom znachenii Srednei Azii v otnoshenii k Rossii," *Russkii Vestnik*, XLI (October 1862), 706–736. The author was director of the chancellery of the Ministry of Finance.

Grigoriev, Vasilii Vasilevich, "Russkaia politika v otnoshenii k Srednei Azii, istoricheskii ocherk," *Sbornik Gosudarstvennykh Znanii*, I (1874), 233–261. Covers the period up to 1850.

3. *The Russian Conquest of Bukhara and Khiva*

A. G. Serebrennikov, ed., *Turkestanskii krai. Sbornik materialov dlia istorii ego zavoevaniia*, 14 vols. (Tashkent, 1912–1916), is an indispensable documentary collection. Only vols. 1–8 (covering the period 1839–1852) and 17–22 (1864–1866) were published; of the latter group, only vols. 17–19 (January 1864-July 1865) are available in the United States. D. I. Romanovskii, *Zametki po sredne-aziiatskomu voprosu* (St. Petersburg, 1868), available in translation as *Notes on the Central Asiatic Question* (Calcutta, 1870), is invaluable not only for the views of Kaufman's predecessor but for the appendix containing many documents not found elsewhere. The standard secondary work on the conquest is M. A. Terentiev, *Istoriia zavoevaniia Srednei Azii*, 3 vols. and atlas (St. Petersburg, 1906), the bulk of which was written in the 1870's. The author participated in some of the events described, including the war against Bukhara in 1868 and the delimitation of the Russo-Bukharan boundary in the following year. Also valuable is the same author's adamantly anti-British *Russia and England in Central Asia*, 2 vols. (Calcutta, 1876), a translation of the Russian edition (St. Petersburg, 1875). A. L. Popov, "Iz istorii zavoevaniia Srednei Azii," *Istoricheskie Zapiski*, IX (1940), 198–242, is a significant contribution. N. A. Khalfin's two studies, *Politika Rossii v Srednei Azii* (1857–1868) (Moscow, 1960) and *Prisoedinenie Srednei Azii k Rossii* (60–90e gody XIX v.) (Moscow, 1965), are useful but add little new. J. A. MacGahan, *Campaigning on the Oxus, and the Fall of Khiva* (New York, 1874), is a vivid eye-witness account by the *New York Herald*'s correspondent.

4. *Bukhara and Khiva under the Russian Protectorate to 1885*

A. Primary Sources and Contemporary Works

Two sources of considerable interest for the protectorates, although dealing mainly with the government-general of Turkestan, are K. P. von Kaufman, *Proekt vsepoddanneishago otcheta po grazhdanskomu upravleniiu i ustroistvu v oblastiakh Turkestanskago general-gubernatorstva, 7 noiabria 1867—25 marta 1881 g.* (St. Petersburg, 1885), and F. K. Giers, *Otchet revizuiushchago, po Vysochaishemu poveleniiu, Turkestanskii krai, Tainago Sovetnika Girsa* (St. Petersburg, 1883). Two relevant memoirs are D. A. Miliutin, *Dnevnik 1873–1882*, 4 vols. (Moscow, 1947–1950), and G. P. Fedorov, "Moia sluzhba v Turkestanskom krae (1870–1906 goda)," *Istoricheskii Vestnik*, CXXXIII (1913), 786–812; CXXXIV (1913), 33–55, 437–467, 860–893.

The most important sources for this period are the reports of official and unofficial visitors to the protectorates. The most valuable of these are:

Arandarenko, G., "Bukharskiia voiska v 1880 g.," *Voennyi Sbornik*, October 1881, pp. 341–367. The author was commandant of the Samarkand Uezd.

———— "Darvaz i Karategin," *Voennyi Sbornik*, November 1883, pp. 140–159; December 1883, pp. 303–319.

———— "V gorakh Darvaza-Karategina," *Vostochnoe Obozrenie*, July 14, 1883, pp. 9–10; July 21, 1883, pp. 9–10.

Bonvalot, Gabriel, *De Moscou en Bactriane* (Paris, 1884) and *Du Kohistan à la Caspiènne* (Paris, 1885). Journal of a French scientific expedition in 1881.

Burnaby, Captain Fred, *A Ride to Khiva* (London, 1876). The author was an English officer on leave who went to Khiva purely for the sport of it.

Capus, Guillaume, *A travers le royaume de Tamerlan* (Paris, 1892). The author was Bonvalot's companion in 1881.

———— and Gabriel Bonvalot, "Rapport sur une mission scientifique dans l'Asie centrale," *Archives des Missions Scientifiques et Littéraires*, 3rd series, X (1883), 277–311.

Gloukhovsky [Glukhovskoi], A., "Captivité en Boukharie," *Bulletin de la Société de Géographie*, 5th series, XVI, September 1868, pp. 265–296. The author was a member of the ill-fated Struve mission to Emir Muzaffar in 1865; this account is probably an abridged translation of A. Glukhovskoi, "Plen v Bukhare," *Russkii Invalid*, 1868, Nos. 97–100, which is unavailable in this country.

———— "Zapiska o znachenii Bukharskogo khanstva dlia Rossii i o neobkhodimosti priniatiia reshitelnykh mer dlia prochnogo vodvoreniia nashego vliianiia v Srednei Azii," excerpt in *Khrestomatiia po istorii SSSR*, vol. III (1857–1894), 2nd ed. (Moscow, 1952).

Iavorskii, Doctor I. L., *Puteshestvie russkago posolstva po Avganistanu i Bukharskomu khanstvu v 1878–1879 gg.*, 2 vols. (St. Petersburg, 1882–1883).

Kostenko, L., "Gorod Khiva v 1873 godu," *Voennyi Sbornik*, December 1873, pp. 321–340.

———— *Puteshestvie v Bukharu russkoi missii v 1870 godu* (St. Petersburg, 1871). The author was a member of Nosovich's mission; parts of this book first appeared as the following three articles:

———— "Puteshestvie russkoi missii v Bukharu, v 1870 godu," *Voennyi Sbornik*, October 1870, pp. 249–260.

———— "Opisanie puteshestviia russkoi missii v Bukharu v 1870 godu," *Voennyi Sbornik*, December 1870, pp. 381–410.

———— "Gorod Bukhara v 1870 godu," *Voennyi Sbornik*, December 1870, pp. 411–425.

———— *Turkestanskii krai*, 3 vols. (St. Petersburg, 1880).

Krestovskii, Vsevolod V., "V gostiakh u emira bukharskago. Putevoi dnevnik," *Russkii Vestnik*, February 1884, pp. 469–532; March, pp. 113–154; May, pp. 5–75; June, pp. 608–659; July, pp. 49–110; August, pp. 478–559. Later published in book form under the same title (St. Petersburg, 1887). The author was a member of the Wittgenstein mission in December 1882—January, 1883.

Kun, A. L., "Poezdka po Khivinskomu khanstvu v 1873 g.," IRGO, *Izvestiia*, X (1874), 47–58.

———— "Ocherki Shagrisebzskago bekstva," IRGO, *Zapiski po Otdeleniiu Etnografii*, VI (1880), 201–237. The author accompanied Abramov's 1870 expedition.

Lansdell, Henry, *Russian Central Asia, Including Kuldja, Bokhara, Khiva and Merv*, 2 vols. (London, 1885). The travels in 1882 of an English clergyman whose purpose was the dissemination of religious literature.

Moser, Henri, *A travers l'Asie centrale* (Paris, 1885). The author was a Swiss silk manufacturer.

Petrovskii, N. F., "Moia poezdka v Bukharu," *Vestnik Evropy*, March 1873, pp. 209–248. The author was an agent of the Ministry of Finance.

Putiata, Captain, "Ocherk ekspeditsii v Pamir, Sarykol, Vakhan i Shugnan 1883 g.," SMPA, X (1884), 1–88.

Schuyler, Eugene, *Turkistan. Notes of a Journey in Russian Turkistan, Khokand, Bukhara, and Kuldja*, 2 vols. (New York, 1876). Account of a trip made in 1873 by the American consul general in St. Petersburg.

Stremoukhov, N. P., "Poezdka v Bukharu," *Russkii Vestnik*, CXVII (1875), 630–695. A trip made in 1874.

Tatarinov, A., *Semimesiachnyi plen v Bukharii* (St. Petersburg, 1867). The author was, like Glukhovskoi, a member of the 1865 Struve mission.

Terentiev, M., "Turkestan i turkestantsy," *Vestnik Evropy*, September 1875, pp. 65–112; October, pp. 499–529; November, pp. 142–172.

The following works are of interest primarily for their contributions to geographical knowledge of Bukhara and Khiva:

Arkhipov, Captain, "Voennaia rekognostsirovka ravninnoi chasti Bukharskago khanstva, proizvedennaia v 1883 g.," SMPA, X (1884), 171–238.

Beliavskii, Colonel, "Izsledovanie puti ot zaliva Tsesarevicha (Mertvyi Kultuk) cherez Ust-iurt do Kungrada, proizvedennoi v 1884 g.," SMPA, XV (1885), 1–89.

Bykov, Captain, "Ocherk doliny Amu-dari," SMPA, IX (1884), 34–73. Account of the expedition of 1877–1879 sponsored by the Grand Duke Nikolai Konstantinovich.

Gedeonov, Captain, "Astronomicheskiia opredeleniia punktov v Zakaspiiskoi oblasti, Khivinskom i Bukharskom khanstvakh, v 1884 godu," IRGO, *Izvestiia*, XXI (1885), 199–202.

Gedroits, Prince A. E., "Predvaritelnyi otchet o geologicheskikh izsledovaniiakh na sukhikh ruslakh Amu-dari," IRGO, *Izvestiia*, XVIII (1882), 77–105. Expedition sent out in 1879–1880 by the Ministry of Ways of Communication.

Gelman, Kh. V., "Izsledovanie proryvov reki Amu-Dari, obrazovavshikhsia vo vremia eia razliva letom v 1878 godu," IRGO, *Zapiski Kavkazskago Otdela*, X (1879), Supplement to No. 3, 1–77. Expedition sponsored by Tiflis in 1877–1878.

———— "Ot Krasnovodska do Khivy," *Vestnik Evropy*, August 1882, pp. 697–707. Journey in November–December 1878.

Grodekoff, Colonel N., *Colonel Grodekoff's Ride from Samarcand to Herat* (London, 1880). A translation of N. I. Grodekov, *Cherez Afganistan* (St. Petersburg, 1880).

———— "Poezdka iz Samarkanda cherez Gerat v Afganistan (v 1878 godu)," *SMPA*, V (1883), 58–107.

Grum-Grzhimailo, G. E., "Ocherk pri-pamirskikh stran," IRGO, *Izvestiia*, XXII (1886), 82–109.

Ivanov, D. L., "Puteshestvie na Pamir," IRGO, *Izvestiia*, XX (1884), 209–252. The author was a member of the 1883 Pamir Expedition, dispatched by Governor General Cherniaev and led by Captain Putiata.

———— "Shugnan," *Vestnik Evropy*, June 1885, pp. 612–658; July, pp. 48–97.

Kaulbars, Colonel Baron A. V., "Nizovia Amu dari, opisannyia po sobstvennym izsledovaniiam v 1873 g.," IRGO, *Zapiski po Obshchei Geografii*, IX (1881), 1–630. The author was sent by Kaufman to explore the delta during the Russian occupation of Khiva.

Kosiakov, P. E., "Putevyia zametki po Karateginu i Darvazu v 1882 godu," IRGO, *Izvestiia*, XX (1884), 589–613. The author was Regel's topographer in 1882.

Kostenko, L., "Ot Khivy do Kazalinska," *Voennyi Sbornik*, November 1873, pp. 151–166. Trip in August 1873.

Maev, N. A., "Doliny Vakhsha i Kafirnigana," IRGO, *Izvestiia*, XVII (1881), 179–192. Elorations in 1879.

———— "Geograficheskii ocherk Gissarskago kraia i Kuliabskago bekstva," IRGO, *Izvestiia*, XII (1876), 349–363. The 1875 Hisar Expedition.

———— "Marshruty i zametki po iuzhnym chastiam Bukharskago khanstva," IRGO, *Izvestiia*, XIV (1878), 361–386. Explorations in the spring of 1878.

———— "Putevyia zametki o Bukharskom khanstve," *Voennyi Sbornik*, August 1877, pp. 296–307. Trip to Kitab and Shahr in February–March 1877.

———— "Rekognostsirovka gornykh putei v Bukharskom khanstve," IRGO, *Izvestiia*, XV (1879), 87–99. Explorations in the spring of 1878; a continuation of "Marshruty i zametki."

———— "Stepnye puti ot Karshi k Amu-dare," IRGO, *Izvestiia*, XVII (1881), 166–178. Explorations in 1880.

Matveev, Colonel, "Poezdka po bukharskim i avganskim vladeniiam v fevrale 1877 g.," *SMPA*, V (1883), 1–57. Travels in late 1878; the date in the title is in error.

Nazirov, Lieutenant, *Marshrutnoe opisanie puti ot g. Mesheda v gorod Chardzhui* (St. Petersburg, 1883). Journey in the spring of 1882.

Oshanin, V. F., "Karategin i Darvaz," IRGO, *Izvestiia*, XVII (1881), 21–58. Trip to Karategin in 1878.

Petrov, G. M., "Putevyia zametki 1884 g.," *SMPA*, XXI (1886), 53–102.

———— "Zametki o dorogakh iz Chardzhuia v Karki, Kelif, Guzar i Karshi 1885 g.," *SMPA*, XXI (1886), 102–110.

Regel, A. E., "Poezdka v Karategin i Darvaz," IRGO, *Izvestiia*, XVIII (1882), 137–141. Explorations in 1881.

———— "Puteshestvie v Shugnan," IRGO, *Izvestiia*, XX (1884), 268–274. Explorations in 1882–1883.

Severtsov, N. A., "Orograficheskii ocherk Pamirskoi gornoi sistemy," IRGO, *Zapiski po Obshchei Geografii*, XIII (1886), 1–384. Expedition of 1879.

Sobolev, L. N., "Geograficheskiia i statisticheskiia svedeniia o Zeravshanskom okruge," IRGO, *Zapiski po Otdeleniiu Statistiki*, IV (1874), 161–718.

———— "O postepennom dvizhenii peskov k g. Bukhare," IRGO, *Izvestiia*, IX (1873), 259–265.

———— "Obzor dostupov k Khivinskomu khanstvu i kratkiia svedeniia o nem," *Voennyi Sbornik*, May 1873, pp. 127–164.

———— "Zametki o Gissarskikh vladeniiakh i o srednem techenii Surkh-abdari," IRGO, *Izvestiia*, IX (1873), 307–314.

Sorokin, N. V., "Ocherki iz puteshestviia po Srednei Azii," Kazan University, *Uchenyia Zapiski*, January–April 1882, section two, pp. 1–39. Grand Duke Nikolai Konstantinovich's expedition to the Amu-Darya basin, 1877–1879.

———— "Puteshestviia v Sredniuiu Aziiu i Frantsiiu v 1878 i 1879 godakh," Kazan University, *Izvestiia i Uchenyia Zapiski*, 1881, No. 1, pp. 3–100.

Stoletov, N. G., "Amu-Darinskaia ekspeditsiia," IRGO, *Izvestiia*, X (1874), 321–323.

"Svedeniia o puti v Sredniuiu Aziiu, cherez Mertvyi Kultuk, po Ust-Urtu i Amu-Dare," *SMPA*, IX (1884).

Syrovatskii, S., "Putevyia zametki o Khivinskom khanstve," *Voennyi Sbornik*, November 1874, pp. 127–158.

Trotter, Captain Henry, "On the Geographical Results of the Mission to Kashghar, under Sir T. Douglas Forsyth in 1873–74," *The Journal of the Royal Geographical Society*, XLVIII (1878), 173–234. Contains information on Shugnan and Roshan.

Zubov, N., "Verkhnee i srednee techenie sudokhodnoi Amu," IRGO, *Zapiski po Obshchei Geografii*, XV (1886), 1–59. Explorations conducted by Grand Duke Nikolai Konstantinovich's expedition in the summer of 1879.

B. Secondary Works

Richard A. Pierce, *Russian Central Asia 1867–1917* (Berkeley, 1960), is now the standard work on the government-general of Turkestan but is not very helpful on Bukhara and Khiva. The same is true of the important early Soviet work by P. G. Galuzo, *Turkestan—koloniia* (*Ocherk istorii Turkestana ot zavoevaniia russkimi do revoliutsii 1917 goda*) (Moscow, 1929). Zeki Validi Togan, *Turkestan Today*, an unpublished English translation of the author's *Bügunkü Tür-*

kili (Türkistan) ve yakin Tarihi (Istanbul, 1942–1947) in the library of the Russian Research Center at Harvard University, deals with the protectorates as well as the government-general but is continually inaccurate or misleading with respect to Bukhara and Khiva.

There are a number of excellent Soviet monographs, based on research in the archives, of value both for this period and for the years after 1885. S. P. Pokrovskii, "Mezhdunarodnye otnosheniia Rossii i Bukhary v dorevoliutsionnoe vremia i pri sovetskoi vlasti—do natsionalnogo razmezhevaniia sredne-aziatskikh respublik," SAGU, *Biulleten,* XVI (1927), 39–58; XVII (1928), 31–57, is indispensable for the series of formal agreements concluded between Russia and Bukhara, beginning with the 1868 treaty. Three studies by B. I. Iskandarov are valuable for Russo-Bukharan relations as well as for conditions within the protectorate, especially central and eastern Bukhara: *Iz istorii Bukharskogo emirata (Vostochnaia Bukhara i Zapadnyi Pamir v kontse XIX veka)* (Moscow, 1958); *Vostochnaia Bukhara i Pamir v period prisoedineniia Srednei Azii k Rossii* (Stalinabad, 1960); and *Vostochnaia Bukhara i Pamir vo vtoroi polovine XIX v.,* 2 vols. (Dushanbe, 1962–1963).

Internal conditions in central Bukhara are also the subject of Sh. Iusupov, *Ocherki istorii Kuliabskogo bekstva v kontse XIX i nachale XX veka* (Dushanbe, 1964), and N. A. Kisliakov, "Ishan—feodal Vostochnoi Bukhary," Akademiia Nauk SSSR, Tadzhikistanskaia baza, *Trudy,* IX (1938), 3–27. Bukhara's capital is treated in O. A. Sukhareva, *Bukhara XIX–nachalo XX v. (Pozdnefeodalnyi gorod i ego naselenie)* (Moscow, 1966). Administrative and fiscal aspects of the emir's government are explored in two excellent monographs by A. A. Semenov, *Ocherk ustroistva tsentralnogo administrativnogo upravleniia Bukharskogo khanstva pozdneishego vremeni* (Stalinabad, 1954) and *Ocherk pozemelno-podatnogo i nalogovogo ustroistva b. Bukharskogo khanstva* (Tashkent, 1929). A. P. Savitskii, "Materialy k istorii Amu-Darinskogo otdela," SAGU, *Trudy,* new series, LXII (1955), 67–84, is of great value for Khiva.

A good survey of the geographical exploration of the khanates is P. P. Semenov, *Istoriia poluvekovoi deiatelnosti Imperatorskago Russkago Geograficheskago Obshchestva 1845–1895,* 3 vols. (St. Petersburg, 1896), especially chs. 31 and 32. Russia's work in mapping Bukhara and Khiva is covered in two articles by Ch. V. Galkov, "Trianguliatsionnye raboty v Srednei Azii (iz istorii Turkestanskogo voenno-topograficheskogo otdela)" and "Semochnye i kartograficheskie raboty Turkestanskogo voenno-topograficheskogo otdela," *Izvestiia Uzbekistanskogo filiala Geograficheskogo Obshchestva SSSR,* II (1956), 123–133, and III (1957), 57–94.

5. Anglo-Russian Relations and the Protectorates

A. Primary Sources and Contemporary Works

The most valuable sources are the British Blue Books on Central Asia and Afghanistan, published in the official *Parliamentary Papers* between 1873 and 1895, and the Russian foreign ministry's documentary collection, *Afganskoe razgranichenie: Peregovory mezhdu Rossiei i Velikobritaniei 1872–1885* (St.

Petersburg, 1886). Also of interest are Baron Alexandre Meyendorff, ed., *Correspondance diplomatique de M. de Staal (1884–1900)*, 2 vols. (Paris, 1929); Lord Augustus Loftus, *Diplomatic Reminiscences 1862–79*, 2 vols. (London, 1894); Agatha Ramm, ed., *The Political Correspondence of Mr. Gladstone and Lord Granville 1868–1876*, Camden Society, 3rd series, vols. LXXXI–LXXXII (London, 1952) and *The Political Correspondence of Mr. Gladstone and Lord Granville 1876–1886*, 2 vols. (Oxford, 1962).

Among the contemporary works the following are useful:

Alikhanov-Avarskii, M., "Zakaspiiskiia vospominaniia 1881–1885," *Vestnik Evropy*, September 1904, pp. 73–125; October, pp. 445–495.

Andreev, "Otchet chinovnika osobykh poruchenii Turkestanskago okruzhnago intendantstva kollezhskago sovetnika Andreeva, soprovozhdavshago v 1884 g. 17-i Turkestanskii lineinyi batalion iz Petro-Aleksandrovskago v Merv," *SMPA*, XV (1885), 148–182.

Boulger, Demetrius Charles, *Central Asian Portraits* (London, 1880).

———— *Central Asian Questions* (London, 1885).

———— *England and Russia in Central Asia*, 2 vols. (London, 1879).

Kostenko, L., "Istoricheskii ocherk rasprostraneniia russkago vladychestva v Srednei Azii," *Voennyi Sbornik*, August 1887, pp. 145–178; September, pp. 5–37; October, pp. 139–160; November, pp. 5–35.

Lessar, P. M., "Mervskie khany. Polozhenie Merva i Ateka v kontse 1882 g.," *SMPA*, VI (1883), 62–82.

———— "Peski Kara-kum, puti soobshcheniia Zakaspiiskoi oblasti s Khivoiu, Mervom i Bukharoiu 1883 g.," *SMPA*, VI (1883), 83–121.

Martens, M. F., *La Russie et l'Angleterre dans l'Asie centrale* (Ghent, 1879). The author, a Russian professor of international law, attempts to prove that the 1869–1873 negotiations established Afghanistan as an independent and neutral state in which Britain had no special rights.

Rawlinson, Major General Sir Henry, *England and Russia in the East* (London, 1875).

Veniukov, M. I., "Ocherk mezhdunarodnykh voprosov v Azii," *Russkii Vestnik*, February 1877, pp. 511–559; April, pp. 473–503.

B. Secondary Works

The most valuable are:

Alder, G. J., *British India's Northern Frontier 1865–95, A Study in Imperial Policy* (London, 1963).

Khan, Mohammad Anwar, *England, Russia and Central Asia (A Study in Diplomacy) 1857–1878* (Peshawar, 1963).

Prasad, Bisheshwar, *The Foundations of India's Foreign Policy*, vol. I (1860–1882) (Calcutta, 1955).

Also of interest are the following:

Aitchison, Sir Charles, *Lord Lawrence* (Oxford, 1892). Very pro-Lawrence.

Ghose, Dilip Kumar, *England and Afghanistan* (Calcutta, 1960). Deals with the period 1876–1887.

Gopal, S., *The Viceroyalty of Lord Ripon 1880–1884* (Oxford, 1953).

Habberton, William, *Anglo-Russian Relations Concerning Afghanistan 1837–1907* (Urbana, 1937).

Khalfin, N., *Proval britanskoi agressii v Afganistane (XIX v.–nachalo XX v.)* (Moscow, 1959).

Shteinberg, E. L., *Istoriia britanskoi agressii na Srednem Vostoke* (Moscow, 1951).

Sykes, Brigadier General Sir Percy, *A History of Afghanistan*, 2 vols. (London, 1940).

Thornton, A. P., "Afghanistan in Anglo-Russian Diplomacy, 1869–1873," *Cambridge Historical Journal*, XI (1953–55), 204–218.

———— "The Reopening of the 'Central Asian Question,' 1864–9," *History*, XLI (1956), 122–136.

Tikhomirov, M. N., *Prisoedinenie Merva k Rossii* (Moscow, 1960).

6. Bukhara and Khiva, 1885–1917: General

A. Primary Sources and Contemporary Works

The basic source for the government-general in this period also contains valuable information on the protectorates: K. K. Pahlen, *Otchet po revizii Turkestanskago kraia*, 19 parts (St. Petersburg, 1909–1911). Count Pahlen's reminiscences of his 1908–1909 inspection tour of Central Asia, written entirely from memory in 1922 and not very reliable, have been translated and published as *Mission to Turkestan* (London, 1964). The most valuable contemporary surveys of Russian Turkestan and the khanates are:

Geier, I. I., *Turkestan*, 2nd ed. (Tashkent, 1909).

Grulew, M., *Das Ringen Russlands und Englands in Mittel-Asien* [*Russland in Asien*, vol. X] (Berlin, 1909). A new edition of M. V. Grulev, *Sopernichestvo Rossii i Anglii v Srednei Azii* (St. Petersburg, 1900).

Masalskii, Prince V. I., *Turkestanskii krai* [V. P. Semenov-Tian-Shanskii, ed., *Rossiia, Polnoe geograficheskoe opisanie nashego otechestva*, vol. XIX] (St. Petersburg, 1913).

Extremely useful, despite their bias and frequent inaccuracies, are the works of Logofet:

D. N. Logofet, *Bukharskoe khanstvo pod russkim protektoratom*, 2 vols. (St. Petersburg, 1911).

———— "Cherez Bukharu (Putevye ocherki po Srednei Azii)," *Voennyi Sbornik*, January 1907, pp. 231–246; February, pp. 215–232; April, pp. 231–244; July, pp. 215–234; September, pp. 199–214.

———— "Cherez Bukharu (Putevye ocherki po Srednei Azii)," *Voennyi Sbornik*, January 1910, pp. 187–218; February, pp. 189–212; March, pp. 243–262; April, pp. 253–270; May, pp. 235–254; June, pp. 229–250; July, pp. 228–250; August, pp. 187–228; September, pp. 219–232; October, pp. 199–218; November, pp. 241–254; December, pp. 223–236.

———— *Na granitsakh Srednei Azii. Putevye ocherki*, 3 vols. (St. Petersburg, 1909). The third volume describes the Bukharan-Afghan border.

———— *Strana bezpraviia. Bukharskoe khanstvo i ego sovremennoe sostoianie* (St. Petersburg, 1909).

————— V *gorakh i na ravninakh Bukhary* (St. Petersburg, 1913).

Of minor value for the protectorates, although a work of fundamental importance for the study of Russian Central Asia in general, is the official publication *Aziatskaia Rossiia*, 3 vols. and atlas (St. Petersburg, 1914). Other contemporary surveys are:

Krahmer, Gustav, *Russland in Mittel-Asien* [*Russland in Asien*, vol. II] (Leipzig, 1898).

Semenov, M. P. de, *La Russie extra-européenne et polaire* (Paris, 1900).

Skrine, Francis Henry, and Edward Denison Ross, *The Heart of Asia, A History of Russian Turkestan and the Central Asian Khanates from the Earliest Times* (London, 1899). Descriptive as well as historical; based on a brief visit in 1898 and on the published accounts of such earlier visitors as Khanykov and Schuyler; contains many factual errors.

The following memoirs are very useful:

Dukhovskaia, Varvara, *Turkestanskiia vospominaniia* (St. Petersburg, 1913). The author was the widow of Governor General S. M. Dukhovskoi (1898–1901).

Polovtsoff, A., *The Land of Timur* (London, 1932). Reminiscences of Turkestan and Bukhara at the turn of the century by a government official.

Tcharykow, N. V., *Glimpses of High Politics* (London, 1931).

Vitte, S. Iu., *Vospominaniia*, 3 vols. (Moscow, 1960).

A major source of information is the literature produced by official and unofficial visitors to the khanates. The more valuable of such works are:

Curtis, William Eleroy, *Turkestan: The Heart of Asia* (New York, 1911). Visit by an American journalist in the spring and early summer of 1910.

Curzon, George N., *Russia in Central Asia in 1889 and the Anglo-Russian Question* (London, 1889). Based on a trip in the fall of 1888; extremely valuable, especially for the building of the Central Asian Railroad.

Dobson, George, *Russia's Railway Advance into Central Asia* (London, 1890). The author, a London *Times* correspondent, was one of a group of foreigners invited by General Annenkov to witness the inauguration of the Central Asian Railroad in the spring of 1888.

Galkin, A., "Kratkii ocherk Bukharskago khanstva," *Voennyi Sbornik*, November 1890, pp. 176–179; December, pp. 400–425.

Heyfelder; Doctor O., "Buchara nach und vor der Transkaspischen Eisenbahn," *Unsere Zeit* (Leipzig), 1888, No. 10, pp. 339–355. The author was chief medical officer to the troops who built the Central Asian Railroad; he returned to Old Bukhara in 1887 to establish a medical practice and organize a native hospital.

Kordes, Johannes, "In Buchara," *Deutsche Monatsschrift für Russland* (Reval), III (1914), 417–432.

Nechaev, A. V., *Po gornoi Bukhare. Putevye ocherki* (St. Petersburg, 1914). Journey in summer of 1908.

Olufsen, O., *The Emir of Bokhara and His Country* (London and Copenhagen, 1911). Travels of a Danish explorer in the late 1890's.

Pokotilo, N. N., "Ocherk bukharskikh vladenii na levom beregu r. Piandzha 1886 g.," *SMPA*, XXV (1887), 267–278.

————— "Puteshestvie v tsentralnuiu i vostochnuiu Bukharu v 1886 godu," *IRGO, Izvestiia*, XXV (1889), 480–502.

Poslavskii, P., "Bukhara," *Voennyi Sbornik*, November 1891, pp. 237–268; December, pp. 452–486. Description of the emir's capital in 1886–1888.

———— "Bukhara. Opisanie goroda i khanstva," *SMPA*, XLVII (1891), 1–102.

Rocca, Félix de, *De l'Alaï à l'Amou-Daria* (Paris, 1896). The author was a member of the 1893 Russian Pamir Expedition who returned by way of Karategin, Darvaz, and the Amu-Darya.

Semenov, A. A., "Po granitsam Bukhary i Afganistana," *Istoricheskii Vestnik*, LXXXVII (1902), 961–992; LXXXVIII (1902), 98–122. Trip in 1898.

Shubinskii, P. P., "Nedavniaia tragediia v Bukhare," *Istoricheskii Vestnik*, XLVIII (1892), 466–475.

———— "Ocherki Bukhary," *Istoricheskii Vestnik*, XLIX (1892), 118–142, 363–389, 620–648; L (1892), 99–123. The author, a Cossack captain and an apologist for the emir's government, was in Bukhara in June 1891.

Taranetz, A. Ia., "Poezdka v Bukharu," *Istoricheskii Vestnik*, CXXXII (1913), 1019–1038.

Varygin, M. A., "Opyt opisaniia Kuliabskago bekstva," IRGO, *Izvestiia*, LII (1916), 737–803.

Z. Z., "Poezdka v Bukharu," *Moskovskiia Vedomosti*, January 23, 1886, pp. 4–5.

Travel accounts of less value for this study include:

Baturin, Rear Admiral, "Otchet ob ekspeditsii v verkhove r. Amu-Dari (1894 g.)," *SMPA*, LXIV (1896), 246–277.

Beliavskii, Lieutenant Colonel, "Opisanie obrekognostsirovannago uchastka, zakliuchaiushchago na sebe proidennye puti v predelakh Shaar-sabiz, Guzarskago bekstva i chasti nagornoi Derbentskoi vozvyshennosti," *SMPA*, LVII (1894), 87–153.

Bonvalot, Gabriel, *Du Caucase aux Indes à travers le Pamir* (Paris, 1888). The author passed through Bukhara in the fall of 1887.

Bookwalter, John W., *Siberia and Central Asia* (London, 1900). An Ohio businessman's visit in 1898.

Boutroue, Alexandre, *En Transcaspie. Notes de Voyage* (Paris, 1897).

Durrieux, A., and R. Fauvelle, *Samarkand. La bien gardée* (Paris, 1901).

Evarnitskii, D. I., *Putevoditel po Srednei Azii, ot Baku do Tashkenta* (Tashkent, 1893).

Fedorov, Colonel, "Statisticheskii ocherk Guzarskago bekstva i chasti Kelifskago," *SMPA*, LVII (1894), 154–207.

Gaevskii, I., "Kurgan-Tiubinskoe bekstvo," RGO, *Izvestiia*, LV (1919–23), No. 2, 14–67.

Galkin, Colonel, "Kratkii voenno-statisticheskii ocherk ofitserov Generalnago Shtaba Turkestanskago voennago okruga v 1889 godu v Bukharskom khanstve i v iuzhnoi chasti Samarkandskoi oblasti," *SMPA*, LVII (1894), 1–42. A summary of the work of military exploring parties led by Beliavskii, Fedorov, Gintyllo, Lilienthal, Stetkevich, Vasiliev, and Vereshchagin, *q.v.*

———— "Voenno-statisticheskii ocherk srednei i iuzhnoi chastei Surkhanskoi doliny, 1889 g.," *SMPA*, LVII (1894), 364–384.

Gelman, Kh. V., "Nabliudeniia nad dvizheniem letuchikh peskov v Khivinskom khanstve," IRGO, *Izvestiia*, XXVII (1891), 384–415.

Gintyllo, Captain, "Svedeniia po intendantskoi chasti, sobrannyia v Bukharskom khanstve v mae i iiune 1885 g.," *SMPA*, XXI (1886), 1–53.

Graham, Stephen, *Through Russian Central Asia* (New York, 1916). Trip in summer of 1914.

Grulev, M. V., "Nekotoryia geografiko-statisticheskiia dannyia, otnosiashchiiasia k uchastku Amu-Dari mezhdu Chardzhuem i Patta-Gissarom," IRGO, *Izvestiia Turkestanskago Otdela*, II (1900), No. 1, 5–87.

Holbrook, Frederick, *Through Turkestan and the Caucasus* (Brattleboro, Vt., 1916).

Jefferson, Robert L., *A New Ride to Khiva* (London, 1899).

Korolkov, B. Ia., "Karatagskoe zemletriasenie 8 oktiabria 1907 goda," IRGO, *Izvestiia Turkestanskago Otdela*, IX (1913), 44–65.

Krafft, Hugues, *A travers le Turkestan russe* (Paris, 1902).

Leclercq, Jules, *Du Caucase aux Monts Alaï* (Paris, 1890).

Liliental, Captain, "Gissarskoe i Kabadianskoe bekstva, 1889 g.," *SMPA*, LVII (1894), 285–322.

Lipskii, V. I., *Gornaia Bukharà*, 3 parts (St. Petersburg, 1902–1905). Botanical and geological explorations during the summers of 1896, 1897, and 1899.

Markov, Evgenii, *Rossiia v Srednei Azii. Ocherki puteshestviia*, 2 vols. (St. Petersburg, 1901). Travels in the early 1890's; part of the book was previously published as "Na Oksus i Iaksarte (Putevye ocherki Turkestana)," *Russkoe Obozrenie*, January, February, March, April, November, and December 1893.

Matveev, Colonel, "Kratkii ocherk Bukhary 1887 g.," *SMPA*, XXXVI (1888), 1–8.

Meakin, Annette M. B., *In Russian Turkestan* (New York, 1915).

Novitskii, V. F., "Poezdka v khrebet Petra Velikago letom 1903 goda," IRGO, *Izvestiia*, XL (1904), 1–30. A geological trip to Karategin and Darvaz.

Obruchev, V. A., *Po goram i pustyniam Srednei Azii* (Moscow, 1948). The author's scientific journeys in 1886–1888.

———— "Zakaspiiskaia nizmennost. Geologicheskii i orograficheskii ocherk," IRGO, *Zapiski po Obshchei Geografii*, XX (1890), No. 3, 1–271. The author's work took him into the Bukharan part of the Zarafshan Valley.

Perowne, J. T. Woolrych, *Russian Hosts and English Guests in Central Asia* (London, 1898).

Phibbs, Isabelle Mary, *A Visit to the Russians in Central Asia* (London, 1899).

Proskowetz, Doctor Max von, *Vom Newastrand nach Samarkand* (Vienna, 1889).

Puare, Captain, "Opisanie dorogi ot Guzara do Kerki," *SMPA*, LVII (1894), 208–216.

Rickmers, W. Rickmer, *The Duab of Turkestan* (Cambridge, Eng., 1913). Travels in Bukhara, 1896–1906.

Rozhevits, R. Iu., "Poezdka v iuzhnuiu i sredniuiu Bukharu v 1906 g.," IRGO, *Izvestiia*, XLIV (1908), 593–656.

Serebrennikov, Captain, "Ocherki Shugnana," *SMPA*, LXX (1896), 1–52.

Shoemaker, M. M., *Trans-Caspia. The Sealed Provinces of the Czar* (Cincinnati, 1895).

Shvarts, F., "Astronomicheskiia, magnitnyia i barometricheskiia nabliu-

deniia, proizvedennyia v 1886 godu v Bukhare, Darvaze, Karategine, i v Ze-
ravshanskoi, Ferganskoi i Syr-Darinskoi oblastiakh," IRGO, *Zapiski po Obshchei
Geografii*, XXV (1893), No. 3, 1–56.

Sitniakovskii, N. F., "Popytki k ischisleniiu narodonaseleniia v gor. Bukhare," IRGO, *Izvestiia Turkestanskago Otdela*, I (1898–1899), No. 1, 77–85.

———— "Zametki o bukharskoi chasti doliny Zeravshana," IRGO, *Izvestiia
Turkestanskago Otdela*, I (1898–1899), No. 2, 121–314.

Snesarev, Lieutenant Colonel, "Vostochnaia Bukhara (voenno-geografiche-
skii ocherk)," *SMPA*, LXXIX (1906), 1–148.

Stein, Aurel, *On Ancient Central-Asian Tracks* (New York, 1964; repr. of
1933 ed.). Travels of a British archeologist in eastern Bukhara during World
War I.

Stern, Bernhard, *Vom Kaukasus zum Hindukusch* (Berlin, 1893).

Stetkevich, Captain, "Basein Karatag-dari. Voenno-statisticheskii ocherk
1889 g.," *SMPA*, LVII (1894), 234–284.

Ukhtomskii, Prince Esper, *Ot Kalmytskoi stepi do Bukhary* (St. Petersburg,
1891).

Vannovskii, Captain, "Izvlechenie iz otcheta o rekognostsirovke v Rushane
i Darvaze 1893 g.," *SMPA*, LVI (1894), 73–125.

Vasiliev, Captain, "Kratkoe statisticheskoe opisanie Karategina," *SMPA*,
XXXIII (1888), 8–53.

———— "Statisticheskie materialy dlia opisaniia Bukhary. Bekstvo Shira-
badskoe i chast Baisunskago. 1889 g.," *SMPA*, LVII (1894), 399–402.

Vereshchagin, Captain, "R. Amu-Daria mezhdu g.g. Kerki i Kelifom v
predelakh Bukhary i pribrezhnye puti. Rekognostsirovka 1889 g.," *SMPA*,
LVII (1894), 48–86.

Woeikof, A., *Le Turkestan russe* (Paris, 1914). Trip made in summer,
1912.

B. Secondary Works

In addition to the works listed under 4B. above, the following monographs
are of value for this period:

B. I. Iskandarov, *O nekotorykh izmeneniiakh v ekonomike Vostochnoi
Bukhary na rubezhe XIX–XX vv.* (Stalinabad, 1958). A much broader treatment than the title suggests.

Kisliakov, N. A., *Patriarkhalno-feodalnye otnosheniia sredi osedlogo selskogo
naseleniia Bukharskogo khanstva v kontse XIX–nachale XX veka* (Moscow,
1962).

Madzhlisov, A., *Karategin nakanune ustanovleniia sovetskoi vlasti* (Stalinabad, 1959).

7. Bukhara and Khiva, 1885–1917: Special Topics

A. The Central Asian Railroad and Abd al-Ahad's Succession

De Lesseps' scheme for a Calais-Calcutta railroad is described in A. Stuart, "Le
chemin de fer central-asiatique projeté par MM. Ferdinand de Lesseps et

Cotard," *L'Explorateur* (Paris), II (1875), 396–399, 417–422, 445–449, 476–480, 496–498. The author was an engineer in de Lesseps' employ. Also useful is R. Radau, "Les routes de l'avenir à travers l'Asie," *Revue des Deux Mondes*, 3rd period, XVI (1876), 386–421. Abd al-Ahad's succession is narrated in "Vosshestvie na bukharskii prestol novago emira," *Pravitelstvennyi Vestnik*, April 24/May 6, 1886, p. 2. In the following years this official newspaper continually reported on the activities of the rulers of the khanates, both at home and on their visits to Russia.

B. Changing Legal Relationships

S. P. Pokrovskii, "Mezhdunarodnye otnosheniia Rossii i Bukhary" (listed under 4B. above), is indispensable. I. F. Abramov, ed., *Polozhenie ob upravlenii Turkestanskago kraia* (Tashkent, 1916), is a valuable guide to the mass of legislation and government directives pertaining to the protectorates. The legislation itself is contained in the following collections:

Polnoe sobranie zakonov Rossiiskoi imperii. Sobranie vtoroe (1825–1881), 55 vols. (St. Petersburg, 1830–1884); Sobranie tretie (1881–1913), 33 vols. (St. Petersburg, 1885–1916).

Sbornik deistvuiushchikh traktatov, konventsii i soglashenii, zakliuchennykh Rossiei s drugimi gosudarstvami i kasaiushchikhsia razlichnykh voprosov chastnago mezhdunarodnago prava, 4 vols. (St. Petersburg, 1889–1896); vols. I and II, 2nd ed. (St. Petersburg, 1902–1906).

Sobranie uzakonenii i rasporiazhenii pravitelstva, izdavaemoe pri Pravitelstvuiushchem Senate, 159 vols. (St. Petersburg, 1863–1917).

Svod zakonov Rossiiskoi imperii, 16 vols. (St. Petersburg, 1914–1916).

C. The Political Agency and the Russian Settlements

The Russian foreign ministry's *Ezhegodnik* (*Annuaire diplomatique*) for the years 1886–1916 is indispensable for the development of the political agency, changes in personnel, and the decorations bestowed on Russian diplomats by the emir. A. P. Fomchenko, *Russkie poseleniia v Bukharskom emirate* (Tashkent, 1958), is a superficial treatment of the Russian enclaves.

D. The Bukharan Jews

The basic sources are Ia. I. Gimpelson, ed., *Zakony o evreiakh*, 2 vols. (St. Petersburg, 1914–1915), and L. M. Rogovin, ed., *Sistematicheskii sbornik deistvuiushchikh zakonov o evreiakh* (St. Petersburg, 1913). Secondary works include:

Ben-Zvi, Itzhak, *The Exiled and the Redeemed* (Philadelphia, 1957).
Encyclopaedia Judaica, vol. IV (Berlin, 1929).
Evreiskaia Entsiklopediia, vol. VIII (St. Petersburg, 1911).
The Jewish Encyclopedia, vol. III (New York, 1902).
Loewenthal, Rudolf, "Les Juifs de Boukhara," *Cahiers du Monde Russe et Soviétique*, II, January–March 1961, 104–108.

—— *The Jews of Bukhara* (Washington, 1961).

Slousch, N., "Les Juifs à Boukhara," *Revue du Monde Musulman*, VII (1909), 402–413.

The Universal Jewish Encyclopedia, vol. II (New York, 1940).

E. Economic Development

In addition to the general sources and surveys listed under 6A. above, the basic contemporary works are:

Gubarevich-Radobylskii, A., *Ekonomicheskii ocherk Bukhary i Tunisa* (St. Petersburg, 1905).

Klem, V., "Sovremennoe sostoianie torgovli v Bukharskom khanstve. 1887 g.," *SMPA*, XXXIII (1888), 1–7. The author was secretary and dragoman of the political agency, 1886–1893, and director of the Third Political (Central Asiatic) Section of the foreign ministry, 1914–1917.

Kovalevskii, A. N., *Zapiska k proektu Khivinskoi zheleznoi dorogi* (Petrograd, 1915).

Ruma, L. L., ed., *Kaspiisko-aralskaia zheleznaia doroga v ekonomicheskom otnoshenii* (St. Petersburg, 1914).

Other contemporary works are:

Abramov, K. A., "Karatigenskoe vladenie," IRGO, *Izvestiia*, VI (1870).

Charykov, N., "Zapiska o mestnykh putiakh soobshchenii, podlezhashchikh uluchsheniiu v interesakh razvitiia russkoi torgovli v bukharskikh vladeniiakh," *SMPA*, XV (1885), 182–193.

Kostenko, L., "Khivinskoe khanstvo v selsko-khoziaistvennom otnoshenii," *Voennyi Sbornik*, April 1874, pp. 373–388.

Krauze, I. I., "O khivinskom zemledelii," IRGO, *Izvestiia*, X (1874), 40–46.

Masalskii, Prince V. I., *Khlopkovoe delo v Srednei Azii (Turkestan, Zakaspiiskaia oblast, Bukhara i Khiva) i ego budushchee* (St. Petersburg, 1892).

Pokrovskii, V. I., ed., *Sbornik svedenii po istorii i statistike vneshnei torgovli Rossii*, vol. I (St. Petersburg, 1902).

Shakhnazarov, A. I., *Selskoe khoziaistvo v Turkestanskom krae* (St. Petersburg, 1908).

Terentiev, M. A., *Rossiia i Angliia v borbe za rynki* (St. Petersburg, 1876).

Among the Soviet studies the following four are of exceptional usefulness:

Iuferev, V. I., *Khlopkovodstvo v Turkestane* (Leningrad, 1925).

Riabinskii, A., "Tsarskaia Rossiia i Bukhara v epokhu imperializma," *Istorik Marksist*, 1941, No. 4, pp. 3–25.

Sadykov, A. S., *Ekonomicheskie sviazi Khivy s Rossiei vo vtoroi polovine XIX–nachale XX vv.* (Tashkent, 1965).

Tukhtametov, T. G., "Ekonomicheskoe sostoianie Bukharskogo emirata v kontse XIX i nachale XX vekov," Akademiia Nauk Kirgizskoi SSR, Institut Istorii, *Trudy*, III (1957), 151–183.

Other Soviet works include:

Akhmedzhanova, Z. K., "K istorii stroitelstva Bukharskoi zheleznoi dorogi (1914–1916 gody)," *Obshchestvennye Nauki v Uzbekistane* (Tashkent), April 1962, pp. 29–38.

Aminov, A. M., *Ekonomicheskoe razvitie Srednei Azii (so vtoroi poloviny XIX stoletiia do pervoi mirovoi voiny)* (Tashkent, 1959).

Iskandarov, B. I., "Proniknovenie russkogo kapitala v severnye raiony Tadzhikistana i Bukharskogo emirata," in A. L. Sidorov, ed., *Ob osobennostiakh imperializma v Rossii* (Moscow, 1963), pp. 166–175.

Lyashchenko, Peter I., *History of the National Economy of Russia to the 1917 Revolution* (New York, 1949).

Narzikulov, I. K., *Kratkie svedeniia o dorevoliutsionnoi kustarnoi promyshlennosti Tadzhikistana* (Stalinabad, 1957).

Vekselman, M. I., "K voprosu o proniknovenii inostrannogo kapitala v ekonomiku Srednei Azii do pervoi mirovoi voiny," *Obshchestvennye Nauki v Uzbekistane,* July 1961, pp. 31–36.

F. Cultural Development and Native Reform Movements

On the limited cultural awakening in Bukhara at the end of the nineteenth century, Z. Radzhabov, *Iz istorii obshchestvenno-politicheskoi mysli tadzhikskogo naroda vo vtoroi polovine XIX i v nachale XX vv.* (Stalinabad, 1957), is very useful. Less so is Ibragim Muminov, *Iz istorii razvitiia obshchestvenno-filosofskoi mysli v Uzbekistane kontsa XIX i nachala XX vv.* (Tashkent, 1957). Sadriddin Aini, *Vospominaniia,* translated from Tadjik by Anna Rozenfeld (Moscow, 1960), affords an interesting glance backward by one who lived under the emirs. Also interesting are the same author's "Korotko o moei zhizni" in vol. one of his *Sobranie sochinenii,* 4 vols. (Moscow, 1960–1961), and several of his works of fiction, particularly the autobiographical "Staraia shkola" in vol. four. G. N. Chabrov, "Iz istorii poligrafii i izdatelstva literatury na mestnykh iazykakh v dorevoliutsionnom Turkestane (1868–1917 gg.)," SAGU, *Trudy,* new series, LVII (1954), 77–95, is a valuable monograph. Arminius Vámbéry, *Western Culture in Eastern Lands, A Comparison of the Methods Adopted by England and Russia in the Middle East* (New York, 1906), is critical of Russia while taking for granted the beneficial influence of Western culture in the East.

For the Bukharan Djadids, both of the following articles are indispensable: I. I. Umniakov, "K istorii novometodnoi shkoly v Bukhare," SAGU, *Biulleten,* XVI (1927), 81–98, and A. N. Samoilovich, "Pervoe tainoe obshchestvo mlado-bukhartsev," *Vostok,* I (1922), 97–99. Also helpful are:

Arsharuni, A., and Kh. Gabidullin, *Ocherki panislamizma i pantiurkizma v Rossii* (Moscow, 1931).

Hayit, Baymirza, *Turkestan im XX. Jahrhundert* (Darmstadt, 1956). Factually unreliable.

Khodzhaev, Faizullah, "Dzhadidy," *Ocherki revoliutsionnogo dvizheniia v Srednei Azii. Sbornik statei* (Moscow, 1926), pp. 7–12.

———— "O mlado-bukhartsakh," *Istorik Marksist,* I (1926), 123–141.

Klimovich, Liutsian, *Islam v tsarskoi Rossii* (Moscow, 1936). Very hostile to the Djadids.

Mende, Gerhard von, *Der nationale Kampf der Russlandtürken* (Berlin, 1936).

Piaskovskii, A. V., *Revoliutsiia 1905–1907 godov v Turkestane* (Moscow, 1958).

Vakhabov, M. G., "O sotsialnoi prirode sredne-aziatskogo dzhadidizma i ego evoliutsii v period velikoi oktiabrskoi revoliutsii," *Istoriia SSSR*, 1963, No. 2, pp. 35–56.

Zenkovsky, Serge A., *Pan-Turkism and Islam in Russia* (Cambridge, Mass., 1960).

G. Internal Troubles in Bukhara and Khiva

On the 1910 riots in Bukhara a comprehensive and reliable contemporary account is A. Dzhidzhikhiia, "O poslednikh sobytiiakh v Bukhare," *Voennyi Sbornik*, May 1910, pp. 207–222. A recent view is A. Kh. Khamraev, "K voprosu o ianvarskikh sobytiiakh 1910 goda v Bukhare," SAGU, *Trudy*, LVII (1954), 65–75. The Duma debates and reports on the Bukharan problem in the last years before World War I are in Gosudarstvennaia Duma, *Stenograficheskie otchety*, Third and Fourth Dumas.

On the internal troubles in Khiva on the eve of the 1917 Revolution, the most valuable single source is "Khiva, Rossiia i Turkmeny (Istoricheskaia spravka)," *Turkmenovedenie* (Ashkhabad), 1930, No. 1, pp. 15–19, containing a report written in January 1916 by V. F. Minorskii, diplomatic attaché to the governor general of Turkestan. Other works are:

Fedorov, E., *Ocherki natsionalno-osvoboditelnogo dvizheniia v Srednei Azii* (Tashkent, 1925).

Istoriia Turkmenskoi SSR, 2 vols. in 3 (Ashkhabad, 1957).

"Khiva i Rossiia (K istorii vosstaniia khivinskikh Turkmen v 1916 godu)," *Turkmenovedenie*, 1929, No. 6–7, pp. 42–43.

Kovalev, P. A., "Krizis kolonialnogo rezhima i 'reformy' Kuropatkina v Turkestane v 1916 godu," SAGU, *Trudy*, LVII (1954), 31–63.

——— "Pervaia mirovaia voina i nazrevanie revoliutsionnogo krizisa v Uzbekistane v period 1914–1916 g.g.," SAGU, *Trudy*, new series, LXII (1955), 5–32.

Piaskovskii, A. V., ed., *Vosstanie 1916 goda v Srednei Azii i Kazakhstane. Sbornik dokumentov* (Moscow, 1960).

Rosliakov, A. A., *Revoliutsionnoe dvizhenie i sotsial-demokraticheskie organizatsii v Turkmenistane v dooktiabrskii period (1900-mart 1917)* (Ashkhabad, 1957).

Sokol, Edward Dennis, *The Revolt of 1916 in Russian Central Asia* (Baltimore, 1954).

8. Bukhara and Khiva, 1917–1924

A. Documentary Collections

Browder, R. P., and A. F. Kerensky, *The Russian Provisional Government 1917. Documents*, 3 vols. (Stanford, 1961).

"Bukhara v 1917 godu," *Krasnyi Arkhiv*, XX (1927), 78–122.

Dimanshtein, S. M., ed., *Revoliutsiia i natsionalnyi vopros. Dokumenty i materialy*, vol. III (Moscow, 1930).

Dokumenty vneshnei politiki SSSR, vol. II (1919–1920) (Moscow, 1958).

Godovoi otchet NKID k VIII Sezdu Sovetov (1919–1920) (Moscow, 1921).

Inostrannaia voennaia interventsiia i grazhdanskaia voina v Srednei Azii i Kazakhstane, 2 vols. (Alma-Ata, 1963–1964).

"Iz dnevnika A. N. Kuropatkina," *Krasnyi Arkhiv*, XX (1927), 56–77.

Iz istorii grazhdanskoi voiny v SSSR. Sbornik dokumentov i materialov, 1918–1922, 3 vols. (Moscow, 1961).

"Iz istorii natsionalnoi politiki Vremennogo Pravitelstva (Ukraina, Finliandiia, Khiva)," *Krasnyi Arkhiv*, XXX (1928), 46–79.

Kommunisticheskaia partiia Sovetskogo Soiuza v rezoliutsiiakh i resheniiakh sezdov, konferentsii i plenumov TsK, 2 vols., 7th ed. (Moscow, 1953).

Lenin, V. I., *Polnoe sobranie sochinenii*, 55 vols., 5th ed. (Moscow, 1958–1965).

Mashitskii, A., ed., "Materialy po istorii bukharskoi revoliutsii," NKID, *Vestnik*, 1922, No. 4–5, pp. 122–136.

Pobeda oktiabrskoi revoliutsii v Uzbekistane. Sbornik dokumentov, vol. I (Tashkent, 1963).

Revoliutsionnoe dvizhenie v Rossii posle sverzheniia samoderzhaviia (Velikaia oktiabrskaia sotsialisticheskaia revoliutsiia. Dokumenty i materialy) (Moscow, 1957).

Sbornik deistvuiushchikh dogovorov, soglashenii i konventsii, zakliuchennykh R.S.F.S.R. s inostrannymi gosudarstvami, 5 vols. (Moscow, 1921–1923), and vol. I, 2nd ed. (1924).

Sezdy sovetov Soiuza SSR, soiuznykh i avtonomykh sovetskikh sotsialisticheskikh respublik. Sbornik dokumentov 1917–1937 g.g., 7 vols. (Moscow, 1959–1965).

Shapiro, Leonard, ed., *Soviet Treaty Series*, 2 vols. (Washington, 1950–1955).

Stalin, I. V., *Sochineniia*, 13 vols. (Moscow, 1946–1951).

Triumfalnoe shestvie sovetskoi vlasti (Velikaia oktiabrskaia sotsialisticheskaia revoliutsiia. Dokumenty i materialy), 2 vols. (Moscow, 1963).

Turkmenistan v period inostrannoi voennoi interventsii i grazhdanskoi voiny 1918–1920 gg. Sbornik dokumentov (Ashkhabad, 1957).

B. Memoirs

Bailey, F. M., *Mission to Tashkent* (London, 1946).

Blacker, L. V. S., *On Secret Patrol in High Asia* (London, 1922). Both Bailey and Blacker were British officers on assignment in Russian Central Asia during 1918–1919.

Etherton, P. T., *In the Heart of Asia* (London, 1925). The author was British consul general and political resident in Sinkiang during the civil war in Russia.

Fedko, N., "Mirnye peregovory," in *Oktiabrskaia sotsialisticheskaia revo-liutsiia i grazhdanskaia voina v Turkestane. Vospominaniia uchastnikov* (Tashkent, 1957), pp. 478–482. Negotiating the Treaty of Takhta with Khiva, March–April 1919.

Gudovich, A., "Na pomoshch," in M. Gorkii *et al.,* eds., *Voina v peskakh. Materialy po istorii grazhdanskoi voiny* (Moscow, 1935), pp. 276–289. The rescue of Kolesov's troops.

Khodzhaev, Faizullah, *K istorii revoliutsii v Bukhare* (Tashkent, 1926).

Kolesov, F., and A. Bobunov, "Vosstanie v Bukhare," in Gorkii, pp. 231–275.

Malleson, Sir Wilfrid, "The British Military Mission to Turkistan, 1918–1920," *Journal of the Royal Central Asian Society,* IX (1922), 96–110.

Saïd Alim Khan, *La voix de la Boukharie opprimée* (Paris, 1929).

Skalov, G., "Khivinskaia revoliutsiia 1920 goda," *Novyi Vostok,* III (1923), 241–257.

Vostrikov, N., "Voenno-revoliutsionnye sobytiia v Amu-Darinskom otdele i Khorezme," in *Oktiabrskaia sotsialisticheskaia revoliutsiia i grazhdanskaia voina v Turkestane,* pp. 483–496. Events of the spring of 1919.

Zaitsev, I. M., *V zashchitu ot klevetnikov* (n.p., 1922).

C. Secondary Works

Aleskerov, Iu. N., *Interventsiia i grazhdanskaia voina v Srednei Azii* (Tashkent, 1959).

Aliev, A., *Velikii oktiabr i revoliutsionizirovanie narodov Bukhary* (Tashkent, 1958).

Babakhodzhaev, A. Kh., "Iz istorii bukharsko-afganskikh otnoshenii 1920–24 gg.," Akademiia Nauk UzSSR, *Izvestiia,* social science series, 1960, No. 4, pp. 8–13.

———— *Proval agressivnoi politiki angliiskogo imperializma v Srednei Azii v 1917–1920 gg.* (Tashkent, 1955).

———— *Proval angliiskoi politiki v Srednei Azii i na Srednem Vostoke* (1918–1924 gg.) (Moscow, 1962). A revised and enlarged version of the author's *Proval angliiskoi antisovetskoi politiki v Srednei Azii i na Srednem Vostoke* (1921–24 gg.) (Tashkent, 1957).

Boersner, Demetrio, *The Bolsheviks and the National and Colonial Question* (1917–1928) (Geneva, 1957).

Carr, E. H., *The Bolshevik Revolution,* 3 vols. (New York, 1951–1953).

Castagné, Joseph, "Le Bolchevisme et l'Islam: I—Les organisations soviétiques de la Russie musulmane," *Revue du Monde Musulman,* LI (1922), 1–254.

Degtiarenko, N. D., *Razvitie sovetskoi gosudarstvennosti v Tadzhikistane* (Moscow, 1960).

Dervish, "Bukharskaia sovetskaia narodnaia respublika," *Zhizn Natsional-nostei,* January 1923, No. 1, pp. 195–200.

Ellis, C. H., *The British "Intervention" in Transcaspia 1918–1919* (Berkeley, 1963).

Ferro, Marc, "La politique des nationalités du gouvernement provisoire," *Cahiers du Monde Russe et Soviétique*, II (1961), 131–165.

Glovatskii, O., *Revoliutsiia pobezhdaet* (Tashkent, 1930).

Gurko-Kriazhin, V. A., "Angliiskaia interventsiia 1918–1919 gg. v Zakaspii i Zakavkaze," *Istorik Marksist*, II (1926), 115–139.

Inoiatov, Kh. Sh., and D. A. Chugaev, "Pobeda narodnykh revoliutsii i obrazovanie narodnykh sovetskikh respublik v Khorezme i Bukhare," *Istoriia SSSR*, 1966, No. 2, pp. 66–83.

Ishanov, A. I., "Pobeda narodnoi sovetskoi revoliutsii v Bukhare," in *Materialy obedinennoi nauchnoi sessii po istorii narodov Srednei Azii i Kazakhstana v epokhu sotsializma* (Tashkent, 1957).

—— *Sozdanie Bukharskoi narodnoi sovetskoi respubliki (1920–1924 gg.)* (Tashkent, 1955).

Iskandarov, B. I., "Bukhara v 1918–1920 gg. (Likvidatsiia Bukharskogo emirata—ochaga angliiskikh interventov i rossiiskoi kontrrevoliutsii v Srednei Azii)," Akademiia Nauk Tadzhikskoi SSR, *Trudy*, XIX (1954), 3–67.

—— "Podgotovka Anglii bukharskogo platsdarma dlia interventsii v sovetskii Turkestan (1918–1920 gg.)," *Istoricheskie Zapiski*, XXXVI (1951), 32–63.

Istoriia grazhdanskoi voiny v Uzbekistane, vol. I (1918–1919) (Tashkent, 1964).

Istoriia sovetskogo gosudarstva i prava Uzbekistana, vol. I (1917–1924) (Tashkent, 1960).

Kunitz, Joshua, *Dawn Over Samarkand. The Rebirth of Central Asia* (New York, 1935).

Levin, A. G., "Finansy Khorezma," *Novyi Vostok*, IV (1923), 250–257.

Makarova, G. P., "Borba Bukharskoi kommunisticheskoi partii za ustanovlenie sovetskoi vlasti v Bukhare," in *Velikii oktiabr. Sbornik statei* (Moscow, 1958), pp. 483–512.

Mashitskii, A., "K istorii revoliutsii v Bukhare," NKID, *Vestnik*, 1921, No. 3–4, pp. 24–37; No. 5–6, pp. 70–83.

Mukhammedberdyev, K., *Kommunisticheskaia partiia v borbe za pobedu narodnoi sovetskoi revoliutsii v Khorezme* (Ashkhabad, 1959).

—— "Oktiabrskaia revoliutsiia i ustanovlenie sovetskoi vlasti v Khorezme (1917 g.–fevral 1920 g.)," in *Velikii oktiabr*, pp. 456–482.

Nemchenko, M., *Natsionalnoe razmezhevanie Srednei Azii* (Moscow, 1925).

Nepesov, Gaib, *Iz istorii khorezmskoi revoliutsii, 1920–1924 gg.* (Tashkent, 1962).

—— *Velikii oktiabr i narodnye revoliutsii 1920 goda v severnom i vostochnom Turkmenistane* (Ashkhabad, 1958).

Park, Alexander G., *Bolshevism in Turkestan 1917–1927* (New York, 1957).

Pipes, Richard, *The Formation of the Soviet Union*, 2nd ed. (Cambridge, Mass., 1964).

Ramzin, K., *Revoliutsiia v Srednei Azii v obrazakh i kartinakh* (Tashkent, 1928).

Rawson, A., "Unhappy Bokhara," *The Asiatic Review*, XX (1924), 34–41, 219–224.

Safarov, G. I., *Kolonialnaia revoliutsiia* (*Opyt Turkestana*) (Moscow, 1921).

Shek, L. K., "Iz istorii sovetsko-bukharskikh otnoshenii (1917–1920 gg.)," SAGU, *Trudy*, LXXVIII (1956), 105–128.

Shikhmuradov, O. O., and A. A. Rosliakov, eds., *Ocherki istorii kommunisticheskoi partii Turkmenistana* (Ashkhabad, 1961).

Soloveichik, D., "Revoliutsionnaia Bukhara," *Novyi Vostok*, II (1922), 272–288.

Ullman, Richard H., *Anglo-Soviet Relations, 1917–1921: Intervention and the War* (Princeton, 1961).

Vinogradova, A., "Khorezmskaia sovetskaia narodnaia respublika," *Zhizn Natsionalnostei*, January 1923, No. 1, pp. 181–194.

Zevelev, A. I., *Iz istorii grazhdanskoi voiny v Uzbekistane* (Tashkent, 1959).

Notes

Introduction

1. Although its precise definition is still a source of fruitful debate, modernization essentially involves:
(1) Acceptance by a society's rulers of secular and rationalist *intellectual* attitudes that emphasize both the possibility and the desirability of man's increasing his knowledge of, and control over, his environment
(2) An *economic* revolution, resulting from the massive application of post-Newtonian scientific technology to agriculture, transportation, communications, and industry, and characterized by
 (*a*) A dramatic rise in per capita production
 (*b*) A wholesale shift of manpower from agriculture to industry
 (*c*) The formation of a market economy embracing virtually all producers
(3) A *social* revolution in response to both the demands and opportunities created by the economic revolution, consisting of
 (*a*) Achievement of unprecedented levels of urbanization and geographical and social mobility
 (*b*) Formation of a new, nonhereditary elite of technical, managerial, and professional talent
 (*c*) Development of mass literacy and widespread opportunities for extensive formal education
(4) Creation of new *political* patterns, involving
 (*a*) Participation of the general public in political life through elections, plebiscites, or membership in political parties
 (*b*) A centralized and bureaucratic (in the Weberian sense) administrative machine
 (*c*) An expansion of governmental activity in the areas of health, education, and welfare
2. Geoffrey Wheeler, *The Modern History of Soviet Central Asia* (London and New York, 1964), pp. 159ff. For a Westerner's impressions on the modernization of the emir of Bukhara's former capital in the two decades before 1958, see Fitzroy Maclean, *Back to Bokhara* (New York, 1959), pp. 110–111.

Chapter 1. The Setting

1. From west to east the major oases are: the Merv oasis on the lower Murgab River, the Khivan oasis on the lower Amu-Darya or Oxus River, the lower and

middle Zarafshan River (including Bukhara and Samarkand), and the middle and upper Sir-Darya or Jaxartes River (from the town of Turkestan to the Fergana Valley). The Eurasian Steppe, which borders Central Asia on the north, is a broad prairie extending for over 2500 miles from the Altai Mountains on the frontier of Mongolia to the Carpathians in southeastern Europe.

2. On Central Asia as the northeast march of Iran, see Arnold J. Toynbee, *A Study of History* (London, 1935–1961), II, 138–150. Some of Central Asia's nomadic conquerors ruled the area from their homes on the steppe, while others immigrated en masse into the oases and were gradually absorbed by the sedentary population.

3. The settled population of Central Asia has been Moslem since the Arab conquest at the beginning of the eighth century. The Uzbegs were converted to Islam over a century before their invasion of Central Asia.

4. The term Uzbeg was political rather than ethnic in origin. For the Uzbegs and Shaibanids prior to their invasion of Central Asia, see *Istoriia Uzbekskoi SSR* (Tashkent, 1955–1956), I, Pt. I, 373–377, and René Grousset, *L'empire des steppes*, 4th ed. (Paris, 1952), pp. 469–470.

5. The Kazakhs were a splinter group from the main body of Uzbegs, which formed during the second half of the fifteenth century in the valley of the Chu River around a nucleus of discontented fugitives from the short-lived nomadic empire built by Muhammad Shaibani-khan's grandfather. In the early sixteenth century the Kazakhs occupied the steppe recently vacated by the Uzbegs. (*Istoriia Uzbekskoi SSR*, I, Pt. I, 376–377.)

6. The area of Bukhara after the incorporation of Shugnan and Roshan in 1895 was 217,000 square versts, or 95,480 square miles. (K. K. Pahlen, *Otchet po revizii Turkestanskago kraia* [St. Petersburg, 1909–1911], Part XIX, *Prilozhenie. Materialy k kharakteristike narodnago khoziaistva*, I, Pt. II, 434.)

7. Those of the Zarafshan River, the Kashka-Darya, and the Amu-Darya.

8. The Shirabad, Surkhan-Darya, Kafirnihan, and Vakhsh.

9. Karategin, Darvaz, and Shugnan-Roshan.

10. Pahlen, I, Pt. II, 436. The official Soviet estimate in 1924 was a very low figure of 1.53 million. (*Materialy po raionirovaniiu Srednei Azii* [Tashkent, 1926], I, 149.) A Soviet scholar has recently tried to reconcile this estimate with a figure of two million or over for the turn of the century by suggesting that Bukhara experienced a population loss of at least 25 percent during the troubled period 1917–1922, but such a loss hardly seems credible. (N. A. Kisliakov, *Patriarkhalno-feodalnye otnosheniia sredi osedlogo selskogo naseleniia Bukharskogo khanstva v kontse XIX–nachale XX veka* [Moscow-Leningrad, 1962], p. 19.)

11. Prince V. I. Masalskii, *Turkestanskii krai*, in V. P. Semenov-Tian-Shanskii, ed., *Rossiia, Polnoe geograficheskoe opisanie nashego otechestva*, XIX (St. Petersburg, 1913), p. 349. In Russia at this time the urban population constituted a similar proportion of the total—9 percent in 1858, 13 percent in 1897. (Alexander Kornilov, *Modern Russian History* [New York, 1943], II, 129–131.)

12. D. N. Logofet, *Bukharskoe khanstvo pod russkim protektoratom* (St. Petersburg, 1911), I, 186; Masalskii, p. 349; O. A. Sukhareva, *Bukhara XIX*

—*nachalo XX v.* (Moscow, 1966), pp. 98–103. There are widely varying estimates for most Bukharan towns. Some estimates of the capital's population run as high as 150,000. O. Olufsen (*The Emir of Bokhara and His Country* [London, 1911], p. 562) gives only 25,000 for Karshi. A. Gubarevich-Radobylskii (*Ekonomicheskii ocherk Bukhary i Tunisa* [St. Petersburg, 1905], pp. 33–34) puts Karshi, Shahr-i Sabz, and Chardjui in the 6,000–10,000 range.

13. Masalskii, pp. 362, 367; *Istoriia Uzbekskoi SSR*, I. Pt. II, 135; Gaib Nepesov, *Velikii oktiabr i narodnye revoliutsii 1920 goda v severnom i vostochnom Turkmenistane* (Ashkhabad, 1958), pp. 3–4; Mary Holdsworth, *Turkestan in the Nineteenth Century* (London, 1959), p. 3. The Sarts, who constituted the majority of the population in all the large towns of Central Asia, were a composite ethnic group, basically Iranian but with a large admixture of various Turkic elements and Turkic-speaking. In this study Soviet practice is followed and the Sarts are classified as Uzbegs.

14. The best account of the central government is A. A. Semenov, *Ocherk ustroistva tsentralnogo administrativnogo upravleniia Bukharskogo khanstva pozdneishego vremeni* (Stalinabad, 1954). For a good description of provincial government, see I. I. Geier, *Turkestan*, 2nd ed. (Tashkent, 1909), pp. 187–190.

15. After the Russian conquest and the consolidation of the emir's hold over central and eastern Bukhara, completed by 1895, the number of begliks was stabilized at twenty-seven. They were distributed as follows: sixteen in the west (Nurata, Karakul, Kabakli, Chardjui, Burdalik, Kerki, Kelif, Karshi, Chirakchi, Kermine, Ziaddin, Khatirchi, Yakkabah, Shahr-i Sabz, Kitab, and Guzar) and eleven in central and eastern Bukhara (Shirabad, Baisun, Hisar, Denau, Kurgan-Tübe, Baldjuan, Kulab, Kabadiyan, Karategin, Darvaz, and Shugnan-Roshan). (Logofet, I, 240.) Some former begliks, such as Saridjui and Yurchi, had by 1895 been incorporated into neighboring provinces.

16. Emir Muzaffar (1860–1885) had been beg of Kermine during his father's lifetime. His eldest son, Abd al-Malik, was beg of Karshi until 1868, and his other sons served as begs in Chardjui, Hisar, Kermine, Guzar, Karshi, and Chirakchi. Abd al-Ahad, Muzaffar's fifth son, was beg of Kermine from 1871 until he succeeded his father.

17. See, for eample, A. V. Nechaev, *Po gornoi Bukhare. Putevye ocherki* (St. Petersburg, 1914), pp. 74–75.

18. Logofet, I, 247–251.

19. For the clerical hierarchy, see Semenov, *Ocherk ustroistva.*

20. The area of Khiva after the Russian conquest in 1873 was 54,700 square versts, or 24,068 square miles—one fourth the size of Bukhara. (Pahlen, I, Pt. II, 452).

21. Estimates ran all the way from 506,000 (Geier, p. 9) to 1,100,000 (L. L. Ruma, ed., *Kaspiisko-aralskaia zheleznaia doroga v ekonomicheskom otnoshenii* [St. Petersburg, 1914], Appendix, pp. 26–27). The official Soviet estimate in 1924 was only 461,000. (*Materialy po raionirovaniiu Srednei Azii*, II, 64.)

22. Colonel G. I. Danilevskii, "Opisanie Khivinskago khanstva," IRGO, *Zapiski*, V (1851), 100; Masalskii, p. 352.

23. *Istoriia Uzbekskoi SSR*, I, Pt. II, 148.

24. A. N. Kovalevskii, *Zapiska k proektu Khivinskoi zheleznoi dorogi* (Petrograd, 1915), p. 22; Olufsen, p. 220. Urgench, sometimes called New Urgench, must be distinguished from Kunya-Urgench, the ancient capital of Khwarizm.

25. Masalskii, p. 361.

26. For Khiva's government, see Danilevskii, pp. 133–134; L. Sobolev, "Obzor dostupov k Khivinskomu khanstvu i kratkiia svedeniia o nem," *Voennyi Sbornik*, May 1873, pp. 158–159; Masalskii, p. 750.

27. The Khivan begliks were Pitniyak, Khazarasp, Khanki, Urgench, Koshkupir, Khazavat, Kiyat, Shah-abat, Tashauz, Ambar-Manak, Gurlen, Mangit, Klich-Niyaz-bau, Kipchak, Porsu, Ilyali, Kunya-Urgench, Khodjeili, Chumanai, and Kungrat. In addition, there were two districts, Bish-arik and Kiyat-Kungrat, each ruled collectively by several *naibs* (Uzbeg tribal elders). (Masalskii, p. 750.)

28. Arminius Vámbéry, *Travels in Central Asia* (London, 1864), pp. 434–437. The khans of Central Asia recognized the Ottoman sultan-khalif's theoretical suzerainty because they gained prestige among their subjects from serving as his lieutenants, honorary cupbearers, and constables. Turkey was too distant to pose any threat to their independence.

29. *Istoriia Uzbekskoi SSR*, I, Pt. I, 434. For speculation on cultural links between Khwarizm and the early Slavs, see George Vernadsky, *The Origins of Russia* (Oxford, 1959).

30. This summary of Russian aims is taken from S. V. Zhukovskii, *Snosheniia Rossii s Bukharoi i Khivoi za poslednee trekhsotletie* (Petrograd, 1915), pp. 116–154.

31. For statistics on Russian trade with Bukhara, Khiva, and Kokand in 1851–1867, see M. K. Rozhkova, "Iz istorii torgovli Rossii so Srednei Aziei vo 60-kh godakh XIX v.," *Istoricheskie Zapiski*, LXVII (1960), 193.

32. A. L. Popov, "Iz istorii zavoevaniia Srednei Azii," *Istoricheskie Zapiski*, IX (1940), 200.

33. Popov, pp. 204–205; N. A. Khalfin, *Politika Rossii v Srednei Azii 1857–1868* (Moscow, 1960), pp. 120–123.

34. H. C. Rawlinson, *England and Russia in the East* (London, 1875), pp. 149–159. The first Englishmen to visit Bukhara since Jenkinson in the sixteenth century were William Moorcroft and George Trebeck, who spent five months there in the spring and summer of 1825. They both died on the return trip in northern Afghanistan. They were followed early in 1832 by Rev. Joseph Wolff, the eccentric missionary to the Jews. Lieutenant Alexander Burnes visited Bukhara only two months later, followed by Captains Charles Stoddart in 1838 and Arthur Conolly in 1841. Wolff traveled to Bukhara again in 1844 to learn the fate of Stoddart and Conolly; he established that Emir Nasr Allah had executed them in 1842. Khiva was visited by Captain James Abbott and Captain Richmond Shakespeare in 1840. See William Moorcroft and George Trebeck, *Travels in the Himalayan Provinces of Hindustan and the Panjab; in Ladakh and Kashmir; in Peshawar, Kabul, Kunduz, and Bokhara*, 2 vols. (London, 1841); Joseph Wolff, *Travels and Adventures of the Reverend Joseph Wolff, D.D., LL.D.*, 2nd ed., 2 vols. (London, 1860–1861); Lieut. Alexander Burnes, *Travels into Bokhara*, 3 vols. (London, 1834); Rev. Joseph Wolff, *Narrative of a Mission to Bokhara*, 2 vols. (London, 1845); Capt. James Abbott, *Narrative of a Jour-*

ney from Heraut to Khiva, Moscow, and St. Petersburgh, 2 vols. (London, 1843).

35. Popov, pp. 201–202; Khalfin, pp. 49–54.

36. Popov, pp. 202–203.

37. Statement by E. P. Kovalevskii, director of the Asiatic Department of the Ministry of Foreign Affairs, in Popov, p. 204. This and all subsequent translations are my own. Khanykov got no farther than Herat, for Dost Muhammad, faithful to his English allies, refused to allow the Russian mission to proceed to Kabul. (Khalfin, pp. 115–116.) For both the Ignatiev and the Khanykov missions of 1858, see N. A. Khalfin, *Tri russkie missii* (Tashkent, 1956).

38. Popov, p. 207.

39. Popov, p. 210; Khalfin, *Politika Rossii*, pp. 141–142, 146, 158.

40. Popov, p. 211.

41. Popov, p. 212; *Istoriia Uzbekskoi SSR*, I, Pt. II, 87–88.

42. Khalfin, *Politika Rossii*, p. 94; Popov, p. 211.

43. Gorchakov to Alexander II, October 31, 1864, in A. G. Serebrennikov, ed., *Turkestanskii krai. Sbornik materialov dlia istorii ego zavoevaniia* (Tashkent, 1912–1916), XVIII, 165–172.

44. The text, in both the original French and English translation, is in "Central Asia, No. 2 (1873)," pp. 70–75, *Parliamentary Papers* (1873), LXXV. Gorchakov's circular was never officially communicated to foreign governments, but the British foreign office obtained a copy in December 1864 from N. P. Ignatiev, Russian ambassador at Constantinople, and the text was published several months later in three government-inspired St. Petersburg newspapers. (A. P. Thornton, "The Reopening of the 'Central Asian Question,' 1864–9," *History*, XLI [1956], 127, 129–130.)

45. Loftus to Granville, April 16, 1872 [N.S.], in "Central Asia, No. 2 (1873)," p. 58.

46. Before the extension of the telegraph to Tashkent in 1873 it took almost one month to send a dispatch from Tashkent to Orenburg, which was connected by wire to St. Petersburg. It thus took about two months for Tashkent to send an inquiry to St. Petersburg and receive an answer.

47. Lenin's *Imperialism: The Highest Stage of Capitalism*, written in 1916, relies heavily on the classic statement of the economic interpretation in J. A. Hobson, *Imperialism: A Study* (London, 1902). A recent, thorough refutation of Hobson and the economic interpretation is D. K. Fieldhouse, "Imperialism: An Historiographical Revision," *Economic History Review*, 2nd ser., XIV (1961–1962), 187–209. An excellent case study, which finds the economic interpretation unsatisfactory, is R. Robinson and J. Gallagher, *Africa and the Victorians* (London and New York, 1961).

48. A. L. Sidorov *et al.*, eds., *Istoriia SSSR*, II, 2nd ed. (Moscow, 1965), 165.

49. V. A. Zorin *et al.*, eds., *Istoriia diplomatii*, v. I, 2nd ed. (Moscow, 1959), 819.

50. P. I. Lyashchenko, *History of the National Economy of Russia to the 1917 Revolution* (New York, 1949), p. 355. This is a translation of the 1939 Soviet edition.

51. Zorin, I, 819. The most thorough of the many recent Soviet restatements

of the economic interpretation of the conquest is Khalfin, *Politika Rossii v Srednei Azii*.

52. A Soviet historian recently raised this possibility by subjecting the traditional Leninist version of the conquest to rigorous criticism. M. K. Rozhkova (*Ekonomicheskie sviazi Rossii so Srednei Aziei, 40–60e gody XIX veka* [Moscow, 1963], ch. 7) concludes that economic motives played a subsidiary role in the formation of Russia's Central Asian policy. St. Petersburg pursued its own political aims and was not guided by the interests of the Russian bourgeoisie. Rozhkova's attack has been rebuffed, both implicitly in the 1965 revision of the official Soviet college textbook on Russian history (Sidorov, *Istoriia SSSR*, II), which continues to propound the traditional interpretation, and explicitly by Khalfin, who charges in his latest work (*Prisoedinenie Srednei Azii k Rossii* [60–90e gody XIX v.] [Moscow, 1965], p. 39) that Rozhkova "underestimates the significance of economics."

53. Russian textile manufacturers had previously depended on English yarn. (Lyashchenko, pp. 333–335.)

54. Rozhkova, "Iz istorii torgovli Rossii," p. 194.

55. E. V. Bunakov, "K istorii snoshenii Rossii s sredneaziatskimi khanstvami v XIX veke," *Sovetskoe Vostokovedenie*, II (1941), 23.

56. Rozhkova, "Iz istorii torgovli Rossii," p. 191.

57. Popov, p. 209.

58. Rozhkova, "Iz istorii torgovli Rossii," pp. 194–195.

59. *Ibid.*, p. 189. Cotton textiles continued to grow in importance among Russian exports to the khanates, accounting for 68 percent of the total value of such exports by 1867. (Rozhkova, *Ekonomicheskie sviazi Rossii*, p. 66.)

60. Popov, p. 199.

61. *E.g.*, Iu. A. G[agemeister], "O torgovom znachenii Srednei Azii v otnoshenii k Rossii," *Russkii Vestnik*, XLI (October 1862), 706–736. Hagemeister, who was director of the Chancellery of the Finance Ministry, 1858–1862, recommended that the government advance the frontier to the upper Sir-Darya, gain a firm foothold on the Amu-Darya, and establish consulates and trading posts in the khanates. (G[agemeister], pp. 735–736.)

62. Popov, p. 209; Rozhkova, *Ekonomicheskie sviazi Rossii*, pp. 148, 151, 153–154.

63. Rozhkova, *Ekonomicheskie sviazi Rossii*, pp. 156–157.

64. Rozhkova, "Iz istorii torgovli Rossii," p. 206.

65. Rozhkova, *Ekonomicheskie sviazi Rossii*, p. 151.

Chapter 2. The Reduction of Bukhara

1. The statement of Russian policy is taken from Gorchakov to Kryzhanovskii, February 23, 1865, in A. G. Serebrennikov, ed., *Turkestanskii krai. Sbornik materialov dlia istorii ego zavoevaniia* (Tashkent, 1912–1916), XIX, 81–84.

2. Decree of the Minister of War, February 12, 1865, in Serebrennikov, XIX, 59.

3. Cherniaev to Poltoratskii, January 22, 1865, in Serebrennikov, XIX, 33.

4. Kryzhanovskii to Cherniaev, February 25, 1865, in Serebrennikov, XIX, 88.

5. Cherniaev to Kryzhanovskii, May 2; Lewenhof [acting commander of the troops of the Orenburg military *krai*] to Miliutin, May 22; in Serebrennikov, XIX, 146, 163–164.

6. Cherniaev to Kryzhanovskii, May 11, in Serebrennikov, XIX, 153.

7. Cherniaev's report of August 6, 1865, in D. I. Romanovskii, *Zametki po sredne-aziiatskomu voprosu* (St. Petersburg, 1868), p. 171.

8. Cherniaev to the Emir of Bukhara, May [10?], 1865, in Romanovskii, p. 176.

9. Cherniaev to Kryzhanovskii, May 13, in Serebrennikov, XIX, 156.

10. Kryzhanovskii to Lewenhof, June 5, in Serebrennikov, XIX, 192.

11. Cherniaev's report of August 6, 1865, in Romanovskii, p. 171. This report included for the first time the full text of Cherniaev's May letter to Muzaffar. An abbreviated version, minus the important sections, was included in Cherniaev to Kryzhanovskii, June 11, 1865, in Serebrennikov, XIX, 205.

12. Cherniaev to Kryzhanovskii, June 11, July 7, 1865, in Serebrennikov, XIX, 201–202, 245.

13. Cherniaev to Kryzhanovskii, July 7, 1865, in Serebrennikov, XIX, 252.

14. Kryzhanovskii to Stremoukhov, May 24, 1865, in Serebrennikov, XIX, 167–168. Gorchakov left to Kryzhanovskii's discretion the question of when to forward the letter containing the demands to Bukhara. (Gorchakov to Kryzhanovskii, June 5, in Serebrennikov, XIX, 193.) When, or whether, it was sent is not known.

15. N. A. Khalfin, *Politika Rossii v Srednei Azii 1857–1868* (Moscow, 1960), p. 217.

16. Muhammad-shah-biy [the Bukharan dignitary in charge of relations with Russia] to Cherniaev, [June 1865], in Serebrennikov, XIX, 274–275; Cherniaev's report of August 6, 1865, in Romanovskii, p. 171.

17. Cherniaev to Kryzhanovskii, June 26, 1865, in Serebrennikov, XIX, 273. N. A. Verevkin, acting commander of the Sir-Darya line, reported that Cherniaev had notified him that the emir was planning to attack Tashkent and the Sir-Darya line. (Verevkin to Kryzhanovskii, July 2, in Serebrennikov, XIX, 272–273).

18. Kryzhanovskii to Miliutin, July 13 and 15, in Serebrennikov, XIX, 265–268, 270–272.

19. M. A. Terentiev, *Istoriia zavoevaniia Srednei Azii* (St. Petersburg, 1906), I, 323.

20. Emir of Bukhara to Cherniaev, Safar, 1282 A. H. [June–July 1865], in Romanovskii, p. 163, and Serebrennikov, XIX, 273–274; Cherniaev's report of August 6, 1865, in Romanovskii, pp. 171–172.

21. Cherniaev to the Emir of Bukhara [early July 1865], in Romanovskii, p. 177; Cherniaev to Kryzhanovskii, July 12, in Serebrennikov, XIX, 263.

22. Kryzhanovskii to Miliutin, July 19, in Serebrennikov, XIX, 280.

23. Gorchakov to Miliutin, July 23, in Serebrennikov, XIX, 283.

24. Miliutin to Kryzhanovskii, July 24 and 29, in Serebrennikov, XIX, 284, 293.

25. Terentiev, I, 324; Kryzhanovskii to Miliutin, July 30, 1865, in Serebrennikov, XIX, 294–295.

26. Khalfin, p. 208. Kryzhanovskii formally proclaimed Tashkent an independent state in September 1865. (A. L. Popov, "Iz istorii zavoevaniia Srednei Azii," *Istoricheskie Zapiski*, IX [1940], 214.)

27. Khalfin, pp. 218–219.

28. A. Tatarinov, *Semimesiachnyi plen v Bukharii* (St. Petersburg, 1867), p. 32. Another briefer account of the Struve mission was published as Gloukhovsky, "Captivité en Boukharie," *Bulletin de la Société de Géographie*, 5th series, XVI (September 1868), 265–296. Both Tatarinov and Glukhovskoi were members of the mission.

29. Terentiev, I, 328–329.

30. Cherniaev's report of January 12, 1866; Emir of Bukhara to Cherniaev; in Romanovskii, pp. 179, 181.

31. Terentiev, I, 330–331.

32. Cherniaev to the Emir of Bukhara, in Romanovskii, p. 186.

33. This Hungry Steppe was formerly an arid waste between the Sir-Darya and Djizak and is now the site of immense irrigation works constructed under both the tsars and the Soviets. It is not to be confused with the larger Hungry Steppe between Lake Balkhash and the lower Sir-Darya.

34. Terentiev, I, 331–334; Khalfin, p. 221.

35. For these instructions, see Terentiev, I, 336–337.

36. Khalfin, p. 221.

37. Romanovskii, p. 42.

38. Terentiev, I, 338–339, 343; Romanovskii, p. 186.

39. Romanovskii, p. 59.

40. Romanovskii, p. 65.

41. Romanovskii, p. 76.

42. Romanovskii, p. 91.

43. Excerpts from Glukhovskoi's memorandum, which was published as *Zapiska o znachenii Bukharskogo khanstva dlia Rossii i o neobkhodimosti priniatiia reshitelnykh mer dlia prochnogo vodvoreniia nashego vliianiia v Srednei Azii* (St. Petersburg, 1867), are included in *Khrestomatiia po istorii SSSR*, 2nd ed. (Moscow, 1952), III, 316–317. Other parts of the memorandum are summarized in Popov, pp. 217–218.

44. Khalfin, p. 216.

45. Romanovskii to the Emir of Bukhara, [August 1866]; Emir of Bukhara to Romanovskii, August 1866; in Romanovskii, pp. 228, 229.

46. Kryzhanovskii to the Emir of Bukhara, September 1866, in Romanovskii, p. 270; S. P. Pokrovskii, "Mezhdunarodnye otnosheniia Rossii i Bukhary v dorevoliutsionnoe vremia i pri sovetskoi vlasti—do natsionalnogo razmezhevaniia sredne-aziatskikh respublik," SAGU, *Biulleten*, XVI (1927), 48.

47. Khalfin, p. 224; Terentiev, I, 363.

48. Terentiev, I, 370–372, 382–383; Romanovskii, pp. 99–100.

49. Miliutin to Kryzhanovskii, November 1, 1866, in Popov, p. 215.

50. Popov, p. 215.

51. Bisheshwar Prasad, *The Foundations of India's Foreign Policy* (Calcutta, 1955), I, 27; Mohammad Anwar Khan, *England, Russia and Central Asia, 1857–1878* (Peshawar, 1963), pp. 108–111.

52. Terentiev, I, 386–387.

53. Law of July 11, 1867, *PSZ* (1867), No. 44,831.

54. The text is in K. K. Pahlen, *Otchet po revizii Turkestanskago kraia* (St. Petersburg, 1909–1911), Part X, *Kraevoe upravlenie*, 11–12. The authority to wage war is not specifically mentioned (contrary to Terentiev, I, 383–384) but is certainly implied. Miliutin later claimed that he had requested Kaufman's appointment. (D. A. Miliutin, *Dnevnik 1873–1882* [Moscow, 1947–1950], IV, 132.)

55. Stremoukhov to Heiden, July 29, 1867, in Popov, p. 217.

56. Terentiev, I, 387–388. Kryzhanovskii had dropped his demand of the previous September for a war indemnity, which confirmed that he had used the indemnity merely as a pretext for further conquest.

57. Kaufman to Stremoukhov, September 16, 1867, in Pokrovskii, XVI, 51.

58. Terentiev, I, 402.

59. Reports from Constantinople by N. P. Ignatiev, ambassador to Turkey, of September 12 and October 3, 1867, cited in Pokrovskii, XVI, 49, and Terentiev, I, 405–406.

60. M. A. Terentiev, *Russia and England in Central Asia* (Calcutta, 1876), I, 45.

61. Terentiev, *Istoriia zavoevaniia*, I, 399–400; Terentiev, *Russia and England*, I, 45.

62. The text is in *Pravitelstvennyi Vestnik*, October 31/November 12, 1872, p. 1.

63. An interesting account of the Russian conquest, written by Muzaffar's official court historian, is Mirza Abdal Azim Sami, *Tarikh-i salatin-i mangitiia* (*Istoriia mangytskikh gosudarei*) (Moscow, 1962), having both the original Persian and a Russian translation. Sami's work, written in secret in 1906–1907, is bitterly anti-Russian as well as highly critical of the favor shown by nineteenth-century emirs to low-born people and Shiites at the expense of the old Uzbeg tribal aristocracy.

64. Terentiev, *Istoriia zavoevaniia*, I, 406–407, 402; Terentiev, *Russia and England*, I, 46, 49.

65. Pokrovskii, XVI, 51.

66. Terentiev, *Istoriia zavoevaniia*, I, 423–424. The text of the commercial convention is in *Pravitelstvennyi Vestnik*, October 31/November 12, 1872, p. 2. See Appendix 1 for an English translation. Kaufman at first considered creating a separate khanate of Samarkand, to be ruled under Russian protection by Saiyid Abd Allah, Muzaffar's nephew and enemy. Abd Allah, however, proved to be a puppet of the begs of Shahr-i Sabz, who were as hostile to Russia as to Bukhara. After the suppression of the revolt in Samarkand at the beginning of June, Kaufman decided to subject the city to direct Russian control. (Terentiev, *Istoriia zavoevaniia*, I, 428, 471.) During the summer he came under strong pressure from the foreign ministry and the emperor to return Samarkand to Muzaffar, but Kaufman finally persuaded Alexander II to keep the city. (N. A. Khalfin, *Prisoedinenie Srednei Azii k Rossii* [Moscow, 1965], 282–284.)

67. Terentiev, *Istoriia zavoevaniia*, I, 428–430. The text of the May 23 supplementary peace conditions is in S. V. Zhukovskii, *Snosheniia Rossii s Bukharoi i Khivoi za poslednee trekhsotletie* (Petrograd, 1915), Appendix I.

68. Terentiev, *Istoriia zavoevaniia*, I, 472–473.

69. Terentiev, *Istoriia zavoevaniia*, I, 473.
70. Such was the opinion of the famous orientalist V. V. Bartold (*Istoriia kulturnoi zhizni Turkestana* [Leningrad, 1927], p. 227).
71. Kaufman to the Emir of Bukhara, June 12, 1868, in Pokrovskii, XVI, 49.
72. Terentiev, *Istoriia zavoevaniia*, I, 474.
73. For example, M. V. Nechkina, ed., *Istoriia SSSR*, II, 3rd ed. (Moscow, 1954), 545; V. A. Zorin et al., eds., *Istoriia diplomatii* (Moscow, 1959), I, 820; *Istoriia tadzhikskogo naroda* (Moscow, 1963–1965), II, Pt. II, 135.

Chapter 3. The Consolidation of Russia's Position in Bukhara

1. *Pravitelstvennyi Vestnik*, October 31/November 12, 1872, p. 2; Eugene Schuyler, *Turkistan* (New York, 1876), II, 309–310, 277—278; M. A. Terentiev, *Russia and England in Central Asia* (Calcutta, 1876), I, 139, 141–142.
2. S. P. Pokrovskii, "Mezhdunarodnye otnosheniia Rossii i Bukhary," SAGU, *Biulleten*, XVI (1927), 46–47.
3. V. V. Bartold, *Istoriia kulturnoi zhizni Turkestana* (Leningrad, 1927), p. 238.
4. Pokrovskii, XVI, p. 46.
5. A. L. Popov, "Iz istorii zavoevaniia Srednei Azii," *Istoricheskie Zapiski*, IX (1940), 219.
6. K. P. von Kaufman, *Proekt vsepoddanneishago otcheta po grazhdanskomu upravleniiu i ustroistvu v oblastiakh Turkestanskago general-gubernatorstva, 7 noiabria 1867–25 marta 1881 g.* (St. Petersburg, 1885), p. 68; Popov, p. 219. Although the foreign ministry managed to postpone indefinitely imperial ratification of the 1868 treaty with Bukhara, this minor victory neither forced Kaufman to return Samarkand nor had the slightest effect on relations with Muzaffar, since Kaufman never informed him that the treaty had not been ratified. (N. A. Khalfin, *Prisoedinenie Srednei Azii k Rossii* [Moscow, 1965], pp. 283, 285, 290n, 293–294.)
7. M. A. Terentiev, *Istoriia zavoevaniia Srednei Azii* (St. Petersburg, 1906), I, 476–478; Arminius Vámbéry, *History of Bokhara* (London, 1873), pp. 414–415.
8. Zeki Validi Togan, *Turkestan Today* [unpublished English translation of A. Zeki Velidi Togan, *Bugünkü Türkili (Türkistan) ve yakin Tarihi* (Istanbul, 1942–1947) in the library of the Russian Research Center, Harvard University], p. 280; Bartold, p. 229.
9. Stremoukhov to Kaufman, December 28, 1868, in Popov, p. 219.
10. Popov, p. 220; Terentiev, *Russia and England*, I, 72–73.
11. Terentiev, *Istoriia zavoevaniia*, I, 478.
12. Terentiev, *Istoriia zavoevaniia*, I, 476, 478–481.
13. Terentiev, *Istoriia zavoevaniia*, I, 480–481.
14. B. I. Iskandarov, *Vostochnaia Bukhara i Pamir v period prisoedineniia Srednei Azii k Rossii* (Stalinabad, 1960), pp. 56–57, 171–176; Bartold, p. 229.
15. G. A. Arandarenko, "Darvaz i Karategin," *Voennyi Sbornik*, November 1883, p. 148; Terentiev, *Istoriia zavoevaniia*, I, 482; Terentiev, *Russia*

and England, I, 84–86; Bartold, pp. 229–230; B. I. Iskandarov, *Vostochnaia Bukhara i Pamir vo vtoroi polovine XIX v.* (Dushanbe, 1962–1963), I, 143–144.

16. Terentiev, *Russia and England*, I, 86.

17. Buchanan to Clarendon, March 22, 1870 [N.S.], "Central Asia, No. 2 (1873)," p. 35, *Parliamentary Papers* (1873), LXXV. Miliutin may have told this to Buchanan merely to allay British suspicions over Bukhara's expansion.

18. Terentiev, *Istoriia zavoevaniia*, I, 482.

19. Popov, p. 227.

20. Buchanan to Clarendon, March 22, May 4, 1870 [N.S.], "Central Asia, No. 2 (1873)," pp. 36, 41.

21. Buchanan to Clarendon, December 1, 1869, February 21, 26, 1870 [N.S.], "Central Asia No. 2 (1873)," pp. 19, 29, 31. On September 2, 1869 [N.S.], in Heidelberg Gorchakov had told Clarendon, the British foreign secretary, that the emperor intended to return Samarkand to Bukhara. (Clarendon to Buchanan, September 3, 1869 [N.S.], "Central Asia, No. 2 [1873]," p. 9.)

22. Kaufman's offer was reported by Miliutin to Buchanan on February 13/25. (Buchanan to Clarendon, February 26, 1870 [N.S.], "Central Asia, No. 2 [1873]," p. 31.)

23. Terentiev, *Russia and England*, I, 88; L. F. Kostenko, *Puteshestvie v Bukharu russkoi missii v 1870 godu* (St. Petersburg, 1871), pp. 102–103.

24. Terentiev, *Istoriia zavoevaniia*, I, 486; Kostenko, pp. 71–72.

25. Kostenko, pp. 72–73; Terentiev, *Istoriia zavoevaniia*, I, 485–486.

26. Kaufman to Gorchakov, August 16, 1870, in Popov, p. 231.

27. Kaufman, p. 12.

28. The first request was in October 1868 after the defeat of Abd al-Malik and the capture of Karshi by the Russians.

29. The term Russian Turkestan is used in this study to designate the central oblasts of the government-general of Turkestan: Sir-Darya, Samarkand, and (after 1876) Fergana. From 1867 to 1882 Semirechie, and from 1898 to 1917 both Semirechie and Transcaspia, were included in the government-general, but these two oblasts are not here comprehended by the term Russian Turkestan.

30. Terentiev, *Russia and England*, I, 92–94; Terentiev, *Istoriia zavoevaniia*, I, 499–509; D. N. Logofet, *Strana bezpraviia* (St. Petersburg, 1909), pp. 15–16. St. Petersburg was not informed of Kaufman's intervention against Shahr-i Sabz until it was all over. (Khalfin, p. 292.) Muzaffar's son and successor made peace with Djura-beg in 1906 in Tashkent and granted him 200,000 rubles as compensation for the loss of Shahr-i Sabz. (D. N. Logofet, *Bukharskoe khanstvo pod russkim protektoratom* [St. Petersburg, 1911], II, 254). In 1917 Djura-beg's son was living in Tashkent as a retired colonel and wealthy landowner; in May of that year he served as a delegate to both the All-Russian Moslem Congress in Moscow and the All-Russian Peasant Congress in Petrograd. ("Iz dnevnika A. N. Kuropatkina," *Krasnyi Arkhiv*, XX [1927], 75–76.)

31. Terentiev, *Istoriia zavoevaniia*, I, 486–487; Terentiev, *Russia and England*, I, 96–99.

32. Buchanan to Granville, July 26, 1871 [N.S.], "Central Asia, No. 2 (1873)," p. 54.

33. Terentiev, _Russia and England_, I, 100–101. According to Schuyler, II, 308, both begs of Shahr-i Sabz were involved. In general, Terentiev was a more accurate reporter than Schuyler. In at least two previous cases the Russians had turned over Bukharan bandits to the authorities in the khanate. (Bartold, 231.)

34. Terentiev, _Russia and England_, I, 102; L. N. Sobolev, "Geograficheskiia i statisticheskiia svedeniia o Zeravshanskom okruge," IRGO, _Zapiski po Otdeleniiu Statistiki_, IV (1874), 268; N. Petrovskii, "Moia poezdka v Bukharu," _Vestnik Evropy_, March 1873, p. 218.

35. Sobolev, pp. 338–339; Kaufman, pp. 247–248.

36. Mohammad Anwar Khan, _England, Russia and Central Asia_ (Peshawar, 1963), pp. 124–127.

37. Terentiev, _Russia and England_, I, 104; Terentiev, _Istoriia zavoevaniia_, I, 487.

38. Petrovskii, pp. 214–215, 226, 229, 242. For Glukhovskoi's comments on Bukhara's espionage system, see A. Gloukhovsky, "Captivité en Boukharie," _Bulletin de la Société de Géographie_, 5th series, XVI (September 1868), 274, 287. For Nosovich's similar experiences in 1870, see Kostenko, p. 63.

39. Petrovskii, pp. 246–247.

40. Kostenko, pp. 56–57, 72.

41. Kostenko, pp. 40–41, 50, 79; Terentiev, _Istoriia zavoevaniia_, I, 485, 487; Petrovskii, pp. 225–226, 243, 248.

42. Terentiev, _Istoriia zavoevaniia_, I, 480.

43. Kostenko, p. 94; Terentiev, _Istoriia zavoevaniia_, I, 487; Petrovskii, pp. 243–244.

44. Schuyler, II, 311.

45. Muzaffar sent envoys to Khiva to demand the extradition of Abd al-Malik after the suppression of the latter's revolt, and to inform the khan of his conquest of Hisar in late 1869. (Terentiev, _Russia and England_, I, 161–162; Terentiev, _Istoriia zavoevaniia_, II, 66.)

46. Terentiev, _Istoriia zavoevaniia_, I, 487; Terentiev, _Russia and England_, I, 103–104; Khan, p. 126. Terentiev's version, probably devised to save face for Muzaffar, implies that the man in question was not an official envoy and misrepresented the emir's views.

47. Ignatiev to Stremoukhov, January 25, 1873, in E. L. Shteinberg, _Istoriia britanskoi agressii na Srednem Vostoke_ (Moscow, 1951), pp. 115–116.

48. Pokrovskii, XVI, 53–54.

49. Pokrovskii, XVI, 55–56.

50. All dates in this section, unless otherwise indicated, are given according to the Gregorian calendar or New Style because diplomatic correspondence from the West was dated thus.

51. Bisheshwar Prasad, _The Foundations of India's Foreign Policy_ (Calcutta, 1955), I, 7–12, 23–27; Khan, pp. 43–46, 108–111, 124–127.

52. Shir Ali succeeded his father in 1863 but was soon faced with the

revolt of two of his half-brothers, Azim and Afzal, and of Afzal's son Abd ar-Rahman. With help from Bukhara, the rebels seized the northern part of the country and Kabul itself in the spring of 1866, and Shir Ali took refuge in Herat. Early in 1867 Lawrence became alarmed at reports that Shir Ali was seeking aid from Russia. (Sir Charles Aitchison, *Lord Lawrence* [Oxford, 1892], pp. 178–183.) Afzal did in fact contact Tashkent in June 1867 with an offer of friendship and commercial relations. (Khan, p. 81.)

53. A. P. Thornton, "Afghanistan in Anglo-Russian Diplomacy, 1869–1873," *Cambridge Historical Journal*, XI (1953–1955), 204–206; A. P. Thornton, "The Reopening of the 'Central Asian Question,' 1864–9," *History*, XLI (1956), 131–133; H. C. Rawlinson, Memorandum on the Central Asian Question, July 20, 1868, "Afghanistan, No. 1 (1878)," p. 38, *Parliamentary Papers* (1878–1879), LVI.

54. Government of India, Foreign Department, to Northcote, September 3, 1867, "Afghanistan, No. 1 (1878)," pp. 20–21. The sphere of influence was the most indefinite of the methods used by nineteenth-century imperialist powers to stake out claims. The assertion of a sphere of influence was a political, not a legal, act, which gave the imperialist power no rights over the territory but merely signified that it regarded the territory as closed to the ambitions of any other power, with a possible view to converting it into a protectorate or colony later.

55. Northcote to Lawrence, December 26, 1867, Lawrence's memorandum, November 25, 1868, "Afghanistan, No. 1 (1878)," pp. 25–26, 61; Khan, p. 134.

56. Government of India, Foreign Department, to the Duke of Argyll [Gladstone's secretary of state for India], January 4, 1869, "Afghanistan, No. 1 (1878)," pp. 43–45.

57. Clarendon to Buchanan [British ambassador to Russia], March 27, 1869, "Central Asia, No. 2 (1873)," p. 1.

58. Thornton, "The Reopening of the 'Central Asian Question,' " p. 122.

59. Gortchakow to Brunnow, February 24/March 7, 1869, "Central Asia, No. 2 (1873)," p. 3.

60. Clarendon to Rumbold [British chargé d'affaires in St. Petersburg], April 17, 1869, "Central Asia, No. 2 (1873)," p. 4. The map Clarendon referred to (Edward Weller's "Persia, Afghanistan and Beloochistan," published by George Philip and Son no later than 1863) actually depicted only the Merv oasis as belonging to Khiva, with the rest of the region between the Hindu Kush and the Amu-Darya divided among Bukhara and a number of independent khanates: Balkh, "Koondooz," etc. The map reflected the situation before 1860, when Dost Muhammad extended Afghanistan's borders to the Amu-Darya. The lack of accurate geographical information complicated the task of the diplomats: on June 2 Gorchakov and Rumbold debated the question of whether the territory south of the Amu-Darya belonged to Bukhara, as Gorchakov argued (his reason for rejecting the line of the river as proposed by Clarendon), or to Khiva, as London insisted. (Rumbold to Clarendon, June 2, 1869, "Central Asia, No. 2 (1873)," p. 6.) Four years later Gladstone was still pleading with the foreign office to "give or

get us some recent and trustworthy map of the Central Asian district." (Gladstone to Granville, April 13, 1873, in Agatha Ramm, ed., *The Political Correspondence of Mr. Gladstone and Lord Granville 1868–1876* [Camden Society, 3rd series, LXXXI–LXXXII; London, 1952], II, 381.)

61. Clarendon to Buchanan, September 3, 1869, "Central Asia, No. 2 (1873)," p. 10.

62. Government of India to the Duke of Argyll, June 3, 1869, in Prasad, I, 42–44.

63. Rumbold to Clarendon, June 2, 1869; Buchanan to Clarendon, July 28, 1869; Clarendon to Buchanan, September 3, 1869; "Central Asia, No. 2 (1873)," pp. 6, 8, 10.

64. Forsyth to Buchanan, November 2, 1869, "Central Asia, No. 2 (1873)," pp. 13–14.

65. Forsyth to Buchanan, November 5, 1869, "Central Asia, No. 2 (1873)," p. 16.

66. Buchanan to Clarendon, February 8, 1870, "Central Asia, No. 2 (1873)," p. 28.

67. Loftus to Granville, November 12, 1872, "Central Asia, No. 2 (1873)," p. 62.

68. Granville to Loftus, November 23, 1872, "Central Asia, No. 2 (1873)," p. 62. Six years later Granville pointed out to Gladstone that in effect when Britain claimed the Amu-Darya as the boundary of Afghanistan, "the idea of a neutral zone was abandoned." (Granville to Gladstone, September 30, 1878, in Agatha Ramm, ed., *The Political Correspondence of Mr. Gladstone and Lord Granville 1876–1886* [Oxford, 1962], I, 81.)

69. Kashgar in 1872 signed a commercial treaty with Russia identical to those concluded by Russia with Bukhara and Kokand.

70. Buchanan to Clarendon, November 5, 1869; Loftus to Granville, November 27, 1872; "Central Asia, No. 2 (1873)," pp. 14–15, 64; Gortchakow to Brunnow, December 7/19, 1872, "Central Asia, No. 1 (1873)," pp. 6, 9, 11, *Parliamentary Papers* (1873), LXXV. The presence of a number of political refugees on both sides of the Amu-Darya created a potentially explosive situation. In addition to the former beg of Kulab, Muzaffar's rebellious son Abd al-Malik was living in Afghanistan during this period. At the same time the dispossessed mir of Badakhshan was living in exile in Hisar, and in late 1869 the Afghan emir's nephew and enemy, Abd ar-Rahman, took refuge in Bukhara, whence he moved to Tashkent.

71. Thornton, "Afghanistan in Anglo-Russian Diplomacy," p. 215. Loftus had been advising London for some time that Russia would send an expedition against Khiva at the first favorable opportunity. (Lord Augustus Loftus, *Diplomatic Reminiscences 1862–79* [London, 1894], II, 16–18.) Neither Gladstone nor Granville shared the concern voiced in the press, in Parliament, and in Calcutta over Russia's conquest of Khiva; both saw Russia's advance in Central Asia as a repetition of Britain's experience in India. (See the exchange of notes between Granville and Gladstone, December 24–25, 1873, in Ramm, ed., *Political Correspondence 1868–1876*, II, 433–434.) The duke of Argyll was more blunt: "About Central Asia, I am so bored by it that it is all I can do to give it any attention." (Argyll to Granville, January 9, 1872, in Khan, pp. 243–244.)

72. Gortchakow to Brunnow, December 7/19, 1872, "Central Asia, No. 1 (1873)," pp. 2, 6, 9, 11.

73. Gortchakow to Brunnow, January 19/31, 1873, "Central Asia, No. 1 (1873)," p. 15.

74. D. A. Miliutin, *Dnevnik 1873–1882* (Moscow, 1947–1950), I, 183–184; Gortchakow's memorandum, April 5/17, 1875, "Central Asia, No. 1 (1878)," pp. 39–40, *Parliamentary Papers* (1878), LXXX.

75. Gortchakow to Schouvaloff, February 3/15, 1876, "Central Asia, No. 1 (1878)," pp. 68–69. For the British interpretation of the 1873 agreement, see: Government of India, Foreign Department, to the Duke of Argyll, June 30, 1873, "Afghanistan, No. 1 (1878)," pp. 103, 106–107; Hamilton [India Office] to Lord Tenterden [permanent undersecretary for foreign affairs], June 22, 1875, and memorandum of the Earl of Derby [Disraeli's foreign secretary], October 25, 1875, "Central Asia, No. 1 (1878)," pp. 43, 59.

Chapter 4. The Conquest of Khiva and the Treaties of 1873

1. M. K. Rozhkova, "Iz istorii torgovli Rossii so Srednei Aziei v 60-kh godakh XIX v.," *Istoricheskie Zapiski*, LXVII (1960), 193.

2. M. A. Terentiev, *Istoriia zavoevaniia Srednei Azii* (St. Petersburg, 1906), II, 60.

3. Minutes of Special Committee, January 4, 1865, in A. G. Serebrennikov, ed., *Turkestanskii krai. Sbornik materialov dlia istorii ego zavoevaniia* (Tashkent, 1912–1916), XIX, 4–5.

4. A. L. Popov, "Iz istorii zavoevaniia Srednei Azii," *Istoricheskie Zapiski*, IX (1940), 223–224.

5. M. A. Terentiev, *Russia and England in Central Asia* (Calcutta, 1876), I, 168–170.

6. Popov, p. 225.

7. Terentiev, *Russia and England*, I, 176–177.

8. Popov, pp. 224–225.

9. Popov, pp. 224, 230.

10. Terentiev, *Istoriia zavoevaniia*, I, 481–482.

11. Terentiev, *Russia and England*, I, 188–189.

12. Popov, pp. 230–231.

13. Terentiev, *Russia and England*, I, 182–183, 189–191, 193; Terentiev, *Istoriia zavoevaniia*, II, 66–68.

14. Stremoukhov to Kaufman, March 6, 1870, in Popov, p. 231.

15. Popov, pp. 231–236.

16. Terentiev, *Russia and England*, I, 201–203.

17. Terentiev, *Istoriia zavoevaniia*, II, 68, 73; Loftus to Granville, March 19, April 3, 1872 [N.S.], "Central Asia, No. 2 (1873)," pp. 57, 58, *Parliamentary Papers* (1873), LXXV.

18. Terentiev, *Istoriia zavoevaniia*, II, 73–74; Loftus to Granville, April 3, 1872 [N.S.], "Central Asia, No. 2 (1873)," p. 58.

19. Robert Michell, "Khivan Mission to India," *The Geographical Magazine*, II (1875), 177–178; Mohammad Anwar Khan, *England, Russia and Central Asia* (Peshawar, 1963), pp. 199–200.

20. Popov, pp. 236–237; Bisheshwar Prasad, *The Foundations of India's Foreign Policy* (Calcutta, 1955), I, 71–75. The text of the treaty is in *Pravitelstvennyi Vestnik*, October 31/November 12, 1872, p. 2.

21. G. J. Alder, *British India's Northern Frontier 1865–95* (London, 1963), pp. 49–51; Terentiev, *Russia and England*, I, 286–288.

22. Terentiev, *Istoriia zavoevaniia*, II, 77–80; Loftus to Granville, November 27, 1872 [N.S.], "Central Asia, No. 2 (1873)," p. 63.

23. Popov, p. 238.

24. Schuyler to Hamilton Fish [American secretary of state], December 21, 1872 [N.S.], *Papers Relating to the Foreign Relations of the United States* (1873), II, 767.

25. Terentiev, *Istoriia zavoevaniia*, II, 112.

26. Terentiev, *Istoriia zavoevaniia*, II, 174, 251–261.

27. Terentiev, *Istoriia zavoevaniia*, II, 262–263.

28. Terentiev, *Istoriia zavoevaniia*, II, 263; V. V. Bartold, *Istoriia kulturnoi zhizni Turkestana* (Leningrad, 1927), p. 235; *Pravitelstvennyi Vestnik*, September 28/October 10, 1873, p. 2.

29. J. A. MacGahan, *Campaigning on the Oxus, and the Fall of Khiva* (New York, 1874), pp. 310–311; Terentiev, *Russia and England*, I, 217–218; Terentiev, *Istoriia zavoevaniia*, II, 264.

30. The American diplomat Eugene Schuyler claimed that the Tashkent detachment's thirst for military glory had not been satisfied because of their late arrival before the khan's capital in May. (Eugene Schuyler, *Turkistan* [New York, 1876], II, 354–355.) A. A. Weinberg, who succeeded K. V. Struve as Kaufman's diplomatic attaché at the end of 1873, argued that the campaign against the Yomuts was necessary in order to establish Muhammad Rahim's authority, on the analogy, presumably, of General Abramov's occupation of Karshi in 1868 and of Shahr-i Sabz in 1870. The Yomuts, however, were not at the time in rebellion. (Terentiev, *Istoriia zavoevaniia*, II, 278.) Terentiev himself believed there was no justifiable reason for the expedition. (*Istoriia zavoevaniia*, II, 279.) J. A. MacGahan, the *New York Herald* correspondent who accompanied the expedition, claimed that the Turkomans could not be trusted to keep the peace once their Uzbeg overlords had been defeated by Russia, and that the Uzbegs of Khiva would be conciliated and bound to Russia by Kaufman's reduction of their unruly subjects and neighbors. (MacGahan, pp. 353–354.)

31. Terentiev, *Istoriia zavoevaniia*, II, 267–270; MacGahan, pp. 349, 355, 358–408.

32. Terentiev, *Istoriia zavoevaniia*, II, 281–282, 284.

33. Kaufman's draft arrived in St. Petersburg on July 6. (D. A. Miliutin, *Dnevnik 1873–1882* [Moscow, 1947–1950], I, 89–90.) Either just before or just after this date the draft treaty was published at Tashkent in the official *Turkestanskie Vedomosti*, presumably on Kaufman's authority. (Schuyler, II, 363–364; Lord Loftus, *Diplomatic Reminiscences* [London, 1894], II, 106.) The governor general's boldness made it very difficult for Alexander II to do anything but approve the treaty as it stood, although there is no reason to suppose that he wanted the terms altered. Alexander approved the treaty and returned it to Kaufman before the formal signing. (Loftus, II, 105; MacGahan, p. 416.)

34. The khan's throne was placed in the Kremlin. (Terentiev, *Istoriia zavoevaniia*, II, 265; V. V. Stasov, "Tron khivinskikh khanov," *Vestnik iziashchnykh iskusstv*, IV [1886], No. 5, 405–417.) The documents that Kaufman seized are described in P. P. Ivanov, ed., *Arkhiv khivinskikh khanov XIX v.* (Leningrad, 1940).

35. See Chapter 3 for the discussion of a new treaty with Bukhara in 1871–72. A similar new treaty with Kokand was considered at the same time. (Popov, p. 237.) The text of the Khivan treaty is in *Pravitelstvennyi Vestnik*, November 30/December 12, 1873, p. 1. See Appendix 2 for an English translation.

36. "A protectorate arises when a weak State surrenders itself by treaty into the protection of a strong State in such a way that it transfers the management of all its more important international affairs to the protecting State." (L. Oppenheim, *International Law, A Treatise*, I, 7th ed. [London, 1948], 173–174.)

37. *Pravitelstvennyi Vestnik*, November 30/December 12, 1873, p. 1; Terentiev, *Istoriia zavoevaniia*, II, 286; Gortchakow's memorandum, April 5/17, 1875, "Central Asia, No. 1 (1878)," p. 38, *Parliamentary Papers* (1878), LXXX.

38. Bartold, p. 235; K. P. von Kaufman, *Proekt vsepoddanneishago otcheta* (St. Petersburg, 1885), pp. 248–249, 251–252.

39. Terentiev, *Russia and England*, I, 107–111; Eugene Schuyler, "Report on Central Asia," March 7, 1874 [N.S.], *Papers Relating to the Foreign Relations of the United States* (1874), p. 826.

40. *Pravitelstvennyi Vestnik*, November 4/16, 1873, p. 2. The text of the treaty is in the issue of December 18/30, 1873, p. 1. See Appendix 3 for an English translation.

41. S. P. Pokrovskii, "Mezhdunarodnye otnosheniia Rossii i Bukhary," SAGU, *Biulleten*, XVI (1927), 57.

Chapter 5. The Stabilization of Khiva and the Expansion of Bukhara

1. J. A. MacGahan, *Campaigning on the Oxus, and the Fall of Khiva* (New York, 1874), pp. 409–410.

2. Petro-Aleksandrovsk was over 425 miles (an eleven- or twelve-day journey) from Tashkent, and about 325 miles from Kazalinsk. No road or telegraph line ever linked Petro-Aleksandrovsk across the desert wastes to the rest of Russian Turkestan. From the late 1880's the town was connected to Chardjui (250 miles upriver) on the Central Asian Railroad by road, telegraph, and steamboat, so that all communication with the rest of Russia was conducted via Chardjui.

3. M. A. Terentiev, *Istoriia zavoevaniia Srednei Azii* (St. Petersburg, 1906), II, 299–300.

4. Terentiev, II, 302–305; Eugene Schuyler, *Turkistan* (New York, 1876), II, 371–372.

5. Terentiev, II, 305–307.

6. Schuyler, II, 376–377.

7. Transcaspia was under the jurisdiction of the viceroy of the Caucasus, 1869–1890. The year 1864 had marked the end of the wars in the Caucasus and the beginning of the campaigns in Central Asia. Henceforth military glory and

rapid promotion were to be found east of the Caspian Sea rather than in the Caucasus.

8. Terentiev, II, 308–309.

9. Terentiev gave this contemporary opinion on the diversion of the Amu-Darya to the Caspian: "In order to effect this, it will probably be necessary to stop up all the irrigation canals which at present spring from the river and carry off an immense volume of water on to the fields of the Khivan oasis. If this be done, agriculture would be ruined, and the khanate would become a desert, but in view of the inestimable benefits to Russia, the interests of Khiva must necessarily be sacrificed." (*Russia and England in Central Asia* [Calcutta, 1876], I, 222.) Terentiev at the same time advocated the occupation of Bukhara in order to secure its markets for Russia and to shut out English goods. ("Tur-kestan i Turkestantsy," *Vestnik Evropy*, November 1875, p. 172.)

10. Ivanov to Kaufman, August 30, 1876, in Terentiev, *Istoriia zavoevaniia*, II, 309–311.

11. Terentiev, *Istoriia zavoevaniia*, II, 311–313.

12. Terentiev, *Istoriia zavoevaniia*, III, 3.

13. Terentiev, *Istoriia zavoevaniia*, II, 314–315. The European situation to which Kaufman referred was the Eastern crisis; the Russo-Turkish War of 1877–1878 broke out one month later.

14. A. P. Savitskii, "Materialy k istorii Amu-Darinskogo otdela," SAGU, *Trudy*, new series, LXII (1955), 76.

15. Terentiev, *Istoriia zavoevaniia*, II, 315.

16. F. K. Giers, *Otchet revizuiushchago, po Vysochaishemu poveleniiu, Tur-kestanskii krai, Tainago Sovetnika Girsa* [St. Petersburg, 1883?], pp. 107, 103.

17. The khan of Khiva later maintained a consul at Petro-Aleksandrovsk be-ginning in the 1890's. (O. Olufsen, *The Emir of Bokhara and His Country* [London, 1911], p. 191; A. Woeikof, *Le Turkestan russe* [Paris, 1914], p. 210.)

18. Some of the embassies, including all those sent by Bukhara to the Rus-sian capital, were purely ceremonial. In late 1873 Bukhara was invited to send an embassy to St. Petersburg to receive imperial thanks for the emir's support in the Khivan campaign. (G. P. Fedorov, "Moia sluzhba v Turkestanskom krae [1870–1906 goda]," *Istoricheskii Vestnik*, CXXXIII [1913], 811–812.) Muzaffar sent another ceremonial embassy, including several of his own sons, to St. Peters-burg in November 1876. (D. A. Miliutin, *Dnevnik 1873–1882* [Moscow, 1947–1950], II, 116.) He also sent an embassy to Tashkent in October 1882 to con-gratulate Cherniaev on his appointment as governor general after Kaufman's death. (Vsevolod V. Krestovskii, "V gostiakh u emira bukharskago. Putevoi dnevnik," *Russkii Vestnik*, February 1884, pp. 469–470.)

19. N. P. Stremoukhov, "Poezdka v Bukharu," *Russkii Vestnik*, June 1875, p. 659.

20. V. V. Bartold, *Istoriia kulturnoi zhizni Turkestana* (Leningrad, 1927), p. 243.

21. Krestovskii, June 1884, p. 630.

22. S. P. Pokrovskii, "Mezhdunarodnye otnosheniia Rossii i Bukhary," SAGU, *Biulleten*, XVII (1928), 32.

23. Pokrovskii, XVII, 32–33.

24. Stremoukhov, p. 690. Yet Stremoukhov refused to interfere in the case

of a Bukharan Uzbeg who claimed that his two daughters had been sold into slavery, on the ground that it was an internal matter. (Pp. 655–656.)

25. B. I. Iskandarov, *Vostochnaia Bukhara i Pamir vo vtoroi polovine XIX v.* (Dushanbe, 1962–1963), II, 99–100; Henry Lansdell, *Russian Central Asia, Including Kuldja, Bokhara, Khiva and Merv* (London, 1885), II, 185.

26. Pokrovskii, XVII, 32–34.

27. Pokrovskii, XVII, 53. Pokrovskii deals only with Bukhara, and no reference can be found to the subject of criminal jurisdiction over Russians in Khiva in this period. It is highly probable that the same interpretation was placed on article sixteen of Khiva's treaty, which was identical with article fourteen of the Bukharan treaty.

28. Giers, p. 270.

29. N. F. Petrovskii, "Moia poezdka v Bukharu," *Vestnik Evropy*, March 1873, p. 233.

30. Pokrovski, XVI, 56; Gabriel Bonvalot, *Du Kohistan à la Caspiènne* (Paris, 1885), p. 195.

31. "Svedeniia o puti v Sredniuiu Aziiu, cherez Mertvyi Kultuk, po Ust-Urtu i Amu-Dare," *SMPA*, IX (1884), 45. Narazim beglik was later abolished.

32. G. Arandarenko, "Bukharskiia voiska v 1880 g.," *Voennyi Sbornik*, October 1881, p. 360. Arandarenko reported 5,000 cavalrymen at Chardjui but he was obviously in error, for the entire Bukharan cavalry was not that large. The figure of 500, estimated the previous year by Captain Bykov ("Ocherk doliny Amu-dari," *SMPA*, IX [1884], 69–70), is undoubtedly more accurate.

33. Bonvalot, pp. 187–189, 191–193, 196, 203–208; Lansdell, II, 216–217; Henri Moser, *A travers l'Asie centrale* (Paris, 1885), pp. 204, 206, 218.

34. Bartold, pp. 218, 238; Schuyler, II, 311–312.

35. In November 1876 N. K. Giers, Stremoukhov's successor as director of the foreign ministry's Asiatic Department, protested to the British ambassador over a reported Afghan invasion of Darvaz. Giers described Darvaz and Karategin as "independent," "vassal" states of Bukhara. (Giers to Loftus, November 19/December 1, 1876, "Central Asia, No. 1 [1878]," pp. 93–94, *Parliamentary Papers* [1878], LXXX.)

36. A. Madzhlisov, *Karategin nakanune ustanovleniia sovetskoi vlasti* (Stalinabad, 1959), pp. 17–21.

37. B. I. Iskandarov, *Vostochnaia Bukhara i Pamir v period prisoedineniia Srednei Azii k Rossii* (Stalinabad, 1960), p. 194.

38. V. F. Oshanin, "Karategin i Darvaz," IRGO, *Izvestiia*, XVII (1881), 52–53; Captain Pokotilo, "Ocherk bukharskikh vladenii na levom beregu r. Piandzha 1886 g.," *SMPA*, XXV (1887), 271–272; L. F. Kostenko, *Turkestanskii krai* (St. Petersburg, 1880), III, 295; Iskandarov, *Vostochnaia Bukhara i Pamir vo vtoroi polovine XIX v.*, I, 147–149.

39. See, for example, the works of A. L. Kun listed in bibliography. Kun accompanied Abramov's 1870 expedition against Shahr-i Sabz and the 1873 Khivan expedition. In April 1873 the Imperial Russian Geographic Society proposed a whole series of problems on which information was to be collected during the Khivan campaign. ("Voprosy predlagaemye Imperatorskim Russkim Geograficheskim Obshchestvom pri izsledovanii Khivinskago khanstva i sopredelnykh s nim stepei," IRGO, *Izvestiia*, IX [1873], 43–73.)

40. P. P. Semenov, *Istoriia poluvekovoi deiatelnosti Imperatorskago Russkago Geograficheskago Obshchestva 1845–1895* (St. Petersburg, 1896), II, 799–813, 817–823. See also works by Kh. V. Gelman, Captain Bykov, N. V. Sorokin, and Prince A. E. Gedroits listed in bibliography.

41. Semenov, II, 747–751, 769, 772–773, 815, 824. See also works by Maev, Matveev, and N. Zubov listed in bibliography.

42. Semenov, II, 769–770, 778, 781–789. See also works by Oshanin, Regel, P. E. Kosiakov, D. L. Ivanov, and Captain Putiata listed in bibliography.

43. G. Arandarenko, "V gorakh Darvaza-Karategina," *Vostochnoe Obozrenie*, July 14, 1883, p. 9.

44. Captain Gedeonov, "Astronomicheskiia opredeleniia punktov v Zakaspiiskoi oblasti, Khivinskom i Bukharskom khanstvakh, v 1884 godu," IRGO, *Izvestiia*, XXI (1885), 201; Ch. V. Galkov, "Trianguliatsionnye raboty v Srednei Azii (iz istorii Turkestanskogo voenno-topograficheskogo otdela)," *Izvestiia Uzbekistanskogo filiala Geograficheskogo Obshchestva SSSR*, II (1956), 124, 127–129, 132; Galkov, "Semochnye i kartograficheskie raboty Turkestanskogo voenno-topograficheskogo otdela," *Izvestiia Uzbekistanskogo filiala Geograficheskogo Obshchestva SSSR*, III (1957), 63–65, 69, 74–75, 78.

45. MacGahan, p. 138; Captain Fred Burnaby, *A Ride to Khiva* (London, 1876), p. 329; Gabriel Bonvalot, *De Moscou en Bactriane* (Paris, 1884), p. 268; Moser, p. 11.

Chapter 6. Anglo-Russian Relations and the Pacification of the Turkomans

1. Granville to Loftus, January 7, 1874 [N.S.], in Lord Loftus, *Diplomatic Reminiscences* (London, 1894), II, 297–304.

2. Bisheshwar Prasad, *The Foundations of India's Foreign Policy* (Calcutta, 1955), I, 150. Kalat was in fact transformed into an Indian native state in October 1876, while its northern districts, bordering on Afghanistan, were annexed to British India as British Baluchistan. Kashgar was reconquered by China in 1877–1878.

3. Prasad, I, 181–182, 177, 130–131, 151; Mohammad Anwar Khan, *England, Russia and Central Asia* (Peshawar, 1963), pp. 245, 281. For Kaufman's correspondence with Shir Ali, see "Central Asia, No. 2 (1873)" and "Central Asia, No. 1 (1878)," *Parliamentary Papers* (1873), LXXV and (1878), LXXX.

4. Governor General of India to Salisbury, May 3, 1877 [N.S.], "Central Asia, No. 1 (1878)," p. 111. In the fall of 1880 after the end of the Second Anglo-Afghan War, St. Petersburg informed the British that Kaufman had been instructed to cease all direct contact with Kabul, but as late as the following June London was convinced that his correspondence with the Afghan emir was continuing. (S. Gopal, *The Viceroyalty of Lord Ripon, 1880–1884* [Oxford, 1953], p. 32.)

5. In October 1876 Disraeli had toyed briefly with the idea of striking a military blow against Russia in Central Asia, a project which Lytton enthusiastically supported. (Khan, pp. 232–240.)

6. M. A. Terentiev, *Istoriia zavoevaniia Srednei Azii* (St. Petersburg, 1906), II, 428, 431, 434–435.

7. If the kush-begi's claim in 1882 was true, Bukhara had already played a small role in the Eastern crisis by rejecting Turkey's overture for an alliance against Russia just before the outbreak of the Russo-Turkish War. (V. V. Krestovskii, "V gostiakh u emira bukharskago. Putevoi dnevnik," *Russkii Vestnik*, July 1884, p. 73.)

8. Terentiev, II, 436.

9. Terentiev, II, 439; L. Kostenko, "Istoricheskii ocherk rasprostraneniia russkago vladychestva v Srednei Azii," *Voennyi Sbornik*, November 1887, pp. 5–6.

10. I. L. Iavorskii, *Puteshestvie russkago posolstva po Avganistanu i Bukharskomu khanstvu v 1878–1879 gg.* (St. Petersburg, 1882–1883), I, 53, 375.

11. Terentiev, II, 543–544; V. V. Bartold, *Istoriia kulturnoi zhizni Turkestana* (Leningrad, 1927), pp. 240–241.

12. The exchange of envoys between Bukhara and Kabul during 1871–1878 is reported in "Central Asia, No. 1 (1878)," pp. 97–98, 160, 192. N. P. Stremoukhov noted the presence of an Afghan embassy at Shahr-i Sabz in May 1874. ("Poezdka v Bukharu," *Russkii Vestnik*, June 1875, pp. 641–642.) Colonel N. I. Grodekov, en route from Tashkent to Herat, reported an Afghan embassy at Kitab in October 1878. (*Colonel Grodekoff's Ride from Samarcand to Herat* [London, 1880], pp. 5–6.) Doctor Iavorskii saw a Bukharan embassy at Mazar-i Sharif in Afghan Turkestan in February 1879 and an Afghan embassy at Bukhara in the following month. (Iavorskii, II, 213, 369–370.)

13. Terentiev, III, 2–3; N. A. Khalfin, *Prisoedinenie Srednei Azii k Rossii* (Moscow, 1965), pp. 334–335.

14. Terentiev, III, 43, 46, 98, 132, 210. The route via Bukhara and Merv would have been more direct, but the Merv Turkomans blocked the way.

15. Terentiev, III, 143, 216. *Istoriia narodov Uzbekistana* (Tashkent, 1947–1950), II, 418, alleges, but without documentation, that Muhammad Rahim unsuccessfully approached Kabul for an alliance against Russia in 1881 in return for Khiva's submission to Afghanistan. Such an approach would not have been impossible but is highly unlikely in view of the khan of Khiva's attitude of resignation after 1873 and especially of Russia's victories over the Turkomans.

16. P. M. Lessar, "Mervskie khany. Polozhenie Merva i Ateka v kontse 1882 g.," *SMPA*, VI (1883), 63–64; M. N. Tikhomirov, *Prisoedinenie Merva k Rossii* (Moscow, 1960), p. 97. Tikhomirov (p. 98) states that Yusuf died in October 1881, but this is in error. In August 1882 Yusuf received Lessar, who placed his death in October of that year. (Lessar, pp. 64, 66.) Tikhomirov also claims that Yusuf's successor, Abd ar-Rahman, was sent out a month after Yusuf's death. Ronald F. Thomson, the British minister at Teheran, reported early in 1883 that Abd ar-Rahman had recently arrived in Merv to succeed the late Yusuf-beg. (Thomson to Granville, February 9 and March 9, 1883 [N.S.], "Central Asia, No. 1 [1884]," pp. 68, 75–76, *Parliamentary Papers* [1884], LXXXVII.) Thomson's report thus confirms Lessar's account.

17. Tikhomirov, pp. 98–100, 126–127.

18. Bartold, p. 237. According to Bartold, Abd ar-Rahman had been acting on instructions from Khiva, but this is doubtful.

19. Tikhomirov, pp. 218, 127–128; M. Alikhanov-Avarskii, "Zakaspiiskiia vospominaniia 1881–1885," *Vestnik Evropy*, September 1904, pp. 106–109. In December 1883 Alikhanov-Avarskii saw Ata-djan-beg's commission from the khan of Khiva, bearing Cherniaev's approval, signature, and seal.

20. Khalfin, p. 360; Sir Edward Thornton [British ambassador to Russia] to Giers, February 29/March 12, 1884, *Afganskoe razgranichenie: Peregovory mezhdu Rossiei i Velikobritaniei 1872–1885* (St. Petersburg, 1886), Pt. II, 44. As early as 1877 the geographer Veniukov had written in support of Khiva's claims to Merv. (M. I. Veniukov, "Ocherk mezhdunarodnykh voprosov v Azii," *Russkii Vestnik*, April 1877, p. 483.)

21. Khalfin, pp. 362–364; Tikhomirov, p. 152; Alikhanov-Avarskii, p. 109.

22. Tikhomirov, p. 138.

23. Lieutenant Alexander Burnes, *Travels into Bokhara* (London, 1834), II, 215–216.

24. A. E. Regel, "Puteshestvie v Shugnan," IRGO, *Izvestiia*, XX (1884), 273; Captain Putiata, "Ocherk ekspeditsii v Pamir, Sarykol, Vakhan i Shugnan 1883 g.," SMPA, X (1884), 75–79.

25. Vlangali memorandum, "Central Asia, No. 2 (1885)," pp. 2–3, *Parliamentary Papers* (1884–1885), LXXXVII. In transmitting the memorandum to Granville, Thornton reported that Vlangali had presented it to him on December 17/29. (Thornton to Granville, December 31, 1883 [N.S.], "Central Asia, No. 2 [1885]," p. 1.) Vlangali's memorandum was also published in *Afganskoe razgranichenie*, pp. 28–30, where it is dated December 19.

26. G. J. Alder, *British India's Northern Frontier* (London, 1963), pp. 182–186, 189–191.

27. Alder, pp. 195–198; Giers [Russian foreign minister] to Staal [Russian ambassador to Britain], July 6, 1884, in Baron Alexandre Meyendorff, ed., *Correspondance diplomatique de M. de Staal, 1884–1900* (Paris, 1929), I, 43–44.

28. Alder, p. 197; Gopal, p. 42. Two years later, after Kabul had thwarted British efforts to explore the upper Amu-Darya for the purpose of a possible future demarcation of frontiers, Viceroy Dufferin warned Abd ar-Rahman that Afghanistan would have to take responsibility if Russia again raised the question of Shugnan. (Alder, pp. 200–203.) Contemporary Soviet historiography on the Shugnan question shows less judiciousness than faithfulness to current Russian foreign policy objectives. The interpretation in vogue is that the Afghans, traditional friends of Russia, were not to blame for the seizure of Shugnan and Roshan, now a part of the Tadjik SSR. Rather, imperialistic Britain urged Afghanistan to commit this act of aggression and supplied the necessary arms and money. Britain was motivated by a desire to divert Afghanistan's attention from India's northwest frontier, where Afghans were subject to Britain's oppressive rule. This refers obliquely to the current dispute between Afghanistan and Pakistan over the Pathans, Afghan tribes living in northwest Pakistan. Yet in fact the Pathans were not effectively brought under British control until the 1890's. For the Soviet interpretation, see B. I. Iskandarov, *Vostochnaia Bukhara i Pamir vo vtoroi polovine XIX v.* (Dushanbe, 1962–1963), I, 182, 220–221; Iskandarov, *Iz istorii Bukharskogo emirata* (Moscow, 1958), p. 86; N. Khalfin, *Proval britanskoi agressii v Afganistane (XIX v.-nachalo XX v.)* (Moscow, 1959), pp. 136–138. It is true that Afghanistan received arms and an annual subsidy from Britain, but this does not mean that they were intended specifically for use in Shugnan. As for Khalfin's argument that Abd ar-Rahman could not have violated the 1873 Anglo-Russian agreement without Britain's knowledge, Abd ar-Rahman was never a mere puppet of British policy, and Britain's re-

turn in 1880 to the policy of nonintervention in Afghanistan left him free to pursue his own aims. Khalfin's only evidence is a report of April 1884 from a frontier commandant in the Zarafshan Okrug to Tashkent that English envoys had proposed to Kabul the subjugation of Shugnan. Such reports, however, very often consisted of unsubstantiated rumors circulating among the local population or brought by travelers.

29. Putiata, p. 79.

30. Memorandum of the foreign ministry to Thornton, June 9, 1884, *Afganskoe razgranichenie*, p. 66.

31. Granville to Thornton, April 29, 1884 [N.S.], "Central Asia, No. 2 (1885)," p. 27; Thornton to Giers, June 13/25, 1884, "Central Asia, No. 2 (1885)," p. 50 (also in *Afganskoe razgranichenie*, p. 68).

32. Granville to Loftus, October 17, 1872 [N.S.], "Central Asia, No. 1 (1873)," p. 1, *Parliamentary Papers* (1873), LXXV.

33. Giers to Thornton, June 23, 1884, "Central Asia, No. 2 (1885)," pp. 55–56 (also in *Afganskoe razgranichenie*, pp. 78–82).

34. Granville to Thornton, August 6, 1884 [N.S.], "Central Asia, No. 2 (1885)," p. 70; Thornton to Giers, August 1/13, 1884, *Afganskoe razgranichenie*, p. 90.

Chapter 7. The End of an Era

1. N. P. Stremoukhov, "Poezdka v Bukharu," *Russkii Vestnik*, June 1875, p. 643.

2. Doria to Derby [British foreign secretary], July 13, 1875 [N.S.], "Central Asia, No. 1 (1878)," p. 45, *Parliamentary Papers* (1878), LXXX.

3. M. I. Veniukov, "Ocherk mezhdunarodnykh voprosov v Azii," *Russkii Vestnik*, April 1877, p. 487; Captain Putiata, "Ocherk ekspeditsii v Pamir, Sarykol, Vakhan i Shugnan 1883 g.," SMPA, X (1884), 80; Henri Moser, *A travers l'Asie centrale* (Paris, 1885), p. 187.

4. Kaufman adopted a similar policy toward the Moslem schools and other native institutions of Russian Turkestan. (Richard A. Pierce, *Russian Central Asia, 1867–1917* [Berkeley, 1960], pp. 213–214.)

5. K. P. von Kaufman, *Proekt vsepoddanneishago otcheta* (St. Petersburg, 1885), pp. 9, 133–134, 349, 352.

6. Putiata, p. 82:

7. Kaufman, pp. 133, 311, 351–353.

8. M. A. Terentiev, *Istoriia zavoevaniia Srednei Azii* (St. Petersburg, 1906), III, 330.

9. Gabriel Bonvalot, *Du Kohistan à la Caspiènne* (Paris, 1885), p. 168. L. F. Kostenko (*Turkestanskii krai* [St. Petersburg, 1880], III, 296) had already predicted in 1880 that Muzaffar's death would be followed by civil turmoil necessitating Russian intervention.

10. B. I. Iskandarov, *Iz istorii Bukharskogo emirata* (Moscow, 1958), pp. 73–74.

11. F. K. Giers, *Otchet revizuiushchago, po Vysochaishemu poveleniiu, Turkestanskii krai, Tainago Sovetnika Girsa* (St. Petersburg, 1883), pp. 459–460;

V. V. Krestovskii, "V gostiakh u emira bukharskago. Putevoi dnevnik," *Russkii Vestnik*, May 1884, pp. 57–61.

12. Stremoukhov, p. 688. Abd al-Ahad is often called Muzaffar's fourth son, but this designation properly belongs to Abd Allah Fattah-khan. (Arminius Vámbéry, *History of Bokhara* [London, 1873], pp. 416–417; M. A. Terentiev, *Russia and England in Central Asia* [Calcutta, 1876], I, 78–79). Abd Allah Fattah was born in 1857, two years before Abd al-Ahad. P. P. Shubinskii ("Ocherki Bukhary," *Istoricheskii Vestnik*, XLIX [1892], 119–120) calls Abd al-Ahad the fourth son and gives his year of birth as 1857, but lists four other sons, including Abd Allah Fattah, as having been born up through 1857. The Russian foreign ministry's yearbooks and the *Pravitelstvennyi Vestnik* later placed Abd al-Ahad's birth in 1859.

13. Krestovskii, August 1884, p. 552.

14. Iskandarov, pp. 87, 72, 89.

15. D. N. Logofet, *Bukharskoe khanstvo pod russkim protektoratom* (St. Petersburg, 1911), II, 169, 171–172, 177.

16. Logofet, II, 175–176; V. V. Bartold, *Istoriia kulturnoi zhizni Turkestana* (Leningrad, 1927), p. 243.

17. *Istoriia Uzbekskoi SSR* (Tashkent, 1955–1956), I, Pt. II, 144.

18. Giers, p. 189.

19. Krestovskii, May 1884, pp. 41–42.

20. Krestovskii, May 1884, pp. 24, 41–44, 56.

21. Moser, pp. 148–150, 182. Moser's date for the emir's consent, November 2, is presumably New Style.

22. S. P. Pokrovskii, "Mezhdunarodnye otnosheniia Rossii i Bukhary," SAGU, *Biulleten*, XVII (1928), 42.

23. Stremoukhov, pp. 691–692.

24. N. Charykov, "Zapiska o mestnykh putiakh soobshchenii, podlezhashchikh uluchsheniiu v interesakh razvitiia russkoi torgovli v bukharskikh vladeniiakh," *SMPA*, XV (1885), 191.

25. Arminius Vámbéry, *Travels in Central Asia* (London, 1864), pp. 187–190; "Bukharskii emir i ego poddannye," IRGO, *Izvestiia*, II (1866), 64–65.

26. L. F. Kostenko, *Puteshestvie v Bukharu russkoi missii v 1870 godu* (St. Petersburg, 1871), p. 96; Eugene Schuyler, *Turkistan* (New York, 1876), II, 83–85; Stremoukhov, pp. 641–642, 682. A generation later Muzaffar's own court historian, writing with a venomous pen, characterized his former master as arrogant and egotistic, licentious and depraved. (Mirza Abdal Azim Sami, *Tarikh-i salatin-i mangitiia* [Moscow, 1962], p. 120.)

27. Stremoukhov, pp. 682, 686–687, 692. Stremoukhov estimated Muzaffar's harem at 1000 wives and concubines. Shubinskii (p. 120) gives the more credible figure of 4 wives and 150–200 concubines.

28. Stremoukhov, p. 641.

29. G. Arandarenko, "Bukharskiia voiska v 1880 g.," *Voennyi Sbornik*, October 1881, p. 367.

30. Moser, p. 154.

31. Logofet, II, 176–177.

32. Bartold, p. 241; Krestovskii, March 1884, p. 136; Moser, p. 78.

33. Giers, p. 102.

34. Krestovskii, May 1884, p. 44; Moser, p. 157; Shubinskii, p. 133.

35. N. Petrovskii, "Moia poezdka v Bukharu," *Vestnik Evropy*, March 1873, p. 241; Stremoukhov, p. 643; Krestovskii, July 1884, p. 73. Muhammad-biy was born in northeastern Persia. Captured as a boy by Turkoman raiders and sold into slavery in Bukhara in 1820, he gradually rose to high office in the service of Nasr Allah and Muzaffar. Muhammad-biy and his son each married one of Muzaffar's discarded concubines. The "biy" designated Muhammad's rank in the secular hierarchy. These ranks were, from highest to lowest: atalik, kush-begi, divan-begi, parvanachi, inak, dadkha, biy, ishik-aka-bashi, toksaba, mirakhur, karaul-begi, djibachi, mirza-bashi, chukhra-aka-bashi, and bahadur. (A. A. Semenov, *Ocherk ustroistva tsentralnogo administrativnogo upravleniia Bukharskogo khanstva pozdneishego vremeni* [Stalinabad, 1954], pp. 60–61.) These ranks were not directly related to any particular offices, although the highest dignitaries and the begs customarily held one of the seven highest ranks. Thus, the incumbent of the *office* of kush-begi, as in Muhammad-biy's case, did not necessarily hold the *rank* of kush-begi. Muhammad-biy's son, Muhammad Sharif, was Muzaffar's zakatchi-kalan, and his grandson, Astanakul-inak, was beg of Karshi and subsequently of Chardjui. A more distant relative was beg of Ziaddin, and others were scattered throughout the bureaucracy.

36. Krestovskii, July 1884, pp. 66–67. Karataev was credited with having saved the lives of Struve and Glukhovskoi in 1865. (Stremoukhov, pp. 668–669.)

37. J. A. MacGahan, *Campaigning on the Oxus, and the Fall of Khiva* (New York, 1874), pp. 278, 280; Captain Fred Burnaby, *A Ride to Khiva* (London, 1876), pp. 308, 323.

38. Bonvalot, pp. 226–231, 235.

39. Bartold, p. 235; Bonvalot, p. 220.

40. Guillaume Capus, *A travers le royaume de Tamerlan* (Paris, 1892), pp. 360, 363.

41. Lieutenant Alexander Burnes, *Travels into Bokhara* (London, 1834), I, 277.

42. Kostenko, *Puteshestvie v Bukharu*, pp. 69–70; Stremoukhov, p. 676.

43. O. Olufsen, *The Emir of Bokhara and His Country* (London, 1911), p. 538; Fitzroy Maclean, *Back to Bokhara* (New York, 1959), p. 113. Jules Leclercq, a French tourist in Bukhara at the end of the 1880's, reported that the clock was stopped at 11:45, and no one in the khanate knew how to repair it. (Jules Leclercq, *Du Caucase aux Monts Alaï* [Paris, 1890], pp. 95–96.)

44. Stremoukhov, pp. 651–652; Kostenko, *Puteshestvie v Bukharu*, p. 56; Krestovskii, May 1884, pp. 48–49. The details of Osman's life are far from clear. Stremoukhov gives his real name as Aleksei Iakovlev; Krestovskii says that it was Popov and that he commanded the Bukharan army for twenty-three years. Arandarenko (p. 347) claims that Osman took command only after the defeat at Irdjar on May 8, 1866.

45. Kostenko, *Puteshestvie v Bukharu*, p. 105.

46. Stremoukhov, p. 651.

47. Arandarenko, p. 361.

48. Henry Lansdell, *Russian Central Asia* (London, 1885), II, 21–22.

49. Putiata, pp. 83–86.

50. Logofet, I, 252; Colonel Matveev, "Kratkii ocherk Bukhary. 1887 g.," *SMPA*, XXXVI (1888), 6.

51. Arandarenko, p. 365.

52. Stremoukhov, pp. 630–631.

53. Moser, p. 139.

54. I. L. Iavorskii, *Puteshestvie russkago posolstva po Avganistanu i Bukharskomu khanstvu v 1878–1879 gg.* (St. Petersburg, 1882–1883), II, 37.

55. Putiata, p. 38; Krestovskii, May 1884, p. 30.

56. Bartold, p. 241; Moser, p. 157; Krestovskii, March 1884, p. 148.

57. Lansdell, II, 31; Iavorskii, II, 302–378; Capus, p. 316.

58. Kostenko, *Puteshestvie v Bukharu,* p. 85; Stremoukhov, pp. 643, 655, 683–684; Gabriel Bonvalot, *De Moscou en Bactriane,* pp. 106–112, 117, 156–157; Lansdell, II, 10, 20, 82–83, 159, 490; Capus, p. 132; Moser, p. 166.

59. Burnaby, p. 315; Lansdell, II, 270.

60. G. N. Chabrov, "Iz istorii poligrafii i izdatelstva literatury na mestnykh iazykakh v dorevoliutsionnom Turkestane (1868–1917 gg.)," SAGU, *Trudy,* new series, LVII (1954), 79–80; Bartold, p. 237. The Russians had established a printing press at Tashkent in 1868, but Muhammad Rahim's was the first local publishing venture. (Edward Allworth, *Central Asian Publishing and the Rise of Nationalism* [New York, 1965], pp. 10–12.)

61. Moser, pp. 239, 251, 255–256; Bonvalot, *Du Kohistan à la Caspiènne,* p. 232.

62. Burnaby, pp. 320–321; Lansdell, II, 312.

63. Terentiev, *Istoriia zavoevaniia Srednei Azii,* III, 270; Moser, p. 271. The Mennonite immigrants to Khiva probably numbered 2000–3000. Terentiev gives the figure of 500 families, while Moser reported 400 individual settlers at Tashauz alone.

64. Robert L. Jefferson, *A New Ride to Khiva* (London, 1899), pp. 288–294.

65. In February-March 1884 a government commission headed by General Count N. P. Ignatiev had rejected a proposal to unite Transcaspia to the government-general of Turkestan because it feared that Bukhara and Khiva could not long retain their autonomy if surrounded by a single administrative unit. (Pierce, p. 62.)

Chapter 8. Russo-Bukharan Relations Transformed

1. George N. Curzon, *Russia in Central Asia in 1889 and the Anglo-Russian Question* (London, 1889), pp. 274, xii.

2. Arminius Vámbéry, *Travels in Central Asia* (London, 1864), p. 407; Eugene Schuyler, *Turkistan* (New York, 1876), I, 219–220. The trip by caravan from Orenburg to Bukhara took approximately five days longer, to Khiva five days less, than the journey to Tashkent. (M. K. Rozhkova, *Ekonomicheskie sviazi Rossii so Srednei Aziei* (Moscow, 1963), pp. 76–77.)

3. Rozhkova, pp. 82–86.

4. Curzon, p. 35; A. Stuart, "Le chemin de fer central-asiatique projeté par MM. Ferdinand de Lesseps et Cotard," *L'Explorateur,* II (1875), 396–397; Schuyler, I, 224.

5. D. A. Miliutin, *Dnevnik, 1873–1882* (Moscow, 1947–1950), I, 181, and III, 177.

6. The Tsesarevich Bay route, which would connect by sea with Astrakhan, was proposed by A. A. Grotenhelm, commandant of the Amu-Darya Otdel, and

surveyed in 1881–1882 at the order of General G. A. Kolpakovskii, acting governor general of Turkestan. (M. A. Terentiev, *Istoriia zavoevaniia Srednei Azii* (St. Petersburg, 1906), III, 230–232.) The Orenburg route would connect with steamboats on the Aral Sea. (Miliutin, III, 177.)

7. Curzon, pp. 37, 41–43; *SMPA*, IX (1884), 189–191.

8. Terentiev, III, 232, 239; Henri Moser, *A travers l'Asie centrale* (Paris, 1885), pp. 58–59; A. S. Sadykov, *Ekonomicheskie sviazi Khivy s Rossiei vo vtoroi polovine XIX–nachale XX vv.* (Tashkent, 1965), pp. 85–86.

9. Curzon, pp. 44–45.

10. S. P. Pokrovskii, "Mezhdunarodnye otnosheniia Rossii i Bukhary," SAGU, *Biulleten*, XVII (1928), 44–45.

11. N. V. Tcharykow, *Glimpses of High Politics* (London, 1931), pp. 197–198; Pokrovskii, XVII, 45, 48. Charykov unaccountably dates the protocol July 18/30.

12. Pokrovskii, XVII, 44; Tcharykow, pp. 198–199, 208.

13. *Pravitelstvennyi Vestnik*, April 24/May 6, 1886, p. 2.

14. An eyewitness account of these events is in Z. Z., "Poezdka v Bukharu," *Moskovskiia Vedomosti*, January 23, 1886, pp. 4–5. The new emir later rewarded his uncle Astanakul with the rank of kush-begi and the begship of Hisar. (D. N. Logofet, "Cherez Bukharu," *Voennyi Sbornik*, February 1910, pp. 205–206; June, p. 243.) Abd al-Ahad retained Muhammad-biy in the office of kush-begi until the latter's death in 1889.

15. Tcharykow, pp. 203–204; Terentiev, III, 358.

16. Guillaume Capus, *A travers le royaume de Tamerlan* (Paris, 1892), p. 311; Gabriel Bonvalot, *Du Caucase aux Indes à travers le Pamir* (Paris, 1888), pp. 191–192; Sadriddin Aini, *Vospominaniia* (Moscow, 1960), p. 778; Logofet, January 1910, pp. 201–202.

17. *PSZ* (1885), No. 3274. In his memoirs, written in exile more than a third of a century later, Charykov claimed that by the summer of 1884 St. Petersburg had already decided to establish the political agency and, when he left to assume his post of diplomatic attaché in Tashkent in July of that year, he carried a dispatch for General Rosenbach advising him of the government's decision. (Tcharykow, p. 189.) However, Pokrovskii (XVII, 50) states that the final decision to establish the political agency came as a consequence of the railroad. There is no apparent reason to have delayed the creation of the post for a year and a half if the decision was in fact taken in 1884. Writing so long after the event, Charykov may have been betrayed by his memory, particularly since the foreign ministry was advocating the creation of a political agency in the spring of 1884. Pokrovskii, an unusually reliable authority, worked directly from the archives, although on this point he offers no documentation.

18. Pokrovskii, XVII, 52.

19. "Vremennoe polozhenie ob upravlenii Zakaspiiskoi oblasti," article 6, February 6, 1890, SU, March 16, 1890, No. 256. During 1890–1898 the commandant of the Transcaspian Oblast was directly responsible to the minister of war, instead of to the governor general of the Caucasus as he had formerly been. In 1898 Transcaspia was incorporated into the government-general of Turkestan.

20. Law of May 12, 1893, *PSZ* (1893), No. 9595.

21. Pokrovskii, XVII, 50–51.

22. Yearbooks of the Russian foreign ministry, 1886–1916.

23. Tcharykow, pp. 163–164, 190, 200–202, 206. Charykov was to gain international notoriety in 1911 when, as ambassador to Turkey, he launched the "Charykov kite," a proposal that Turkey open the Straits to Russian warships and join a Balkan League directed against Austria-Hungary in return for a Russian guarantee of Turkish territory in Europe.

24. Pokrovskii, XVII, 50; Curzon, p. 152. The imported silver was also minted into local money in Bukhara and used in 1887 to pay the unskilled native labor hired to build the railroad. (Tcharykow, p. 209.)

25. Terentiev, III, 359. The railroad bridge built over the Amu-Darya at Chardjui in 1887 was a rickety wooden structure, which the train, traveling at a snail's pace, took half an hour to cross. A steel bridge finally replaced the earlier one at the turn of the century.

26. Tcharykow, pp. 209–210.

27. Curzon, pp. 154–155.

28. T. G. Tukhtametov, "Ekonomicheskoe sostoianie Bukharskogo emirata v kontse XIX i nachale XX vekov," Akademiia Nauk Kirgizskoi SSR, Institut Istorii, *Trudy*, III (1957), 165.

29. Curzon, pp. 156, 168–169.

30. Esper Ukhtomskii, *Ot Kalmytskoi stepi do Bukhary* (St. Petersburg, 1891), p. 202. Ukhtomskii, who visited the khanate in 1889, wrote that the agency moved to New Bukhara in 1890. But P. P. Shubinskii, a more reliable authority because he was in Bukhara in June 1891, reported that the agency had moved earlier that year. ("Ocherki Bukhary," *Istoricheskii Vestnik*, XLIX [1892], 126.)

31. B. I. Iskandarov, *Iz istorii Bukharskogo emirata* (Moscow, 1958), pp. 90–92; Vlangali to Staal, May 6/18, 1886, in Baron Alexandre Meyendorff, ed., *Correspondance diplomatique de M. de Staal* (Paris, 1929), I, 299.

32. Terentiev, III, 355. The Aral Sea Flotilla, established in the early 1850's, was disbanded in 1882.

33. Terentiev, III, 358.

34. Z. Radzhabov, *Iz istorii obshchestvenno-politicheskoi mysli tadzhikskogo naroda vo vtoroi polovine XIX i v nachale XX vv.* (Stalinabad, 1957), p. 100.

35. Ministry of War to Governor General of Turkestan, October 28, 1886, in Iskandarov, p. 26.

36. D. N. Logofet, *Strana bezpraviia. Bukharskoe khanstvo i ego sovremennoe sostoianie* (St. Petersburg, 1909), p. 124; Terentiev, III, 359.

37. Terentiev, III, 357; D. N. Logofet, *Bukharskoe khanstvo pod russkim protektoratom* (St. Petersburg, 1911), I, 218, 203.

38. Curzon, pp. 124–125; Terentiev, III, 360; George Dobson, *Russia's Railway Advance into Central Asia* (London, 1890), pp. 39–41, 229–230.

39. Earl of Rosebery [British foreign secretary] to Sir R. B. D. Morier [ambassador to Russia], February 12, 1886 [N.S.], Ridgeway to Rosebery, May 16, 1886 [N.S.], "Central Asia, No. 2 (1887)," pp. 20–21, 84, *Parliamentary Papers* (1887), LXIII.

40. Iskandarov, pp. 88–93.

41. Pokrovskii, XVII, 36. The first grant was made to Mazov & Co., a large Orenburg firm, which received 2,700 acres, tax-exempt for twelve years, on the

right bank of the Amu-Darya across from Chardjui. (Pokrovskii, XVII, 37; Tukh-tametov, p. 158.)

42. Pokrovskii, XVII, 37.

43. Pokrovskii, XVII, 37.

44. A. P. Fomchenko, *Russkie poseleniia v Bukharskom emirate* (Tashkent, 1958), p. 14.

45. Tcharykow, p. 198. The station was named Kagan.

46. Pokrovskii, XVII, 47.

47. Pokrovskii, XVII, 48. The text of the protocol is in Logofet, *Strana bez-praviia*, pp. 218–221, and S. V. Zhukovskii, *Snosheniia Rossii s Bukharoi i Khivoi za poslednee trekhsotletie* (Petrograd, 1915), Appendix IV.

48. Pokrovskii, XVII, 47. Pokrovskii dates the draft of the regulations May 3, 1887, but probably means 1888. The text of the appendix is in Logofet, *Strana bezpraviia*, pp. 221–224.

49. This principle was reaffirmed in 1890 in a note to article one of the Provisional Statute on the Administration of the Transcaspian Oblast, which specifically reserved to the jurisdiction of the governor general of Turkestan the "inhabited points in the riverine zone along the left bank of the Amu-Darya," *i.e.*, Chardjui and Kerki. (*SU*, March 16, 1890, No. 256.)

50. Pokrovskii, XVII, 57.

51. The authority of the governor of New Bukhara was subsequently enlarged to cover all Russians in Old Bukhara and in the railroad zone, which extended for two thirds of a mile (one verst) in either direction from the railroad. (Fomchenko, p. 18; Logofet, *Strana bezpraviia*, p. 180; V. V. Bartold, *Istoriia kulturnoi zhizni Turkestana* [Leningrad, 1927], p. 251.)

52. Félix de Rocca, *De l'Alaï à l'Amou-Daria* (Paris, 1896), p. 325; Logofet, *Bukharskoe khanstvo*, I, 185; Fomchenko, pp. 14–17; Shubinskii, L (1892), 123; K. K. Pahlen, *Otchet po revizii Turkestanskago kraia* (St. Petersburg, 1909–1911), Pt. VIII, *Nalogi i poshliny. Organy finansovago upravleniia*, p. 229. Fomchenko (p. 17) mistakenly declares that Termez was never considered a Russian settlement.

53. Tcharykow, p. 219. The text is in Zhukovskii, Appendix V.

54. Further regulations on the production of wine by Russians in Bukhara were approved by the governor general on December 15, 1893. The text is in Logofet, *Strana bezpraviia*, pp. 232–234.

55. Pokrovskii, XVII, 53–54. Consular jurisdiction in Persia and Turkey was exercised as follows: Russians committing crimes other than capital ones against other Russians, natives, or subjects of a third power were tried on the spot by the Russian ambassador, minister, chargé d'affaires, or consul. In cases of capital crimes the accused was sent to the nearest Russian frontier province for trial.

56. *PSZ* (1887), No. 4498. The Samarkand Oblast replaced the old Zaraf-shan Okrug in the administrative reform of 1886 in Russian Turkestan.

57. Pokrovskii, XVII, 54.

58. *PSZ* (1888), No. 5194.

59. Pokrovskii, XVII, 55. Charykov's tremendous workload, coupled with an attack of malaria, resulted in a nervous breakdown in the summer of 1889. He went on sick-leave, first to Samarkand Oblast and later to St. Petersburg and Paris, and never returned to his post. (Tcharykow, pp. 218–222.)

60. *PSZ* (1889), No. 5994.

61. *PSZ* (1893), No. 9424.

62. *PSZ* (1894), No. 10690.

63. *PSZ* (1894), No. 10100.

64. *PSZ* (1896), No. 12412.

65. Pahlen, Pt. II, *Sudebnyia uchrezhdeniia*, pp. 64, 69.

66. Logofet, *Bukharskoe khanstvo*, I, 336.

67. Pahlen, Pt. II, *Sudebnyia uchrezhdeniia*, p. 24. The Samarkand okrug court replaced the Samarkand oblast court after the judicial reform of 1898 in Turkestan.

68. Dobson, p. 321.

69. Francis Henry Skrine and Edward Denison Ross, *The Heart of Asia. A History of Russian Turkestan and the Central Asian Khanates from the Earliest Times* (London, 1899), p. 383.

70. F. K. Giers, *Otchet revizuiushchago . . . Turkestanskii krai, Tainago Sovetnika Girsa* (St. Petersburg, 1883), p. 333.

71. "Polozhenie ob upravlenii Turkestanskim kraem," June 12, 1886, *PSZ* (1886), No. 3814. This statute replaced the "temporary" statute of 1867.

72. *PSZ* (1888), No. 5203.

73. *PSZ* (1892), No. 8464. On March 15 of the following year the governor general received the complementary power to recall to Russia from Bukhara and Khiva any Russian subjects against whom charges were brought by the political agent or the commandant of the Amu-Darya Otdel. (*PSZ* [1893], No. 9425.)

74. I. F. Abramov, ed., *Polozhenie ob upravlenii Turkestanskago kraia* (*Sv. Zak. t. II, izd. 1892 g., po prod. 1912, 1913 i 1914 g.g.*) *s raziasneniiami Pravitelstvuiushchago Senata* (Tashkent, 1916), p. 36.

75. In the late 1890's the railroad was transferred to the Ministry of Ways of Communication. (Skrine and Ross, pp. 313–315.)

Chapter 9. The Protectorate Completed: Russia and Bukhara

1. L. Kostenko, "Istoricheskii ocherk rasprostraneniia russkago vladychestva v Srednei Azii," *Voennyi Sbornik*, August 1887, p. 148.

2. Lt. Col. P. Poslavskii, "Bukhara. Opisanie goroda i khanstva," *SMPA*, XLVII (1891), 6, 96, 102.

3. Evgenii Markov, *Rossiia v Srednei Azii* (St. Petersburg, 1901), I, 376. Lessar, a civil engineer by training, had seen a decade of service in Central Asia before his appointment to the political agency. He had explored the route of the Transcaspian Railroad for General Annenkov in the early 1880's and served on the Anglo-Russian commission that delimited the Russo-Afghan boundary in 1886–1887.

4. George N. Curzon, *Russia in Central Asia in 1889 and the Anglo-Russian Question* (London, 1889), pp. 249, 281.

5. S. P. Pokrovskii, "Mezhdunarodnye otnosheniia Rossii i Bukhary," *SAGU, Biulleten*, XVII (1928), 48.

6. A. Gubarevich-Radobylskii, *Ekonomicheskii ocherk Bukhary i Tunisa* (St. Petersburg, 1905), pp. 166–168.

7. Gubarevich-Radobylskii, p. 170; D. N. Logofet, *Bukharskoe khanstvo pod russkim protektoratom* (St. Petersburg, 1911), II, 181.

8. Gubarevich-Radobylskii, pp. 168–169, 171; S. V. Zhukovskii, *Snosheniia Rossii s Bukharoi i Khivoi za poslednee trekhsotletie* (Petrograd, 1915), Appendix VI; *Pravitelstvennyi Vestnik*, January 16/28, 1893, p. 2; Pokrovskii, XVII, 48–49. Pokrovskii does not mention the trip to Russia, but it was fully covered in the January 1893 issues of *Pravitelstvennyi Vestnik*.

9. K. K. Pahlen, *Otchet po revizii Turkestanskago kraia* (St. Petersburg, 1909–1911), Pt. VIII, *Nalogi i poshliny. Organy finansovago upravleniia*, p. 250; Gubarevich-Radobylskii, p. 163. The text of the kush-begi's note is in Zhukovskii, Appendix VI.

10. Pahlen, Pt. VIII, *Nalogi i poshliny*, pp. 254, 257; Pahlen, Pt. XIX, *Prilozhenie. Materialy k kharakteristike narodnago khoziaistva*, I, Pt. II, 486; D. N. Logofet, *Strana bezpraviia* (St. Petersburg, 1909), pp. 131–133.

11. Rear Admiral Baturin, "Otchet ob ekspeditsii v verkhove r. Amu-Dari (1894 g.)," *SMPA*, LXIV (1896), 246–248. Customs posts were established at Kerki, Bassgin, Kelif, Chushka-Guzar, Patta-Hisar, Aivadj, Sarai, Chubek, and Bogorak. Patta-Hisar, later Termez, was the seat of the Central Customs Administration. For a vivid description of the posts at Chubek and Sarai in 1898, see A. A. Semenov, "Po granitsam Bukhary i Afganistana," *Istoricheskii Vestnik*, LXXXVIII (1902), 98–105. The frontier zone in which the Russians operated at first extended 7 versts (4.6 miles) back from the river, but by 1914 it had been widened to 21 versts (13.9 miles). (Pokrovskii, XVII, 49.)

12. Z. Radzhabov, *Iz istorii obshchestvenno-politicheskoi mysli tadzhikskogo naroda* (Stalinabad, 1957), p. 68.

13. Gubarevich-Radobylskii, p. 171.

14. B. I. Iskandarov, *Iz istorii Bukharskogo emirata* (Moscow, 1958), p. 22. As estimated by Lessar, the army's annual cost was 1.3 million rubles. (Iskandarov, p. 21.) In 1880, however, Arandarenko had estimated the army's cost at 2.3 million rubles out of a total state budget of 6 millions. (G. Arandarenko, "Bukharskiia voiska v 1880 g.," *Voennyi Sbornik*, October 1881, p. 366.)

15. V. V. Bartold, *Istoriia kulturnoi zhizni Turkestana* (Leningrad, 1927), p. 233.

16. P. Poslavskii, "Bukhara (Kratkii istoricheskii ocherk)," *Voennyi Sbornik*, December 1891, p. 486.

17. Iskandarov, pp. 20–21, 23.

18. M. Grulew, *Das Ringen Russlands und Englands in Mittel-Asien* (Berlin, 1909), p. 91.

19. Russia had already assumed *political* responsibility for Bukhara's defense in the negotiations of 1869–1873 with Great Britain.

20. Pokrovskii, XVII, 51–52; Gubarevich-Radobylskii, pp. 164–165.

21. Pokrovskii, XVII, 52.

22. G. J. Alder, *British India's Northern Frontier* (London, 1963), pp. 218–219, 221–222.

23. P. P. Semenov, *Istoriia poluvekovoi deiatelnosti Imperatorskago Russkago Geograficheskago Obshchestva, 1845–1895* (St. Petersburg, 1896), III, 1111.

24. B. I. Iskandarov, *Vostochnaia Bukhara i Pamir vo vtoroi polovine XIX*

v. (Dushanbe, 1962–63), I, 281–282; Alder, pp. 223–225, 245. The valley of the Vakhan-Darya constituted the eastern part of the province of Vakhan. Although Vakhan was subject to Afghanistan from 1883, Kabul's authority was nonexistent in this remote region.

25. Alder, pp. 216, 225, 228–229; William Habberton, *Anglo-Russian Relations Concerning Afghanistan, 1837–1907* (Urbana, 1937), pp. 59–60.

26. Sir Robert Morier [British ambassador to Russia] to Giers, January 13/25, 1892, in Baron Alexandre Meyendorff, ed., *Correspondance diplomatique de M. de Staal* (Paris, 1929), II, 158.

27. Alder, pp. 240–241, 245–251, 263–278.

28. Habberton, pp. 64–65; Sir Percy Sykes, *A History of Afghanistan* (London, 1940), II, 174–175, 352.

29. M. A. Terentiev, *Istoriia zavoevaniia Srednei Azii* (St. Petersburg, 1906), III, 414. Upon assuming the post of political agent, Charykov first learned that Bukhara held territory on the left bank of the Pandj. In April 1886 Acting Governor-General Grodekov sent Captain N. N. Pokotilo to verify this fact and collect as much information as possible on the area in question. Out of regard for the 1873 agreement, Pokotilo was forbidden to visit the left bank. During the summer he followed the right bank of the Pandj to the frontier of Roshan and then returned via Garm to Shahr-i Sabz. (N. N. Pokotilo, "Puteshestvie v tsentralnuiu i vostochnuiu Bukharu v 1886 godu," IRGO, *Izvestiia*, XXV [1889], 480, 492, 495.) Astanakul's description of southern Darvaz is borne out by that of Pokotilo, who called it a barren, mountainous land where the population was confined to the bank of the Pandj and to mountain gorges, and where arable land, food, and work were very scarce. (Captain Pokotilo, "Ocherk bukharskikh vladenii na levom beregu r. Piandzha 1886 g.," SMPA, XXV [1887], 267–269.)

30. The text of the agreement is in *Parliamentary Papers* (1895), CIX.

31. Sykes, II, 183; Iskandarov, *Vostochnaia Bukhara i Pamir vo vtoroi polovine XIX v.*, I, 306–307.

32. O. Olufsen, *The Emir of Bokhara and His Country* (London, 1911), pp. 13, 23, 70.

33. Iskandarov, *Iz istorii Bukharskogo emirata*, pp. 93–97.

34. Gubarevich-Radobylskii, p. 155.

35. Pahlen, Pt. XIX, *Prilozhenie*, I, Pt. II, 466; Pokrovskii, XVII, 38.

36. Logofet, *Bukharskoe khanstvo*, II, 70–71.

37. Pokrovskii, XVII, 38–39. Persian was still the court language in the Central Asian khanates in the late nineteenth century, although the use of Uzbeg was increasing.

38. PSZ (1893), No. 9883. In 1897 the Russian paper ruble was made freely convertible into gold at par and at the same time devalued by one third. Previous to this the paper ruble had been worth only 66–67 kopeks in gold, the silver ruble even less.

39. PSZ (1893), No. 10002; Pahlen, Pt. XIX, *Prilozhenie*, I, Pt. II, 466–467.

40. Pahlen, XIX, 467, 470; Pokrovskii, XVII, 38; Logofet, *Bukharskoe khanstvo*, II, 71. According to V. I. Masalskii (*Turkestanskii krai* [St. Petersburg, 1913], pp. 347, 554) the khan of Khiva had already been forbidden to mint tangas in 1892.

41. Logofet, *Bukharskoe khanstvo*, II, 71; Gubarevich-Radobylskii, p. 155.

42. Pokrovskii, XVII, 39–40.

43. Pokrovskii, XVII, 40.

44. Pokrovski, XVII, 41. The text of the letter, dated April 22 and repeating all the above points, is in Zhukovskii, Appendix VII.

45. Gubarevich-Radobylskii, p. 156; Logofet, *Strana bezpraviia*, pp. 106–107; Masalskii, p. 554; *Istoriia narodov Uzbekistana* (Tashkent, 1947–1950), II, 406.

46. Pahlen, Pt. XIX, *Prilozhenie*, I, Pt. II, 467–470, 491; A. S. Sadykov, *Ekonomicheskie sviazi Khivy s Rossiei vo vtoroi polovine XIX–nachale XX vv.* (Tashkent, 1965), pp. 131–132. Sadykov claims that the khan secretly minted tangas after 1908 but that nevertheless there was more Russian money than Khivan in circulation in the khanate by 1913.

47. Gubarevich-Radobylskii, pp. 181–182; Logofet, *Strana bezpraviia*, p. 124; Logofet, *Bukharskoe khanstvo*, II, 190–191; Bartold, p. 244.

48. Logofet, *Bukharskoe khanstvo*, I, 203–205; Bartold, p. 248. Logofet claimed that the road was so bad that wheeled traffic could use it only in an emergency, but Bartold reported that it carried considerable traffic.

49. B. I. Iskandarov, *O nekotorykh izmeneniiakh v ekonomike Vostochnoi Bukhary na rubezhe XIX–XX vv.* (Stalinabad, 1958), p. 51.

50. George Dobson, *Russia's Railway Advance into Central Asia* (London, 1890), p. 269; Logofet, *Strana bezpraviia*, p. 112.

51. Logofet, *Bukharskoe khanstvo*, I, 229; *Aziatskaia Rossiia* (St. Petersburg, 1914), Atlas, Map No. 58a.

52. Pokrovskii, XVII, 43. A Russo-Bukharan agreement in 1912 regulated the operation of the Old Bukhara telegraph office; the emir paid for its maintenance and received half the revenues. (*PSZ* [1912], No. 36540.)

53. Pahlen, Pt. VII, *Oroshenie*, pp. 26–28, 152, 440.

54. *Istoriia narodov Uzbekistana*, II, 401–402; A. P. Fomchenko, *Russkie poseleniia v Bukharskom emirate* (Tashkent, 1958), p. 10.

55. Gubarevich-Radobylskii, pp. 178–179; *PSZ* (1902), No. 22259.

56. Itzhak Ben-Zvi, *The Exiled and the Redeemed* (Philadelphia, 1957), p. 82. *The Jewish Encyclopedia* (New York, 1901–1906), III, 295, gives an approximately correct figure of 4,000–5,000 Jews for the capital, but a greatly exaggerated total of 20,000 for the entire khanate. Arminius Vámbéry (*Travels in Central Asia* [London, 1864], p. 372) estimated 10,000 for Bukhara, including Samarkand, before the Russian conquest.

57. Henry Lansdell, *Russian Central Asia* (London, 1885), I, 521, 590; V. V. Krestovskii, "V gostiakh u emira bukharskago," *Russkii Vestnik*, May 1884, pp. 61–62.

58. Law of July 4, 1833, paragraph 6, *PSZ* (1833), No. 6304; law of December 29, 1842, *PSZ* (1842), No. 16385; law of April 29, 1866, *PSZ* (1866), No. 43247. The governor general of Orenburg was authorized to naturalize Central Asian Jews upon evidence of their good character and to register them in the border towns of the Orenburg Krai. They were to enroll in the merchant guilds and be subject to the general laws pertaining to Russian Jews. This provision was subsequently extended to the government-general of Turkestan, and the authority of the governor general of Orenburg was transferred in the 1880's to the Minister of Internal Affairs and the governor general of Turkestan. The

privilege of naturalization was specifically confirmed to Central Asian Jews as late as 1889. (Law of March 6, 1889, *PSZ* [1889], No. 5827.)

59. Pokrovskii, XVII, 34; *Evreiskaia Entsiklopediia* (St. Petersburg, 1908–1913), VIII, col. 207.

60. *Encyclopaedia Judaica* (Berlin, 1928–1934), IV, col. 1127.

61. *PSZ* (1889), No. 6039. The same law, however, confirmed the right to own property to "Jews who have been settled since time immemorial in the Turkestan Krai, as well as their descendants." Bukharan Jews were placed on an equal legal footing with other foreign Jews, who were in effect forbidden to own real property in Russia. (See "Svod zakonov o sostoianiiakh," 1899 edition, 1912 supplement, article 828, note 2, *Svod zakonov Rossiiskoi Imperii* [St. Petersburg, 1914–1916], IX.)

62. Pokrovskii, XVII, 34.

63. Ia. I. Gimpelson, ed., *Zakony o evreiakh* (St. Petersburg, 1914–1915), II, 844; Pokrovskii, XVII, 35.

64. Pokrovskii, XVII, 35.

65. L. M. Rogovin, ed., *Sistematicheskii sbornik deistvuiushchikh zakonov o evreiakh* (St. Petersburg, 1913), p. 226.

66. Pokrovskii, XVII, 35.

67. Sovet Ministrov, *Osobyi Zhurnal*, January 28, 1910, p. 2.

68. Sovet Ministrov, *Osobyi Zhurnal*, January 28, 1910, pp. 2–3. Although a pale for Russian Jews in Turkestan was never legally enacted, one did exist, perhaps based on a broad interpretation of the law of 1866 on naturalization.

69. Law of June 5, 1900, *PSZ* (1900), No. 18743.

70. Law of January 16, 1906, *PSZ* (1906), No. 27250; law of December 22, 1908, *PSZ* (1908), No. 31310.

71. Governor General Samsonov argued before the Council of Ministers on January 28, 1910, "the strict application of the law [of June 5, 1900] would require the expulsion from the Turkestan Krai of a significant number of Bukharan Jews," and noted that the law in question "was motivated, among other things, by a desire to rid Turkestan of Bukharan Jews, as a bad element." The Council confirmed, however, that under the new law Bukharan Jews could still live in the designated border towns. (Sovet Ministrov, *Osobyi Zhurnal*, January 28, 1910, pp. 1–2, 5.) The *Evreiskaia Entsiklopediia* (VIII, col. 207) declares that from 1910 Central Asian Jews who could prove residence prior to the conquest were confined to the Turkestan pale, and that Jews who were Bukharan subjects had to leave the government-general altogether. Ben-Zvi (p. 78) says that in 1911 Samsonov ordered all Bukharan Jews in Turkestan to return to the khanate.

72. Gimpelson, II, 831, 844; *Evreiskaia Entsiklopediia*, VIII, col. 207.

73. N. Slousch, "Les Juifs à Boukhara," *Revue du Monde Musulman*, VII (1909), 402; Sovet Ministrov, *Osobyi Zhurnal*, January 28, 1910, pp. 2, 5.

Chapter 10. Economic Development

1. I. I. Geier, *Turkestan* (Tashkent, 1909), pp. 76, 193, 201, 210; N. F. Petrovskii, "Moia poezdka v Bukharu," *Vestnik Evropy*, March 1873, p. 228; K. K. Pahlen, *Otchet po revizii Turkestanskago kraia* (St. Petersburg, 1909–

1911), Pt. XIX, *Prilozhenie. Materialy k kharakteristike narodnago khoziaistva,* I, Pt. II, 443–445; Eugene Schuyler, *Turkistan* (New York, 1876), II, 79; I. L. Iavorskii, *Puteshestvie russkago posolstva po Avganistanu i Bukharskomu khanstvu v 1878–1879 gg.* (St. Petersburg, 1882–1883), II, 41.

2. Geier, pp. 192–193, 196, 211; N. A. Maev, "Marshruty i zametki po iuzhnym chastiam Bukharskago khanstva," IRGO, *Izvestiia,* XIV (1878), 384; Maev, "Geograficheskii ocherk Gissarskago kraia i Kuliabskago bekstva," IRGO, *Izvestiia,* XII (1876), 359.

3. Captain Putiata, "Ocherk ekspeditsii v Pamir, Sarykol, Vakhan i Shugnan 1883 g.," *SMPA,* X (1884), 87; Pahlen, I, Pt. II, 442; N. N. Pokotilo, "Puteshestvie v tsentralnuiu i vostochnuiu Bukharu v 1886 godu," IRGO, *Izvestiia,* XXV (1889), 498–499; V. F. Oshanin, "Karategin i Darvaz," IRGO, *Izvestiia,* XVII (1881), 48; G. A. Arandarenko, "Darvaz i Karategin," *Voennyi Sbornik,* November 1883, p. 154; Geier, pp. 183–184.

4. Geier, pp. 184–185, 192; Colonel Matveev, "Poezdka po bukharskim i avganskim vladeniiam v fevrale 1877 g.," *SMPA,* V (1883), 24, 28; Oshanin, pp. 47–48.

5. Geier, p. 76; L. L. Ruma, ed., *Kaspiisko-aralskaia zheleznaia doroga v ekonomicheskom otnoshenii* (St. Petersburg, 1914), Appendix, pp. 77, 82; G. I. Danilevskii, "Opisanie Khivinskago khanstva," IRGO, *Zapiski,* V (1851), 124–125, 128–129.

6. Arminius Vámbéry, *Travels in Central Asia* (London, 1864), pp. 329–331; Vámbéry, *Sketches of Central Asia* (London, 1868), p. 128; L. Kostenko, "Gorod Khiva v 1873 godu," *Voennyi Sbornik,* December 1873, p. 333; Henri Moser, *A travers l'Asie centrale* (Paris, 1885), p. 258.

7. Pahlen, I, Pt. II, 449; V. I. Masalskii, *Turkestanskii krai* (St. Petersburg, 1913), pp. 550, 651; A. Gubarevich-Radobylskii, *Ekonomicheskii ocherk Bukhary i Tunisa* (St. Petersburg, 1905), pp. 97, 101–102.

8. M. K. Rozhkova, "Iz istorii torgovli Rossii so Srednei Aziei v 60-kh godakh XIX v.," *Istoricheskie Zapiski,* LXVII (1960), 193.

9. Gubarevich-Radobylskii, p. 91.

10. V. Klem, "Sovremennoe sostoianie torgovli v Bukharskom khanstve. 1887 g.," *SMPA,* XXXIII (1888), 3; Gustav Krahmer, *Russland in Mittel-Asien* (Leipzig, 1898), p. 149; A. Riabinskii, "Tsarskaia Rossiia i Bukhara v epokhu imperializma," *Istorik Marksist,* 1941, No. 4, 15–16. Prices for Central Asian cotton on the Moscow market rose 74 percent during 1891–1914, which was partly responsible for the increase in value of Bukhara's trade with Russia. (See V. I. Iuferev, *Khlopkovodstvo v Turkestane* [Leningrad, 1925], pp. 150–152.)

11. L. F. Kostenko, *Puteshestvie v Bukharu russkoi missii v 1870 godu* (St. Petersburg, 1871), p. 54; Petrovskii, pp. 236, 240; Schuyler, II, pp. 94–95; N. P. Stremoukhov, "Poezdka v Bukharu," *Russkii Vestnik,* June 1875, p. 666; Henry Lansdell, *Russian Central Asia* (London, 1885), II, 88–89; N. Charykov, "Zapiska o mestnykh putiakh soobshchenii, podlezhashchikh uluchsheniiu v interesakh razvitiia russkoi torgovli v bukharskikh vladeniiakh," *SMPA,* XV (1885), 185; Guillaume Capus, *A travers le royaume de Tamerlan* (Paris, 1892), p. 314.

12. Klem, pp. 3–4.

13. Dr. O. Heyfelder, "Buchara nach und vor der Transkaspischen Eisen-

bahn," *Unsere Zeit*, 1888, No. 10, 344; B. I. Iskandarov, *O nekotorykh iz-meneniiakh v ekonomike Vostochnoi Bukhary na rubezhe XIX–XX vv.* (Stalina-bad, 1958), pp. 38–40; William Eleroy Curtis, *Turkestan: The Heart of Asia* (New York, 1911), p. 129.

14. *Istoriia narodov Uzbekistana* (Tashkent, 1947–1950), II, 409.

15. IRGO, *Izvestiia*, XI (1875), 240.

16. V. V. Krestovskii, "V gostiakh u emira bukharskago," *Russkii Vestnik*, August 1884, p. 506.

17. Charykov, pp. 190–193.

18. D. N. Logofet, *Strana bezpraviia* (St. Petersburg, 1909), pp. 118, 212, 171–172, 180–181; Logofet, *Bukharskoe khanstvo pod russkim protektoratom* (St. Petersburg, 1911), II, 191.

19. Pahlen, Pt. VIII, *Nalogi i poshliny*, pp. 208–209, 229–230.

20. B. I. Iskandarov, *Iz istorii Bukharskogo emirata* (Moscow, 1958), pp. 47–48.

21. Pahlen, Pt. VIII, *Nalogi i poshliny*, pp. 230–234; Pahlen, Pt. XIX, *Prilozhenie*, I, Pt. II, 486–487.

22. A. A. Semenov, *Ocherk pozemelno-podatnogo i nalogovogo ustroistva b. Bukharskogo khanstva* (Tashkent, 1929), pp. 45–46.

23. N. V. Khanikoff, *Bokhara: Its Amir and Its People* (London, 1845), p. 212; Vámbéry, *Travels in Central Asia*, pp. 424–427; Petrovskii, p. 238; Schuyler, II, 70; Stremoukhov, p. 664; Capus, p. 314; George N. Curzon, *Russia in Central Asia in 1889* (London, 1889), p. 189; Charykov, p. 183.

24. In 1883 the zakatchi-kalan reported that Bukhara's total foreign trade was 35 to 40 million rubles a year. (Krestovskii, July 1884, p. 77.)

25. Kostenko, *Puteshestvie v Bukharu*, pp. 97–99; Petrovskii, pp. 222, 240; Kostenko, "Gorod Khiva v 1873 godu," p. 334.

26. Charykov, p. 184; Curzon, p. 284. A similar ban imposed in 1868 had been temporary. (M. K. Rozhkova, *Ekonomicheskie sviazi Rossii so Srednei Aziei* [Moscow, 1963], pp. 99–100.)

27. Krestovskii, July 1884, p. 91; Klem, p. 2.

28. Figures derived from statistics in Klem, p. 3.

29. Gubarevich-Radobylskii, pp. 105, 124.

30. Riabinskii, p. 16; Klem, p. 3.

31. Gubarevich-Radobylskii, pp. 104–105. Since established tastes proved difficult to change, Indian tea continued to dominate the Bukharan market until 1917. (B. I. Iskandarov, "Proniknovenie russkogo kapitala v severnye raiony Tadzhikistana i Bukharskogo emirata," in A. L. Sidorov, ed., *Ob osobennostiakh imperializma v Rossii* [Moscow, 1963], pp. 173–174.)

32. Figures derived from statistics in Gubarevich-Radobylskii, p. 124.

33. Figures derived from statistics in Riabinskii, p. 16. The figure of 96.5 percent given by Riabinskii for imports is based on a typographical error in his table of statistics.

34. Geier, pp. 159, 166; Hugo Stumm, *Russia in Central Asia* (London, 1885), p. 351; Masalskii, p. 545; Pahlen, Pt. XIX, *Prilozhenie*, I, Pt. II, 460.

35. Captain H. Spalding, trans., *Khiva and Turkestan* (London, 1874), p. 219; A. S. Sadykov, *Ekonomicheskie sviazi Khivy s Rossiei vo vtoroi polovine XIX–nachale XX vv.* (Tashkent, 1965), p. 69.

36. Mary Holdsworth, *Turkestan in the Nineteenth Century* (London, 1959),

p. 25. Sadykov (pp. 72, 75) notes a tripling in Khiva's exports by weight in the first decade after the building of the railroad but gives the surprising figure of 4.43 million rubles for the total value of Russo-Khivan trade in 1899—roughly the same as his figure for the early 1880's.

37. George Dobson, *Russia's Railway Advance into Central Asia* (London, 1890), pp. 370–371; Pahlen, Pt. XIX, *Prilozhenie*, I, Pt. II, 459; Masalskii, p. 545; Geier, p. 166.

38. Prince V. I. Masalskii, *Khlopkovoe delo v Srednei Azii* (*Turkestan, Zakaspiiskaia oblast, Bukharà i Khiva*) *i ego budushchee* (St. Petersburg, 1892), p. 155.

39. Pahlen, Pt. XIX, *Prilozhenie*, I, Pt. II, 456–457, 460.

40. Gubarevich-Radobylskii, pp. 85, 115; Logofet, *Bukharskoe khanstvo*, I, 218–221; Pahlen, Pt. XIX, *Prilozhenie*, I, Pt. II, 459; Ruma, Ekonomicheskaia zapiska, pp. 5–7.

41. Pahlen, Pt. VIII, *Nalogi i poshliny*, p. 235.

42. Pahlen, Pt. VIII, *Nalogi i poshliny*, pp. 235–236.

43. Pahlen, Pt. VIII, *Nalogi i poshliny*, pp. 236–237; Sadykov, pp. 117–122.

44. Pahlen, Pt. VIII, *Nalogi i poshliny*, p. 237.

45. Ruma, Statistiko-ekonomicheskie ocherki, pp. 148–149.

46. Colonel Beliavskii, "Izsledovanie puti ot zaliva Tsesarevich (Mertvyi Kultuk) cherez Ust-iurt do Kungrada, proizvedennoe v 1884 g.," SMPA, XV (1885), 32.

47. In 1887 Bukhara had ninety native merchants with a capital of 20,000 to 100,000 rubles each, and ten with a capital of 100,000 to 500,000 rubles. (Klem, p. 3.)

48. M. A. Terentiev, *Rossiia i Angliia v borbe za rynki* (St. Petersburg, 1876), p. 57; Rozhkova, "Iz istorii torgovli Rossii," pp. 193, 195; T. G. Tukhtametov, "Ekonomicheskoe sostoianie Bukharskogo emirata v kontse XIX i nachale XX vekov," Akademiia Nauk Kirgizskoi SSR, Institut Istorii, *Trudy*, III (1957), 156; Holdsworth, p. 25.

49. V. I. Pokrovskii, ed., *Sbornik svedenii po istorii i statistike vneshnei torgovli Rossii* (St. Petersburg, 1902), I, 274; Iuferev, pp. 53–54.

50. Schuyler, I, 295; *Aziatskaia Rossiia* (St. Petersburg, 1914), II, 278; M. A. Terentiev, *Istoriia zavoevaniia Srednei Azii* (St. Petersburg, 1906), III, 366; Iuferev, pp. 86, 138–139, 146; Klem, p. 3; Tukhtametov, p. 156; A. M. Aminov, *Ekonomicheskoe razvitie Srednei Azii* (*so vtoroi poloviny XIX stoletiia do pervoi mirovoi voiny*) (Tashkent, 1959), p. 150; Gubarevich-Radobylskii, p. 96; Pahlen, Pt. XIX, *Prilozhenie*, I, Pt. II, 441, 453; Ruma, Supplement, pp. 11–12; Holdsworth, p. 25. The statistics on Khivan cotton exports vary. Sadykov (pp. 62, 72) gives somewhat different figures, indicating that Khiva's cotton exports exceeded 200,000 puds annually before the building of the railroad, and 500,000 puds by the late 1890's.

51. Iskandarov, O nekotorykh izmeneniiakh, pp. 28–29.

52. Pahlen, Pt. XIX, *Frilozhenie*, I, Pt. II, 441, 450; Geier, p. 80; Curtis, p. 307. The cultivation of native cotton became somewhat more profitable after a special machine to pick this variety was invented by a Mr. Gardner of the Brown Gin Company of New London, Connecticut, who had been hired for the purpose by a group of Bukharans. (Curtis, p. 308.)

53. Iuferev, p. 67; Masalskii, *Turkestanskii krai*, p. 460.

54. Stremoukhov, p. 671; Tukhtametov, pp. 157–159. See also Gubarevich-Radobylskii, p. 59; Geier, p. 192; Pahlen, Pt. XIX, *Prilozhenie*, I, Pt. II, 441.

55. I. Gaevskii, "Kurgan-Tiubinskoe bekstvo," RGO, *Izvestiia*, LV (1919–1923), No. 2, 38.

56. Tukhtametov, pp. 159–160.

57. Iskandarov, *O nekotorykh izmeneniiakh*, p. 34; Iuferev, pp. 138–139.

58. A. N. Kovalevskii, *Zapiska k proektu Khivinskoi zheleznoi dorogi* (Petrograd, 1915), p. 36; *Istoriia Turkmenskoi SSR* (Ashkhabad, 1957), I, Pt. II, 196; *Istoriia narodov Uzbekistana*, II, 419. During 1873–1915 Bukhara increased her cotton exports to Russia by six and a half times; Khiva in the same period increased hers by over thirty times.

59. Pahlen, Pt. XIX, *Prilozhenie*, I, Pt. II, 440, 443, 445. Pahlen gives the total of arable land as 2,900,000 desiatinas, of which one third was always fallow because of the three-field system; 986,000 desiatinas were given over to wheat, and only 75,000 to cotton.

60. Iuferev, pp. 130, 138; Aminov, p. 143. In absolute terms, Fergana on the eve of World War I had more than three times the cotton acreage of Bukhara and produced five to six times as much cotton. (*Aziatskaia Rossiia*, II, 277; Iuferev, pp. 138–139.)

61. Masalskii, *Khlopkovoe delo*, p. 149.

62. Ruma, Appendix, pp. 73–75.

63. Masalskii, *Khlopkovoe delo*, p. 149.

64. Masalskii, *Khlopkovoe delo*, pp. 142–143.

65. Gubarevich-Radobylskii, pp. 61–74.

66. Pahlen, Pt. XIX, *Prilozhenie*, I, Pt. II, 441, 446.

67. Riabinskii, p. 7.

68. Tukhtametov, pp. 170–171. The geographic distribution of cotton-ginning mills in 1916 was twelve in New Bukhara, four in Kerki, three each in Chardjui, Kermine, and Termez, two each in Kizil-Tepe, Ziaddin, and Zerabulak, and one each in Karakul, Old Bukhara, Gizhduvan, and Djilikul. The oil-pressing mills were located at New Bukhara, Chardjui, and Termez. By comparison, Russian Turkestan had 201 cotton-ginning mills in 1914. (Iuferev, p. 49.)

69. Riabinskii, p. 7; Ruma, Appendix, pp. 92–95; A. P. Fomchenko, *Russkie poseleniia v Bukharskom emirate* (Tashkent, 1958), pp. 14–15; Pahlen, Pt. XIX, *Prilozhenie*, I, Pt. II, 321; Gubarevich-Radobylskii, p. 67; Logofet, *Strana bezpraviia*, p. 145.

70. Masalskii, *Khlopkovoe delo*, p. 154; Geier, p. 82; *Istoriia Uzbekskoi SSR* (Tashkent, 1955–1956), I, Pt. II, 325.

71. Pahlen, Pt. XIX, *Prilozhenie*, I, Pt. II, 455.

72. Ruma, Appendix, p. 96.

73. A. V. Piaskovskii, *Revoliutsiia 1905–1907 godov v Turkestane* (Moscow, 1958), pp. 26–27; *Istoriia grazhdanskoi voiny v Uzbekistane*, I (Tashkent, 1964), 266; *Istoriia Uzbekskoi SSR*, I, Pt. II, 326.

74. Pahlen, Pt. XIX, *Prilozhenie*, I, Pt. II, 333–334.

75. The text of these regulations is in Logofet, *Strana bezpraviia*, pp. 234–239.

76. Tukhtametov, pp. 173–174; Iskandarov, *O nekotorykh izmeneniiakh*, pp. 61–72.

77. Iskandarov, *O nekotorykh izmeneniiakh*, pp. 30–31.
78. Riabinskii, pp. 4–5; *Istoriia Uzbekskoi SSR*, I, Pt. II, 310–311.
79. Sadykov, pp. 150–158.
80. Riabinskii, p. 11.
81. Iskandarov, *O nekotorykh izmeneniiakh*, p. 25. Andronikov was an adventurer who cultivated close relations with members of the court and government for his personal gain. When for several months in late 1915 he enjoyed the favor of Rasputin and the empress, he wielded considerable power.
82. Riabinskii, pp. 9, 11; Ruma, Appendix, p. 93; *Istoriia narodov Uzbekistana*, II, 406.
83. Riabinskii, pp. 5, 10–11. Several other concessions were granted during this period. In July 1913 A. V. Glushkov and D. F. Konev received 5,000 desiatinas at Aivadj; two years later A. N. Kovalevskii received 28,680 desiatinas at Kerki and 5,619 at Kelif in return for his services in building the Bukharan Railroad. (Riabinskii, pp. 5, 10–11.) In Khiva several very large concessions were also granted to Russians during 1912–1913. (Sadykov, pp. 138–139.)
84. Riabinskii, pp. 10–12.
85. Iskandarov, *O nekotorykh izmeneniiakh*, pp. 25–26.
86. Riabinskii, p. 20.
87. Iskandarov, *O nekotorykh izmeneniiakh*, p. 104.
88. V. V. Bartold, *Istoriia kulturnoi zhizni Turkestana* (Leningrad, 1927), p. 244; Tukhtametov, pp. 166–167; Logofet, *Bukharskoe khanstvo*, I, 209, 228; Gubarevich-Radobylskii, pp. 86, 120; Pahlen, Pt. XIX, *Prilozhenie*, I, Pt. II, 476; Masalskii, *Turkestanskii krai*, pp. 571, 585; Z. K. Akhmedzhanova, "K istorii stroitelstva Bukharskoi zheleznoi dorogi (1914–1916 gody)," *Obshchestvennye Nauki v Uzbekistane*, April 1962, p. 29; Riabinskii, p. 12. The text of the kush-begi's letter is in S. V. Zhukovskii, *Snosheniia Rossii s Bukharoi i Khivoi za poslednee trekhsotletie* (Petrograd, 1915), Appendix VIII.
89. PSZ (1913), No. 39936.
90. Riabinskii, p. 13.
91. Akhmedzhanova, pp. 30–34.
92. M. I. Vekselman, "K voprosu o proniknovenii inostrannogo kapitala v ekonomiku Srednei Azii do pervoi mirovoi voiny," *Obshchestvennye Nauki v Uzbekistane*, July 1961, p. 35.
93. Tukhtametov, p. 169.
94. *Aziatskaia Rossiia*, II, 549.
95. Ruma, Supplement, p. 6; Kovalevskii, pp. 7–8, Sadykov, pp. 140–143.
96. Pahlen, Pt. XIX, *Prilozhenie*, I, Pt. II, 476; Masalskii, *Turkestanskii krai*, p. 585; Sadykov, pp. 87–88, 139–140.
97. Tukhtametov, p. 167. Logofet (*Bukharskoe khanstvo*, I, 228) proposed a similar route. An extension from Termez to Hisar and Stalinabad (Düshambe in the days of the emirs and Dushanbe after 1962), thence to Kurgan-Tübe and Kulab, was built between the World Wars.

Chapter 11. Bukhara Between Two Worlds

1. V. I. Masalskii, *Turkestanskii krai* (St. Petersburg, 1913), p. 347. As an American visitor to Russia's Central Asian colonies at the end of the 1890's noted, "Unlike some nations, she does not send to her newly acquired posses-

sions a favored class only, to enjoy the emoluments of office or the dignity of administering their civil and political affairs," but she peoples each new possession "with her industrial classes, who engage in every branch of trade and agriculture." (John W. Bookwalter, *Siberia and Central Asia* [London, 1900], p. 431.)

2. D. N. Logofet, *Bukharskoe khanstvo pod russkim protektoratom* (St. Petersburg, 1911), I, 185–186; *Aziatskaia Rossiia* (St. Petersburg, 1914), I, 178. Logofet also noted in 1910 the presence of some three thousand Russian Kazakhs who had migrated to Hisar, Kulab, and Kurgan-Tübe begliks.

3. Masalskii, pp. 339, 653, 655; I. I. Geier, *Turkestan* (Tashkent, 1909), pp. 201, 206, 217; A. P. Fomchenko, *Russkie poseleniia v Bukharskom emirate* (Tashkent, 1958), pp. 14–17; L. L. Ruma, ed., *Kaspiisko-aralskaia zheleznaia doroga v ekonomicheskom otnoshenii* (St. Petersburg, 1914), Appendix, p. 93; Karl Baedeker, *Russia* (Leipzig, German and French editions of 1901 and after); G. N. Chabrov, "Iz istorii poligrafii i izdatelstva literatury na mestnykh iazykakh v dorevoliutsionnom Turkestane (1868–1917 gg.)," SAGU, *Trudy,* new series, LVII (1954), 81, 88. In 1906 the four settlements had a total of six Russian elementary schools with an enrollment of three hundred pupils.

4. Masalskii, p. 653; D. N. Logofet, *Na granitsakh Srednei Azii. Putevye ocherki* (St. Petersburg, 1909), III, 118; Aurel Stein, *On Ancient Central-Asian Tracks* (New York, 1933, repr. 1964), p. 275.

5. O. Olufsen, *The Emir of Bokhara and His Country* (London, 1911), p. 343; Geier, pp. 205–206; T. G. Tukhtametov, "Ekonomicheskoe sostoianie Bukharskogo emirata v kontse XIX i nachale XX vekov," Akademiia Nauk Kirgizskoi SSR, Institut Istorii, *Trudy,* III (1957), 172; George N. Curzon, *Russia in Central Asia in 1889* (London, 1889), pp. 189, 191; William Eleroy Curtis, *Turkestan: The Heart of Asia* (New York, 1911), p. 166.

6. See, for example, J. T. Woolrych Perowne, *Russian Hosts and English Guests in Central Asia* (London, 1898), and Isabelle Mary Phibbs, *A Visit to the Russians in Central Asia* (London, 1899). Foreigners required special permission from the Russian government to visit Bukhara and further permission from the emir's government and the political agency to travel beyond the limits of the railroad zone. (W. Rickmer Rickmers, *The Duab of Turkestan* [Cambridge, 1913], p. 111; A. V. Nechaev, *Po gornoi Bukhara. Putevye ocherki* [St. Petersburg, 1914], p. 13.) Kerki, Termez, and the posts along the Afghan frontier were completely forbidden to foreigners. (Regulations of June 29, 1902, in I. F. Abramov, ed., *Polozhenie ob upravlenii Turkestanskago kraia* [Tashkent, 1916], p. 248.)

7. Geier, p. 205; Olufsen, p. 518. Baedeker's guidebooks warned tourists against visiting the mosques of the capital because of the fanaticism of the population.

8. Nechaev, p. 29.

9. George Dobson, *Russia's Railway Advance into Central Asia* (London, 1890), p. 239n; Félix de Rocca, *De l'Alaï à l'Amou-Daria* (Paris, 1896), p. 394; Varvara Dukhovskaia, *Turkestanskiia vospominaniia* (St. Petersburg, 1913), pp. 64–65; A. Polovtsoff, *The Land of Timur* (London, 1932), pp. 107–108; Count K. K. Pahlen, *Mission to Turkestan* (London, 1964), pp. 65, 67. Except for the

emir's palace, Kermine was a town untouched by Western influence. (Geier, p. 207.)

10. Olufsen, p. 326; V. V. Bartold, *Istoriia kulturnoi zhizni Turkestana* (Leningrad, 1927), p. 246.

11. G. P. Fedorov, "Moia sluzhba v Turkestanskom krae (1870–1906 goda)," *Istoricheskii Vestnik*, CXXXIV (1913), 460–462, 874–877; F. H. Skrine and E. D. Ross, *The Heart of Asia* (London, 1899), p. 384; Olufsen, pp. 174–175; Dukhovskaia, p. 63. On Abd al-Ahad's trip in December 1892 and January 1893, see *Pravitelstvennyi Vestnik*, December 11/23, 1892, p. 3; December 29, 1892/ January 10, 1893, p. 3; January 3/15 through January 29/February 10, 1893.

12. Dukhovskaia, pp. 50, 54, 64.

13. See the yearbooks of the Russian foreign ministry, 1891–1906, and Pahlen, pp. 29–30.

14. *Pravitelstvennyi Vestnik*, February 25/March 9, 1894, pp. 1–2; D. N. Logofet, *Strana bezpraviia* (St. Petersburg, 1909), p. 158; N. V. Tcharykow, *Glimpses of High Politics* (London, 1931), p. 207.

15. See, for example, Fedorov, p. 448.

16. Olufsen, p. 392.

17. This incident was related by Murkos' student, A. A. Semenov, in *Ocherk ustroistva tsentralnogo administrativnogo upravleniia Bukharskogo khanstva pozdneishego vremeni* (Stalinabad, 1954), p. 9.

18. In the 1888 protocol on the Russian settlements in Bukhara, Abd al-Ahad is referred to as "High Eminence." He is called "Illustriousness" by the *Pravitelstvennyi Vestnik* in 1893 and also in the kush-begi's letter consenting to the customs unification in 1894. The term "Highness" is used in the 1901 monetary agreement. See also Bartold, p. 245.

19. P. P. Shubinskii, "Ocherki Bukhary," *Istoricheskii Vestnik*, XLIX (1892), 133; Bartold, p. 245; *Istoriia narodov Uzbekistana* (Tashkent, 1947–1950), II, 407.

20. Bartold's claim (p. 243) that Charykov, Lessar, and Ignatiev functioned much like English residents at the courts of Indian princes is an exaggeration, since the Russian political agent in Bukhara never held that much power.

21. Logofet, *Bukharskoe khanstvo*, I, 20. A. S. Somov, political agent in 1911–1913, had served as secretary of legation in Bucharest and Teheran and consul general in Seoul. His successor, A. K. Beliaev (1913–1916), had seen service in five Russian consulates in the Ottoman Empire, rising from secretary and dragoman at Erzerum to consul general at Saloniki. The last political agent, A. Ia. Miller (1916–1917), had been consul general in Tabriz, Persia, and Urga, Outer Mongolia.

22. Logofet, *Bukharskoe khanstvo*, II, 182–184. Abd al-Ahad moved away from his capital primarily to escape from the turbulent and fanatic clergy. (Semenov, p. 68; Geier, p. 207.)

23. Logofet, *Strana bezpraviia*, pp. 6–7. The governors general frequently traversed Bukhara on the railroad but never visited the other parts of the country until 1903, after which date several governors general visited Kerki and Termez. (K. K. Pahlen, *Otchet po revizii Turkestanskago kraia* (St. Petersburg, 1909–1911), Pt. X, *Kraevoe upravlenie*, pp. 53–55; Bartold, p. 244.)

24. *Revue du Monde Musulman*, III (1907), 552.

25. A. Gubarevich-Radobylskii, *Ekonomicheskii ocherk Bukhary i Tunisa* (St. Petersburg, 1905), pp. 147, 149; B. I. Iskandarov, *Iz istorii Bukharskogo emirata* (Moscow, 1958), pp. 50–51; Logofet, *Strana bezpraviia*, pp. 52, 54; Tukhtametov, p. 182; M. Grulew, *Das Ringen Russlands und Englands in Mittel-Asien* (Berlin, 1909), p. 90.

26. In December 1913 V. O. von Klemm, director of the foreign ministry's Third Political (Central Asiatic) Section, reported that Abd al-Ahad's son and successor, Emir Alim, had on deposit in the Russian State Bank 27 million rubles, and another 7 million in private Russian banks. (Semenov, p. 9.)

27. Semenov, p. 9; Bartold, p. 247.

28. Logofet, *Bukharskoe khanstvo*, II, 88.

29. S. Iu. Vitte, *Vospominaniia* (Moscow, 1960), I, 419; Logofet, *Bukharskoe khanstvo*, I, 234; *Pravitelstvennyi Vestnik*, February 2/15, 1910, p. 1. Pisarenko served Abd al-Ahad's successor as court physician also. (*Pravitelstvennyi Vestnik*, May 12/25, 1911, p. 3.)

30. Major cholera epidemics struck Bukhara in 1871–1872 and 1893. (Eugene Schuyler, *Turkistan* (New York, 1876), I, 148–149; Sadriddin Aini, *Vospominaniia* [Moscow, 1960], pp. 451–454.) In the summer of 1889 a malaria epidemic killed thousands of Bukharans, including three of the emir's five sons. (Shubinskii, p. 137; Dobson, p. 247; Gubarevich-Radobylskii, p. 179.) On rishta, see Geier, p. 202; D. I. Evarnitskii, *Putevoditel po Srednei Azii, ot Baku do Tashkenta* (Tashkent, 1893), p. 61; Curtis, p. 128.

31. Aini, pp. 596–599; Gubarevich-Radobylskii, p. 180; Bartold, p. 248.

32. Doctor O. Heyfelder, who had served as chief medical officer to the troops who built the Central Asian Railroad, established himself in Old Bukhara in 1887 and several years later helped to found a native hospital there. By 1912 this hospital was treating 28,000 patients annually, although an American visitor in 1910 described it as being in poor condition and grudgingly supported by the emir. (Curzon, pp. 194–195; Dobson, pp. 246–247; Fomchenko, p. 28; Curtis, p. 158.) A Russian woman doctor also opened a practice in Old Bukhara at the turn of the century. (Aini, p. 878.) For services provided by hospitals in the Russian settlements to natives, see Logofet, *Bukharskoe khanstvo*, II, 142.

33. Tcharykow, pp. 204–206; Shubinskii, p. 126; Rocca, pp. 431–432; Rickmers, p. 104. There is much difference of opinion as to when the practice of hurling criminals from the Great Minaret was abandoned, but early in Abd al-Ahad's reign is the most probable date. Although Bartold (p. 245), declares that the last such execution may have taken place in 1884, Curzon (p. 179) reports three such executions in the years 1885–1888. Two American visitors reported that the minaret was used for executions as late as 1894 or even 1907, but neither is a very reliable source on any subject on which he did not have first-hand information. (M. M. Shoemaker, *Trans-Caspia. The Sealed Provinces of the Czar* [Cincinnati, 1895], p. 106; Curtis, p. 151.)

34. Skrine and Ross, pp. 377–378; Curzon, pp. 184–185; Dobson, pp. 255–257; Olufsen, pp. 336–337; Perowne, pp. 137–138; Geier, pp. 210–211; Rickmers, p. 474; Pahlen, *Mission to Turkestan*, pp. 69–71. One example of extreme barbarity was the treatment meted out in 1888 to the assassin of Muhammad Sharif, the divan-begi, son of the kush-begi, and Abd al-Ahad's favorite.

The emir ordered the assassin delivered according to ancient custom to the victim's relatives, who tied him to a horse's tail, dragged him in this manner through the streets of the capital until he was barely alive, then crushed his hands and feet and threw him to be eaten by the dogs beyond the city wall. (P. P. Shubinskii, "Nedavniaia tragediia v Bukhare," *Istoricheskii Vestnik,* LXVIII [1892], 472–475; Curzon, pp. 179–180.)

35. Logofet, *Strana bezpraviia,* p. 36.

36. Ia. Ia. Liutsh, the political agent in 1902–1911, reported in February 1909 that the five million rubles paid annually in land taxes by the Bukharan peasantry was four times the amount paid by the peasants of Russian Turkestan, although Russian Turkestan had twice as many inhabitants. (Governor General of Turkestan to Minister of War, February 1909, in Z. Radzhabov, *Iz istorii obshchestvenno-politicheskoi mysli tadzhikskogo naroda* [Stalinabad, 1957], pp. 73–74.)

37. In April 1900 the political agent reported to Tashkent that several men had come to the emir from Baldjuan to make a formal complaint against their beg. Abd al-Ahad rejected their complaint and made an example of two of the petitioners by ordering them to be given seventy-five blows each. Upon their return to Baldjuan the beg ordered an additional thirty-nine blows for each of the men. (B. I. Iskandarov, *Vostochnaia Bukhara i Pamir vo vtoroi polovine XIX v.* [Dushanbe, 1962–1963], II, 39.) From 1877 to 1905 Kulab had nineteen begs. In the period 1905–1910, according to Liutsh, Kulab had five begs, while Hisar, Shirabad, Kabadiyan, and Baldjuan each had three. (M. A. Varygin, "Opyt opisaniia Kuliabskago bekstva," IRGO, *Izvestiia,* LII [1916], 743; Radzhabov, p. 134.)

38. See, for example, the case reported by N. P. Stremoukhov ("Poezdka v Bukharu," *Russkii Vestnik,* June 1875, p. 683.)

39. For the Vose uprising, see Iskandarov, *Iz istorii Bukharskogo emirata,* pp. 75–82, and K. Z. Mukhsinova, "Novoe o vosstanii Vose," *Obshchestvennye Nauki v Uzbekistane,* October 1963, pp. 52–55.

40. Logofet, *Strana bezpraviia,* pp. 50–51. In 1889, for example, the beg of Kelif called on the Russian troops to suppress a peasant revolt. (B. I. Iskandarov, *O nekotorykh izmeneniiakh v ekonomike Vostochnoi Bukhary na rubezhe XIX–XX vv.* [Stalinabad, 1958], pp. 87–88.)

41. Iskandarov, *Iz istorii Bukharskogo emirata,* p. 99. Political Agent Ignatiev shortly afterward prevailed upon the emir to remove the beg of Kulab, whose despotism had provoked the exodus.

42. Radzhabov, p. 176. Zeki Validi Togan (*Turkestan Today* [Istanbul, 1942–1947], p. 311) claims that Donish also accompanied Abd al-Ahad to Alexander III's coronation, and Tukhtametov (p. 164) says that Donish was a member of a Bukharan embassy sent to St. Petersburg in 1889 to thank the emperor for the Central Asian Railroad. On Ahmad Donish, see B. G. Gafurov, *Istoriia tadzhikskogo naroda,* 2nd ed. (Moscow, 1952), I, 414–416; Radzhabov, Ch. II; K. Iuldashev, "O sotsialno-ekonomicheskikh vozzreniiakh Akhmada Donisha," *Obshchestvennye Nauki v Uzbekistane,* October 1963, pp. 55–58; Baymirza Hayit, *Turkestan im XX. Jahrhundert* (Darmstadt, 1956), pp. 34–35. The Persian text of Donish's "Short History of the Mangit Emirs of Bukhara" was published in Stalinabad in 1960 by the Tadjik Academy of Sciences.

43. The madrasa was a privately endowed seminary or college, usually attached to a mosque. The course of studies, given by mudarrises appointed by the kazi-kalan, took twenty years or longer to complete, and graduates were eligible for positions in the clerical hierarchy as kazis, ulemas, muftis, mudarrises, etc. The madrasas of the Bukharan capital were famous throughout the Turkic-speaking world for their religious orthodoxy, drawing students from as far away as Kazan and Sinkiang. Students from Transcaspia, however, were strongly discouraged from attending Bukharan or Khivan madrasas because the Russian authorities in that oblast regarded the institutions as hotbeds of fanaticism and anti-Russian feeling. (Pahlen, Pt. VI, _Uchebnoe delo_, 125, 131.)

44. Gafurov, I, 416, 436; Radzhabov, pp. 208–216; Aini, pp. 399–401, 778–779; O. A. Sukhareva, _Bukhara XIX–nachalo XX v._ (Moscow, 1966), p. 267. Sadriddin Aini, the celebrated Tadjik author of the Soviet period who was active in the Bukharan reform movement, testified in his memoirs to the important role played by Donish's writings in his own intellectual awakening during the 1890's, while he was a student in a Bukharan madrasa. (Aini, pp. 252–265, 402–415, 771–798.)

45. Geier, p. 29; Serge A. Zenkovsky, _Pan-Turkism and Islam in Russia_ (Cambridge, Mass., 1960), p. 76. Aini confirmed by his own experience the observations of visitors from Khanykov to Olufsen on the worthlessness of a maktab education; when he graduated, he could read only the books he had learned by rote in school and no others. (Aini, p. 103.) Aini's experiences in a Bukharan maktab are the basis for his short story "The Old School," published in Russian translation in Sadriddin Aini, _Sobranie sochinenii_ (Moscow, 1960–61), IV.

46. A. V. Piaskovskii, _Revoliutsiia 1905–1907 godov v Turkestane_ (Moscow, 1958), p. 99.

47. I. I. Umniakov, "K istorii novometodnoi shkoly v Bukhare," SAGU, _Biulleten_, XVI (1927), 83; A. N. Samoilovich, "Pervoe tainoe obshchestvo mladobukhartsev," _Vostok_, I (1922), 97; Hayit, pp. 40, 118. In July 1914 a group of Bukharan merchants unsuccessfully petitioned the political agent to use his influence to help establish a new-method school in Bukhara. They cited the need for a knowledge of elementary mathematics, geography, and Russian in dealing with Russians and other foreigners in the khanate. (Umniakov, pp. 93–94.)

48. See, for example, Aini, _Vospominaniia_, p. 435. On October 12, 1883, _Tardjuman_ had proudly announced on page one that Crown Prince Abd al-Ahad had honored it with a subscription. (Liutsian Klimovich, _Islam v tsarskoi Rossii_ [Moscow, 1936], p. 212.) This gesture undoubtedly signified curiosity about one aspect of Russian life rather than support for Gasprinskii's ideas.

49. Piaskovskii, pp. 116–117, 186, 196, 204–205, 237, 267. Of a total industrial proletariat of almost thirteen hundred in the khanate, Chardjui had eight hundred. (Piaskovskii, p. 27; Fomchenko, p. 32.)

50. Piaskovskii, pp. 281, 289–290.

51. Piaskovskii, pp. 292–294. In early December 1905 Chardjui was occupied by loyal troops from Transcaspia. The revolutionary tide was ebbing, although there were sporadic outbreaks in the khanate over the next eight months —a workers' strike in New Bukhara on January 9, 1906, to commemorate the first anniversary of Bloody Sunday; a strike in New Bukhara's cotton-ginning mills on February 20; a May Day strike in Chardjui; a mutiny in the garrison

at Termez on June 4; and a sailors' mutiny at Chardjui on July 12. (Piaskovskii, pp. 316, 320, 378–379, 385, 406, 426.)

52. Umniakov, pp. 82–87, 91–92; Hayit, p. 118.

53. Faizullah Khodzhaev, "Dzhadidy," *Ocherki revoliutsionnogo dvizheniia v Srednei Azii. Sbornik statei* (Moscow, 1926), p. 8; Piaskovskii, p. 543; Umniakov, p. 87.

54. The statutes and bylaws of the society are printed in A. Arsharuni and Kh. Gabidullin, *Ocherki panislamizma i pantiurkizma v Rossii* (Moscow, 1931), pp. 133–135.

55. Umniakov, p. 88; Samoilovich, p. 98. Togan (p. 432) says the society was founded on November 7, 1910, but Hayit (p. 118) gives the date as December 2.

56. Samoilovich, pp. 98–99.

57. Samoilovich, p. 99; Umniakov, pp. 90–93.

58. There is some confusion as to the formal relationship between the two societies. Samoilovich (p. 99) says that the Constantinople group had members in Bukhara. Togan (p. 432) and Hayit (p. 119) claim that Fitrat and several other original members of the Bukharan group went to Constantinople in 1910 and founded the Society for the Dissemination of Knowledge as a branch of the Society for the Education of Children. The statutes of the Constantinople group, however, are dated 11 Shawwal 1327 A.H., *i.e.*, late October 1909—more than a year before establishment of the Bukharan group and also before the arrival of Fitrat and the others in Constantinople.

59. Umniakov, p. 88; Hayit, p. 42.

60. *Pravitelstvennyi Vestnik*, December 29, 1910/January 11, 1911, p. 3.

61. See, for example, the account of his first visit to Russia after his accession in *Pravitelstvennyi Vestnik*, May 12/25 through May 24/June 6, 1911. When the Red Army captured Alim's villa between Old and New Bukhara in September 1920, among the Russian volumes in the library were the works of Tolstoy, Dostoevsky, Belinsky, and Nekrasov. In another part of the villa were discovered piles of receipts in connection with the purchase of girls for Alim's harem. (A. Mashitskii, "Materialy po istorii bukharskoi revoliutsii," NKID, *Vestnik*, No. 4–5 [1922], 123–124.)

62. Umniakov, pp. 89–90, 93. Public support for the schools in Kerki and Shahr-i Sabz prevented their closing, despite the emir's orders. (Faizullah Khodzhaev, "O mlado-bukhartsakh," *Istorik Marksist*, I [1926], 130.)

63. Zenkovsky, pp. 90–91.

64. Sadriddin Aini, "Korotko o moei zhizni," *Sobranie sochinenii*, I, 50; Samoilovich, p. 99.

65. A. Riabinskii, "Tsarskaia Rossiia i Bukhara v epokhu imperializma," *Istorik Marksist*, 1941, No. 4, p. 24.

66. Umniakov, p. 93; Aini, "Korotko o moei zhizni," pp. 49–55.

67. Faizullah Khodzhaev, secretary of the Bukharan Communist Party in the 1920's and a former Djadid, stoutly defended the thesis that the Djadid movement rested on the intelligentsia rather than on a particular economic class (the bourgeoisie), although he conceded that the movement coincidentally expressed the interests of its allies, the commercial capitalist class. (Khodzhaev, "O mlado-bukhartsakh," pp. 126, 128; Khodzhaev, "Dzhadidy," pp. 10–11; Khodzhaev, *K istorii revoliutsii v Bukhare* [Tashkent, 1926], pp. 6, 9–12.)

Stalinist historiography condemned the Djadids as reactionary bourgeois nationalists. The current Soviet line, countering attempts in the Central Asian republics to rehabilitate Djadidism, makes a spurious distinction between Djadidism—"the nationalist ideology of the local bourgeoisie . . . out of touch with the masses of the people . . . the ally of tsarism and the Russian bourgeoisie" —and what it calls "the progressive representatives of culture—the teachers, writers and poets of the colonial period, who in the past were also labelled Djadids. Their activity reflected the interests of the workers, and they were themselves essentially democrat-enlighteners, although, possibly, they called themselves Djadids." (M. G. Vakhabov, "O sotsialnoi prirode sredne-aziatskogo dzhadidizma i ego evoliutsii v period velikoi oktiabrskoi revoliutsii," *Istoriia SSSR*, 1963, No. 2, pp. 35, 39–40, 56.)

Chapter 12. Nonintervention under Attack: Russia and Bukhara

1. M. Grulew, *Das Ringen Russlands und Englands in Mittel-Asien* (Berlin, 1909), pp. 95–96.

2. A. Gubarevich-Radobylskii, *Ekonomicheskii ocherk Bukhary i Tunisa* (St. Petersburg, 1905), pp. 150–151, 163–164, 192–193.

3. V. V. Bartold (*La Découverte de l'Asie* [Paris, 1947], p. 290) characterizes Logofet's works as unscientific and notes that despite his long residence in the khanate Logofet never learned the local languages. A. A. Semenov (*Ocherk ustroistva tsentralnogo administrativnogo upravleniia Bukharskogo khanstva pozdneishego vremeni* [Stalinabad, 1954], p. 18) calls Logofet's 1911 book "pretentious, very often confused and unscientific, expounding on many aspects of former Bukharan life, including also the administrative system of Bukhara in the most recent period, about which the author had very confused ideas, despite his prolonged residence in the khanate." Logofet borrowed freely from Grulev and Gubarevich-Radobylskii.

4. D. N. Logofet, *Strana bezpraviia* (St. Petersburg, 1909), pp. 7–8.

5. Logofet, pp. 25–26, 153, 168–170. In 1906 the governor general forbade any Russian in Turkestan to accept gifts from Bukharan officials, and in 1908 Governor General Mishchenko refused presents from the emir. In 1910 the Senate prohibited anyone in government service from receiving gifts from the emir, but the order was never enforced. (Logofet, p. 165; Logofet, *Bukharskoe khanstvo pod russkim protektoratom* [St. Petersburg, 1911], II, 189; V. V. Bartold, *Istoriia kulturnoi zhizni Turkestana*, [Leningrad, 1927], p. 243; *Istoriia narodov Uzbekistana* [Tashkent, 1947–1950], II, 409.)

6. Logofet, *Strana bezpraviia*, pp. 7–10, 72, 171–178, 212–213.

7. Logofet's elaborate plan of reform, which drew heavily on Lessar's 1891 proposals, is in his *Bukharskoe khanstvo*, II, 298–324.

8. See, for example, Logofet, *Strana bezpraviia*, p. 213; Logofet, *Bukharskoe khanstvo*, I, 14–15, 17–18, 20.

9. V. I. Masalskii, *Turkestanskii krai* (St. Petersburg, 1913), pp. 346n, 560.

10. Cartoon reproduced in Liutsian Klimovich, *Islam v tsarskoi Rossii* (Moscow, 1936), p. 210.

11. I. I. Umniakov, "K istorii novometodnoi shkoly v Bukhare," SAGU, *Biulleten*, XVI (1927), 88.

12. Serge A. Zenkovsky, *Pan-Turkism and Islam in Russia* (Cambridge, Mass., 1960), p. 87.

13. M. A. Varygin, "Opyt opisaniia Kuliabskago bekstva," IRGO, *Izvestiia*, LII (1916), 802–803.

14. The population of Roshan declined by 50 percent in the first ten years of Afghan occupation. (Captain Vannovskii, "Izvlechenie iz otcheta o rekognostsirovke v Rushane i Darvaze v 1893 g.," *SMPA*, LVI [1894], 76.)

15. B. I. Iskandarov, *Iz istorii Bukharskogo emirata* (Moscow, 1958), pp. 102–107.

16. Iskandarov, *Vostochnaia Bukhara i Pamir vo vtoroi polovine XIX v.* (Dushanbe, 1962–1963), I, 346.

17. Iskandarov, *Iz istorii Bukharskogo emirata*, pp. 103–104. Iskandarov here dates Ignatiev's report to Dukhovskoi in February 1898, but Dukhovskoi became governor general only at the end of March 1898. Iskandarov's own narrative sequence indicates that February 1899 is meant, and he dates the report February 6, 1899, in *Vostochnaia Bukhara i Pamir vo vtoroi polovine XIX v.*, II, 144.

18. Ignatiev's report of June 3, 1899, in Iskandarov, *Iz istorii Bukharskogo emirata*, p. 108.

19. Iskandarov, *Iz istorii Bukharskogo emirata*, p. 109.

20. Iskandarov, *Iz istorii Bukharskogo emirata*, p. 105.

21. Iskandarov, *Iz istorii Bukharskogo emirata*, pp. 109–111, 130.

22. Iskandarov, *Iz istorii Bukharskogo emirata*, pp. 111–118; Z. Radzhabov, *Iz istorii obshchestvenno-politicheskoi mysli tadzhikskogo naroda* (Stalinabad, 1957), p. 108.

23. Iskandarov, *Iz istorii Bukharskogo emirata*, pp. 101–103, 118–120.

24. Iskandarov, *Iz istorii Bukharskogo emirata*, pp. 122–126; Iskandarov, *O nekotorykh izmeneniiakh v ekonomike Vostochnoi Bukhary na rubezhe XIX–XX vv.* (Stalinabad, 1958), pp. 134–135. The 1905 settlement was preserved down to the 1917 Revolution. Conditions in the western Pamirs improved somewhat under Russian administration.

25. A. Dzhidzhikhiia, "O poslednikh sobytiiakh v Bukhare," *Voennyi Sbornik*, May 1910, pp. 213–215.

26. Dzhidzhikhiia, p. 216; Logofet, *Bukharskoe khanstvo*, II, 209–210.

27. Dzhidzhikhiia, pp. 217–218. Five hundred Bukharans were killed on both sides during the rioting. (Logofet, *Bukharskoe khanstvo*, II, 274.)

28. Dzhidzhikhiia, p. 218; Logofet, *Bukharskoe khanstvo*, II, 210–211.

29. Dzhidzhikhiia, pp. 219–221; Logofet, *Bukharskoe khanstvo*, II, 281–282; *Pravitelstvennyi Vestnik*, February 2/15, 1910, p. 1.

30. Umniakov, p. 86. Nasr Allah was a Sunnite; Russian protection enabled the emir to abandon the traditional policy of using Shiites of Persian descent in high office to counter the power of the Uzbeg aristocracy. (A. Kh. Khamraev, "K voprosu o ianvarskikh sobytiiakh 1910 goda v Bukhare," SAGU, *Trudy*, LVII [1954], 73.) Khamraev's article marked a shift in the Soviet interpretation of the 1910 disorders, which had been characterized in 1950 as the beginning of a popular movement against the feudal order. (*Istoriia narodov Uzbekistana*, II, 414.) Khamraev attacked this interpretation as a "politically harmful idealization." He pictured the riots as an attempt on the part of the Sunnite members of the clerical-feudal ruling class to involve the masses in the

power struggle within the ruling class and thereby divert them from pursuing the class struggle against feudalism.

31. Radzhabov, pp. 134, 139. The statement in A. I. Ishanov, *Sozdanie Bukharskoi narodnoi sovetskoi respubliki (1920–1924 gg.)* ([Tashkent, 1955], p. 23), repeated in *Istoriia Uzbekskoi SSR* ([Tashkent, 1955–1956], I, Pt. II, 322–323), that in July 1916 Russian troops occupied the capital of Bukhara in order to protect the emir's government and restore order is without foundation. Ishanov's mention of General Lilienthal seems to indicate that the events of January 1910 have been confused with the native revolt of 1916 in the government-general of Turkestan and the oblasts of the Kazakh Steppe. The only way that the revolt of 1916 affected Bukhara was in the action of the Russian and Bukharan authorities to apprehend suspected supporters and agents of the rebels. (A. V. Piaskovskii, ed., *Vosstanie 1916 goda v Srednei Azii i Kazakhstane. Sbornik dokumentov* [Moscow, 1960], pp. 59, 64, 103, 139–140, 719n, 721n). Soviet historiography has recently attempted to characterize a peasant uprising in Karategin in July 1916 as an "anti-feudal movement" and an "integral part" of the "progressive" Central Asian revolt of 1916. (A. Madzhlisov, *Karategin nakanune ustanovleniia sovetskoi vlasti* [Stalinabad, 1959], p. 104. See also Madzhlisov's remarks at an historical conference in Tashkent in 1954 (*Materialy obedinennoi nauchnoi sessii, posviashchennoi istorii Srednei Azii i Kazakhstana v dooktiabrskii period* [Tashkent, 1955], pp. 383–388). Although perhaps encouraged by the revolt in Russian Turkestan, the Karategin uprising was a purely local affair over local grievances and was suppressed without Russian intervention.

32. A. Riabinskii, "Tsarskaia Rossiia i Bukhara v epokhu imperializma," *Istorik Marksist*, 1941, No. 4, pp. 18–19; Ishanov, p. 34.

33. Riabinskii, pp. 19–20.

34. Riabinskii, p. 21; Ishanov, p. 36.

35. Ishanov, pp. 36–37.

36. Radzhabov, p. 66.

37. Gosudarstvennaia Duma, *Stenograficheskie otchety*, Third Duma, 5th Session, IV, 2265–2266. The committee's report is in Gosudarstvennaia Duma, *Stenograficheskie otchety*, Third Duma, 5th Session, Prilozheniia, I, No. 114. The new law placed under the jurisdiction of the justices of the peace of the Amu-Darya Otdel all civil and criminal cases in Khiva involving a Russian national or a Christian alien. (PSZ [1912], No. 37,565.)

38. The committee's report is in Gosudarstvennaia Duma, *Stenograficheskie otchety*, Fourth Duma, 2nd Session, Prilozheniia, X, No. 884.

39. Gosudarstvennaia Duma, *Stenograficheskie otchety*, Fourth Duma, 2nd Session, V, 1355–1357.

Chapter 13. Nonintervention Abandoned: Russia and Khiva

1. V. I. Masalskii, *Turkestanskii krai* (St. Petersburg, 1913), p. 347; L. L. Ruma, ed., *Kaspiisko-aralskaia zheleznaia doroga v ekonomicheskom otnoshenii* (St. Petersburg, 1914), Appendix, pp. 26–27.

2. Masalskii, p. 754; *Istoriia narodov Uzbekistana* (Tashkent, 1947–1950), II, 420.

3. *Pravitelstvennyi Vestnik*, August 21/September 3, 1910, p. 2. Isfendiyar

was still referred to as "Illustriousness" on his trip to Russia in May–June 1911 (*Pravitelstvennyi Vestnik*, May 27/June 9, 1911, p. 2), but by January 1917 he was "Highness" (A. P. Savitskii, "Materialy k istorii Amu-Darinskogo otdela," SAGU, *Trudy*, new series, LXII [1955], 83).

4. *Istoriia narodov Uzbekistana*, II, 418.

5. A. Kun, "Poezdka po Khivinskomu khanstvu v 1873 g.," IRGO, *Izvestiia*, X (1874), 54.

6. K. K. Pahlen, *Otchet po revizii Turkestanskago kraia* (St. Petersburg, 1909–1911), Pt. XIX, *Prilozhenie*, I, Pt. II, 466–467.

7. Masalskii, p. 557.

8. *Istoriia narodov Uzbekistana*, II, 420.

9. *Pravitelstvennyi Vestnik*, August 21/September 3, 1910, p. 2; *Revue du Monde Mussulman*, XII (1910), 357.

10. Savitskii, pp. 79–80, 83–84; *Pravitelstvennyi Vestnik*, April 7/20, 1911, p. 3. The Djadid movement had already reached Khiva toward the end of Muhammad Rahim's reign; by 1908 there were four new-method schools in the khanate, but they did not last long. (A. N. Samoilovich, "Pervoe tainoe obshchestvo mlado-bukhartsev," *Vostok*, I [1922], 98.) By early 1911 there was not a single new-method school left in Khiva. (*Pravitelstvennyi Vestnik*, April 7/20, 1911, p. 3.)

11. Zeki Validi Togan, *Turkestan Today* (Istanbul, 1942–1947), pp. 316–317; *Istoriia Uzbekskoi SSR* (Tashkent, 1955–1956) I, Pt. II, 326; Samoilovich, p. 98; Baymirza Hayit, *Turkestan im XX. Jahrhundert* (Darmstadt, 1956), p. 144.

12. *Pravitelstvennyi Vestnik*, April 7/20, 1911, p. 3.

13. "Khiva, Rossiia i Turkmeny (Istoricheskaia spravka)," *Turkmenovedenie*, 1930, No. 1, pp. 16, 18; *Istoriia Turkmenskoi SSR*, I, Pt. II (Ashkhabad, 1957), 198–199, 347.

14. "Khiva, Rossiia i Turkmeny," pp. 16, 18.

15. A. A. Rosliakov, *Revoliutsionnoe dvizhenie i sotsial-demokraticheskie organizatsii v Turkmenistane v dooktiabrskii period (1900–mart 1917)* (Ashkhabad, 1957), pp. 231–232; *Istoriia Turkmenskoi SSR*, I, Pt. II, 347; "Khiva, Rossiia i Turkmeny," p. 16; Gaib Nepesov, *Velikii oktiabr i narodnye revoliutsii 1920 goda v severnom i vostochnom Turkmenistane* (Ashkhabad, 1958), p. 20. Compare the very misleading and wholly inaccurate account of the 1912–1913 revolt in Hayit, pp. 144–145.

16. Rosliakov, p. 232; "Khiva, Rossiia i Turkmeny," pp. 18, 16.

17. E. Fedorov, *Ocherki natsionalno-osvoboditelnogo dvizheniia v Srednei Azii* (Tashkent, 1925), pp. 49–51; Nepesov, p. 12; P. A. Kovalev, "Krizis kolonialnogo rezhima i 'reformy' Kuropatkina v Turkestane v 1916 godu," SAGU, *Trudy*, LVII (1954), 53. Fedorov says the extortion of money from Isfendiyar began in 1911; Nepesov gives 1914. The earlier date is most unlikely since neither Lykoshin nor Samsonov was ever charged with having received any of the money.

18. Nepesov, p. 20.

19. "Khiva, Rossiia i Turkmeny," pp. 16, 18. In current Soviet historiography Djunaid-khan is depicted as a paid agent of Turkey and indirectly of Germany. (*Istoriia Uzbekskoi SSR*, I, Pt. II, 328; *Istoriia Turkmenskoi SSR*, I, Pt. II, 380; Rosliakov, p. 239.) Earlier, however, he was characterized as the leader of a popular, antifeudal, and anti-imperialist movement. (N. Fioletov, "Bukharskoe

i Khivinskoe khanstva i otnosheniia ikh s Rossiei," *Istoricheskii Zhurnal*, 1941, No. 3, p. 71.)

20. Fedorov, p. 50; Nepesov, p. 21.
21. "Khiva, Rossiia i Turkmeny," pp. 16–17.
22. "Khiva, Rossiia i Turkmeny," pp. 17–19; Nepesov, p. 21.
23. "Khiva, Rossiia i Turkmeny," p. 17.
24. Savitskii, p. 75.
25. "Khiva, Rossiia i Turkmeny," p. 18. The bulk of this article consists of Minorskii's report of January 14, 1916, entitled "A note on the situation in Khiva," which reviews events in the khanate since the start of the troubles in 1912.
26. Nepesov, pp. 21, 23; *Istoriia Turkmenskoi SSR*, I, Pt. II, 383–384.
27. *Istoriia Turkmenskoi SSR*, I, Pt. II, 384; "Khiva i Rossiia (K istorii vosstaniia khivinskikh Turkmen v 1916 godu)," *Turkmenovedenie*, 1929, No. 6–7, p. 42; P. A. Kovalev, "Pervaia mirovaia voina i nazrevanie revoliutsionnogo krizisa v Uzbekistane v period 1914–1916 g.g.," SAGU, *Trudy*, new series, LXII (1955), 19; K. Mukhammedberdyev, *Kommunisticheskaia partiia v borbe za pobedu narodnoi sovetskoi revoliutsii v Khorezme* (Ashkhabad, 1959), pp. 44–45.
28. Nepesov, pp. 22–23; *Istoriia Turkmenskoi SSR*, I, Pt. II, 384; "Khiva, Rossiia i Turkmeny," p. 15. During the Central Asian revolt of 1916, which began shortly after Khiva was pacified, Russia kept an anxious eye on Djunaidkhan's whereabouts. In August he was reported to have returned to Khiva from Persia, but early in November the Russian police in Transcaspia learned that the Afghan government had prevented him from leaving Afghanistan. (A. V. Piaskovskii, ed., *Vosstanie 1916 goda v Srednei Azii i Kazakhstane. Sbornik dokumentov* [Moscow, 1960], pp. 431, 459.)
29. Fedorov, p. 49; Nepesov, p. 12. When Kuropatkin requested permission to examine Kolosovskii's bank deposits, the Ministry of Finance refused on the grounds that the secrecy of bank accounts was protected by law. (Kovalev, "Krizis kolonialnogo rezhima," p. 53.)
30. Extracts from the text of the agreement are in Savitskii, pp. 83–84.

Chapter 14. The Provisional Government and the Protectorates

1. Two exceptions were the Poles and the Finns, whose right to independence and political autonomy, respectively, the Provisional Government quickly recognized. For the various Russian attitudes toward the national problem, see Richard Pipes, *The Formation of the Soviet Union*, 2nd ed. (Cambridge, Mass., 1964), pp. 29–34, and Marc Ferro, "La politique des nationalités du gouvernement provisoire," *Cahiers du Monde Russe et Soviétique*, II (1961), 142–143.
2. S. M. Dimanshtein, ed., *Revoliutsiia i natsionalnyi vopros. Dokumenty i materialy* (Moscow, 1930), III, 72. One-man leadership was restored in Turkestan's colonial administration by the definitive law of August 26, which placed the Turkestan Committee under a commissar general. He, rather than the committee as a whole, was now charged with the government of Turkestan, including "the administration of the frontier affairs of the krai and direct relations with the emir of Bukhara and with the khan of Khiva." (R. P. Browder and

A. F. Kerensky, eds., *The Russian Provisional Government 1917. Documents* [Stanford, 1961], I, 421.)

3. Miller to Ministry of Foreign Affairs, March 13, 1917, "Bukhara v 1917 godu," *Krasnyi Arkhiv*, XX (1927), 80n; Dimanshtein, III, 72.

4. Miliukov to Provisional Government [March 14–16, 1917], *Revoliutsionnoe dvizhenie v Rossii posle sverzheniia samoderzhaviia* (*Velikaia oktiabrskaia sotsialisticheskaia revoliutsiia. Dokumenty i materialy.*) (Moscow, 1957), p. 436.

5. *Pobeda oktiabrskoi revoliutsii v Uzbekistane. Sbornik dokumentov* (Tashkent, 1963), I, 30, 35; A. I. Ishanov, *Sozdanie Bukharskoi narodnoi sovetskoi respubliki* (Tashkent, 1955), pp. 38–39.

6. Turkestan Committee to Kerensky [Minister of Justice], June 7, 1917, *Pobeda oktiabrskoi revoliutsii*, I, 129; Miller to Miliukov, April 15, "Bukhara v 1917 godu," p. 96; Ishanov, pp. 47–50.

7. A. A. Rosliakov, *Revoliutsionnoe dvizhenie i sotsial-demokraticheskie organizatsii v Turkmenistane* (Ashkhabad, 1957), p. 248; Gaib Nepesov, *Velikii oktiabr i narodnye revoliutsii 1920 goda v severnom i vostochnom Turkmenistane* (Ashkhabad, 1958), pp. 26, 33; *Pobeda oktiabrskoi revoliutsii*, I, 86, 165; *Istoriia tadzhikskogo naroda* (Moscow, 1963–1965), II, Pt. II, 252; A. P. Fomchenko, *Russkie poseleniia v Bukharskom emirate* (Tashkent, 1958), pp. 44–46, 49.

8. Ishanov, p. 38. A report on August 31 from the procurator of the Samarkand okrug court to his superior at Tashkent noted that at Termez, where the soviet was supported by the soldiers but not the civilian population, the soviet and the municipal government refused to recognize each other. (*Pobeda oktiabrskoi revoliutsii*, I, 265.) In the wake of Kornilov's abortive coup in Russia, the New Bukhara Soviet formed a Committee to Save the Revolution, which on September 2, over the strong opposition of the New Bukhara Executive Committee, proposed to tax the propertied classes in order to create a fund to combat the counterrevolution. (Vvedenskii to Turkestan Committee, August 30, September 2, 1917, *Pobeda oktiabrskoi revoliutsii*, I, 258, 273.)

9. A. Mashitskii, "K istorii revoliutsii v Bukhare," NKID, *Vestnik*, 1921, No. 5–6, p. 78; Faizullah Khodzhaev, *K istorii revoliutsii v Bukhare* (Tashkent, 1926), pp. 18–19.

10. Miller to Ministry of Foreign Affairs, March 9, 1917, Kuropatkin to Ministry of Foreign Affairs, March 10, Emir of Bukhara to Ministry of Foreign Affairs, March 10, "Bukhara v 1917 godu," pp. 79–80.

11. Z. Radzhabov, *Iz istorii obshchestvenno-politicheskoi mysli tadzhikskogo naroda* (Stalinabad, 1957), pp. 429–430.

12. Klemm [director, Central Asiatic Department] to Miller, March 19, *Pobeda oktiabrskoi revoliutsii*, I, 40–41. Klemm had headed this department since before World War I.

13. Miller to Miliukov, March 18, Miller to Ministry of Foreign Affairs, March 20, "Bukhara v 1917 godu," pp. 81–82.

14. See Miller's telegrams of March 22–26 to the foreign ministry, "Bukhara v 1917 godu," pp. 83–87.

15. Miller to Ministry of Foreign Affairs, March 31, *Revoliutsionnoe dvizhenie v Rossii*, pp. 447–448.

16. Kuropatkin to Miliukov, March 24, Miller to Ministry of Foreign Affairs, March 30, "Bukhara v 1917 godu," pp. 84, 88.

17. Miller to Ministry of Foreign Affairs, March 25, "Bukhara v 1917 godu,"

p. 86; Miller to Ministry of Foreign Affairs, March 31, *Revoliutsionnoe dvizhenie v Rossii,* pp. 447–448.

18. See Miller's telegrams of March 30 and April 5 to the foreign ministry, "Bukhara v 1917 godu," pp. 87–88, 90.

19. The text of the manifesto is in A. Mashitskii, "Materialy po istorii bukharskoi revoliutsii," NKID, *Vestnik,* 1922, No. 4–5, 128–129. Khodzhaev (p. 20) dated the manifesto March 17 (O.S.), and his error has often gone unnoticed (*see* Radzhabov, p. 430, and Baymirza Hayit, *Turkestan im XX. Jahrhundert* [Darmstadt, 1956], p. 121). Mashitskii incorrectly gives the Western equivalent of 28 Jumada II, 1335 A. H., as September 8, 1918.

20. Khodzhaev, pp. 12, 15–17, 21–23; Sadriddin Aini, "Korotko o moei zhizni," *Sobranie sochinenii* (Moscow, 1960–1961), I, 58–59; Miller to Miliukov, April 9 and 10, "Bukhara v 1917 godu," pp. 91–92. Hayit's account of the events of April 1917 in Bukhara (pp. 122–123) is confused and unreliable. His reference to the kush-begi's summoning of a madjlis on April 7 is obviously based on events in Khiva, not Bukhara.

21. Khodzhaev, pp. 23–24; Miller to Miliukov, April 9, "Bukhara v 1917 godu," p. 91; Aini, pp. 63–67. Khodzhaev's estimate of five to seven thousand participants in the Djadid demonstration is undoubtedly much inflated. Aini, a moderate Djadid who boycotted the demonstration but was nevertheless arrested and whipped, later used his experiences as material for his novels *Dokhunda* and *Raby.*

22. Miller to Colonel Slinko [Samarkand Oblast Commissar], April 9, *Pobeda oktiabrskoi revoliutsii,* I, 58; Miller to Miliukov, April 9 and 10, Miller to Ministry of Foreign Affairs, April 10, "Bukhara v 1917 godu," pp. 91–92; Aini, pp. 68–70.

23. Miller and Shulga to Miliukov, April 10, Miller to Ministry of Foreign Affairs, April 11, Miller to Miliukov, April 13, "Bukhara v 1917 godu," pp. 91, 93, 101; "Iz dnevnika A. N. Kuropatkina," *Krasnyi Arkhiv,* XX (1927), 76.

24. Khodzhaev, pp. 26–29.

25. Miller to Miliukov, April 15, "Bukhara v 1917 godu," pp. 95–96; Khodzhaev, pp. 29–30. Mashitskii's assertion ("K istorii revoliutsii," No. 5–6, pp. 79–82) that the Young Bukharans escaped from the citadel by holding Miller, Shulga, and Vvedenskii as hostages is unsupported by any evidence.

26. Miller to Ministry of Foreign Affairs, April 10, Miller to Miliukov, April 15 and 16, Chirkin [Miller's successor] to Ministry of Foreign Affairs, April 22 and 24, Young Bukharan Committee to Miliukov, April 25, "Bukhara v 1917 godu," pp. 92, 94, 96, 98, 102, 104, 105.

27. Ishanov, p. 43; Vvedenskii to Ministry of Foreign Affairs, May 8, June 9, Chirkin to Ministry of Foreign Affairs, May 2, July 1, 14, and 20, Miller to Miliukov, April 16, "Bukhara v 1917 godu," pp. 97–98, 108–110, 116, 118–120.

28. Vvedenskii to Ministry of Foreign Affairs, April 21, June 9, Chirkin to Ministry of Foreign Affairs, April 24, May 9 and 31, June 1, July 14, "Bukhara v 1917 godu," pp. 102–103, 110, 115–117, 120. The begs and amlakdars objected to being put on regular salaries, so the scheme was dropped (A. A. Semenov, *Ocherk ustroistva tsentralnogo administrativnogo upravleniia Bukharskogo khanstva pozdneishego vremeni* [Stalinabad, 1954], p. 11).

29. Vvedenskii to Ministry of Foreign Affairs, May 11, Chirkin to Ministry of Foreign Affairs, May 9 and 15, "Bukhara v 1917 godu," pp. 110–112.

30. See the telegrams sent to Petrograd on April 16–17 by Miller, Chertov, and representatives of Russian firms in Bukhara, "Bukhara v 1917 godu," pp. 96–97, 99.

31. Shchepkin [Chairman of the Turkestan Committee] to Miliukov, April 17 and 19, Preobrazhenskii to Miliukov, April 23, "Bukhara v 1917 godu," 100–103; "Iz dnevnika A. N. Kuropatkina," p. 76. Chirkin had served as the foreign ministry's diplomatic attaché in Tashkent in 1914–1915.

32. Vvedenskii to Ministry of Foreign Affairs, April 21, Shchepkin to Miliukov, April 28, Miller to Miliukov, April 15, "Bukhara v 1917 godu," pp. 94, 101–102, 106.

33. Chirkin to Ministry of Foreign Affairs, April 25, 28, and 30, May 5 and 29, June 20, Shchepkin and Preobrazhenskii to Ministry of Foreign Affairs, May 10, Vvedenskii to Ministry of Foreign Affairs, May 11, June 9, "Bukhara v 1917 godu," pp. 104, 106–109, 111–112, 114–117.

34. Chirkin to Ministry of Foreign Affairs, July 5 and 13, "Bukhara v 1917 godu," pp. 118–119; "Iz dnevnika A. N. Kuropatkina," p. 70.

35. Chirkin to Ministry of Foreign Affairs, August 7, Elpatievskii to Ministry of Foreign Affairs, October 9, "Bukhara v 1917 godu," pp. 121–122.

36. Chirkin to Ministry of Foreign Affairs, May 24, "Bukhara v 1917 godu," p. 114.

37. In mid-July Chirkin confessed to Petrograd that he felt helpless to prevent the return to office of Burhan ad-Din; compromise was the only way to preserve order, and the preservation of order was the only feasible aim of Russian policy in Bukhara at the time. (Chirkin to Ministry of Foreign Affairs, July 14, "Bukhara v 1917 godu," p. 120.)

38. Chirkin to Ministry of Foreign Affairs, April 22 and 25, May 2, "Bukhara v 1917 godu," pp. 102, 104, 108–109; Khodzhaev, pp. 30–33.

39. Gaib Nepesov, *Iz istorii khorezmskoi revoliutsii, 1920–1924 gg.* (Tashkent, 1962), pp. 75–79; Joseph Castagné, "Le Bolchevisme et l'Islam," *Revue du Monde Musulman*, LI (1922), 204.

40. Nepesov, *Iz istorii khorezmskoi revoliutsii*, pp. 78, 80–81; *Velikaia oktiabrskaia sotsialisticheskaia revoliutsiia. Khronika sobytii 27 fevralia–25 oktiabria 1917 goda* (Moscow, 1957–1961), I, 413.

41. Nepesov, *Iz istorii khorezmskoi revoliutsii*, p. 81.

42. The commission was headed by Lieutenant Colonel B. P. Trizna, commissar of Sir-Darya Oblast. Cossack Lieutenant Prince Misostov represented the Turkestan Krai Soviet, and Kh. Iumagulov represented the Turkestan Moslem Central Council or *Shura* (*Pobeda oktiabrskoi revoliutsii*, I, 131). Iumagulov's recollections of the mission are in *Zhizn Natsionalnostei*, August 10, 1920, p. 2.

43. Nepesov, *Iz istorii khorezmskoi revoliutsii*, p. 83; memorandum from Turkestan Committee to Minister of War, September 13, 1917, "Iz istorii natsionalnoi politiki Vremennogo pravitelstva (Ukraina, Finliandiia, Khiva)," *Krasnyi Arkhiv*, XXX (1928), 71–72. This article (pp. 72–79) contains the texts of the statute for the commissariat and the fundamental laws.

44. The commissar, who was to be appointed or dismissed by the minister of war upon recommendation of the Turkestan Committee, was to report on developments in Khiva to Tashkent in brief every three months, and in detail annually. He was also responsible for defending the legal rights and interests of Russians in the khanate, who were to continue to enjoy complete extraterritoriality.

45. I. M. Zaitsev, *V zashchitu ot klevetnikov* (n.p., 1922), p. 2.

46. Nepesov, *Iz istorii khorezmskoi revoliutsii*, pp. 83–84; *Pobeda oktiabrskoi revoliutsii*, I, 321, 334, 393, 452, 460, 468, 472, 525.

47. "Iz istorii natsionalnoi politiki Vremennogo pravitelstva," p. 71n.

Chapter 15. The Bolshevik Revolution and the Independence of the Khanates

1. Marx's support for Polish nationalism was an exception, motivated by his desire to weaken in any way possible that "barbarous" bulwark of reaction, tsarist Russia.

2. *Kommunisticheskaia partiia Sovetskogo Soiuza v rezoliutsiiakh i resheniiakh sezdov, konferentsii i plenumov TsK*, 7th ed. (Moscow, 1953), I, 40. The German version of the London Congress proceedings substituted "self-determination" (*Selbstbestimmungsrecht*) for "autonomy," and it was in this form that the term entered the vocabulary of Russian Marxism. My discussion of Bolshevik nationality policy relies heavily on E. H. Carr, *The Bolshevik Revolution* (New York, 1951–1953), I, 412–428, and Richard Pipes, *The Formation of the Soviet Union* (Cambridge, Mass., 1964), pp. 32–49.

3. Carr, I, 258.

4. V. I. Lenin, "On the Manifesto of the Armenian Social Democrats" (February 1, 1903), *Polnoe sobranie sochinenii*, 5th ed. (Moscow, 1958–1965), VII, 105.

5. I. V. Stalin, "On the Road to Nationalism" (January 12, 1913) and "Marxism and the National Question" (1912–1913), *Sochineniia* (Moscow, 1946–1951), II, 286, 312–313.

6. Lenin, "The National Question in Our Program" (July 15, 1903), VII, 234; "Theses on the National Question" (June 1913), XXIII, 315; "Resolution on the National Question" (September 1913), XXIV, 59; Letter to S. G. Shaumian (November 23, 1913), XLVIII, 235.

7. Stalin, II, 286.

8. Lenin, XXIII, 314.

9. Lenin, "Critical Remarks on the National Question" (fall 1913), XXIV, 130.

10. Lenin, "On the Right of Nations to Self-Determination" (spring 1914), XXV, 287.

11. Lenin, "The Revolutionary Proletariat and the Right of Nations to Self-Determination" (October 1915) and "The Socialist Revolution and the Right of Nations to Self-Determination" (March 1916), XXVII, 63, 255–257, 261.

12. Pipes, p. 41.

13. In a moment of optimism in 1913 Lenin briefly envisioned a state based on "democratic centralism," *i.e.*, a unitary state with regional and local self-government where warranted by economic, social, or ethnic peculiarities. (Lenin, XXIV, 144.)

14. Lenin, "Resolution on the National Question" (for the Seventh Party Conference) (April 1917), XXXI, 440; Stalin, "Report on the National Question" (to the Seventh Party Conference) (April 29, 1917), III, 53.

15. Lenin, "The Development of Capitalism in Russia" (1899), III, 595; Preface to "Imperialism, The Highest Stage of Capitalism" (April 1917), XXVII,

302; Speech to First All-Russian Congress of Soviets (June 4, 1917), XXXII, 274; "Summation of the Discussion on Self-Determination" (fall 1916), XXX, 34; Speech on the national question (April 29, 1917), XXXI, 436–437.

16. See, for example, the Declaration of the Rights of the Peoples of Russia, signed by Lenin and Stalin, in *Izvestiia*, November 3, 1917, p. 4; Stalin's speech on November 14 to the party congress of the Finnish Social Democrats, in Stalin, IV, 4.

17. Stalin, "Reply to Ukrainian Comrades" (December 12, 1917) and Report on the national question to the Third Congress of Soviets (January 15, 1918), IV, 8–9, 31–32.

18. *Pobeda oktiabrskoi revoliutsii v Uzbekistane* (Tashkent, 1963), I, 313–314, 320, 324, 330, 341, 358–359, 363, 374–376, 381, 438, 492, 530–531, 541–544, 549, 572, 578; A. I. Ishanov, *Sozdanie Bukharskoi narodnoi sovetskoi respubliki* (Tashkent, 1955), p. 54; A. P. Fomchenko, *Russkie poseleniia v Bukharskom emirate* (Tashkent, 1958), pp. 53–54; B. I. Iskandarov, "Bukhara v 1918–1920 gg.," Akademiia Nauk Tadzhikskoi SSR, *Trudy*, XIX (1954), 4–5.

19. Iskandarov, p. 11.

20. Iskandarov, pp. 12–13; L. K. Shek, "Iz istorii sovetsko-bukharskikh otnoshenii (1917–1920 gg.)," SAGU, *Trudy*, LXXVIII (1956), 108; Faizullah Khodzhaev, *K istorii revoliutsii v Bukhare* (Tashkent, 1926), p. 41.

21. Pipes, p. 175. Recent Soviet historiography maintains, but furnishes no proof, that during the winter of 1917–1918 Bukhara was allied with Kokand as well as with Ataman Dutov, Afghanistan, Britain, and counterrevolutionaries within Soviet Turkestan. (Iskandarov, pp. 11–12; Shek, p. 107; Ishanov, p. 60.)

22. Khodzhaev, pp. 40, 35–38. Fitrat's program was adopted by the Young Bukharan central committee in late January 1918 but not published until two years later. The text of the program is in S. M. Dimanshtein, ed., *Revoliutsiia i natsionalnyi vopros* (Moscow, 1930), III, 354–359.

23. Khodzhaev, pp. 41–46; F. Kolesov and A. Bobunov, "Vosstanie v Bukhare," in M. Gorkii et al., eds., *Voina v peskakh. Materialy po istorii grazhdanskoi voiny* (Moscow, 1935), pp. 238–240; Iskandarov, pp. 13–14. My account of Kolesov's campaign is based on Khodzhaev, pp. 46–53; Kolesov and Bobunov, pp. 241–272; A. Gudovich, "Na pomoshch," in Gorkii, pp. 282–288; Iskandarov, pp. 14–17.

24. I. I. Umniakov, "K istorii novometodnoi shkoly v Bukhare," SAGU, *Biulleten*, XVI (1927), 95. Osman-beg's son was at the same time appointed divan-begi. (O. A. Sukhareva, *Bukhara XIX–nachalo XX v.* [Moscow, 1966], 269.)

25. The text of the treaty is in Umniakov, pp. 96–98. In May 1918 the Fifth Turkestan Congress of Soviets condemned Kolesov for his bad judgment in launching the campaign against Bukhara, and Kolesov admitted his responsibility. (A. I. Zevelev, *Iz istorii grazhdanskoi voiny v Uzbekistane* [Tashkent, 1959], p. 76.) In the 1930's Kolesov tried unconvincingly to put the blame for the humiliating conclusion of the campaign on alleged counterrevolutionaries in the Tashkent regime who misled him into making peace with the emir and returning to deal with Turkestan's problems rather than using the troop reinforcements to settle with Bukhara. (Kolesov and Bobunov, pp. 273–275.) A recent Soviet attempt to present Kolesov's campaign as a successful rebuff of Anglo-Bukharan aggression against Tashkent (Gaib Nepesov, *Iz istorii khorezmskoi revoliutsii* [Tashkent, 1962], p. 96) contrasts sharply with a candid Bolshevik admission a generation

ago that the campaign and the ensuing peace treaty constituted "a defeat for the revolution." (O. Glovatskii, *Revoliutsiia pobezhdaet* [Tashkent, 1930], p. 24.)

26. I. M. Zaitsev, *V zashchitu ot klevetnikov* (n.p., 1922), p. 2.

27. Nepesov, p. 88.

28. Zaitsev, pp. 2–3; Nepesov, pp. 89–90; *Istoriia grazhdanskoi voiny v Uzbekistane* (Tashkent, 1964), I, 128–130. Zaitsev escaped from a Tashkent prison on July 1, fought under Ataman Dutov from April 1919 until March 1920, and then fled to China.

29. *Zhizn Natsionalnostei*, April 20, 1919, p. 1; Nepesov, pp. 96–97.

Chapter 16. The Civil War and the Second Russian Conquest

1. *Zhizn Natsionalnostei*, July 20, 1919, p. 1. Tashkent had on April 1 appointed a diplomatic representative to the emir's court, and on July 12, 1918, Bukhara established a permanent embassy in Tashkent. (L. K. Shek, "Iz istorii sovetsko-bukharskikh otnoshenii," SAGU, *Trudy*, LXXVIII [1956], 110–111.)

2. Memorandum of telephone conversation between members of Central Executive Committee of Turkestan Republic and Commissar of War, June 12, 1918, *Inostrannaia voennaia interventsiia i grazhdanskaia voina v Srednei Azii i Kazakhstane* (Alma-Ata, 1963–1964), I, 42–44, 338–339.

3. C. H. Ellis, *The British "Intervention" in Transcaspia 1918–1919* (Berkeley, 1963), pp. 27–28, 113. In December 1918 Bukhara again failed to respond to an approach from Askhabad.

4. Shek, p. 112.

5. On the British intervention, see Richard H. Ullman, *Anglo-Soviet Relations, 1917–1921: Intervention and the War* (Princeton, 1961), Ch. XI; Ellis, *The British "Intervention."*

6. Ellis, pp. 80–81.

7. B. I. Iskandarov, "Bukhara v 1918–1920 gg.," Akademiia Nauk Tadzhikskoi SSR, *Trudy*, XIX (1954), 24; Ellis, pp. 113, 141–144, 154.

8. F. M. Bailey, *Mission to Tashkent* (London, 1946), pp. 212–215, 238–239, 260; L. V. S. Blacker, *On Secret Patrol in High Asia* (London, 1922), pp. 159–161; Ellis, pp. 75, 154. For the Soviet version of Britain's military aid to Alim, which accepts the rumors as true, see Iskandarov, p. 26; A. I. Ishanov, *Sozdanie Bukharskoi narodnoi sovetskoi respubliki* (Tashkent, 1955), p. 64; *Istoriia grazhdanskoi voiny v Uzbekistane* (Tashkent, 1964), I, 289.

9. *Inostrannaia voennaia interventsiia*, I, 514; Iskandarov, p. 27; Shek, p. 115.

10. *Inostrannaia voennaia interventsiia*, I, 481, 499; Pechatnikov [Tashkent's plenipotentiary in the khanate] to Bukharan government, [June] 1919, *Turkmenistan v period inostrannoi voennoi interventsii i grazhdanskoi voiny 1918–1920 gg. Sbornik dokumentov* (Ashkhabad, 1957), p. 375. Land contact between Turkestan and European Russia had been reestablished in February 1919.

11. *Turkmenistan v period interventsii*, pp. 213–214, 216–219; *Inostrannaia voennaia interventsiia*, I, 386–387; Iskandarov, pp. 30–32; Ishanov, pp. 66–67; Shek, pp. 116–118.

12. Ishanov, p. 68. The Bukharan government had unsuccessfully demanded

the evacuation of Russian troops during the Soviet retreat in Transcaspia in November 1918. (Shek, p. 113.)

13. Bailey, pp. 174–175; Shek, p. 117; A. Mashitskii, "K istorii revoliutsii v Bukhare," NKID, *Vestnik*, 1921, No. 3–4, p. 35.

14. Order from the Revolutionary Military Council of the Transcaspian Front, September 2, 1919, *Inostrannaia voennaia interventsiia*, II, 257.

15. Malleson to Emir Alim, 21 Ramadan, 1337 A.H. [June 20, 1919], in A. Mashitskii, "Materialy po istorii bukharskoi revoliutsii," NKID, *Vestnik*, 1922, No. 4–5, pp. 129–131.

16. By late September, when Kolchak approached Bukhara and Khiva with offers of an alliance against Moscow (Ishanov, p. 67; Iskandarov, pp. 27–28), his forces had been driven back to the line of the Tobol-Irtysh rivers in western Siberia, so that an alliance with him could have held little attraction for the khanates. His letters to the emir and the khan, which were intercepted by the Communists, have nevertheless been used in Soviet propaganda and historiography as evidence of the collusion of all anti-Communists during the civil war (see, for example, the posters reproduced in K. Ramzin, *Revoliutsiia v Srednei Azii v obrazakh i kartinakh* [Tashkent, 1928], Chs. X, XI).

17. I. V. Stalin, "One Immediate Task" (April 9, 1918) and Speech to conference on formation of a Tatar-Bashkir Soviet Republic (May 10), *Sochineniia* (Moscow, 1946–1951), IV, 76, 87; V. I. Lenin, Report on party program (March 19, 1919), *Polnoe sobranie sochinenii* (Moscow, 1958–1965), XXXVIII, 158–159.

18. *Zhizn Natsionalnostei*, February 23, 1919, pp. 1–2; March 2, p. 1; June 1, p. 1; August 17, p. 2.

19. Faizullah Khodzhaev, *K istorii revoliutsii v Bukhare* (Tashkent, 1926), pp. 54–55, 58–59.

20. A. P. Fomchenko, *Russkie poseleniia v Bukharskom emirate* (Tashkent, 1958), p. 55; *Inostrannaia voennaia interventsiia*, I, 109–110; O. O. Shikhmuradov and A. A. Rosliakov, eds., *Ocherki istorii kommunisticheskoi partii Turkmenistana* (Ashkhabad, 1961), pp. 106, 143–144.

21. G. P. Makarova, "Borba Bukharskoi kommunisticheskoi partii za ustanovlenie sovetskoi vlasti v Bukhare," *Velikii oktiabr. Sbornik statei* (Moscow, 1958), pp. 488–489; Iskandarov, p. 34; *Istoriia sovetskogo gosudarstva i prava Uzbekistana*, I (1917–1924 gg.) (Tashkent, 1960), p. 138. Poltoratskii, who had been a typesetter in New Bukhara at the time of the February Revolution, was one of the founders and leaders of the New Bukhara Soviet and became a Bolshevik while attending the First All-Russian Congress of Soviets in June 1917. (Iskandarov, p. 9.)

22. Iskandarov, pp. 34–35; Makarova, pp. 491–492.

23. Khodzhaev, pp. 51–53; Mashitskii, "K istorii revoliutsii," No. 5–6, p. 76; Baymirza Hayit, *Turkestan im XX. Jahrhundert* (Darmstadt, 1956), pp. 40–41, 129; Iskandarov, p. 17. In March 1918 the emir terminated all Russian land concessions, which were then attacked by Bukharan mobs.

24. Shek, p. 114; Khodzhaev, p. 57.

25. *Zhizn Natsionalnostei*, July 20, 1919, p. 1; A. I. Ishanov, "Pobeda narodnoi sovetskoi revoliutsii v Bukhare," *Materialy obedinennoi nauchnoi sessii po istorii narodov Srednei Azii i Kazakhstana v epokhu sotsializma* (Tashkent, 1957), p. 89.

In 1917, as a result of the revolution's disruption of the Russian economy, Bukharan cotton production had dropped from its record wartime level back to the 1913 figure. (V. I. Iuferev, *Khlopkovodstvo v Turkestane* [Leningrad, 1925], pp. 138–139.) The decline in cotton acreage and production in Russian Turkestan was even greater.

26. Iskandarov, pp. 34–35; Ishanov, "Pobeda narodnoi sovetskoi revoliutsii," p. 90; Ishanov, *Sozdanie Bukharskoi respubliki*, pp. 70–71; Makarova, p. 493.

27. Gaib Nepesov, *Iz istorii khorezmskoi revoliutsii* (Tashkent, 1962), pp. 97–100; K. Mukhammedberdyev, "Oktiabrskaia revoliutsiia i ustanovlenie sovetskoi vlasti v Khorezme (1917 g.–fevral 1920 g.)," *Velikii oktiabr*, p. 464.

28. Nepesov, pp. 111–117; *Zhizn Natsionalnostei*, April 20, 1919, p. 1. The sources are in disagreement as to whether Abd Allah was Isfendiyar's older or younger brother.

29. Mukhammedberdyev, p. 464; *Istoriia grazhdanskoi voiny v Uzbekistane*, I, 237–241; Nepesov, pp. 117–123.

30. Nepesov, pp. 124–126, 129; K. Mukhammedberdyev, *Kommunisticheskaia partiia v borbe za pobedu narodnoi sovetskoi revoliutsii v Khorezme* (Ashkhabad, 1959), pp. 81–82; N. Fedko, "Mirnye peregovory," and N. Vostrikov, "Voenno-revoliutsionnye sobytiia v Amu-Darinskom otdele i Khorezme," *Oktiabrskaia sotsialisticheskaia revoliutsiia i grazhdanskaia voina v Turkestane. Vospominaniia uchastnikov* (Tashkent, 1957), pp. 479–480, 493–495.

31. Nepesov, pp. 132–134.

32. Nepesov, pp. 135–137, 142–143; *Inostrannaia voennaia interventsiia*, I, 139, and II, 500–501.

33. Mukhammedberdyev, "Oktiabrskaia revoliutsiia," pp. 467–468; Mukhammedberdyev, *Kommunisticheskaia partiia*, p. 89.

34. *Izvestiia*, October 10, 1919, p. 2; Resolution of the Fourth Congress of the CPT, October 7, 1919, *Inostrannaia voennaia interventsiia*, II, 485.

35. Shikhmuradov and Rosliakov, pp. 164–165; *Inostrannaia voennaia interventsiia*, II, 486, 491–492, 502; Nepesov, pp. 156–158, 160.

36. *Inostrannaia voennaia interventsiia*, II, 493–495; Mukhammedberdyev, *Kommunisticheskaia partiia*, pp. 135–137.

37. Mukhammedberdyev, *Kommunisticheskaia partiia*, pp. 122, 131–134; Nepesov, pp. 161–167.

38. G. Skalov, "Khivinskaia revoliutsiia 1920 goda," *Novyi Vostok*, III (1922), 253–254; Nepesov, pp. 167–170; Mukhammedberdyev, "Oktiabrskaia revoliutsiia," pp. 478–479; *Inostrannaia voennaia interventsiia*, II, 498, 504, 610. The text of the 1920 constitution of the Khorezmi People's Soviet Republic, as amended in 1921 and 1922, is in *Sezdy sovetov Soiuza SSR, soiuznykh i avtonomykh sovetskikh sotsialisticheskikh respublik. Sbornik dokumentov 1917–1937 g.g.* (Moscow, 1959–1965), II, 503–508, 514–521, 526–543.

39. Shikhmuradov and Rosliakov, pp. 171–172.

40. *Zhizn Natsionalnostei*, February 15, 1920, p. 4; Iskandarov, p. 49; Frunze to Lenin, April 14, 1920, *Inostrannaia voennaia interventsiia*, II, 595; Ishanov, *Sozdanie Bukharskoi respubliki*, pp. 58–59.

41. Emir Amanullah to Emir Alim, 25 Muharram, 1338 A.H. [October 20, 1919], in Mashitskii, "Materialy po istorii," pp. 134–135; Ishanov, *Sozdanie Bukharskoi respubliki*, pp. 68–69; Frunze to Lenin, April 14, 1920, *Inostrannaia voennaia interventsiia*, II, 594–595; Frunze to Lenin, May 23 and 27, *Iz istorii*

grazhdanskoi voiny v SSSR. Sbornik dokumentov i materialov, 1918–1922 (Moscow, 1961), III, 556–558; Commissariat of Foreign Affairs to Lenin, May 20, in Ishanov, "Pobeda narodnoi sovetskoi revoliutsii," p. 92.

42. Lenin, "Preliminary Draft of Theses on the National and Colonial Questions" (June 5, 1920), XLI, 166–167; *Inostrannaia voennaia interventsiia,* II, 507; Emir of Bukhara to Chicherin, June 8, 1920, Chicherin to Emir of Bukhara, June 24, *Dokumenty vneshnei politiki SSSR,* II (Moscow, 1958), pp. 586–587n. Frunze's and Kuibyshev's speeches were published in the Tashkent *Izvestiia,* June 22.

43. Frunze to armies of the Turkestan front, June 24, 1920, *Inostrannaia voennaia interventsiia,* II, 319–320.

44. Frunze to Turkestan Commission, June 30, 1920, in Ishanov, "Pobeda narodnoi sovetskoi revoliutsii," p. 94; Frunze to Commander-in-Chief RSFSR, July 12, Frunze to Lenin, end of July, Politburo to Revolutionary Military Council of the Turkestan Front, August 10, *Inostrannaia voennaia interventsiia,* II, 508–509, 513–515.

45. Khodzhaev, pp. 64–65, 71; Sadriddin Aini, "Korotko o moei zhizni," *Sobranie sochinenii* (Moscow, 1960–1961), I, 74; Mashitskii, "K istorii revoliutsii," No. 5–6, pp. 72–74; Ishanov, "Pobeda narodnoi sovetskoi revoliutsii," p. 96.

46. Mashitskii, "Materialy po istorii," pp. 124–125; Shikhmuradov and Rosliakov, p. 173.

47. Khodzhaev, pp. 75–76; Makarova, p. 504; *Inostrannaia voennaia interventsiia,* II, 515n, 518, 696.

48. Shikhmuradov and Rosliakov, p. 175; Frunze to troops of the Turkestan front, August 25, 1920, Turkestan Commission to Central Committee, August 26, *Inostrannaia voennaia interventsiia,* II, 515–518. Despite the efforts of the Young Bukharans and the BCP, the revolt was not a mass movement. Glovatskii (pp. 31–32) admitted a decade later, "the broad masses of the peasantry did not take an active part in the revolt itself. With the exception of the Chardjui uprising, the peasantry at best was sympathetic to [the revolution], as in Kitab and Shahr-i Sabz, and at worst fought against the revolution on the side of the feudal class, as in Old Bukhara and Karshi."

49. *Inostrannaia voennaia interventsiia,* II, 522–523; Makarova, pp. 505–507; Iskandarov, p. 59; Bailey, p. 271; I. I. Umniakov, "K istorii novometodnoi shkoly v Bukhare," SAGU, *Biulleten,* XVI (1927), 93.

50. Khodzhaev, p. 76; *Iz istorii grazhdanskoi voiny,* III, 855.

Chapter 17. Bukhara and Khiva as Soviet Satellites

1. I. V. Stalin, "The Policy of the Soviet Government on the National Question in Russia," *Sochineniia* (Moscow, 1946–1951), IV, 351–355; Richard Pipes, *The Formation of the Soviet Union* (Cambridge, Mass., 1964), pp. 229, 252–253.

2. Pipes, pp. 253–254.

3. Stalin, "The October Revolution and the National Policy of the Russian Communists" (November 6–7, 1921), V, 114.

4. Treaty of Alliance between RSFSR and KhPSR, September 13, 1920, articles 1–2; Treaty of Alliance between RSFSR and BPSR, March 4, 1921, prologue and article 1. The texts of these two treaties are in *Sbornik deistvuiushchikh dogovorov, soglashenii i konventsii, zakliuchennykh R.S.F.S.R. s ino-*

strannymi gosudarstvami (Moscow, 1921–1923), I, 17–22, and II, 7–11. English translations of many of the treaties between Russia and the Central Asian people's republics are in Leonard Shapiro, *Soviet Treaty Series* (Washington, 1950–1955), I.

5. The 1920 treaty of alliance with Khorezm, articles 3–5; 1921 treaty of alliance with Bukhara, articles 7, 9.

6. Provisional Treaty between RSFSR and BPSR, November 6, 1920, *Inostrannaia voennaia interventsiia i grazhdanskaia voina v Srednei Azii i Kazakhstane* (Alma-Ata, 1963–1964), II, 555–556; 1921 treaty of alliance with Bukhara, article 13. The transfer of the flotilla occurred in September 1921. (Gaib Nepesov, *Iz istorii khorezmskoi revoliutsii* [Tashkent, 1962], pp. 224–225.)

7. Turkestan Commission's resolution of June 26, 1920, *Iz istorii grazhdanskoi voiny v SSSR* (Moscow, 1961), III, 563–564.

8. The 1920 treaty of alliance with Khorezm, articles 18–19, 21; Economic Agreement between RSFSR and KhPSR, September 13, 1920, article 4. The text of the economic agreement is in *Sbornik deistvuiushchikh dogovorov*, I, 23–26.

9. Nepesov, pp. 223–224, 236–237, 256.

10. Decision of Tashkent conference of Russian and Bukharan officials, September 5, 1920, *Iz istorii grazhdanskoi voiny*, III, 582; 1921 treaty of alliance with Bukhara, articles 5, 14; Economic Agreement between RSFSR and BPSR, March 4, 1921, articles 9, 12–13. The text of the economic agreement is in *Sbornik deistvuiushchikh dogovorov*, II, 12–14.

11. The 1920 treaty of alliance with Khorezm, articles 6–7, 17, 20; decision of Tashkent conference, September 5, 1920, *Iz istorii grazhdanskoi voiny*, III, 580–581; Provisional Military and Political Agreement between RSFSR and BPSR, October 1920, *Inostrannaia voennaia interventsiia*, II, 551–552; 1921 treaty of alliance with Bukhara, articles 2, 6; Economic Agreement between RSFSR and KhPSR, June 29, 1922, articles 5–7; 1921 economic agreement with Bukhara, articles 3, 7, 10–11; Economic Agreement between RSFSR and BPSR, August 9, 1922, articles 4–5. The texts of the 1922 economic agreements with Khorezm and Bukhara are in *Sbornik deistvuiushchikh dogovorov*, IV, 13–14, 9–10.

12. *Iz istorii grazhdanskoi voiny*, III, 564, 581; K. Mukhammedberdyev, *Kommunisticheskaia partiia v borbe za pobedu narodnoi sovetskoi revoliutsii v Khorezme* (Ashkhabad, 1959), pp. 199–200; Baymirza Hayit, *Turkestan im XX. Jahrhundert* (Darmstadt, 1956), p. 149; 1920 treaty of alliance with Khorezm, articles 13, 15; 1921 treaty of alliance with Bukhara, articles 11–12.

13. Stalin, "The October Revolution," V, 114–115.

14. Nepesov, pp. 190–191, 197–198, 200, 202, 216; Mukhammedberdyev, pp. 200–203; *Godovoi otchet NKID k VIII Sezdu Sovetov (1919–1920)* (Moscow, 1921), pp. 71–72.

15. Nepesov, pp. 203–204, 209–211, 264, 269; Mukhammedberdyev, pp. 206, 208, 210–215; Kh. Sh. Inoiatov and D. A. Chugaev, "Pobeda narodnykh revoliutsii i obrazovanie narodnykh sovetskikh respublik v Khorezme i Bukhare," *Istoriia SSSR*, 1966, No. 2, p. 77.

16. Nepesov, pp. 204–209, 212–215; *Sezdy sovetov Soiuza SSR, soiuznykh i avtonomykh sovetskikh sotsialisticheskikh respublik. Sbornik dokumentov 1917–1937 g.g.* (Moscow, 1959–1965), II, pp. 498–500, 509–512, 514–521. In July

1922 a Kirgiz [Kazakh] bureau was added to TsIK. In October 1923 the Fourth Khorezmi Kurultai of Soviets added a Karakalpak section; the new constitution adopted at the same time provided for the election of members of each of the three national minority sections of TsIK by conferences of representatives of their respective nationalities. In Bukhara similar sections within TsIK were established for Turkomans (September 1921) and Kazakhs (November 1923). The Fourth Bukharan Kurultai of Soviets in October 1923 went further and approved the formation of a separate Turkoman region, comprising the former Chardjui and Kerki begliks, to be governed by its own TsIK. (*Sezdy sovetov SSSR*, II, 523–524, 564–566, and VII, 23–33, 59–60.)

17. Inoiatov and Chugaev, p. 78; Geoffrey Wheeler, *The Modern History of Soviet Central Asia* (London and New York, 1964), p. 121; Hayit, p. 157. The party soon recovered but did not regain its former numerical strength.

18. A. Mashitskii, "K istorii revoliutsii v Bukhare," NKID, *Vestnik*, 1921, No. 5–6, p. 75n; Inoiatov and Chugaev, pp. 80–81; Hayit, pp. 132–133. Abd al-Kadir Muhiddin later held a prominent position in the government of the Tadjik SSR. He was executed in 1937.

19. In the western Pamirs, administered by Russia since 1905, local committees loyal to the Provisional Government assumed power in April and May 1917 and repudiated Bukharan sovereignty. Soviet authority was not established in the region until November 1918, when the anti-Communist elements in the Russian garrison at Khorog withdrew to India. The western Pamirs changed hands again in October 1919, when Basmachis led by a Russian colonel seized control. After the Basmachis' departure for India in May 1920 and a brief restoration of Bukharan rule in June, Soviet authority was definitively established. (*Istoriia tadzhikskogo naroda* [Moscow, 1963–1965], II, Pt. II, 256–257; III, Pt. I, 34–36, 62, 66–67.)

20. F. M. Bailey, *Mission to Tashkent* (London, 1946), p. 299; Pipes, p. 256.

21. Joseph Castagné, "Le Bolchevisme et l'Islam," *Revue du Monde Musulman*, LI (1922), 227–228; D. Soloveichik, "Revoliutsionnaia Bukhara," *Novyi Vostok*, II (1922), 281–283; Pipes, pp. 256–258; Hayit, p. 140.

22. Pipes, pp. 258–260; N. A. Kisliakov, "Ishan—feodal Vostochnoi Bukhary," Akademiia Nauk SSSR, Tadzhikistanskaia baza, *Trudy*, IX (1938), 25–27.

23. *Istoriia sovetskogo gosudarstva i prava Uzbekistana* (Tashkent, 1960), I, 162, 165–166; Nepesov, pp. 238, 247.

24. Stalin, Speech at the fourth conference of the Central Committee of the RCP(b) with workers of the national republics and oblasts (June 12, 1923), V, 330–332. Stalin's figures were probably exaggerated for dramatic effect, since a recent Soviet study claims that only 32 percent of the Khorezmi party membership was purged, leaving 584 members. (Nepesov, p. 254.)

25. *Istoriia sovetskogo gosudarstva*, I, 171–175; Hayit, p. 141; *Sezdy sovetov SSSR*, VII, 41, 67. Fitrat was released in 1924, joined the Uzbeg SSR Commissariat of Education, and taught at the universities of Samarkand and Tashkent. He disappeared after being arrested in 1938. Faizullah Khodzhaev became premier of the Uzbeg SSR in 1924, was executed in 1938, and rehabilitated in 1965–1966. (Hayit, p. 142; Edward Allworth, *Uzbek Literary Politics* [The Hague, 1964], p. 115; *Central Asian Review*, XIV [1966], No. 3, pp. 206–207.)

26. Stalin, V, 142, 151.

27. The new constitution proclaiming Khorezm a soviet socialist republic is

in *Sezdy sovetov SSSR*, VII, 23–33; the resolution of the Fifth Kurultai of Soviets, effecting the same change in Bukhara, is in VII, 74–75. The experience of the Khorezmi and Bukharan People's Soviet Republics in moving from "feudalism" to "socialism" in four years is currently being turned to political advantage in the Soviet Union, as proof that "backward countries with the help of the victorious proletariat of more advanced countries" can bypass capitalism and attain socialism directly. (Inoiatov and Chugaev, pp. 66, 75; A. I. Ishanov, "Narodnaia sovetskaia respublika—perekhodnaia forma k sotsialisticheskoi gosudarstvennosti," *Obshchestvennye Nauki v Uzbekistane*, February 1965, pp. 9–19.)

28. V. I. Iuferev, *Khlopkovodstvo v Turkestane* (Leningrad, 1925), pp. 138–139; *Istoriia sovetskogo gosudarstva*, I, 170; Soloveichik, p. 279. The figures for cotton production in Soviet Turkestan closely parallel those for the people's republics.

29. Nepesov, pp. 283–290. The Bukharan kurultai had given proof of the persistence of old attitudes in August 1922, when it proclaimed its "sacred duty" to liquidate the Basmachi revolt in central and eastern Bukhara, which it denounced as contrary to the Sharia and causing the destruction of mosques and madrasas. (*Sezdy sovetov SSSR*, II, 587.)

30. Nepesov, pp. 291–292; *Central Asian Review*, XIII (1965), No. 3, p. 225. Djunaid-khan found asylum in Afghanistan in 1929, where he died nine years later.

31. *Izvestiia*, March 28, 1923, p. 3; *Pravda*, April 1, p. 1. For the Central Asian Economic Council, see T. K. Kasymov, "Iz istorii organizatsii i deiatelnosti Sredneaziatskogo ekonomicheskogo soveta," *Obshchestvennye Nauki v Uzbekistane*, February 1963, pp. 19–26.

32. Agreement between RSFSR and Bukharan and Khorezmi Republics on the Administration of the Amu-Darya Flotilla, April 30, 1923, *Sbornik deistvuiushchikh dogovorov*, V, 5; Customs Agreement between RSFSR and BPSR, May 31, 1923, *Sbornik deistvuiushchikh dogovorov, soglashenii i konventsii, zakliuchennykh s inostrannymi gosudarstvami*, I, 2nd ed. (Moscow, 1924), pp. 317–320. In contrast to the inclusion of Bukhara in the Russian customs frontier in 1894, the 1923 agreement established a true customs union with a single tariff schedule.

33. Stalin, "On the Immediate Tasks of the Party in the National Question" (February 10, 1921), V, 23. For his definition of a nation, see Stalin, "Marxism and the National Question" (1912–1913), II, 296–297.

34. Stalin, "National Factors in Party and State Affairs" (January–February 1923), V, 189.

35. As early as June 1920 Lenin had toyed with the idea of dividing Russian Turkestan into three national regions: "Uzbekia, Kirgizia and Turkmenia." ("Remarks on a project of the Turkestan Commission" [June 13, 1920], *Leninskii sbornik* [Moscow, 1924–1959], XXXIV, 326.)

36. For the resolutions of the Khorezmi and Bukharan kurultais of soviets, approving the liquidation of their respective republics, see *Sezdy sovetov SSSR*, VII, 35–36 and 72–73. For a detailed account of the steps by which national delimitation was effected, see A. A. Gordienko, *Sozdanie sovetskoi natsionalnoi gosudarstvennosti v Srednei Azii* (Moscow, 1959), pp. 156–184. The Tadjik ASSR became a union republic in 1929; in 1932 Karakalpakia became an ASSR and was transferred to the Uzbeg republic.

Glossary of Russian and
Central Asian Terms

Aminana Sales tax on purchases by a wholesaler from a producer
Amlakdar Administrator of a subdivision of a beglik
Atli-bashi Local military governor in Khiva under Djunaid-khan
Batcha Boy trained as a dancer and entertainer
Beg Governor of a beglik
Beglik Province, subdivision of a khanate
Darya River
Desiatina Russian land measure equal to 2.7 acres
Divan-begi Finance minister and treasurer (Bukhara); prime minister (Khiva)
Guberniia Russian province
Hakim Governor of a beglik (Khiva)
Heradj Harvest tax
Ishan-rais Chief of police and supervisor of morals
Katta-türa Crown prince
Kazi Moslem judge
Kazi-kalan Chief justice and head of the clerical hierarchy
Khalat Native gown
Kopek 1/100 of a ruble
Krai Russian frontier region
Kurultai Congress
Kush-begi Prime minister (Bukhara); administrator of northern half of the khanate (Khiva)
Madjlis Parliament
Madrasa Traditional Moslem seminary or college
Maktab Traditional Moslem elementary school
Mir Governor of a beglik (eastern Bukhara)
Mudarris Professor in a madrasa, usually a mufti
Mufti Jurisconsult, neither judge nor lawyer
Mullah Learned man, member of the clerical estate
Nazir Minister or commissar
Oblast Russian province or subdivision of a government-general

Okrug	Russian province, military district, or judicial circuit
Otdel	Military district or subdivision of an oblast or okrug
Pud	Russian measure of weight equal to 36.1 pounds
Rais	Police chief
Ruble	Russian monetary unit equal to $0.51 in 1914
Sharia	Moslem religious law
Tanga	Bukharan or Khivan silver coin worth fifteen to twenty kopeks
Tilla	Bukharan gold coin equal to eighteen tangas; Khivan gold coin equal to nine tangas
Uezd	District, subdivision of an oblast, okrug, or guberniia
Ulema	Moslem theological scholar
Zakat	Tax on movable property, customs duty
Zakatchi	Collector of the zakat
Zakatchi-kalan	Chief collector of the zakat

Index

Russian Research Center Studies

* Out of print.
† Publications of the Harvard Project on the Soviet Social System.
‡ Published jointly with the Center for International Affairs, Harvard University.

DATE DUE

10/31			
GAYLORD			PRINTED IN U.S.A.